# PRINCIPLES OF
# PSYCHOLOGY

# PRINCIPLES OF PSYCHOLOGY

### BY J. R. KANTOR

PROFESSOR OF PSYCHOLOGY, UNIVERSITY OF INDIANA

## VOLUME II

1926

NEW YORK   ALFRED · A · KNOPF   LONDON

# FOREWORD

In completing our survey of psychological phenomena we are more than ever convinced of the correctness of the hypothesis we are testing. We deem it fairly well demonstrated that both the origin and the operation of psychological facts are summed up and completed in the interactions between psychological organisms and the objects stimulating them. In Chapter XXVII we have attempted to show how these interactions, in connection with the general conditions associated with them, exhaust the phenomena of the development and operation of psychological facts.

As we have indicated in the Preface (Volume I), our hypothesis has been applied not only to phenomena ordinarily considered in psychological treatises, but to some which are seldom handled and to others which are handled not at all. In this connection we may call attention in the present volume to Chapters XVII, on Wishing and Desiring; XX, on Intellectual Responses; XXIII on Language; XXIV, on International Behavior, and XXX, on Psychopathic Conduct. For these chapters we make the claim, perhaps not immodestly, that in their treatment of the activities of persons in contact with the surrounding stimuli we have given for the first time an adequate presentation of the data involved as distinctly psychological phenomena. Also in observing strictly the actual behavior of individuals we have isolated distinct differences between Thinking and Problem Solving (XXI), and Reasoning Responses (XXII).

If psychological phenomena are actually stimulus-response interactions, we appreciate in consequence all the more keenly the incompleteness with which much of the material has had to be handled. Our descriptions could hardly be detailed enough to bring out the fundamental facts involved in the operation of the various types of behavior. Accordingly we merely offer suggestions and do not in any sense exhaust the necessary details.

On the other hand, those who consider scientific descriptions to be necessarily abstract may find some cause for complaint in the concreteness of our handling of the various subjects. Such individuals may even think that our descriptions merely amount to practical records of events occurring, instead of the representation of laws or principles. Such differences of opinion are natural and even inevitable. Our study indicates very forcibly, however, that the data of the psychology when treated as natural phenomena can be esteemed only as the very intimate and detailed facts of stimulus-response interactions. It may be added, too, that whatever such detailed and concrete descriptions may lack in the appearance of profundity is, we believe, more than compensated by the validity of the descriptions and the understanding they afford of psychological phenomena.

J. R. K.

June, 1925.

# CONTENTS

## CHAPTER XVI

## CHAPTER XVII

## CHAPTER XVIII

## CHAPTER XIX

## CHAPTER XXIX

## CHAPTER XXX

# CHAPTER XVI

## EMOTIONAL ACTIVITIES AS NO-RESPONSE BEHAVIOR SEGMENTS

Emotional behavior consists essentially of interruptive forms of action stimulated by rapidly changing circumstances and in all cases involves various slight or intense general organic and visceral processes.[1]

General Description of Emotional Conduct

Probably the most obvious observation made in studying emotional conduct is that the primary occurrences in such action are the confusion and excitement which disrupt the behavior that ordinarily takes place when the emotion-exciting stimulus appears. When we attempt to describe the specific characteristics of an emotional act we are profoundly impressed with this condition of disrupting chaos and inhibition of action. We may look upon the emotional person as one who is practically paralyzed for a moment; he appears to undergo a dissociation of his reaction systems, so that he remains powerless and helpless until his responses are reconstituted. This reconstitution may be superficially described as a refocussing of the person toward some definite object. Essentially, emotional conduct is a momentary condition of "no response," since there appears to be a complete cessation of all directed responses to surrounding conditions. In point of fact, it is this disruptive chaos which definitely distinguishes the milder emotional activities from the numerous classes of affective or feeling behavior to which they otherwise display a striking resemblance.

In detail, it might be pointed out that emotional conduct consists of a definite type of failure to perform an expected form of adjustment or adaptation upon the basis of surrounding conditions and the individual's reactional biography or previous behavior history. Whenever it is possible for the person to make the expected or necessary response to the stimulating condition, there is no emotional disturbance.

In studying emotional conduct it is of cardinal importance to notice that such activities constitute distinct forms of disruptive disorganizations of responses, for there are others that may lay claim to such a descriptive term, such as the responses involving a dimming or absence of the differentiation factor or the anomalous reactions symptomatic of atrophy or injury of a muscular, glandular, or neural element.

[1] The material of this chapter is based upon an article entitled "An Attempt toward a Naturalistic Description of Emotions," published in the Psychological Review, 1921, 28, No. 1 and 2.

1

Again, by disruptive conduct we cannot mean action in which the stimulus object is absent nor activity in which for some reason the precurrent attention or perception reaction systems fail to operate and thus cause a disturbance or a failure of conduct.

Although the disruptive chaos may be taken as the definite mark of differentiation between emotions and other forms of behavior, it should not be considered in any sense an exhaustive description. In the actual delineation of a concrete emotional situation we must include many other essential features, although chief reliance is finally placed upon the absence of a focussed adaptation or adjustment. When we thus take cognizance of all the factors in a behavior situation, it becomes impossible to confuse emotional conduct with the hypnagogic dissociations in which the person is temporarily cut off from his surroundings, or with the attention shift in which there is a momentary lack of focussed action preparatory to an orderly reconstitution of reaction systems which is, in turn, preparatory to a change in behavior. If we were always to give as full a description of each instance and type of behavior as possible, we might avoid the mistakes that now are most flagrantly made, namely, the confusing of emotions with exciting or arousing feelings, passions, sentiments, and habits of affective response, or identifying as something else actions which are emotional in character.

Lest someone inject into the description of emotional behavior any teleological notion concerning the lack of response, we might suggest once more that the assumption of such a lack of a response system is based directly upon the immediate facts of the emotional situation. In any specific emotional circumstance the contextual stimuli and the associated activities that occur, clearly indicate that a particular kind of stimulus-response correlation is a significant factor in the segment of behavior under observation, and especially if we consider the developmental history of the individual. In most, if not in all instances, we can determine with little chance of error what the person may be expected to offer in the way of an organized and directed activity in a particular situation.

We are guarded from the injection of any sort of teleological factor into the description of emotional behavior by the consideration that no order and regularity marks the occurrence of such conduct. Thus such disruptive actions are at times exceedingly harmful and interfere considerably with the person's intercourse with his surroundings. In other cases, they may serve as preparatory actions for later conduct, or in general they may facilitate the operation of succeeding action.

Specific Characteristics of Emotional Behavior Segments    Looking more minutely into the actual behavior occurrence that takes place in emotional conduct, we discover a very definite characteristic condition. Namely, emotional activity consists of behavior segments in which the consummatory or final responses do not or cannot occur while the rest of the response pattern is definitely performed. It is in this sense that we call emotional activity "no-response" action. The no-response phase clearly refers only to the consummatory or final action, whether an effective or knowledge response, and positively not to the other factors (reaction systems) of the response pattern. In other words, the attention and perceptual phases of emotional behavior segments cannot be followed by the overt, effective, or other final reaction system.

Considerable light is reflected upon the character of emotional behavior segments when we consider that the lack of stimulus-response integration ordinarily occurs under conditions making it impossible for the person to develop response systems with which to adapt himself to such circumstances.

Emotional responses, then, are not organized reaction systems of any sort. That is to say, emotions are not names for definite reaction systems constituting factors in the reactional equipment of individuals. In no sense, therefore, can it be said that we are prepared to make specific disruptive reactions to definite objects of stimulation. In the case of various informational or habit activities, on the other hand, the organism does have definite potential response systems in its functional equipment. Thus, for example, the verbal stimulus "who was the victor at Salamis?" or the perceptual presentation of the word "loan" in stenographic notes, will bring out definite overt responses which were acquired at a previous time and are called into action by the present stimulation. This is not so, however, in the case of emotional behavior in which no definite response system is functioning. What really happens to the person in the emotional situation in the absence of what, from a reactional standpoint, may be called a required response system, is that he is thrown back upon any available behavior resources. In the most turbulent situations he can substitute only visceral reflexes. Such behavior we may call the elemental emotions. In contrast with this condition, that is to say, in the more typically human situations,[1] the person replaces the required response system with one serviceable in some similar circumstance (he laughs when caught in a socially disapproved act, as though it were a deliberate joke), or with some response previously associated with the required act in this particular environing condition (he smiles instead of answering a question).

The failure of the consummatory or final reaction system to operate in the emotional behavior segment completely accounts, we believe, for the utter irregularity and disorder of emotional action. Ordinarily, the definiteness and regularity, as well as the predictability of an action, depend upon the specific correlation of a definite final reaction system with precurrent reaction systems and with some particular

[1] By the terms elemental and human the writer means to point out a difference in behavior circumstances, illustrated by a person coming upon a dangerous animal in a wood, or by being informed of a legacy that has been bequeathed.

stimulus.  Whenever the organism performs a definite final response system of some sort, preceded by its appropriate precurrent reaction and subject to excitation by a specific stimulus, we may expect an orderly and more or less compact act or pattern of response.  Even here, of course, the act is spontaneous and variable, provided the context or setting of the stimulus is modifiable.  This sort of situation is well illustrated by the web-spinning of spiders in which the slight modifications of the context of the stimuli make possible the hardly perceptible differences in web-spinning.  In human informational and habit modes of action a somewhat greater invariability and non-conformity to type are introduced by the greater possibilities of variation in the stimuli or in their settings.  It is clear, therefore, that notwithstanding the latitude for irregularity of behavior supplied by the variability in the stimulus or its setting, there is a fundamental and describable regularity in all of our behavior which comprises organized response patterns.  All this order and regularity is entirely and completely lacking in emotional behavior segments.

Moreover, this lack of a final response system makes it possible for us to understand why the only basis for predicting the behavior of a person in the emotional situation is a knowledge of the influence of the surroundings at the moment.  Indeed it is only because the surroundings can determine the intensity of the person's dissociation that we are able to describe, however inadequately, the comparatively large segment of behavior which includes the emotional act.

To the writer it seems that the absence of a definite response system in emotional behavior explains the following facts.  Furthermore, unless there are other satisfactory means of accounting for these facts, they tend to support the hypothesis that an emotional act is essentially a "no-response" phase of behavior.  The facts are: (1) the impossibility of an onlooker's specifying what sort of emotion a person is experiencing from any observation of the individual aside from the emotional circumstances; and (2) the hitherto complete failure of psychologists to make any satisfactory classification of emotional acts; (3) Furthermore, is it not the absence of a response system in emotional behavior and its replacement by reflexes, which make it easy for psychologists to misinterpret emotional acts, and to look upon them as mere bodily "changes" or "expressions" of invisible states of mind? (4) again, it appears that only "no-behavior" conduct could induce psychologists to interpret emotions as the awareness of organic changes or to look upon the substituted visceral reflexes as instincts which protect the organism, pending the arousal of awareness of what is to be done in the situation.  (5) Finally, the view that the same emotions are found in the animal world as in human action equipment may be traced to the fact that psychologists were observing in the human organism, not definite reactions, but replacement responses which do, in part, resemble the simple organized activities of animals.

If in each case of emotional conduct the fundamental principle is the absence of a certain response system, the question arises as to how to distinguish between the more and the less violent emotional activities. Here, as elsewhere in the investigation of emotions, the only safe and sufficient guide is the consideration of the specific conditions under which the behavior occurs. As we have already pointed out, the person may be found lacking a response system in a situation in which the greatest immediate need for definite action seems to dissociate him so completely that he is left with only his simplest elementary behavior, while in other situations events do not occur so suddenly, nor are the circumstances so pressing as to bring about even a very marked surface confusion. In the milder situation there is, in fact, only a slight difference between the activity interrupted by the emotion-exciting stimulus and the resumed occupation after the emotional period is over. Consequently, the milder sorts of emotion seem to merge with the non-emotional situation in which a definite response is merely delayed or is inhibited because of the person's lack of attention to a certain stimulus, or because of a momentary failure of perception.

We have now to consider briefly the stimuli conditions in emotional behavior segments. Immediately we might suggest that a general descriptive condition prevails. That is to say, the objects or situations with which the person is in contact do not perform any definite stimulational function for a consummatory or final reaction, although they operate very effectively in stimulating the person to perform attention and perception reactions. It is because the stimuli objects do perform certain functions and not others, that we may be fairly certain as to what consummatory response can be expected in any given case. In considering the stimulational functions of the objects and situations to which emotional responses are made, we must not overlook the fact that what is true for the overt stimuli of the more elemental reactions, is likewise true for the substitutional stimuli objects which, for the most part, elicit more subtle and refined emotional activities.

As a distinctive segment of psychological activity, an emotional act can not only be separated from its preceding and succeeding contextual correlatives, but can also be analyzed into its functionally constituent phases. The latter analysis is possible in spite of the generally confused character of such behavior segments. Although emotional behavior segments can be distinguished from the preceding and succeeding activities, possibly this type of action more than any other, can be described most expediently in terms of other related activities which, along with the distinct emotional segment, constitute a complex behavior situation. Accordingly, we may analyze an emotional behavior situation into four distinct behavior segments. These we may refer to as (1) Pre-Emotional Behavior Segments, (2) Emotional Behavior Segment Proper, (3) First Proximate Post-Emotional Be-

Systematic Analysis of an Emotional Behavior Situation

havior Segments, and (4) Second Proximate Post-Emotional Behavior Segments. We shall describe these different behavior segments in order.

(1) Pre-Emotional Behavior Segments

Because emotional conduct involves such a complex confusional action it is well to point out that almost always some of its characteristics may be traced to the fact that it immediately follows some other activity of a different type. For example, a pre-emotional behavior segment may be one in which an individual is so preoccupied with some thought as he crosses a meadow, that when the animal which later proves to be the stimulus for an emotional reaction, makes its appearance, there occurs a decided shift in the behavior circumstances of the acting individual. At all events, we must observe that the emotional behavior segment proper always appears to the observer as a unique and remarkable type of action.

(2) Emotional Behavior Segment Proper

The actual emotional behavior segment is like any other, with two notable and characteristic exceptions. In the first place, there is of course no final reaction system coördinated with the precurrent reaction systems in the response pattern. In the second place, there is present a great mass of visceral and general organic functioning which serves as replacement actions operating in the absence of an organized, consummatory reaction system. Other differences, of course, must also exist, but none with such marked identifying characteristics. The various precurrent reaction systems and the replacing organic action may all be advantageously discussed separately.

Attention reactions precurrent to the operation of the rest of the emotional behavior pattern are usually rapid and rather sudden actualizations of stimuli. For in the more intense emotional situations, at least, the stimuli objects appear rather suddenly and frequently with overwhelming force. We may point out also that there exist extreme variations in the reconstitutive character of the individual's attentional conduct, so that sometimes he is unable to perform another attentional act for a considerable period. In other cases the attention reconstitution is not so long in occurring. Generally speaking, the time of attentional reconstitution depends directly upon the intensity of the behavior segment.

The perceptual phase of the emotional behavior segment is an act of simple apprehension which in a given case may be an implicit appreciation of danger or safety. As an incipient response system, a perceptual reaction of danger involves uneasiness, excitement, trembling, and unpleasantness, all of which are reminiscent of a previous condition of the individual in actual danger, which condition is preserved and revived in vestigial form. In a degree, the perceptual phase of the emotional situation is a direct preparatory response for some specific act which is to follow. When, as sometimes happens, the exigencies of the situation prevent the occurrence of the consummatory or final act, as for example, when one is confronted by a dangerous animal under conditions affording no means of escape, or when an appropriate act has never been acquired for the present frustrating and baffling circumstances, then the cataclysm or seizure which is the emotional phase proper is instantaneously irrupted.

At this point it is worth noting why we have been deliberately assuming that the responses of emotional behavior segments must be regarded as patterns of response. Unless the emotional response were a pattern with definite precurrent reaction systems and a place for a final reaction system, there would be no chance for an emotional activity. In short, were the emotional reaction merely a single, direct, reaction system, it would never involve the typical, confusional, disruptive activity always found in emotional conduct.

In the more subtle and refined emotional activities we naturally expect to find some implicit reaction systems. Accordingly, the ideational antecedent of the emotional behavior pattern, as compared with the perceptual anticipatory phase of emotional action, is a more refined and more vague vestige of an original danger or other response; it is brought into operation through another stimulus serving as a substitution for the original danger situation. The statements just made presuppose an idea to be a definite act which incipiently, and in many cases symbolically, repeats a previously direct and overt adjustment, or what was in a former time a precurrent or preparatory activity, such as reading something, or hearing imparted information. In the case of such an antecedent act, the emotional behavior is much milder. The organism does not, as a rule, get so much out of hand as when the emotional situation is preceded by a coarse perceptual reaction.

It must be understood, however, that the violence of an emotional activity is entirely owing to the surrounding circumstances, so that the emotion following an ideational process may possibly be far more turbulent than one preceded by a perceptual activity.

In the absence of the consummatory phase of the emotional reaction pattern, we can describe the emotional act only as a process of disintegration of the series of response systems constituting the individual at the moment. In effect there is a total inhibition or suppression of all activity so far as any overt adjustmental response is concerned. Essentially, the emotional factor is a phase of behavior in which there is lacking a coördinate stimulus-response process ordinarily resulting in a definitely directed act. When such a direct act occurs, it may be looked upon as a consummatory response initiated by the precurrent perceptual or ideational action; and we call the pattern of response a volitional or habitual adjustment. Contrariwise, typical commotional seizure and chaos directly result from the non-operation of a consummatory reaction when its appropriate antecedent has functioned. According to our hypothesis, therefore, an emotion is intrinsically a negative form of behavior, although it may serve to induce or to accelerate another adjustment.

Because every psychological act is the reaction of an organism, it is an invariable law that whenever a stimulus fails to produce its appropriate response, the organism is forced to resort to a substitution or replacement act. We have already suggested that in the most striking emotional situations the replacement acts are interoceptive reflexes. Hence we find an almost universal emphasis upon organic processes as prominent factors in emotional behavior. Naturally there is a great difference in the amount and intensity of such organic activity when the elemental behavior sometimes called violent emotions is compared with the human or cultural conduct usually referred to as the subtle or tender emotions.[1]  In the latter case it is universally true that, whether the stimulus is perceptual or ideational, some measure of direct adjustment is always possible, and therefore there is less organic functioning.

If we accept as a fact the difference between the elemental and cultural emotions, we may then permit our specification of some of the conditions in the more violent and pervasive emotional action to stand as a type. Moreover, we assume that the descriptions will hold for the more refined and subtle activities with a variation merely in the degree of intensity of the action and in their organic components. First, we note that the replacing organic activities involve vascular and visceral processes of all sorts. There are disturbances of the digestive secretions, respiration, contraction of blood vessels, acceleration or retardation of the heart-beat, induction of various secretions, etc. Very frequently we also find as substitutes for definite focussed responses, imperfectly articulate cries which in most cases answer to the description of groans or screams better than to language. Still other substituted actions are the numerous random activities of the skeletal muscles, sometimes becoming so exaggerated in emotional behavior that persons assume poses of cataleptic rigidity or simulate the choreic twitchings and convulsions of St. Vitus dance. It is while performing these extreme replacement actions in emotional conduct that the person reaches almost a purely biological status.

(3) First Proximate Post-Emotional Behavior Segments
Following very closely upon the emotional activity proper, the person begins an act which is directly conditioned by the stimulating circumstances which surround him at the moment. Now the stimulus object initiating the post-emotional behavior segment may be some thing or condition, such as the fence toward which escape might be directed, or a meaning action stimulating the person to lie still and play "possum." Again it might possibly be some combination of the two, as in recalling that a place of asylum exists near by. Whatever the stimulus may be, the type of response depends upon the circumstances which initiated the emotional activity in the first place, since we are here observing what is, after all, a definite and restricted event. In the case of a primary emotion the activities are large overt responses involving the external skeletal muscles, as in fighting, running, and jumping. It is in such cases that the preceding definite emotional conditions may be of service. In the secondary or social emotional

---

[1] Not sentiments or diffused feelings.

situations the transition from the state of suspense and confusion is more gradual. In fact, the whole emotional situation is more closely related to other activities than is true in the case of the primary emotions; in other words, the specific emotional action is decidedly less marked off from preceding and succeeding segments of behavior.

The directed responses following an emotional situation are, then, very rigidly determined by the surrounding stimulating objects and in practically all types of emotional conduct are at first diffuse and not especially well directed for the needs at hand. The recovery is indefinitely more rapid, however, for the cultural emotions since, in these cases, as we have already seen, the organism is never shaken to reactional or personality foundations. In all cases, however, it must be noted that when some definite activity (post emotional) once begins, the emotional action proper has ceased to exist. This directed act or adjustment must be regarded as a consummatory act following a precurrent response which is not identical with the anticipatory phase of the emotional act. From the standpoint of the stimulus, therefore, it is a new and not merely a delayed reaction. So disparate are the emotional acts and the adjustments which follow them that in any given emotional circumstance the presentation of a new stimulus, no matter how remote from the emotional situation, strikingly curtails the emotion. Such a situation is well illustrated by the case of a student suffering an emotional confusion while he is being orally examined, but who recovers immediately upon attempting to make some reply, however unsuited it may be. It need hardly be added that unless the emotional behavior segment is followed by another emotional behavior segment, as when the person performs serial emotional responses, the succeeding post-emotional behavior segment will include a definitely organized final or consummatory reaction system.

At this point we might indicate that very frequently the post-emotional behavior segment or the reconstituting behavior of the person consists of some momentarily acquired reaction system which develops under the stress of the moment and the particular situation. Possibly this type of behavior recovery occurs more frequently under the auspices of the social than the more elemental situations. In cases in which the reconstituting activity is of the momentarily acquired type, the emotional situation in its details serves as the stimulus.

Very frequently the emotional behavior situation carries over to another behavior segment. The latter is described as the realization act which may have the emotional behavior segment as its stimulus. In general, we discover here that the person is stimulated by his escape or by some other result of his emotional action to sum up to himself either verbally or not, the character of his predicament and his manner of escaping from it. In the older literature on emotions it was probably this action which was interpreted erroneously as the mental emotion which succeeded the operation of an emotional expression.

**(4) Second Proximate Post-Emotional Behavior Segments**

As a precautionary detail it might be suggested once more that the three behavior segments that we have included in the emotional situation along with the emotional behavior segment proper are not necessarily and indispensably factors of the description. They are added to the account of emotions mainly for purposes of completeness. Furthermore, it should be remarked that, especially in the subtler emotion situations, the emotional activity practically always involves considerable affective behavior of many forms, determined in detail by the type of emotional activity transpiring. These affective responses may be stimulated by the visceral replacement of the emotional behavior segments, by the individual's general behavior conditions or by the specific surrounding circumstances of the emotional situation. In no case are the affective activities (reaction systems) integral portions of the emotional behavior segment, although they can hardly be regarded as not closely connected with the total emotional situation. In fact, affective activities are very intimately related to emotional behavior of all sorts, and in many cases may be the preceding instead of the succeeding activities.[1]

**Distinction of Emotions from Non-Emotional Feeling Behavior**

The strict observation of actual responses under different conditions of stimulation indicates very clearly that a wide difference exists between the disruptive types of emotional action and various forms of feeling behavior which are frequently called by the same name. Few accomplishments in psychology are more desirable than the isolation and examination of the distinguishing features of the great mass of activities which has been indiscriminately thrown together through the intellectualistic influence of subjectivistic psychology. Let us note that the necessity of reviewing the facts of affective behavior is intimately bound up with a naturalistic attitude. In the first place, not until this attitude became established was it deemed necessary to give much attention to the detailed analysis of human behavior. Again, this naturalistic view is of great advantage to us in the study of feeling behavior, since it serves to prevent our being misled by the conception of a presumed operation in various different circumstances of some form of common mental content symbolized by such a word as Fear or Anger.

In reply to the question whether there is any feature of behavior which distinguishes the emotions from other kinds of feeling conduct, we may refer to the suggestion made in the chapter on Feelings, namely, the criterion of the presence or absence in the act or behavior segment of an organized response system. If this criterion is valid and employed as a guide in the investigation of human activity, we should be able to distinguish emotions not only from all other feel-

[1] In spite of the intermixture of emotional behavior with affective and other reactions the emotional behavior segment is still quite isolated when compared, for example, with intricate intellectual behavior segments. Doubtless this is accounted for by the unique "no-response" character of the emotional behavior segment.

ing behavior as a class, but also from each type of activity in the class.

Especially is it necessary to mark off the emotions sharply from the *passions*, which constitute a very different form of behavior. Unlike the emotions, the passions consist of organized response systems which in some form operate continuously, whether or not the original stimulating object is present. The passions, as exemplified by love and hate, are the prolonged functioning of organized response systems kept active by the periodic appearance of the original stimulus or by some substituted stimulus-object, such as a letter or some other token. Moreover, between the intervals of direct or substituted stimulation by the original object of love or hate, the person is constantly responding in a characteristic feeling manner, thereby inducing much self-stimulation. Thus, a person who acquires a passion for another individual or for an object, begins to respond with some form of implicit feeling activity and becomes cheerful, hopeful, happy, or enthusiastic, depending upon specific circumstances.[1] Clearly, when we observe the person responding to the absent object of passion, that is, when he responds with the protracted implicit feeling activity, we cannot possibly confuse such behavior with the momentarily explosive emotional reaction. On the other hand, when we compare with an emotion the more violent and focussed passion responses performed in the presence of the stimulating object, probably the only crucial criterion is that the passion acts do, and the emotional acts do not, involve definite organized reaction systems. However unsatisfactory the description of passion acts may be at the present time, there is no doubt that they constitute a genuine chapter in the psychology of feeling.

The emotions must also be clearly distinguished from the *sentiments*, which are essentially prescriptive and limiting types of activity developed under the influence of social approval. Sentiment acts are directed forms of responses usually resulting in some definite kind of complex social conduct. Illustrative of the sentiments are the activities of modesty, cleanliness, and charitableness. A sentiment is a preferred act of acquiescence or readiness to do or to have done certain definite complex things. Again, sentiments are in a genuine sense latent and intermittent responses, and the specific acts may involve much implicit or thought activity. As compared with sentiments, passions are for the most part direct and specific responses to stimuli. Passion acts being more elemental and explicit, they are also more closely integrated with immediate, surrounding conditions, while sentiments are more generalized reaction systems having a larger range of exciting stimuli.

---

[1] The extreme importance of the situation to which responses are made is well brought out in these activities; we observe also the intermingling of different forms of feeling reaction in the same segment of behavior. We find considerable alternation between different behavior segments and especially between emotions and diffuse feelings.

Unfortunate, indeed, is the confusing of emotional conduct with *diffuse feeling behavior,* which occurs when the term emotions is employed as a general blanket for all sorts of feeling activity. The diffused feeling acts are responses to prolonged conditions involving desire, achievement, or frustration. They are responses to objects and conditions definitely recognized as having a particular character, beauty,[1] goodness, wisdom, etc. On the basis of definite external situations in which the person finds himself we can trace out particular forms of responses that may be described or denoted as reactions of regret, remorse, relief, elation, cheer, enthusiasm, disappointment, admiration, patience or impatience, happiness, excitement, shock, depression, and an indefinite number of other affective responses. In all these cases more or less continued effects are brought about in the person through some contact with particular objects in specific settings. It appears in each case that the whole individual is involved for a considerable period of time, so that any particular feeling is distributed over all the reaction patterns of the person. In worry, for example, the individual seems overwhelmed by a certain environing condition and keeps up a continual process of self-stimulation, thereby reinforcing the worry. We find also the constant tendency to hark back to the feeling stimulus as a point of reference. Thus, when we are worried about an impending calamity and read of someone's success, we connect ourselves with that situation and feel more deeply concerning our own affairs. In a general way, the diffuse feelings are implicit phases of all the activities of the person while he is in an affective condition.

In a similar manner we may compare emotional conduct with each of the different individual types of affective behavior segments.[2] While in every case we find the criterion of organized versus disruptive activity marking off the two kinds of behavior, other more specific criteria may be discovered. The latter, however, do not supply us with clear-cut lines of demarcation either between feelings and emotions or between the different specific forms of each large type division.

Great as are the difficulties of description and differentiation encountered in even the slightest penetration into the maze of emotional and feeling responses, they can be amply accounted for by the meagre exploration which has been made into the psychology of feelings. The absence of accurate investigations in this domain is manifested by the fact that the interpretation of feeling conduct is based less upon facts of concrete reactions than upon the habits of popular speech. The futility of such interpretation is clear when it is noted that no feeling term in popular use refers to a type of response be-

[1] Sometimes referred to as the emotional life of art.

[2] For descriptions of the affective reactions, see Vol. I, Chap. XII. It is in the hope that we may catch an additional illuminating if fleeting glance at the character of feeling actions and their differences from emotional activities that we brave a repetition of our descriptions.

longing exclusively to a single class of psychological reactions. But although we have yet to begin the isolation of the various classes of feeling behavior, the differentiation of emotional conduct from the various other forms of feeling conduct appears plausible and worth while.

One of the effects resulting from the growing influence which biological theories began to exert upon psychology in the middle of the last century, was the conception that emotions are definite adaptational reactions which promote the conservation of the individual. This assumption of the self-preservative character of emotional conduct is closely linked with the idea that emotions are inherited forms of response. Not the least surprising, then, is the fact that the utilitarian doctrine of emotional behavior is more prescriptive than descriptive, and brings in its train results that are most remarkable. *The Utility of Emotional Behavior*

Even the most careful observer of emotional behavior necessarily comes to the conclusion that some features of emotional action must be adaptational and useful. In particular, this is the case with the glandular secretions so prominent in emotional situations. But what right have we to base our conclusions upon a limited number of features? What of the looseness of the bowels, the retching and vomiting, the violent heart-beat and the innumerable other symptoms of emotional shock? Are these, too, of use in the organism's adaptations? And is there anything in the nature of a psychological act which prohibits us from considering the glandular reflexes as entirely fortuitous occurrences in the total complex pattern of response?

Further indications of the invalidity of the utilitarian theory come to light when we consider that in the cultural emotions organic functions are not nearly so prominent, and apparently do not produce energy-giving secretions. It is hardly convincing to say that in these secondary emotions the organic reflexes are not present because they are not needed, for in so saying one clearly makes utility synonymous with presence, and in consequence assumes that which is to be established since, as a matter of fact, even when the organic activities are present, their utility is questioned.

Unfortunately the apparent serviceability of various strongly excited organic activities under certain circumstances has induced several writers to indulge in much indifferent speculation concerning the general utility and survival character of emotions. Aside from the question whether these writers are observing emotions at all,[1] the objectionable feature of such speculation is the implication that organisms possess general mechanisms with definite purposive functions to meet specific unfavorable circumstances. The consequence of holding such a view is that it inevitably results in the overlooking of such a fact as, for example, the substituted character of the or-

[1] Note the grouping of phenomena—pain, hunger, fear, rage.

ganic processes which is not compatible with such a preconception.

The writer submits that, on the whole, observational evidence does not support the view that emotional disruptive shock is always or, even in most cases, beneficial to the organism, either at the moment of its occurrence or in the long run. As a record of fact, all that the study of emotions enables us to say is that under certain circumstances the emotional behavior is apparently a useful reaction in the sense that it makes possible a very rapid and immediate response which is necessary at the time. But, in quite as many cases, the dissociating and disruptive character of emotional acts is very harmful to the organism and is not infrequently the cause of its death. What chance would a person have in a difficult situation if he were deprived even for a moment of the opportunity to offer a definitely centered and directed response to a pressing stimulus object or circumstance? It is evident, then, that emotional behavior is not always serviceable activity. Consequently we must summarily reject any utility interpretation, especially since such an interpretation appears to be based, not upon actual observation, but upon belief in a teleological mental force or some sort of entelechy manifesting itself in physiological conduct.

**The Classification of Emotions**
Judging from our description there can be, strictly speaking, only one kind of emotional behavior. That is to say, emotions constitute a class or type of action. The most obvious means, therefore, of classifying the various emotional activities is to correlate them with the exact circumstances under which they occur. While the extreme complexity of these stimulating circumstances militates against our attaining at present any well rounded and compact classification, such a correlation serves to give some behavior-content and meaning to the various divisions. Moreover, to describe an emotional act under the circumstances in which it occurs is to give it its stimulus-response setting and to keep our classification from resembling an enumeration of specific faculties.

The problem of ordering and arranging emotional acts involves us in precisely the same difficulties as the classification of thinking or of other complex acts. In each case, however, the attempt to specify the exact circumstances under which the person is responding will give us an insight into the operation of human reactions, besides helping us to understand the precise details involved in building up reaction systems. For instance, a comprehensive behavioristic study of the more subtle or refined emotions will afford us some appreciation of the intricate details of social behavior and the social modification of human action. Further, unless we plan to make such a comprehensive study of emotional activity we can find little promise of obtaining additional information about it, by a mere analysis, say, of the secretory functions which play a prominent part in emotional acts as well as in other types of behavior. There would be considerable value in such an analysis if the glandular secretions were regarded as integrated parts of response systems replacing acts that for the time being could not be correlated with their usual, stimulating circumstances. It is scarcely scientific wisdom, however, to place one's hope for the classification of emotional conduct, as some writers do, entirely in the physiological factors of behavior, to the neglect of the other components and of the stimulating conditions of the whole response.

Of cardinal importance for the classification of emotional conduct is knowledge of the fact that whenever we persistently cling to a name as though it were something more significant than a symbol, we inevitably falsify essential facts. Perhaps in no other domain of psychological science do names mean quite so little or work so much harm as they do in the study of emotions. It is not surprising, then, that the literature on the subject amply reveals many difficulties of description and interpretation because such terms as fear, anger, joy, and sorrow are presumed to represent unique sorts of psychological facts. The truth of the matter is that these names, as commonly used, stand not only for genuine emotional reactions but also for various other complex human responses, such as feelings, besides symbolizing simpler organized responses of animals and infants. Furthermore, let us not forget that besides standing for widely different forms of actual behavior, the names found in the writings on emotions are presumed to represent mental states, each of which has a variety of expressions. Because names are so treacherous in the psychology of emotions, the needs of the science demand that a closer examination be made of the behavior which is to be classified, and that less attention be given to conventional terminology.

The description of psychological phenomena must always be incomplete unless to our report of the facts of stimulus and response we add also the conditions under which the latter interact. The necessity of investigating the precise conditions which influence responses appears from the fact that all reactions depend upon the conditions of the individual and the character of the surroundings as much as upon the bare presence or absence of reaction systems and stimuli. In the case of the emotional situation the disruptive chaos can obviously be avoided by the substitution of an overt response for one that is lacking, provided the surroundings are propitious and the person is prepared for such an emergency. The hunter who, in a general way, knows what to do when an animal appears and is equipped to deal with such a situation, is not expected to perform emotional action. Furthermore an individual equipped with reaction systems fitting into a particular situation may more easily than others reconstitute his behavior conditions when the emotional shock is over.

*Conditions Determining the Occurrence of Emotional Reactions*

Although there is great difficulty in specifying the exact determining conditions of emotional conduct, it is possible, however, to isolate a few factors which have a contributory effect in bringing about or preventing an emotional response. We may call these, respectively, personality and stimulating conditions, inasmuch as they refer primarily to the condition of the person or of the surroundings.

First and foremost of such conditions is (a) the individual's psychological equipment. A person thoroughly equipped with response patterns for the various situations in which he finds himself is not very likely to be thrown into a no-response situation. The student who has previously prepared himself in his learning task is much less likely to suffer a surprise emotion when confronted with a difficult examination. (b) Closely related to the previous condition is the individual's speed of reaction. Ordinarily an individual who is not quick to improve upon a situation confronting him will probably be caught in a dangerous or undesirable position. The person who begins to act rapidly in the presence of a dangerous object, possibly to inhibit movement, or to substitute another overt adjustment, is much less likely to suffer disruption of his actions. The person who is clever at repartee seldom if ever suffers embarrassment. In this type of situation, as in some of the elemental situations, self-confidence is an extremely potent factor in the prevention of emotional disturbance. (c) The ability to avoid an emotional shock depends upon the individual's general physiological condition since his capacity to handle his reactional equipment varies with his physiological status. A person who is just recovering from an illness may be for the time being inadequately equipped to grapple with a dangerous natural situation. Similarly, to be overworked, "nervous," or discouraged, results in a special susceptibility to emotional shock. In these cases, as in all others, we must observe that the constitutional condition has direct reference only to the stimulations at hand. Similarly, the present condition of an individual, which is the outcome of an immediately preceding emotional situation, decidedly affects his present emotional conduct. Thus the same or a similar stimulus may now influence the person to suffer no emotional disturbance at all, or to experience a mild rather than a violent seizure.

The stimulational conditions of emotional behavior are, as we might expect, very numerous. (a) One of the outstanding conditions is the familiarity of the person with the stimulating objects and their settings. When stimuli are known and not strange they are less likely to bring about a dissociation or disturbance. One is seldom overawed or overwhelmed by familiar surroundings. In a sense this is obvious when we consider that familiar surroundings imply the development of definite integrations of stimuli and responses. (b) Prominent as a contributory factor to social emotions is the presence of certain persons; a reproof or a *faux pas* in the presence of some relative, or of a loved, admired, or feared individual, often results in emotional behavior which otherwise would not occur. In general, the emotional disturbance is conditioned by the setting of the stimulus object, so that while the person may know what response to make to an object under certain circumstances, he may have no response for it in its present setting. (c) Thus it follows from the character of the conditions of emotional behavior that a potent preventive of emotional seizure is frequent contact with any given situation and especially with a situation which, through recent experience, has shown itself capable of inducing an emotional disturbance.

(d) Although emotional conduct does not involve the operation of definite equipmental reaction systems, but rather the failure of such activities to operate, still we may trace a conditioning influence upon emotional conduct to the person's social development. Not only does the social or cultural development influence the mode of operation of the more refined emotional activities, but it also conditions whether or not a particular kind of emotional action shall occur at all. The latter point is well exemplified in the observation that children develop only gradually to the point of performing the kind of no-responses that convention expects of them.

From our description of emotional activity it is obvious that there is no room in such an analysis for what is popularly called the "expression of an emotion." But this is not to deny that certain phases of the person's activity while performing emotional behavior, especially of the more refined type, merit the designation of "expressions." In view, therefore, of the prevalence of the faulty conception of emotional expressions we may consider briefly what is probably the basis for such a doctrine, a procedure that will undoubtedly throw some further light upon the nature of emotional activities and especially of those features which may properly be called expressions.

*Emotions and Expression*

In our first approach to the popular doctrine of emotional expression, we observe that it is based upon the false dichotomy to which we have referred, namely, that which is derived from the old animatistic psychology and which presupposes that emotional activity can be divided into an inner state called the emotion proper, and an outer expression of it, mainly conceived as a bodily activity or process. This type of conception requires no comment here further than the statement that this is the most fragile basis for the establishment of any kind of doctrine.

Again, the doctrine of expression is based upon the observation that emotional reactions at times, though not very frequently, may be stimuli for other activities, both for post-emotional activities which are part of the emotional situation, and for other acts. These other activities are the ones which are looked upon as the expressions of the actual emotional responses. Doubtless it is an attempt at a very extreme form of interpretation that can produce such a result as this. Furthermore, it is really feeling responses, rather than emotional conduct, which usually constitute the stimuli for other reactions.

Another probable basis for the origin of the conception we are discussing is the observation that very frequently feeling reactions, and less frequently emotional activity, have a conditioning influence upon other types of reactions. Accordingly the original conditioning feeling or emotional response is believed to be an "emotion," while the conditioned reactions are thought of as the expressions of the emotion.

An additional foundation for the expression hypothesis is the fact that in the case of emotional reactions we have, as we have indicated, a great mass of by-play activities in the form of replacement responses. It is these by-play reactions that are translated into the expressions, whereas some other feature of the emotional behavior is considered to be the internal emotional act which is expressed.

Finally, we might indicate that the expression doctrine is founded upon more specific forms of by-play reactions which actually constitute integral features of affective reactions, such as facial and other gestures. These we might look upon in some sense as more specialized by-play activities, or as specific features of the effects that objects produce in individuals rather than as visceral and general organic reflexes. In no case, of course, can we regard these activities as anything but actual responses forming parts of particular kinds of behavior segments.

**Emotions in Animals and Infants**

In considering every type of psychological phenomenon we find it expedient, whenever possible, to make a comparative study of the particular form of reaction. It is always worth while to compare the activities of adult individuals with those of infants and children. Also, much information concerning a particular type of instance of reaction is gained from a comparison of such activity in the human individual with that of infrahuman animals. This comparative study is especially important in the case of emotions, since a great many errors are current concerning the performance of emotional reactions by animals.

Especially since Darwin's time, when the continuity of species became the dominant motive in the biological domain, the view has prevailed that man's emotions are really vestigial remnants of the emotions which his animal ancestors had acquired. As a consequence, animals are presumed to perform various emotional activities which, because of their organization and development, they, in common with infants, obviously cannot have. The ascribing to animals and infants of such complex reactions as can be acquired only in a long social experience, is probably owing to the fact that some psychologists read back into the actions of children and animals certain motives and conditions of behavior which they find in themselves. How illegitimate such a proceeding is, may be judged from the fact that a critical observation of actual responses made to stimulating circumstances convinces us not only that animals never have any social emotions, but also that they seldom, if ever, develop to the stage of performing even elemental emotional behavior.

Since the present status of psychological opinion concerning emotions in animals has its roots in the Darwinian influence upon psychology, it would not be amiss to digress at this point in order to trace the growth of the conception that man and animals perform the same types of psychological actions. First, let us observe that Darwin accepted the underlying biological similarity between the human and the animal organism as the basis for a correlation between the expressions of emotions in the two cases. What seemed to be similar "expressions" were then taken to refer to similar mental states. What Darwin and the other writers overlooked was the fact that they were observing, not expressions of mental states, but rather direct responses to specific stimuli. They, however, named these responses by applying conventional terms,[1] and in this way animals began to be endowed with all types of emotions, and other sorts of reactions, especially feelings. Finally, this mode of thinking developed to the extent that Darwin [2] could write that "man himself cannot express love and humility by its external signs, so plainly as does a dog." Clearly we have here as flagrant a piece of anthropomorphism as one would care to find, even in as culpable a writer as Darwin is in this direction.[3]

In spite of the unsound foundation of the view that animals readily perform emotional behavior, psychologists generally accept the doctrine that present-day human conduct is continuous with that of the lower animals, with the implication that emotions are persisting potencies which operate as properties of men and animals.[4] Here is evidence that about as much violence can be done to scientific facts by the uncritical acceptance of a doctrine of continuity as of a doctrine of discontinuity. A careful study of actual behavior discloses definite continuities in the activities of man and animals which are occasioned by similar organizations and common external surroundings, but there are none the less quite as definite discontinuities between the two types of organisms due to disparities of biological and psychological development and differences in surroundings. It is safe to say that at the point of emotional behavior, observation discloses indefinitely more discontinuity than continuity.

But let us turn to actual observations themselves, for we must not dismiss the problem without an attempt to examine some types of animal behavior which appear to bear some resemblance to emotional activity in human beings. Consider the action of the chipmunk stimulated by approaching footsteps while he is calmly nibbling at some garden green. Immediately there is a start and shift of position while the animal turns to face squarely the approaching object; then it scampers toward its hole. Now, much as the activity just described may resemble an emotional situation, a careful examination

[1] What can be meant by "insulting" a monkey? Darwin, *Expressions of the Emotions*, p. 137.

[2] Loc. cit., p. 10.

[3] One is strongly reminded here of Darwin's violent assumptions concerning the exalted æsthetic development in animals, as described in connection with his theory of sexual selection.

[4] When not based upon observed facts such a doctrine would, of course, be a metaphysical proposition.

of the details indicates no breakdown of stimulus-response coördination. The start observed is nothing but the ordinary change of attitude we find in all attention responses. In fact this attention start, which superficially appears similar to an emotional phase of behavior, is always present, in addition to the emotional phase in all actual emotional conduct; and in sequence it precedes the emotion-initiating perceptual or ideational process. Far from proving the presence of emotional behavior in animals, the attention-start points to the possibility of describing whatever activity we find in animals in their ordinary surroundings by reference to the practically full complement of foundation response systems with which they adapt themselves. The animal is uninterruptedly performing such acts as the attention-start during each hour of its active life, and this fact would seem to indicate that these responses are due to a definite form of response system.

Similarly we often observe the activities of rats in experimental procedures in which they seem to break down in their behavior and either sit or lie down in a violently vibrating and trembling fit. While such behavior may plausibly fall within the range of an exceedingly elementary sort of emotional activity, it is a very doubtful example of genuine no-response conduct as we have described it. We do not believe that these activities are failures of stimulus-response coördinations to operate. Rather, we consider such actions to be entirely organic in their operation. We may add further that if one insists upon calling them emotions, they must be considered as absolutely different types of phenomena than human, no-response activities.

Considerable extenuation for the misinterpretation of facts respecting emotions in animals is discovered in the confusion of feelings and emotions by those who ascribe emotional conduct to animals. Without doubt the infrahuman animals perform elementary feeling responses and it is these that are called emotions. But even here a protest must be made against ascribing to animals the performance of sorrow, love, humility, and similar reactions.

The problem of emotions in infants reveals a similar dearth of condition capable of giving rise to emotional disturbances. The study of infants demonstrates the absence in the conduct histories of young children of the characteristic chaotic or no-response conditions with the replacement of necessary action by visceral and other reflexes. This condition is, of course, a decidedly temporary one, for as soon as any considerable development of reactional biography takes place, the stage is set for emotional behavior. As a matter of actual practise, however, it is rare that an infant who is not yet able to walk about and take care of itself alone should come into emotional stimuli situations. With children who do take care of themselves much of the true emotional activities may be performed but even here not very frequently.

Throughout our exposition we have made frequent references to the fact that emotional activities may be divided into two classes, namely, the elemental reactions performed under primarily natural conditions, and the more subtle and refined activity, constituting the individual's action in a more primarily human or societal setting. In the present section we wish to point out that in both of these general classes of emotional activities the acts may be more or less violent in operation. Accordingly, we might consider all of the emotional activities that a person performs as placed upon a unilinear intensity scale. Emotional activities of both the elemental and social sort may be looked upon as differing in strength of performance and intensity. It must be added, further, that because of the unlimited number of different possible situations in which both the elemental and societal emotional activities may occur, all degrees of intensity of emotional activity may actually be discovered to operate.

Types of<br>Emotional<br>Activities

In order to indicate some of the different degrees of intensity we might suggest the names of some of the societal, emotional activities which correspond to the elemental, emotional actions popularly called fear, rage, anger, etc. We may mention here the activity of being stunned, shocked, "struck dumb," abashed, surprised, disappointed. These different names may not only serve to indicate intensity degrees of societal emotional conduct found in different classes, but also each may itself be taken to refer to a different degree of intensity of societal activity in a specific class.

Emotional activities are not exceptions to the rule that all complex psychological phenomena have been historically subject to a great many misinterpretations. Emotional reactions especially have been regarded as connected in some way with the putative powers designated by the name of instincts. Hence they were thought of as internal forces outwardly expressed by instinct action, or as "mental" reverberations of conflicts between "instincts." In all of these views little justice has been done to emotional activities, first, as actual modes of action of the psychological individual, and secondly, as actual cases of no-response behavior.

Some<br>Misconcep-<br>tions Con-<br>cerning<br>Emotional<br>Conduct

By far the most glaring misconception concerning emotional conduct is that which makes such behavior consist of permanent entities which are transmitted from parent to offspring. This conception is a legacy that psychology has acquired from the tradition of biological abstractionism. We immediately face the question as to what is inherited and how. From the standpoint of animatistic psychology, one might say, of course, that a permanent state of mind may be inherited, but what bearing can such an assertion have upon the problems of objective psychology? When we confine our study to definite facts of behavior and reject the conception of emotion-cause and its manifestations, we find no specific kind of chaotic condition which is a permanent acquisition of the person and arousable to action by various sorts of stimulating objects or conditions. There are some who might say that the inheritance of emotions means that the individual is so constituted that he will suffer dissociation when put under certain kinds of stress.  How informing is this statement?  Is it not on a par with the assertion that the human individual is born to think, to perceive, to wear clothes, as well as to undergo various other experiences?

The doctrine of diuturnal inheritable emotions must inevitably make emotions into entities of some sort.  For consider that the doctrine requires nothing less than that a person should be equipped with some innate powers manifesting themselves in complex and peculiar activities in emotional situations.  Not the least objectionable consequence of the entity interpretation is that it implies a parallelism or an interactionism which always means an obscuring of actual events in human behavior.  An emotion comes to be either a cause, an effect, or an accompaniment of bodily activities.  Instead of describing emotional behavior, and indeed all other phenomena of the psychological domain, as actual organismic responses to specific stimulating circumstances, the attempt is made to describe behavior as manifestations of putative powers, or of certain substances resident in the individual.  In consequence the names of emotions, as well as of other classes of behavior, are hypostatized as unique qualities of mind.  The subjectivistic psychologist of emotions treats the behavior he studies much after the fashion in which the older ethicist handled the social activities he dealt with, and so fear, love, and anger became "properties" of the individual in a manner similar to that of the "virtues."

If anything can be clearly discovered from the observation and description of emotional behavior it is this: that such behavior occurs only under definite, external conditions and can therefore be described only in terms of such conditions.  The specific movements of, and changes in the individual are direct effects of definite external circumstances and are not expressions of innate and continuous entities.  This fact is, of course, no more true for emotions than for any other sort of behavior, but it requires special mention here, because the tradition has grown up that emotions are peculiar forces or tendencies which manifest themselves in many singular ways.  This is in effect making emotions, or the instincts presumed to operate with them, into final causes or primary principles of behavior of which the various activities of the human individual are the effects.

An excellent illustration of this attitude is the reiterated assertion that love, including all the acts referred to under this term, is the manifestation of a hidden force called the sexual instinct.  This sex-love situation admittedly constitutes a crucial instance because of the pervasiveness of sex behavior, but a critical examination of the facts involved offers sufficient evidence that every specific activity which we find in this series of behavior segments can be described without invoking any transexperiential causative factor.  The wide prevalence and constant occurrence of certain forms of behavior can be readily accounted for on the basis of incessant stimulation. Consequently, in the presence of all the multifarious sex stimulations, both social and physiological, constantly surrounding us, it would be very remarkable if there existed less sex activity in the form of actual sex behavior and discussion than we now find.

Among the conditions unwittingly or traditionally designed to induce sex stimulation are the divergent apparel, work, duties, virtues of men and women, all of which have developed with an uncanny inclination towards the emphasis of sexual differences. Moreover, modern civilization has tended more and more to make of woman a sex object, a stimulus to sex reaction. Possibly the reader will find just here a justification of the belief that a sex instinct-emotion is responsible for such social development as we have suggested. But is it of advantage to psychology, we might ask, to compromise our interpretations with a hopeless bias of immutable final causes, in view of the fact that we can readily convince ourselves of the existence of definite empirical facts to account for the kind of society that we have developed? Any critical investigation of differential phases of civilization as represented by different geographical, national, and temporal conditions, discloses enough verifiable economic, social, and religious motives to account for the peculiarities of our complex social behavior,

And now we must consider the biological facts of sex, those most potent sources of confusion in psychological investigations. Because the biological factors which condition psychological reactions are so imperious in their influence and so constant in their operation they have been repeatedly misinterpreted. Instead of being described as essential factors in organismic reactions they have been made into vital forces or purposes. Now it is obvious that the biological organization of the person, as the pre-psychological matrix of all human behavior, exerts great influence upon conduct, but it is just as obvious that the biological sex factors are simple stimulus-response activities. To consider the comparatively simple biochemical processes which operate as components in psychological reactions, as causes or representatives of vital causes, is to do violence to critical observation. Furthermore, it is not incorrect to say that the biological factors of sex, at the level of human psychological development, serve among many others as subordinate influences of behavior. Are we beyond understanding how physiological sex activity provides secondary excitements to behavior originally induced by primary interpersonal sex stimulation? And what of the numerous sex-gland and other reflexes which serve as important stimuli to sex behavior, both implicit and overt? Are these reflexes to be interpreted as anything but natural consequences of the metabolic conditions of the individual at the time? For if they are the results of such definite physiological processes, and who can doubt the fact, then they are, of course, the effects of immediately occurring and verifiable biological processes, and not the manifestations of mysterious instincts. Most infelicitous is the confusion of the directly observable biological processes which serve as stimuli for psychological behavior, with hidden forces which have no actual existence aside from their name.  Must we not conclude then, that the biological factors of sex, the sex structures and their functions, merely provide a foundation and a means for the operation of sex behavior, while the sex reflexes serve only as concrete stimuli for various kinds of reactions?

To believe that all the complex human sex actions are the manifestations of a sex-instinct-emotion is comparable to attributing the standing-up reactions of a child to an upright instinct, although in the latter case only the slightest amount of critical observation reveals that it is not because he has a standing-up instinct that the child is induced to acquire standing-up reactions, but because in addition to his peculiar biological structure he is living in a standing-up world.  All the objects and their settings are standing-up objects and it would be really impossible for the child to develop otherwise.  Here as elsewhere, of course, one can invoke an absolute teleological factor and say that an ultimate cosmic purpose has brought it about that the child should be born into a standing-up world.  But such a proposition contains its own answers.

If we have succeeded in making it at all plausible that the intricate emotional and feeling behavior of the sex type is to be interpreted primarily, if not exclusively, in terms of definite surrounding circumstances and the behavior equipment of the individual, it must appear that the same situation would be true in the case of other feeling behavior such as anger, grief, and fear.  In each case, the specific phases of the behavior event can be correlated with a stimulating object or condition.  The names given to the events denote concretely occurring phenomena and not ends which are being worked out through prearranged machinery.  Unfortunately, psychologists have been in the habit of considering emotional responses as innate, feeling activities much after the fashion in which they have thought of instincts as innate, knowledge, or effective action processes.  And this condition prevails in spite of the fact that every observation of fear or anger behavior strongly suggests that no matter what action occurs, it is a direct function, in a mathematical sense, of changes that are taking place in the psychological environment of the individual.

What is more natural than that a person should attempt to strike back when struck and, if prevented by being held, that he should kick, cry, and seek other means of releasing himself and doing damage to his opponent?  This whole activity may be called an anger stimulus and response situation, but in no sense must we speak of the striking out, the breath holding, the snarling and the crying as "emotional manifestations" of an anger "emotion."  Can there be any other explanation than that the variable and unpredictable occurrences in an emotional situation are the results of a series of specific external stimulations?  When the name of the total behavior stands for an actual emotional reaction, is it not derived from the mere fact that an emotional factor is included, although that factor is of the briefest duration? For the most part, however the actions taking place in the total situation can be analyzed into volitions, habits, perceptual responses, etc. Do psychologists mean by an "emotion" anything more than some event hypostatized through the medium of a name?

In the study of emotional activity and affective behavior a peculiar condition has existed in recent decades. On the one hand, such study has led workers on these types of activity to stress somatic and general bodily factors, while on the other, emotional and feeling reactions have been considered as the most elusive inner and subjectivistic phenomena not readily amenable to the ordinary methods of investigation.

This condition is excellently illustrated by the so-called James-Lange theory of emotions, the main point of which turns about the problem of harmonizing the directness and immediacy of emotional conduct with the apparently necessary cognition of what sort of act should occur. The pre-Jamesian view was interpreted in the following manner. The stimulus object excites a mental state (emotion) which is followed by an appropriate bodily expression. Not unlike his predecessors James was a mentalist, and consequently thought of an emotion as a "state of mind," but he saw clearly the necessity of connecting it very closely with overt activities if the description was to be at all in consonance with the facts. As a result, James was led to assert that the emotion proper follows the bodily expression.

Now although the James-Lange theory does fair justice to a number of the actual facts in emotional behavior, it involves, however, a number of fundamental errors and confusions. Among the facts that it takes account of are the immediacy and directness of organic happenings and the more or less closely subsequent simple realization of what has transpired, or the elaborate knowledge of the character of the stimulus object or situation.

The primary difficulty with such a view as James', however, is that it perpetuates the intolerable animatistic tradition insofar as it makes emotional conduct consist of an "emotion" in the form of a "mental state" feeling of organic changes, while the "bodily" or organic functioning is presumed to be the expression of the emotion.

Closely connected with this primary error and as a means of carrying it out, is the confusion of the different behavior segments. In the first place, the upholders of the James-Lange theory confuse the second post-emotional behavior segment of our description with the emotional action proper, by thinking of it as the essential feature (mental component) which is presumed to follow the operation of the organic or visceral factors.

In the second place, the visceral reflexes, which are really replacement actions, are considered to be positive reactional features instead of the grossest sort of substitutes for an action that is precluded from

26

occurring.   It is the belief that these replacement reflexes are positive
direct responses which is at the basis of the conception of the utilitarian character of emotional behavior.

As a final comment upon the perspectival background of the study
of emotional phenomena, we might say that although from a quite
early period the descriptions of emotional and affective conduct carried within them the germs of an objective psychology, such activities
have nevertheless seemed to resist any genuine naturalistic description.   The study of emotional behavior constitutes in a genuine way
one of the actual historical beginnings of a behavioristic attitude in
psychology.

# CHAPTER XVII

## WISHING, DESIRING, AND KINDRED FORMS
## OF RESPONSES

**General
Nature of
Desire Re-
sponses**

In studying the psychological facts of desiring and kindred conduct, we propose first to describe in a preliminary way all the specific
types of such behavior included in this chapter under the simple term
of desire or desiring behavior.  In thus treating wanting, wishing, and
similar conduct, we will determine the general characteristics distinguishing such behavior from other types of psychological phenomena.
After this general description we will indicate some specific differences
between the particular and distinct forms of desiring conduct, such
as wanting, longing, yearning, etc.  As will appear in the sequel, this
plan is not unrecommended by various considerations of expediency.

An important general feature of desiring conduct is that, as specific
reactions, such behavior consists essentially of decidedly implicit reaction systems to objects, persons, and conditions of all sorts.  Desiring reactions are consequently always mediate activities.  They involve the intervention of substitute stimuli between the acting person
and the adjustment stimuli objects and conditions.  Such reactions
always symptomatize a detachment of the individual from the adjustment stimulus, so that his action upon that object is prevented,
inhibited, or delayed.  The substitution is not necessarily due to the
absence of the adjustment stimulus object.

On the contrary, the adjustment stimuli objects are very frequently
present and in immediate spatial contact with the acting person.  In
many cases the objects and conditions constituting the stimuli of our
most intense desiring reactions are in plain sight of and in easy approach to the acting person, but he can nevertheless react to them only
in an implicit way.  He may desire some object, wish he had it or desire to make some changes in its activities.  Now from the standpoint
of implicitness and so far as the details of the responses to the stimulus
object are concerned, all of these actions are on a par with retrospect-
ing or musing.

The fact that the desiring individual while performing implicit
reactions is very often in immediate proximity to the desired object
is extremely important.  For this circumstance informs us adequately
concerning some behavior details involved in desiring reactions.
Among these details we observe the thorough participation of the person in the action which he is performing.  In some types of desiring
behavior the person may be exerting himself considerably, performing

28

many external and visible movements, as well as organic and visceral actions of various sorts. So numerous in fact are his apparent surface actions and so intense may his response be, that in many cases it is fair to call the desiring responses semi- instead of fully implicit actions. This is especially the case when they are stimulated by exceedingly intolerable conditions, which require modification or the person's removal to more desirable circumstances.

Howsoever active the person may be in the performance of certain desiring reactions, such activity as desiring behavior never reaches the condition of actual effective behavior. To be more concrete, desiring conduct does not constitute any action upon objects in the form of changing or manipulating them in any way, although obviously desiring responses may be very intimately connected with effective activity.

An essential qualitatively distinguishing mark of desiring reactions is that they constitute shifting status responses. Namely, they consist of actions describable as unstable and shifting with respect to their coördinate stimuli objects. Hence, they may be considered as tense and even incipient acts looking toward the modification and manipulation of objects (creating, improving, or destroying), the effecting of some change in their relations (possibly disposing of them), or the performing of some mutual action with respect to them (playing or living with them).

Our description of desiring reactions has sufficiently indicated, then, that such behavior frequently and perhaps usually constitutes very intimate and personal responses. They are exceedingly personal in the sense that they are peculiar to a specific individual since they involve particular stimulating objects which can be desiring stimuli only for certain persons under given conditions. In the case of desiring situations we find a greater emphasis than in almost any other behavior circumstances upon the varying possibilities that exist between the natural properties of objects and their stimulating functions. Many large classes of desiring actions (the idiosyncratic type) cannot occur at all with some individuals who are simply never aroused to desire certain things. The mode and intensity of desire responses also vary with respect to particular objects and conditions.

Desiring reactions are intimate also in the sense that they involve, in many cases, at least, the intimate operation of the entire individual, including his organic activity. Many desiring reactions and especially the more elementary types go deeply into the person's response factors. It is the latter types that exhibit very profound organic and general visceral functioning. In this way they simulate the affective responses, although they are on the whole very different forms of behavior. In more complicated responses we may expect, of course, to find such organic or visceral factors less prominent although they may still be actually operating in the specific reaction systems.

Still another important characteristic of desiring responses is that they are decidedly continuous or prolonged. They require time in which to operate. In every case it can be clearly observed that they go on for a definite period of time. Their length and duration naturally depend upon the fact that a condition of satisfaction is involved; some kind of object or thing must be obtained; some change in an object or condition must be brought about in order to complete or carry out one's action. In general, desiring action tends to relieve the tension and the instability of relations between the person and the stimulus object. The individual must be able to proceed from the stage of general arousedness and perhaps uneasiness which the substitution stimulus incites, to some definitive form of contact with the adjustment stimulus, whether it be the same actual object or some other. Generally speaking, then, the length and specific type of the desiring act depend upon the availability of the satisfying object or condition, and the ease and rapidity with which the individual can perform the act which results in satisfaction or finally, perhaps, upon whether the person is removed from contact with the substitution stimulus. An unsatisfied desire that can never be really satisfied by a change of action with respect to the adjustment stimulus, may continue only so long as the person remains in proximity to the substitution stimulus.

Whatever duration a desire reaction has, whether it is definitively satisfied or temporarily appeased, it is considered to have a definite temporal limit. In either case the action is finished and complete. Just what this point signifies may be seen from the fact that in cases in which the desiring reactions are definitively satisfied, the activity is entirely terminated and is not in any sense revivable, although the individual may again perform desiring reactions with respect to the same object.

Analysis
of Desire
Reaction
Systems

That desiring reactions constitute many types of specific responses to desiderata of various sorts, we have already suggested. We may add further that the specific instances within the general types vary greatly between certain limits, which means that the specific reaction systems for desiring conduct cover a large variety of forms. However, we may still indicate in a more or less abstract manner the essential characteristics of desiring reaction systems.

Prominent in desiring reaction systems are the cognitive or discriminative factors, which operate not only in the complex desiring responses but likewise in the simple ones. Even in performing comparatively simple desire reactions, one may wish very decidedly for a particular thing with certain qualities, so we must assume that an important place is occupied in every instance by the discrimination factor in the desiring reaction system.

When the desired object substitutes for itself the discrimination refers, of course, to the qualities and conditions of the object with which the person is in immediate contact. When desiring reactions are stimulated by some object other than the desideratum, then the appreciation of the qualities of the latter (and sometimes also its relation to the substitute stimulus) becomes, in addition to an identification of the qualities of the substitute object, an element in the reaction system.

With respect to the attention factor in desiring reaction systems, we might indicate that it too is of a specialized form. It tends practically always toward a deliberate direction of the person toward desiderata. Very seldom, if ever, are things desired because they force themselves upon the individual. Rather the person actualizes objects into desire stimuli as the result of considerable previous development of action with respect to the desired objects.

As conspicuous features in many forms of desiring reactions we find various affective factors. In many instances, desiring reactions approach in descriptive character the same type of action that we call affective or feeling responses. In other cases, there is very little likeness present. In fact a decided similarity may be noted between many types of desiring activity and the more colorless intellectual actions.

The receptor mechanisms in desiring reaction systems function primarily in the contacts of the reacting individual with the objects serving as the substitute stimuli for the desiderata, whether or not the latter are the same as the substitute stimuli. When the substitute stimuli are concrete objects, we can fairly definitely trace out the number and the specific types of receptor mechanisms operating in the desire reaction. On the other hand, when the desire stimulus is some organic need or condition, the receptor mechanisms cannot be so definitely discovered.

Since desiring reaction systems are frequently similar to affective unit responses we expect them to include the vigorous operation of glandular mechanisms. This is especially true for the desiring types called cravings. In the desires for food and sex objects and for alimentary and sexual satisfaction we may isolate with exactness and certainty the particular glandular mechanisms operating in specific desiring reaction systems.

On the whole, the muscular mechanisms of the external skeletal types of action have a minor place in desiring reaction systems. This is true even though in the total behavior segment the person exerts considerable muscular effort.

The most important point to be noted with respect to neural mechanisms is that in the craving and appetite forms of desire activities, the autonomic neural functions play a very considerable rôle along with the central neural mechanisms. In other desiring reaction systems the autonomic functions are of course not so prominent.

We might suggest once more that the types of desiring reaction systems are very numerous and that in attempting an analysis of them we can do no more than mention the striking variations and similarities found in a comparison of desiring behavior with other varieties of psychological action.

Strictly speaking the term desire stands for a specific type of reaction system. When this reaction system operates in behavior segments it is usually such a prominent factor in the total activity that it gives the name to the whole segment. In other words we may look upon it as a desire segment of behavior. This is not to deny, of course, that in some behavior segments the desire reaction system is overshadowed by some other type of reaction system. This, however, is the exception rather than the rule.

Behavior segments of the desire sort may be divided into two distinct classes. First, we have the behavior segments in which the desire reaction system constitutes a precurrent or anticipatory reaction system, in the sense that it precedes, and perhaps determines, what the following reaction system will be. That is to say, in a given behavior segment we locate (a) the attending reaction system to a stimulus object, (b) the perceiving of it, (c) a desiring response with respect to it and (d) the act of securing the object, or obtaining the means to secure it. It is the desiring reaction system that determines the operation of the act of securing or attempting to secure the object in question.

On the other hand, the desiring reaction system in a behavior segment may serve as a final or consummatory activity. Here is an object which the individual attends to and perceives and, so far as the particular behavior segment is concerned, an object which he vainly desires to possess. The responding individual fully appreciates that he cannot further perform a reaction with respect to the object in question, even though that reaction signifies in the final analysis merely a change of status of the individual with respect to the object. In spite of the inevitable futility of the action the person none the less desires the object. In the latter situation we must think of the desiring activity as a consummatory response and not as a precurrent or anticipatory activity.

Reverting to desiring reaction systems as precurrent phases of behavior segments, we may point out that a large number of types of such precurrent desiring reactions may be isolated in various desire behavior segments. In the first place, as in our illustration, we have desiring reactions precurrent to effective responses. In these cases the individual desires something which he wishes to touch, manipulate, possess, or toward which he wishes in some other way to perform some effective response.

In other situations the desiring reaction system is precurrent to informational reactions. The final response then in the behavior segment is an informational activity of some sort which is led up to and determined by a desiring reaction system. This information may refer to some specific knowledge about an object or situation which may or may not lead to further performative responses or it may be general, theoretical or orientational activity having no connection with performative behavior.

Another type of desiring behavior segment is that in which the precurrent, desiring, reaction system anticipates or determines the operation of some sort of affective response. Such situations are illustrated by desiring activity which leads to acts in which the consummatory response is the enjoyment of some thing or some situation. These final activities, again, may or may not be further connected with performative activities of some sort.

With respect to consummatory desire responses we may say that they represent the final or the completed stages of behavior segments, which may be preceded by any and every type of antecedent reaction. They may follow simple attention and perceptual reaction systems or responses to objects in the immediate surroundings of the person, or reactions to organic stimuli located in the individual's own organism.

More complicated consummatory desire reaction systems are found in behavior segments where the final desiring responses are preceded by ideational reaction systems of various types. Here the person's desire is determined by knowledge concerning the desiderata, or he desires something as a result of a problem solving activity or because of a complex decision or reflection with respect to the desired object. Similar complex consummatory desire reaction systems also follow complicated affective responses. On the whole, in these situations we find more abstract and subtle desiring reactions than in the consummatory desire responses preceded by simple attentional and perceptual reactions.

Because of the extreme prominence and prolonged character of desire activities in the lives of human beings, we find that they not only constitute particular momentary adaptations to immediate surroundings but also that they have a place in many of our complicated behavior situations. In short, desire behavior segments assume a large place in typical human behavior. This is true not only of complicated desire actions; mere cravings in their humanly conditioned character also play a large rôle in a person's adaptations. A considerable amount of our action is based directly upon or is influenced by desires. Either they condition the occurrence of some activities or modify the manner, time, or place of their happening. *The Place of Desires Behavior Segments in Behavior Situations*

Human striving toward some goal or end has always a firm foundation in various kinds of desires. The attempt to achieve some different condition or to modify one's self may be traced back to, or found to be conditioned by, the person's various desires. In general, the activity of aiming at some different, higher, or better form of existence involves desires developed as specific responses in the form of dissatisfaction, ferment, or general instability of behavior status with respect to the particular surroundings of the individual. In other words, desiring reactions may be considered to be the essential details of activities which constitute transforming behavior conduct which operates to modify or to bring more or less change in the surroundings of the psychological organism.

Similarly, we find that desire plays a strong part in more specific behavior situations. In almost every case where such relationship is possible our beliefs are strongly influenced by our desires with respect to specific objects and general situations. It is a very common observation that what we believe and the direction in which our beliefs are inclined, are influenced to a considerable extent by things and conditions desired by us, both when such desires are and are not known to us. Again, the type of knowledge we have concerning particular objects, and the degree of interest we display in acquiring specific information about them, are strongly conditioned by our desires respecting the particular object or some more general situation. Throughout the entire gamut of human conduct there are infinite illustrations to be found which demonstrate how imposing a place desiring behavior segments command in our complicated behavior situations.

**Differentiation of Desiring Activity from Purposive Conduct**

Desiring behavior bears some very close resemblances to other types of action. It is consequently very important to indicate the differences between these similar activities. In the chapter on affective conduct we have already had occasion to distinguish between feeling and desiring reactions. A similar differentiation must be made here between purposing and desiring actions which likewise possess many common elements. Such a comparative study appears essential when we consider that some of the primary traits of both desiring and purposing behavior, namely, their prolonged character and peculiar connection with their respective stimuli objects and conditions, make it easy for us to mistake the form and operation of one for those of the other.

First, we might consider that in spite of the fact that desiring actions appear to influence the person and his conduct over a long period of time, as is the case with purposing behavior, nevertheless the analysis of the desiring behavior situation indicates that it is quite definitely limited in time. In contrast with desiring actions purposive behavior is practically indefinite in its duration. We do not mean to imply that desiring reactions may not require a long time for their performance or that purposing actions cannot be concluded in a brief space of time. The point to be noted is that, by comparison, purposive action is not confined to stated temporal limits.

Very closely connected with the comparison of purposing and desiring conduct just discussed is the fact that desiring reactions always consist of behavior segments of a simple or complex type, whereas purposing conduct constitutes simple or complex situations. In each case the activities under discussion may belong to larger behavior situations but the fact remains that in the case of purposing activities, the situations always comprise a more extensive scope of behavior.

A cardinal distinction between desiring and purposing action refers to the comparative primacy of the stimulus or the response factors in the respective activities. In desiring activity the reactionistic emphasis is upon the response rather than upon the stimulus or the stimuli conditions. The individual is bent upon securing something or upon modifying a condition which is not satisfactory to him. Whatever control the stimulus object or situation exercises upon the desiring person, is due entirely to reactional factors based upon his behavior equipment and previous experience with the same object or similar objects. That is to say, things exert an influence upon the person primarily because he is interested in them or desires them, and not because they possess dominating qualities or characteristics.

Contrariwise, in purposive action since the emphasis is upon the stimulus situation, the individual performs prolonged behavior which is determined mainly by the character of the conditions and the hold they have upon him. For instance, he may be controlled by certain stimuli entirely against any desire of his own. It is this emphasis of the stimulating conditions in purposive conduct that makes such activity into situations rather than restricted behavior segments.

Because purposive activity is conditioned by the character of the stimuli situations rather than by the individual's reactional conditions we naturally find that on the reaction side it is not so definitely localized as desiring behavior. Even though the stimulus object of the desire reaction may be a condition which cannot be removed in any direct way, and therefore is involved with a complex series of actions on the part of the person, the entire behavior circumstances are nevertheless fairly definitely isolable and describable. In the case of purposive conduct, on the contrary, and especially in every complex situation the reactional factors in the behavior circumstance cannot very well be isolated.

For instance, the person may be carrying out a very large plan or purpose which itself may be inadequate, but because it represents an attempt to modify his present situation it can be called a single form of action. The indefiniteness and unlocalizability of purposing behavior is possibly due to its frequent negative character; that is, the purpose may be removal from or avoidance of some condition or circumstance. The negative character of behavior is, however, not limited to purposing activities.

In still other ways desiring reactions may be differentiated from purposive conduct. It is easily recognized that desiring behavior is much more personal and intimate than purposive conduct. This condition follows from the fact that desiring reactions are more intimately related to the person's status and needs than to the requirements of the stimuli. For this reason, desiring reactions are more definitely focussed upon the individual's activities than upon the results to things which is true of purposive conduct.

We note once more that desiring reactions may or may not require other activities in order to be carried out. Purposing reactions, on the other hand, are always at the basis of other acts; that is, they require the performance of additional activity in order to be accomplished themselves. But desiring acts need not be thought of as connected with any further acts at all. Indeed, when they are so connected they may be considered as the results or effects of other actions. This is not true of purposing action, which is itself the condition or cause of the happening of other kinds of behavior. Another way to state this difference is that the acts connected with desiring responses are means to bring about satisfaction of desires, while actions connected with purposing responses are performed as ends or as the results of conditions initiated by the purposing reaction.

The comparative nature of desiring and purposing behavior may be well indicated by pointing out that every complicated desiring reaction is convertible into a purposing response. This means that the stimulus for every complicated desire may become functionally a general purpose for the carrying out of which many subordinate activities are necessary. Thus, even so simple a desire as that for some particular kind of food may, depending upon the availability of the adjustment stimulus and the energy expended in obtaining it, constitute an elaborate purposing behavior situation, in the sense that many acts are performed and many conditions overcome in satisfying the desire. This transforming of a desiring into a purposing behavior is further illustrated by the complex case of the person who desires to be well thought of. Such a general response to a social stimulus involves numerous series of discriminating responses to things and situations. A large general difference between desiring and purposing activity issues from our comparison, namely, that whenever a desiring action develops into a purposing act we find that the desire response itself becomes the stimulus for the carrying out of many subordinate actions, all of which serve as parts of the general response to satisfy the desire.

In general, desiring activities may become purposing responses when the desires are not satisfied. When the individual desires some object which is important to him or some change of vital significance in circumstances, those stimuli conditions may themselves become of primary importance in behavior situations. Consequently, the individual is controlled by the stimuli objects, and the center of the whole activity is changed from the original desire response to the stimulus object or situation. In this manner the entire behavior becomes transformed in character, taking on the characteristics of the purposive situation.

When we turn to the distinctly stimulational factors in desiring and purposing conduct, we also find important differences of various kinds. Primary among these differences is the fact that in purposing behavior segments the stimuli objects and conditions exert a more or less general influence over the individual's action, and determine his performance of many diverse kinds of behavior. Desiring stimuli, on the contrary, serve merely to arouse a specific form of want or wish.

Thus the stimuli for purposing activity are much less definitely located than those for desiring behavior. This is true partly for the reason that the stimuli objects and conditions of purposing activity are circumstances of greater magnitude and importance to the reacting individual than those of desiring activity. On the whole, they are also less tangible objects and situations than desire stimuli. So definitely may desiring behavior stimuli be located that they are sometimes found to consist of changes and modifications inside the person's own organism. This is seldom, if ever, the case in purposive behavior.

Finally, when the stimuli for desiring reactions become so imperative, by virtue of difficulty in carrying out responses to them, that they resemble the behavior situation of the purposive type, they may still be differentiated from the latter. And how? Because purposing stimuli induce the operation of effective responses whereas desire stimuli, no matter how intense, elicit only non-effective behavior. In point of fact the more intense and pressing the stimulus, the more decidedly implicit the desiring response.

Three distinct stimuli problems for desiring behavior may be isolated. One of these refers to the type of objects which constitute desiderata. The second concerns the specific operation of desiring stimuli, while the third involves the question as to their varying intensities.

**Stimuli for Desiring Behavior**

With respect to things serving as stimuli for desiring reactions, it may be said that objects, situations, circumstances, conditions, persons, etc., in short, any type of thing or condition that can serve as a psychological stimulus at all, may operate to arouse desire and kindred forms of responses. Whatever objects possess qualities, attributes, or properties usable in any way or intrinsically worth while or agreeable may constitute stimuli for desiring or wanting responses. Such reactions refer to possession, change, removal or other conduct with respect to objects and their qualities or properties.

It must be distinctly understood that tangible objects of all sorts are considered only a single type of desiring stimuli. Intangible objects of every variety, and impossible or non-existent conditions or situations likewise serve to elicit desires. Desire reactions may have for their adjustment stimuli one's lost and misspent youth, the city of God, the golden age, in fact anything that can be verbally or symbolically substituted for. Whether a person desires primarily tangible or intangible, possible or impossible things, is a matter of specific individual differences and the factors that such differences entail.

Acts of the desiring person or of some other individual or group of individuals provide further desiring stimuli. We may consider as adjustment stimuli, the crossing of the street, the ability to read, write, add, or the performance of some other kind of action. In more complex situations adjustment stimuli for desiring conduct may be the wish to achieve some complex end or result through action of a particular type.  A good example of an action serving as a substitute stimulus is a hunger reflex which calls out a desiring or craving response either to some certain kind of food or to food in general.  In this situation the substitute stimulus may arouse a reaction either directly to the adjustment stimulus object, or through the intermediation of some other kind of implicit action such as the idea or thought of the food.  In this general type of situation the interoceptive reflex stimulus may operate in conjunction with some stimulation by an object in the general external surroundings of the person.  Among the acts of other persons that stimulate desire responses in us are the good opinion and admiration that they maintain with respect to us, as well as their carrying out of our directions and requests.  Also one may desire or wish that another person perform less complex acts with respect to oneself, something, or object.

Persons themselves and their characteristics stimulate all sorts of desire and wish reactions.  Individuals stimulate others to desire contact with them in various ways, for instance, to have intellectual, social, personal, sexual or domestic relations with them.

Among the conditions constituting prominent forms of desire stimuli we place economic conditions and circumstances in an outstanding position.  Closely following these are political and domestic situations of all types which the reacting individual wishes or desires to have effectively modified in order to make for more comfortable and more convenient conditions.

Goals or ends, whether consisting primarily of concrete conditions and situations or of intangible ideals, serve to stimulate the individual to perform many different types of desire and wishing reactions. The more concrete of such stimuli situations call out responses of a definite desiring and wishing sort, whereas intangible desiring stimuli are correlated with longings and yearnings, whether or not sharply defined, to the individual himself.

An important question with respect to all stimuli objects for desiring conduct concerns their relative isolability.  In many cases the stimulus object operates so as to arouse a desire response entirely uncomplicated by other objects or situations.  In still other instances, however, desiring stimuli are closely interrelated with other types. In fact, the stimulus object may be so intimately associated with other objects that the person, in addition to being stimulated to desire this object, is at the same time aroused to perform other reactions. When I desire to purchase a particular kind of utensil I may be simultaneously stimulated to make many inquiries and to visit many shops in order to satisfy the desire.[1]  This interconnection between stimuli provides a basis for distinguishing between different kinds of desiring

---

[1] The responses additional to the desire reaction are clearly connected with the latter.  Otherwise we should have the ordinary situation in which an object calls out more than one kind of action, that is to say, performs several stimulational functions.

stimuli objects.' Thus we differentiate between goal and goalless desire stimuli. Goal stimuli involve two conditions, only one of which is found in the goalless type. The first condition is that they elicit desire reactions that lead to specific satisfaction, and the second, that they necessitate a complex of behavior to bring this satisfaction about. Only goal desire stimuli possess both conditions, while all desire stimuli have the first. It may be added here that all of the behavior involved in goal stimulation may be performed in contact with a single object. To illustrate, the desiring reaction may be satisfied by merely taking and retaining the desired object.

Since desiring responses are implicit activities and therefore are performed in contact with objects having a double stimulational function (adjustment and substitute), it follows that the stimuli operate differently. We find that in simpler cases the same natural objects, persons, or situations serve both functions. In other words, some particular object stimulates a desire for itself. Some object not possessed by the individual may stimulate him to desire to appropriate it as his own.

It is in more complicated situations that we find different objects and situations serving the two stimulational functions. For instance, undesirable or unsatisfactory conditions surrounding an individual constitute the stimulus for the desiring of a better condition. Just what objects or conditions can serve to arouse desiring reactions to other objects or conditions depend upon innumerable specific factors. A mere resemblance or a slight similarity between two different objects or some condition involving the combined operation of the two objects or situations upon the person at some past time may serve to arouse a desiring reaction.

A very important observation in connection with the dual stimulational function in desiring behavior segments is that the substitute stimulus may actually and directly arouse a desiring reaction which leads the person, once he is stimulated, to desire not the arousing object but the thing for which it substitutes. Were it not that the person's desire is actually directed toward the adjustment stimulus object, the exciting object would not be a substitute. Frequently, because of the potency of an exciting stimulus to arouse a desiring action, the substituting stimulus object determines which object shall be desired as well as arousing a desire for it. Seeing my friend injured by another person, I desire not only to avenge him but to perform the avenging in a particular way. Naturally, the influence of the stimuli here is derived from the behavior equipment possessed by the desiring person as well as from the conditions under which the action occurs.

Desiring reactions are rather singular with respect to the great influence exerted upon their stimuli objects by the settings or the milieu in which they function. Always less definite forms of behavior than effective activity, desiring responses are more extensively conditioned by various surrounding circumstances. In other words, great relativity prevails with respect to the desirability of objects so far as calling out desiring reactions is concerned. Things, and especially articles of wearing apparel, do not appeal to us nor call out desiring reactions unless they are popular and worn by many people, or unless they are exclusive and worn by only a few. The probability that an object or situation will elicit desiring responses depends, in many cases, upon how far removed it is from our present intellectual or effective behavior condition, since we are frequently prone to magnify the value and merits of things not available or believed to be not available for our purposes.

**Degrees of Intensity of Desiring Reactions**    Desiring responses of the same general type are subject to differentiation on the basis of the degree of intensity with which they operate. Within any one type, desiring reactions may be represented upon a scale of action starting from indifferent behavior with respect to some object or condition to very intense conduct stimulated by the same object. Not only do such stimuli arouse a person to desire something but the more intense of them stimulate him to work for its satisfaction. While one is acquiring a desiring reaction to certain objects, the objects not only take on the desiring stimulational function but also the capacity to force the individual to seek satisfaction of the desire. It is such intense desiring reactions that in popular psychology are designated as willing action. A person acting in this way is popularly thought of as exhibiting the will to do or get something.

So intense and powerful do desiring reactions become at times that they may take complete possession of the individual and dominate his entire activities. In such instances the person is so completely absorbed by his desire for some object that he cannot think of anything unrelated to the desideratum.

The degrees of intensity characteristic of desiring reactions have their sources in different conditions. For instance, the intensity may be due to the character and properties of the stimulus object or situation. Wealth and social position in a pecuniary society possess irresistible properties of an inherent sort that stimulate exceedingly intense desires. On the other hand, the intensity may depend upon circumstances not intrinsic to the desiderata but closely connected with the latter. Perhaps the possession of the object is of extreme importance in carrying on some type of work or in enhancing the acting person's prestige.

The source of the intensity of desiring reactions may also be located in the personality make-up of the individual. Persons of the enthusiastic type, when in contact with things which favor desiring action, become aroused to desire particular objects with extraordinary intensity. Similarly, specific conditions of the person not only augment but make inevitable the intensive operation of desire responses. The desire for food or particular kinds of food is especially intensified when the person is hungry as compared with situations in which hunger is not a potent factor.

It may be superfluous to remark that the degree of intensity with which desiring responses operate depends entirely upon the nature of the reacting persons and the particular situations involved. This point is again suggested, however, in order to indicate that the statements made about desiring reactions refer to behavior of a particular character which operates more or less intensely because of specified conditions. It is quite a different problem that is concerned with the conditions determining whether desiring actions shall operate at all. To the study of this problem we devote our next section.

Desiring reactions, because of their personal and intimate character, are subject to a number of conditions which affect their occurrence. These conditions may be subdivided into reactional (personality) and stimulational types.

Conditions Influencing Desiring Reactions

Our first consideration concerns the reactional conditions of desire. It is at once clear that desiring responses are to a considerable extent determined in their occurrence and character by the individual's behavior equipment. Such equipmental influences, for example, may be due to the individual's possession of particular knowledge concerned with desiderata, intellectual attitudes of approval or disapproval, and the capacity to imagine things with respect to the desiderata and the performance of desiring behavior, etc.

Knowledge of the existence of things and of conditions capable of serving as adjustment stimuli is an essential factor in the operation of desiring reactions. What we do not know or do not know about we cannot desire. Quite necessary is cognizance of the nature and uses of things in order to desire them either in general or to fill some specific need. Frequently it is precisely the lack of knowledge concerning things which makes them appear desirable. Knowledge also influences desire by virtue of the individual's awareness of his needs.

Again, in many instances desire for things depends upon one's capacity for obtaining them. Oftentimes the impossibility of obtaining desired things or of securing them within a stated period inhibits desiring reactions; on the other hand, such incapacity may itself be a factor in desiring. In other instances the presence or absence in the individual's equipment of various affective responses to particular objects has a very decided influence upon his desiring reactions to such objects.

Additional important reactional conditions which influence desiring behavior are found in the more general behavior equipment acquired by deliberate training or casual past experiences. Among such equipmental influences we find interests of all sorts, as well as a variety of character traits derived from the individual's previous contacts with objects. Thus, an individual who has acquired in his equipment coveting and envying responses of various sorts is stimulated by various things and persons to perform many desiring activities. Similarly, the acquisition in the person's reactional biography of likes, dislikes, and preferences of given types later determine whether or not he desires particular objects.

Nor must we overlook in an individual's cultural development and surroundings the many conditioning circumstances that aid in determining the occurrence and nature of desiring activities. In such cultural development are built up the various evaluations of objects, the attitudes which lead to the choice of certain things, and the endowment of them with properties of desirability. Such culturalization likewise results in the acquisition of various conformities of approval and disapproval of things and actions, which in turn have an exceedingly potent influence upon the desiring of such objects.

Institutional conditions such as custom, law, and public opinion decidedly alter our desiring reactions. They not only severally and totally condition the availability of desiderata which can be reacted to, but also make things undesirable by restrictions and mandates of recognized sorts. When the state demands it, men vie with one another in the intensity of their desire to die for a great cause. It is a most interesting phenomenon that the mere prohibition of alcoholic beverages in a state or community induces not only desires but tremendous cravings for alcohol.

Not only equipmental factors but also immediate behavior circumstances condition desiring conduct. For example, memorial activity in an outstanding manner influences desiring behavior. For manifestly, unless one recalls having seen or having otherwise been in contact with certain objects, he cannot develop or perform desiring reaction with respect to them. In the same way the performance of some planning or other thinking reaction, or an action constituting the exercise of some present or immediate interest, affects what we desire. To sum up, almost any action may indicate or bring out a need which results in the performance of some form of desiring behavior.

Let us turn now to the stimulational conditions of desiring reactions. Whether or not we have desires, or desire a certain object necessarily depends upon the presence of such an object in our surroundings or in our past contact with this or a similar type of object. Such dependence of the individual's behavior upon his stimuli surroundings is, of course, typical of all psychological conduct; but it has especial significance here, since desiring actions are somewhat detached actions and therefore always primarily reactional in character. So much is true for momentarily acquired and momentarily operating desire responses. For the operation of desiring reactions which function in a definitely secondary manner, however, that is, without the presence of the desideratum, the importance of this point must be still more strongly emphasized.

A great many desiring reactions are momentarily acquired and The Origin and Development of Desire momentarily occurring. They constitute reactions developed in some immediate situation through the first contact of the person with a desirable or valuable object. The desire to touch, seize, possess, or otherwise change one's reactional status toward some specific object may have no previous history beyond the immediate situation. The mere act of attending to and identifying some valuable or desirable thing results at once in a desiring response. To be sure, this behavior circumstance depends upon the individual's reactional biography, but there are no specific influences from the person's development to affect this particular incident. In other words, it may be an entirely accidental and unlooked-for occurrence.

Most frequently such momentarily acquired desires last only as long as the individual is in contact with the desired object. As soon as his attention is attracted elsewhere or as soon as he is called upon to perform an action to some other thing, his desiring response to the previous stimulus object disappears. In fact, he may never again desire that or a similar thing.

Desire responses in other situations constitute a type of action requiring an appreciable time for its development. The desiring response, when it is once fully established, may have behind it a record of cumulative effects which are summed up in the present desire response. It may be thought of, then, as having been gradually learned or acquired over a period of time. Once it is initiated, it may be considered a more or less permanent equipmental activity. It is this kind of action more than any other type of desire that most closely resembles purposing activity. Furthermore, desiring reactions of this type may also function as the stimulus for genuine purposing activity, although in themselves they are decidedly nothing more than desiring actions. Developed desires, therefore, at least as long as they endure, may properly be called desire attitudes. On the desiring level they compare with intellectual and affective attitudes.

On the whole, since the developed and attitudinal forms of desiring reactions are related to goals, they are more prominent factors in arousing the person's psychological activities than are other desires. In addition, they are probably on the whole more insistent upon satisfaction. Not only does the stimulating object put the person into a state of unbalanced reactional status with respect to it, but it also induces him to perform some action in order to change this condition.

As we have just indicated, the operation of desire reactions may be Satisfaction of Desires divided into two general forms. On the one hand, we have the reaction of desiring or wanting something which may have no issue in conduct. If the desire is intense, the person finds himself in a very uneasy state, but nothing further may occur in his conduct with respect to the stimuli objects. The satisfaction of such desires, in other words, is a very indefinite process. Frequently it is impossible to accomplish such satisfaction at all because the object may not be available or may be subject to further control by the person, or because such satisfaction is incompatible with one's interests, character equipment, religious vows, political oaths, or general mode of living.

Contrasting with this form of operation, other desiring reactions call for a definite satisfaction and effective outcome. For this reason some desires are prolonged and continue in operation until they are satisfied. Such satisfaction then constitutes a definite point of termination of the desiring activity. As we must of course expect, the mode of satisfying any specific desire varies with the character of the desiring response and its stimulus object. When the stimulus is some concrete thing, the securing of it comprises the satisfaction of the desire. Similarly, when some unsatisfactory condition is the stimulus, its modification or removal brings about the desired satisfaction.

Some desiring reactions belonging to the type which demand satisfaction cannot, however, be satisfied. In other words, certain desiring responses which ordinarily can be brought to a satisfactory conclusion cannot, because of unusual conditions, be made to constitute a proper balance between the person and the stimulus object. In consequence, such desires constitute essentially prolonged activities with no definite termination. They are merely interrupted in their operation while the person is outside the range of the substitute stimuli—a break in contact which does not constitute a definite carrying out of the desire action. When any decided change in the person's responses occurs, it amounts to a dulling or complete cessation of the specific desiring or wanting activity through a change in the person's behavior equipment and especially his interests, knowledge, etc. Not seldom the impossibility of satisfying a desire is fraught with extremely harrowing and rending torture, the continuation of which cannot but lead to despair and depression, if not to utter disaster.[1]

From the nature of desiring actions it is clear that in most cases the satisfaction of desires depends upon the knowledge and information which the desiring person may have with regard to his desires and to the objects stimulating them. Accordingly, in many instances the person is satisfied with respect to his desires although the actual stimulating conditions are not at all changed. It follows, then, that in many cases only an apparent gratification is obtained with respect to unchanged conditions or conditions constituting aggravations of the original desire situations. A case in point is the person who desires to purchase some article and through lack of information is satisfied with purchasing a decidedly inferior article, or even one that will thwart him in the purpose for which it was purchased. A

[1] A splendid literary description of such a condition under unusual circumstances is found in France's sketch of *Paphnutius* in *Thais*.

similar behavior situation is that in which the person misconceives the character of his desires even to the point of not really desiring what he deems himself to be most desirous of, and accordingly is either unable to satisfy his desires at all or to satisfy them without difficulty.

Intimate and pervasive as desiring conduct is in the total series of the person's behavior, we naturally expect such activities to be closely interrelated with other types of action. Corresponding to the influences we have indicated which other behavior, e. g., knowing and affective responses, exerts upon desires, we may now suggest how some of these other activities are conditioned by desires. Also at this point, we may consider the simple coincidence in operation of desiring and other actions without any special effect of one type upon the other. **Influence of Desires Upon Other Activities**

First, let us consider the single coincidental operation of desiring ,and other types of action. Here we suggest that desiring conduct takes its place among general psychological activities exactly as any other type of behavior. Thus desiring reactions are autonomous activities depending upon contacts of the person with surrounding stimuli objects and conditions without necessarily influencing other actions or being influenced by them. In spite of the fact that they may be very intimately bound up with other kinds of action, they may at the same time be independent and operate upon their own account.

In turning to those desiring responses which exert considerable influence upon other actions we will first mention the activities most closely related to desires. These, we may readily ascertain, are actions of an effective sort that function in carrying the satisfaction of desires to a conclusion. Among such actions we find all sorts of specific responses suitable to the concrete surrounding objects and conditions which make for the consummation of the individual's desires. But let it not be supposed that only effective responses serve here. Thinking, planning, and reasoning of all varieties and complexities operate to carry out desiring reactions. Whatever the other reaction may be, it is very definitely and closely conditioned, first by the desiring response, and then by the aforementioned surrounding conditions. It is the latter which effectively condition the details of the actions connected with the desiring behavior. Naturally desiring reactions influence not only responses necessary to satisfy the desires, but also actions which might interfere with the consummation or satisfaction of the desire. Thus they may affect reactions connected with them only in a negative way.

Desiring reactions similarly influence responses which are not necessarily connected with them. Merely because the person desires certain things, he is interested in similar objects and therefore goes out of his way to see them or to perform some other reaction to them. Desires have more specific influences upon other unrelated action when they are thwarted or otherwise made impossible of consummation or satisfaction. An especial connection may be traced here between desiring actions of various sorts and affective responses. How desire responses influence thinking, believing, reasoning and similar forms of complex behavior, is a story often told by psychologists.

**Modality of Desiring Reactions** To appreciate more fully the character of desiring conduct, it is necessary to point out that it partakes of all the various modalities which characterize any kind of psychological activity. This point is especially worthy of note in view of the fact that desiring reactions have such great influence upon other behavior. What we learn in detail from such a consideration is that desiring reactions, even when they are unknown to the reacting individual, are frequently potent in their conditioning effect upon other actions.

Probably the modes of desiring activity that most effectively influence other behavior are the subreactionalistic types. In these actions the individual is stimulated to desire something which he sees or knows about, but without being aware of the desire. Thus, such desiring responses may have an insidious and uncontrollable effect upon many other forms of conduct.

Desires may be automatistic in character. The person often performs reflex desires aroused by the mere presence of desiderata of various types. These desiring reactions may also have a potent influence upon other behavior, both simple and complex. For example, they may condition immediate judgments and choices concerning particular things which the individual is about to purchase or ask for. Most suggestive in this connection are the simple reflex, sex desires and their influence upon various forms of action.

Reactionalistic desires likewise constitute a large part of the person's wishes and wants. Here the individual definitely reacts to his own responses aroused by various desiderata. Such desires operate with the person's full appreciation of the objects desired and of his action in desiring them.

When there is a question of the desiring person's capacity in carrying out the reaction, or of the effect which the satisfaction or lack of satisfaction may have upon him, then we are fairly certain to have subpersonalistic modes of action. In these cases the desires are definitely attached to the person who is himself as much reacted to in the desire situation as the desiderata; in fact, we may consider the desiring person as a part of the setting of the desiderata.

The most definite of the personalistic desires are naturally those in which the individual himself is the center of the desiring situation. Frequently the question arises as to what one should desire, and as to the kinds of desires one should have. Plainly, in this instance, the person who performs the action is the primary stimulus of the behavior segment. Such desiring reaction may be called voluntary or choice actions.

Pursuant to our suggestion made in the early part of this chapter that we first study desiring conduct as a general type of psychological activity, reserving for a later section the analysis and description of its specific types, we may now turn to the latter consideration. Upon first approaching this task we discover that there are innumerable types of desiring conduct and that the attempt to analyze and specifically describe them with any degree of adequacy brings us up sharply against almost insuperable difficulties. Accordingly, we have adopted the same pragmatic procedure found useful upon previous occasions, for example, in the study of feeling behavior. That is, we have taken several terms which have a more or less definite symbolic connection with specific forms of desiring conduct and have used them as representative of distinct types of desiring action. While in this procedure we have found it expedient to employ names having popular currency, we have been obliged to give them special significance. Hence, in our description they take on fairly technical meaning.

The attempt to organize desiring conduct into classes indicates at once a great number of possible criteria which may be employed in developing such a classification. For our purposes we have divided into three distinct classes all the different criteria we shall use. In other words, we have attempted to consider desiring conduct from the standpoint of its types of characteristics. In consequence we find that the criteria for the description of desiring behavior may be taken from (1) the type of stimulus, (2) the nature of the response details, and (3) the possibility and mode of satisfaction. We may consider these in turn.

The first type of stimulus criterion refers to the kind of thing that elicits the desire response. Is the stimulus an act, an object of some sort, a condition or circumstance, etc.? Again, the stimulus criterion may involve the question whether the object is definite or indefinite. In many cases desiring responses have stimuli which are positive, definite, and tangible objects or conditions. In others, the stimuli may be very indefinite and intangible. A third stimulus criterion concerns the closeness of connection between the person and the stimuli objects—whether the stimulus object is immediately present or absent. Or the closeness of connection between the stimulus and acting individual may refer at times to the problem whether the adjustment stimulus is clear enough and sufficiently known to the individual to exercise potent functions in the behavior situation, or whether the adjustment stimulus is merely suggested by the substitution stimulus.

An exceedingly important and significant problem on the response side arises with respect to the character of desiring responses, namely, whether the reaction is so personal as to involve organic and very simple physiological details, or whether it is a more or less impersonal action with little or no suggestion of organic or physiological functioning. A second response criterion includes the problem whether the response is apparent to the observer, to the person himself, or

Classification and Types of Desiring Behavior

some other individual, or whether the action is inapparent to the observer, and is thus very subtle in its operation. A third response criterion leads us to inquire whether the desiring activity may be classified as universal, that is, one depending upon the biological organization of the individual, or whether it is cultural behavior and so dependent upon institutional stimuli of various sorts.

Of the satisfaction criteria we may also enumerate a series, the first of which logically refers to the question as to whether satisfaction of desire is possible at all. It is quite evident that some of our desiring responses cannot be satisfied, whereas others can very easily and readily be gratified. In other instances the criterion refers to the question whether the person himself can or cannot bring about the satisfaction of the desire or whether he requires the aid of someone else. Closely connected with this type of satisfaction is the problem whether the desire is carried out directly with respect to the stimulus object, or whether some other intervening action is necessary for the accomplishment of the satisfaction. An additional criterion concerns the problem whether satisfaction can actually or only probably be achieved.

On the basis of various combinations of these different specific criteria we may organize in a more or less logical arrangement a series of classes of diverse, desiring conduct. Despite the precariousness of the classification, the different types enumerated actually refer to concrete adaptations of the person to specific desiderata.

Cravings    Craving responses are very striking as types of desiring behavior. They are essentially implicit actions which prominently involve definite organic and visceral factors. Because of their gross and visible character they simulate overt behavior. Quite naturally the stimuli for craving reactions involve particular conditions of the organism's own functioning. Hunger, thirst, and similar conditions serve as stimuli to desire food, drugs, or sex objects, which can be operated upon, manipulated, eaten, drunk, etc., to the end that the satisfaction of the craving behavior is brought about. Thus the essential fact in craving actions is that they are desires for action, for the performance of a particular activity. In other words, they represent the person's desires to exercise or make use of his own organism with especial reference, of course, to some particular desideratum as stimulus and as immediate occasion for such specific action. Accordingly, craving activities may sometimes appear to constitute a condition of the organism rather than definite, responsive activities. This situation prevails of course in case the craving response is mild in its operation and is manifested only in subtle behavior. Further, we might observe that craving activities may be decidedly prolonged in their operation, depending upon the time required to make the stimuli objects available and thus to satisfy the desires. In some cases, of course, the satisfaction of the craving activity does not require any considerable time, especially if the craving is stimulated by the immediate presence of the desired object.

Insofar as they involve exceedingly prominent organic factors, appetites also very closely resemble craving action. A point of difference, however, is quite apparent. Cravings we regard as desires for the performance of action. Appetites, on the other hand, we look upon as desires for particular kinds of things, viz., sexual objects, food, etc. That is, the appetites stress the nature of the stimuli objects rather than the performance of an action, and the stimuli objects themselves stand out in sharper relief. For example, in appetite activities there is not only an emphasis on food but on some particular kind of food. Hence the appetite is always a specific desire and not merely a general craving. **Appetites**

The very fact that the stimuli conditions are stressed in the operation of appetite desires makes these desires more dependent. In consequence they are more periodic in their occurrence as the reacting person comes into regular contact with the desiderata which arouse them. The periodicity of the appetites is further influenced by the circumstance that the substitute stimuli are frequently various time factors, as in the case of the appearance of certain objects at conventionally determined intervals, the alternation of the seasons, etc. Such periodicity receives reinforcement from the fact that prominent substitute stimuli for appetites are the person's own visceral reflexes (sexual, alimentary) which, upon functioning, arouse appetite desires for particular objects.

A distinct variant of the appetite responses, though on the whole intimately related to them morphologically, are hankering forms of desire. These differ from the appetites in that the stimuli objects are not in such close contact with the individual, so that while he knows in general what it is that he desires, he is at a loss to determine the specific desideratum that stimulates the desiring behavior.

To the same extent that physiological or organic functioning is present in cravings, it is absent in universal desires. In other words, the reaction systems do not consist of physiological reflex factors, nor do the stimuli for universal desires constitute factors within the organism itself. Universal desires, then, are not so intimate in their functioning as either the appetites or the cravings. They do not relate the person nearly so closely with his immediate surroundings and in general they may be considered as somewhat detached from his organic needs. What, then, is their specific character? First, these actions are more indicative of the person's status with respect to comforts and conveniences than to sheer necessities. It follows, then, that they lay claim to the term universal, not because they are direct functions of the person's biological make-up, but rather because what the person desires is related more to his biological make-up than to any other feature of the behavior situation. We must insist, however, that univer- **Universal Desires** sal desires are definitely based upon the person's biological organization, although the actual desiring conduct may have complex cultural features in its origin and development.

Among the universal desires are the wishes and wants relating to shelter, health, and well-being, that is, a general provision against injury and exposure. Stimuli for universal desire-reactions comprise possessions of all sorts, children, companions, food objects, and sex pleasures or enjoyments. In short, universal desiring reactions are not in particular either desires for action, or primarily desiring responses to things, but they may be either the one or the other, or combinations of both. On the whole, the adjustment stimuli for desiring reactions are more vague and indefinite than those of either appetites or cravings. Usually, too, they are substituted for by objects and situations other than the actual desiderata.

**Idiosyncratic Desires**  By reason of their origin and general reactional character, we place in a distinct class a series of reactions called idiosyncratic desires. In detail we have here desires peculiar to given individuals on the basis of their reactional biographies and their unique present behavior circumstances. It is certain that every person responds in unique personal ways to various objects. He desires things that perhaps no other person desires, or if others do desire the same kind of things, the correspondent desires have demonstrably developed as coincidences, without any relationship between them. The characteristic variations in idiosyncratic desiring, therefore, are due directly to the influence of the individual's past experience.

What specific things are desired in this type of desiring behavior situation depends to a considerable extent upon the tastes, likes, and dislikes that the person has developed in his various contacts with stimuli surroundings. Likewise, idiosyncratic desires are founded upon the private knowledge, information, and general intellectual attitudes of the desiring person.

In similar fashion, the mode of satisfying idiosyncratic desires is also a matter which can be determined only by concrete studies of the specific individuals involved. It must be observed, however, that such individualistic modes of satisfying desires constitute integral features of the specimen reactions in the idiosyncratic classification.

**Cultural Desires**  Many desiring reactions are cultural. Indeed, for many individuals the preponderance of desiring activity is performed through the influence of the specific institutional surroundings in which they live. As a member of a given cultural group a man is constantly dominated by certain institutions which determine that he shall perform certain types of desire and for particular sorts of objects.

The individual culturalized in a certain way desires to obtain various positions in his group. He desires to be respectable and well thought of, and in general to possess the social and economic virtues approved and prescribed by the members of his cultural community.

Not only conditions are desired through cultural influence, but also objects of all sorts. Such determined desires reflect the status of particular groups with respect to tastes, knowledge, and other community responses. As we may also expect, the cultural control of desires has an inhibitory and repressive effect upon the individual's desire conduct. In this negative way society exercises a powerful influence upon the desiring life of man.

Recognizing, then, the control which groups exercise, or attempt to exercise, over their members, we find that the general problem of cultural desires is considerably illuminated. In various group situations one may or may not have certain desires. When certain tabooed desires are developed they must be suppressed or altogether eradicated. Thus we have the epicureanisms, asceticisms, puritanisms, and other social behavior conditions and personality developments insofar as they involve specific desiring conduct.

**Wishing**

The term wishes sums up a class of desiring activities chiefly characterized by the person's inability to satisfy them. They cannot be gratified primarily because their adjustment stimuli are constituted of certain, inevitable circumstances which the person desires to have changed. For instance, he may wish that he had not done some act which now he regrets or deplores. Or he may wish to possess something—wealth, the esteem of his friends, or success in some venture— all of which are denied him. The mockery of life is such that many of the desiderata of our wishes are things and events that no longer exist or which cannot be recalled or repeated.

We hardly need to add that wishes are capable of operation in all varieties and degrees of intensity. In each instance the intensity is a direct function of the type of object wanted and its availability for the satisfaction of the desire. As we have already indicated, any type of object or situation may be the adjustment stimulus for a wishing response. In the main the desiderata are fairly concrete objects and situations which for the individual do not equal in importance the desiderata of other types of desiring behavior.

In general, our wishes are cast either in a cultural or in an idiosyncratic mould. Furthermore, while they are on the whole reactionalistic or personalistic in nature, they may in rare instances be unknown in their operation to the reacting individual.

**Yearning**

Much more than wishes, yearning responses represent desires of a very intimate and personal sort. Like wishes, however, yearnings cannot be satisfied. We do not imply that yearning behavior is completely precluded from satisfaction; rather the consummation may be very long drawn out or exceedingly problematical. Quite in harmony, then, with the character of yearnings their desiderata or stimuli objects are very personal objects or conditions wanted by the individual. Accordingly, whatever indefiniteness attaches to such desiderata is entirely due to the individual's failure to secure them or in some other form to satisfy or consummate the yearning. Because of the intensity of the desire and the probability of its satisfaction, yearning responses constitute exceedingly passive and hopeless activity. The individual may be described as pining because of the lack of satisfaction. This situation is clearly portrayed when the person yearns for such a desideratum as the personal affection of some other individual.

**Longing**    Longing and yearning reactions are very similar. These two represent activities which are extremely problematic with respect to their satisfaction. Hence they may constitute exceedingly intense activities on the part of the acting individual. Longing responses, however, unlike yearning reactions, have as their stimuli conditions desiderata which are only vaguely appreciated by the individual, and are therefore not such definite objects and conditions. As a consequence, instead of being directly stimulated by some specific desired object or condition that cannot be secured, the longing individual is, to a great extent, aroused by various lacks and needs which substitute for, and elicit responses to, fairly vague desiderata. Typical of this type of behavior is the adolescent's longing for love or for a fairly abstract condition of happiness or peace. Frequently we find individuals wistfully desiring or longing for equitable economic conditions or some past golden age.

On the whole, longing activities are probably the most radically implicit of all desiring behavior. For the most part they are morphologically inapparent, so that the longing individual is able to conceal his activity. Not until a decidedly depressive condition is induced in the longing person is it apparent to observers. For this reason both longing and yearning desires simulate attitudes rather than immediate performances more than any other types of desiring behavior.

**Wanting**    When an individual wants something, he is stimulated by specific and completely circumscribed contacts with objects, which thereupon become desiderata and stimulate desiring responses. Wanting reactions, therefore, are essentially desires of occasion. Objects become desiderata for a particular moment because of some use or need for them. Hence immediately upon using the object, the individual finds that it no longer possesses the stimulational function necessary to arouse a desiring response with respect to it. Wanting reactions may also be considered desiring responses which are not only immediately satisfied, but which do not become desiring reactions unless the objects capable of satisfying them are present as the stimuli for the desire in the first instance.

An excellent example of this type of behavior is the situation of a workman who, in the process of repairing a certain mechanism, must employ a number of different kinds of tools. As soon as the occasion arises, he is stimulated to desire a particular one of these instruments. Perhaps the desire is satisfied in a moment or two and is thus terminated. Or, on the other hand, the individual may perform whole series of desiring reactions in a very brief space of time.

To enhance our present description we may add that wanting responses may be entirely accidental and unrelated to any other behavior circumstances. Consider the individual who happens to be in a wood and who quite accidentally observes from a distance a new species of bird. Immediately he responds with a desire to see the bird more clearly—a desire which not only has an extremely accidental origin but which may be very quickly and permanently terminated.

In commendation of our classification of desiring responses it may be said that we have achieved a fairly accurate description of some of the different ways in which desiring reactions are performed. Certainly such a brief enumeration of desiring behavior is far from adequate. Completeness must be sacrificed here for brevity. Suffice it to add that there are many terms such as hoping and trusting, which, although taken very definitely to signify reactions other than strictly desiring responses, are likewise examples of desiring types.

In traditional psychological literature desiring behavior has been very much neglected. Unfortunately, with the recent increase in information and interest concerning this type of behavior, the conception of it has for the most part been pronouncedly out of harmony with its actual character and the way in which it operates.

*Some Common Misconceptions Concerning Desire Behavior*

In particular, two faulty conceptions seem to prevail. In the first place, the term "desire" is used to signify processes or powers in the individual which tend to make him reach out for or desire certain objects or things. The more obvious and intense desiring responses especially are considered forces which influence action in the same way that the instincts of current, evil repute are presumed to do. Probably the greatest objection to such a misinterpretation is that it interferes with the conception of desiring actions as very concrete activities which occur when the person is in contact with various objects and individuals which may, in the normal course of events, become desiderata.

A second misconception is very similar to the first with one exception, however. That is, these powerful forces which are presumed to condition the individual's actions are said to reside in some organ or in some biological function. This conception was developed as a corrective to the former crude notion, although not even with the greatest indulgence can we say that it describes more truly the actual facts of human desires. No less, therefore, than the original force conception does this physiological view prevent the study of desire behavior as the actual psychological activity that it is.

# CHAPTER XVIII

## IMAGINATION REACTIONS AS CREATIVE CONDUCT

**General
Nature of
Imagina-
tion
Reactions**
Imagination reactions are essentially types of behavior in which the person transforms or in some way modifies objects and conditions stimulating his activity. But we must note that the detailed manipulative and transformative imagination responses to stimuli objects are performed not primarily because such transformations and changes are specifically indicated by the objects or conditions themselves, but rather because they are ways and means by which the individual may exercise his own intellectual, æsthetic, or technical equipments. This means that in detail the particular imagination responses are primarily prompted by personality or equipmental conditions rather than by circumstances of present behavior. Thus immediate desires, conceptions, or beliefs may be the source and origin of imagination action.

Imagination behavior is so extensively equipmental action that the specific responses, even in complex artistic behavior, may be aroused to activity even by comparatively extraneous conditions such as poverty or the promise of reward. The stimulus object itself only in general elicits the action here called the imagination response. To a certain extent, therefore, the object itself is merely the material for action supplying the occasion for imaginative conduct. A convincing illustration is the activity of the artist. It may be a piece of marble that stimulates him to sculp a figure but the actual creational behavior is determined by entirely different things—by the artistic conception, for example. The piece of marble does to some extent condition the character of the finished figure but insofar as it conditions the size and shape, it functions not as a direct stimulus to action but only as a setting.

Clearly the general problem here centers about the identity or character of the stimuli for imagination behavior. One may ask whether so slight a stimulus function performed by an object may really be called a stimulus function at all. It is true that there is considerable incertitude on this point. To acknowledge this, however, is merely to allude to the primacy and originality of imagination behavior. It is tantamount to pointing out the great disproportion between the stimulational and reactional functions in this type of conduct.

Obviously this description of creational conduct does not preclude the fact that the stimulus for transforming some object may be a property or condition of that object. This is very frequently the case, as for example, when an industrial technician requires to have a machine changed because of faulty performance or some improper adaptation to the requirements of production. Certainly, in this instance, the manipulative and transformative behavior is definitely prompted by the defect or insufficiency of the object. And yet if this is a situation requiring imagination behavior, consider how small a proportion of the actual details of the creative or transformative action is directly stimulated in this way. Notwithstanding the fact that this is among the simplest and least creative imagination behavior situations, all its minutiæ of behavior are the direct functions of the person's creative capacities, and in consequence depend upon his reactional biography and intimate present reactional equipment. It is in this type of situation that a stimulus object is made into an imaginative product.

Possibly we ought to consider that in this latter instance there are always two reactions. The first, stimulated by the defect in the machine, is the act of starting to correct the defect. The precise act of finally bringing about the correction is another response, namely, the intimate imagination reaction conditioned by the individual's knowledge and skill. This latter action, insofar as it occurs in a particular way, is conditioned much more by the person's own behavior equipment than by conditions surrounding him.

Generally speaking, imagination responses from the standpoint of product of action can be divided into two great divisions of behavior. On the one hand, they are principally recombining in character. The reacting individual recombines and reorganizes parts of objects or whole objects into new wholes. Essentially, this means the contrivance of new relationships between the elements or parts, so that the reconstituted object or condition is very different from the constituent elements. In the second division of imagination behavior the reactions are more generative in nature. They result in action products which bear a much slighter resemblance to the original material than in the former instance and in which, furthermore, the spontaneity of the individual is more marked. That is, he contributes more to the final object or situation as compared with the original material, than is true in the case of combinative imagination.[1]

Imagination activity is creative behavior. This proposition is just as true when the activity is combinative as when it is generative. That is to say, the person creates and develops new types of things, processes, and conditions, or new modes of responding to them, partially on the basis of his previous reactions and experiences and partially on the basis of a cumulative or developing technique of creativeness. The generative process of cumulative creative action is illustrated by the development of artistic behavior. In the first in-

---

[1] No one will of course confuse this distinction with the animatistic tradition of *combination of ideas* versus mere *reproduction* of them.

stance, artistic development issues presumably from the mere copying or reproduction of an object, and gradually approaches the development of new creations, perhaps bearing no resemblance to anything with which the creator has been overtly or actually in contact. Most assuredly it is impossible for anything to be created completely *de novo*. We would like to point out, however, that the creation of an angel or a griffin is certainly in no sense a reproduction of something that one has actually observed. And these conventional objects are not in the slightest degree comparable in their creation, with an original work of art. The connection is utterly lost when comparing these objects with complex ideas as imagination products.

To no mean extent imagination reactions are behavior types which unify and enlarge the person's behavior surroundings and the occasions for his actions with respect to those surroundings. Instead of merely adapting himself to objects as they are, he remakes his situations and forces them into a condition better suited to his purposes.[1] In this sense the transformations he effects in his environing circumstances are based upon and conditioned by some sort of pattern or ideal which as yet does not exist in the particular situation but which may be developed, or one which perhaps may not exist at all.

To this general description of imagination behavior we are obliged to add that the manipulative and creative activity need not result in any positive production. In other words, the action of the individual and not the product, or the result of such activity, is the point to be stressed. The significance of this proposition may be well indicated and illustrated by the fact that there are many degrees of completeness possible in imagination products. This apparent observation makes plausible the proposition that in some cases there need not be even the beginnings of a product. We may therefore distinguish between what may be called executive and non-executive imagination behavior. The latter is the type which does not result in any product either because from the nature of the activity no product is necessary or possible, or because it has not yet begun to be worked out.

In formulating a general account of what takes place when an individual performs imagination or creative conduct, we may isolate a number of essential factors. First we refer to the interest, conception, or purpose prompting the particular manipulation of things. These reactional features are based upon the previous stimulation of persons during the course of their development and training. When acquired, these activities are put into action by direct stimulation of various objects or situations, or by their qualities and conditions. Next we may consider the actual manipulational actions to tangible objects by means of tools of various sorts and the employment of specialized techniques. The latter are equipmental factors or depend

1 Cf. Vol. I, Ch. IV, "Division on Inventive and Creative Conduct."

upon such factors. Or they may be immediate actions themselves or actions involving the use of instruments and materials. The objects undergoing manufacture or change may along with other things used in the process be regarded as materials for creative action.

When the objects are complete or the work upon them is done they may be looked upon as products. In some cases these products are the adjustment stimuli which have been known in greater or lesser detail before they have been produced. At other times, they are developed without having been known beforehand. In this case the materials, as they are actually handled, perform some of the stimulational functions in the behavior situation. In all of this work, of course, the appropriate stimuli objects, settings, and occasions for the constructive action influence and guide the behavior.

From the general nature of imagination responses we can readily see that the instances of their specific operation cover a wide range of types of human activities and situations. In their simplest form, they comprise purely overt manipulations of objects by way of rearrangement and distribution. Such simple imaginative behavior is definitely or immediately stimulated by circumstances directly forcing themselves upon the individual's attention. In the actual process of responding, however, the expression of the person's tastes and distastes, likes and dislikes, desires and aversions, knowledge and ignorance, etc., is clearly visible. Through the instrumentality of his reactional equipment, he arranges and reconstructs gross objects and situations in his surroundings to suit special occasions and certain felt needs.

*The Operation of Imagination Reactions*

In other, and perhaps more complicated situations, the person recreates the surroundings or practically creates new conditions, but in a purely implicit manner. It is precisely this type of operation of imagination responses that has given rise to the statement that certain acts are performed exclusively in a person's own mind. As examples of such purely implicit actions we may suggest the development of plans for revenge and retribution. To make most certain that such imagination reactions are purely implicit, we need only refer to those that are, on the whole, results of the desire for revenge or for the accomplishment of some purpose, rather than the actual performance of an action upon some surrounding object or individual.

Generally speaking, the purely implicit creative conduct appears to be more passive than the other type but this is, of course, only an apparent characteristic. One may be just as active while performing the constructive behavior of day dreaming or other phantasy action as when performing effective responses. On the whole it may be true that effective action is the more fatiguing and onerous but this is not a thoroughgoing difference between the two types. When the problem of the importance of behavior is taken into account, the apparently passive and subtle constructive action may appear to have the advantage. For among the passive actions are numbered whatever is creative in the form of artistic and other kinds of appreciation.

Probably, imagination responses operate for the most part however, as combinations of both overt and implicit types of action. This statement is made in view of the fact that most imagination reactions function in fairly serious situations. The person's reconstructive ability must, therefore, closely conform to stimuli objects and situations. In the development of a plan of action, in drawing and painting a picture, or in designing a mechanical thing or process, we utilize a great number of combinations of overt and implicit action. The precise way in which the two types are combined and the way in which they function, depend of course upon the specific reactional conditions.

In studying the details of the operation of imagination responses we discover immediately that they are conditioned not only by the individual's general equipment and his reactional status at the time, but also by a number of specific reactional occurrences. We may even say that imagination responses are based upon the operation of a series of simpler reactions.

In the first place, we may consider the function of recall responses. No complicated form of imagination can operate without numerous implicit responses to conditions and actions which the individual has previously performed or with which he has been in contact. It is precisely in these memorial reactions that the source material for creative activity is found—for the designing of a new bridge, the invention of a new machine or process, or the making of a painting or a piece of sculpture.

Depending upon the complexity of the imagination behavior the person may be called upon in carrying out the action to perform some problem solving activities of a simple or more complex sort. Constructive changes in surrounding objects require experimental manipulation of them, based both upon accepted general principles and various immediate trial and error procedures.

Abstracting responses are likewise called into frequent use. For the purposes at hand in the imagination situation it is necessary to abstract various factors from past and present situations and objects in order to perform the creative action demanded by the present imaginative circumstances. Again it is necessary to analyze our previous reactions, objects, and situations, partially for the purpose of making the abstractions of which we have just spoken, and partially as a direct method for the accomplishment of some creative reaction. Furthermore, as the nature of imagination responses would seem to indicate, such actions are based upon a very elaborate series of syntheses. The more complicated the situations, the more important and frequent the basic synthetic reactions involved. These may be overt recombinations of things, or implicit connections between different objects.

Nor can one invent new objects or circumstances unless he makes use to a considerable extent of analogical situations. Therefore the isolation and recognition of analogies or likenesses between various things and situations are of great importance. These, of course, are more common in situations where some kind of mechanical or other type of useful object is created, but they play a part in the construction of the most novel and remote works of art. Very characteristic also of every imaginative behavior segment is the process of symbolization. A symbol itself represents a creational activity and product but in the development of any kind of complex invention or work of art, symbols are used as stepping stones to the performance of more complex types of creative behavior. Thus it may be said in general that imagination responses in their various operations involve practically every other type of psychological activity.

Reflection upon the various types of operation of imagination or creation behavior brings us to a consideration of the relative importance of certain modes of behavior for creative accomplishment. Some actions are of greater advantage to the person than others in the performance of imagination behavior. In a sense they fit more aptly and are more serviceable as component responses. We have already seen that implicit responses of the imagery type are especially adaptable to the performance of imagination actions. This is naturally true because imagery behavior proves very easy to manipulate.

But even imagery forms of response do not begin to approach verbal and linguistic action in providing a workable basis for imagination responses. This fact is almost obvious when we recall that words and language reactions constitute the freest and most facile of all the reactions we perform. No matter how difficult it may be to overcome a situation in any overt and direct manipulative manner, we can always handle it verbally. We can discuss or describe it even if we cannot change it. Furthermore, language reactions constitute the most fertile source of substitute stimuli. For by means of language we can substitute for any object or condition with which we can have any sort of contact, and in addition, make the most complex analyses or syntheses of things. By means of language we can create not only the situations we know exist and with which we have no opportunity to be in touch, but also the most impossible thing or situations. Words enable us to perform feats that are absolutely beyond human capacity. Literature and general cultural records of human action are eloquent in their testimony to the capacity of man to create, either in his own image or in the image of other things, animals, causes, forces, and gods. By means of words and linguistic behavior in general, a person can remake things to suit his own heart's desire. In this connection it is relevant to recall the creations of the story teller, the scientist, the philosopher, and the theologian.

Doubtless it has already appeared from our study that imagination responses are behavior segments rather than mere reaction systems.

Imagination Conduct Exclusively Behavior Segments

In other words, they are not precurrent or preliminary to some other feature of a reaction pattern which would give its name to the total behavior segment. On the contrary, imagination reactions are themselves always patterns or responses connected with their own unique stimuli objects. This is true whether or not the action results in a definite product. It is probably not necessary to emphasize this point when the responses constitute overt manipulations of things. But the same conditions prevail, however, when the responses are the most tenuous of implicit activities. Moreover, when a product of the imagination reaction exists, there seems no justification for the assumption that imagination activities are merely preliminary to other responses. But this is in no sense a denial that an imagination action may be closely related to some other action as, for example, when creative activity is involved in solving a problem.

To be sure in many instances imagination responses are followed by some further action but we should always insist that this further activity constitutes a new behavior segment, in addition to and following up, the imagination response.[1] In just this point we find a criterion for differentiating imagination responses from some implicit reactions which in morphological character are very similar to imagination behavior. The implicit responses, however, are unmistakably preliminary or precurrent to some other action. In brief, their whole character is conditioned by the fact that they are intended to be preliminary to further behavior. Illustrative of such precurrent reactions resembling imagination responses are the various imagery types of implicit action which serve as reference responses in memorial problem solving activities. A notion of how different they are from the creative responses which constitute the imagination pattern is to be seen from the fact that the implicit reaction systems themselves are very frequently elements in imagination response patterns. Such is always the case when imagination responses are implicit in character or when they involve implicit reactions.

**Degrees of Conditioning of Imagination Responses**    Such eminently spontaneous forms of action as imagination responses may definitely be expected to vary in the degree with which they are conditioned by external circumstances. Some of these activities are conditioned by surrounding objects and situations to no greater extent than is necessary to effect the person's stimulation. In other cases imagination reactions are controlled at every point by the qualities and circumstances of the surrounding objects. By far the least conditioned of all imagination responses are those stimulated by conditions within the individual's own organism. As examples of the latter, we may cite the elaborate constructive actions performed under the stimulation of hunger reflexes when imagining oneself partaking of a sumptuous banquet.

Generally speaking, the degree of conditioning to which imagina-

---

[1] It is clear, we assume, that these actions are not the manipulations which result in the making of an imagination product.

tion reactions are subject depends entirely upon the functional cir-cumstances under which they operate. It depends upon the kind of stimulating conditions that are present, that is to say, upon the problem to be solved, the adjustment to be made, or the work to be done, as well as upon the capacity of the individual to perform spontaneous, constructive activities, or to be aroused to reconstruct or to reorganize his surroundings. The nature of this conditioning of constructive action is very well illustrated by technical or mechan-ical inventive conduct which we may consider the typical form of controlled imagination. The principal fact to be noted here is that the specific manipulation of things and conditions and the particular ways of employing information and techniques of various sorts are all conditioned by the nature of the situation. In other words, the inventive activity represents an attempt to achieve some particular type of result based upon specifications supplied by the stimulus situation. Naturally enough, controlled activity consists to a great extent of various sorts of overt actions as, for example, the develop-ment of models and tentative drawings. The overt actions, however, are not limited to the more controlled imagination reactions but are found likewise in the case of the less conditioned. Overt responses, however, are typical and even indispensable for the more conditioned type whereas the less conditioned free imagination responses may lack any morphologically overt actions whatsoever.

In decided contrast with the mechanical, inventive type of imagina-tion is the creative conduct of literary production or sheer phantasy. Indulging in such action, the person constructs simple or exceedingly complex things with a minimum of conditioning by surrounding objects and events. Very noticeable then is the freedom and spon-taneity of action that is checked very little by specification and in-dicated necessities. The products of such behavior, moreover, bear only the slightest resemblances to things with which the person has been in contact.

Correlating somewhat with the extent of the conditioning of imagi-nation responses is the apparent degree of activity of the responding person. Thus, when the imagination response is conditioned to the greatest extent, the person appears most active. He must definitely conduct himself in a manner dictated and provided for by the speci-fications of the task at hand or by the general conditions of the sur-roundings. On the other hand, when the stimulus situation imposes few conditioning factors upon the imagination activity, the individual is ostensibly very passive. Accordingly, literary artists frequently describe their method of work as merely a process of recording what is already worked out for them. Similarly, imaginative writers are frequently, if not always, regarded as visionaries and dreamers, a re-sult of the fact that their work is considered akin to the passive per-formances of night- or day-dreaming activities.

Such passive creating of things indicates how much the imagination responses are relatively constituted of implicit and inapparent, or overt and apparent responses. In the more active instances of the creative forms of conduct, the person performs a definitely larger proportion of overt and effective acts than in more passive imagination situations where a general predominance of implicit and inapparent actions are discoverable. Such prevalence of implicit responses may be roughly correlated with the number of externally conditioning elements which guide and control the constructive action.

Impressive is the fact that no matter how free and unconditioned by surrounding circumstances the constructive action is, thus occasioning apparently passive responses, these responses are passive morphologically only. From the standpoint of results produced and the importance of action we must consider such behavior as very active indeed.

The limitation of restraints upon creative conduct may itself be a factor in the facility and value of such behavior. This freedom, even in the case of imagination responses which are conditioned by definite needs and problems, greatly enhances such behavior and makes it more productive. Because of the greater freedom in action, the so-called functionally passive imagination acts allow the individual to cover a wider sweep of conditions and to construct much more easily and actively with relation to things in which he is interested. For example, in scientific imagination the freer the scope of the individual's insight into and manipulation of conditions, by virtue of his equipment and training, the more serviceable the hypothesis which he is thereby enabled to construct.

**Influences upon Imagination**
No normal human being in actual contact with the ordinary conditions of human life fails to perform some imagination reactions. But it is clear that their specific forms, intensity, and range differ with different individuals and vary for one individual at different times. We might then consider some of the conditions responsible for these variations.

In the first place and primarily, imagination reactions depend upon the person's behavior equipment. The ability to reconstruct things or to create new ones is a direct function of the type of behavior equipment possessed. Through lack of acquired behavior equipment some individuals cannot possibly imagine things and conditions that are exceedingly important in certain situations, while other persons can perform these actions with ease and dispatch. Similarly, what the new creation will be is determined to a very considerable degree by the person's information, desire, and skill reaction systems acquired in his past contacts with objects and conditions similar to those which constitute his present imagination stimuli. It is such behavior equipments which lie at the bottom of the analogical details that comprise the immediate creative responses.

To be more specific, we may say that unless one has considerable information concerning particular things, he is unable to perform creative reactions with respect to them. The capacity, then, for creative activity is directly contingent upon the individual's past experience, and his intimate reactional biography. We may safely assert, therefore, that our most creative acts must have a basis in some actual prior experience.

We do not mean to intimate, however, that the kind of equipment necessary for creative reactions need be essentially the result of actual effective contacts with certain objects. They may have been acquired through various degrees of mediation. That is, we can obtain the necessary equipment for creative reactions merely by reading or by hearing tales about the things to which we are reacting. This point is made more clear when we remember that so far as our most complex actions are concerned, we need be only remotely connected with our stimuli objects. For instance, most of the facts and events of science, history, and geography must be obtained through a very indirect method. Consider that in the realm of science, for example, the specialist in a particular field, such as chemistry, has probably discovered himself only a modicum of novel facts and has been in contact with very few original situations. Most of his information is therefore dependent upon reading or other secondary sources of contact.

If we consider the reactional equipment of the individual, developed in his behavioristic biography as the more permanent influence upon imagination responses, we must likewise accord a prominent place to the immediate behavior circumstances as equally important influences. In other words, from the behavioristic or person's side of the situation, the reactional equipment is the more important influence upon imagination reactions. But no matter how well equipped an individual may be to perform imagination responses, their actual performance is definitely contingent upon the circumstances making constructive behavior necessary and even possible. So we must grant an equally significant position in the imagination situation to the stimuli circumstances and conditions.

Howsoever spontaneous and original imagination responses may be, they must await occasion to be called forth. It is for this reason that the history of invention records numerous claimants to priority for particular inventions. This is as true for mechanical types of imagination responses as for intellectual forms. There are always several or many individuals who claim to be originators of the same machine, idea, or process. Time and place, as well as specific mechanical or ideational conditions, are exceedingly important factors in imagination behavior.

An influence of no small significance upon our imagination reactions is the individual's independence of the situation in which he is behavioristically involved. It is a general principle that con-

structive behavior calls for a distinct freedom of action.[1]  The person
must for the time being be relieved from the necessity of performing
an immediate effective response with respect to the stimulus object.
Imaginative or creative actions require time for the various necessary manipulations.  Moreover, the individual must be so removed
from the immediate necessity of performing a definite response
that he can be spontaneous and draw upon his equipmental resources for ideational and skill responses in order to accomplish the
desired results.

How the freedom and autonomy of the person is utilized in imagination reactions is well illustrated by various dream activities.
Observe that the optative condition for dreaming is the relaxed waking
state, when we are free from the impulsion of immediate tasks, or
the sleeping state in which we are almost completely out of contact
with our ordinary complex surroundings.

Our emphasis with regard to the marked autonomous condition of
the person in performing imagination responses is not intended as a
denial of the fact that imagination or constructive reactions operate
very frequently under the person's needs or other utilitarian circumstances.  It is undoubtedly true, of course, that the inventive form
of imagination is especially influenced by the need for some modification in machinery, or for new ways of handling things in industrial
techniques.  Our early example of imagination responses to the machine situation illustrated this point.  But here the utilitarian character of the imaginative situation does not at all detract from the fact
that the invention or construction involves an autonomy of conduct,
a freedom from the pressure of immediate responses such that the person can manipulate and experiment both overtly and implicitly, both
apparently and inapparently, to the end of bringing about a new or
very different sort of behavior product.

In a larger sense the autonomy of the imagining person implies a
general period of freedom and leisure affording ample opportunity
to cultivate ideas, perform experiments, and in other ways learn to
accomplish transformative actions.

Let us now pass on to the element of practise in imaginary conduct.
It is impossible to maximize the importance of practise as a factor
in the ability not only to perform imagination responses, but also
to carry out such behavior.  As in all other cases of psychological
action the effectiveness of constructive conduct depends upon the
experience of the individual in doing that particular type of thing.
The more experience one has in transforming one's surroundings or
making things, the more easily can such action be performed.  The
more adept an artist is in the development of new conceptions and in

---

[1] Here is the source of what genuine basis there is for making imagination
behavior into play activity.  Some feature of play activity is undoubtedly
imaginative action and some imaginative action is play, but surely these two
types of behavior do not exactly coincide.

the invention of manners, forms, and styles of executing those conceptions, the more certainly is his imaginative conduct traceable to many trials and experiments with the elements involved. It is for this reason that we find the person's best type of constructive activity accomplished in particular kinds of situations, namely, those which represent the reacting person's specialty.

In like fashion a particular individual's imagination reactions are conditioned and influenced by the strength and vividness of his implicit behavior. The capacity to construct objects and situations of various sorts depends upon how strongly objects in general serve as substitute stimuli for the performance of implicit responses. For certain persons objects serve as substitute stimuli only when they are deliberately connected with other objects. On the other hand, some people are readily capable of making one thing stand for another; they see all sorts of similarities and resemblances among various objects and are able to project in them the materials for manipulations which finally result in the transformations and rearrangements constituting the constructive activities of the imagination type.

Individual factors of another sort of implicit response must also be emphasized. The person's adaptability to the use of imagery in specific situations adds greatly to his general capacity to perform creational conduct. The painting of pictures or the composition of music, for example, depend upon the ability of the person to perform visual, auditory, and other kinds of image actions.

It must be mentioned finally that of no mean importance as a conditioning detail which influences creative activities is the individual's own measure of expressiveness. Creational conduct depends to a great extent upon a superior kind of activity. General expressiveness and abundance of action, when controlled, can be led into the direction of creative or imaginative conduct. The expressiveness of which we speak can perhaps be most readily and frequently observed in the form of linguistic and verbal sedulity. Expressiveness of all degrees we find manifested in conversational and literary articulation. It is not sufficient that some persons have various experiences, develop ideas, and undergo feelings of sundry types; they must make them known to others.

Who can doubt that the fame of thinkers or writers is a direct function of the extent to which they express themselves, whereas the lack of renown of those who are further advanced in thought and accomplishment is due to their disinclination to inform the world of their achievements. Be this as it may, our interest is of course in the fact that expressiveness and assiduity are the basis not only of such celebrity as we have indicated, but also of the actual standing and merit of the thinkers and performers themselves. Artists, scientists, and philosophers gain their places through the expressiveness and alertness of their behavior. In sum, expressive behavior is responsible for the person's seeking out information, perfecting himself in various feats and performances and in general participating in all kinds of experiences.

Now in many particulars such expressiveness not only influences but constitutes the actual creative conduct of the individual. Expressive activities stimulate and make necessary all sorts of inventive and originative conduct as directed and conditioned by the individual's surrounding circumstances or interest. It is such expressive traits as characterize creators of things and developers of ideas, which in general, enable them to initiate changes in things by the transmission to them of a velocity in a particular direction. While expressiveness is undoubtedly only one of a fairly large number of influences upon creative conduct, it is a very important factor in all of the activities of the novelist or innovator.

**Sources of Imagination Reactions** The starting-point of imagination behavior may be located either in the surroundings of the individual or in his behavior circumstances and conditions. These sources of creative activity may be looked upon as energizing circumstances, which initiate and facilitate the operation of imagination conduct. In surveying the former source first, we find that certain additional changes must be made in some object or condition in order that it may be dominated and prevented from exercising a controlling influence upon us. The contrivance of a footpath across a stream gives ample opportunity for the play of simple forms of constructive action. In the actual day's work the adaptation of specific tools to particular uses (which often means a unique handling of them) cannot be excluded from the realm of imaginative situations. From such simple work conditions imagination reactions proceed to the invention of entirely new tools and machines designed to carry out newer techniques of work.

The sources for imagination reactions in the relations of one person with others are innumerable. In the various needs to please our friends we must exercise our most effective ingenuity in planning and performing creative conduct. Again, in the numerous rivalries and coöperations with our fellow-beings in all the diverse dealings we have with them, whether in justifying our intentions, our acts, or ourselves, or in making such conduct necessary on their part, lie the sources of complicated acts of imagination.

Turning from the sources that originate primarily in the person's environing conditions and circumstances, we pass on to the sources residing in the various activities of the person himself. Now, these sources are not limited to any specific type of the person's actions, but are discoverable equally in his affective, desiring, or in his intellectual behavior, as well as in other types. To begin with some very elementary activities, we may suggest that acts tending toward the satisfaction of hunger and the securing of shelter, especially when the means of accomplishing these purposes are unavailable, may lead the individual to create means for the exigencies at hand. In elaborate situations constructive behavior comprises the contriving of techniques to bring about the furtherance of the person's activities. In all such situations it must be assumed, of course, that the person has acquired the capacity to perform imagination responses. Indeed, it is only when he possesses this capacity that such intricate situations serve to initiate creative conduct.

Coming to more complicated activities which supply occasion for the performance of imagination responses, we might consider desiring activities. Every conceivable sort of desire for any kind of condition or object, if only it be intense enough, may become the primary condition for the development of creative conduct as a means of satisfying the desire behavior.

The affective life and action of the person affords an additional and fertile source of imagination responses. Consider only the operation of creative conduct developed by the various fear and depression situations in which one may find himself. A no less fertile imaginative source is found in the joyous and exuberant behavior aroused by favorable, pleasant, and beautiful conditions. A notion of just how replete affective behavior situations are for the development of imagination responses may be gathered from the fact that such situations are involved very closely with a great deal of æsthetic activity. Many poems, pictures, and symphonies are initiated and developed in all their creational intricacies from the sort of affective reactional situations we have been indicating. In many cases, as some believe, creative behavior arises from affective situations as a witting or unwitting effort of the person to perpetuate his affective responses and conditions. Undoubtedly imaginative actions operate in other instances merely as enlargements upon affective experience.

Intellectual activity, with its train of immediate problem solving and more general orientational adjustments, provides a great many occasions for the performance of the type of constructive behavior we are considering. In order to meet the many problematic situations calling for thinking and reasoning, the individual must construct things, techniques, and processes to the end of carrying out the solution of such problems. Here there is ample play for the exercise of constructive activities. Similarly, inventions and innovations of all kinds are occasioned by the need of the individual to obtain for himself a general orientation with respect to his surroundings. In detail such orientational constructions consist of various hypotheses and explanations designed to account for the existence of certain conditions and circumstances and the changes taking place in them. Furthermore, in the activities of explaining and accounting for strange and complex things and conditions, creative responses are indispensable. Such explanations may merely be inventions to rationalize conditions or to justify actions done or left undone, or they may be the development of hypotheses and theories for the more consequential purpose of providing intellectual orientation among all the various natural and cultural objects among which one lives and works.

To discuss these various sources of creative conduct is to arrive more or less directly at the fact of imagination action as sublimation. By this term we mean that various actions or conditions of the person may be turned into the direction of imaginative conduct. Thus the feeling action aroused by a beautiful object or the sex response prompted by another person may become the immediate cause or stimulus for the performance of a creative activity. Thus it is frequently said that artists find inspiration for some of their aesthetic activity in persons they love, or in the love behavior itself. Doubtless this view is correct, whether the action involved consists of reflex action or more complex conduct. Another sort of sublimation source is that in which the development of new ideas may be traced to the person's striving to achieve some sort of superiority.

Generally speaking, creative activities are or may be motivated by the individual's need to express himself in the sense of giving vent to his desires, feelings, ambitions, thoughts, or strivings with respect to his surroundings. Such use of imagination responses may result in the conception and execution of creative products of every type and in every medium. A source and use of creative conduct coming between the actual everyday adaptation or work situation and play and artistic endeavors, is that in which it is necessary for the person to change his general orientation. He may find it urgent to escape from some kind of intolerable situation (whether it be actual or not). Here the creative activity serves to a great extent to provide the individual with various sorts of compensations which remove him from his condition. A person who is inefficient in some respect, either anatomically, economically, socially, or intellectually, may create for himself a situation in which these disabilities are removed and in which all the circumstances of his life are left edifying and inspiring.

**Development and Training of Imagination**    The development of imaginative behavior begins very early in the life of an individual. In point of fact, under ordinary circumstances there is no time in the life of a person so conducive to the development and performance of imagination reactions as the early period of childhood with its fairly care-free and protected conditions. Upon reflection, of course, it appears immediately that the earliest forms of imagination reactions are the unconditioned types. It is also clear that they consist entirely of new ways of moving, turning, walking, running, looking, and, in general, direct manipulating experiments with things at hand. On the whole, the period of infancy is a time in which the individual has nothing to do but to express himself, to externalize his reactions, to test out his properties and capacities with respect to things. This condition is of course based upon the biological fact of maturation. In other words, the individual performs elementary inventive action as phases in his ripening development. Throughout all this period the infant spontaneously discovers in himself and in surrounding objects new capacities, new ways of acting, as they become possible through his development. At this time there is little or no urgency observable in the surroundings: practically no demands of any sort are made upon the infant by environing situations. Most of the complicated things the organism must do by way of direct adaptation to its surroundings are performed by parents or nurses.

Upon arriving at the stage of conventional play the child is stimulated by objects of all sorts which must be handled in particular ways. Toys have rather fixed and unchanging properties of their own. The manipulation of them consequently involves contrivings and inventings fairly well conditioned by the stimuli objects. This is especially the case when the toys consist of parts requiring organization into patterns and combinations. At this point the child develops very definite inventive and constructive reactions in order to deal effectively with the play surroundings. In these situations imagination reactions may be said to have their origin in play activities.

Furthermore, in childhood the individual is informed of things which he has not seen. Tales are told to him about strange and interesting objects such as animals, fairies, mechanical things, and events. The child, therefore, learns of the existence of many things which he has not witnessed and which not only are not available but are also very different from the things which he has seen. He then proceeds to develop them by means of the materials he has at hand. Now comes the great evolution of language activities. The child, being told fairy tales and stories of various sorts, begins to perform creative reactions for himself and to enlarge upon things he has seen or heard. Thus he combines them in various ways, adding size, shape, and color. From this stage on, through more and more manipulative practise and through the acquisition of knowledge and other behavior equipment that can be employed as integral factors, imagination reactions develop to their fullest constructive capacity.

Cultural and disciplinary stimuli of all sorts provide at this stage of the individual's career many occasions for the origin of constructive behavior. Very frequently the child finds himself obliged to invent justifications for acts he has performed, and to excuse behavior frowned upon by his elders. This is also the period for the imaginary appropriation of objects which the child desires but does not possess, and for the magnification of his own and his parents' power when the exigencies of playmate rivalries make such action expedient or desirable.

The training of imagination consists, we may say, of the multiplication of contacts of the originating person with varieties of things and conditions. Naturally, the work of constructing, whether it be implicit or overt, may be criticized and controlled to the end of improving it. This sort of imagination training is illustrated by the criticism of the art student by his teacher. The critic stimulates the individual not only to develop his manipulation by improving his drawings, color combinations, or the technique of modeling, but also to better his general conceptions and plans of the work. Frequently the constructive phase is considered to be the primary one. We must amend this idea, however, by suggesting that all phases, overt manipulations as well as implicit construction of plans, are of equal importance from a strict psychological standpoint. When we reach the stage of actual aesthetic appreciation, the equal importance of all phases is readily estimated.

**Stimuli for Imagination Responses**  From the nature of imagination responses we may readily surmise that their stimuli are practically always very complex. Moreover, it is clear that the stimuli are generally situations rather than mere objects or persons. Whenever an object or person, however, does perform the stimulus function for some creative action, it serves to suggest and imply that some change or modification is required or feasible rather than to elicit some immediate or standard form of response.

Briefly, creative behavior segments comprise two types of stimuli. On the one hand, we have objects suggesting or calling out direct, modifying manipulations resulting in a production which again suggests by its new appearance or character further modifying and creational responses. This serial process may continue for a considerable period of time or until some desired or required product is finally obtained. If we have here a substitute stimulational function at all, we must think of both the substitute and adjustment functions as inhering in the same object or situation. On the one hand, the object functions to indicate or imply the need for change and transformation, and on the other, it points to the changes required or desired.

In every case, of course, the precise modes in which the stimuli operate depend upon the particular individual who is acting. Objects and situations which to one person suggest hardly anything in the way of a need for change or the manner in which the change should be made, to another individual suggest the most intricate and complex creative effects. What we have been saying naturally applies to the simpler type of imagination stimuli, although the reactions indicated by the stimuli may vary from mere rearrangement and change to the most thoroughgoing recreation.

The second type of imagination stimulus shows plainly the clear substitutional character. We can point with unfailing precision to distinctly different things serving the two stimulational functions. Very frequently the substitute stimulus has no manner of direct relationship to the adjustment stimulus or the product. The former merely calls out the response that we have so often indicated is worked out on the basis of the individual's creational activity. Or possibly the substitute stimuli first call out a creative reaction quite appropriately called a conceptual product which may mark the completion of the imagination activity. In other instances the conceptual response may be considered to be only a partial adjustment or creative response which is to be completed by the execution of the conception upon some type of material. In such imagination situations the conceptual response may function as a partial stimulus to elicit the operation of the executory phase of the reaction pattern.

Probably in no situation do the settings of stimuli objects play so prominent and important a rôle as they do in the case of imagination behavior segments. These settings serve in a peculiar and effective way to provide suggestions for the detailed manipulations and creations which constitute imagination responses. In other words, the occasions and circumstances under which imagination stimulation takes place exert a considerable influence upon the course and development of the whole creative action.

We have already implied that particular objects perform a variety of imaginative stimuli functions. The incompleteness and insufficiency of objects stimulate us to imagine them in finished form. Parts of things and situations induce us to create the absent or missing portions or features. Things in ruin invite us to recreate them or recast them in a more complete mould. Especially conducive to the development of imagination behavior are those things which are novel, mysterious, beautiful, impressive, unattainable, sublime, etc.

Prominent among the situations stimulating creative conduct are various lacunae in our knowledge. Such gaps in our information actively stimulate us to acquire cognitional equipment concerning the particular things in question. Similarly, all our various personal relations with other individuals, especially as they emphasize deficiencies and unsatisfactoriness, are effective agents in suggesting means of improving and overcoming such relationships.

As in all cases of psychological reactions, imagination responses differ among individuals in both amount and intensity. Beyond this we also find more unique forms of individual differences which really consist of types of specialization with respect to imaginative processes and situations. We discover, for example, that individuals who perform very striking creative behavior in the field, say, of poetry, cannot perform creative responses of a mechanical type. The individual especially creative in the field of mechanical activity may, on the other hand, not be able to accomplish much in a literary or intellectual situation. *Individual Differences in Imagination*

For instance, in the poetic field the constructive behavior of a person may be restricted to some particular form of verse. He may write well in one medium and not in another. Or he may be very adept in writing about a particular thing but not about all things. This type of individual difference also takes into account the fact that persons differ in the degree to which they excel in a large number of creative activities. Similar individual differences are discernible in all other fields of constructive behavior. Mechanical inventors and intellectual creators are likewise restricted to particular sorts of attempts and accomplishments. A man who can invent an adding machine is not necessarily capable of producing an electrical contrivance, and vice versa.

Referring back to our study of the influences upon creative conduct, we may trace the bases for such individual differences to the intimate behavior equipment of the creating individual and his reactional biography. These divergent equipments acquired through varying reactional biographies account for the different ways in which creative conduct functions as specific responses of the acting person.

Quite as important determinants of imaginative individual differences are the specific momentary occasions which provide actual stimuli for the performance of imagination responses. Most decidedly we must look upon the earliest or original reactional capacity of performing creative actions as momentarily acquired behavior. But, in addition, the entire matrix of imaginative situations, with their intimate and specific stimuli indicators for the performance of detailed manipulations and constructions, must come from a momentarily presented and momentarily developed situation. This means to say that imagination conduct may be considered to be in part at least contingential behavior.

**Inspiration and Originality as Forms of Creative Conduct**

Because of various specific conditions surrounding every individual instance of creative conduct and especially its more complex types, we find that it acquires salient characteristics sufficient to warrant special naming and description. Two of these we select for treatment because of their unique traditional interest and equally traditional misapprehension. Of these two, inspirational conduct involves primarily a temporal factor which lends the activity a very striking aspect. Superficially the person appears to be accomplishing on the spur of the moment an exceedingly complex action which, however, could not really be so achieved were it not for some definite preceding activity. Originality, on the other hand, constitutes a type of imagination behavior which seems to imply magical powers on the part of the acting individual, whereas in reality his actual performances grow out of a series of definite conditions that usually lead inevitably to the final results.

Inspirational action involves on the surface a seemingly immediate constructive action very different from the behavior directly preceding and following the condition of inspiration. Also the product of the action is presumed to be very unlike any other resulting from the person's responses. When we examine the situation closely what we actually discover is that the person is not doing something which has no antecedent phases, but rather that he is now able to perform some type of creational reaction which for a time seemed suspended and impossible of occurrence. To a certain extent the phenomenon of inspiration consists of a release of the person's creative activity. In the final analysis, therefore, inspiration turns out to be merely a peculiar form of creational behavior. Of what does this peculiarity consist? Of nothing more, we might answer, than the suddenness or unex-

pectedness of the final imagination release and the consequent constructive behavior. In other words, the person inspired to do
something, has been stimulated by some kind of situation but for the
time being is actually unable to perform the creational response.
After a period of brooding and ruminating upon the situation, however, the response may finally occur. Very frequently the inspiration
consists of the final release of the creative activity by the appearance
in the situation of a new phase or a new angle of the stimulus which
was previously invisible but which is now brought into focus by the
process of ruminating and so-called incubation. These latter processes consist for the most part of subtle implicit manipulations of the
stimulational factors which are involved in the specific creational action under discussion.

The subtle preperformative activities which constitute a phase of
inspirational creative conduct and which are so difficult to observe,
may be readily investigated when the constructive activity is of the
overt and effective type. The person who is attempting to put together a complex anatomical model, for example, may be checked at
some point in the performance of this action and then, after looking
around, discovers some hook to which must be attached a part of the
model. At the instant when he first comes across this hook which
is a key to the situation at hand, he seems overwhelmed by the discovery and is inspired to do the thing which for a time he was unable to
do. Precisely the same situation prevails when the constructional
activity is an implicit one, but here the new stimulus situation which
happens to be a reaction of the person himself, is not so clearly evident. It is the latter type of situation that has led to the popular
mystification concerning the process of inspiration.

One other feature of the inspirational type, namely its affective
accompaniments, is exceedingly worthy of inspection, chiefly because
of the light it throws upon the general character of imagination responses. Because of the checking of the creative action and its consequent suddenness or unexpectedness of release, the person frequently
undergoes at the same time a decided feeling experience. It may involve a suffusion of the whole organism and be so intense as to appear
to shake the individual completely. Furthermore, the person may
undergo a very intense feeling reaction as a result of his final success
in performing an important creative action. Accordingly, many cases
of inspirational creative conduct lend a concrete foundation to the
popular tales concerning the intense fire and passion of constructive
behavior and the deep penetration of reality which attends the creating passion when one is performing inspirational conduct.

Originality, therefore, as a quality of the creating individual and a
characteristic of a particular sort of imaginative conduct, differs considerably in its actual identity and operation from the popular conception of the type of fact and with which it is confused. In short,
that individual is most original who has had the largest series of con-

tacts with things. As a consequence he has acquired the technique of isolating similarities and dissimilarities and thus is enabled to manipulate things and their qualities implicitly as a necessary basis for constructing reactions. The originality of a person consists, then, of a more thorough and comprehensive series of contacts with things rather than of an absence of such reactional relations with them. It should not be inferred, however, that original behavior demands that one have actual first contacts with things. On the contrary, some individuals through reading and other such indirect sources have far more intensive contacts with things than others who are in actual connection with them.

**The Relation of Imaginative Activities and Intelligence**        A question of considerable importance arises with respect to the relation of intelligence and imagination. Is one subordinate to the other? Are they interdependent? Or do they represent two distinct types of action?

At first glance, it seems that in general the greater the degree of one's intelligence the more apt one is to perform creational activities. This is no doubt a fact. Yet is it true that, unless a person is intelligent, he cannot perform creational action? Our answer is a decided negative. The performance of creational action is possible even when the individual is not capable of any high degree of intelligent activity. For example, as our exposition has revealed, an infant performs very many creational or imaginative reactions in spite of the fact that he has not yet reached a very high degree of intelligence. Now we must not overlook here that possibly the same infant, when it has acquired more intelligence through a general increase of behavior equipment, can perform more elaborate and useful imaginative reactions. But still the absence of intelligent behavior in any considerable degree does not prevent the individual from performing imaginative responses.

Some further commonly known facts throwing light on the relationship of intelligence and imagination are the popular observations that the highest type of constructive individual, especially when his imagination is of the artistic or æsthetic type, is not especially intelligent. That is to say, if intelligence is considered as the capacity to do certain things, it is frequently discoverable that artists are hopelessly lacking in ability to do some things which are apparently needed for purposes of practical adjustment. This statement is not intended to imply that we accept the conventional belief that an artist is subnormal with respect to economic and social conditions. On the contrary, what we are trying to point out is that imagination reactions may be exceedingly specialized, so that the possession of a large and useful series of imagination responses does not guarantee the presence of a complete equipment of intelligent reactions.

So far, then, we may conclude that while constructive conduct as a type of psychological behavior is fairly independent of intelligent conduct, still the capacity of the person to perform constructive action may be greatly enhanced by intelligent behavior. It may be added also that the effectiveness gained by intelligence in the performance of imagination activity concerns the more complex types of imaginative behavior.

To look at the relationship from the opposite standpoint we find that the capacity to perform constructive or imaginative action is a prime factor in the development and operation of intelligent reactions. When the person is able to reconstruct his stimulating situations, he will be able to extricate himself from difficult conditions and in general succeed in solving problems and in meeting new situations. Here the relationship between the two types of action is plainly reversed. We must indicate, therefore, that in spite of the fact that imagination conduct is not absolutely essential for the performance of intelligent actions the former is of considerable value for the adequate and effective performance of the latter. In general, we may say that a very close relationship exists between intelligent and imaginative activities, especially when complex psychological conduct is in question.

Creative conduct, even its complex forms, occurs in all modalities. We may imagine things which are in full and vivid contact with ourselves and our surroundings as stimuli. Contrariwise, we perform creative actions while farthest removed from, and very remotely connected with, the activating stimuli objects. Naturally imagination activities of the more complex sort operating as reactionalistic, subreactionalistic, etc., are the purely implicit type. Elaborate performances of this kind are most familiar in dream life.[1] The important point to observe here is that imaginative actions need not operate with the knowledge and intention of the acting person.

*Witting and Unwitting Imagination*

The probably familiar observation just made serves as an introduction to the fact that frequently the person finds himself reacting to objects which were really created by himself as though they were actually existing in their natural state. In everyday language this is spoken of as the confusion of unreality with reality. Such situations constitute the essential conditions for hallucinations of all sorts. What actually happens is that the individual is dealing with some situation involving objects, persons, or information, to which he has added some elements by means of his own creative efforts.

Such confusion is possible because imagination reactions may be unwittingly performed. Thus at times a person is unable to distinguish between the objects or situations of which he has some real knowledge, and a similar object that he has in part or wholly created. Abundant illustrations of this sort of phenomena are found in the reports of different witnesses of the same events. The variations in particulars that such eyewitnesses report are most remarkable. A more extreme form of this confusion of the existing and the created

[1] But this must by no means be taken to imply that all dreams are imagination activities.

is found in the experience of artists concerning what they see or hear. By far the most exaggerated form is the phenomena we find in the strongly absorbed poet,[1] the insane, or individuals otherwise alienated. All these persons do not distinguish between the facts in nature to which they react and those same facts to which they have added a considerable portion by their own constructive behavior.

Children, and in general those who have no or little behavior equipment of certain types, are prone to confuse the actual and the imagined. This fact doubtless accounts for much infantile behavior which parents consider strange and to which they react with the strongest disapproval. Once the child has created a property for a thing, either some natural object or some related event or person, he has no hesitation in giving it his staunchest support of belief, or in apprising others of its existence. In all this, of course, the unwitting performance of constructive actions has a very prominent place.

Strangely enough, we find the same conditions prevailing in the most rigid scientific thinking and action. Many a scientist who accepts a certain hypothesis or theory concerning some fact accepts as an actual objective datum some thing which he has in large or great part himself invented. Here again the unwitting performance of creative conduct proves to be the causal agent or the primary contributory condition to which the whole occurrence is attributable.

**Classification of Imagination Activities**

In approaching the problem of classifying imagination reactions we are immediately brought face to face with the same general question of criteria we have already met in studying other behavior segments. First we must ask, what shall be the logical ground of the organization? In the case of imagination reactions we might consider the stimulating situations, namely, base our classification upon the kinds of objects which constitute the adjustment stimuli. For instance, are we performing reactions to æsthetic, technical, or philosophical objects or situations? Or, we might organize the behavior on the basis of whether it is unconditioned or conditioned, and if the latter, how much and in what way. In the question whether the constructive action is more controlled and mechanical we already find an emphasis on the substitute stimuli factors in contrast to the freer behavior in which the responses are more prominent. The products of the action provide still another criterion. Here the question is whether the results of the behavior comprise a new or transformed object, situation, or process, or whether the result of the behavior is another action. Again, our classification basis may be the kind of material used in engendering the product, or the place at and purpose for which it is contrived or fashioned. Since the matter of product of action has hitherto received but meagre treatment in our study, we will stress that as the primary basis of our classification, giving slighter emphasis to the other factors.

---

[1] Shelley, for example. It is said, he was very apt to confuse the products of his fancy with those of his actual surroundings.

For the most part we place under this rubric constructions that con- **Phantasy** stitute rebuilding and transformations of the reacting person's immediate surroundings. The products of phantastic imagination are conditions and situations which provide more pleasant or more endurable living conditions, refuges for escape from intolerable circumstances. Such transformations may constitute genuine plans for actual changes in one's surroundings. As such, they are actual preliminary developments preceding definite modifications of one's condition. On the other hand, the products of this constructive activity may have very little relation with actual things and conditions surrounding the reacting individual. He may be performing such imagination reactions only for the amusement it affords him or because he is dissociated from his actual surroundings. It is here that we must place the activities of the dreamers who build for themselves worlds of their own, worlds but slightly related to those in which their creators really live. It is the confusion of this kind of behavior with artistic creation that is the root of the erroneous conception that æsthetic imagination is an instrument for release from troubles and for the satisfaction of desires.

So far as constructive materials for phantastic imagining are concerned, it appears from the nature of the case that the most common forms are the person's own acts, and especially those of the implicit type. All manner of phantasy creations can be made from implicit actions. A close second among types of phantasy creational material is verbal action. From words and in terms of words all sorts of imaginative constructions and transformations are produced.

It would be a great error, however, to suppose that the most recondite materials cannot be manipulated in performing phantastic imagination responses. The complicated mechanical inventions of alienated individuals who attempt to solve the problem of perpetual motion and the aberrant drawings and paintings of abnormal persons eloquently testify to this fact.

The scientific type of imagination resembles, to a considerable ex- **Scientific** tent, the more utilitarian form of phantasy, especially in the fact that **Imagination** both may be considered processes for the recreating of surroundings. These two types, however, differ very markedly. Whereas at least some forms of phantasy are extremely free, in the case of scientific imagination the conditions are always fairly imperative and circumscribed. The constructions of science are therefore dictated by the actual conditions surrounding the situation in which the scientific work is being done. In this case, too, the individual is not only conditioned by the immediate situations of the problem at hand, but by relevant facts and information already developed and standardized. It is for this reason that scientific imagination must emphasize knowing rather than doing, although the underlying motive is the solution of practical problems leading to the control and modification of actual surrounding situations.

The products of scientific imagination may therefore be considered to be of two sorts. The first or immediate are changes and modifications in the circumstances and surroundings as dictated by the needs and requirements of everyday life. The second and less immediate products, which may be considered preliminary or instrumental to the development of the first, are hypotheses and theories created for the purpose of transforming crude facts into more controllable and standardized conditions and circumstances.

Materials for scientific creation of the first and immediate type are of course the situations or conditions which stimulate the performance of imaginative reactions. These may be considered as problems of all sorts, including living and working conditions that are not satisfactory or require improvement as well as objects and events arousing curiosity and interest. The materials used for the construction of hypotheses and theories are ideas and knowledge that have been previously developed or acquired and now constitute the traditional stock of scientific information.

**Philo-sophic Imagina-tion**

For the most part the results of philosophic imagination reactions are created hypotheses, modes of explanation of things, or ways of interpreting conditions. Such products enable the person to achieve a larger and more secure orientation with respect to the particular kinds of data with which he is occupied.

Generally speaking the activities referred to as the work of the philosophic imagination are freer and less conditioned in their operation than are scientific creative actions which they otherwise resemble. Because philosophical enterprises, as compared with scientific, are not so specialized the individual's activity is not determined by some particular detail for an immediate purpose. Hence the philosophic interest is a much broader one. Also the range of things dealt with is larger and provides occasion for a greater breadth of creative action. It must be noted, however, that philosophic imagination demands careful and critical attention to actual facts.

Materials for the activities of philosophic imagination are afforded by precisely the same things and conditions which provoke scientific creation, namely, the same general types of problems but presented, however, in a more abstract way.

**Linguistic Imagina-tion**

The field of language provides a fertile source for the development of a great many creative reactions. In considering only the everyday uses of language, we find in the descriptive and narrational uses of speech many occasions to perform original actions. The products here may be definitely classified as metaphors, similes, and other types of figures of speech. But this series of creational linguistic products by no means exhausts the list of original linguistic reactions. Others are particular and peculiar means that individuals have of saying things, referring to objects and events, or expressing their feelings, wants, and desires, etc.

Among the more complex products of linguistic imagination are the literary forms and objects comprising poems, narratives, plays, and other compositions. How large a place linguistic products occupy among human creations may be gathered from the fact that they constitute the materials for the most popular of the arts, namely, the literary and the dramatic.

Since the linguistic activities of persons are primarily cultural in character it appears that such actions are more restricted and conditioned in their operation than are other forms. Accordingly, creation in the field of language is much more the originality of use and of transformation than of new development. Also, here as in the case of intellectual originality, there is ample room for negative action. Just as in the intellectual field, in which a person may be original merely by not believing what others of his school believe, or what other schools adhere to, so in the case of language a person may be creative and original by avoiding what is currently done and by leaning toward other ways of doing things.

Typical products of the religious imagination are conditions and situations affording a refuge and relief from undesirable and intolerable living conditions and circumstances. This statement is especially true of the results of creative efforts in the religious field so far as they concern conventional materials. For the most part the traditional products of religious imagination consist of descriptions of governing powers who offer rewards and punishments, and of places where the distasteful conditions of ordinary life find sharp contrast. Also, much religious creation constitutes descriptions of what one might do in order to live a happier or better life than the customary one. Religious Imagination

Quite common are the religious, creative functions directed to the development of schemes or methods of justifying a certain religious tradition and making it appear plausible in view of actual facts discovered around us. Such justifying and rationalizing invention is an extension of the same type of psychological processes which function in all sorts of myth making. Myths, in general, may be considered inventions developed to represent or symbolize the attitudes of people of a particular social status, or account for things of particular interest or appeal.

The products of the more individualized religious reactions are descriptions of conditions which extend beyond human facts and conditions of the actual world. For instance, religious imagination of the individual type involves the solution of problems that are not susceptible to solution by ordinary methods of reflection and investigation.

Clearly the materials of religious creation consist primarily of verbal actions. For the products of such creative effort cannot comprise more substantial textures. Because of the verbal medium the development of conventional religious inventions and constructions has a greater or lesser temporal continuity. Hence the later religious constructions are contrived from and fashioned out of earlier forms.

As a final type of material for religious invention we must mention the various sorts of action which constitute religious forms and practices. Ways of worship as specific kinds of action can be manipulated and reconstructed to constitute different and newer modes of behavior, although such activities are not such fertile sources of creative conduct as other types of human conduct.

**Technical Imagination**

Processes of all sorts susceptible of employment in everyday life, in industry, commerce, and in the arts, as well as objects of all kinds, tools and machines, constitute the main tangible results of technical imaginative behavior. All of the varieties of situations that constantly surround persons in their various cultural environments supply abundant stimuli to elicit inventive reactions of innumerable sorts. Among these may be mentioned a host of social and economic conditions which symptomatize the needs and requirements of a community as well as the resources for satisfying such needs. The same group of general conditions also sets the pace for the work of imagination and constitutes conditioning and limiting influences upon the types and numbers of articles and processes developed.

With respect to limiting conditions which operate in technological imagination activities, we must not ignore the industrial and commercial conventions and customs constituting the tried and accepted practices prevalent in such situations. So effective are such determinants that in most cases it is difficult to overcome the resistance of these traditional prejudices. Hence the effective barrier they form against the progress of creative activities.

When we seek the materials for technical manipulations and trials we find them in the innumerable existing methods of work and technical processes. These result in the development and contrivance of new ways of doing things and of instruments and machines for accomplishing work of particular sorts. Technical imagination, though primarily a type of activity operating in circumstances concerned with work, is by no means limited to such situations. It finds numerous uses and applications in every field of human activity.

**Æsthetic Imagination**

The æsthetic imagination has always appeared as the most striking domain of constructive behavior. This condition has prevailed not only because the activities of the æsthetic imagination display to us the most active and unhampered, as well as the most complex creations of all the situations in which imaginative action occurs, but also because the plasticity of the material affords unmistakable results in the form of new objects. Landscapes and people are actually recreated through painting; characters are recreated through sculpture and through literary art.

That aesthetic imaginative activity is a work of creation and contrivance of new things, is proved clearly by the fact that such activity represents a performance of the acting individual in which he expresses his own personal behavior equipment, including his likes, tastes, and conceptions of things. As a consequence such activity is free and unobstructed, conditioned only by the individual's proficiency, his experience, and the media through which he carries out his conceptions or reflects his intellectual and aesthetic attitudes.

Great opportunity for creative action is further made possible in the field of æsthetic imagination by the fact that the products are not conditioned by the necessities and limitations of use and convenience. Whereas in other forms of constructive activity the person must be quicker in his performance, because of the possible applicability and serviceability of the product, in the case of art production no such conditions have any decisive effect upon the work or its results. Even when the artistic activities are to be applied within the limits of a given space or occasion, the restrictions placed upon the creative powers of the acting individual are at a minimum.

Of materials for artistic activity there is an inexhaustible list. Consider only the color, sound, taste and smell activities; the design; the stone, wood, bronze, and other materials; the words, phrases and literary forms in which artistic effect is consummated. The materials for statues, pictures, poems, stories, musical compositions, etc., are innumerable. But these constitute only one general type of artistic material; the other comprises various kinds of actions. Among the latter are the attitudes and other reactions that the person develops towards the objects around him. Here we place all the ideas and conceptions which in everyday language are spoken of as embodied and expressed in the color, stone, composition or design, etc., of the artistic product. Not only are the person's own conceptions such material for manipulation and development, but other individuals' ideas also are employed as a basis for artistic activity.

Not uncommon is the creation of unique products in the form of ideals of conduct to which persons later more or less strictly conform. We do not mean that these ideals as imagination products are found only in the moral domain; but they are exceedingly well represented in moral situations. In a genuine sense, moral ideals as products of imagination conduct are very like hypotheses and theories which are the products of scientific creation action. In more concrete form we may consider moral imagination products as actions performed under prescribed conditions and verbally constituted prescriptions as to what should be done under given circumstances. Available materials for moral imagination activities are, however, not limited to the conventional morals, ideals, and prescriptions, but reside also in the person's idiosyncratic modes of conduct, as well as in his knowledge of and desire for particular kinds of action bearing the moral stamp. *Moral Imagination*

For the most part, moral imagination is exceedingly restricted and displays a lack of freedom and innovation that is most peculiar for creative conduct. Ethical imagination is hedged about by restricting customs of all sorts, by economic conditions and circumstances, and perhaps even more so by the conflicting interests of persons and associations of a given locality and community.

**Political and Social Imagination**

Although the world of political and social activities is not an extremely fertile field for imaginative behavior it still exhibits activities of a creative type. On the whole the products of such imagination behavior are concerned with slight modifications in administrative procedure and in social order and arrangement. Such products may be said in general to be situations and conditions rather than objects of any sort.

Probably social and political imagination is even more definitely restricted than moral imagination. This is especially true since the tangible political products are actually designed for practical use. Indeed they place social and political imagination upon the border line between creative and merely adaptive action. However, in the case of conceptual creations which range from the most fanciful and impractical to the most definitely applicable situations, the creative activities of the political and social domain may be very like those of other departments of human action.

Aside from the conceptual and verbal materials used for such manipulative and transformative operations, the things upon which the reacting person has to work are existing political and social situations and conditions. Their insufficiencies and defects stimulate attempts toward improvement and modification to the end of creating newer and better situations.

With the suggestion of these specimen types of imaginative behavior we have a series of fair examples of the different ways in which our creative actions operate. It has already been noted that creative action is performed more or less successfully in every one of our domains of human conduct. In some cases conditions are such that free creative action is not only prompted by prevailing conditions but is easily accomplished. In other instances only the slightest amount of transformation of the surroundings appears possible. One further suggestion is desirable, namely, that while certain types of products are more closely connected with certain situations than with others they are not exclusively connected with them. Thus, for example, while things or processes primarily constitute the products of one type of situation they may be developed in others also. On the whole, it must be noted that the products, mode of stimulation of the performance, type of performance, etc., are all factors of specific situations and depend upon them.

That imagination behavior is essentially a type of reaction process is a truth that has been frequently stressed. But the idea that imagination is a creative process, although based, doubtless, upon the observation of actual creational behavior in art and mechanical invention, has not resulted in the conception of this creational process as a definite form of concrete activity. On the contrary it has usually been conceived of as a mysterious kind of impalpable occurrence.

If we refer only to ideas current in our own day we find that the creative action observable in art is attributed to some superexperiential urge or power which it is possible for only a few peculiarly gifted individuals to possess. A variant of this idea is the conception of some mysterious entity connected with the individual in which these urges are located or from which they spring. This type of viewpoint includes the psychoanalytic doctrines according to which creative power is an expression of some kind of subconscious or unconscious mind from which ideas and conceptions arise and which are later worked out in some specific medium. It is hardly necessary to comment upon such views, except to say that they belong to a domain of intellectual endeavor entirely different from that of objective psychological facts and theories. In general, the views which make creative processes into mysterious happenings simply forego the difficult analysis of the intricate observable and inferred behavior facts. Moreover, they completely ignore the evolution of such behavior in the life of the person through his many contacts with the objects and occasions of his creative and constructive conduct.

Not all traditional views have dallied with such a weird procedure, but they have been equally removed from the facts af actual creational behavior. For example, we have the theory that imagination phenomena always consist of purely mental activity as compared with the tangible movements and actions of the biological organism. These pure types of psychological processes are called images.

That imagination has to do only with imagery behavior is a view that may be traced back to a psychological period in which only mentalities came into consideration. No bodily or biological phenomena were considered at all. Accordingly it was found necessary to distinguish the materials which represented the stable and the generally real from the internal fluctuating states of mental existence. Most frequently, of course, images were regarded as vestiges or remnants of the more solid and reliable mental states called sensations. At any rate the images were considered to be derived in some way from sensations. In more recent literature such a view is well represented in the work of Taine (*On Intelligence*, 1872), which follows the tradition

83

of David Hume and James Mill. Now because of this derivative form, imagination was frequently regarded as not wholly a reliable or dependable form of mentality. Imagery, it was thought, dealt with falsifying conditions and unrealities. It was also very closely related to abnormalities and deficiencies of psychological activity. When such a theory is made to deal with sheer mentalities of a particular sort we can of course do nothing but reiterate our complete disseverance from it. This attitude is just as binding upon us when the mentalities are thought of as connected with bodily or physiological facts as when no connection is postulated.

We submit, however, that even if by images one means implicit action, and by implicit action definite objective behavior, this theory is far removed from the conception that imagination consists of actual transforming and creating conduct. For as we have indicated in the present chapter, the essential fact is the creative conduct, no matter of what general type. To make imagination consist exclusively of inapparent action would be to overemphasize one type of behavior, howsoever genuine and important, and totally exclude others of equal value. From the standpoint of the imagery conception of imagination it is quite a novel view that imagination activity is the creative response to any type of thing or action which is so manipulated and treated as to be transformed into something new.

A variant of the imagery conception is the theory that imagination involves the creative type of imagery as distinguished from the mere reproductive sort which, with the former, constitute the two forms of such mental occurrences. A brilliant representative of this theory is Ribot (*Essay on the Creative Imagination*, 1906). While this work stresses the creational factor, no closer approach is made to the conception of imagination as the performance of objective transforming action than we have indicated in speaking of the general imagery theory.

In view of our statement that imagination has always been considered in its relation to artistic and constructive action it is probably anomalous that the admission of biological factors into discussions of imagination has had so peculiar an outcome. It is quite remarkable to find a psychologist who assumes that imagination has a stimulational organ not directly or at all connected with external objects. In a very crude form imagination phenomena were thought to be aroused by internal or cerebral, instead of peripheral, factors. James' statement in the chapter on Imagination in the *Principles* is typical. The biological viewpoint did not add anything valid to the description of imagination behavior but merely resulted in the contriving of an extraordinary conception of neurology.

It remains to be said that probably the best materials for the perspective of imagination behavior can be found in descriptions of literary and mechanical productions written from the standpoint of the biography of the constructing individual. It is in the study of these materials that one discovers the sources and the development of particular imagination products. Typical of such materials are the illustrations found in the work of Paulhan (*Psychologie de l'Invention*, 1901).

# CHAPTER XIX

## REMEMBERING AND FORGETTING

Memory activities or memorial conduct constitute behavior segments in which the final reactions are definitely delayed or postponed. Such delay or postponement is due to the fact that either (1) the adjustment stimulus is no longer present when the response is made and consequently must be substituted for (that is to say, a substitute stimulus-object or condition serves to call out the delayed reaction or response phase of the memory behavior) or (2) the stimulus object itself is again available after a period of unavailability. In the latter case, although the unavailability or absence may be an exceedingly brief one, we must still look upon the effective stimulus-object as a substitute for the adjustment stimulus, which in this instance may be the same object in a different temporal setting. Accordingly memory actions constitute a special class of implicit behavior segments.

We may characterize memorial behavior segments more accurately perhaps by referring to them as suspended or continuous reactions. Probably the latter description is more to the point. The fundamental characteristic of true memory reactions is that they start at some particular time, continue through another time interval which constitutes a less active or suspended stage, and are finally brought to completion in a third, and active stage.[1] Or when this last part of the reaction does not occur we have the opposite fact, namely, forgetting. The main emphasis in all cases, however, is on the fact of temporal continuity despite the circumstance that there is a middle period of indiscernible action between the two more active phases. The emphasis on the continuity of memory reactions is made, first, because there is a period of apparent non-action before the final phase of the memory act is executed, and secondly, because we are dealing with the actual behavior of a person covering a period of time. Consequently the phases or partial acts might erroneously be considered as independent, discontinuous activities. That a memory behavior segment is a single continuous action, no matter how long a time is required for its transpiration, is clear from the fact that a memory reaction goes on from one period to another. It begins, for instance, at the moment we make an engagement with someone and ends when we actually meet the person at the appointed time and place.

We find it exceedingly helpful to study memory reactions in a

---

[1] The hypothesis presented here was first published in an article entitled, Memory: A Triphase Objective Action, Journal of Philosophy, 1922, 29, 624–639.

practical way as concrete, actual responses.  This enables us to see how it is possible for a person to continue an identical memory activity throughout a whole series of time periods.  For example, he may make an engagement, and keep it at some later time, while also doing other things, both at the time when the engagement is being made and kept, as well as between the two periods.  This situation is similar to the case of a person who is going somewhere and in the same time interval greets a friend on the way.  When we consider that the person can actually stop to chat with his friend, the hypothesis of the temporal continuity of a memory action is strengthened rather than weakened by the analogy between these otherwise very different sorts of behavior.

While we naturally choose for illustrative purposes types of memorial behavior which lend themselves advantageously to the presentation of our conception, we still insist that the case of memory stands no differently with respect to informational reactions than grosser sorts of behavior.  Here we must be more careful, however, to avoid mere language habits and informational learning which are quite different sorts of phenomena from memory action.

A memory reaction, it follows then, cannot be studied and understood without a consideration of the behavior from the standpoint of all of the time periods involved.  We observe the distinct existence of three such periods, namely, (1) the inceptive, (2) the between stage, and (3) the consummatory stage.  Three phases of a unit action correspond to these three time units, to wit, (1) the projection or initiatory phase, (2) the middle phase, and (3) the recollective or consummatory phase.  The middle phase, because of its relative invisibility and submerged operation, may be practically neglected, although it is a genuine phase of all memory behavior.  Although in general descriptions of memory we disregard the middle phase, it is presupposed in both the projection and recollective phases.  Accordingly, the brief examination of each of the two end phases in our opinion will reveal evidence not only that a memory behavior segment requires a definite time interval for its operation, be it minutes or months, but also that a memorial response consists of a single, triphase, continuous action.

Whenever we start a memory reaction it is invariably implied that the reaction will be continued or suspended until some specified, posterior time.  The immediate act is initiated in order that some related action shall occur.  We make engagements in order to keep them; we memorize in order to recite after some longer or shorter intervening time interval.

Furthermore, the intervening phase of action, which superficially appears as no action whatever, must in fact be looked upon as a positive mode of psychological adaptation, since memory behavior necessitates this interval between the initiation of the action and its final consummation.  A moment's reflection regarding the inhibition of reaction reveals the actual character of the suspended memory phase, especially since here the consummatory phase is only temporarily inhibited or postponed. After signing the contract the waiting for the expiration of ninety days to pay the amount nominated in the bond is very much a part of the total memory action involved. A definite disturbance or anomaly in memorial conduct occurs when this middle stage does not remain passive. Think how annoying it is when one agrees to appear and explain, for example, the wrong parking of a car and the projected action cannot be properly inhibited and is thus implicitly preperformed. Such a reaction need not be unpleasant as, for example, when a young woman preperforms implicitly the projection action of entertaining her first caller. Either case well illustrates the character of the phase of action in question.

When the final or completion phase of a memory behavior segment operates, its mode of action is conditioned by, and implies the functioning of, the middle phase. The final action occurs only after a suitable given period which is conditioned by the stimulating circumstances of the entire behavior.

The two terminal actions are incomplete and insignificant unless they are inextricably intercorrelated with the strict implication of the middle part of the action. In fact, while the three phases appear morphologically distinct they are not at all distinct functionally.[1]

Another important point for the understanding of memory behavior and one which argues further for its continuous character is the fact that it involves very close connections between specific responses and the particular stimuli coördinated with them. A given stimulus must directly elicit a specific name or a specified act of some nonverbal sort. No substitution of response, no new act not previously begun and postponed may now occur, or we are either not remembering or are remembering faultily and ineffectively. With respect to directness of connection between stimuli and responses, memorial behavior differs from thinking (another type of delayed behavior) in that the latter action, when it occurs, may be indefinitely determined or conditioned by an anterior trial and error procedure.

To the important points which we have just made concerning memory behavior segments, namely, that they operate between two definite end-time points, and that throughout this time a particular coördination of stimulus and response is operating, we may now add a third point, namely, that the time during which the continuous memory action operates may be more or less prolonged. That is to say, even when memory reactions are intentionally projected they may operate finally only after some indefinite time period.

[1] This reflection gives rise to the query whether the third phase is really independent of the other two, or whether it should be interpreted as part of the first. In either interpretation the fact stands out with certainty that this part of the memory conduct is a definite mode of action.

This situation is illustrated by the case of a person who is memorizing some material for an examination although he is not fully informed as to when that examination is to take place.

The continuous or postponing character of memorial reactions appears plausible enough when such delayed behavior is autonomous (that is, when the memory act is the only adjustment or adaptation in question). The postponent character is equally present when the memory behavior is a necessary precursor to another act. In other words, even when the memory action is only preliminary to further conduct, the postponed or continuous functioning is an integral feature of the total behavior situation. This point is essential in illuminating the general character of memory behavior, namely, that memorial reactions constitute definite types of psychological action in the sense that they comprise either preliminary recalling of information upon which further action is based, or complete adaptations, as in reminiscence. In this connection it is well to point out that, once the second active phase of a behavior segment is operating, the additional problem arises as to whether there will be a forward-looking result or merely a backward-looking one, that is, one that merely refers back to or repeats the projection stage of memory.

Corresponding to the precurrent and final character of memorial reactions are their simple and complex characters. Plainly, the precurrent reactions are by far the simpler of the two types. In fact, the complex, final, memory behavior segments are replete with all sorts of component responses many of which, if functioning alone, are far removed from the description and name of memory behavior.

**Memory Behavior Contrasted With other Types**    The fact that memorial reactions are delayed and consequently require substitution stimuli constitutes the essential criterion for distinguishing such reactions from, say, perceptual responses. But why contrast memory with perception? We answer, because it has been traditionally held that, since in perceptual behavior we react to whole objects although we are in direct contact only with some phase or quality of them, we must therefore have a memory reaction in each perceptual response. Now we hold that because of the complete absence in perceptual behavior of the continuous and temporally distributed features of memory action, the two are totally unlike.

Let us recall that the fundamental feature of perceptual responses is the fact that a specific differential reaction is called out by a specific stimulus-object or condition and that any change in the stimulus-object or its setting results in a corresponding change in the perceptual reaction system. Of course, it is quite true that the reaction now made to a perceptual object is one that was built up in many cases to a whole object, only part of which now calls out the original response, but which in no wise involves any memory response. We do not ordinarily remember that a book we perceive has such and such features on the side we cannot now see, although this contact with the book may involve, as in every other perceptual situation, definite memorial behavior. The truth of this observation appears when we take the case of say, an orange or other particular object to which we react without having been in contact with it before. The act in this illustration is a perceptual one but cannot be a memory action because in the former case we are reacting to an object with a reaction system developed to certain qualities (size, shape, color) present among others (taste, weight, texture), etc., whereas in the case of memory the original object is not present at all but is substituted for. Moreover, in the case of memory we have a delayed or postponed reaction. Because memory depends upon a substitute stimulus the reaction is never exactly like a former one and even while it continues to be performed is gradually fading. Also, due to the fact that a number of different absent objects may be reacted to simultaneously, our memorial responses may be exceedingly unreliable. When faulty perceptual reactions (illusions) occur they are due to entirely different conditions, although some imperfect perceptual reactions (hallucinations) may be accounted for on much the same basis.

Two types of situations are implied, therefore, in our conception of memorial behavior. In the first place, there is no room in our description for the sorcerous reinstatement of mental states in the remembering mind through a mysterious association of ideas, a process usually made still more mysterious by means of various forms of imaginary neurology. And in the second place, we abjure the notion that memory behavior consists merely of a reaction system previously acquired, functioning later whenever the adjustment stimulus is presented. The latter is merely a general property or condition of psychological organisms and is the basis for all psychological responses, not merely of memory behavior. Moreover, such a reaction process is much simpler than that involved in memory and cannot possibly be confused with the delayed or postponed reaction system. Let us observe then, that memorial behavior cannot be identified with either habit responses or with learning. The former are behavior segments constituting closely integrated responses and stimuli so that the appearance of the stimuli immediately arouses the correlated responses. Indeed, habits when characterized from the standpoint of the promptness and immediacy of the total response are almost opposite in type to memory behavior.

Now with respect to learning reactions, besides being merely a coördination of responses and stimuli, they result presumably in a more or less permanent acquisition. This is actually the usual condition, whereas memory in a unique sense is a temporal affair which is designed to operate for a specific period of time or for some specific occasion. As a matter of fact, the rather unusual learning known as cramming or sheer mechanical memorizing universally acclaimed as the most incompetent form, answers much more to the description of memory than any other kind. While memorial action with its definite projection and temporary continuity of action is far removed from the repetitive connection of a response and a stimulus, the two types of action are the same when the repetition is regarded as a deliberate form of projection of action for future use. This is true when I memorize a verse for recital at tomorrow's banquet. In this case when the delayed action is performed it is an exact duplicate of the projected action.

Furthermore, whereas learning involves a single coördination between stimuli and responses, memorial behavior comprises a special combination of the given responses with both adjustment and substitute stimuli. Moreover, the coördination of learning responses and stimuli are presumed to operate periodically when the original stimulus reappears, while memory reactions function continuously until the temporal end period. Naturally learning reactions may involve memorial behavior. In fact, complex learning actions always do comprise some memory operations, but they are not identical with memory reactions. In the same sense learning behavior may include many other kinds of reactions, for example, thinking, reasoning, perceiving, imagining, willing, etc. Our distinction at this point also must not be understood as a denial that sometimes, in order to project an action or in order to remember, we must set about to learn something. But this behavior acquisition is in no sense an essential feature of memorial conduct.

Incidentally, we may here enter a caveat against the assumption that memory responses represent elementary organic or physiological processes which are frequently referred to nowadays as mnemic processes. Besides confusing memory conduct with an empty abstraction, which is really not concerned either with physiological activities or psychological behavior, this assumption leads us to overlook the tremendously complex conditions which are involved in every memory situation. Almost any memorial response indicates a large series of human conditions and circumstances, adaptational needs, and evironmental stimuli, all of which in their combination and interaction play a part in the projection and recall phenomena of memory.

Finally, as in the case of imagination behavior, we must be careful to distinguish the complex interaction of the person with his surrounding stimuli objects (essentially the fact of memorial conduct), from merely implicit behavior. Memory conduct always implies a mass of behavior content which is not necessarily involved in mere implicit conduct while, on the other hand, on the morphological side

**The Psychological Foundations of Memorial Conduct** memorial behavior may comprise a great deal of effective action which is impossible in the case of implicit conduct.

Of the six elementary principles of psychological activity two are especially involved in the operation of memory conduct. These two are modifiability and delay of reaction. Besides these, memory ac-

tions are developed upon the general psychological process of association.

What we may speak of as the general capacity factor in memory
conduct is directly and very definitely based upon the psychological
principle of modifiability.  In the performance of memory actions
the individual must, by modifying his previous conduct, be able to
perform new types of action to meet new circumstances.  When a
person projects a future response he is modifying in a sense some
older or some present conduct by making it operate under new stimuli
and new behavior circumstances.  Furthermore, this newly continued
mode of action must persist for a given period until the recollective
phase of the activity transpires.  For the most part, of course, this
modifiability of action refers to the rearrangement and reorganization of responses with different stimuli objects and conditions.

Delay of reaction is a very obvious factor in the behavior segment
in which a previous projection produces a later recollection.  It need
only be remarked therefore that the memory forms of conduct constitute the most prominent and unique type of delay in psychological
activities.

A number of points marking the particular dependence of memory
upon associational processes may well be pointed out.  In the first
place, memory conduct is primarily and essentially a matter of connecting up specific responses with stimuli objects.  This means that
no peculiar powers need be invoked to account for the fact that an
activity can be projected and later performed.  Chief of the peculiar
explanations of memory conduct to be thus precluded is the one which
relies upon the hypothetical and even imaginary functioning of the
nervous system.  Secondly, since the associational basis indicates a
series of specific and genuine contacts with stimuli objects, we can
account for the exact occurrences which take place when one remembers or forgets.  Furthermore, since the more complex memory activities involve definite reorganization of response and stimulus factors, the rôle of associational processes in memory conduct must be
patent.

While we are pointing out the grounding of memory conduct in
associational behavior it should be recalled that memory activity is
not the same as the ordinary connection or association of a response
with a stimulus, much as the actual operation of projection and recall
phases of memory depend upon simple processes of connection and
interconnection of responses and stimuli factors.  For example, contrary to the habits of everyday speech, it is not psychologically proper
to say that we "forget how to swim" or "play the piano."  These
situations do not involve memory activities; rather, they involve skill
and capacity responses (namely, the organization and association of
responses and specific stimuli) and are lacking in the definite projection feature typifying memory behavior.

Throughout the whole series of thousands of memory reactions we

**Projective or Antici- patory and Recollec- tive Memory**

can trace a functional difference which may be selected to divide memory reactions into two broad types. These we will name (1) projective and (2) recollective memory respectively. The first type is characterized by the fact that its operation depends primarily upon the responsive or personal element in the stimulus-response coördination and circumstance; that is to say, the initiation of the act occurs to a considerable extent because of the needs, interests, and desires of the person. The second type, on the other hand, depends somewhat more definitely upon the stimulating conditions. Because of the intensity or unusual character of a particular event in which the person partakes, the memory activity is initiated and operates continuously. The extreme forms of this type of memory are those cases in which, because of a frightful experience, any slightly similar situation recalls, sometimes in a shocking manner, the original event. Obviously, this distinction is a relative one but it is sufficiently observable in practise to provide a criterion.

Another and even more relative distinction between projective and recollective memory may be introduced. We may separate them on the basis of an apparently more prominent operation of the initiatory and consummatory phases of the total behavior. In the projective type, the action appears to involve more prominently the initiation or projection of a memory behavior, while in the recollective form the important factor seems to be the recalling phase or what is popularly called remembering. Naturally, in each case both phases must be equally present in the memory situation. Since we are dealing with continuous action, the apparent prominence of one or the other phase may be only seemingly a difference but for purposes of classification, at any rate, we accept the distinction as an actual practical difference in memory behavior types. We proceed, then, to discuss the two types of memory action separately.

**Projective Memory Acts**

In this class we might consider two types (a) the intentional and (b) the unintentional projective memory response.

By intentional projective memory we mean the actions in which the person purposely postpones, suspends, or projects a response into the future. This is illustrated by the situations in which the person makes an engagement, or arranges for some future action, or memorizes some information to be used at a future date.

The varying degrees of explicitness with which activities are projected for future performance throw light upon the entire set of memory facts. This explicitness refers to the definiteness with which the person postpones his action to some future time. In some cases the individual plans to continue and to consummate an action in a specified temporal period. For example, when making an engagement he starts an action at a given point in time expecting to culminate it at some precisely determined future period. The entire memory activity, then, is temporally located between two definitely given points. Quite at the opposite extreme to this concrete form of memory behavior is the case in which, while we are definitely initiating a continuous response, we do not exactly locate the point of its completion. The precise determination of that period remains more or less in abeyance. A typical illustration of this situation is the development of some information with the intention of using it at a later but not specified date. Much college and professional education represents this kind of memorial behavior. We acquire knowledge in order to project it for future application but just when it will be applied, if applied at all, remains unknown.

Between these two extremes we find various modifications of indeterminateness of memorial responses. For example, we agree in perfectly good faith to call upon our friend but not until some situation arises (which we may really hope will occur) to consummate a continuous activity that we now initiate. Again, the student who prepares to offer certain answers to questions, although he does not know when the examination will occur, illustrates the same form of moderately indefinite memory projection.

Unintentional projective memories refer to situations in which the person is not spontaneously concerned with the memory action; he is either disinterested or influenced merely by a group convention, although he himself, rather than the stimuli, plays the predominant rôle in the total behavior segment. Typical of such memory reactions is the casual information behavior which involves the acquisition of memory materials through mere contact with things.

Under the rubric of recollective memory behavior we include three types, namely, (a) casual remembering or reminiscence, (b) direct recollection, and (c) memorial recovery.

*Recollective Memory Acts*

By casual remembering, we mean the kind of activity in which some unimportant and even obscure stimulus starts off a train of memory actions to absent things and events. The whole procedure is unconditioned by any need, interest, or necessity, but once the process is started it gains momentum and proceeds apace. Each element referred to serves to arouse a further factor. On the whole, the response is passive at the time and no special practical value accrues to the person, although much amusement or depressive uneasiness may result. That is to say, the ongoing of the activity may be of tremendous importance in stimulating the person. So far as the surrounding objects are concerned, however, no change in them need be effected. Again, the whole procedure may be greatly facilitated by the individual's relaxed and inactive condition. We cannot at this point refrain from mentioning again that the action represents a consummation of stimulus and response connection previously organized.

In direct recollection the need to have some information or to recover a lost article stimulates the operation of a consummatory phase of a memory behavior. Here the primary emphasis is upon the recall for the purpose of achieving some practical result, although when the initiatory phase of the action was started there was no emphasis upon the person's participation in the situation. This type of memory is well illustrated by the recollection of a witness in a court trial, though in this particular case the memory behavior may not result in any apparent direct consequences. The criterion, however, for this kind of memory remains the instrumental recollective character of the activity.

In contrast with the type of memory just discussed, memorial recovery represents activity in which the consummatory phase is made to operate primarily for the purpose of the action itself rather than to effect some change in surrounding objects. The aim is to produce a modified condition in the person, for example, the removal of a weight from one's conscience as in ritualistic confession or in medical psychoanalysis. It was in connection with this capacity to re-live experiences that Aristotle developed his theory of æsthetic Catharsis.

**Informational and Performative Memory Acts**

Implicit in our distinction of memory behavior just discussed, as well as in the rest of our description, lies another differentiation which we must point out. It is, namely, the distinction between memory acts constituting some actual work to be done (performative) and memory behavior that merely adapts the person to some past event or action (informational). In the latter case, the person may merely know something about past conditions. In some instances, of course, the information memory reaction is a preliminary step to a future action dated from the time of the last or consummatory period of the informational memory behavior segment, but in this case we assume that the new action belongs to a different behavior segment. The whole distinction we are making hinges upon the functional character of the behavior segment in which the memory action plays a part. Thus, memorizing might be considered as a memory action midway between the informational and performative sort.

To a considerable extent we may use the distinction we have just made as a differentiation between the cases in which we are definitely aware of the operation and purpose of the entire act (informational), and the cases in which we remember without definitely employing memory activity to bring about a necessary or desirable further performative result. It is only proper to add here that informational memory may involve a maximum of awareness while performative memory can be so extremely lacking in awareness or intention that it may be characterized by the popular term subconscious.

**How Memory Reactions Operate**

The operation of memory responses consists primarily of the functioning of the two more definitely observable of the three phases described in an earlier part of this chapter, to wit, the initiatory and consummatory stages.

**The Initiatory or Projective Phase**

In general, this phase consists of the connecting up of three things or of organizing a tripartite association. This association connects up some act with an adjustment and a substitute stimulus. In different situations one or the other of these features stands out more prominently. For example, in some cases the association of the response with the adjustment stimulus is most prominent. This is true, for example, when the delayed memory response consists of making an engagement (typical projective response). Again, in other instances, the association between the adjustment and substitute stimuli seems to be most prominent, as is true whenever we employ a mnemonic system. When we remember the number of days in a month by means of a verse, the verse constitutes the substitute stimulus and the days of the months the adjustment stimulus. In still other cases the connection between the response and the substitute stimulus appears most prominent. This occurs when an engagement response seems to be associated with the day of the week rather than with the person, situation, or event to which we are preparing to adjust ourselves.

This summary statement is obviously the barest sort of outline of the initiation of a continuous or memory reaction. In fact, a fuller content description would necessarily include details concerning the nature of the specific future act involved, besides the description of the exact objects, persons and events which serve as the adjustment and substitute stimuli.

The significance and importance of the triple association is not only plain but necessarily follows from the general nature of memory action. Because the behavior is projected and to be completed later when the adjustment stimulus is no longer present, it is essential that connections be made between what is to be the consummatory action and other stimuli capable of arousing the response to the adjustment stimulus. But in order that one object or condition should be capable of substituting for another object or condition, it is necessary that the two be connected with each other as well as with the projected act. The entire process of connection here referred to is merely the ordinary process of psychological association.

The performance of the delayed phase of the memory reaction occurs when the reacting person comes into contact with a substitute stimulus. Possibly the contact with the substitute stimulus is a definitely arranged affair, as when we employ a memorandum book for the purpose, or it may consist of a very casual contact. In either case we must regard the substitute stimulus function as a unique type of fact inasmuch as in memorial conduct the substitute stimulus has been definitely and sometimes even deliberately connected with both the adjustment stimulus and the correlated response. The ordinary substitute stimulus is not so definitely or closely connected with an adjustment stimulus and most frequently has only a very remote connection with the response factor. *The Consummatory or Recollective Phase*

The whole matter of the consummation of a memory act is well illustrated by the fact that forgetting is a direct function of the degree of deliberateness characterizing the person's contact with the substitute stimulus. This point is also illustrated by the fact that the possibility of remembering is a function of the number of substitute stimuli connected with the adjustment stimulus. The more substitute stimuli that function in any specific situation the more probable it is that the memory response will operate or that there will be no forgetting.

The reason why a memory response is more likely to occur when there are many substitute stimuli than when there are few is because there is then greater possibility of contact between the person and the stimuli. That is to say, the adjustment stimulus is more thoroughly represented. This fact of making possible the operation of the consummatory phase of a memory reaction or in short, remembering at all, is usually referred to as retentiveness. The fact that certain information is retained depends upon the number of objects with which it is connected.

In the performance of memory behavior segments a series of specific forms of operation may be observed. These forms involve primarily either the stimulus or the response and may be described as follows:

**Stimulus Forms**     In some instances one object or event operates throughout the whole behavior segment. Here the substitution and the adjustment stimuli are both located in the same object, as for example, when I am reminded by someone's presence to tell him something I previously agreed to tell him or through seeing an object I remember to do something to it. Probably this form of memory action is most common in the segments we have agreed to name recollective reactions.

At other times another object becomes the adequate stimulus. In these segments, an object other than the one to which the response is to be made, initiates the consummatory phase of the response. This form of memory may safely be called the typical sort. Undoubtedly it constitutes a larger series of actual memory behavior segments than any other form, and comprises the most effective of our memory behavior. The range of objects that can serve to arouse the memory reaction makes possible its being carried over great stretches of time and place. A striking example of the power of such memory actions is supplied in the operation of the extremely complex behavior in which we use printed and other symbolic records to stimulate the functioning of memory reactions.

**Reaction Forms**     Many of our memory reactions operate through a postdated functioning of the same reaction system or response pattern. That is to say, we are aroused to remember by the original projected action which is connected with a specific stimulus, whether it be the same or a different object. Illustrative of this form of memory reaction is the recalling of a name, a date, or any type of information. The effectiveness of the reaction depends entirely upon the literalness with which the original projected act operates after its period of actual delay. Possibly this type of response does not comprise the most important of our memory reactions, since we include here the whole series of rote memory responses.

A great number of our memory responses do not necessarily involve a simple exact repetition of a specific reaction system.  Rather, more or less freedom is possible in the action because of the operation of different or partially different reaction systems.  The reason for this circumstance is that these types of memory behavior represent adaptations to cultural objects or conditions and not to specific physical objects.  Nor are these reactions very definite direct adaptations, such as going to a certain place at a given time; instead they involve situations in which a novel or constructive action carries out the purpose of the situation.  The projection and later furtherance of a scientific investigation, the execution of a literary or other artistic commission, insofar as they involve a projection and later operation of a memory reaction, all illustrate the extreme forms of memory reactions of the present class.  From these more complex substitutable responses we may trace a descending series which runs down to substitute reactions and differs very little in morphological character from the action operating at the time the memory behavior is in the projection stage.

Psychologists have always assumed that memory behavior essentially and intimately involves recognition.  The relationship is indeed a close one.  Recognition, however, is not exclusively a feature of memorial conduct.  Perceptual reactions are no less intimately connected with recognition behavior.  That recognition reactions, however, have historically been presumed to be most closely connected with memory is accounted for, we believe, by the fact that in complex memorial behavior, recognition assuredly occupies a very strategic and prominent position.  Unless we are to leave our present description in too fragmentary a form we must indicate the exact operation of the recognition function in memory.

Recogni-
tion and
Memorial
Conduct

But first let us point out why recognition appears to be so prominent a factor in such behavior.  Both the clue and solution are found in the continuous and prolonged character of memory reactions.  In other words, there must be some marks or signs relating the second phase to the first.  The second or middle phase, although an integral part of the memory behavior segment, may still be wholly or in part detached from the first or projection phase of action.  Now, aside from the essential or universal fact that the two phases must occur in order that a memory act may be completed, it is frequently necessary that the person performing the action should appreciate overtly the connection between the two phases.  How often this overt appreciation of the continuity of the memory behavior must occur depends upon the general overtness of the memory action.  That is to say, whenever the person is fully aware of a need for the operation of a memory reaction, the recognition factor is essential.  Incidentally we observe two related points.  In the first place, not all types of memory behavior require a recognition factor, in fact, only the more elaborate sorts do.  And secondly, the recognition feature exists in different degrees.  It remains for us now to describe briefly the process of recognition and to indicate how it varies in its operation.

Recognition in general is, of course, a type of meaning reaction,[1] that is to say, the final action to a stimulus is preceded by a determining action which lends color and direction to the succedent or final act.  Because a memory action involves a minimum of two operations (projection and consummatory) and also two stimuli (adjustmental and substitute) the stage is well set for the performance of recognition action.  To illustrate with the simplest case, when the substitute stimulus appears there may occur a single direct response to the adjustment stimulus; here we have memory without recognition.  But if in this behavior segment some implicit or overt response either necessarily or fortuitously precedes the reaction to the adjustment stimulus, we assume that the individual recognizes either the reaction or the object to which the reaction is made.  In other words, the substitution stimulus-object becomes a sign for whatever thing we presume is signified (act or adjustment object).  As in every other case of meaning behavior the recognition factors are to a considerable extent, though of course not exclusively, implicit and verbal reactions.  Possibly the latter are most characteristic in memory behavior.  The functioning of exclamatory reactions in memorial recognition is very familiar, "I see" being a frequent meaning reaction.  None the less potent, however, are subvocal language responses.

Besides the appreciation by the person that the stimulus-object initiating his memory behavior, and the stimulus-object (substitution) operating in the culmination of the act are related to each other and to the act, there are still other factors involved in the more complex forms of recognition.  In addition, the individual may realize his own place in the total memory situation.  That is to say, the person himself becomes an additional stimulus, or more frequently, functions as the setting of one or more of the stimuli involved.  The most complex form of recognition occurs when the individual continues to project himself into every feature of the continuous memorial response.  It is in such cases as these that the person's own responses constitute a good share of the memory behavior and thus directly condition its continuity features.

Now we might point out that in complex recognitive memorial reactions the person plays a part in the total behavior not only when the recollective phase operates, but also in the initiatory phase.  Instead of appreciating that the response has in fact been continued, has reached culmination and that the final response has fulfilled its purpose, he may likewise appreciate the necessity for and the actual occurrence of a projection act.  Recognition of the nature and needs of projecting a response to be later consummated depends, of course, upon previous experiences with similar situations.

In discussing the place of recognition in memory conduct we have incidentally been pointing out that memory reactions are divisible

[1] Cf. Vol. I, Chapter XIII.

into various modes. At the very apex of the modalities we find memory reactions which involve the most explicit recognition features. Such a memory behavior segment belongs to the personalistic [1] mode of behavior. Other memory behavior segments belong to the simpler modes including those in which the individual himself and his actions constitute no further feature of the situation beyond that of a mere performer of a response to a stimulus. Memory conduct of a mode close to the personalistic is that in which the recognition action, although present is either not appreciated at all or is not fully appreciated by the reacting individual.

In descriptions of memory behavior the specifications of stimuli and stimulational conditions appear to be of more significance than in other types of action, although stimuli are of necessity integral factors in all psychological acts. In the first place, because memory behavior consists essentially of the interconnection of responses with adjustment and substitute stimuli, the stimuli are more uniquely phases of the total behavior segment. The reader will recall that memory conduct, instead of constituting acts whose importance consists of what is done to things, really constitutes a connection between responses and stimuli. Hence projection, retention, and recall are all relational acts. In the second place, since memory behavior comprises three distinct phases operating at different times, the stimuli features implying the relational character of such reactions loom large. And finally, because memory reactions are responses of occasion so that combinations of responses function together, the stimuli obtrude themselves upon the student who attempts to analyze such behavior. For example, when taking an examination the fact that we are undergoing examination is in general a stimulus for memory behavior, while the specific ideas or facts recalled are elicited by the particular questions asked which we may call the substitute stimuli for the objects and events around which the examination is centered. *Stimuli for Memorial Reactions*

Granting, then, that the stimuli actors are exceedingly conspicuous in descriptions of memory behavior, we will proceed to separate these stimuli into two divisions. The first is concerned with the enumeration of some of the more prominent forms of adjustment stimuli, and the second with the kinds of objects and conditions serving as substitute stimuli for the retentive and recollective phases of memory behavior.

The adjustment stimuli objects for memory, that is to say, the stimuli objects remembered, may consist of almost any kind of thing which can serve as a stimulus at all. We may remember objects of all sorts, the places in which we saw them, the people who possessed them, and the time periods during which we had our original, projective contact with them. Similarly, events of all possible types are reacted to memorially. Almost any event in which we have participated, in which we are interested, or which is expected to occur in the future

[1] Cf. Vol. I, Chap. IV, Section 3.

and is brought to our attention through some association with a substitute stimulus, may be remembered. Conditions, whether they affect us or others, events or happenings of every type whether they existed or occurred in the remote or in the immediate past are reacted to more or less frequently. Certain types of personal conditions, such as sickness or some extreme happiness, poverty or deprivation, may constitute so frequent a stimulus for memory reaction that they comprise almost constant stimuli to behavior.

Actions of all types and descriptions are prominent also as memory stimuli. These comprise acts we have performed ourselves (e. g., acts which involve remorse) or activities performed by other individuals (kindness, harmful acts) that we have observed or been apprised of. Noteworthy also are abstract objects and imaginary situations. Once these have become objects to which we have responded they may be memorially reacted to at some later time.

As a final instance of adjustment stimuli objects for memorial conduct we suggest words, language and in general conversation which in the practical affairs of life constitute prominent factors in our memory behavior segments.

When we ask what kind of objects and conditions serve as substitute stimuli for memory conduct we find that here, too, the field is unlimited. Under proper conditions almost any object, event or condition may serve in this substitutive capacity.

Any object connected with something to which we respond in its absence may serve to arouse a response to that non-present object. This is true not only of objects in the ordinary sense but of all kinds of things contrived to arouse memory conduct. Written records are of especial significance in arousing recollective responses to things, conditions, and events which have already occurred, or in referring to conditions or acts (promises) which have been made in the past to forecast some action in the future. A vast number of mnemonic systems of all sorts may be considered as illustrating the function of things in arousing memory or recollective behavior. And what is true of objects themselves is likewise true of the settings of objects or events. A time object, or place setting may arouse an individual to respond to some object previously connected with that setting. As we have pointed out [1] the capacity with which some objects, events, or persons function as substitute stimuli to elicit responses to other events is conditioned entirely by the association facts of frequency, recall, etc.

In actual human intercourse a very large number of our substitute stimuli functions are performed by persons. This is true for several reasons. First, so much of our behavior involves contacts with persons that they may substitute for one another as memory stimuli. Moreover, because considerable memory activity consists of informational reactions the stimuli thereto comprise personal contacts including language activities. In general, language behavior in all of its

[1] Cf. Chapter on Association, Vol. I.

forms constitutes a very fertile source of substitute stimuli for an enormous variety of memorial activities.  Not to be excluded are the linguistic activities of the persons themselves who perform the memory conduct.

The importance of linguistic actions in calling out memory responses to things suggests that no less a rôle is played by actions in general.  Both our own actions and those of others, by their resemblances and similarities or previous contextual relations, elicit responses to absent objects and actions to which they are behavioristically related.  Gestures of all sorts are especially significant in this, connection.  Equally effective are cravings, desires, and feelings which immediately cause the individual to recollect some person, event, or circumstance.  Another familiar situation of this sort is that in which some implicit response, say a "tune running through one's head," or a visual image of some sort, especially when it is itself aroused by some unknown stimulus object, arouses a "memory" of an opera or of the person with whom we attended it, or some picture or an event connected with it.

In our present sampling of memory stimuli we have not attempted to discriminate between types of objects functioning in primarily projective or recollective activities, although in actual practice this distinction is exceedingly important.  Furthermore, we may again be reminded that in almost any situation the same actual object may operate both as an adjustment and as a substitute stimulus.  In other words, the appearance of an object may remind us of some experience or contact we had with it at a prior time.

Genuine memorial conduct is probably not so commonly or so frequently performed as is generally supposed.  Nevertheless there is no question that such behavior is an essential feature of all typically human conduct.  Precisely because memory behavior is so interwoven with the general texture of complex psychological activities it is no easy matter to isolate it from the rest of the intricate behavior matrix in which it is involved.  Nevertheless, because it is possible to single out the general functions of such activity, as a general type of behavior, and set them up for objective inspection we are able to study their connections with other behavior to which they are inextricably interrelated.

In thus evaluating memory conduct we may point out that such behavior is essentially a process of organizing the individual's capacities and bringing about a continuity in his behavior life, especially upon the more complex (societal) levels.  In short, memory responses enable us to adapt ourselves to a much larger field of objects and events than is immediately present in our surroundings.  Not only is the scope of our behavior enlarged in space, but we can extend our adaptations into time.  This allows us to make use of our past experiences in a most effective way, giving us a capacity to organize and arrange our behavior in the most economical and serviceable manner.

**The Place and Function of Memorial Behavior**

By being able to remember what things and conditions exist elsewhere than in one's immediate surroundings one is more effective in adapting oneself, besides having a general capability to know things, and to build up a body of knowledge and information. Here memorial conduct is operating in the verbal or linguistic organization of events and facts. Also this capacity to respond to things when not immediately present (recollecting memory) enables individuals to communicate, to have intercouse one with another. Memory functions, then, in a general sense are typically human reactions making, perhaps more than any other single type of response, for the specific human quality of the organism. Were it not for memory it would be impossible for us to develop such distinctly human forms of behavior as language, thinking or imagination, or to have literature, science, etc.

How, we may ask, could we without memory connect different periods of time, or make continuous the different intervals of time, and so connect past with present events? This ability in turn gives the individual the power to project these events into the future in order to control them, and to make predictions for scientific and practical purposes. The control that memory gives us is well illustrated by the fact that we can adapt ourselves to events that have not yet happened, but which we can predict will transpire, by remembering some event or series of events which has occurred under somewhat similar circumstances.

Summing up the especially significant features of memory conduct, we may say that by means of memory functions we become better oriented among the total series of conditions in which we live. Because of the absolute complication of all our human action by memory responses it is impossible to realize how utterly chaotic and disconnected our actions would be, were it not for the organizing capacity we derive from the operation of memory action. Of course it cannot be said that memorial reactions are responsible for bringing about this connection of our experiences; rather, in thus making a logical abstraction of memory functions, it is possible to indicate their relative place in the entire scheme of interrelated human activity insofar as this activity involves the orientation of the person to the totality of his surroundings.

Nothing is plainer than the fact that in the performance of memory conduct we find the authentic basis for the empirical facts of personal identity, as known and appreciated by the individual himself.[1]

[1] We say here personal identity "as known and appreciated by the individual himself" because we are abstracting only one feature of the fact of personal identity (his witting connection with things) from others. Among these other facts are, in the first place, the actual continuity of the person as a psychological organism existing and responding throughout the course of his actual life; and in the second place his continuity in function and behavior by being a part of a large set of concrete events of which his actual surroundings (things and persons) constitute another part.

None other than this fact of personal identity is at the basis of all responsibility as found in voluntary conduct, and in purpose action, (as illustrated by voluntary, creative, and other types of behavior). Indeed the memory activities of the individual set him off in his own knowledge as a continuous practical entity differentiated from, and interacting with, all of the various facts with which he is in contact.

We have already suggested the importance of this empirical fact of self identity in intimating that it is the center of responsibility.   How precarious this appreciation of personal identity may be is observed in the fact that although a person may perform some work of the most complicated sort and produce a product of remarkable properties, he is yet unable to connect it with himself.   Everyone recalls the anecdote attributed to literary and musical artists who have exclaimed, while reacting to a product of their own creation, that they wished they themselves might have produced it.   Only after consulting some form of evidence can such individuals realize that the art product they are appreciating was created by themselves.   Our point therefore is that in the fact of projecting and of later performing activities, in other words in keeping these different reactional situations in their genuine continuity, the psychological fact of personal identity is discoverable.

Let the reader be aware that we are suggesting here nothing but the witting interconnection of the individual with his adjustment and substitutional stimuli.   The fact of personal identity depends entirely upon the interconnection between the individual and these two stimulational functions.   This circumstance is exemplified by the illustration of the individual who is told to get two electric lamps but can recall only that he was told to get two things.   What they are he cannot say.   The activity of purchasing such objects has not been one of his activities for a very long time so that actual personal identity is impossible because of the importance of part of his surroundings in serving as a substitutional stimulus for a reaction to the adjustment stimulus (in this case the lamps).   Clearly observable, then, in this illustration is the interconnection between the facts of personal identity and memorial behavior.

Assuming that memory constitutes one of the characteristic forms of human behavior we may next turn to the study of the specific place which memory actions occupy in some of our important behavior situations.   Let us note that the operation of the delay function which organizes our experiences is absolutely essential for any thinking or intellectual response of any degree of complexity.   For does not the significant feature of thinking consist of the extension of the individual's contact with objects and events all of which are not immediately present?   In fact, the solution of a problem, and the prominent features of thinking reactions, involve a comparison of conditions now existing with those of a previous period.

Again, our recent survey of imagination behavior has shown that such a free interconnection of the person with various objects and persons depends precisely upon the possibility of projecting action. Namely, it is impossible for us to construct any object or situation unless we have previously had some contact with it. If we have created the impression that memory responses are basic to the general organization of the person in his complex surroundings, we have already indicated the place of memory behavior in reactions of play, in artistic, economic, and social responses. The whole connection between memory responses and other forms of behavior is perhaps most strikingly revealed when we consider the part that memory plays in learning, both the acquisition of information and skill.

**Memorial Conduct as Autonomous or Dependent Behavior Segments**     Among the mass of memory activities some consist of behavior segments which are parts of larger behavior segments or situations that are not essentially of the memory type. Others are distinctly memorial behavior segments which include a few or many non-memorial actions. These latter behavior segments, however, are manifestly memory behavior situations.

Let us consider the former type first. A memorial reaction may be a process of remembering an object or its location in order to perform some further activity in connection with it. Here the memory action serves as a definite precurrent response to another action that is not memorial in character. This actual segment of behavior therefore forms a much larger type of activity than the memorial action. The latter is only a part or phase of the whole situation. The larger activity may involve the carrying out of some project of a business or engineering sort, or the playing of some game. The main point is that whatever the activity is, memorial responses in such instances serve only in an incidental or an essential way to promote the project and to bring it to a final conclusion. The memory reactions are themselves dependent or subordinate actions.

Or memorial responses serve as precurrent responses to final actions which are memorial in character. In carrying out a memory behavior segment, that is, one in which the final or consummatory reaction involves the performance of a final response that has been previously projected, some or many particular memorial responses may precede the memory action.

On the other hand, we may think of the memorial reaction as the autonomous and primary behavior. Accordingly when the behavior situation requires, the person performs a considerable number of actions necessary to carry out the memorial conduct. These may themselves be memory actions to a certain extent or they may be responses of an entirely different sort. Thus, a complex memorial behavior segment includes the handling of books and instruments, the study of charts, the searching of records, and other similar actions. In many cases the latter activities operate not only in the actual performance of the memorial action but also in its verification. To make sure that I am actually performing the informational response I projected some time ago, it may be necessary for me to consult some records of the object or event which is the stimulus for the memory action.

This distinction between autonomous and dependent memorial behavior segments brings up the general problem of the complexity of such behavior. In some cases memory reactions are very simple, involving only one or at most a few reaction systems. In other instances they consist of a large group of complex reaction patterns. The simplest type naturally includes those memory reaction systems which function as precurrent or anticipatory responses in a larger segment of behavior whether it is or is not of the memorial type, whereas complex memorial reactions comprise those in which the whole behavior pattern may be designated as memory. Now, as we may well suppose, the complexity as well as the autonomy or dependence of a memorial behavior segment is contingent upon the general stimuli conditions of the action as a whole, that is to say, upon the actual type of adaptation that the individual is making at the time under a particular set of circumstances.

An indefinite number of morphologically different reaction systems are performed by the memorially responding individual. They may be implicit, overt, partially implicit, or combinations of these widely different types.

Morphological Variations in Memory Reactions

Ordinarily, the initiatory or consummatory phases of memorial activities may be either implicit or overt in form. When such initiatory phases are implicit we observe the individual project a certain kind of action which for some reason he cannot perform at the time. Possibly the objects and circumstances constituting the stimuli for the projected and finally performed action are not available for immediate contact.

In similar fashion the activities of revery and daydreaming, of reliving past experiences or responding to things and conditions not at present existing in the behavior environment of the individual, involve non-effective and inapparent implicit activities. Naturally they can be accompanied by apparent or effective (overt) reactions.

Leaving the purely implicit form we turn to those complex memory types that occur in terms of partially implicit responses, namely verbal or language reactions. Illustrative here is the informational response. In complex scientific work especially the individual memorial reactions tend to fall into distinctly symbolic and verbal forms. To a great extent this type of memory behavior succeds the original contact with the things responded to. It follows, therefore, that whenever the original thing, object, or event responded to is of an abstract sort, the response has to be wholly implicit or verbal, i. e., partially implicit.

Quite different types of memory situations demand definite overt and even effective reactions such as writing or drawing in various forms. The projection of actions, as in planning a campaign of behavior, may require a great deal of manipulative handling of objects.

A mechanic, in arranging the order of bolts, washers, etc., which he must remember to fit together, needs to perform considerable manipulation of this type. Similarly, the later consummations of memorial actions frequently require overt and effective responses. The action of going from one place to another or of removing an object from one place to another may constitute an integral feature of a memorial behavior segment. Or whenever the person is required to take an oral or written examination the opportunity for the performance of overt memory behavior is palpably present.

Not only are overt and effective responses performed in memorial conduct of a manipulative type but they are also found in more abstract forms of situations. Students of science required to deal with exceedingly abstract phenomena often find it useful in remembering, to make drawings, copy figures, and employ other overt reactional devices along with and sometimes in substitution for verbal descriptions or some other purely implicit form of action.

Of quite another sort of overt, consummatory response is the affective memorial reaction. Many of our memory responses are cast in the mould of a feeling response which marks the culmination of a continuing action previously begun. We often plan to remember or act over some pleasure or grief when occasion shall permit. In such activities the affective reaction is a response to a situation or condition which originally called out the pleasurable or grieving reaction. Thus the consummatory memory action is not an accomplishing or fulfilling act but one which involves reliving an action from the past. Incidentally we may point out also that such activities offer considerable contrast with intellectual responses, namely, those in which the memorial consummation consists of some informational reaction to an object or situation.

**Do Animals Perform Memorial Conduct?** The question as to whether animals have memory has been considerably modified since the time that it was first asked. At first, when memory was interpreted as an association of ideas in the mind, animals were of course excluded from the class of beings possessing the capability of remembering. Later, during the period of the influence of biology on psychology, a period which can be summed up for our purposes as the time when the barrier between human and infrahuman behavior was thought to be broken down, a different conception prevailed. At that time the processes of memory were reduced to the acquisition by the organism of specific overt responses and their retention. In other words, memory was described as a particular case of motor habit. As an alternative, memorial conduct was divided into two types of process, one the motor habit type, and the other an ideational form, quite in the original sense referred to. In this latter period of biopsychological thinking, animals were said to have memory responses, at least of the motor memory form.

It is not very clear on this basis whether animals were actually believed to perform memory responses or not, although writers on the subject professed such a belief. It is questionable whether memorial conduct can be so ascribed to animals. That the retentivity mentioned was probably not actual memory behavior appeared from the fact that the motor habit idea of memory was extended to the concept of memory as the property which an organism possessed for preserving its own conditions. In this sense, at least, all organic objects were endowed with conservational powers, or with the mnemic properties for conserving changes and modifications in their experiences (contacts with things).

Now, from the standpoint of memory as a projection or continuous reaction, another attitude toward the present problem is demanded. Genuine memorial activities, with the more or less deliberate projection of actions which are later to be performed, appear beyond the range of animal conduct. In all probability, however, it may be said that some of the higher types of infrahuman animals do possess memorial responses but they are of a rather simple form. The latter hardly go beyond the slighter types of recollective memory.

From our standpoint it is manifestly unfair to compare human individuals with infrahuman animals since the performance of behavior is part of a general complexity of facts which is highly different for organisms so varied in evolutionary development and ontogenetic history as human beings and animals. But yet it may not be entirely futile to indicate that the animal lives in the present with no regard for past or future events. It is in contact with no stimuli other than those to which it is responding at any precise moment.

Individuals vary in the way they react memorially no less than in the performance of any other kind of psychological action. Although such individual differences exist with respect to all forms of memorial conduct they are more readily observed and described in the realm of informational behavior. Accordingly it is possible not only to point out specific kinds of such differences, but also to inquire how they have come about and how they have become modified. **Individual Differences and Training of Memory**

At once we observe that if memorial conduct involves the projection of an action or the starting off of a continuous response, the general capacity for doing so and in what form, depend upon several definitely isolable factors. They depend upon the behavior equipment of the individual, his general experience, as well as his immediate reactional perspective. These considerations stress again the fact that memory cannot be regarded as a general kind of action; it is always a definite concrete process depending upon specific conditions. And so the temptation to believe that the experience of memorizing in some particular connection is a sure warrant for more effective memory operation in other connections is manifestly unfounded. Of course, there may be many similarities among the different situations which would influence the transfer of memory capacity from one kind of situation to another. But we can never overlook the fact that memorial responses vary according to the individual and his experience. Only in the exact proportion that two individuals have developed the same behavior equipment and interact with the same situations will they have the same kind of memorial responses.

In general, we may sum up individual differences as we find them in informational situations under two headings. One refers particularly to the stimulus and the other to the response feature of the behavior. With respect to the former, some individuals more easily remember certain types of material, for example, mathematical information, while others more easily remember historical facts. Some have greater capacity for business material, others for academic matters, etc., Some people remember events with greater facility than objects seen or facts heard.

The response phases present like variations. Certain individuals learn (project) slowly and retain well; some attain rapidly and do not remember over a long period of time, while the behavior of others constitutes varying combinations of the different memory phases.

Individuals differ markedly with respect to the general effectiveness of their memorial conduct. This means that they vary more or less in one or more, or perhaps all of the modes of activity which constitute efficient memory behavior. The general sufficiency by means of which objects and situations are related to one another in their psychological environment, the rapidity with which memorial responses are initiated, the length of time during which the material is retained, and the rapidity and accuracy of the culmination of the reactions are widely dissimilar in different individuals. All these elements determine the general serviceability of the material retained and the way in which memory responses are made.

Nor are we prone to perform our memory acts in a common way. Some individuals perform many and important memorial responses without the use of any tools (pencil and paper, for example) while others cannot do so. Similarly some persons perform their memorial reactions to a great extent in terms of implicit responses or vocal behavior though others do not pursue this method. Extremely wide variations are exhibited by persons who can perform many actions implicitly (as in mental arithmetic) in contrast to those who have acquired no such technique. On the whole those who perform a large part of their continuous behavior in terms of implicit responses find many of their substitute stimuli among their own reactions.

Of all these dissimilarities some of the most easily recognized are those between younger and older persons. They are especially manifest in the process ordinarily called disintegration of memory. For one thing, abstract ideas constitute a larger part of the older persons' memorial behavior equipments. Again they have better memory for events which occurred a long time past. And above all, older persons exhibit a gradual disappearance of the capacity to perform memorial reactions of various forms, a loss of function that may comprise very definite stages.

At one period in the development of psychology the question as to whether or not one could improve his memory was much debated. Such a problem arises only when memory is regarded as a peculiar innate capacity and as such it was then considered. The whole process of memory was treated as a matter of connecting specific ideas with one another, and these in turn with brain elements and processes. Thus memory was not described as a specific reactional activity at all. Therefore, because the neural organization, which was presumed to determine the individual's memorial capacities, was a fixed quantity, memorial ability came to be considered unalterable. When, however, memory is considered a fact of actual adaptation to stimuli, the possibility of its being trained and improved may be taken for granted. The only problem is the method to be employed in the training and improvement. We have already by implication touched on all of these points. Here we have merely to indicate the outstanding conditions involved in memory training.

Firstly, the training of memory consists in the acquisition of a large number of reactions to the kind of stimuli that one wishes to remember. Also, since the culminating stage involves the operation of substitute stimuli, we must in our memory training attach the original responses to as many of these substitute stimuli as possible. Moreover, because of the large rôle that recognition plays in memory action, we must be alive to situations in which we initiate the continuous response. Many concrete suggestions as to how this may be brought about are available. We need to make our learning situations very vivid, to repeat constantly the information we are acquiring, and to learn to use specific tools (reference works, slide rules, etc.) for the projection and final operation of the delayed memorial responses.

Since memorial conduct is delayed behavior and depends for its operation upon substitute stimuli, it is probably more than other psychological phenomena, subject to slight or extreme variations in occurrence. The different forms of these variations may be profitably considered under two heads. At the outset, we find specific memorial actions lacking entirely when the person simply does not remember things or events. This form of abnormality which may be designated by the name of amnesia or obliviscence is obviously the most striking as well as the most typical. It is the most striking because of the total failure of a projected response to operate while, on the other hand, it is the most typical because only when there is a potentiality to forget or a possibility of the non-operation of the projected action can we have a failure of memory or of remembering.

The second type of defect of memory is that in which the continuous behavior operates, but functions very ineffectively with respect

Abnormalities of Memory

to the behavior needs of the individual in particular situations. A notable illustration is the common phenomenon of remembering after having forgotten. That is to say, an action continues beyond the time to which it is projected, and is performed only after some further time has elapsed.

Let us now consider in greater detail the total non-functioning of memory reactions. The abnormality may be localized at different points in the behavior segment. It is possible that the person is unable to project his reactions properly, so that as a result no consummation of the memorial act can occur. Because of the character of the stimuli objects or events few, if any, connections can be made between them and other things that might serve as substitute stimuli. Accordingly, we find that failures of memory constitute dysreactions to particular stimuli objects, specific events, particular things or persons, and types of things seen or heard, etc. The degree of memorial abnormality is necessarily correlated with the number and general distribution of objects and conditions to which the person finds himself unable to respond. The most serious abnormalities are those in which memorial incapacities are very widespread, total, or general. In all these cases we assume that memorial dysreactions are traceable to the character of the stimuli objects or situations and their settings.

Possibly the abnormality of the projective phase may be accounted for on the basis of the person's conditions, both reactional and hygienic. When an individual is ill, dispirited, or injured, he is unable to project responses in a manner which fits him to perform them later. Or the failure may be due to the person's being so intimately related to and absorbed in some thing or task that he does not effectively project his reactions to other things, although he is decidedly in contact with them.

When the amnesia is traceable to reactions or hygienic conditions the abnormality is localizable in time from the standpoint of the beginning and end of the condition centering in the shock or injury. Accordingly, differentiation is made between amnesia which begins at the time of injury and extends to a definite period called anterograde amnesia, and obliviscence which continues more or less indefinitely and is called continuous and retrograde amnesia,[1] consisting of a lack of memory reactions from some given period prior and up to the injury.

Leaving the projection abnormalities we turn to defects of the consummatory phase. Persons may suffer from the non-functioning of an adequately projected response because of the absence of substitute stimuli or because of their failure to operate. The latter condition is illustrated by the following example. "A" and "B", after entering a department store, separate and go to different

---

[1] The conditions referred to by these terms in the medical or psychiatric literature are not confined to actual memory facts but include knowledge and language also.

counters.  After "A," who has only recently opened a charge account at this store, purchases some article which is to be charged and sent, he goes to meet "B" at the other counter which happens to be a book section.  While there, "A" is attracted to an expensive book.  Fumbling for the currency with which to pay for it, "B" suggests that it be charged to his account and "A" agrees.  Although it is only twenty minutes after he has charged the first article, "A" does not find the situation an adequate substitute stimulus for remembering that he himself has a charge account.  Probably the non-operation of the substitute stimulus can be traced to the fact that, before opening an account with this firm, "A" had been able to take advantage of "B's" account in making purchases.  The consummatory phase of memory action may also fail to operate because of interfering reactional or hygienic conditions.

To this brief statement concerning the non-functioning of memorial actions we need only add that while, in general, we insist that the precise details of the situation depend upon the particular individual and his behavior situation, there are observable certain uniformities of memorial abnormalities.  For example, we all fail to react to recent stimuli events before we do so with respect to more remote stimuli events.  Also abstract stimuli continue to call out reactions after responses to more concrete stimuli fail to occur.  Likewise illustrative of this general condition of memory actions is the more or less uniform deterioration of memory behavior in old age.  At this time memory for nouns or names appears to fail, while responses to adjectives, verbs, etc., still operate.

Up to this point we have been stressing the total lack of memorial behavior.  We come now to the defective functioning of memorial reactions.  All too frequently some important or unusual event with which the person has been in contact forces itself upon and dominates him.  One may be unable to forget the death of a friend or relative even though it may not only cause much grief but actually interfere with one's daily activities.  Similarly, once having participated in some horrible circumstance, even remote objects and conditions serve to arouse responses to it.  The abnormality therefore is a failure to forget or to inhibit an undesirable response.  Otherwise described the difficulty is a too vivid recollection of an event which, even though it be remembered, should not produce so violent and disturbing a response.

Closely connected with the latter memorial defects are the familiar disturbances of memory in which the person experiences an immediate and overflowing recollection of events, or remembers some isolated happening of which he has not thought for a long time or perhaps ever before.  Perhaps the person has suffered a reactional disturbance incidental to the accident of barely escaping death or of merely fearing some accident.  As a consequence, he goes over and over a great many events of his past life and relives his ambitions and strivings.

It is generally believed that the same thing happens to dying persons. When only one event is recalled it may be the sudden remembering of a happening in early childhood. What is important to be noticed is the way in which a certain substitute stimulus calls out a memorial response having no immediate relation to the behavior context of the person. Not infrequently this recollective condition is induced because, along with the existence of the required substitute stimulus, the person is in a reactional readiness for such recalling, as when he has no special activity to perform.

Under the name of paramnesia are listed various falsifications of objects and misinterpretations of actions. Frequently objects are falsified by the collective addition to them of details they do not possess. In like fashion, the report of an event is filled out with items one has not actually observed in the projection period. Thus we have a definite infidelity of recollection. Again we have situations in which the individual wrongly orients objects to which he reacts recollectively. He may remember to have seen something at a place and a time in which it was not there at all. In the field of writing innocent plagiarism is often indulged in. One remembers as one's own some statement or story that has been read or heard.

Misinterpretation of memorial conduct in its turn tempts the individual to believe that he remembers things he has really just heard for the first time. In other words, at the ordinary time of projection of response it appears to such an individual that it is the period of culmination of an already projected reaction. The person is certain that he remembers seeing or hearing some particular thing, whereas he is actually in contact with it for the first time. This is only one of many types of memorial defects centered about some form of mistake or uncertitude. Another type to be cited is that exemplified by a person who believes that he is not remembering something although he actually is remembering it. Or, he may be in doubt as to whether or not any memorial conduct is taking place.

Finally, we may mention the instance in which a person projects a response to some object, and later performs it, but fails to appreciate the fact. For example, an individual orders a book to be later delivered but when it arrives, is certain that he has never had anything to do with it until he finds the record of the order.

Let us pause a moment to exclude from the list of memorial irregularities some conditions thought to be memorial defects but which are really not. This will help us to understand both the abnormal and the normal occurrence of memory behavior. Among these non-memory defects is the condition referred to as ' being forgetful.'' What is popularly called being forgetful is certainly a genuine behavior fact but it is not in any sense a fact of memory conduct. To be forgetful really means that we are acting in certain situations in a way that is not serviceable for that circumstance. In other words, our response is different from the reaction we should be performing or that we are expected to perform. It does not, however, refer to the fact that we have projected a response which we have not carried to the consummatory stage, nor that we have failed to project a response when such activity was necessary. Exactly what happens is that we either neglect or disregard the necessity of making a projection or that we refuse to make it. Neither in this manner of not performing certain responses through neglect nor in a voluntary act of refusing to perform them do we find memory conduct. The latter situation is suggested in the advice sometimes offered "just to forget something." But this advice does not refer to memorial behavior. In its more naive form it is merely an admonition not to do a particular act, such as to worry or get excited. In its more sophisticated form it suggests that the individual keep away from certain stimuli in order to avoid performing certain kinds of reactions.

Each one of these three phases of a memory action, namely, the initiatory, "between," and consummatory phase is conditioned first in its occurring at all and then in its particular way of occurring. Such influences condition not only the functional and morphological characteristics of the memory response but also its functional ease and readiness. **Factors Influencing Memory Reactions**

But in the very act of asserting that specific concrete situations affect memory conduct we indicate at the same time that it is not possible to describe or even enumerate these influences. For they are different in each specific memory act. Certainly it is impossible to generalize upon the circumstances. What remains, then, is to mention some outstanding general influences which at the same time will serve to reinforce the idea of the concrete human character of memorial behavior. Such a procedure necessarily involves some repetition of points already made in our exposition, since in describing such action we have already had to mention influences upon it.

The stimulus and response organization of facts found so useful in other parts of this work may be employed here also. As a matter of fact, both the stimulus and response types of influences may be further divided into general and more special influences, the former primarily conditioning whether or not the action shall occur at all, the latter influencing the precise form the action assumes.

Salient among the general stimulational influences are the conditions referred to as the person's needs, that is to say, the great mass of reactional requirements forcing the person to perform memorial conduct. To recover an object one is interested in, one must remember its relation to other things. It is only in specific instances, however, that we look upon the need as a stimulus for the projection of memorial conduct. It is true that the necessity to pay a bill or to call upon a certain person is the empirical cause of the initiation and final performance of a memory action. Furthermore, without the presence of such needs all through the time interval involved, the act may be initiated but not finally consummated. That a memory action in all its phases may occur, stimuli occasions in the form of all sorts of objects and conditions must surround the person.

Such need and requirement conditioners of memorial conduct comprise all sorts of human circumstances. They may be purely natural phenomena, the existence of things, events, or persons in the individual's behavior milieu which call for continuous types of action. In the same manner conventional and cultural conditions of all varieties operate in this connection.

Besides needs or conditions demanding that one remember to do things (whether performative or informational), we must include as conditions the suggestiveness of objects and situations. At certain times we perform memory conduct merely because conditions casually suggest and lead to such action. Here also it may be added that the presence of the suggestion must be continuous in some form either because the actual object or situation perdures or is substituted for by something else.

Of equal influence are the striking and extraordinary situations which stand out from their contexts and force themselves upon us in such a way that they control our memorial behavior. To these types of influences we have already referred in studying abnormalities of memory. In milder form they operate in normal memory situations.

Among reactional influences we note first the general organization of the person's reactional equipment. His general behavior make-up, his knowledge and information concerning objects and conditions determine what and how he remembers and whether he remembers at all. Similarly, our interest in facts leading to the desire to remember plays an important rôle. Things we want to remember, other things not preventing, will be remembered. Sometimes, of course, the desire to remember something produces the opposite result; it may lead to easier forgetting. Booksellers who serve members of the bar notice how a lawyer handling a certain case successfully projects to the time of the trial a great deal of informational behavior concerning a subject which is ordinarily very remote from his interests. After this time the information is promptly sloughed off. But in some of the abnormal conditions we have mentioned, on the other hand, the need and desire to forget some unpleasant event or to remember some pleasant one influence the situation in the opposite direction from that desired.

As in most cases of psychological phenomena the stimuli and response conditions operate in conjunction. Thus we may suggest here influences of the frequency and recency of contacts of the specific stimuli and responses involved. If we have frequently or recently performed a particular response we find that it is likely to recur. These facts are implied in the elementary phenomena of psychological association. Another very decided feature here is the process of interference. If we are attempting to project too many responses at the same time, the probability is that the responses will interfere with each other. This phenomenon is illustrated by the fact of retroactive inhibition.    If after having projected a response, we very soon afterwards attempt to project some other form of memory reaction, we find at the time of culmination of the first memory response that it has been very seriously interfered with.    Sometimes this later projection does not interfere with the first one but on the contrary serves to better the memorial action.    This all depends upon the similarity and other qualities of the different types of material involved, and on the hygienic conditions of the person at the time.

Another combination stimulus and response condition is the relaxation of the individual, a condition very favorable for the recollection type of memory.    Certainly it is very conducive to day dreaming or the indiscriminate recollection of events.    When such a relaxation condition, however, is a positive distraction or a possible dissociation from the stimulus it is extremely unfavorable for the operation of memorial responses.

Nowhere in the literature of psychology is memory action treated as an intimate mode of response to very specific features of the person's actual surroundings (persons, events, and conditions). This is undoubtedly a serious circumstance if one is tolerant toward the view that concrete stimulus or response interactions are closely connected with, or compose the intimate details of memorial responses. Accordingly our emphasis upon specific acts of persons as the data of psychology is even more significant in this chapter than in others.

Notwithstanding the fact that psychologists have not looked upon memorial behavior as the concrete adaptations of individuals, it is still true that in the field of memorial conduct the conception that the phenomena involved consist completely or essentially of mentalistic processes has not been completely accepted. Memorial behavior has frequently been handled as action even though this action has been considered to be mere motor responses or motor habits. That memory behavior was frequently taken to be action is shown by the prevalence of the almost universal belief that Ebbinghaus in his work on nonsense syllables (published in the volume on Memory, Eng. trans. 1913) was definitely experimenting on memory conduct. It is hardly to be supposed that otherwise a study primarily concerned with experiments on verbal habits of a serial type should become so signal a part of the traditional literature on the subject of memory. It may be added, however, that Ebbinghaus thought of memory as the impression, retention, association and reproduction of ideas, and that he and others thought of the motor action as accompanying or manifesting mental processes.

The description of memory in this work differs markedly (as we have suggested) from the conception of motor habit. Memorial conduct is analyzed and emphasized as an important dynamic process which plays a large and unique part in human life. Memory, then, is not mere motion or movement. While the motor habit conception of memory is to be commended because it replaced mentalistic states or processes, it does not symbolize adequately the intricacies and complexities of memorial conduct. The motor habit viewpoint is no less objectionable in its implication that memory constitutes a conservational process rather than the intimate interaction of a person with the human objects and circumstances surrounding him.

It is an interesting, though certainly not an anomalous circumstance, that only in an early form of psychological thinking abandoned long ago as false and unscientific was there an approach (crude

116

and partial as it was) to a factual statement of memory conduct. It was the old faculty psychologists (for example Wolff, *Psychologia Empirica*, 1732, etc.) who thought of memory conduct as the action of individuals. This conception that persons perform memorial action commends their views beyond many more recent ones. Of course the older psychologists knew nothing of stimuli and responses. Moreover, their explanatory principles reverted to a substantial soul resident in man and in which these faculties inhered.

So crude a psychological view naturally could not persist. Hence the historical records inform us that memory came to be considered a process independent of substantial mind or soul in which it could inhere. In short memory was considered as a state of consciousness. This is the period in which association, like the principle of gravitation in physics, became a principle explaining how the ephemeral states of consciousness could persist and be revived. The revival was explained of course as the bringing into consciousness (or the mind) of one idea by another idea. Presumably the two ideas together constitute the mind or each successively does so.

Now this sort of thinking led to two types of conception, the frailty of each of which is patent. On the one hand, we have the notion of a mental process which waxes and wanes. On the other, some form of mental stuff is conserved and stored away. How many errors and obstructions have been brought into psychology by such conceptions! These descriptions of revivals, wanings, and storehouses can only, by an exercise of extreme charity, be called figures of speech. They are indeed hardly that. What factual occurrences can be actually referred to by the ideas and expressions of something retained or lost, by impressions made, by fixations accomplished, or by experiences recalled? As we have had occasion to see in our notes to the chapter on Association (Vol. I), the neural theory advanced to support and make plausible the revivals and storehouses has contributed nothing solid to psychological science.[1]

It is impossible to pass without comment the recent revival of the storehouse and conservation theories of memory in their most phantastic form. This is the psychoanalytic view of the unconscious as an entity in which mental elements are stored up, either to be revived, or to play havoc generally with the individual. That such a theory can prevail at all is probably to be explained by the fact that its adherents employ it to misinterpret some compelling facts with which the orthodox psychologist does not usually concern himself. A salient example is the familiar case in which the individual continues to suffer a behavior disturbance which was initiated by an incident long since forgotten. Now, in this case as in all others, at least part of the situation is immediately accounted for by the operation of substitute stimuli.

[1] Think only of the notion that amnesia is caused or paralleled by loss or degeneration of neural cells.

This suggestion applies to all of the phases of actual memorial recovery. What is left is probably the mere fact that a reaction system previously acquired now operates when its appropriate or coördinate stimulus is present. In addition such a situation may contain elements which depend upon the dissociated character of the individual. In other words, when a person is in a situation representing detachment from his present stimuli surroundings he is very likely to respond with behavior that belongs to a past period or in general his reaction equipment may be called out by objects which ordinarily are not attended to. We cannot neglect, either, the fact that what is considered a resuscitation from the pit of the unconscious is nothing more than the immediate building up of some reaction presumed to be thus recovered. Certainly the external aspects of the organismic theory of memory are greatly enhanced when they are contrasted with this unconscious memory doctrine.

As a last item in the perspectival placing of the present exposition of memory we may point out that memorial conduct does not exclusively constitute cognitive orientational reactions, as the traditional literature implies. Of a certainty in many instances, and in the lives of thinkers probably in most cases, memorial activities are indubitably cognitive in character, but this situation is by no means inevitable. Memorial activities may just as well be phases of practical performative conduct far removed from any ideational circumstance.

# CHAPTER XX

## THE NATURE OF INTELLECTUAL REACTIONS

Intellectual reactions are attitudinal types of behavior. They are adjustments or adaptations of the individual which occur in situations in which the stimuli objects and events offer him an opportunity to take a decided stand or attitude toward them. In many cases, too, the stimuli objects and conditions are of such a nature that the person is obliged to assume some cognitive position,[1] either for the purpose of performing a further type of reaction to the objects or as a part of a large general orientational mode of behavior. The essential feature of such reactions is that the individual performs a response to the stimulus object or event in the form of a personal action or attitude. This action, to be sure, does not constitute a performance upon the object. The object is not manipulated in order to insure the individual maintenance or protection; nor does the individual transform it in order to make it fit into new or different circumstances. On the contrary, he merely develops some sort of critical or judgmental attitude toward it. Conditions, objects, persons, or events which excite our curiosity or wonder, stimulate us to guess and assume something about them, to doubt or believe in their existence or otherwise to become reactionally placed or attitudinized concerning them, in short to assume some positive intellectual relation to them.

Intellectual reactions, accordingly, are decidedly of the mediate sort. In consequence the person may be very far removed from any sort of intimate contact with the stimuli objects or situations. Intellectual responses are therefore non-effective in character. No manipulation or any type of direct immediate contact is necessary. This may be due to the fact that the objects and conditions cannot be handled, or cannot be directly known and are consequently in contact with the person only through his reading or being told about them. Thus intellectual reactions are to a great extent implicit although they need not always be so. The specific reaction systems involved are of the inapparent type. But this is not an inevitable characteristic. We stress this point concerning their inapparent nature chiefly to indicate their personal and removed character. The degree of inapparentness depends upon the intricacy of the specific intellectual conduct, as well as upon the type of development and personality equipment of the reacting individual.

The Problem of Intellectual Reactions

---

[1] Poverty of language dictates the use of configurative and spatial metaphors as descriptive. They will not, it is hoped, be taken to refer to anything else than actual responses in accordance with the emphasis in this treatise.

Intellectual attitudes and postures are apparently related closely to the knowledge type of general orientation conduct, especially in the sense that the person assumes a relationship to stimulating objects. Nevertheless, there are a number of distinct differences which rather sharply distinguish the two types of behavior. In a certain sense the individual and his action are stressed more in intellectual responses. The adjustment is more intimate and personal; the individual adjusts himself by bringing about a relation between himself and the stimuli objects. He insists upon taking a stand toward them and to a great extent, also, a certain type of stand. In other words, the intellectual response depends more upon the person's peculiar equipment and experience than is true in mere cognitive responses. Also in the case of knowledge reactions the response is barely established. As compared with intellectual behavior therefore they do not constitute so prolonged or lasting a type of occurrence. Moreover, the orientation depends upon the person's direct or indirect contacts with the qualities and conditions (origin, existence, development) of things. Intellectual responses, on the other hand, require no objects. The reaction may be one of accepting, or taking a position with respect to, the probable or possible existence of an object or the probable nature of its qualities if it does exist. That is to say, intellectual conduct may be completely and exclusively referential; when it is, it has no parallel in the knowledge field of action.

Of these intellectual responses there exist a great many individual types, among which we may number attitudes, beliefs, opinions, suppositions, appreciation, criticism, evaluation, etc. The particular type in each case depends, of course, upon the precise stimuli conditions of the behavior segment, upon the degree of definiteness or probability, the lack or presence of evidence, the availability or obscurity of causes and conditions, etc. If it is impossible to *know* a certain thing, if we have not enough evidence about it to be sure of our knowledge concerning it, then we can react to it only in a belief manner. If certain information relative to some foreign political situation is withheld from us, we can have only vague suppositions with respect to it. Of a somewhat different nature are such intellectual responses as opining and conjecturing. In performing these reactions the stimuli objects may be immediately present but their incompleteness is such that the intellectual reaction is an intimate personal one, more or less independent of the stimuli objects.

**Differentiation of Intellectual Reactions from Other Psychological Behavior** The non-effective and somewhat passive character of intellectual reactions from the standpoint of stimuli objects, and the fact that, howsoever different from other types of action they may be, they are still frequently intermixed with these other types, suggest the necessity of differentiating intellectual reactions from actions superficially resembling them. In most cases, of course, it is hardly likely that these different types of activity will be confused, but on the whole the attempt to make the detailed differentiation will undoubtedly help us in our understanding of all the different types of action involved.

First, let us point out the essential variations between intellectual reactions and feeling attitudes. In some cases the two types are so closely related superficially that we are in danger of concluding that the contacts of the person with stimuli objects are approximately the same in both cases. The main difference between them so far as contact with stimuli is concerned reverts to differences in the morphological character of the reaction systems involved. In contradistinction to feeling attitudes, intellectual responses do not necessarily involve any definite organic (glandular) or visceral changes. Intellectual responses are merely cases of appreciating and accepting certain qualities in objects and noticing changes in these qualities. Further, intellectual responses are thoroughly cold-blooded in the sense that they involve no palpitation or libration of the individual. In affective attitudes such phenomena are invariably present. Intellectual responses are accordingly never so absolutely intimate as feeling responses. Consequently, they may be verbal or propositional in character and, as such, involve a practical minimum operation of the organism and its organic factors.

Because intellectual responses are intimate modes of behavior they bear a close resemblance, in this respect, to affective conduct. But the resemblance is only an external one. Intellectual responses are intimate in quite another sense. They are intimate because, unlike feeling reactions, they are founded and depend upon the person's behavior equipment and intimate reactional biography. Feeling responses on the contrary are relatively conditioned more by the character of the stimuli and are in consequence more common. When intellectual responses are performed in a similar manner by different persons it is because of similarities in these individuals' reactional history and verbal and propositional character.

So much for the differences between feeling attitudes and intellectual reactions when the stimuli are objects definitely present. When we recall that intellectual responses are stimulated by conditions and probabilities, the differences are magnified. It is impossible, in fact, to perform any feeling responses to such situations. Here is involved not merely the performance of implicit responses, which are of course equally possible in the case of feeling reactions, but also the assumption of some attitudes with respect to an indefinite, uncertain, and perhaps improbable, circumstance.

We may concern ourselves next with the relation between intellectual responses and desiring reactions to which the former also bear resemblance. In the case of desiring behavior it is very clear that the attitude reaction, if it is not one of manipulation and effective contact with stimuli, is invariably a substitution for such action or a preparation for it. In performing intellectual reactions, however, persons are much more indifferent to the stimuli and always less active with respect to them.

Intellectual reactions are likewise to be distinguished from thinking and reasoning, although the latter are very much like them in their common orientational features. Intellectual responses differ from thinking action in that they need not involve any further behavior than the assumption of an intellectual stand toward something. Clearly the person performing thinking responses may be involved in a reactionally more effective way with stimuli objects or conditions. Usually the specific thinking actions precede some more definitely manipulative or performative action. Planning, as a type of thinking action, anticipates further practical activity. Intellectual responses comprise nothing more than merely approving or disapproving of some thing or action.

In a similar way we may differentiate between intellectual responses and reasoning action. In general the latter typically represents a more active and expert determination of the intellectual position the person should take toward things, rather than the mere assumption of such an attitude. For this reason we consider reasoning activities, as well as thinking responses, more intimately related to the stimuli objects and situations than is the case with intellectual responses.

Finally, we must distinguish intellectual reactions from the more permanent type of behavior equipment designated as intellectual habits. Intellectual responses must be considered to be momentarily occurring and contingential reactions. They are immediate responses to stimuli objects and conditions. Their duration is regarded as a function of the length of time during which the stimuli objects are present in the behavior surroundings of the individual. They are not more or less permanent behavior traits which are intimately integrated with specific stimuli objects and conditions such that the presence of the latter calls for a more or less static type of intellectual response. Howsoever such reactions are influenced and conditioned by intellectual habits, they are still very different from these habits. No matter how long stimuli are in contact with the individual his intellectual responses to them are very different from such habit responses as intellectual vacillation, dogmatism, dogmatic openmindedness, permanent discipleship or subserviency, etc.[1]

**Analysis of Intellectual Behavior Segments**    The responses of intellectual behavior segments are activities of occasion. They are unique processes adapting the individual either to more or less stable stimuli objects and conditions, or to stimuli objects lacking such fixed qualities. Precisely because the stimuli objects are not constant, however, and because the intellectual responses are primarily reactional in character (being attitudes or postures of the individual), they may last for a long time. They are subject, of course, to modification. Intellectual reactions, however, must not be considered as equipmental. They are functions of immediate situations and

---

[1] In this connection, as in so many others, we must guard against confusing different types of behavior because of similarity of verbal designation.

do not represent permanent organizations of particular stimuli and responses.

Because of these various characteristics of intellectual actions, it is important to study their origin and development. Their character and duration depend decidedly upon their genesis and modification. Intellectual responses must be looked upon as products of situations; as such they can be best understood.

Intellectual behavior segments, we may suggest, originate in many different ways. For some reason or other the person becomes curious about an object and develops an opinion or assumption concerning it. Again he is told something about a particular object or situation without having had any previous interest in or knowledge of the object's existence. He is thus induced to develop beliefs and opinions concerning it. In other instances an individual's interest in, or his necessary contact with, an object induces him to develop intellectual attitudes with respect to related objects or circumstances. In still other cases, as is true of scientists and artists, it devolves upon the individual to develop and entertain opinions and beliefs about particular subject matters. In all of these cases while the individual may find it necessary to develop and have opinions of certain sorts, the necessity for performing such action does not lie directly in the character of the stimulus object but in the nature of the circumstances connected with it. In detail, the character of the substitution stimulus points to and directs the individual toward the adjustment stimulus for the intellectual reaction. We may now turn to a more detailed discussion of the response and stimulus factors of intellectual behavior segments.

Among the innumerable types of specific response factors of intellectual reactions we find widely differing modes of contact between the individual and the stimuli objects. Some of the responses we may call analogical. The person may take an intellectual stand toward some present stimulus object in a manner analogous to the response he makes to some other object. This fact may be due to similarity between the two things. Again, the present reaction may be one in which the person refers the present stimulus to some other object or event which is referred to as a standard. Here the unique response that occurs is merely a variant from one usually coördinated with the stimulus standard. In other intellectual responses the person discovers some differences in the various features of a present object. This may consist of a more subtle reference to some standard stimulus object than was true in the preceding case. Intellectual responses also consist of the appreciation or determination of a comparison between two things immediately present. In addition, the specific character of intellectual responses in some instances consists of cognitive attraction toward an object or withdrawal from it.

With respect to the response factors, the question arises as to whether intellectual responses consist of precurrent or consummatory reaction systems. Such a question is invariably answered in favor of the consummatory type. Intellectual reactions are final activities and are not precurrent to other types of behavior. When the individual forms an opinion or develops a belief the behavior segment is complete and finished. This does not mean in any sense that these reactions cannot be the basis of, or preliminary to, other and perhaps more effective forms of behavior. Our point is merely that, the intellectual behavior segment itself is an autonomous action. Whenever it is connected with some other type of activity, we are dealing with two entirely different kinds of behavior segments.

We may observe, however, that the intellectual behavior segment operates either in a comparatively simple or in a complex way. In the simpler reaction the attention and perceptual precurrent responses are immediately followed by the intellectual attitude as a final response. In other cases, however, before the final intellectual reaction occurs a large amount of precurrent behavior takes place, which may be regarded as leading to the consummatory intellectual response. A belief or opinion reaction may be preceded by a considerable amount of preliminary activity which serves as an aid in forming the final intellectual orientation. Very frequently, although not always, we can correlate intellectual responses with intelligent modes of behavior on the basis of the presence and amount of precurrent activity involved in specific behavior segments. Those comprising precurrent responses constitute more intelligent activity on the whole than those containing few or no anticipatory reaction systems.

Intellectual reaction systems may be roughly divided into two large types on the basis of the particular kinds of relationship between the reacting individual and the stimulus object. In the one type we find the person in close contact with the stimulus object. There is an intimate connection between the adjustment and substitute stimuli operating in the behavior segment. This is the case whenever the intellectual response is made to an object immediately present. Since intellectual reactions are primarily reactional or attitudinal in nature the person is always more or less remote from actual contact with the object. Accordingly, when the object to which the intellectual responses are made is immediately present we find that it performs both substitutional and adjustmental functions. By comparison with these types of reactions, in which the adjustment and substitutional functions are performed by the same object, we have responses in which the two functions are quite disparate, existing in widely separated objects, or in some cases adjustment objects not actually existing at all. Such is true in the case of the intellectual responses of doubting or believing.

The specific reaction systems of intellectual behavior segments are, therefore, of both the implicit and overt type. While the final reactions are always implicit, since they constitute a removed and detached attitude toward things, the total behavior segment may possibly involve many overt or even manipulative reaction systems. Obviously this is especially true in the case of those behavior segments in which the final reaction is performed after considerable precurrent preliminary reaction. For instance, the intellectual reaction of the textile expert in accepting or rejecting some cloth on the basis of a set standard, occurs only after he has handled the fabric, tested it, etc.

So far as the stimuli for intellectual reactions are concerned, we have already observed that they are of two types, the substitute and the adjustment. Generally speaking, of course, we can perform intellectual reactions to any type of object, person, or situation. All of the different sorts of facts and events which constitute our surroundings stimulate us to develop opinions, beliefs, and assumptions. But, as is not true in other cases, the stimuli here may consist of unknown, indeterminate and even non-existing objects.

It might be well to specify that, so far as the substitute functions are concerned, intellectual stimuli consist primarily of objects and conditions standing for and pointing to other objects, conditions, propositions, and information constituting evidence and symbols of the adjustment stimuli.

The types of adjustment stimuli objects for intellectual reactions consist of the origin and relations of things, their existence and value, which must be assumed or believed to exist in particular ways and certain degrees. Additional adjustment stimuli objects comprise relations between the person and other persons or other things, e. g., one may believe himself to be an exceedingly important factor in some industrial organization.

From the fact that intellectual behavior consists of attitudes toward various types of stimuli, and also that it represents extremely complex forms of action, it follows that there is an intimate relationship between verbal and linguistic responses, and intellectual behavior. In point of fact, many intellectual reactions transcend the simpler inapparent forms of implicit behavior and occur in the more visible and palpable manner of statement as terms and propositions. This intricate behavior of a linguistic type is required to formulate attitude reactions and in general to take behavior positions with respect to objects. Not only is the operation of intellectual conduct interwoven with language factors, but its actual development is also. To develop a belief or an opinion concerning the existence or function of some complex phenomenon is an activity which cannot operate without the performance of a great many linguistic responses. *Linguistic Factors in Intellectual Conduct*

This is especially true for the large class of intellectual activities which persist for some time. These attitudinal reactions simulate intellectual habits and equipment. For their operation language responses are absolutely indispensable. Because we develop our more stable and intricate intellectual attitudes through interpersonal association, these attitudes must be referred to by means of language activities. The building up and propagation of any belief or opinion, whether developed by some single individual or by several, is achieved only through the performance of innumerable language activities. Our intellectual behavior of this type is thoroughly shot through with linguistic factors.

In order to appreciate properly the relationship between language and intellectual behavior we must distinguish very carefully between the linguistic conduct which constitutes the attitude itself or its embodiment, and the language activity which functions when [1] some other person is referred to it. It is only in the communicative situation that we have genuine language reactions. The actual formulation or development of these attitudes does not necessarily represent true language situations. Whatever language activities are involved at this stage function more effectively than implicit responses, whether imagal or verbal. They are not, therefore, indirect reactions as is the case with genuine language.[2] It is likewise urgent to differentiate here elementary verbal reactions, belonging to the class of implicit behavior, from terms and propositions constituting a more elaborate form of linguistic psychological conduct. The language factors involved in the use of terms may even include language elements that are not reactions but stimuli, although they must be equally intimate factors of intellectual behavior, namely, crystallizations of genuine verbal responses. In this sense, object or stimulational linguistic factors operate as knowledge and concept-objects. This last point is illustrated by the use of words standing for abstractions, as in the case of the whole terminology concerning atomic theory. Similarly, more popular behavior beliefs and opinions concerning religious matters cannot be developed or entertained without the medium of linguistic elements that are not at the time definite language responses.

**General Conditions of Intellectual Behavior**

Whether we think of our intellectual reactions as particular instances of an individual's adaptation to specified stimuli or as general types of complex behavior, we find certain specific conditions governing their operation in each case. Ordinarily our intellectual actions are subject to a series of circumstances that make them occur in a very specialized way. In anticipation of our detailed treatment of particular intellectual conditions we will enumerate first some general influences which determine to a great extent the detailed features of intellectual conduct and mark it off as belonging to some particular type.

In the first place, our intellectual reactions to things are definitely determined by the character of those things. Practical situations demand an entirely different intellectual process than do theoretical circumstances. Whether the stimulus object is a knowledge element, a thing or a condition, materially affects the character of the intellectual action involved. Similarly, the tangible or intangible char-

---

[1] Popularly spoken of as a communication of an idea.
[2] Cf. Chapter XXIII, p. 209.

acter of stimuli objects or situations alters the particular intellectual response performed. Both of these influences are closely connected with the question as to whether the stimuli situations are problematic or definite. Here the complexity and general form of the response depend upon whether the object eliciting the reaction is itself present or must be substituted for. In the latter case the adjustment stimulus objects may be doubtful or improbable.

Again, the kind of intellectual activity that occurs and its particular character is based upon the number of objects involved. To a single object the reaction is probably a direct evaluation or approval, whereas the behavior segment, including many stimuli objects and conditions, calls for an intellectual attitude of discrimination and comparison. When things constitute the stimuli, their newness or novelty and the degree of their difference from objects with which we have recently or frequently been in contact, means that we perform a more complicated and difficult form of intellectual response. Also involved here is a large number of preliminary reactions, as compared with the case in which objects are familiar and related to others to which we have heretofore responded.

Obviously the importance and seriousness of stimuli objects affect the type of intellectual reaction which they arouse. In some situations, when the stimulus object is not of much concern, our intellectual response consists of guessing or supposing. Situations of more momentous import call forth intellectual attitudes characterized by more cautious development and operation.

Whether the adjustment stimulus is one that has already occurred or is presently transpiring, or whether it is some action or situation which may occur or be expected in the future, are considerations which materially alter the character and mode of operation of intellectual behavior. Intellectual reactions may thus have an intrinsic temporal factor or, in some other way bespeak the type of specific adaptation which is being performed.

Besides the conditions issuing from the character of the stimulus and the general behavior situations there are those which have more to do with the reacting person and his intimate circumstances. Foremost among these conditions is the individual's general behavior equipment. The larger the equipment of knowledge reactions, skills, and capacities the more easily and more expertly are intellectual responses developed. The intellectual behavior under such circumstances is more positive, more effective and, in general, more dependable, in the particular situations for which the behavior equipment is applicable. This type of condition is more saliently involved than any other in the intellectual attitudes which are idiosyncratic and based upon deliberation and understanding of the behavior situations.

It is exceedingly instructive to observe how the behavior equipment of an individual, especially his more lasting desires and interests, influences his intellectual reactions, even though not always to their advantage from the standpoint of the stimuli conditions involved. The behavior equipment serves not only as a mode for the development of intellectual attitudes toward things, but serves also to magnify and overemphasize the nature of the stimuli. This situation is strikingly illustrated in circumstances which are not expected to be advantageous to the individual and to his general adaptational conduct. For example, in the field of scientific work we find that a person whose behavior equipment inclines him toward experimentation may seriously have his intellectual conduct affected by this fact. He may develop wrong attitudes toward phenomena which are not subject to experimentation. He may disbelieve in their existence or their value. Or he may develop false attitudes toward the work of other individuals as it concerns such data because it does not follow his preconception as to its nature. A physicist may disparage the work of a biologist, or the experimental biologist may look with disdain upon his fellow worker who is more interested than he in field problems.

On the other hand, the individual whose personality equipment and behavior circumstances are more theoretical in character may develop similar disserviceable attitudes toward certain phenomena and toward the work of other individuals occupied with factual particularities. This untoward influence of personality equipment upon one's intellectual reactions is illustrated in every branch of human activity. Some individuals must perforce develop and foster intellectual attitudes of an idealistic sort although, because of the circumstances involved, this may actually prove to be a type of sentimentalism, instead of a solid attitude toward the particular world of things concerned.

Our intellectual behavior toward persons as individuals is also seriously affected when conditioned by our immediate behavior. Thus, to judge a man a good scholar or brilliant worker because we like him personally is far from a valuable and effective intellectual response. Similarly, to believe a student brilliant merely because we are pleased and flattered by his acceptance of our own attitude does not imply that we have appropriately adapted ourselves to him as a stimulus object.

At other times, after we have acted out a fear or dread response, we inevitably assume a decidedly different intellectual position with respect to some intellectual stimulus. Patently this influence will be more marked when the affective response is closely connected with the stimulus object for the intellectual response. Such variations in influence are likewise due to the degree of intensity of the affective action. Intellectual responses may in this way be differentiated from each other on the basis of the kind of behavior conditions which have influenced them. They may be further differentiated upon the basis of the kind of activities, if any, which they in turn condition or influence.

Likewise the character and operation of intellectual responses depend upon the person's reactional biography and previous training, as well as his general experience. The particular type of previous contacts which an individual has had exert a very great influence upon his readiness to develop intellectual behavior and upon its expertness and efficacy. Knowledge and experience bearing upon particular situations to which we perform intellectual responses are, however, no guarantee that the response is appropriate for, and adequate to, the stimuli situations. Very frequently the stand we take is influenced more by fairly extraneous circumstances. A person may even enumerate all the wrong attitudes to be avoided in a particular situation and yet adopt some or even all of them.

Outstanding among the determiners of intellectual reactions are the cultural conditions under which the individual lives. The particular qualities of an individual's beliefs, opinions, and other behavior attitudes are leavened by the kinds of institutions with which he has been in contact. One does not expect the attitudes of persons living under Oriental auspices to coincide very closely with those developed under Occidental institutions. Similarly, we discover intellectual attitudes among people who have had contact with scientific institutions, which are entirely different from the attitudes of people who have never had such contacts. Generally speaking, it is this type of intellectual reactions that is painlessly performed under the auspices of the original cultural surroundings. For the most part the reactions performed under these circumstances are comparatively durable, matching the intransiency of the institutions. Hence they are almost of the order of intellectual habits.

Another example of this type of influence is involved in our admiration for a country similar to the one in which we live. Again, to perform intellectual reactions to manners and customs of people on the basis of the cultural circumstances to which we are accustomed does not add to our success in adapting ourselves to such things. All students of human phenomena must appreciate the difficulties and necessities of the intellectual detachedness required here.

No less important than any of the other influences upon intellectual conduct are the individual's hygienic and general health conditions. Everyone is familiar with the fact that more favorable and generous attitudes are taken by individuals in a state of well being, than when suffering from some malfunction. Naturally hygienic and health influences interlock with favorable and unfavorable social conditions which also assist in the formation of intellectual orientation.

It remains to be added that our enumeration of influences upon intellectual conduct has been confined to strictly psychological conditions. This procedure is partially justified by the fact that since we are dealing with intellectual reactions the influences of social, economic, religious, and military conditions and circumstances operate for the most part as secondary influences, in that they first condition behavior fundamental to the intellectual activities. We wish to point

out, however, that whether direct or secondary the influence is none
the less potent.

As we have already indicated, our present survey of conditions influencing intellectual conduct may be used as a basis for differentiating among specific intellectual behavior types. We may now direct
our attention to a discussion of these chief types.

Believing activities constitute behavior segments in which the responses are primarily implicit reactions to uncertain and ambiguous
stimuli situations. Believing behavior accordingly consists of the acceptance or rejection of the existence, nature, or probability of events
or propositions. It essentially comprises an attitude of assent or acquiescence, of dissent or demurral. Despite the fact that the stimuli
conditions are uncertain and ambiguous, these behavior activities are
decidedly positive forms of intellectual action. The individual definitely and, in some cases, deliberately accepts some fact or proposition
as existent or true, although the fact in question is not clearly known
or fully appreciated. It is chiefly this ambiguous character of the
stimulus condition which elicits the particular activity of acceptance
or rejection. As we shall presently have occasion to see, the precise
degree of acceptance or rejection depends upon the extent of uncertainty and ambiguity in the stimulating conditions. The basis for
such acquiescence or incredulity is, of course, evidence or authority
in the form of substitute stimuli representing the objects, conditions,
or propositions which constitute the adjustment stimuli.

Believing reactions are always unique responses that belong intimately to a particular situation. They never comprise, then, a general form of action (or state as the older psychologists would have it)
which involves different specific stimuli.[1] The acceptance or rejection
attitude is an absolute function of particular situations prompting
the belief behavior. This is true chiefly because believing is interconnected with so many details that it cannot have any general characteristics.

Provided that a believing reaction is a unique and definite attitude
of the person, it will not be plausible to say that believing action
represents mere readiness to act. It is undoubtedly true that believing is a very definite criterion of the readiness with which we are
prepared to perform some kind of response. We may say that we
believe the fact [2] or proposition upon which we are ready to act. Let
us observe, however, that we are describing here two different forms
of behavior. In the first instance, we are concerned with the acceptance of a proposition or fact. In the case of acting upon a belief, we
are dealing with another act which depends upon the first one and by
which the character of the first may be determined. Under no circumstances may we forget that we are considering here two distinct
types of action. To neglect this distinction leads us into the predica-

[1] Called content by the older intellectualistic psychologists—
[2] Something about it, or that it exists, perhaps.

ment of including fearing, knowing, and desiring as similar readinesses to act, for they just as certainly as believing, may also be the forerunners of action.[1]

Of the decided characteristics of believing reactions none is more striking than their tendency toward interrelation and system-forming. Because they are reactions to ambiguous and indefinite stimuli of all sorts they are interconnected with or at least influenced by other beliefs. This characteristic is remarkable precisely because the beliefs are such unique and particularized forms of behavior. Not only are the beliefs developed to a great extent through this interrelational condition, but their force and positiveness are buttressed and established by the fact that they do or do not belong to a system of circumstances of which a part has already been accepted. The assent or dissent accorded to propositions or events is conditioned in great part by the system of related believing responses that we have previously performed.

How are beliefs established? Upon what basis do we perform these intellectual acceptance or rejectance responses? First, there must be evidence or authority of some sort. Thus, our belief reactions are adaptations to adjustment stimuli (events or propositions) upon the basis of some sort of substitution stimulation in the form of authority.

When the stimuli conditions are facts, the belief is mediated by evidence of some sort. This evidence may be part of the event we believe is happening or it may be some information or sign of an event which is to follow based upon something that has already taken place. Depending upon the person, his experiences, and interest in the situation, an individual believes more or less strongly in anything, by virtue of the available substitute stimulation. It is upon this basis that believing behavior varies so considerably in the degree of intensity with which the individual accepts or rejects the existence of some fact. The validity and satisfactoriness of the belief must be decided by the individual's contact with, and appreciation of, the character of the substitution stimuli and their relation to adjustment objects or events. It must be remarked here that the substitution stimuli may consist of events similar to the adjustment stimuli events, but which have occurred in the past and of which the person has heard. It is not necessary that he should have personally been in contact with such events or situations.

When knowledge or propositional objects constitute the adjustment stimuli for belief responses, the substitute stimuli take the form of some sort of communication or announcement. Here the firmness or the intensity of the intellectual acceptance or rejection attitude de-

[1] The reader will recall here the question of Sully who objects to Bain's conception that when a thing is such as to make us act on it we believe it. Sully asks, "but how about past things, or remote things, upon which no reaction of ours is possible? And how about belief in things which check action?" Cf. James, *Principles*, Vol. II, p. 322.

pends upon the person's confidence in the truth or falseness of the propositional substitute stimulus. Such confidence is, of course, fostered by the absence of any proposition contradictory to the substitute stimuli and derived either from the individual's own experience or from an informant or authority. Belief attitudes are further supported by prejudices of all sorts which constitute part of the personality equipment of the individual performing the belief action. In such cases the prejudice both induces and supports belief as well as maintains it along with the behavior equipments of the individual.

Among the specificities of believing reactions both to events and propositions are the differences between individuals. Some do and others do not accept as authority the statements of those who share some knowledge in common with them, no matter how remote it may be from the present situation. Again, some behavior proposition is rejected when supported by a person who really is trustworthy. How many people accept "psychic" phenomena because some authority in physics has vouched for such supposed events. Believing reactions are sometimes founded upon the authority of some one who knows only a slight fact which is unknown to the believer.

Believing responses as intellectual reactions are precarious and dependent. They may be further thought of as not requiring investigation. Now it is not merely the fact that the adjustment stimuli facts cannot be investigated which gives these responses the particular character of belief. For, clearly, believing responses may be followed by an investigation. But in that case the belief response serves merely as a stimulus of a problematic sort which influences a further investigative act. The investigation itself is not a part of the belief in question. When, however, this investigation is an integral part of the individual's adaptation, then the activity must be designated by some other name because it constitutes a very different form of conduct. It may be knowing or some type of orientation but should never [1] be called believing.

Concerning the functional character of the stimuli for believing reactions we have already made the suggestion that they must be divided into the adjustment and substitute form. In this case also the relationships between the two types of stimuli are exceedingly important, for the strength of the belief depends upon how closely knit the stimuli are. Among the particular kinds of objects which constitute adjustment stimuli for believing reactions, facts and events as well as propositions and informational materials are very prominently represented. The inclusion of events and facts must be stressed in view of the prevalent opinion that belief is an activity belonging exclusively to informational situations. This opinion originates, of course, among the logicians who stress propositions and information generally. As a matter of fact, when we think in terms of specific accept-

[1] This does not exclude the possibility that believing responses may follow acts of rationalization or even uncritical inference.

ance and rejection activities constituting the specific responses of a believing type, no kind of circumstance or situation is, *ipso facto*, excluded from the rôle of an adjustment stimulus. When situations and events are the stimuli for belief, it is the probability or improbability of their existence or occurrence that form the stimulus. The point here discussed becomes more evident when we consider that even objects themselves are the stimuli for believing reactions. Since believing responses are intellectual attitudes of rejecting or accepting, it follows that believing is a response to the existence of a thing or person in the present, past or future. Furthermore the actual stimulus may be the presence or absence in an object of some particular quality. Obviously, in the case of a psychological attitude, it is not absolutely requisite that the stimulus object have actual existence. What is involved, is the reaction to such existence or non-existence. It is recalled, of course, that so far as the psychological fact is concerned, the non-existence of a thing to which we react does not imply the absence of a cause for this action, for that is found in the object, proposition, or information constituting the substitute stimulus.

Among the substitute stimuli for believing reactions we find a large representation of information and knowledge factors. But this by no means exhausts the list of things serving a substitute function. In addition, objects, events, etc., may stimulate beliefs in other objects, conditions, etc., and even in propositions.

When the substitute stimuli are closely connected with the adjustment stimuli the resulting belief is acceptable and firm. This, however, depends upon the individual's appreciation of the close connection between the two stimuli. When the connection is appreciated by the reacting individual the substitute stimulus, whether an event or information which is part of another event, may constitute the strongest basis for a firm believing action to the adjustment stimulus.

Coincident with the strikingly different auspices under which believing behavior takes place, we find peculiar instances of its occurrence. In brief, these particular intellectual reactions appear to have descriptive properties different from most types of believing behavior. Many times this peculiarity of belief is due to its performance by an individual who is living under peculiar circumstances, or who has particular needs.

*Types of Believing Reaction*

For the most part we may differentiate these peculiar and striking forms from the more usual type of believing action on the basis that the ordinary kind constitutes fairly deliberate and perhaps intelligent attitudinal reactions of persons. On the contrary, the more peculiar form of belief consists of irrational and sometimes irresponsible actions not closely related to the evidence or authority of the substitutional stimuli.

First we may refer to believing behavior which may be called vacillating. Here the individual performing the reaction is so out of touch with the evidence or substitution of the adjustment stimulus, or so little appreciates the connection between the two, that his believing action of acquiescence or recusancy occurs in rapid alternation. Such quick succession of one way of believing and another produces believing action of a very unstable character.

Conspicuous as a distinct form of belief is the persistent acceptance of certain information in spite of the fact that the person has never had any evidence upon which to base his reaction. Or sometimes, long after the basis has disappeared, he still persists in his former belief. In such instances the activity of believing comprises to a considerable extent the inability to recognize or the refusal to accept the fact that the basis for the belief has disappeared.[1]

Our next type of believing reactions consists of those which are not exclusively intellectual but in which the individual is at the same time performing affective responses to the stimuli objects and situations. Typical instances are enthusiastic beliefs. In the first place they require a minimum of evidence or authority. In the second place, they are very tenaciously persisted in. This is true chiefly because the substitute stimulus consists of the individual's affective condition. Striking examples of these powerful types of believing are ordinarily referred to as faith. In other words, the individual accepts a positive and affirmative intellectual attitude toward things because of accompanying affective conditions. The lover who earnestly believes in the faithfulness of his mistress may persist in this behavior merely because of the pleasantness derived from entertaining such a belief. Belief in a Deity is often based very decidedly upon the satisfaction one gains from the belief. Here the substitute object or proposition that stimulates and supports the belief is not so much an affective activity of the individual as it is some advantage or interest the circumstances hold for him. Believing action may likewise have desires or wants as well as information or evidence as substitute stimuli. The desire for some thing or condition stimulates us to accept or reject as existing, possible, or true, some thing, event, or proposition.

Belief responses connected with other types of actions, especially affective behavior, are very numerous. In all of these cases the belief is tinged with pleasantness or unpleasantness, excitement or tranquillity, elevation or depression, etc. Unfortunately the poverty of speech does not permit easy naming of these activities. It remains only for us to refer to our own behavior in which subtle implicit acceptances and rejections of facts or propositions are tinged and shaped by affective responses.

Our exposition of the character of believing behavior has already implied that it varies widely in its modalities. Some beliefs are intellectual attitudes deliberately assumed with strict regard to and

---

[1] Russian literature is replete with striking examples of individuals whose behavior consists primarily of such unfounded and persistent believing, e. g., Goncharov's *Oblomov* and Chekhov's *Liaharev* in the short story *On The Road.*

appreciation of the character of the evidence or the worth of the report which constitutes the substitute stimulus. In other instances, the intellectual attitude comes to the individual quite unwittingly and insidiously. We may then think of the person as playing an exceedingly passive part in the performance of the action. This apparent passivity of the reacting person is sometimes a feature of serious and important behavior situations. That this eventuality is possible is due of course to the general character of believing behavior. It is instructive, then, to notice that people often do not know the ground of their belief though it may be solid ground nevertheless. For instance, the individual's social and natural surroundings determine what intellectual attitudes he should assume when the appropriate stimuli present themselves. Between these two extreme modes of believing we find innumerable types of variations. We may further suggest that these varying modalities partake of both cognitive and voluntary characteristics. Not only may the belief attitudes be assumed knowingly or unknowingly; they may also be chosen and preferred.

It is evident that believing activities are performed upon all levels of human conduct. Intellectual attitudes are assumed with respect to probable conditions and circumstances in all phases of everyday life. We have beliefs concerning ourselves and our intimates and their qualities and relations. The uncertainties of our moral and social surroundings prompt us to take various intellectual positions with respect to them. Probably the most familiar level and source of believing activity is the domain of religious conduct. These different levels may be further characterized as concrete and abstract, or practical and theoretical. On the former levels the data and the propositions comprising the stimuli are generally less strict as evidence and less rigid as propositions than is true on the latter strata.

Behavior segments in which the stimuli are so confused and ambiguous that the person cannot either reject or accept them, we call doubting. While the intellectual attitude which constitutes the response of doubting is a positive form of adaptation, we may still describe it as, in a sense, a suspension of action. As in the case of believing, doubt behavior segments have events, conditions, and propositions as their stimuli. When the adjustment stimulus is some kind of event, the evidence or information concerning it is not sufficiently conclusive or authoritative to lead either to acceptance or rejection. Similarly, when a proposition serves as the adjustment stimulus, the information or authority relating to it is not sufficiently acceptable or rejectable to form the basis for a more positive attitude toward the stimulus in question. **Doubting Behavior**

The situations just suggested may be regarded as involving a mild form of doubting reaction. In a way they simulate the more striking and extreme forms of doubting. In the latter cases, however, the evidence or information constituting the stimuli for the behavior is positively conflicting so that the resulting reaction is hesitant and suspended.  Doubting behavior may be so extreme that its performance is fraught with the most excruciating torture for the individual. This situation occurs, of course, when the stimuli objects or situations toward which the intellectual response is made are of great import and moment to the individual.[1]

Not all doubting situations are of such extreme personal consequence; nor are doubting behavior segments unusual occurrences. Every human life is constantly filled with conduct of this sort.  All situations involving critical, intelligent, and discriminative behavior are replete with perplexing doubt.  Scientific work of all sorts offers numerous circumstances and conditions calling for doubting.  Not only is doubting the beacon of the wise in practical matters of everyday life but it is also a critical organon of scientific action.  All serious action and thought must be safely grounded, to be safe at all, in the psychological activities of judicious doubting.

Disbe-
lieving

Quite a distinct type of behavior segment is that describable as disbelieving, the positive intellectual act of rejecting a fact or proposition.  When the stimulus is indefinite and ambiguous the person is stimulated by the substitute stimulus to perform an apophatic response.  The individual may actually reject the basis for taking an assenting attitude toward some object.  Or the act of disbelief may be influenced and fostered by conditions extraneous to the evidence or authority of the substitute stimuli which represent the adjustment stimuli involved.  To appreciate thoroughly the positive nature of intellectual disbelieving we must sharply distinguish it from unbelief that may be regarded as contrary to believing.  Situations in which the activity of disbelieving occur are unique and decidedly different from either believing or unbelieving situations both from the standpoint of the stimuli conditions involved and the individual performing the action.  In short, disbelieving activities are uniquely rejectional in character while believing involves an assent.  Disbelieving differs from unbelief or non-believing, which, to a certain extent, can be considered negation of action in that it is a positive intellectual attitude of refusing to assent to a proposition, or to accept it as evident or valid.  It is therefore not a mere lack or default in belief. Likewise, disbelieving may be the rejection of an estimate or value of some person or of his abilities, as well as a turning back of a proffered datum or proposition.

Opining
Reactions

Opining in an essential way comprises both implicit and overt reactions to events and propositions toward which the person is unable to develop a complete and assuring attitudinal reaction.  Opining situations are, however, not necessarily ambiguous.  Accordingly they vary from believing circumstances in that the things to which the opining adaptation is made need not be regarded as intrinsically indeterminate nor unavailable for complete orientation.  In the case of

[1] A classic illustration of doubting behavior is described in Strindberg's play called "The Father."

believing reactions, it will be recalled, the stimuli are problematic events and situations, that is to say, totally unknown.[1] Whatever uncertainty and incompleteness of response is present in opining behavior is due more to the reactional deficiencies of the person than to the nature of the stimulational conditions themselves. Intellectual conduct of the opining type, therefore, comprises substitutions and compensations for behavior equipment deficiencies. For instance, when a person is lacking in the number and expertness of his contacts with particular stimuli objects and conditions, the mode of reaction he is able to perform is quite inadequate to the necessities of the stimuli in question. Thus the best compensation that the individual can achieve is to perform an opining intellectual response.

In serious situations, such as scientific investigation, as well as in other more practical and common circumstances, the necessity of responding with opining behavior instead of more definite and certain action is caused by a lack of technique enabling one to arrive at a more certain attitude concerning the facts and events in question. In other cases, the performance of an opining response instead of a reaction of complete intellectual orientation may be due to the person's inability to appreciate the evidence concerning the existence of a fact, or to his failure to have such evidence recorded and preserved. Again, opining intellectual conduct may possibly substitute for a more certain form of reaction when the individual lacks confidence in the authority of the person making the assertion or presenting the proposition with respect to the stimuli concerned.[2]

Our emphasis on the substitutional and uncertain character of opining responses should not lead us to overlook the value of such activity when positively considered. The utility of opining responses is not to be minimized since, as a matter of fact, in the actual situations in which they occur, they function as exceedingly intricate and adequate adaptations. Our scene of complex intellectual behavior is after all very complicated and difficult and hence the necessity to act is imperious. Consider only the situation in which a physician is called upon to make a difficult diagnosis. The importance and value of such an opining form of behavior cannot be overestimated. Out of the performance of opining behavior of a large and varied sort, along with other kinds of action, such as cognitive and orientational responses, issues the basis for intelligent trial and error procedures and experimentation. Furthermore, the larger the number of opining responses the person performs, the greater the opportunities and pos-

----

[1] The strict psychological fact is quite different from the logical or practical situation. What is enough knowledge for practical action or logical inference may be altogether insufficient for an intimate psychological response.

[2] Altogether, opining behavior is extremely idiosyncratic. What may be a sufficient adjustment stimulus for a person's knowledge reaction at one moment is at another time nothing more than opinion for him. It is a matter of accumulated knowledge about some adjustment stimulus or a willingness to go on or be satisfied with less.

sibilities of performing other reactions, both independent of and dependent upon the opining intellectual response.

Opining conduct may, of course, be either exceedingly simple or very complex. In each case the actual type depends upon the character of the stimuli and also upon the complexity of the personality, as well as his reactional biography. Simple opining reactions are founded upon partial knowledge reactions and also upon simple affective reactions which the individual performs with respect to the stimuli. Complex opining responses, on the contrary, may be grounded upon far more intricate contacts of the individual with his stimulational circumstances. Such activity may involve a number of inferring reactions although the behavior as a whole must not be considered a product of deliberate investigative contacts with objects. For, if the latter fact were possible, the type of activity ensuing would be a more certain and definite type of intellectual behavior.

With respect to stimuli for opining reactions, we have already implied that these may be more directly in contact with the individual than is true, for example in the case of believing responses. Thus overt opining reactions are not only possible but very frequent. The detailed range of stimuli conditions or facts prompting the occurrence of opining responses is also much greater than in the case of believing. This range comprises all sorts of conditions and facts of a natural sort and in addition includes literary, scientific, ethical, and æsthetic phenomena. Nor are propositions of all sorts excluded from the stimuli which elicit opining responses. In the latter case the individual reacts more or less directly to a statement, or more generally speaking, to the linguistic conduct of an individual.

When we consider the worth of opinions as psychological phenomena, we must evaluate them on the basis of the person's behavior equipment and experience. In actual practice we find that the most valuable and valid opinions are those formed with respect to objects and conditions with which the individual is in constant and intimate contact. A natural scientist, for example, has adequate opinions concerning the phenomena of his domain and can not have any better opinion about religious phenomena than, say, a lawyer, unless the individual has made a study of human phenomena and especially human behavior of a religious type. Otherwise his opinions as adequate modes of adaptations to religious stimuli cannot be of great value. We do not overlook in this connection the transference from one field to another of a critical and calm attitude, which immediately implies an advantage on the part of the individual possessing it.

Convincing Reactions    The intellectual act of being convinced occurs only after a process of consideration or persuasion. Thus the final conviction reaction takes place in behavior segments containing considerable preliminary argument and reflection. The attitude of conviction comprises either a simple behavior segment, in which case the essential convincing reaction system is the final response following the precurrent reaction systems which lead up to the determined action; or the conviction act consists of a number of behavior segments, the last member of the series including the acceptance and satisfying reaction system.

The intellectual attitude of being convinced is essentially a behavior situation in which the response is stressed as the more striking feature. That is to say, the essential quality lies not in the nature of the stimuli objects to which adaptation is made but rather in the circumstances of the person performing the reaction. The stimuli situations need not be problematic nor indefinite. They may only be necessary to bring about an attitude on the part of the reacting individual. He may require an examination of the stimuli objects in order to arrive at a settled position, or in addition, argument and proof may be imperative. Obviously, in the former case the attitude is achieved by the individual's own exertion and action while in the latter some other individual needs to take a part in the process. In both instances, the investigation or presentation of evidence or authority serves as the cumulative stimulation for the acceptance of the fact or determination of the attitude. In this sense, then, when one does not become convinced of something at the beginning, it may mean that the lack of conviction is due to ignorance of the situation and not to doubt or disbelief about it.

Our description of the conviction attitude has indicated so far that the formulation of such an intellectual response comprises both effective and non-effective components. The proportion of each and the specific relationship between them depend upon the particular behavior circumstances involved. Similarly once conviction behavior is developed, it may operate either in situations where further action is necessary or desirable and hence follows, or where no such further activity occurs. In the latter case, the fact that the person is convinced of something involves only a change in his cognitive orientational relationship to things and does not carry over to effective action of any sort.

These intellectual reactions, like most of the others, involve adjustment and substitution stimulation. The adjustment objects include things of all sorts so far as their existence, origin, and value are concerned. In the case of events, the probability and method of their occurring are the factors to which the person adapts himself. Likewise other persons are responded to with reference to their existence, ability, character, and human qualities. Prominent among such stimuli objects is the behavior of the person himself in the sense of whether he should or should not do something.

Linguistic activities are very striking substitute stimuli involved in bringing about conviction. To a remarkable extent conviction behavior is interpersonal in character. Hence the development of the stand taken implies a great deal of interpersonal stimulation and response. Accordingly, the element of authority and its influence upon the person to be convinced is exceedingly significant. Investigation of circumstances and events not involving mutual personal interaction supplies alternative modes of reaching conviction as compared with those involved only with argument and debate. Whatever types of substitute stimulation are involved, either alone or together, they are not so much representative of adjustment objects as of the attitude to be adopted.

Influences upon conviction behavior are very similar to those operating upon other forms of intellectual conduct with the difference, however, that in the case of conviction they are more directly concerned with the person. For the most part conviction involves knowing a new way of acting with one's previous action and behavior equipment. In more complex conviction behavior situations, demonstrations afford the development of new knowledge and information concerning the adjustment stimuli in question. Affective behavior or situations are not excluded from influencing the development and operation of conviction behavior.

**Cognitive Attitudes** Under this heading we list a series of intellectual attitudes which come closest to and may be compared with orientational behavior of the knowing type. Namely, the individual takes an orientational stand with respect to objects and conditions that may or may not be in direct contact with him at the time. These activities are of course non-performative and non-effective in character. Accordingly, it is expedient to compare them with the knowing responses which they resemble.

Cognitive attitudes are more passive than ordinary knowing reactions. We look upon ordinary knowing reactions as decidedly active responses that are orientational rather than performative. The intellectual attitudes we are now describing are in this sense mere passive stands which the individual assumes toward the stimuli in question. Another basis of distinction between these two types of behavior is that knowing reactions are directed toward the qualities of objects and things. It is for this reason that we regard them as active responses. In the case of intellectual reactions the responses are based to a great extent upon the individual's behavior equipment and his reactional experience with respect to stimuli. The intellectual stand therefore depends in great measure upon how much one knows or has learned concerning the stimuli objects. It appears, then, that intellectual responses are to a great extent founded upon cognitive orientations which have previously occurred. In this sense cognitive attitudes are secondary reactions to knowledge stimuli as compared with knowledge or cognitive orientation responses. It follows from this fact that intellectual responses may be, as we have suggested, dependent more upon behavior equipment than upon the objects to which the reactions are made.

Compared with knowledge responses, cognitive attitudes are performed also upon the basis of various sorts of knowledge habits. What kind of intellectual cognitive attitudes one takes toward objects depends upon the types of intellectual or knowledge habits included in the individual's behavior equipment. The intellectually servile or disciple personality, the dogmatic person, and the original thinker, each differ in the intellectual, cognitive stands they take toward the same facts, even when other conditions are equal.

Contrasted also with ordinary knowledge reactions, cognitive attitudes are activities of more lasting character. We look upon knowledge responses as immediate and momentary reactions to things that are present, whereas cognitive attitudes, as we have been indicating, constitute somewhat continuous reactions. The latter, however, must not be confused with intellectual or knowledge habits which comprise more or less permanent forms of behavior integrated with specific stimuli objects.

Since intellectual attitudes of the cognitive type simulate ordinary cognitive responses we suggest that the particular forms they take constitute modes of behavior similar to those found in knowing behavior segments. In the case of intellectual cognitive attitudes, the stand the individual takes toward things consists possibly of a differentiation of one object from another. A more definite stand with respect to a stimulus consists of the identification of the object or fact. In all of these activities so far mentioned the objects stand out from other things, because of the particular emphasis of their qualities resulting from the person's previous contact with them. In more complicated intellectual attitudes the stand taken by the individual toward some object or fact is a direct and immediate comparison of the present stimulus object with others.

Cognitive attitudes as specific reaction systems comprise predominantly non-effective and inapparent modes of responding. Usually also they are exceedingly subtle modes of adaptation. In other cases, however, cognitive intellectual attitudes may be performed entirely in verbal or linguistic terms. So far as stimuli are concerned, they may be objects and events of all types as well as propositions and informational facts.

Judgment attitudes are intellectual responses of an implicit or overt type. They consist essentially of an evaluation of a stimulus object or event. The position or stand taken in these activities comprises the predication or attribution of qualities or significance to things or persons. To a certain extent we might consider a judging response as one which interprets an object or event. Stimuli objects or situations are characterized by way of the person becoming connected with them in a more or less intimate way. Intellectual actions of the judging type may be considered as responses which ascribe particular qualities to stimuli instead of discovering these qualities in them. A very effective behavior method of taking a judgment stand with respect to objects is to refer them to particular conditions or circumstances or to assign them to specific places in a scale of merit or significance.

**Judgment Attitudes**

All possible qualities, conditions, and merits are found among the ascribed characteristics. We may judge a thing by predicating of it value, hardness, malleability, etc. Or we may ascribe to an individual innocence, brilliance, guilt, handsomeness, and so on. Concerning events we assign them to the frequent, or singly occurring type of phenomena, to the unusual, or the common.

In this type of intellectual behavior, as well as in others, it is possible to specify that the qualities, conditions, and significance ascribed to, or predicated of, things constitute the position taken by the individual toward the stimuli on the basis of his equipment and reactional experience. Whatever a person judges a thing to be is based upon an immediate mode of action and not upon any technical ascertainment of what the stimuli objects and conditions are. Here we may add that the ascription of qualities and significance is possibly dependent upon the cultural or conventional attitudes of the person's various human groups. The intellectual stand taken by the individual may be determined more by the influence exerted upon him of his culturalization than by his own equipmental behavior or reactional history. In all of these judgment attitudes the determining influence of the objects may operate solely upon an analogical foundation. The mere fact that the present stimuli objects or situations resemble other objects can serve as the exclusive stimulational basis for the type of intellectual reaction concerning them.

It is hardly necessary to add that judgment reactions in their intimate morphological character are inapparent and subtle modes of response. Nor is it impossible to underestimate the influence of this type of ascriptional and predicative reaction on most all of the other complicated reactions the individual performs. We might add that, for the most part, the responses here are direct action upon the stimuli objects whether they are immediately present or are substituted for by some other object. When the subject of report of conversation, these intellectual reactions are very intimately related to linguistic behavior. Such intellectual attitudes are of course not essentially the subject of report or conversation.

Expecting Responses

A form of intellectual attitude of quite a distinct type is the implicit behavior performed with respect to some event or action that is to occur in the future. The event or activity constituting the stimulus is not a problematic event, but one of definite certainty. To a considerable extent the occurrence of the event has been definitely foreshadowed but cannot otherwise be reacted to except by the implicit response of expectation and anticipation. It is within the range of possibility that the reaction here is primarily a response to the date and mode of the event's occurrence rather than to the nature of the occurrence itself. The fundamental point, then, is that the stimulus has in it the character of futurity and not at all of possibility or probability.

The type of intellectual response to which we are now referring may be in morphological detail a verbal or other type of implicit reaction which is definitely stimulated by some substitute stimulus closely connected with the adjustment stimulus.

Intimately related to the kind of intellectual reactions just discussed but not involving any element of futurity are the responses called guessing and conjecturing. These activities are primarily reactions to single stimuli objects, situations, and conditions that are indefinite but not problematic. They are merely incomplete. We may consider these responses as direct overt activities which, however, because of the incompleteness of the person's contact with the stimulus object or situation, are attitudes of a tentative and provisional sort. This does not mean that the intellectual action is not complete and finished in itself. It merely describes the kind of action occurring with respect to the stimuli involved. The full significance of the tentative and provisional character of the response is appreciated when we consider the place of such activity in situations where further important behavior is necessary. Obviously, actions based upon guessing and conjecture attitudes toward things cannot be as effective and certain as activity dependent upon some more definite and complete form of intellectual attitude.

Guessing and Conjecturing Behavior

Hypothesizing responses partake of some of the characteristics of both expecting and guessing intellectual conduct. The hypothesizing individual takes an attitude or position with respect to the character, origin, or change in a thing which is appreciated as decidedly provisional, tentative or temporary. The attitude implies, therefore, that new developments will bring about a change in position with respect to the stimulus, either because it is expected to change or because new information about it is expected to become available. Namely, a distinct element of futurity is involved which upon actualization may result in a complete reversal of position or surrender of one's stand without its necessarily being replaced.

Hypothesizing Attitudes

These responses may be directly overt or implicit and constitute reactions to any and every type of object or situation. We may suggest, too, that while they are entirely different from the thinking reactions of the same name they have a slight surface resemblance to them.

We presently turn to a large series of implicit responses in which certain particular objects with which the individual is in direct contact, constitute the stimuli for an attitude toward something else as the adjustment stimulus. We may look upon the attitude or stand as a transcendence of the present object or situation in order to attain some other sort of object or condition. In a sense this type of intellectual activity may be regarded as a form of casual or superficial inference. Thus, cloudiness is accepted as a basis for supposing or assuming that it will rain. To call these activities superficial or casual inferences is to point out that the situations are not every serious ones and that the activity is a fairly direct and immediate response and

Supposing and Assuming Responses

therefore does not involve any elaborate investigation, as is the case in true inference.

Supposing and assuming as distinct intellectual attitudes may be differentiated on the basis of the importance of the situation in which they operate and upon the deliberateness of the activity concerned. In the case of supposing, the situation is less serious and of less importance to the individual. In consequence, the person is regarded as being very casually in contact with his behavior situations. When he performs an assuming reaction, on the contrary, we think of him as more seriously involved with the objects and conditions to which he is reacting.

The substitute stimuli functions for these reactions are performed by any sort of object or situation with which the person is directly in contact. The actual object may be a thing, event (especially the latter), as well as an activity of the person. The adjustment stimuli, on the other hand, are also objects and conditions that are very intimately related with the substitute stimuli and are therefore closely connected with the person and his previous contacts with such stimuli.

At the end of this classification, as at the end of so many others in a general psychological work, we must observe that our descriptions of types of behavior are only illustrations. It is possible merely to offer descriptions of a few exemplary and striking forms of the general class of behavior under discussion. And it may only be hoped, though not established, that the choice and descriptions of the acts involved are typical and accurate. In the case of intellectual reactions or attitudes, it is safe to say that the number is very great, for intellectual behavior occurs under many circumstances and with a wealth of varying details depending upon the circumstances and the particular objects involved. This is true for any particular person. How greatly increased are the complications when we consider many persons, some with extensively complex behavior lives. Furthermore, when we take into account the extreme complexity of the behavior equipment of some personalities and the extraordinary range of their reactional experiences, we realize the increasing extent of the number and complexity of their intellectual reactions.

To say that any classification and exposition of intellectual behavior must follow the cue of language for its selective representation, sufficiently indicates its extent and variety. The formulation of types or classes of complex psychological behavior necessarily rests upon the employment of a trivial but useful technique. Namely, we take terms from both popular and scientific language traditions and attempt to make them stand for particular types of actions. Sometimes, as we might expect, such a procedure runs counter to the accepted usage of terms, either because they are deemed to be symbols for other actions, or because they are regarded as having no reference to any special action at all. In the latter case the terms are supposed to be merely synonyms. In this situation, no less than in some others, it is impossible to avoid names that have become conventional descriptions of different but related forms of action. Indeed, were it not for the help that language symbols afford us in the isolation of particular intellectual responses, the work of distinguishing between individual types of such behavior would be fraught with insuperable difficulty.

To name only a few more types of intellectual reaction not more fully treated we may refer to a large number of general attitudes toward particular stimuli objects. We may speak of the intellectual attitude of deliberately regarding and disregarding certain things and their relationship to other things. In this connection may be mentioned also the indifference and ignorance of things because of particular circumstances, and those intellectual responses denotable as the discriminating or rejecting of facts or propositions, as well as the attitude of being intellectually checked and frustrated by stimuli objects calling out these particular responses. Among the exceedingly important intellectual responses are the various interpretation attitudes which are close to the judging and evaluating reactions.

We need only add that almost all intellectual responses occur upon various levels of human activity and not only those we have especially pointed out as so distributed. In most circumstances intellectual reactions are subtly intermingled with other forms of behavior. For instance they occur in conjunction with affective responses, desire actions, etc. Furthermore, in complex situations various different types of intellectual behavior are combined in particular single situations. Also the complex intellectual responses may be said to include and operate upon the basis of simpler non-intellectual reactions. Upon the question as to whether or not intellectual reactions involve other types of action, and upon the number of such subordinate responses, turns the problem of their identification and comparison. Each of these different types of inclusive responses is also to be considered a modifier of the intellectual responses when the latter operate to alter the person's performance of the other type of reaction as well.

Aside from the study of belief the intellectual reactions have hardly been mentioned in recent works on psychology. Even belief is frequently regarded and described as an emotion or form of affective action. As if to compensate for this lack of investigation of a series of exceedingly important psychological activities, belief has frequently been connected with action of some sort, even if belief itself has usually been regarded as a substantive or processal mental state.

Belief was treated especially during the evolutionary period (Bain-Spencer, etc.) as an actional or will mental state marking a readiness on the part of the organism to perform some biological function or activity. Other writers have thought of belief as an emotional mental state going over into action. Still others looked upon it as an intellectual bit of mentality so strongly compelling as to lead to action.

That all these views make belief a mentalistic something is evidence of the impoverished character of the knowledge and investigation concerning this constantly occurring form of behavior. Our exposition, then, of the specific reaction and attitudinal character of these modes of psychological adaptation even goes beyond the insistence that belief is a concrete mode of psychological action. To look upon belief as a specific mode of adaptational response to particular stimuli objects gives it a secure place among the facts of psychological science.

But to describe believing activities in this way is only to emphasize their place among the rest of the intellectual activities. Our exposition has brought out quite clearly that we perform a great number of these intellectual activities and that they vary exceedingly in general description. Furthermore, it is plain that none of them should be confused with a merely cognitive, conative or affective state of the individual even if these terms represented actions of the person instead of psychic substances or mental flashes. Each intellectual response constitutes its own unique form of reactional adjustment of the person to the specific object or condition constituting its coördinated stimulus. Upon investigating these reactional conditions we can discover their detailed characteristics, their complexities, inclusions of similar forms of behavior, and the relationship between these and other types of adaptational response.

One more perspectival landmark may be sighted. We must insist that in all of our descriptions we have been referring to actual immediate responses of individuals and therefore have not been concerned with beliefs, convictions, and other phenomena mentioned in various anthropological and historical writings which consist of actions or products of behavior but which are not psychological in character. Intellectual activities as immediate psychological responses must be separated from data bearing the same name but which are merely statistical, historical facts and not immediate actual behavior. The difference here may be illustrated by an analogous situation. History records that the Americans entered the war in 1917. Here actual behavior is spoken of but it is historical and statistical and not the record of the actual psychological responses of the individuals treated as an aggregate of Americans.

Similarly, the logical actions of assumption, belief, opinion, etc., as crystallizations and derivatives from concrete psychological action must also be differentiated from the personal responses. The logical facts called doubts, beliefs, etc., are conventionalized and handled as data consisting of established wisdom, knowledge, and convictions in various implicit manipulations. In general, then, we must place in their proper perspectival relation opinions and opining, beliefs and believing, doubts and doubting, and all the others, even if we do not have linguistic tools to indicate the differences and the hiatus between them.

# CHAPTER XXI

## THINKING AND PROBLEM SOLVING

**The Nature of Thinking and Problem Solving**    Doubtless among the most complex of human behavior phenomena are the expert and effective adaptations to intricate stimuli situations which we call thinking and problem solving. So complex are the situations in which we think and solve problems that we must adapt ourselves by bringing to bear upon them innumerable behavior products and techniques of previous experiences. It is this procedure which constitutes the essential features of thinking and problem solving. In many ways these types of behavior are the most effective forms of action having to do with the actual manipulation of things and the immediate adaptation of the individual to concrete situations of all sorts. For instance, thinking and problem solving comprise the most technical handling of things through the use of knowledge, skills, and other behavior equipment previously acquired and now applied to the particular new conditions and situations at hand. In quite a unique sense, then, these behavior situations are complex organizations of equipmental and contingential behavior. Here are behavior conditions and circumstances taxing the person's equipment and reactional biography because the stimuli conditions are complex, novel, and compelling. As an ideal circumstance we find here also that the person is performing idiosyncratic behavior in the most effective manner that is ordinarily possible.

So far our description holds of both thinking and problem solving. Between these two forms, however, a number of striking differences exist. Thinking acts comprise a series of behavior segments which result in the person's intimate interaction with situations and objects so that operations upon them are very effective or feasible. Problem solving, as the name implies, consists primarily in overcoming difficulties and problematic situations. The latter type of action may be considered as the more particular and standard form, since the general behavior scene is more restricted and circumscribed. This relative circumscription of behavior techniques and processes is a function of the particularities of the stimuli conditions. Howsoever varied these stimuli circumstances may be in intimate detail, they are all problems of some sort.

In the domain of thinking, on the other hand, we find at least two outstanding divisions of conduct, each comprising a series of distinct and quite widely varying activities. In both divisions the particular actions are in general more fluid and consist of a large series of types.

148

In each division also the particular modes of adaptation are highly un-predictable and are functions of the immediate time and scene.   Of the two divisions of thinking action one includes the expert and com-petent manipulation of things leading to a better acquaintance with and understanding of them.   The other form of handling things con-stitutes more definitely an ascertainment, discovery, and determina-tion of what the person himself should do with respect to certain con-ditions which present themselves or are about to appear upon the behavior scene.

While in both thinking and problem solving we are bound to stress the connection of such expert manipulation of things with other per-formative actions, we should not overlook the fact that both of these kinds of behavior connect with general orientational responses.   In other words, it is not true that thinking and problem solving are con-cerned only with concrete and practical circumstances of the indi-vidual's life.   The results obtained from manipulating the particular stimuli things may be utilized to further and to expand the knowledge or general orientational relation of the individual to these stimuli as well as to other things in his psychological environment.   When this latter situation prevails, both thinking and problem solving activities belong to the more theoretical circumstances of the individual's life.

In order to identify and specify more closely the nature of these complex manipulatory adaptations we must place them in relation to other activities of a somewhat similar order.   Thus as compared with mere knowledge or simple orientation reactions, the types of behavior of the present chapter are exceedingly active and technical methods of handling things.   They involve not mere mediate appreciation of things but the energetic discovery of what they and their properties are and what should or might be done with them.

Thinking and problem solving reactions likewise differ from in-tellectual attitudes in that they involve active discovery and scrutiny of the properties and conditions of things.   In the sense of being concerned always with actually existing objects and circumstances, thinking and problem solving are more akin to knowing responses than intellectual attitudes.   In another sense, however, namely that thinking and problem solving may be distinctly overt forms of contact with stimuli objects, they are more like some of the intellectual re-sponses than they are like knowing or orientational behavior.

If thinking and problem solving are really the intricate adjust-mental activities that we have been indicating, they must involve and include many simpler activities as component factors.   Such is of course the case even to the point that some of the included activities which must be called simpler component functions are themselves exceedingly complex.   In general it may be said, then, that thinking and problem solving not only tax the practically complete equipment catalogue of the person but call for many immediate responses.

Among the latter it is unnecessary to dwell upon the innumerable

Simpler Compo-nents of Thinking and Prob-lem Solv-ing

attentional and perceptual responses which constitute the individual's immediate contacts with the things serving as stimuli for the thinking and problem solving actions. What we must stress are the volitional, voluntary, desiring, and imaginative responses. What concerns the desire and voluntary actions are the practical urges to know and to discover information in order to perform adequately some future action or to satisfy interests in things for their own sake.

Imagination responses are more proximately interinvolved with thinking and problem solving. Such complicated handling of things as these activities require often demands creative activity of both simple and complex varieties. Especially complex problem solving requires the contrivance of techniques and tools or the general transformation of data or situations as a means of overcoming the problematic stimuli. Which particular kind and number of specific component responses will be performed depend, in the final reckoning, upon the particular situation involved. Its character also conditions whether the activity will be mostly influenced by present circumstances or by past experiences through the person's equipment.

## THINKING CONDUCT

**The Nature of Thinking Reactions**

Essentially, thinking consists of the implicit and overt manipulation of things or situations as preliminary processes frequently looking forward to other practically immediate activities. Thus thinking actions as preceding other effective behavior are decidedly anticipatory in character. Or, we might say they are to a great extent instrumental actions that make way for, and provide the details of, some activity or adjustment that is to follow at an appropriate time. The emphasis should always be upon the manipulative activities, since the whole situation in which any thinking conduct occurs is one which demands such preliminary responses. Whatever action follows our planning or deciding to do a certain act, is inextricably dependent upon the previous activity of planning and determining. The importance of the thinking behavior in any situation is manifest from the fact that the anticipated action to which the thinking is preliminary may not even occur; the thinking activity has nevertheless taken place with all the intimate and serious operation of its details. That the manipulation and handling of things is the significant factor of knowing behavior is still more evident when there is no effective action to follow as in the case of thinking in purely theoretical and abstract situations. The manipulations in these situations are all, of course, of abstract and intangible things.

Planning, choosing, and evaluating actions in brief, thinking, are therefore autonomous behavior segments which always operate in specific types of conduct situations. As anticipatory conduct they prepare the individual for the performance of delayed and dependent definitive responses to novel, interesting, and uncertain stimuli objects or conditions originally inducing the individual to act.

In specific instances the actual importance and complexity of thinking behavior is due to the fact that it is a deliberate method of achieving information with respect to what actions should be performed in some intricate form of adjustment to surroundings. Thinking behavior accordingly is not only precautionary but to a great extent critical. Within the range of his knowledge and with respect to his intellectual attitudes of approval and disapproval of particular actions, the thinker weighs and measures his action in terms of contingencies and liabilities of all sorts. Nor is an individual's thinking beyond the influence of his fears and other affective attitudes.

Thinking reactions, as we have already intimated, have one other general function. Briefly, they are complex handlings and investigations of things and situations to the end of ascertaining their character and identity. In these instances we greatly relax our emphasis upon the implicit character of the specific reaction systems involved, for such activities may go on primarily in terms of overt manipulation. But such conduct is not by far the more complex type. The latter for the most part comprises implicit reaction systems. Probably it is the thinking behavior in this division which partakes more of the character of purely orientational or theoretical adaptations. But this is not exclusively nor necessarily the case. We may think just as abstractly about our own behavior as about other things.

By no means can we understand the precise nature of thinking reactions unless we look upon each instance of such behavior as a very specific mode of adaptation to absolutely unique situations. Thinking is never a generalized process; each action belongs to some particular situation in which the individual finds it necessary to perform complex behavior. Emphasis upon the individuality of thinking is expedient because, as a matter of fact, the precise details in each of these behavior situations are indubitably different. A generalized description of such behavior can only be justified as a means of differentiating thinking from other actions. But the actual description of the operation of the behavior must wait upon the specification of the time, place, persons, and environing circumstances involved.

Generally speaking, the process of thinking consists of the collecting of facts and the reactional resources of the individual in order to further the operation of some future act and make it appropriate and effective from the standpoint of the involved stimuli conditions. In detail, thinking activity constitutes the application by the reacting person of knowledge derived from previous contacts with similar or suggested situations, to the behavior problem challenging the individual at the time.

From our description of thinking behavior we note that it comprises both precurrent and consummatory modes of action. This dual determination works out in two distinct ways. In the first place, in simple behavior situations when the person's response consists of

a single complex behavior segment, the thinking activity may be regarded as a series of precurrent reaction systems predating and anticipating a future final activity. In more complicated behavior
situations when the thinking activity is a series of behavior segments,
the essential thinking activity comprises preliminary and anticipatory
behavior segments antedating the performance of the final behavior
segment of the series. Naturally in these complex situations the
final behavior segment may be considered to be either (1) the ultimate
ascertainment of the character of an object or condition, (2) what sort
of further action is feasible, profitable or necessary, or (3) the statement or specification of what we have discovered or should do.

Thinking as a final or consummatory action is therefore in any
case the last number of series of actions including few or many antecedent manipulative activities. The point just made sharply distinguishes genuine thinking from rationalizing. Aside from other differences that may be brought out, namely, its precariousness or significance, rationalizing activity is usually linguistic or the accounting for some action before or after it has been performed. It belongs,
therefore, more to behavior properly denominated proof and argument than to thinking.

**The Opera-
tion of
Thinking
Conduct**
How difficult it is to specify what constitutes the exact operation of
thinking conduct is manifest when we consider that each instance of
its occurrence is a specific adaptational response. Moreover, there
exists an infinite number of different types of situations in which
thinking actions occur. Yet despite the difficulty of offering a general account of how thinking behavior operates, we may still give a
series of suggestions which, taken in their entirety, may be looked
upon as a sort of composite description. Such a description, precisely because of the intricacy and multiplicity of the phenomena involved, is not completely bereft of some pragmatic value in the study
of thinking behavior.

So far as thinking actions are of the response determining type, that
is to say, responses in which we plan or consider the performance of
some future action, it is apparent that to a considerable extent thinking reactions are implicit in character. An important circumstance
here is that it is necessary to make some response to objects and conditions which are not now present and which consequently have to be
substituted for by other objects and conditions. This component of
implicit behavior must be evident also from the fact that to a considerable extent the thinking reactions prefigure some action depending upon a series of contingencies. Again, in many cases the object
upon which the final reaction is to be performed is immediately
present but the thinking individual must anticipate the changes and
consequences he will bring about in the object itself, or the effects of
these changes upon himself. Just what percentage of the reaction
is implicit or overt depends upon the immediate conditions of the
particular objects and situations at hand. So, as we have already

pointed out, we cannot predict what the specific forms of particular psychological adaptations will be.

While implicit behavior in thinking behavior segments is emphasized, it is plain that no complex manipulatory or adaptational behavior such as thinking can go on without many overt activities. The specific description of a thinking response is therefore essentially a delineation of the rôle of each type of action and the relationship between them. Assuming, then, that thinking behavior segments involve an intricate complex of both implicit and overt reaction systems, we might further assume that these distribute themselves in the total behavior according to the particular circumstances present.

Probably the best way to illustrate the operation of thinking reaction systems is to consider a particular instance. Suppose an individual is planning a vacation. Observe that the economic, domestic, geographical, cultural, hygienic, social, and other human circumstances, all conspire to delimit and circumscribe the range of the person's activity. This means, in other words, that in the case of every individual the thinking activity is surrounded by all sorts of limitations and implications, namely, specific stimuli circumstances which narrow and define his behavior. Suppose, then, that the stimuli elicit planning reactions which depend upon the preference for mountains instead of seashore. As part of the planning the individual proceeds to discuss the situation with people acquainted with one or both of the possible places. Probably one might consider this feature of the planning to be both overt and implicit. Among the more implicit forms of activities functioning in such instances are the responses to the places, climate, routes, and costs substituted for in various ways by maps, schedules, etc., as well as the memorial reactions to previous excursions, financial circumstances, etc. Numbered among the overt reactions we find the actual handling of views in prospectuses, drawing up of budgets, the actual work of calculation, the handling of maps, railway guides, etc.

Generalizing the combined overt and implicit reaction systems which operate here, we describe the individual as doing a number of distinct things. In the first place, he carries himself over from one situation to another, whether or not these situations are thought of as simultaneously existing or related to each other in a temporal sequence. In this sense, the individual is making use of his past experiences in order to bring them to bear on present situations. In asking what should be done and how it should be done, he is utilizing his knowledge and beliefs concerning present conditions and their possible connection with the future, and especially the preferred new or strange situation. Again, the individual in his planning activities connects up situations. Here he employs all sorts of cognitional techniques in apprising himself of the possible relationship between his present circumstances and objects and those he is about to encounter. To a great extent such activity consists of analyses of situations, definition of analogies between various sorts of circumstances and the drawing up of a schedule necessary for connecting an immediate behavior situation with a future one, all of course with a direct regard to his impending action.

Still another generalization concerning the complicated interacting of implicit and overt activities may be referred to as the interconnection of means and ends. In great measure the individual is taking account of some possible goal to be reached, with a reference to the means which can illuminate or further this end. Especially effective for this purpose is the functioning of meanings, concepts, and knowledge of all sorts, in order to manipulate the objects which serve as means in carrying out the thinking activity.

In studying a large number of thinking reactions whether planning, deciding, judging or predicting, it is always apparent that the various combinations of implicit and overt activity result either in a positive or negative issue. Not only may the final result of the complex activity constitute an informational response itself but it may also be an inhibition of any further action. In other words, not only is the person's final reaction merely the acquisition of a new idea, the discovery of some new fact, or the attainment of a new understanding, but it may result in inability to act at all on the basis of the planning. In many cases these two types of issue coincide. This occurs precisely because the individual attains through his planning activity some new insight into the circumstances involved so that he cannot go on with any further activity. Not infrequently the failure of further conduct to materialize may be considered as a definite or positive issue of the thinking activity. To illustrate, a person is offered a position in Africa. After planning various ways of getting there and taking up the work, he discovers that the acceptance of the position is not feasible. Now, in spite of the fact that this issue was not a factor in the thinking activity, the result of the action may be regarded as positive.

The intermixture of implicit and overt behavior found in planning belongs also to all other types of thinking. In each specific type, of course, the details vary with the particular behavior circumstances.

Besides the general unorganized modes of conduct that we have been indicating, thinking behavior of various types includes all kinds of special techniques of behavior. The latter, as we might expect, are especially applicable in particular circumstances. For example in the various arts and professions thinking activity may evolve particular sorts of organized methods of working out some future action or of manipulating objects in a complex way.

Practically since the beginning of observations upon thinking, psychologists have connected such behavior with language action. This observation is verified by practically every instance of complex thinking action. For is not language activity an exceedingly potent instrument for the development and operation of thinking behavior of every type and description? It is therefore fitting to point out once again that the linguistic conduct involved in thinking is really morphological rather than functional language. Further, it is timely to observe that the language actions operating in thinking conduct are primarily verbal types which serve as symbols or counters for the handling of absent objects found in the thinking behavior situation. Language responses operate very prominently in thinking behavior segments as instruments for stating possibilities, for recording general conditions, and for drawing up specifications and stating results of thinking conduct.

Thinking reactions may be considered the most distinctly human activities, since they constitute the modes of adaptation which operate in the complex situation characterizing human conduct. For this same reason, of course, they are the most effective types of behavior. And yet they are correspondingly precarious in their operation because they are dependent upon a number of circumstances arising out of the complexity and novelty of the immediate situations. Our present intention is to point out a number of definite conditions involved in the operation of thinking activities. These conditions make them effective responses while at the same time they allow for all of the miscarriages and misoperations of behavior.

Conditioning Factors of Thinking Behavior

Thinking activities, being modes of behavior in which the person brings his behavior resources to bear upon the accomplishment of an adjustment, very prominently involve the behavior circumstances of the individual. The stimuli conditions, of course, are ever present as conditioning factors.

As usual a prominent place must be accorded here to the individual's behavior equipment. Especially important are the knowledge and information equipments. The more facts and information the individual can apply to the behavior circumstances in which the thinking process is involved, the more effective the activity will be. As a matter of fact, unless a certain minimum number of these informational reactions are a part of the available equipment of the person, the thinking activity cannot take place at all. At once another personalistic factor is suggested, namely, sagacity. By this term we understand a fairly definite quality of the individual's behavior which amounts to an effectiveness in dealing with present stimulating circumstances which results from previous experiences with similar reactional conditions. Sagacity, then, is primarily a condition of the individual's behavior depending upon his reactional biography. We do not have here any very special equipmental reaction systems but a very generalized quality of making contacts with stimuli objects on the basis of accumulative reactional experience with similar stimuli circumstances.

We may consider next the conditioning effect of the individual's intelligence upon thinking activity. Whatever equipment the individual has acquired relating to the present stimulating. situation must be utilized with rapidity, carefulness, directedness, as well as the inerrancy resulting from an organization of such equipment, and insight into the appropriateness of particular ways of reacting to the stimuli situation at hand.

No thinking behavior occurs without the conditioning influence of the spontaneity of the acting individual. The reason why the person favors one mode of action rather than another is that he remains alert to the various features of the stimulating circumstances. Moreover, he appreciates and insists upon performing some particular kind of activity with respect to the stimuli which is deemed desirable, suitable, or necessary. A person lacking such spontaneity finds himself without the resources necessary for the performance of the thinking activity, or his behavior is bungling, inept, and generally ineffective.

Obviously, then, thinking activities provide occasion for the greatest operational scope of individual differences. Every thinking situation offers opportunity for the performance of different types of behavior adjustments as well as for a great variability in the effectiveness and dispatch with which these adjustments are carried out. The possibilities of variability in behavior are not only discovered in equipmental differences and experience in handling thinking situations but also in the numerous possibilities of combination of all of these various factors in some specific thinking situation.

Equally complex and important conditioning factors are injected into thinking situations by stimuli objects and circumstances. The possibility of performing thinking activity and the efficiency with which such action is consummated depends upon the novelty and fixity of the present stimuli conditions. No matter how well equipped an individual may be with respect to other thinking situations, if the present thinking stimulational situation precipitates him into a very foreign milieu, his thinking activity is accordingly inadequate. In like manner, the stimulational situation which is too flexible and fluid, and changes markedly while the individual is in the process of performing the thinking activity, results in an ineffective and unsatisfactory thinking adaptation. Another very important condition for thinking is the association of different objects so that some may serve as substitute stimuli for others. This allows the individual greater possibility to include in his thinking activity a large number of objects, the implicit manipulation of which constitutes an optimum condition for the thinking activity.

Some Types of Thinking Reactions

Naturally we expect persons to perform an exceedingly large and equally varied number of thinking responses, for this class of behavior includes the complex performance of actions in all kinds of situations and under all types of circumstances. For illustrative purposes, therefore, we will describe a few of the more common types, assuming that they will represent the entire class of thinking conduct.

Judging

Judging behavior finds the individual definitely evaluating or equating all kinds of stimuli objects and situations. When performing such action the individual is struck by a certain quality or condition of an object and proceeds to make some sort of determination of it. On the other hand, judging may consist primarily of the ascription of some value or quality to an object or situation because of the necessity to make use of it in some particular connection.    Judging is employed also as a process of interpreting objects or conditions for the purpose either of guiding the individual in some future or further action, or as a mere means of achieving some cognitive orientation with respect to some sort of stimulus.    In every case the judging behavior constitutes a process of deliberately endowing an object or situation with a clear and distinct stimulational function.

Whether the judging activity is cast in the mould of an evaluation, a determination, an ascription, or an interpretive activity, the range of behavior, that is, the possibility for contact with objects is very great.    In many of these cases, the judging occurs as a response to the qualities, functions, and relations of objects which constitute the stimuli features of a particular behavior segment at the time.    In other instances, the judging response is a reaction to the possibility or worthwhileness of some action, considered from the point-of-view of a standard or purpose.    In this latter instance, as in the others, the judging behavior may be either a very definite anticipatory action, performed precurrently to some overt form of response, or a consummatory or final activity without any further behavior involved. This fact is apparent when we consider that the judging behavior may have as its stimulus not some action to be performed, but an activity already accomplished, the value of which is now being determined.

Objects, persons and situations may be evaluated according to the way in which they arouse us to desiring, feeling, or thinking actions. Likewise our judgments of things concern the effects that they produce in other persons.    Both of these types of judgments may have future or past implications.    We judge things on the basis of their effects upon us or upon others in the past, or the effects they are likely to have upon us or others in the future.    A similar type of judging is that in which we are the stimuli in the sense that we evaluate the possible effects certain things may exert upon us.

Obviously, then, judging behavior occurs in all types of situations. The details of performance accordingly vary greatly.    Such variations depend upon whether the person judges a thing in order to perform some action upon it.    The mere evaluation or determination of an object, when one is about to purchase it, differs from one's evaluation when selling the same object.    The judgments concerning a thing one is about to change or transform involve an alertness not found in judging actions which exclude operations upon things. The former judging action may be full of hesitation, vacillation, and a general uncertainty entirely lacking in the other case.    Judging behavior differs, of course, in essential details when the action is, and when it is not, irretrievable. In general such qualities of the judging conduct are in degree more extreme when no action other than a classification of things or a cognitive orientation is involved. Again, many varieties of judging behavior are possible when it is more proximately the basis for an orientation, and more remotely a basis for other action through cognitive orientation, than when only one or another of the two features of the combination is involved.

It follows from the great number and variety of judging activities that the specific details of the judgment processes or behavior segment are innumerable. At times the response pattern is quite simple and consists of fairly direct evaluations of things and actions. On the other hand, a judging behavior pattern may involve one or all of the intellectual reactions and general informational responses comprised in the person's intellectual behavior equipment. Other thinking responses such as analyses, and comparisons, besides criticism, etc., figure in the process of evaluation and interpretation. Since in every case our judging action is the concrete behavior of specific individuals, the evaluatory and determining actions cannot be abstracted from the requirements of circumstances in which the person is acting or from his desires and purposes. Judging behavior is complicated by affective and desiring additions of all sorts which are stimulated by the same objects and conditions that call out the judging action.

In making evaluations and determinations the judging person employs a great number of thinking techniques of various sorts. He may have built up certain habits and schemes for the handling of the objects which constitute the stimuli for the judging reaction. Also he finds various investigative methods useful for the purpose of solving a number of problems, such as discovering the prices and merits of various things involved in the judging complex, or investigating the attitudes of persons and their actions with respect to the details of the thinking situation. Whatever special techniques are employed vary, of course, when the judging action is an autonomous behavior segment, or contains other behavior segments, or when it is itself a part of a larger behavior situation.

Individual differences of action in profusion are discoverable in the performance of judging behavior. In short, it is these individual differences that differentiate the good from the indifferent judge. Briefly, the good judge is one whose action is very definitely connected with the conditions making the judgment necessary, with the purposes for which the judgment is made, as well as with the actual qualities and conditions of the stimuli objects. The poor judge, on the contrary, may perform his thinking action with a disgraceful remoteness from the actual stimulus object. When the characteristics of the objects are important, the value of the judgment depends upon whether the individual has kept his action free from extraneous influences which might prevent it from being an adequate response to the actual stimuli objects.

Of all thinking activities, planning behavior is most intimately **Planning** related to some prospective action of the person. Thinking conduct of the planning type consists essentially of the determination of the ways and means of carrying out a particular action or devising the most feasible or satisfactory method of bringing it to its completion. Throughout the entire action the emphasis is upon a prospective action which serves as the definite stimulation for the thinking process. The determination of the character of the act, therefore, or its consequences does not loom large in the total behavior segment. The latter procedure consists primarily of the precurrent and preliminary action of designing or plotting a course of behavior, or projecting the action itself.

It is not to be overlooked that the behavior planned or designed may have further purposes. In other words, the planning or designing of conduct may be preliminary to action which is itself a precursor to some additional action or contemplated enterprise.

The stimulations for planning behavior reside in some object, situation, or circumstance requiring action, change, or modification. An exceedingly important stimulational source of planning behavior issues from the desires, interests, and purposes of the planning individual. Upon the basis of such reactional stimulation the person projects some form of behavior, and specifies and completes the details of its occurrence.

As in all thinking conduct, the precise action performed depends directly upon the immediate conditions and circumstances. In general, however, planning requires to a great extent the obtaining and perfecting of one's knowledge concerning the proposed action and the circumstances necessary for its culmination. Oftentimes one is compelled to study maps, plans, drawings, specifications of all sorts, personal and impersonal data and to carry on other forms of designing, projection and anticipatory action. The actual process of planning accordingly demands a great many implicit and overt actions localized and centering about some particular behavior situation.

Exceedingly simple forms of behavior are the activities called **Analyzing and** analyzing and synthesizing. For the most part they constitute the **ing and** implicit manipulation of objects, conditions, and circumstances in **Synthe-** an effort to divide and dissect them or to organize or integrate them **sizing Be-** as a behavior basis for some sort of attitude or overt action toward **havior** them.

While analyzing and synthesizing actions may occur as autonomous and independent manipulations, they probably transpire mostly as component actions in larger behavior segments. Whether they operate independently or in combinations with other actions, they are always implicit manipulations and not overt and effective responses to things. This is not to deny, of course, that some contributory overt actions do occur, but when they do, they are decidedly auxiliary and partial and merely support and make a place for the implicit manipulations of analysis and synthesis.

Just how intensive analyzing and synthesizing activities are is a direct function of the immediate situation. Likewise, the type of objects that serve as substitute stimuli is determined by the kind of situations involved. To a great extent these substitute stimuli are the immediate objects and situations themselves, but are reinforced by words, drawings and other objects which represent and symbolize the analyzed and synthesized materials.

Illustrations of the analyzing and synthesizing type of thinking behavior appear in the activities of the lawyer studying the record of a case, or the critic investigating the merits or demerits of a play. In all of this activity the implicit manipulations of the objects can well be ascertained together with the motive, purposes, and other personal conditions and influences operating in the behavior situation.

Because of their simplicity, analyzing and synthesizing action requires separation from intellectual attitudes. Such distinction is easy to accomplish since the latter are bare orientational responses not necessarily involving any form of manipulation or other action. Analyzing and synthesizing reactions, however, are primarily manipulative and require a decided handling of stimuli objects.

**Criticizing Behavior** The specific implicit manipulation in criticizing behavior is the determination of the character of an object from the standpoint of a given standard. When we criticize an object, we determine whether and in what degree it has reached, or can be compared with, some criterion. To the extent that the criticized object is not equal to the criterion, the criticism act may be considered inadequate or negative. On the other hand, the criticism may be a declaration that the criticized object surpasses the standard which is set. Criticizing behavior, then, may or may not involve a fixed standard. In most cases of thinking action the standard must be chosen for the particular purposes at hand. Consequently the criteria or standards are wholly arbitrary. Possibly it is the past work of the person that is now being criticized. Or it may be a general standard more or less contrived by the critic himself, or one that is generally accepted or socially acquired. Hence, the thinking process of criticism is an individual affair entirely dependent upon a unique series of circumstances. Clearly the object of criticism, or the stimulus, is not ordinarily an object, but rather an action or attitude of a person; or it may be criticism of one's own or of another's psychological behavior. Although the critical responses are ordinarily unique and personal processes, they can be more or less standardized with respect to particular sorts of situations. For example, art criticism is a more or less standardized procedure among specific groups of individuals.

We have already had occasion to point out that the criticizing type of thinking involves other types of actions as component responses.

For example, criticism of a complex sort necessitates the analysis or synthesis of the materials or the action involved; it includes comparison of a present work with other works or with parts of the same work; it requires judgments, and even predictions with respect to the public taste or the future prevalence of some kind of product.

The predominating factor of our decision and choice thinking is manipulating things in such a way as to arrive at the inhibition of a response to some stimulus object or situation in order to allow some other object to elicit a reaction. Stated more generally, the deciding form of thinking situation includes a pair of fairly definite alternates of conduct, only one of which can become a consummatory action at a given time. In terms of the stimuli objects the question is which stimulus object will be permitted to exercise its stimulational function.

*Deciding and Choosing Action[1]*

Often we are confronted with the problem as to whether or not some action should be carried out in spite of certain unfavorable conditions, as lack of funds, or unpropitiousness of time, etc. Or else balancing conditions present themselves, so that the individual must force one or the other type of action to the front. When deciding and choosing reactions are very simple the person performs a fairly immediate and direct response to simple situations as they present themselves, perhaps on the basis of his general equipment or immediate interests. Contrariwise, in more complex circumstances the behavior pattern involves a very intricate series of preliminary actions before the final or consummatory choice of alternatives results.

In view of the great number of decision and choice reactions which are made and their variation in intricacy, it is clear that they comprise a great many degrees and specific forms of action. It may be asserted, then, that decision and choice reactions cover a large number of types, some of which we may briefly review as illustrating the generalized description of such behavior. Naturally the simpler choice activities contain no great amount of manipulation of things but still they may not readily result in a choice of alternatives or a decision. In many instances, the final performance of some action occurs more or less in spite of the conditions and circumstances presented by the alternative stimuli objects. The action occurs because we are impelled to do something whether or not it will turn out to be the best thing under the circumstances. Or in other cases the reaction goes by default and the person does not decide. As a result some other kind of action takes place or the individual is removed from the present decision situation. Other situations of the same general simple sort present entirely different happenings. The decision occurs very easily and readily without any sort of struggle or hesitation. For example, the individual decides to purchase a certain object merely because it happens to come within his income, or

[1] The term choice refers to the action directed toward stimuli objects while decision implies the response factors.

because such action is dictated explicitly or implicitly by an authority, or is desirable because of some consequences that appear in the perspective of the situation. Now although in such cases the activity occurs without hesitation or conflict, the person may at the same time experience considerable regret because of the necessity of having to find it expedient to make one choice rather than another.

In similar fashion we may point out a number of behavior pictures which sum up the way in which decisions are reached in more complex circumstances. Here also some decisions occur in a very smooth and orderly way after the person has examined conditions and consequences of a very elaborate sort found in the situation. Innumerable possibilities of decision are exhausted on the basis of the facts in the case, and they lead the individual in a certain direction of action. The stimuli objects and their settings point the way to a preference without conflicting with the person's equipment or present purposes. In complex situations of a different mould we discover the decision occurring before the examination of circumstances has been completed. Thus the person summarily consummates his activity and adopts one of the alternatives of action. This completion of the behavior pattern occurs in two distinct ways. In the first place, the final action is brought about by the appearance of a new stimulus condition in the general choice situation, and accordingly the activity is completed. On the other hand, the person himself may determine to end the activity because he is interested in doing something else or decides that it really does not matter which line of action he follows.

Quite another type of decision situation is that in which the conditions or evidence balance and, in spite of himself, the person is left in doubt so that a choice cannot be made. In consequence we find a number of possibilities of behavior. As in the case just preceding, the individual may come to a decision by some sort of new or extraneous circumstances appearing in the general situation. Or he may force a decision because he is unwilling to prolong the agony of hesitation. Thus, he comes to an action more or less in disregard of the balancing factors. A third possibility is that the individual may so prolong his hesitation that the need for action ceases and the choice goes by default.

As a last type of such behavior we quote the case in which the decision is prolonged and delayed because the individual cannot discover in the situation a definite basis for deciding. Not only does one alternative or one of the series of possibilities not outweigh or overbalance the others, but the person is unable to obtain sufficient information about any one to afford him a foundation for an adequate reaction. Nevertheless the individual may be forced to a decision because of the needs of his situation or because he dreads hesitation and indecision. Sometimes this means that no action or no suitable action may occur at all. But in other cases the person feeling a responsibility in the circumstances forces activity by seeking out the availability and character of further possibilities of responses, even to the point of changing the stimuli functions of objects or employing aid in obtaining information with respect to conditions involved. In this way he indulges in an active handling of the circumstances with whatever promptness and dispatch is feasible, and perhaps with a perfect confidence in the quality of his investigations and in the final decision.[1]

With the intention to compensate for the inability to give general principles and exact descriptive pictures of decision behavior, we plan to enumerate a series of circumstances and conditions which result in or influence decision conduct. Our present aim, then, is to classify under appropriate behavior segment rubrics the different conditions that lead to decisions.

As personality influences we suggest the general equipmental traits of individuals. These can be subdivided into intrinsic and extrinsic factors. Under the former heading are listed the person's knowledge, ideals, and interests which have a definite bearing upon the kind of circumstances involved in the decision situation. Less closely involved with the specific details of the decision behavior are the equipmental actions of fears, jealousies, traits of impetuosity or slowness, lethargy or obstinacy which exert no less potent an influence upon acts of decision. Extrinsic factors often determine in a powerful way the direction of our decisions. For instance one admires an attractive person and decides to have further contact with such an individual, but on hearing that person speak in an unpleasant way, the reacting individual immediately modifies his decision reaction.

Among the more immediate reactional influences upon decision thinking we call attention to the acts of understanding and familiarity which the stimuli objects elicit. Thus the individual is enabled to decide concerning the possibility of the necessary action fittting in with what he happens to be doing at the particular time. The congruity of the needed response with the actions the individual is in the course of performing at the time have decided influence upon the outcome of his thinking decision. Similarly, reactions of an affective, desiring, and attentional type which the decision stimuli or their settings elicit, modify the total course of the decision behavior. How attentive one is to the conditions involved, what feelings or desires they arouse, are all potent factors in determining the trend of the individual's thinking.

A quite important place in decision thinking is assumed by the individual's purposive action which takes place while the decision reactions are pending. Upon whether responses to certain objects

---

[1] With these descriptions of the decision and choice-making manipulations of things stated in terms of stimulus and response interaction compare James' mentalistic but otherwise excellent exposition in *Principles of Psychology*, Chapter XXVI.

are or are not compatible with actions already going on as continuous responses to purposive stimuli, depend not only the final outcome of decision behavior but also the smoothness of such action and the length of time required to make the decision. Many conflicts are possible here between actions indicated by one alternative stimulus and the purposes of the person which facilitate or interfere with the occurrence or nature of a decision.

Some account must also be taken of the stimuli objects and situations themselves. Such a procedure is especially necessary in the thinking behavior we call critical and rational, for in such instances the characters and qualities of the stimuli objects with their relative challenge and attractiveness to the individual exert a powerful influence on decision and choice thinking. At this point also we must consider the analogies, similarities, and contrasts to other objects and situations which the present stimuli offer. Nowhere in the whole range of psychological activity are settings of stimuli so potent and significant as in thinking activity. Unfortunately, however, it is impossible to suggest particulars but we might merely intimate the specific circumstances of the decision, such as, the income of the individual, his various economic pressures when economic decisions are in question, and the value and jeopardy of one's employment. Not to be overlooked either are the person's hygienic conditions which may be considered as the setting or part of the setting of the transpiring activity.

Occasions and opportunities which are not essentially psychological in character do not fail to exert a decided influence upon the decision type of thinking. The matter of time in the sense of the propitiousness of action, the question as to how long one has been in the decision circumstance, as well as whether the individual can succeed with some action he is contemplating, and similar extraneous conditions, have much to do with the occurrence of a decision action. Included among such extraneous factors are customs and conventions which have no particular relation to the immediate thinking situation, but still affect its consequences. We decide not to purchase a picture because it is not executed in the prevailing æsthetic mode. Or, we decide not to employ a person because his morals are disapproved of. For the sake of completeness it might be wise to mention the tremendous influence on decisions of behavior and non-behavior factors unknown to the individual at the time. Doubtless some of these factors unknown to the person are included in the various influences we have already enumerated but others of a different type may possibly function in decision conduct.

Abstracting

An exceedingly important and prominent type of thinking behavior is that form of manipulation of things and propositions called abstracting. Not only is it important in itself because it constitutes a familiar and constant form of behavior but also because it plays a large rôle in other kinds of human activity. Whenever we are dealing with objects and conditions which have to be classified for purposes of handling or orientation it is necessary to abstract and isolate their qualities and relations. Two distinct forms of manipulations are in use at this juncture. In the first place, the abstracting type of thinking involves the analysis of things into their constituents, and secondly the drawing out of particular features and qualities or the abstracting of some complete or partial resemblance of qualities to others, with some pragmatic disregard of the residuum of qualities or other features. This process of abstracting thought is definitely founded upon the more elementary procedure of analysis, as we have indicated, and also that of distinguishing and differentiating, etc.

To illustrate the activity of abstracting thinking, we might consider the type of manipulation employed in classifying things. In dividing compounds into acids and bases we abstract some essence or significant quality and set that up as a possessional criterion for the various compounds. All of those substances containing this essence or quality belong to a given class appropriately named, while others fall outside of the class. Naturally the process of abstraction always depends upon some particular interest of the individual or some necessity of a situation in which the person finds himself at the time. Accordingly manipulative abstraction may result in the isolation of some features of objects which really are not parts of their natural constitution. Also the qualities abstracted may be such as to allow for the classification and organization of the same substances and conditions in a number of different classes.

Among the different stimuli objects to which abstraction actions are made we find situations, persons and actions of all types of description. In each case the abstracting feature is different in detail depending upon the particular stimulus which initiates the thinking behavior. In addition, other appropriate thinking actions along with modes of behavior not classifiable as thinking are correlated with the abstracting thinking type.

An equally decided rôle is played by abstracting thinking in the development of general concepts of many diverse types. When so employed the abstracting process is not necessarily a function of an ordering or classifying situation but rather a feature of an identifying and summing up process. As such, the abstracting performance has in it more of an absolute character. Hence the activities are more intrinsic and confined only to the particular objects and situations that are being manipulated in the abstracting form. The results of such activity on the whole are classifiable as orientational behavior rather than manipulations for any further activity even of an abstract or theoretical type.

When predicting behavior operates, objects or situations are so **Predicting** manipulated· that some future circumstance with relation to it is suggested. In·detail the predicting type of thinking comprises such a handling of a situation that it becomes a more or less reliable type of substitution stimulus for some kind of adjustment action constituting a transformation of the objects concerned. In spite of the fact that the emphasis is upon some future happening, so far as the interests of the individual and the activity as a completed process are concerned, the thinking behavior proper must be considered as the manipulation of the stimuli objects.

The precise form of manipulation may consist of an actual examination of objects or conditions, or a survey of them in view of their perspective and related circumstances. In part also the prediction behavior includes an evaluation and interpretation of the circumstances, qualities, and changes taking place in the object constituting the prediction stimulus. Under other circumstances the manipulations require the discovery of analogies and similarities of the present object to other objects with which one has previously been in contact. In other words, in even a summary form of statement we must discover and refer ourselves to an infinite variety of concrete contacts with the objects in order to reveal their characteristics and perhaps work out a number of tests and experiments as a basis of prediction. Such a basis will constitute, then, the substitute stimulus for the circumstances and conditions which we shall consider the adjustment stimulus of the prediction type of thinking.

So far we have spoken only of manipulation of objects which may be regarded as the overt handling of them, or the evaluative and cognitive acquaintance with them as they exist in their present circumstances and relations. To this type of manipulation and orientation we must now add another exceedingly valuable element in prediction, namely, a census-taking or a statistical organization of previous happenings and conditions in which the present object or situation has had a part. Prediction, then, may be based upon an examination of an object in an effort to ascertain its qualities or connections, or upon a summary of the previous happenings which center around the present object or situation.

Turning to a brief survey of the prediction type of behavior segment, we may summarize its character as a more or less complex series of the type of manipulations we have already surveyed. In addition, the final response of the pattern must consist of a statement or proposition, whether or not expressed or recorded by the individual, with respect to the findings which constitute the thinking response to the adjustment stimulus. Upon superficial examination of this type of behavior it might appear that the final statement of prediction is the essential factor in the behavior segment. Such is probably not the case although, as we have intimated, the final reaction of stating what eventuality may be expected in a given situation is an indispensable feature of the total behavior segment.

**Explaining or Explanatory Thinking**

Manipulations of things for the purpose of discovering their nature or the reason for their existence and the implicit manipulation of events as an attempt to account for their occurrence, we call explaining or explanatory thinking. Because of the numerous circumstances in which such thinking behavior occurs, it is obviously impossible to find stable and generalized conditions which can serve for type descriptions of this kind of conduct. We can only suggest some characteristics that may fairly safely be considered as descriptive of explanatory behavior in general.

Foremost and almost exclusively appears the kind of behavior we call correlation. Explanation or explanatory thinking may be reduced to a process of so handling or reacting to objects that one discovers or sets forth correlated conditions. These conditions are intimately and integrally connected with the objects and events constituting the stimuli for explanatory behavior. Or the individual may contrive relations or correlated circumstances which serve for him as explanatory results. When the person has actually discovered intimately connected correlates, the type of explanatory behavior may be called in popular terms objective explanation. On the other hand, if the contrivances of correlation are conditioned more by the individual's interests and necessity than by the actual relationships between the stimuli objects, we refer to the explanatory results as subjective.

In all actual explanatory thinking, especially the complex type, a peculiar intermixture of these two forms of thinking activity is inevitably discovered. As a matter of fact, in complex situations the explanatory thinking is probably never exclusively one or the other type, for almost every case of explanatory thinking is too intricate and involved to make it impossible for the individual to discover the intimate natural relationships. Thus he falls back on contrived ones. On the other hand, no serious explanatory thinking can be indulged in wholly on the basis of one's own contrived relationships among events. The errancy of such contrived explanatory conduct, however, does not prevent it from being indulged in, especially when the stimuli objects are the individual's own conduct. What we really find here is another type of behavior deserving the name of excusing rather than that of explaining or accounting. We notice at once how closely this type of thinking is connected with rationalization activity in which we substitute one conclusion concerning our action for another. In the excusing instance, however, the interest is not in the discovery of some attitude with respect to the situation but rather in an attempt to manipulate the activity to the advantage of the acting person.

A type of thinking behavior very closely related to predicting activity we refer to as estimating. Characteristic of such a process is a kind of preoccupation with stimuli objects and situations, the result of which provides details that are lacking, and in general completes our information concerning the character of particular objects. On the whole estimating thinking is very closely concerned with some future form of conduct. We attempt to perfect or fill out our

Estimating Behavior

information concerning a situation in order to make some use of the result of our manipulation, or in rarer instances, perhaps, merely to further our orientational contacts with things.

Probably the most conspicuous example of estimating is the ascertainment of the time involved in carrying out a particular project, the cost of furthering such a plan, or its product or result. Considering a simple estimating behavior situation, one can supply the details with precision and exactness. In this behavior pattern there are involved all kinds of measurements, stock takings and surveying bearing directly upon the future action or course of conduct. In order to estimate the cost of fencing off a field, we may measure it by approximating the amount of material needed and the time to be consumed in erecting the enclosure. More complex situations require manipulations and calculations of an exceedingly complicated character which are not capable of any sort of definite description.

Speculating and Reflecting Thinking

A considerable portion of our psychological behavior is given to speculation and reflection. Substantially in these forms of thinking we have activities involving an interest in things or events not immediately available for manipulation, either because they have not yet occurred but are impending, or because they have transpired in the past. When such activities consist of implicit manipulations of future events we call the thinking speculative, while the implicit handling of past situations is denoted as reflective. Reflective conduct carries with it, then, the element of retrospection or a looking back at conditions and events.

Speculative thinking may be decidedly practical in the sense that one's implicit handling of the substitute stimuli for future adjustment objects or situations is directed to the achieving of some definite practical result. Or it may be for some vaguer purpose of orientation. In the practical case the responses are made to events with which the individual expects to have some further contact. Illustrations of such speculations are found in the effort to insure oneself against some future possible danger and in wagering something with respect to this future contingency. Contrariwise, our more abstract speculations are prompted merely by our interest in what possible future attitude we may be forced to take toward some stimulus when it eventuates.

Reflective thinking finds the individual reviewing the sort of attitude he should or might have taken toward some situation in view of better consequences that might have ensued. Or the person ponders over how differently he might have acted in a past situation. The more abstract reflecting thinking, whether it concerns the person's own action or the nature and significance of things, may be considered to be a factor of, or the basis for, scientific thinking as compared with thinking behavior of more practical and everyday situations.

In concluding this illustrative survey of types of thinking we must, as is usually the case in psychological descriptions, point out that the differences emphasized between these various forms do not comprise hard and fast demarcations. It must be especially observed that rigid differentiation among types must be waived in view of their interaction in particular behavior situations. In some specific complex thinking acts a large number of the types we have been describing are found closely intermingled. In this sense any type of thinking action may be a component function with intellectual attitudes of still more complex and inclusive thinking behavior segments.

A fairly unique characteristic of thinking behavior, as compared with other complex types of human action, is the possibility for variation in quality. Because of the particular character of thinking activity, namely, that it constitutes close interactions of the individual with particular stimuli situations more or less distantly removed from the person, we find that such complex behavior is, or may be, more or less critical, more or less effective, and more or less important. These variations in quality may be extreme enough to afford a differentiation between critical and entirely uncritical, between completely effective, and ineffective, thinking. The ineffectiveness of thinking can go so far even as to be disturbing and distressing to the interests and aspirations of the individual. Or the thinking activity may be of some importance to the person and his coevals, or of no importance to anyone.

*Varying Qualities of Thinking Behavior*

So far as the critical character of thinking is concerned, the criterion is for the most part the closeness of connection between the responses in their various patterns and the stimuli objects and conditions. In short, when the responses are definitely related to the stimuli, we may call the reactions critical. The implication underlying the criterion is that the smallest number of extraneous influences condition the response of the person. Assuredly, a thinking reaction is more critical when the response is directed toward the conditions at hand. Furthermore, the critical character of thinking, as well as its consequences, depends upon the carefulness with which the stimulating situation is analyzed and placed under the critical scrutiny of the individual. In sum, then, critical thinking occurs when the consummatory adaptations follow from the conditions and objects present. We find, in fact, that the greatest loss in critical power and in accuracy of thinking is due directly to the lack of connection between the person and the substitute and adjustment stimuli. Such lack of connection between the thinker and his stimuli amounts even to actual distortion. That such inexact responses are so profuse and always possible is due, of course, to the fact that thinking comprises detached and implicit manipulation and handling of objects, or in more succinct terms, detached adaptations to things.

Distortions or errors in thinking frequently arise from the intrusion of extraneous objects and conditions so that we react to our active stimuli as though they were something else. Thus we mistake our differences from other people in coloring and in size as variations in human quality. Usually, too, our cultural or ethnic differences are immediately reacted to as though they were inferiorities and superiorities. In general, anatomical diversities are taken to be differences in "mental capacity." Again because learning one sort of poem does not help us to learn another more quickly, we think that we cannot change our native retentiveness. It is uncritical, however, to overlook the possibility of an alternative, namely, that there is no such thing at all as "native retentiveness."

Both the critical quality and the effectiveness of thinking are conditioned by the idiosyncrasy of the person's activity. No thinking can be effective or critical which does not represent the manipulations and handlings of the stimuli situations on the grounds of the individual's equipment and capacities in the particular situation he is handling. Numerous distortions of thinking are possible when the individual reacts to situations on the basis of the attitudes forced upon him or provided by the school in which he studies or the profession of which he is a member. Even in the thinking situations which should be the most critical of all, for example, in science, individuals often think according to the dogmas or learnings of their schools instead of on the basis of their own immediate personal responses to the stimuli at hand.

With respect to the importance of thinking, the quality is determined by the relevancy of the activity in relation to the time and place of its occurrence. Whether or not the thinking occurs early enough to provide a basis for practical or orientational behavior is a question clearly determining its significance. Unless the thinking transpires when it is required and finds its place in the general behavior of the individual it can hardly be of any great importance. The quality of importance attaches to thinking, likewise, if the situation is such that it requires the implicit manipulation and adaptation characterizing thinking conduct.

In general, then, it is possible to formulate a series of requirements making for critical thinking. First, we must be certain of our facts. We must be sure we have adequate and correct information about the conditions to which we are responding and that we have actual data to handle. Such certainty can only arise from a large number of contacts with, and sympathetic study of, comparable situations and thinking reactions to them. Secondly, we must be sure we analyze our facts so that we appreciate all of their implications, the relationships among the elements and the connections among the latter and other things. Special caution is here requisite so that the type of characterization made will be relevant and appropriate to the thinking situation at hand. The obstructions employed must not be too simple or too far removed from the adjustment stimuli objects. Thirdly, one must be confident that the investigation is relevant to the future act for which the thinking processes are in preparation. Fourthly, only a minimum of bias can be allowed in the thinking individual who is working out the reaction.   We refrain from implying total freedom from bias because probably in no case can such prejudice be completely excluded.   So far as possible, however, each individual, object, or situation must be dealt with upon its own merits.   Finally, the critically thinking person must make certain that he is interpreting facts rather than merely fitting them into a scheme.   Further, he must be certain that such interpretations and comparisons of facts are proper and relevant and that his discoveries of analogies are accurate. Otherwise the interpretation cannot possibly be correct or pertinent. In general, variables finding a place in the thinking situation must be worked out and their character or value ascertained.

Our study of the qualities of thinking throws some light upon the question of thinking in animals and children.   With respect to children, observation shows that even at a very early age they perform all kinds of thinking actions, some of which attain to a considerable degree of complexity.   Specific illustrations are here quite unnecessary.   Generally speaking, it appears clear from such observations as one can make that, within the range of their experiences, children can and do perform critical thinking activities.

Whether or not animals can think is a problem that has long engaged the interest of psychologists.   In view of our study of thinking behavior the answer to such a question is readily forthcoming.   If we can include in thinking the mere anticipation of some future action or the simple manipulation of things in an overt or implicit manner, then it is fairly clear that animals, especially the organisms of the more complex type, can and do think.   On the other hand, if we assume that thinking means expert manipulations of absent objects or the comparison and discovery of analogies between present objects and absent ones, then it is clear animals cannot think.   Considerable light is cast upon this general problem by the fact that we are easily convinced in the ordinary day's activity that there are many human individuals who perform few, if any, actual thinking reactions.   Such being the case, it is easy to believe that animals do not perform such reactions at all.

Our study of thinking has already sufficiently emphasized the fact that it is a type of action occurring in every kind of complex human circumstance.   Whenever any complex project is to be carried out or a difficulty overcome—in general, whenever the behavior of the person is itself a tool or an instrument for accomplishing some other action, then thinking behavior transpires. *Stimuli for Thinking Conduct*

Now as we should expect, the stimuli for thinking behavior are in all cases situations and circumstances calling for the type of instrumental behavior we have been surveying.   In detail, such situations cover every conceivable type of object, circumstance, and action.   Especially noteworthy are propositions or knowledge objects stimulating judgment, decision, and other types of thinking behavior.   We might say that any situation which involves any kind of object demanding instrumental or manipulative behavior may serve as a stimulus for thinking reactions.

To the situations constituting the stimuli for thinking behavior may be ascribed a number of particular distinctive qualities. First in prominence are qualities connected with difficulties. In other words, the stimuli for thinking are often difficult or uncertain situations. The question arises as to whether or not an action can be performed, or what sort of conduct can or should be enacted in a particular instance. Again, the person has to choose or decide whether or not he should initiate some particular mode of behavior in light of some specific circumstance or condition. In equal proportion the problems of the stimuli refer to identifications and the character and nature of objects and persons, etc.

Of a different mould is the stimulational quality of indeterminateness characterizing circumstances which prompt the individual to thinking action. In such cases we find the individual stimulated to make a determination concerning the type of stimulational function which an object or circumstance should have for him in a certain situation. Should he allow what he considers an evil but attractive situation to draw him into contact with it, or should he prevent the appealing stimulational quality of the circumstances from prompting him into action? Additional characteristic qualities of thinking stimuli are the appeal, interest, advantages, disadvantages, or challenge of objects and events calling out instrumental types of behavior. While these types of stimulational qualities are not as prominent as some others, they are none the less authentic and take their coördinate place along with the others mentioned.

A further series of qualities of thinking stimuli are suggested by the fact that the behavior segments in which they operate include response patterns making for satisfaction on the part of the acting individual, the accomplishment of certain desirable or necessary activities, the carrying out of intentions and purposes, and the fulfillment of certain ends.

It should be added that the actual adjustment stimuli are not always apparent to the individual but are merely suggested by a substitute object and condition operating in the situation. Indeed the essential characteristic of thinking behavior is its instrumental character which, either by natural circumstance or by contrivance, serves as an instrument to reveal the character of the stimulus object. Quite excellently is this characteristic illustrated when the thinking behavior is a determination of a course of conduct. In this case the instrumental activity results in the discovery or the acceptance of a particular course of action which becomes the adjustment stimulus in the particular instance. The substitute stimulus also may be unknown and unrecognized by the individual. Such a situation possesses comparatively simple activities by means of which the individual starts upon a course or train of thinking without any very definite appreciation of the stimulus that initiated it. It is clear that the simpler types of thinking behavior function upon a sub-reactionalistic level but, nevertheless, may have exceedingly important and striking issues.

It is probably needless to suggest again that the stimulational settings of thinking reactions are exceedingly important in their influence upon the total course of thinking conduct. At the risk of repetition, however, we suggest the point once more in order to signify the great importance of the individual's own conduct as a setting for his thinking stimuli. Especially to be mentioned are the motivational forms of conduct. These condition not only the actual occurrence of thinking but also its special type and course. Pride of rationality often connects itself with the appreciation of the importance of doing things deliberately and judiciously. Again we have the motive of duty, the recognition of the propriety of acting according to the expectation of one's friends and acquaintances. Motivational settings of another character are the refusals of the individual to commit himself lightly to any form of action. In the simplest cases this refusal involves fear of the consequences or dread of commitment to action that probably cannot be revoked. As a last type of thinking behavior setting we must call attention to the obstinacy or stubbornness of the individual who must persist in a line of conduct once he has begun it. Necessarily he is constantly face to face with the problem of deciding and judging what activities will fall in line with the accepted mode of such conduct. On the other hand, a person may be so uncertain of the way in which he should respond that he continually finds the stimuli for his action indeterminate, problematic, etc.

## PROBLEM SOLVING CONDUCT

Problem solving as a type of psychological conduct is uniquely concerned with the disentanglement of the person from some unsatisfactory situation, the resolution of some perplexity, or the overcoming of a difficulty. The emphasis is all upon the kind of behavior one is to pursue with respect to some problem solving stimulus or situation. Even though the problem may be a certain action one is about to perform or should perform, or the achievement of acquaintance with an object, the stress is upon the problem solving and not upon the mere orientation. When the individual performs problem solving activities with respect to his own conduct, therefore, he is concerned not so much with the question of preparing for an action in the light of his knowledge or in view of the expediencies involved, but he is concerned rather with determining whether a certain action can be performed at all or whether the extrication from particular enmeshing

*Problem Solving as a Type of Behavior*

conditions is possible or not.   Equally common is problem solving behavior that is concerned with the discovery of the character of a thing or the course of conduct to follow with respect to it.

In detail, problem solving activity may be considered behavior segments in which implicit and overt reactions are performed as factors in a specialized type of behavior technique for the purpose of solving a problem.   This technique, as we shall later have more occasion to see, involves a series of procedures.   The individual is bent on working out the proper response to the stimulus situation; he performs experiments, and makes use of previous ones for the purpose at hand. On the whole, problem solving action involves a very intimate contact with the stimulational object.   Such intimacy is a direct outcome of the fact that the stimulus for the problem solving activity consists of some kind of need for modifying an environmenal circumstance, that is, some element in the individual's reactional milieu.   The complexity and intricacy of these behavior techniques vary, of course, directly with the circumstances surrounding the problematic stimulus. As a consequence some of the problematic behavior segments include considerable thinking and imagining behavior at various points, especially in the contrivance of the specialized problem solving required by difficult and exacting situations.

**Types and Range of Problem Solving Behavior**   Hardly a situation exists that is not a source of problem solving behavior or that fails to provide occasions for such conduct.   Accordingly, its range is exceedingly large, including the performance of all kinds of problem solving techniques or processes.   For convenience of description we may divide these types into three classes, namely, the practical, theoretical, and indifferent problem solving behavior.

**Practical Problem Solving**   In the performance of such activity the most essential factor is the actual concrete adaptation affording the person's removal from some object or situation impeding his activity or preventing him from making a particular plan or preference action.   That is to say, by means of practical problem solving, the individual attempts to secure for himself better relation to the various features of his surroundings. To a great extent practical problem solving consists of direct manipulation of the objects constituting the stimuli for the behavior.   At least in some cases it occurs in the form of direct effective behavior segments.   Thus the person is able immediately to bring about desired changes in the things to which he is reacting.   So large is the range of problem solving conduct that many times the nature of the problem and the kind of effective reaction necessary for its solution are not appreciated by the acting person.   In such cases it is only the observer who can report that the acting individual has performed a problem solving activity.   From our preliminary survey it follows that practical problem solving divides itself into different types.

Included in the first type are the reactions of pure overt manipulation.   The person arranges objects, such as blocks or figures, on a form or board and proceeds to go through a process of immediate trial and error effective responses until the problem is solved. Various complex situations of this type show the person operating in conditions of chaos or disorder. Some confusion in things stimulates the individual to manipulate the objects concerned in order that they may be brought into some kind of array or sequence. Innumerable complicated situations of the purely effective type of manipulation may be cited, such as the correction of some disturbance in the operation of a machine or an automobile, the putting together of simple puzzles, or the fitting together of a complex anatomical model such as the Auzoux brain model. All of this manipulation and overt conduct with objects must be understood as constituting the primary problem solving action, although it is not the exclusive activity of the individual while he is performing it. We must take for granted here the occurrence of a variety of attentional and perceptual reactions functioning as necessary precurrent responses to the overt manipulation.

Our second type of problem solving situation is that in which the manipulations involve, in addition to overt manipulative actions, the use of tools or instruments which may or may not be immediately available. Besides objects of various sorts that are employed in secondary contacts with other objects, knowledge also plays a part in this type of problem solving. In other words, the problematic situation comprises the operation of implicit behavior toward objects or things not immediately present. These reactions are of course initiated by some phase of the present situation serving as a substitute stimulus for the implicit responses. In general, we might consider that in this type of practical problem solving the means employed to attain some end are more or less extraneous to the contact of the individual with the stimuli objects and situations. That is, the person is not so completely and fundamentally a part of the problematic situation. He stands somewhat aloof from it, and thus the manipulation or conduct does not exclusively consist of his overt behavior. For the most part all of these types of activities are more complex than those in the first class just pointed out. Such behavior may be illustrated by all types of technical and technological activities. Especially typical of such behavior is the employment of tools and instruments for the accomplishment of a desired result in some form of æsthetic behavior. Similar complications of implicit and overt activities are discoverable in almost all of the complicated behavior situations of persons, for example, in their economic and social contacts.

Of a still more complicated mould is our third type of practical problem solving. Such activity entails not only the performance of implicit behavior, but also the employment of definite principles intended to solve problems. This means the utilization of all sorts of knowledge and information acquired during the person's past experiences with similar types of stimuli situations. In many instances the solving of the problem requires the employment of much of the individual's intellectual equipment. Such a situation is illustrated by the problem of the person who committed a certain crime which constitutes the point of departure or the stimulus for the problem solving action. On the basis of the data presented we can eliminate possibilities based on certain principles and frequently make the data point definitely to a particular single solution or set of solutions. Our ability to solve a certain problem may depend upon our knowledge of the principles of psychology, chemistry, or other types of phenomena constituting the complex data in hand. In addition, it may be necessary to employ definite techniques for eliminating possibilities and forcing the situation to yield suggestions for the solution of the problem. At once we think of the methods and techniques of organic or inorganic chemistry or the performances of a complex series of tests in medical diagnosis.

The three fairly distinct types of practical problem solving activity, we may summarize in the following manner. In the first type we have overt manipulation of the objects involved in the problem solving situation. In the second type, the tools and instruments needed for the solution of the problem are not present. Hence the person has to resort to his implicit behavior; and consequently the adaptation is not overt. In the third type there is the use of actual principles as a result of which the person is more expert in the handling of the situation.

Theoretical Problem Solving

An individual who theoretically solves a problem is adapting himself to a type of situation which is ordinarily far removed from the accomplishment of practical purposes or the performing of maintenance behavior. By means of such action we attain the solution of all sorts of problems of a theoretical or abstract type. One of the most extreme examples is the mathematical form of enterprise. Here the stimuli are knowledge objects and not actual needs in the sense in which we have employed the terms in the study of practical problem solving. Rather in the present instance we have a challenge arising from the difficulty of understanding or handling theoretical materials. The person's objects then are knowledge objects in the form of information or elements of a knowledge system which contain some contradiction baffling to the individual or interfering with the cohesion of different forms of knowledge factors. In this type of problem solving our materials and methods are those which may be called theoretical, scientific, or philosophical, as compared with practical problem solving activities. The latter even in the most complex forms extend only to practical or applied scientific problems, methods, and solutions. Quite unlike this type, theoretical problem solving is always consummated in some sort of more or less elaborate orientation of the person to knowledge surroundings and circumstances. The differentiation of these types of action, however, does not imply that they are entirely mutually exclusive. It is quite possible for theoretical problm solving to include the practical form at the point where experimentation is necessary. Also, even in such an abstract type of problem solving as is involved in complex mathematical operations we must allow for practical manipulations, for the actual mathematical equations employed may be considered the direct material which is manipulated in the manner of practical problem solving.

The essential feature of theoretical problem solving is, therefore, the fact that the person manipulates reactions constituting the intellectual stimuli and the intellectual tools required in the performance of the activity. For this reason theoretical problem solving activity may be of two entirely different types. The first, which always consists of a rational and valuable form of activity, starts from information that has been derived from definite observation or record of natural events or activities of various sorts. After the solution of the problem its validity is tested by means of correlation with the original data from which the problem solving started. This type of testing is performed in addition to another checking up of the problem solving activity, namely, a critical determination and review of the processes used with regard to their relevancy to the problem at hand. Such is the method of all valid scientific work.

On the other hand, theoretical problem solving, because it is primarily a manipulation of attitudes and reactional processes, may not possess any observed data of a natural type. On the contrary, it may start from attitudes held by individuals. The typical thinking here is theological, the value and validity of which can only be determined on the basis of the correctness of the methods used. In other words, it cannot be tested on the basis of any relationship between the individual and natural phenomena of any type. And why? Because the stimuli in this case are, of course, always beliefs and other intellectual attitudes constituting the equipment of the person interested in the problem.

Despite our suggestion that problem solving behavior may occur in all types of human situations we have nevertheless, in the course of characterizing such conduct, limited the types to the utilitarian field on the one hand, and the pure orientational on the other. Such a delineation tends to suggest that it is always a serious and consequential type of behavior. Such is, of course, not at all the case. Problem solving occurs in the most trivial and inconsequential situations. During our most irresponsible moments we frequently perform quite intense and involved problem solving activities. Perhaps a fair characterization of this type of action allows for the use of the term "play" in this connection. Thus to do justice to the extensiveness of the range of problem solving activity we must include in its domain non-serious and insignificant situations.

Naturally in the non-serious types of problem solving, individuals accomplish no utilitarian adjustment or intellectual orientation. They may spend considerable time and effort unravelling the source and truth of some bit of gossip concerning individuals remotely re-

*Indifferent Problem Solving Behavior*

lated to them (such as college instructors, screen stars, base ball heroes, etc.). Included in this division also are the various puzzle activities such as the cross-word type, games, etc. In all kinds of language situations, especially in the attempt to formulate a mode of expression which will be tactful, non-irritating and essentially suitable for a particular purpose, much problem solving activity is performed. Now while we characterize this activity as indifferent and play behavior, rather than utilitarian or orientational conduct, we do not intend to imply that such activity as characteristic problem solving is in any sense different in its processes and specific behavior elements from the action found in the most serious instances of such conduct. While no set performances or reaction systems are isolable as problem solving action, the general mode of conduct characterizable as problem solving is the same in the play type as in all the other forms.

Throughout the whole range of problem solving conduct, whether everyday action of a utilitarian or indifferent type, or scientific and consequential behavior we find varying degrees of value and expertness in the performance. No matter what the circumstances are, or the particular stimuli operating in problem solving behavior segments, certain individuals in particular situations, or perhaps in all situations, operate in a more expert, more effective, manner than some others. As in all psychological conduct we observe the operation of virtuosoship and, in general, varying degrees of excellence in the functions constituting problem solving activity.

Techniques and Methods of Problem Solving

Entirely in consonance with our oft repeated proposition that no detailed formula can be organized to sum up and represent the actual behavior going on when a problem is being solved, is the attempt to point out a number of particular processes or techniques which represent the type of action occurring when a person is solving a problem. These particular techniques in their essential details are component behavior elements in the segments constituting problem solving activity. Such component activities vary immensely in the particular situations in which they have a place, although in each case they may be thought of as an organized effort on the part of the person, to unravel the elements of the problematic situation. As such, these techniques may be primarily effective or non-effective (that is, especially implicit action), or various combinations of the two.

One of the obvious techniques of the more overt type is the actual analysis of objects or situations with a view to discover the parts or partial conditions present in the stimulus situation. In this analysis the individual may be immediately motivated by a number of different kinds of circumstances. In some cases the motivation is very clear to the individual. His work of analysis proceeds precisely and directly on the basis of some given plan. In other cases the technique is more or less haphazard in an endeavor to discover what actually might be there. In either event the analytic process may involve the complete reduction of the whole stimulus situation to a series of specific details. To a considerable extent these reduction processes consist of the discovery and selection of points relevant to the significance and character of the problematic situation, as well as to its solution. Thus, for example, in making a diagnosis of a case it is necessary to analyze the situation into details which have some bearing on it, the symptoms, for example, and other facts which complicate the situation but which are not relevant to the solution or determination of the problem. This analysis may be considered to be preliminary to the more direct technique of finding out which phases of a situation lend themselves to manipulation.

In the more implicit types of action, which may be looked upon as secondary analysis, or in dealing with conceptual or representative materials, the same general description of the technique is true. But in the solution of some problematic situation a variant of this technique, which we may call deduction, consists of the individual's application to a specific problematic circumstance of some general principle or knowledge that he has acquired either in similar or in entirely different sorts of circumstances. Thus, the technique used in the solution of any problem involves a determination as to whether the present stimulus situation is an instance of the sort which falls under a general principle or into a specific class. For example, a surgeon has acquired certain techniques or principles of his profession. Now a case must be investigated to determine whether the technique or general principle will be applicable, or in other words, whether the present instance fits under the general principle or the already formulated technique. In its simplest form, the process of deduction constitutes the action of subsumption or classification. Quite true, the classification may be preliminary to a further solution of a problem. Thus, the contractor who has the problem of determining his bid may have to classify the situation as falling under one or some other type of construction job before he can begin the detailed calculation of cost.

A very closely related problem solving technique is that involved in synthesizing elements of a whole situation for the purpose of eliciting information and discovering the implications when the parts of a situation are seen in their organization. On the more implicit side of action we sometimes find it necessary for the individual to relate present conditions to others he has already met with in his experiences. Such a process leads to the synthesizing of a series of data to yield the essential unit of the present situation. To a considerable extent this means the relating of a particular situation or its elements, to knowledge of other facts, or to principles which seem to govern other conditions. The implicit reaction to absent things, as in our illustration, does not represent the exclusive type of deductive process. It may just as well involve only a series of overt responses. The application or reference of some present circumstance or principle to some more general principle, however, has been the traditional meaning assigned to the inductive process.

Synthetic techniques are related to a problem solving method called conduction. In brief such a process affords the bringing together of a number of specific instances which incline the solution of the problem in one particular way rather than in another. Whereas reduction is disorganization for the purpose of solving a problem, conduction is a means of organization for adaptation to some reasoning situation. Before the individual can use some particular method or technique for a solution of a problem he must bring together all the relevant instances in which this technique or method has successfully operated. This process of conduction involves, then, the organization of positive and negative analogies for the drawing up of a balance. Whether one case sufficiently resembles other cases to warrant the use of the same operation is the question asked by the surgeon when handling some peculiar combination of symptoms. The conductive method need not involve the organization of parts to form a whole but may include all kinds of connections. Besides whole-part and part-whole connections of single or similar things, various parts of the same thing may be joined together as also parts belonging to entirely different things or situations.

Problem solving techniques need not necessarily involve the organization or dismantling of facts or elements which normally belong together. Possibly they concern the autonomous relations of elements which perhaps have never been related before. This relational process requires either the overt or implicit assembling of certain phases of the situation for the purpose of performing manipulations upon them, or other activities closely connected with the ulterior problem solving interest. Guiding motives for the technical operation may be contrasts and comparisons between objects, etc.

What is primarily an implicit form of manipulation of factors in a problematic situation we may consider as hypothesizing. Familiar in this connection is what has become known as the *Gedanken experimente*. This is essentially the manipulation of ideas, propositions, and judgments which have bearing upon some problematic situation and an attempt to discover the results insofar as they may have a bearing on some actual problem.

Quite a distinct problem solving technique is the overt or implicit production and reconstruction of the problematic situation at hand. The data comprising the starting point of the problem demand transformation if some further type of action is to be carried on or some kind of intellectual attitude is to be reached. To a certain extent this technique is merely an extension of ordinary thought processes which transform concrete facts into abstract data on the basis of various types of analogies. The reconstructions here may be of all types. As an extreme we may take the creative process just mentioned, namely, that in which we transform concrete objects into abstract ones, or abstract ones into concrete materials.

In scientific work, for example, the production or transformation work consists in changing the original data, which we may call crude facts, into some new kind of facts we call scientific results. The method of procedure depends upon the new kind of condition required. The necessity of the situation in general determines what sort of thing must be brought about from the materials at hand. This suggestion may be used, then, as a criterion for the manipulation of the present objects and conditions during the process of problem solving. The precise manipulation of the data necessitates the employment of all sorts of tools and apparatus until the material is transformed to suit the situation which originally set the problem.

The more strictly implicit or theoretical types of problem solving display much the same sort of technique or procedure as the above type, but the stimulus situation is very different. Present in this situation are the more critical and abstract discoveries ordinarily called inference. We start with certain established facts and determinations or assumptions and from them come to some conclusion with respect to the problem. But throughout the whole process no reference need be made to any concrete fact. The best illustration of this type of action is in the domain of logic in which inferences are made from one set of propositions to another without any specifications as to particular data.

The most complex problem solving situations involve the construction of techniques, in addition to the transformation of circumstances. Now in the simplest form this may mean the development of a new kind of manipulation or a new type of technique in order to change the problematic situation. For example, a surgeon is called upon to develop an entirely new form of operation to combat some particular form of diseased condition. Examples are likewise found in every phase of mechanics in which new types of machines have to be constructed in order that some new kind of work can be carried on. In more abstract and theoretical situations this construction may refer to an hypothesis for the suggestion of a solution of the problem. Here the whole process is most likely implicit, or it may be only temporarily so and later become a concrete form of overt action. Furthermore, the production may consist of the making of a new object or of new ways of considering problems for the testing of suggestions regarding their solution. The present type of construction is especially prominent in laboratory sciences, in which new techniques have to be developed to test solutions of problems. Without doubt the problem solving technique of developing or transforming techniques may be looked upon as the most complex of all problem solving processes. In other words, it requires the most intricate and involved extension of the person's powers and capacities. Even the simplest instance of this type of technique is an extension of the person's capacities for overt action. When the more complex cases are in question we have an extension of the knowledge and thinking behavior limits of the individual.

Probably the most uncertain type of technique is that which involves the exceedingly precarious trial and error manipulation of both the situation involved in the problem solving circumstance and the techniques employed for the purpose. However, when this technique is successful (which means, for the most part, that the manipulations intentionally or accidentally have been closely related to the facts involved), it results in the discovery of some very significant or novel solution. In such fashion entirely new sets of facts or circumstances are unearthed and novel intellectual attitudes toward the immediate problem solving circumstance and related situations are developed.

Obviously the trial and error or experimental technique has a wide range. It may operate in all the various everyday circumstances surrounding the individual which call for problem solving activity. On the other hand, such a technique takes place in rigidly controlled circumstances and here we consider the behavior and the technique as definite scientific experimentation. As such, it is always based upon an hypothesis or assumption, or in general on some type of intellectual attitude which comes to be the guiding principle in the work. When expert and effective the intellectual attitude or hypothesis is firmly grounded upon previous contacts with conditions similar to those involved in the present problem solving situation. In all serious situations the experimental technique may be contrasted with mere empirical observation. It should be pointed out, then, that a series of variations in the experimental technique may occur depending upon the relations between the two variables involved, namely, the factual situation and the intellectual circumstances of the individual. Accordingly some problems are well solved by close reference to the factual situation even though a good hypothesis is lacking, whereas, on the other hand, a good hypothesis may make solution possible despite the fact that the actual circumstances involved are not clearly known.

In our study of techniques of problem solving we have attempted to point out the characteristics of the various techniques considered as distinct processes in problem solving situations. In actual practice it is hardly necessary to add that other distinct forms may be discoverable whenever certain specific problem solving activities occur. Furthermore, we must think of many or all of these different types of techniques as being used in the same particular situations. The value and effectiveness of problem solving activities are functions of the person's success in applying the appropriate methods to the problematic situation with which he is in contact. Some of the worst failures in problem solving may be traced to the attempt to solve problems with techniques which are borrowed from other situations and which are not suitable for the present circumstances.

Before leaving our discussion of the different problem solving techniques, we must make a sharp distinction between what may be called strictly behavioristic or psychological problem solving methods, and organized, scientific, or conventional methods which are employed as instruments of attack upon problem solving situations. For example, we may well distinguish the work of a scientist in thinking out a method for solving a problem as based upon his observations of the involved conditions and upon his own behavior equipment (together with the performance of memorial, imaginative, and other forms of psychological responses) from the employment of analytical tests, as in chemistry, or the use of mathematical formulæ, which at some previous time have been developed and validated either for similar or quite different situations. On the one hand, the techniques (whether ideas or knowledge or manipulatory facts) are external things, in all respects like tools in their form. But the strictly psychological techniques are of another sort. The latter are intimate actions of the person which may or may not involve the use of external tools, for in their functions of course these acts are inseparable from the external tools.

By no means does this deny that such immediate personal activities are, along with other things and activities, the bases of the manipulations of science. They most assuredly are. What we mean to distinguish here are the single events and actions constituting the life of science (as well as other activities) from the products of previous and present actions now constituting the crystallizations and conventions, the common materials of scientific work.

While in each instance of problem solving activity the stimulus is a problem or problematic situation, the range of stimuli is nevertheless exceedingly large. This fact is quite apparent in that the stimuli for problem solving action are always functions of circumstances or situations, instead of the simpler functions of objects or persons. Hence problem solving stimuli are always complex functions, though in each instance they are centered about some decidedly specific thing or event. In general, there are three types of such centering. In the first place, the stimuli may be centered about the person and his conditions. Secondly, the problem may involve the person's relation to objects or other persons, and thirdly, it may be concerned with objects and things.

Stimuli of Problem Solving Behavior

When objects are at the basis of the stimulus function, the problem is most likely to center about the nature or identity of an object. Various types of problem solving activity and techniques are required for its solution. The problem may be what kind of test to apply, how to analyze it, or it may involve the more complex actions of assuming some characteristic for the purposes of testing. Other problems centering about objects as stimuli refer to the cost of things or the way to obtain them. The simplest solutions involve merely the inquiry concerning the matter.  Again, such stimuli comprise the problem of the manner of moving objects from place to place or of transforming them into something else of a more desirable type.  It is not unlikely that the problem solving responses with respect to objects constitute the simplest type.  This is especially true when the object can be directly responded to, as in most of the cases we have suggested.  When these objects are not available for immediate response, however, and have to be substituted for, then the problem solving activity is more complex and reaches a speculative and theoretical level.

Situations of all sorts supply further sources of problem solving stimulation.  To a great extent a person under such circumstances faces the problem as to how he himself can change his relationship to certain undesirable circumstances and thus place himself in a better situation.

Actions, like situation stimuli for problem solving, are to a great extent connected with the conditions and status of an individual. For the most part problematic situations, having their source in actions, force the individual to determine how to accomplish something or what action to perform in order to carry out a desire or ambition. Problems arise as to whether given types of activity should be performed.  This problem solving may be considered somewhat detached from the individual, however, in the sense that he asks whether a certain act is good, proper, or worth while.  Nevertheless, the problem concerns predominately the nature of the consequences of the action with respect to the individual's personal circumstances.  As another illustration of problem solving stimuli activities, we refer to the functions involving beliefs, propositions, or information about facts. Here to a great extent the problem is the discovery of the truth or falsity of a proposition or belief.

Without question the most difficult and pressing stimuli of all those operating in problem solving behavior segments are those in which the conditions, circumstances, or even objects, around which the functions center, are themselves shifting and variable.  In fact we might consider this element of vacillation and shift as a basis and criterion for differentiating among stimuli.  As an example of the kind of problem stimulated by shifting circumstances we propose the discovery or determination of some kind of uniformity or law which sums up variations or degrees of variations in phenomena.  Doubtless it is this type of problem which most taxes the capacity and behavior equipment of the problem solving individual and results, if the behavior is successful, in a new discovery or invention.

We cannot leave this study of the stimuli for problem solving actions without making a distinction between the actual stimuli to problem solving and the material with which the problem solving action is carried out.  Generally speaking, we may say that the stimulus function for problem solving action suggests a doubt or need of some sort which must be satisfied.  This doubt or need may have more or less connection with some particular object, act, or circumstance. That is to say, in contrast to a simple situation in which the stimulus function is a characteristic of an object, in problem solving activity there is a greater difference between the function and the object or thing, in the sense that the stimulus function cannot be said to be a direct characteristic or property of the object.

Assuming that every problem solving behavior situation involves a set of characteristics, such as some difficulty of behavior with respect to the object because of lack of identity, or some rarity due to no previous experience with the stimulus object, we find entirely different methods of behavior approach to the objects and situations constituting problem solving stimuli. For the most part these individual differences are based upon variations in the behavior equipment of individuals. *Individual Differences in Problem Solving*

In the first place, we find differences among individuals in the matter of ability to appreciate the presence of a problem. This difference is based directly upon the person's previous acquaintance with similar situations. Accordingly the person may or may not lack equipment of a certain sort which furthers sensitivity to the presence of a problem. We might consider that here is involved a unique type of intelligence operating in problem solving situations and of course of a specialized sort. For it is hardly probable that an individual will be sensitive to all kinds of problems regardless of the kind of stimuli situations with which they are connected. More specifically we may point out that the ability to see a problem is a matter of process equipment since, if an individual is fitted directly by equipment to see problems, we hardly expect them to be very serious or difficult problem situations.

Secondly, we may consider individual differences in the matter of the approach to the problem once it is known and appreciated. Some persons approach a situation with considerable self-confidence and reliance. They attempt to estimate it immediately and to bring to bear upon it whatever capacities and equipment they have ready; or in the event that they lack such means they prepare at once to devise such equipment. The extreme variation from this type of individual is the person who, after sensing a problem, runs immediately to someone who is presumably an authority for suggestions as to how the problem should be attacked. This variation in problem solving attacks is frequently based upon genuine incapacity and inefficiency. On the other hand, it may be accounted for merely on the basis of a need to work under authority; and while the person may later reveal the possession of technique and general equipment necessary to solve the problem, he is still not self-reliant enough to forego asking for aid.

Next we turn to a great series of individual differences in the actual attack and solution of problems. Here the personal variations are found mostly in the types of techniques employed for problem solving purposes.[1] So great are these differences that they may distinguish the successful and original problem solving person from the one who is not original even if he can solve problems at all. Especially clear are the factors of personal originality and efficiency in the solution of problems, let us say of mathematical or other related or unrelated types. A distinct problem of individual differences concerns the question as to whether a person operates primarily or most successfully with overt manipulatory techniques or with implicit actions. It may similarly be asked whether the person is more at home with behavior or non-behavior tools. Connected with these questions of individual differences in problem solving is the query whether the person operates always or usually in a personalistic way with his stimuli, or whether his problem solving action goes on in a subpersonalistic or other simpler modes also.

At this point we may distinguish between individual variations in problem solving founded upon an idiosyncratic foundation, and those that have at their basis cultural elements. The latter have to do more with generalized methods of problem solving. In other words, individuals approach problems on the basis of their culturalization. A bacteriologist may sense his problem in a practical way and immediately think of a mode of attack which resembles the traditional method of the laboratory in which he was trained. In still larger illustrations we find that problem solving, even of the most rigid scientific type, is institutional in character and frequently is included within narrow nationalistic limits. In the history of thought we have instances of differences between the British type of thinkers who rely very closely upon models, and the Continental type of thinker who works with more abstract tools. Also the historians of philosophy provide us with instances of the institutional empiricism of the British Islands and the more rational characteristics of Continental thought.

[1] We neglect here all variations in personal conduct such as differences in enthusiasm, rapidity and accuracy as being traits of general behavior and therefore somewhat extraneous to the intimate problem solving situation.

# CHAPTER XXII

## REASONING RESPONSES AS INFER-
## ENTIAL ACTIVITIES

Reasoning or inferring behavior consists of fairly abstract and de- The Na-
tached conduct or the technical use of personality equipment and reac- ture of
tional biography to reach a new knowledge, intellectual status, or Reasoning
attitude with respect to some object, information, or condition. In Reactions
many cases this new intellectual status is a confirmation and sub-
stantiation of a previous tentative one. This detachedness and technical use of behavior equipment emphasizes the emersion of the person from and his dominance of the situation in which the behavior
occurs. It means to stress the fact that the person is extremely involved in the behavior features of the circumstances in which the
present responses transpire. Clearly, of course, all this activity is an
attempt to orient or adapt oneself intellectually to specific objects and
circumstances. But the point is that the behavior is primarily a detached and abstract form of action. It is predominantly personal
conduct rather than transformative and effective.

This lack of accomplishing or effective action is an essential characteristic of reasoning activity. Effective action or accomplishment,
however, may occur in connection with reasoning conduct, but only
in a distantly removed form. The total reasoning behavior segment
is completed or consummated with the change and modification of the
person's intellectual status concerning the stimuli of the behavior
situation. Howsoever important, onerous, or difficult such behavior
may be, no further effective action or contact with the stimuli is an
actual feature of the intellectual situation. Assuredly the reasoning
behavior segment may consist of a preparation for some future action,
but in that case it is plain that the following action constitutes an
entirely new series of behavior segments. They are, therefore, phases
or parts of the reasoning behavior pattern. Probably the behavior
segments that are closest and most constantly connected with other
types of responses, in addition to the essential reasoning or inferring
activity, are those that are intimately related to verbal or propositional responses. In these cases in addition to performing inferring
or reasoning conduct, the person asserts in some language form the
result of his action or the way in which it has come about. Such
language activity is clearly independent of the reasoning or inferring
behavior and may either succeed or precede it in the person's series
of actions.

We have stated that reasoning or inferring reactions result in the development of new intellectual attitudes. It must be stipulated, therefore, that these attitudes, when attained, are a distinct type differing from the ordinary intellectual attitudes already studied. Whereas ordinary intellectual attitudes are attained by some sort of direct though not immediate contact with stimuli objects and situations, reasoning attitudes are actually developed through some deliberate process of technical interaction with stimuli objects. Unlike the other types of intellectual behavior, in the case of reasoning it is not the person's attitude but the development of it that is emphasized. Furthermore, this intellectual status or attitude that is reached, whether permanent or impermanent, is derived as a definite operation on the basis of the evidence or propositions that constitute the stimuli situations and which in the literature of traditional logic, are always referred to as the premises. Reasoning and inferring behavior accordingly constitute a definite situation of search and inquiry intended to lead to the development or discovery of a new knowledge and intellectual status. In short, reasoning action constitutes for the most part a technique of conduct or behavior. Its essential fact is a behavior process of quite a particular sort.

We are further cautioned that reasoning behavior must not be too closely related to intellectual activity by the fact that the results of reasoning action may be definite knowledge instead of an intellectual attitude. By means of the intellectual operations comprising the reasoning activities we become better oriented with respect to the objects or circumstances stimulating the reasoning behavior. With direct regard to the stimuli objects this knowledge may be sheer information or a grasp of probabilities, principles, or laws governing or involving some sort of phenomena. It is needless to suggest that the knowledge so reached is very different from the simple orientational responses derived from a direct implicit contact with stimuli objects and situations.

Although the reasoning and inferring action resulting in a new intellectual status comprises a definite or technical mode of activity it is never formal in the sense that any established rules govern its performance. Just what the activity will be depends upon the immediate circumstances involved, as well as the interests and purposes of the acting individual. What is meant by technical behavior, then, is the fact that the reacting individual makes the stimuli objects and conditions into definite symbols capable of serving as bases and landmarks for a large perspectival situation centering about the particular stimuli objects. The new intellectual responses resulting from the reasoning activity involve, therefore, the appreciation of the perspective of the situation along with the new relationship assumed in it by the central stimulational objects. Sometimes this intellectual attitude is reached simply by means of the manipulation of concepts and other implicit behavior elements; at other times a considerable period of difficult trying and experimentation is necessary.

Reasoning responses in some of their features are clearly not unlike problem solving activities. Nevertheless there is a distinct difference between them. Problem solving places the emphasis of the total behavior upon the working out of some kind of solution in the immediate stimuli situation, whether it be the discovery of some kind of characteristic of a thing or the extrication of the individual from some unsatisfactory circumstance. In the case of reasoning, on the other hand, the primary emphasis is upon the attainment of a new type of intellectual status or knowledge orientation with respect to certain conditions or situations. This difference does not mean, of course, that the specific processes in both cases may not be alike in some particular situation, howsoever greatly they may vary in others. That the two types of behavior cannot be confused, however, is evident from the fact that it is possible for each type to be a component form of action in a complex behavior segment bearing the name of the other type of action.

We may distinguish thinking behavior from inferential conduct on the basis that the latter is a decidedly more personal response and not the manipulation of things. Reasoning reactions insofar as they are connected with things make use of them as bases and premises and therefore do not constitute responses directly to the things even though the latter may be implicitly manipulated. Thinking behavior, involving as it does considerable overt handling of things, is the farthest removed from reasoning, for in reasoning, even when tools are used, they are unmistakably extraneous and foreign aids to the actions involved. In addition it may be said that a comparison of thinking and reasoning when they actually occur shows that they vary enormously in specific details.

To avoid a linguistic pitfall in the study of reasoning we propose to exclude from the domain of inferential behavior such action as is represented by the expression, "reasoning with someone." The action referred to here is clearly linguistic or interpersonal and not inferential. Such action constitutes argumentation or rhetoric on the one hand, or convincing behavior on the other. Never does it refer to the genuine and intimate technique of reasoning.

Inferential behavior occurs naturally in all sorts of concrete situations. The intellectual status or knowledge is a response to almost any kind of thing. Possibly it is the outcome of an inferential examination and a survey of particular practical situations. A typical case is the attainment of a conclusion with respect to some condition or situation that might occur concerning some specific natural phenomenon or some observable human fact or relationship. Inferences concerning specific human occurrences or scientific data illustrate this point. In other cases, the intellectual status or conclusion reached may be some sort of abstract conception or proposition derived from the same type of general contact with abstract propositions or situations.  This latter type has for the most part constituted the subject matter of the formal logician.

**Reasoning or Inferential Behavior Segments**

On the response side reasoning behavior segments consist of personal and detached activities of various sorts.  As a consequence such behavior must be primarily implicit.  Although reasoning conduct comprises some of the most complex forms of psychological adaptation to particular objects and circumstances they are for the most part manipulations of informational and knowledge materials.  The person compares, contrasts, and discriminates between features of objects and propositions, which at the time serve as substitute stimuli for the qualities and relations of things constituting the stimuli proper for the achieved or developed attitude.

The specific details of reasoning behavior consist for the most part of the manipulation of concepts which sum up in various ways and at different points the stimulational objects and situations.  By means of these concepts the reasoning individual organizes, relates and otherwise handles and refers to the component phases and elements in the reasoning situation.  In many cases this conceptual handling of the elements in the reasoning action takes the form of an evaluational and even creational development of conditions and circumstances finding a place in the reasoning situation.

Generally speaking, the actual responses in the reasoning behavior pattern constitute a series of knowings, considerations, reflections, and retrospections upon the qualities and conditions of things to the end that a new intellectual attitude is established or developed with respect to them.  This attitude represents a fresh orientational status not only toward things and their relations, values, etc., but also toward the person's own relations and connections with objects.

Just how these responses operate varies considerably in different cases and with different persons, but practically every type of implicit action is involved.  Especially to be mentioned are the functions of the linguistic elements in the development of conceptions for reasoning actions, and for manipulating them afterwards.

As we might expect in the operation of such complex activity as reasoning conduct, the total responses consist of a considerable amount of auxiliary reactions.  Since these auxiliary forms of behavior have a definite place in the response pattern as a whole they anticipate, lead up to, and condition the character of the final reasoning action.  At times such auxiliary responses comprise definite overt manipulations of the objects constituting the stimuli for the reasoning conduct.  For instance, when the stimulus is an object, the manipulation is some kind of effective handling of that object; or if the stimulus is a proposition or set of propositions the overt manipulations involve primarily the handling of documents and evidence objects, etc.  In this manner the response patterns for reasoning activity include a great many overt, partially overt, and implicit actions.  In each case, of course, we need not refer to the presence of attentional and perceptual reactions. The classification of type of reaction systems involved relates only to the essential reasoning factors.

The predominant rôle of the overt or non-implicit reactions functioning in reasoning behavior patterns concerns the preliminary processes of handling the material in order that the person can get into closer contact with it. Such reactions are decidedly contributory to the reactional adjustment, and while they may be necessary for its occurrence they are not essential features of that adjustment.

The inclusion of contributory or auxiliary reaction systems in the reasoning behavior pattern clearly indicates that such intricate behavior as we are describing must consist in its complex forms of a number of component responses. In contrast to the more simple types in which the final reaction is based only upon a simple observation of the stimuli involved, the more complex cases of reasoning conduct require all sorts of involved auxiliary reactions, not excluding elaborate problem solving activities of various kinds.

A characteristic fact about the stimuli for reasoning or inferring reactions is that they consist primarily of situations and relations, and not simply isolated objects. When objects function in the behavior segment they operate as substitutes for themselves in other relations and circumstances, or they constitute symbols or signs suggestive of conditions and circumstances not at present available for observation. Inferential behavior is performed not only with regard to immediate and existing objects and situations but also with regard to events or objects to occur in the future or to be later originated or developed.

In spite of the exceeding complexity of reasoning and inferential activity it is possible to isolate a series of fairly definite processes which may be considered as the actual technical conduct resulting in the development of an intellectual status or new orientation. It must not be assumed, however, that these processes are always independent forms of action. In many instances they constitute simultaneously operating activities in various combinations. Only in the very simplest types of inferential behavior do these processes operate autonomously and thus constitute the total action operative at the time. In attempting to work out the character of these inferential processes we must be warned against the conception that we are dealing here with formal modes of action. Such is not at all the case. It is for this reason that no concrete general description of such processes can be made prior to the actual occurrence of the reasoning behavior. What we are describing are generalized or typified forms of action, the specific details of which cannot be presented. The reason for this situation becomes all the more clear when we note that the behavior circumstances centering around inferential reactions are composed of unique human conditions. It is true, of course, that ordinarily we discover common elements or similar ones in

*Inferential and Reasoning Processes*

various inferential situations but on the whole the conditions are novel. Furthermore, we must consider that because of the different behavior equipments of individuals and their varied general intellectual status the specific forms which the inferential reactions take, depend upon the particular individuals performing the activity. The typified processes operative in inferential reactions we name as follows: (1) inductive behavior, (2) deductive action, (3) conductive reasoning, (4) constructive and evaluational inference and (5) reductive reasoning.[1]

**Inductive Behavior**

By means of the inductive process the individual attains an intellectual position or attitude which has as its stimulus the establishment of a larger fact upon the basis of a series of lesser or smaller facts. This type of inferential behavior may be described as a process of appreciating the origin of a principle or the discovery or creation of a generalization. The attitude here is that of supersumption, the inclusion in a general principle of a set of facts or propositions upon the basis of their belonging to a system. This inclusion is based upon observations and discoveries of the character of their qualities and various relationships. A classical illustration employed in describing the present type of behavior is the establishment of some generalization as the result of particular qualities discovered in a number of different instances. From the fact that the same price is quoted for a certain type of article by a number of different merchants one arrives at the conclusion that there is a combination or some understanding between the different merchants. When this intellectual attitude is expressed by the reacting individual he says something of each object that is true of all of them as a group. In other words, some principle is discovered which characterizes or classifies the whole set of things or instances. With strict regard to the psychological facts involved we must say that in this situation the person acquires or achieves a generalized attitude or knowledge. We are not, of course, interested in the development of a knowledge product which is a public object when it is referred to or couched and embodied in linguistic acts or symbols. This generalized attitude or attitude of generalization may be reached on the basis of one or many observed facts or propositions.

**Deductive Behavior**

The process of subsuming a number of instances under some already known classification or heading we call deduction. The intellectual attitude therefore is one of location or being able to place things in a proper class or division. Propositions or facts are discovered as localizable within the domain of a particular generalization or class. Thus one has on hand a kind of circumstance or situation which is applicable to a whole series of instances and to some particular form of

---

[1] This terminology is intended to serve two purposes. It the first place, we mean to include in our exposition the results of the traditional consideration of reasoning behavior, and secondly, to indicate the indispensable need for additional descriptions of inferring behavior.

description.  In detail, the inferential process of deduction comprises
the discovery or the appreciation that some present object is caused
or can be explained by a particular principle or generalization that
one has already discovered or which has otherwise become part of
the individual's informational equipment.  Our everyday acts with
things bring us constantly into situations in which, when we meet
some particular object and discover some facts about it, we immediately come to the conclusion that we cannot do certain things with it.

Our intellectual response which is established or discovered may **Conductive Reasoning**
be the result of a process of going from one thing to another.  Unlike
the two processes already described, however, conductive reasoning
does not consist of going from a generalized to a particularizd situation, or vice-versa.  Instead it requires the establishment of an attitude by correlating things or propositions which have no whole-
part or large and small relationship.  Representative of such behavior are those attitudes having as their stimuli the mere relation
of things rather than any kind of implication.  We draw a conclusion concerning some object because it is analogous to, or bears
some similarity or statistical relation to some other object or situation
with which we have had some previous experience.  All types of
correlational processes may tend toward inferential attitudes.  We
may establish a relation toward some particular fact, condition, or
object by means of our acquaintance with a similar fact or condition
in some other object or situation.  Again we may reach an attitude
toward a complex feature or aspect of a thing through some simple
object or condition and vice-versa.  These processes are very different
in their characters and may concern all kinds of conditions and situations.  In other words, the attitudes resulting from such processes
have as their stimuli the causes, origins, continuations, names, and
explanations of things.

Still another process finding a place in inferential and reasoning **Constructive and Evaluative Reasoning**
activities is the ascription of a quality to a situation or object on the
basis of previous contacts with similar or related things.  What
actually occurs is the positive development of a class into which
to put a particular thing as the result of the discovery or observation
of its qualities and characteristics.  Necessary for the production
of a class or the development of a new principle with respect to the
stimulus is the employment of the individual's knowledge and other
behavior equipment which he has gradually acquired in his past
contacts with objects and conditions in some way either related or
unrelated to his present stimuli circumstances.

The attitude to which we now turn our attention refers to the **Reductive Reasoning**
development of a negative evaluational attitude with respect to
certain stimuli objects or situations.  Specifically the process is
activity which eliminates and disposes of descriptions and the circumstances of existence of things and situations.  Such a procedure
finally leads to the establishment or development of an intellectual

or inferential status concerning the stimulus objects in question. A knowledge of what the object is, however, or what its positive characteristics are, is not achieved through the process which operates here. The object itself, so far as its conditions and circumstances are concerned, is left in an unfinished or incomplete state.

In our description of the processes involved in reasoning or inferential behavior we have already had occasion to note that they include observing, comparing, and contrasting things in order to attain to the intellectual attitude that is the result of the process. We might add also that they involve obtaining information of an indirect sort by reading and hearing about the stimuli. Such indirect forms of action are involved, of course, with the individual's equipment. In this sense we find that the intellectual attitudes resulting from inferential and reasoning activities are deeply founded not only upon the individual's informational and cognitive equipment but also upon his fears, desires, and hopes that have resulted from his particular contacts during the course of his reactional biography.

**Critical and Uncritical Reasoning** That reasoning activity is a decidedly human form of contact and interaction with stimuli surroundings is quite apparent from our general treatment of this mode of behavior. It may not be amiss, therefore, to point out how our treatment of reasoning conduct contrasts with and displaces some traditional conceptions of both reasoning and inferring action. The assumption is ordinarily made that, whenever a reasoning act occurs, the total activity is critical and thus the results of the action are supposed to be definite, final, and at least more or less fairly competent. This is a mistaken notion, however. Reasoning, as an activity in itself, does not involve being critical or uncritical or even competent. In every instance we must be on our guard lest this quality of critical or uncritical reasoning be injected into the situation by the observer, in spite of the fact that the action of the person may not involve criticism at all. In no case can the reasoning action in itself be any more competent than the degree in which the premises upon which it is based are critically chosen and competently handled. From the standpoint of orientational adaptation we may possibly find that an objective criterion for the critical quality of reasoning may be the coherence and connection between the premises and the operation upon them. But this certainly does not result in any sort of efficiency or adaptation. Witness the well known fact that the reasoning of an insane individual may absolutely follow from, and be a continuation of, the premises with which he starts. But what of the results? In general, we might say that although no definite or universally reliable criterion for criticalness is available one may assert that the competency of the general adaptation provides such a criterion. Now in any practical situation it is impossible to discover such clear cut conditions as would enable us to assert with definiteness that the reaction results in a competent adaptation. Furthermore, in the complex cases of reasoning the results achieved and the methods developed for the solution of a problem are so different from any of the original conditions that any criterion of competency of performance is entirely beside the mark.   To a certain extent when we know what the needs and conditions of the person actually are, we may conclude that the reasoning action is desirable under the circumstances, but this is not by far an application of the criterion of criticalness.

The difficulty of determining the logical and critical character of reasoning behavior is most apparent when we consider the significant fact in such situations, namely, that the person is a product of his cultural circumstances.   Reasoning behavior goes on to a great extent in terms of concepts and abstract behavior tools forged and perfected in a given behavior milieu.   Since it is these tools that the individual must use, clearly his reasoning cannot far transcend in quality the goodness and efficacy of the tools employed.

Further to complicate the problem of the logical and critical character of reasoning behavior is the fact that such conduct does not always involve the complete awareness of the person.   In other words, important reasoning reactions may occur without the knowledge of the acting person.   This proposition, of course, will not hold for reasoning actions occurring in the most complex types of behavior situations.   Probably when the behavior situation is very important or the need for a new critical intellectual attitude is decidedly pressing, the response is action of the fully personalistic type.   Again it is not to be assumed that action transpiring on the reactionalistic, or even a lower level, is not accurate and effective behavior.   Nevertheless the fact that reasoning behavior may consist of unwitting conduct makes way for reasoning action which lacks critical and effective character.

Whether a reasoning action is or is not critical must be judged by a general ensemble of conditions and circumstances.   Hence the criterion is an exceedingly comprehensive one, involving a great many factors which have an essential place in the total situation.   Elements of the criterion are the stimulational conditions, (the reason why one chooses or accepts the premises) the mode of conducting the processes and procedures of the response, and the final results from the standpoint of the premises and the person's general behavior conditions, past, present, and future.   These suggestions are sufficiently plain if not entirely adequate, in view of the absolute relativity of reasoning behavior in all its circumstances and conditions.

Thus we are brought to a consideration of the fact of general levels of reasoning conduct.   Succinctly, what may appear to be a perfectly confident form of reasoning activity under a specific set of circumstances may still prove to be, from the standpoint of another level of human conduct, a very slight and exceedingly valueless form of behavior.   The point here is that in the different levels of human conduct we find more or less complicated conditions in which the behavior occurs, as well as more or less suitable circumstances under which the reasoning activity is initiated. Further we discover in the different levels of reasoning situations more competent adaptations from the standpoint of some criterion or standard applicable to the two cases. Accordingly, we might come to the conclusion in specific instances that under the circumstances a reasoning activity may be all that one could expect and therefore entirely satisfactory in view of what is desirable for the situation. From the standpoint of a higher level of reasoning behavior situations, however, no such affirmative approval may be accorded the reasoning conduct.

**The Range of Reasoning Behavior** As complex and technical as reasoning actions are, they may still find a place in almost every phase of a person's behavior life. Every phase of our daily existence, from the most ordinary contacts with things and persons to highly complex behavior situations, constitutes a fertile source for the performance of all types of reasoning responses. All manner of conditions and situations stimulate the individual to perform actions leading to new orientational attitudes.

In the more common and practical situations new and important things and conditions prompt the individual to draw inferences concerning their character, origin, value, ownership, etc. The motives for performing the inferential orientative behavior may be traced back to the stimulation of the individual by circumstances of a definite economic type. In such practical and everyday situations the necessity of living with people or of maintaining oneself among certain particular circumstances of geographic, social, commercial, or industrial types leads to the development of all sorts of intellectual attitudes through inferential conduct.

The more practical ranges of inferential conduct include also reasoning responses to social, legal, and historical facts and circumstances of every variety and description. Reasoning and inferring conduct motivated by the practical aim of aligning oneself with existing circumstances and their various qualities and significances takes place likewise in the domain of æsthetic and religious circumstances surrounding the individual.

In a far different sphere of the range of reasoning behavior we may place the inferring conduct based upon an abstract motivation of pure orientation without the remotest regard to any practical result or achievement. As such, the inferring responses are decidedly detached and removed from contact with things, aside of course, from being prompted by them. Within this division of the range of inferring action, objects and conditions are transformed and recreated by means of implicit behavior so they may prove to be very different in the final result. A typical instance of such reasoning activity is the performance of abstract inferences from propositions of a generalized sort having no manner of relation to particular facts. This is the domain of the abstract logic of implication in which any abstract relations capable of suitable symbolization are the subject matters handled.

The fact that the range of reasoning responses is exceedingly large and includes all types and conditions of behavior situations in no wise contradicts the fact that, as a matter of course, the ordinary individual performs very little rational behavior. Two points are here to be taken into consideration. In the first place, as compared with the total series of reactions that an individual performs, very few may properly be called rational behavior segments. The number of rational activities therefore is relatively very small. Secondly, even when reactions are rational, in a lesser number of cases they are not rational, as definitely cognitive action. In other words, the situations, in which we knowingly perform rational responses and utilize our own behavior as the technique and tools of reasoning, are, in the absolute sense, exceedingly rare and uncommon.

What passes for reasoning responses in a great many instances are nothing more than rationalizations of various sorts. A rationalization consists essentially of a linguistically expressed or unexpressed excuse or explanation for an activity one has performed or is about to perform. Ordinarily rationalizations are a means of convincing oneself or others that one's action is appropriate and adequate for the circumstances when the act itself might not be at all a critical and effective adaptation. Finding that one likes liver one becomes extremely hygienic in matters of nutrition and explains one's indulgence in this kind of food on the ground that too much muscle meat is not beneficial. This rationalization works in other ways also, when we must eat something we do not like and discover some good reason for doing it. How gloriously and rationally vindicated we are when we discover some authority for an action requiring justification. We tell ourselves that it is our moral duty to give more money for some purpose than we can actually afford, though in reality we are afraid not to contribute to this cause and thus rationalize what may really be an irrational action. To rationalize, then, appears to be the contrived substitution of an intellectual attitude for one that is held but which one finds inconvenient or not approved of. In other cases of rationalization we start by believing some proposition and then searching for and perhaps finding evidences to justify it. Finding ourselves as psychophysicists we discover all sorts of reasons for believing that only to work with psychological abstractions is scientific. Rationalizing turns out to be definitely opposite to reasoning in critical, if not in effective, character. The effectiveness also, is a doubtful quality.

Because reasoning behavior segments are so complex and involve behavior circumstances in which the greatest degree of uniqueness and indefiniteness is found, it follows therefore that it is not easy to localize the conditions and influences governing the performance of the specific behavior segments. However, we may profitably point out certain features of reasoning behavior situations which are fa-

*Conditions and Influences of Reasoning Conduct*

vorable or disadvantageous for the performance of the action. As usual in such circumstances the conditions and influences may be discussed from the standpoint both of the situations involved and the person's behavior.

So far as the stimuli situations are concerned, there must be present data or propositions leading to or allowing for the performance of rational behavior. These data or propositions are found in situations which permit the performance of technical behavior culminating in the development or establishment of new orientational attitudes. Further, these data or propositions must be such that they can be got hold of and appreciated in order that a new intellectual attitude toward them may result from the behavior responses to them. To illustrate, everyone is familiar with the fact that there are certain conditions and problems with respect to which no actual reasoning processes can be performed. What forms of rational conduct can we perform leading to a critical orientational attitude concerning the problem as to why our evolutionary development has resulted in the particular sorts of animals we now have, rather than in some others? Likewise, there can be no genuine reasoning behavior with respect to the problem as to how language was developed or originated. Howsoever fortunate one may be in discovering some data regarding a certain feature or phase of a general fact or situation, such facts or data may contribute little to the performance of rational conduct or the formation of a resulting intellectual reaction.

Conditions of reasoning behavior involving the reacting person's activity may be both favorable and unfavorable for the performance of rational conduct and the achievement of adequate intellectual orientation. We may mention at once the type and amount of behavior equipment the individual possesses which is capable of employment in any present instance. Not only must a reasoning behavior situation presuppose the existence of data or premises, but likewise the individual must have equipment practicable as tools in the development of the new orientational attitude. Such equipment naturally conditions the performances of the rational action at all, or else has a favorable or unfavorable influence upon its outcome. Upon the basis of such equipment the resulting attitude is, or is not, critical or effective. Whether or not the individual's equipment has a favorable influence upon his present performance of rational activity is contingent upon whether his equipment comprises the ability to select relevant details and to examine them thoroughly. It depends further upon the presence of the trait of maintaining an attitude of judicial hesitation until the evidence has been reviewed and thoroughly examined. In this connection we may in no wise overlook the conditioning and influencing importance of the intelligent conduct of the person. No matter how different reasoning responses may be from intelligent action, we should not expect any very effective or valid reasoning to be performed without the aid and support of intelligent behavior. These and other similar traits of action the individual may acquire as permanent reactional equipment serving as effective reactional tools for the performance of valid and critical rational behavior.

Whatever equipment influences the performance of rational behavior, which in all cases must be relevant to specific situations at hand, it can develop only during the course of the reactional history of the individual while in contact with similar behavior circumstances. It is the similarity between present and previous conditions that makes the person's behavior equipment available for service in any immediate situation. This is true because reactional equipment, being so difficult to modify, can only serve a valid function if it is relevant to the situation. Otherwise it interferes with the smooth and adequate performance of behavior with respect to any rational situation with which one may be in contact.

A traditional procedure among psychologists is to mention the unfavorable influence upon rational behavior of an individual's personal interests and bias. Certainly such equipmental prejudices and inclinations shape the processes and results of rational activity and deflect it from the stimuli situations and circumstances. But to this suggestion may be added a more fundamental condition affecting in a none too salutary manner the performance of rational conduct, namely, the overwhelming power exerted by the institutions existing in the person's behavior milieu. It is not unsafe to say that in practically every instance one can guarantee the critical and effective character of rational conduct if one will remove oneself as far as possible from the contaminating influence of the prevailing intellectual institutions found in the group in which one lives. In plainer terms, no rational action can ever be adequate or valid if one merely fits into some formula certain categories of quality and quantity which are presumed to represent the premises or propositions comprising the stimuli situations in rational conduct circumstances. Rather, true rational behavior is idiosyncratic in character. The adequacy with which any sort of rational conduct works is a direct function of the person's responses to the rational behavior situation at hand.

Much more extraneous conditions having their effect upon reasoning behavior are the hygienic circumstances of the person which are common to other types of behavior situations as well. Distractions and excitements usually have a malevolent influence upon reasoning conduct although in rare cases, being aroused, may redound to the advantage of the reasoning activity.

All genuine reasoning behavior situations are particular action events and therefore unique, regardless of the individual who performs the action. Each behavior situation is a novel and uncommon one because it requires a specific and particularized form of reactional procedure. Hence different individuals in performing such reactions inject their personalities into reasoning situations with the consequence

*Individual Differences in Reasoning Behavior*

that the total activity takes on a peculiar stamp and color. What might be considered the same general situation is turned in a particular direction depending upon the particular individual performing the reasoning action. The person under question may approach the problem from a different standpoint, and in general, impose upon it a distinct form on the basis of his likes, dislikes, and general purpose in adapting himself to the situation. A peculiarity of individual difference in reasoning behavior is that, instead of allowing for a fullness of variety and uniqueness, as is the case in situations permitting more uniform action, it makes the responses more constant and uniform than reasoning situations demand. Such uniformity as is introduced consists of the modification of situations on the basis of the person's particular individual equipment and especially upon his information with respect to this and similar situations. It depends upon his experience with such situations, that is to say, it is influenced by the types of procedure which he has previously used in similar circumstances.

Illustrations of the manner in which individual differences of action modify reasoning behavior occur both in the extreme cases in which the question whether or not one reasons at all comes up, and in those situations in which one's reasoning is more or less fixed. It is a common observation that persons of technical or professional training and vocation must perforce throw all situations and reasoning processes into a particular trend. Physicians reason about things and situations as though they were medical cases. Lawyers cast their reasoning about everything into a legalistic mould. Artists or novelists give a particular turn to their reasoning, and all with at least some disregard of the unsuitableness of the action to the subject matter or situations. It is not an unusual circumstance to find scientists inclining their reasoning behavior to accord with the religious training of their youths. The validity of reasoning behavior is sometimes also affected by certain individual differences influencing persons to handle all problems and situations in an effective and industrious way. Thus they immediately attack any situation at hand in a vigorous manner despite the fact that it could obviously be better handled by less efficacious and more judicious methods.

Because reasoning actions are personal and intimate behavior techniques they may be very individually practised despite the fact that the rules of reasoning are often conditioned by cultural circumstances. In other words, the special techniques employed may be the unique performances of particular persons. This is entirely aside from choosing one's premises which will be different from those anyone else might choose. One may have quite an individual theory of reasoning and, in consequence, conduct one's reasoning in that manner rather than in any other. The condition here is similar to one in the field of art. In that domain it is readily seen that one's technique may be absolutely determined by one's general attitude toward art phenomena.

Nowhere in the entire field of psychology has the evil of simplification and abstractionism struck with such force or culminated in such disaster as at the point of thinking, problem solving, and reasoning. What a sad condition prevails in the psychological literature with respect to such complex phenomena. What a beggarly reception and treatment these reactions, which are among the most typically human, have received at the hands of psychologists. To account for this unfortunate situation we must refer ourselves to a deplorable conspiracy of interdependent circumstances.

Foremost among these circumstances is of course the fact that no psychological phenomena were conceived of as the concrete interactions of individuals with the various objects and persons around them. In consequence, no description of the unique complex manipulations of things and actions could be thought of or observed to happen.

And then, so far as thought and reasoning responses were at all included in the domain of psychological phenomena, they were necessarily conceived of as mysterious forms of internal mechanics consisting of spiritistic or mentalistic functions whether or not connected or correlated with brain processes of some sort. What else could we expect on this basis than a failure to distinguish between the various types of cognitive and orientational behavior and the consequent neglect of most of them? What else could happen under such circumstances than the limiting of the range of such behavior as was considered, and the sketchy and inadequate description of them howsoever they were conceived of? That psychologists have not only not discovered many of these forms of action but have also oversimplified those they have found, is amply and unambiguously testified to by the history of psychological study.

Equally potent in conspiring to diminish the scope and significance of the psychology of thinking is the influence of logic upon psychology. So far as thinking and reasoning are concerned, the field of psychology has been dominated and led captive by the logician. The result was of course inevitable. Oversight, limitation, and rigidity of the facts involved naturally followed. This is true not because the logician's subject matter is simpler and more restricted; such is far from the facts. Rather it is true because the logician is interested in an entirely different level of phenomena. Because he deals with completed facts, with static factors insofar as he is at all concerned with behavior, his materials are formal and brief. The logician, as compared with the psychologist, deals with fixed and standard materials. Stimuli objects for psychological thinking and reasoning are objects personally met with in the individual's experience. The objects reacted to in logical behavior are standard objects—objects of knowledge. The psychologist of course must take cognizance of the procedure followed in formal logical action, both because the action here is an abstracted outgrowth and result of the more intimate psychological activities and because the performance at the time is in part psychological. But this is not to overlook the fact that logical action or methodology comprises also behavior which is not thinking or reasoning, as well as institutions or things which are not psychological at all.

Moreover, the logician is interested in thinking which must be approved of or appropriate to the attainment of a particular goal as determined by a certain problem. The psychologist, on the other hand, is concerned purely with responses of particular persons sometimes to trivial and insignificant stimuli. The logician is interested in accomplishments and achievements, that is, social or human performances in the domain concerned with the establishment of truth and reality or the solving of a serious practical problem.[1] It necessarily ensues, then, that when the psychologist follows the lead of the logician in the study of the psychological phenomena of thinking and problem solving, he involves himself in a trivial-making and falsifying enterprise. Instead of treating thinking in all its branches, problem solving and reasoning as concrete overt and implicit interactions of persons and their surrounding objects, the logical influence makes of them symbolic, secondary and conventional actions. This is the case even when they are really regarded as functional activities. As morphological actions they are invariably handled as processes corresponding to remote implicit actions but not as actual contacts with and manipulations of objects. When thoughts are treated as products, they are symbols or signs, public objects, and not intimate actions at all. In the best sense thought is treated as conventional fictions or abstractions from thought or things such as the social contract, $\Pi$, the economic man, $\sqrt{-1}$, etc. It is in the product division of symbolic thinking that

[1] In the following way we may distinguish between social thinking, logical thinking, and the intimate psychological behavior of the same name. The first is really statistical action or the use of action as a tool, rather than performing it as an event. In this case the stimuli data are given and accepted. In this country there is no exception to thinking that the government must be a republic. In logical thinking, as exemplified by scientific work, the premises and background are not given but deliberately and critically accepted as traditions of the knowledge system; such are scientific principles. In strictly psychological thinking actions, the data are elementary and private in accordance with the personal and comparatively unsophisticated character of the responses.

thinking as process comes close to the activities of proving, argument, and debate.

Are we in any sense minimizing the value of these fictions or abstraction products? By no means, for these are among the most valuable tools of thinking and problem solving actions when such activities transpire in abstract or theoretical domains. We must distinguish here, however, between the intimate psychological responses as instruments, and the formal objects or tools employed in the performance of thinking and other complex action. In the field of thinking and reasoning we may distinguish between the intimate behavior of a person and the more formal and descriptive thinking of the logician, just as in the field of language we may distinguish between the speech of the grammarian and the intimate speech behavior of a person.

No perspectival résumé of the situation in this domain can be concluded without referring to the period of functional logical thinking. Let us recall that when the biological influence began to make itself felt in psychology and the mind came to be thought of as a function in the life of animals, thinking was described as the problem solving function. Reasoning, as in the justly famous chapter of James, became the process of satisfying some interest or gratifying some personal curiosity. From this point the transition was easily made to the no less celebrated work of Dewey (How We Think, 1910) in which thinking acquired a decidedly psychological complexion.[1] From this nucleus we may date the entire corpus of tradition according to which thinking is connected with human needs and activities.

But all of this work is functional logic and not a behavior conception of thinking. Accordingly, two general wide divergences may be indicated between such handling of thinking and that contained in the present work. In the first place, since thinking according to the functional logical tradition is regarded as the working out of purposes of individuals, the whole trend of description is practical and overlooks the concrete manipulations of things for the purpose of attaining orientational attitudes and knowledge, in addition to making possible more effective further action. All thinking is accordingly transformed into concrete problem solving. As a matter of psychological fact, however, thinking and especially reasoning may be most abstruse and about the most impossible and improbable events. Thus to save itself from commerce with the transcendental or transcendent, functional logic has conceived of reasoning as well as thinking as phases of problem solving. But in the meantime, from the psychological standpoint are obliterated all the distinctions between

---

[1] Since this is a perspectival and not an historical résumé it is not necessary to go into a discussion of the general psychological and methodological tradition of logic, tracing its descent from Mill.

the numerous particular kinds of thinking, reasoning, and intellectual action, that may or may not have anything to do with genuine consequential problem solving. The attempt to escape this criticism has been made by asserting that thinking occurs when habits are interfered with. In point of fact, however, thinking as it actually occurs sufficiently refutes this formalistic proposition since it actually operates on a large habit or equipmental basis. In this sense, too, the specific autonomous minor thinking activities such as estimating, assuming, speculating, reflecting, etc., have been given no room in the functional logical tradition. Even the functional logical tradition confines itself to conception or meaning, judging, and inference, even though it already represents a withdrawal from the more static phases of formal logic, such as the term, proposition, and syllogism which are presumed to be correlates of the former processes.

In the second place, since this is, after all, functional logic and not psychological activity, there has been no definite escape from the formal and conventional techniques of action. Logic after all merely typifies entire situations. No matter how functional logic may be as compared with absolutistic thought, it always must deal with more or less standard techniques of thinking from a psychological standpoint. The emphasis is upon the thinking as definite processes and not upon momentary and contingential interactions of the individual and particular stimuli objects. From the standpoint of psychology functional logic, as well as the still more formal types, leaves no place for the intimate behavior facts which may be referred to as the striving for personal satisfaction and the agony of defeat in not being able to solve a problem or draw an inference. Yet these among other private activities may have a great effect upon the course and conclusion of thinking and reasoning.

Organismic psychology, because it considers thinking activities in all of their phases as specific modes of interaction with specific stimulational circumstances, stands out as a different view. Its chief merit lies in bringing to light all the varieties of activities that legitimately fall under the general category of thinking. It esteems any kind of action as a member of a certain class merely when the stimulus-response interaction constitutes a particular type of event. We observe, then, that according to the organismic view it is not merely imperative to distinguish between thinking, intellectual conduct, and reasoning whether or not they are serious and consequential behavior, but also to take specific account of the particular occasions for thinking and the corresponding particularities of individual thinking and reasoning conduct.

It might be added that while reasoning behavior has not been neglected as much as thinking, it has especially suffered from the logicizing of the descriptions. This circumstance exists although it was realized long ago that reflective individuals throughout their practical activities constantly perform inferences of all sorts. Probably it is the intensely personal and intimate character of reasoning responses as behavior techniques that makes such actions subject to abstract formulation.

# CHAPTER XXIII

## THE PSYCHOLOGY OF LANGUAGE[1]

The Problems of Language

If we include under the heading of language all of its varieties of expressive and communicative behavior we find that it is not far from our most pervasive form of action. Not a moment of our lives passes without the performance of a great many language reactions either alone or in conjunction with other types of behavior. Consider that language reactions comprise not only speaking and reading but also are essentially involved in such complex behavior as musing, desiring, thinking, dreaming, planning, and willing. In fact, we might say that language responses not only constitute important autonomous adaptations to stimuli but parallel and complement almost all of our complex behavior. In spite of this condition, however, there exists to-day hardly the beginnings even of an adequate analysis of the psychology of language.

Among the important problems in language study is the preliminary isolation of the psychological facts of language from numerous other language forms. Since language constitutes the subject matter of several humanistic sciences, it is extremely necessary to differentiate the psychological facts of language phenomena from other linguistic data. For language is not only a series of specific responses to particular stimuli; it is just as certainly a cultural fact, a matter of historical development, of social custom, etc. Now it is precisely the circumstance that language belongs to different domains of investigation which makes it difficult to keep separate the different approaches to language study, but which at the same time make it so rigorously imperative that such a distinction between different data be observed. Penalties in abundance pursue us when we confound the different types of language data, for then we almost inevitably misinterpret our facts. After such a differentiation we must work out in detail precisely what occurs when psychological language reactions are performed. The solution of these problems leads to the further inquiry concerning the acquisition, development, and classification of the psychological facts of linguistic conduct.

Differentiation of Psychological from Other Language Data

For the reasons we have just indicated, we shall find it most expedient to differentiate the facts of psychological language from (1) the anthropological, (2) philological, and (3) from symbological forms. It is with these types of data that psychological language facts are most intricately interrelated and most deplorably confused.

[1] This chapter is founded upon an article entitled, "An Analysis of Psychological Language Data", published in *Psychol. Rev.*, 1922, 29, 267–309.

Our interest here is probably best served by a brief consideration of the nature of language data with respect to each of these disciplines.

Language from an anthropological standpoint may be considered first as a cultural product exactly like other products of cultural development and practise. As such, language consists of a tool, or a set of distinct tools, useful for particular purposes, as are canoes, arrows, pottery, etc., found among particular groups of human beings. Secondly, the language of a group may be looked upon as a specific kind of action of that group. In this case language activities are actions of particular groups precisely as are their religious ceremonials, their economic conduct, songs, dances, etc. Now, such language activity constitutes the materials of a statistical and descriptive study of the conduct of a group of human beings. Whether the language activities are considered to be cultural products of particular sorts, institutional or cultural entities, or statistical and descriptive action of the various groups, the anthropological interest is to describe the distribution of such cultural features, to trace their origin or development, and the influences of languages upon each other, etc. Anthropological Language Data

It is especially important to distinguish anthropological from psychological language data because anthropological facts obviously come very close to psychological ones. What makes the distinction of psychological language from anthropological language especially confusing is the fact that the data of anthropological language, that is to say, language customs and traditions, constitute genuine though potential phases of psychological behavior segments, to wit, stimuli to language responses. That is to say, it is undoubtedly true that when individuals begin to develop language reactions in infancy this development is subject to the conditioning pressure of language customs and institutions developed by their groups, but until such institutions actually function as stimuli to language reactions they cannot be called psychological facts. Anthropological language activities must therefore be looked upon as abstracted behavior of communities and not as concrete responses of persons to specific stimuli.

Much the same care employed in distinguishing between psychological and anthropological phases of language must be exercised in keeping distinct psychological and philological aspects. For philological data and interpretations are concerned mainly with fixed forms of socially prevalent language institutions, their types, relationships and periodic variation [1] and not at all with the concrete forms of language responses which especially concern the psychologist. And so we may say that the philologist gets no closer to the psychologist's data than does the anthropologist, although the philologist may be exclusively concerned with the facts of some particular language, and not languages as social institutions. That is to say, the philologist may also deal with the institutional stimuli of genuine language reactions but this is only one kind of language fact, and one which, Philological Language Data

[1] As exemplified by such laws as Grimm's, Grassmann's, Verner's, etc.

unless it is contained in an actual response situation, or behavior segment, consists of conventions of speech rather than speech itself. When the philologist's material is not part of a behavior segment, such as the contents of a book when it is not being read, this material may be considered to be merely a physical object. Here we have the various levels of analysis, phonemes, morphemes, semantemes, phrases, sentences, etc. It is not incorrect to say that the philologist is interested in evidences of speech, spoken or written, as well as in standards of speech and is only remotely concerned with the psychological adaptations constituting language behavior, for the latter involves much more than is comprised in customary speech. To be brief, the philologist is essentially interested in fixed modes of phonetic systems and their symbolic representation and not in actual responses to stimuli.

Because the philologist is interested in conventional sounds and their symbolization, his data and interpretations cannot be directly accepted by the psychologist. In the first place, many of the philologist's problems fall outside of the province of psychology since they have developed entirely as historical facts. Among such facts are the problems of gender, the development of inflection or analysis and the absence of words expressing abstract ideas. In the second place, the philologist is moved by his interest in the conventional to exclude interjectional reactions or to think of them as evolutionary prototypes of standardized speech, in other words, to place too great emphasis upon standard words whether as roots or affixes or as combinations of the two. And in the third place, the philologist assumes that language is a vehicle for the communication of ideas through technical and even logical elements, namely, sentences.[1] To accept the philologist's material manifestly would put the psychologist at great disadvantage. It would cause him to overemphasize the crystallized products and results of historical reactions and to pay scant attention to actual present behavior.

**Symbological Language Data** Among other non-language data which must be kept distinct from psychological materials are the logical and symbological facts. Writers in these fields look upon words and language in general as symbols which in their isolation and combination refer to things. The words of a sentence for example may individually be signs for things while a series of words which constitutes a sentence may like-

---

[1] Obviously we cannot stop here to differentiate between the innumerable different attitudes of philologists concerning the motive and function of language. Accordingly we accept the above statement as the most effective contribution of the philologist (cf. Gardiner, "Some Thoughts on the Subject of Language," *Man*, 1919, 19, 2–6, and "The Definition of the Word and the Sentence," *British Journal of Psychology*, 1922, 12, 352–361), without considering the philological attitude that language is thought (mental process) or the duplicate or expression thereof. Furthermore, we must not overlook the fact that since philologists and other students of language are dealing with the same phenomena they must at some point approach the psychological attitude toward language.

wise be considered to be such a symbol.[1]  When the references involve communication (verbal or graphic reactions) the symbols may be regarded as language.  But the symbological and logical study of words and gestures are not essentially concerned with written or spoken acts, for the latter are only specimens of any type of thing which represent or can be substituted for something else.  It is the symbol or sign, as such, which is the subject-matter of this type of inquiry.

Naturally here, as in the case of the other studies which involve language, there is considerable overlapping with psychology but the problems and methods are quite distinct.  For example, when the symbologist is handling linguistic materials he looks upon them as substitutive counters rather than verbal or gestural acts, which may be functional symbols.  For the symbologist a word must have an invariable one-to-one relationship with some other particular thing.  For the psychologist on the other hand, words are only symbols as accidental references to things.  At various stated periods different words or gestures may stand for the same thing while at any given period different language elements may represent the object or referent.

Clearer still is the difference between the two viewpoints with respect to the character of linguistic elements.  Instead of investigating referential stimulus-response activities the symbologist is interested in the differences between the symbolic character of words.  The latter are taken to be either sounds or meanings but each is considered of course to be an object instead of an action.  In general the logician must handle his data as symbolic things rather than acts.

Further problems of the symbologist or logician which distinguish him from the psychologist concern the proper or improper, the adequate or inadequate, symbolization of things by various signs or symbols.  A specialized problem in this connection concerns whether or not the symbols stand for an existent when circumstances require that it should.  In short, the logician is intensely interested in the symbolical use of words.  Again, does the symbol actually refer to something or does it only serve to call out an affective response?  These and other logical problems lead to the question of definition; when are things and events properly defined, properly or adequately symbolized?  Symbols that are actually written or spoken words can only be authentic language by express intention of the individual who uses them.  It is entirely incorrect, therefore, to say from a psychological standpoint that language is "a system of signs, different from the things signified, but able to suggest them," for while this definition does touch some psychological language facts, namely, those in which language acts serve as signs, it excludes essential features

[1] The symbological and logical aspects of language are ably and interestingly treated by Ogden and Richards, *The Meaning of Meaning*, 1923.

of language and replaces them with the data of logic or symbolism.

In striking contrast to all of the above treatments of linguistic phenomena the psychologist must look upon language as a series of intimate actions of particular persons, speaking, reading, listening, gesturing, and interjecting, in short, adaptive responses.   As a student of language the psychologist is not interested in the sheer existence of language or languages even when they are considered to be reactional products.   Nor is he concerned with historical or statistical developments and descriptions of language as they now exist or have existed in the past unless those data are treated as specific activities of individuals to particular stimulation conditions.   To differentiate between psychological and other investigations of language, we might specify that the transmissive and receptive aspects of both spoken and written communicative behavior are on both sides concrete bistimulational actions,[1] and not merely responses to and between persons.   In this sense the psychological fact of language is different from the philological which is merely presumed to be making sounds or gestures which it is intended another person will hear and understand.

In sum, from the psychological standpoint language comprises various sorts of adjustmental behavior, diverse forms of adaptations to surrounding stimuli.   Such reactions in common with other types of psychological response, serve as definite means of accomplishing specific results.   In consequence, for the psychologist language reactions are unique, personal, and sometimes practically serviceable or expressive reactions.[2]   In many ways linguistic conduct may be looked upon as an extension of the person's actions and especially when we think of how much further one can go in written descriptions than in pointing or reciting.   Whatever is common or standard about such behavior is due entirely to the commonness and the institutional character of the stimuli which condition the acquisition of the specific phases of language reactions and call them out when they are acquired.

Linguistic studies provide us with numerous practical criteria to indicate the differences between psychological and other kinds of language.   For instance language students have great difficulty in defining what a word is.[3]   The statement of what a word is in one language breaks down completely when it is made to apply to words in other languages.   Also words from various languages exhibit great differences in form, structure, and function.   The same thing is true,

---

[1] See below, p. 218.

[2] Doubtless it is caution in excess to suggest that this conception has nothing to do with the similarly expressed metaphysical idea of the intuitive and momentarily existing expression of psychic states as developed by a long line of philosophers and philologists including Vico, Herder Hamann, von Humboldt, Steinthal, Croce, etc.   Cf. Croce's treatment of these writers in his *Aesthetic*, 1922.

[3] Cf. Vendreyes, *Language*, 1925, p. 87.

of course, in the case of sentences and various other linguistic units. These variations and incongruities indicate in an unmistakable way the divergence between crystallized grammatical forms and the concrete referential acts of persons.

Another such criterion of the differences between psychological and non-psychological aspects. of language is the lack of permanent identity or the fluctuation of the parts of speech.[1] The actual language activities stop at no formal variants in the functional organization of word types. Similarly, the inevitable illogical character of speech and other linguistic forms indicate the variation between acting in order to adapt oneself, and using instruments that have prescribed functions and conventional existences. Again the incommensurability of written and spoken language in any group or for any person points to particular actions, in the one case, and to structural or logical formalities in the other. Although the latter are also actions, they are describable as following a pattern or demand of custom. This difference is very similar to the variation between affective and logical action.[2] The former is presumed to refer to the specific speaker's participation in language behavior with all his stresses, accents, and gesticulations. Logical action is merely the performance of an action which may be performed by anybody. It is nothing but the passing on of symbols. A similar difference, but one not thought of as being induced in the hearer, is referred to as the distinction between the emotive and the symbolic use of language.[3] In both cases we see the division between specific adaptational acts of individuals and the more solid existence of linguistic institutions.

Because language is so exceedingly difficult to isolate from other actions occurring at the same time, and so complicated in description, it is essential to formulate as clear a criterion as possible with which to distinguish language responses from other kinds of psychological action. Upon reviewing a large number of linguistic facts we arrive at the principle that language reactions are inherently indirect or referential adaptations to stimuli. In order to examine and establish this criterion it is best at first to contrast language reactions with some of the most direct and immediate forms of response. Such direct responses are illustrated by simple performative reflex actions as well as by complex æsthetic reactions to works of art or even by thinking of some thing or person. Such acts have no further reference to present or non-present objects or persons; nothing else but the directly functioning stimulus and response are involved in the behavior segment.

*What are the Psychological Characteristics of Language?*

Generalizing the fact of indirectness of action which characterizes language behavior, we might say that language involves at least two stimuli, the adjustment stimulus (the thing, event, or person talked

---

[1] Cf. *Vendreyes,* loc. cit. pp. 115–136, Sapir, *Language,* 1921, pp. 123 ff.
[2] Vendreyes, pp. 137–154.
[3] Cf. Ogden and Richards, *The Meaning of Meaning,* 1923, Ch. 7.

about, referred or otherwise responded to) and the auxiliary or indirect stimulus (the object, or the act of a person provoking the language action, whether talking, thinking, or some sort of overt behavior).

Now we must be careful to observe here that we are not dealing with two objects having a simple stimulational function but with two distinct stimulational functions, whether or not they are brought out by the same object, both of which events may occur. Moreover, these two stimuli are simultaneously operative in their functioning. This means, of course, that we have two responses both in the case of the speaker and the auditor. In the former instance, there is a reference act (indirect) and a command act, and in the latter a reference act and an understanding (indirect) response. In both cases these two actions constitute the essentially linguistic behavior whatever else the persons may be doing at the time.

Illustrative of the indirectness of language behavior is the ordinary conversation or communication reaction. "A" desires to have a book picked up from the floor; he therefore offers "B" a verbal reference, or gestural stimulus which we may call the auxiliary or indirect stimulus, and which serves as the means to bring about "B's" reaction to the book. The book may be called, for our present purposes, the adjustment stimulus. What is essentially language in this situation is the direct action that "A" performs with respect to the object picked up. The specific means by which the indirect reaction is accomplished, whether through spoken words or pointing gestures, make no difference with respect to the language features of the situation.

Perhaps we can appreciate more clearly the operation of the indirect response when we alter our point of vantage from that of the speaker (or the person who uses language as an instrument to bring about an indirect response to a stimulus object) to that of the hearer or auditor (the person who is involved in the actual carrying out of the reaction). Now while the latter person adjusts himself directly to the adjustment stimulus object, he is involved at the same time in an indirect response to the request or speech stimulus.

But here we can imagine someone saying, "Is this action of picking up the book not a direct response on the part of 'B' to the request of 'A' as stimulus?" We must admit that considerable ambiguity exists here but, we believe, with respect only to the name of the stimulus. For it is probable that "B" is in fact performing a direct action not to "A", but rather to "A's" request. But if the latter is true then, because the action of "A" (the request or command) is a referential act, "B's" response itself cannot but refer to the book. Hence the request is only an auxiliary stimulus. If we do not grant this, then we may still say that the person who gives the command is not like an ordinary natural object in his rôle as stimulus. To an ordinary natural object we can only perform direct action, both when the object serves as substitution and as adjustment stimulus, while the significance of a person as a stimulus lies precisely in the fact that he can refer to things aside from himself by means of conventional signs, which he and those with whom he communicates [1] have developed in common social situations. The two stimuli can be equally well analyzed both when the person talks to himself and when he is reacting to another person. That is to say, when I speak to myself about myself I am both adjustment and auxiliary stimulus to myself as acting person. Again, when I perform a direct reaction to an object, say a fright or startle response to an automobile which barely misses striking me, that object or the accident situation may be both auxiliary and adjustment stimulus for a secondary or indirect reaction. It is possible, of course, that we can react directly to persons as we do to ordinary natural objects but in this case we should not attempt to consider any phase of the situation as language.

While the form of language we have just been discussing and which we name communicative may be called fairly typical, it is not by far the most important or the most widely prevalent of our language behavior. But it is certain, however, that in all behavior properly denominated language we can distinguish the two stimulating situations or circumstances. And upon the particular mode of contact with these two stimuli we can establish the criterion of indirectness for language reactions.

Two types of indirectness or degrees of language reactions may be distinguished upon the basis of what might be considered from a biological, social or utility standpoint as the absence of direct adjustments to stimuli, or perhaps the absence of any overtly adjustmental behavior. For example, language in the form of casual conversation may be considered from a biological standpoint not adaptive at all, while language in the form of instructions or commands may from the same standpoint be regarded as indirectly adaptive. In general, we might name the two degrees of indirect action (1) mediative and (2) referential language. The criterion for distinction is the closeness to a direct response, the referential being the farthest removed. And so we might consider as referential all the language behavior we call ordinary conversation and the exclamatory reactions which substitute for direct reactions. Now, although it is true that in the case of some referential behavior, a direct reaction to a stimulus is out of the question, in the sense that it need never occur (as for example, casual conversation), still the criterion of indirectness is just as valid in such cases as when some direct reaction is possible. Under the division of mediative behavior we can place all the language reactions that are in some form or other connected with direct reactions, that is, those responses which are instrumental in provoking direct action or which are closely associated with it.

*Mediative and Mere Referential Indirect Reactions*

[1] Really all those who use the language.

In practise language responses may be said to be related to direct action in four ways, namely, they may precede, accompany, follow, or substitute for it. It will serve to illustrate the indirect character of language reactions to discuss briefly here the four different ways in which they operate. We find that the language responses that precede, accompany, or follow, direct action belong under the mediative heading, while the substituting type of language reactions we will call referential, in that it need not bear directly upon any direct action.

**Language as Preceding Reactions**

Various forms of preceding language responses may be isolated. A clear-cut case is that in which language is used to induce someone to perform a direct action upon an object. Here we have the ordinary case of instructional or directing language. We may call this a practical or instrumental use of language. In other cases our preceding language may be the overt or expressed wish, hope, or plan to perform an action with respect to a certain stimulus object or situation. While for theoretical purposes there is no difference between this expressive type of language and instrumental speech, in our practical circumstances their variations turn out to be quite significant. And this is true whether or not the preceding indirect language act is or is not followed by direct action. In case the direct action does not occur, or there is a definite certainty that it will not occur, we must place this preceding act in the class of referential language.

**Language as Accompanying Reactions**

To illustrate language as accompanying or simultaneously occurring indirect reactions we may take the case of responding to a picture by way of admiring or disliking it and at the same time voicing or otherwise indicating the nature of our direct response to this object. Here, of course, the direct responses may be the person's own thought or feeling reactions which are accompanied by language behavior.

**Language as Following Reactions**

What in many cases is very close to accompanying reactions may actually be indirect following responses which may be definitely determined by preceding direct responses. Such succeeding indirect responses are exemplified by the act of telling someone what effect some object or situation has had upon one. The student who tells one of his companions of the pangs he suffered during an examination is performing definitely succedent indirect reactions which are quite different from those indirect reactions that we assume to have accompanied the actual examination. To sing by way of glorifying, or to bewail what has happened also comprise indirect succedent responses. Of these succedent responses a large number may be subsumed under the heading of reference language reactions.

**Language as Substitute Reactions**

Let the reader observe that as a matter of fact our four conditions of indirect action resolve themselves into two general conditions, namely, indirect action (1) associated with (preceding, accompanying, or following) other responses, and indirect action (2) substituted for direct action.   Our three aforementioned language types, as we stated at the outset, belong of course under the first or associational heading and now we must illustrate indirect responses which substitute for or replace direct action.   Substitutional language does not influence, or need not necessarily influence, any direct action, while in the associative type of language there may be such an influence.   As an example of a substitute language reaction we may take the case of the person who, instead of rushing into a burning building to rescue a child, merely exclaims in a variety of ways what he sees.   In this sense language reactions may substitute for and represent any kind of action or event that one has participated in, as well as meaning, thoughts, and similar forms of behavior.

The indirectness of language responses as we have been attempting to establish it, can be very readily and very convincingly observed during the formation of language habits by the infant.[1]   The observer must be struck with the differences between the language responses and the necessities and desires of the infant, as well as with the specific responses of the infant in satisfying those wants or of the person who aids in their accomplishment.[2]   The indirectness of the reaction can perhaps be no better established than by the reflection upon the numerous ways in which the language reaction can be carried out, especially if we consider the different language reactions of different groups and the varying language responses of the members of any given group.

Lest our emphasis of the indirectness of language reactions be thought too persistent we proffer the defensive suggestion that because our task here is that of definitely marking off one type of psychological response from other sorts of psychological behavior, we cannot be too exact in our descriptions.   Especially is this true since not only are language reactions, like all other psychological phenomena, specific responses to particular stimuli, but they are not always morphologically different from other types of behavior.   Of a surety when we think of verbal responses as language, we cannot make many mistakes in differentiating what is, from what is not language, but just as surely must we realize that verbal responses are not by far the only kinds of language reaction, nor are indeed verbal reactions always language activities.[3]

With a myriad voices, though with no intention at all, has philological science, as well as popular thought, celebrated the indirectness

[1] See Watson's (aside from the "neurology") excellent statement, *Behavior*, 1914, pp. 329 ff.

[2] It is for this reason no doubt that language reactions are called substitute responses.  We do not believe that substitution is a general characteristic of language reactions although such a description fits well some language types, and especially the talk that substitutes for knowledge and thinking.

[3] For example, naming an object may no more be a language reaction than looking at it, for all the laryngeal processes involved.

of language reactions.[1] This characterization of indirectness has been achieved by looking upon language responses and their graphic representations as symbols of meanings and as indicators of concepts or ideas. To us it is manifest that no matter what view we take concerning the nature of concepts or ideas, we must consider them as forms of implicit or incipient processes. For our own part, of course, meanings, ideas, and concepts are also definite forms of psychological responses. We say that philological science and popular thought do not intentionally make language into indirect behavior, because as a matter of fact the symbolic character of language does not lie in any reference to mental or psychic processes as popular psychology would have it, but rather in the instrumental or mediative function of language responses. Not all language is meaning behavior, but it is true that an exceedingly large amount of our language reactions serves as means or instruments for bringing about or for carrying on other types of action, or otherwise accomplishing our purposes; so that the referential or indirect character of language has been generally observed and recorded.

How such observations were made we may infer from the fact that when anyone speaks of things or events not present, or asks someone to do something, he must surely note that his action is indirect and referential with respect to the absent thing or the thing the other person acts upon. Were it generally appreciated that ideas and concepts are merely implicit reactions to stimuli, that is to say, actual responses, then it might be overtly recognized that language constitutes indirect reactions connected with concepts and ideas as direct responses to the same stimuli objects. But whether concepts, meanings, and ideas are properly or improperly defined in popular psychology, the very fact that they are connected with language indicates clearly that language is fairly universally recognized to be indirect behavior, especially when the popular view concerning ideas and meanings is correctly interpreted, that is, as definite behavior facts.

But here a very important problem presents itself, namely, the connection of language and ideational or thought processes. How are these processes in fact related? Are they perhaps identical? Such an identity indeed suggests itself through the circumstance that both thought and language are mediate activities. Recently this identification has been strenuously urged in an attempt to show that thoughts (concepts, ideas) are not mental substances or psychic processes. Certainly from an objective psychological standpoint, thought cannot be considered as anything but adaptational responses to stimuli. Because of the close relation and apparent similarity between thought and language it will add greatly to our understanding of language to compare the two processes, and if they are not identical to mark lan-

---

[1] For example, when language is thought of as primarily metaphorical or originating in metaphors. Are not metaphors in a sense verbal substitutes for pointing, in the absence of the object pointed to?

guage off definitely from thinking.  To the discussion of this relation between the two kinds of behavior we devote another division of our study.

Because of the multiplicity of occasions for language adjustments and the consequent differences in their variety it is essential to provide some descriptive definiteness and order for such reactions.  Two tasks especially confront us here.  The first is to mark off what are actual language reactions from behavior which may closely resemble language and yet not be language.  And secondly, we must distinguish between totally different modes of definitely established language reactions, for in failing to do this we might exclude from our enumeration authentic language reactions, as would be the case, for example, were we to confine language to merely verbal speech. *Modes of Language Reactions*

First we must point out that only upon a functional basis can we accomplish our first classificatory purposes, namely, the separation of language from non-language behavior.  Even where we find behavior which is morphologically similar to other kinds of unmistakable language activities we must withhold from it the name of language unless it serves a language function.  In other words, it must serve as indirect reactions or adjustments.  Suppose I wish to have my typewriter operate more smoothly but cannot make the necessary changes myself.  I must therefore let my wishes be known to someone who is able to carry them out.  My psychological adaptation is made by means of verbal speech or by pointing. *Morphological and Functional Language*

In contrast to this definite functional operation of language behavior it may happen that I utter perfectly formed words or perform other genuinely linguistic reactions which will not at all serve as instrumental or even indirect adjustmental acts.  These, then, we exclude from the domain of functional language.  An example would be the words we utter as replacement reactions in emotional situations.  Along with the large number of reflexes that replace the absent final reaction system in emotional behavior segments we may utter words, mere verbalizations that are really acquired reflexes which, because of the fundamentally non-adjustmental character of emotional reactions, no more adapt the person to his surroundings than do the reflexes.[1]

Again, the use of words by infants in imitation of bits of conversation overheard also illustrates what is perfect language morphologically, but what at the same time is not in the least language functionally.  It is possible also that words and phrases used by dissociated and otherwise abnormal persons (verbigeration) exemplify morphological similarities to language responses but are certainly not themselves such behavior.

When we turn to other than verbal language reactions the criteria for differentiating between language and other forms of behavior cannot be so well made, since there is not the sharp division here between

[1] Cf. Chapter XVI.

morphology and function that there is in the case of vocal language reactions. But since we assume the criterion of language to be the question whether the person performs an indirect response, we can at least specify what are not language responses. For example, we can distinguish the true language reactions of the infant from its random acts that may be only morphologically language, if language at all. Thus the crying act of an infant may be considered both a definite indirect action serving to communicate to someone the child's uncomfortable situation and an expression of some such discomforting condition. On the other hand, from the language standpoint, the crying may be purely random action along with many other sorts of infant behavior which are merely indications of superabundant energy and in consequence not genuine language at all. The final criterion in every case, if it can be discovered, is the question whether the action is a direct response to a single stimulus, or an indirect response.

Our problem of distinguishing between what we call morphological language and genuine or functional language in the domain of graphic or printed speech is more simple. Here words, sentences, narration, description, etc., may not only not be genuine language in the sense of indirect adaptational responses, but they may even be non-psychological. In this department of language we may have merely symbols serving as records, as well as proverbs and maxims, which unless actually functioning as indirect or referential responses, may be looked upon as social institutions.

At this point it is well to observe that in a great many instances the differentiation between morphological and functional language is not equivalent to a complete rejection of morphological types. Possibly the distinction serves merely to point out some types of language that may become genuine functional linguistic activities. This is certainly the case when we consider vocal sounds as symbols which may at some particular time become language elements, perhaps for some specific group. Also in many instances the written or printed symbols have their specific forms as particularized stimuli correlated with specific modes of actual linguistic responses.

What can we say in this connection of implicit language behavior, since by becoming implicit such behavior loses its function of indirect overt adjustment? To this query we can only answer that we must accept the dictates of hard facts and agree that implicit language is not language, precisely as we say that spending money implicitly or partaking of a meal implicitly is not spending or eating. The criterion employed here is entirely a functional one. The question concerns what is actually done or accomplished. In our opinion we cannot avoid this conclusion, much as we may consent to the proposition that implicit language reactions are morphologically just like overt language responses.

To balance, as it were, this exclusion of a whole class of psychological reactions from the domain of language we must propose the unqualified inclusion of reactions which are frequently not treated as genuine language. This is specifically the case of interjectional reactions. Especially is this exclusion urged by those philologists who attempt either to exclude interjections from language phenomena altogether or to minimize the importance of such behavior. Why they do this is plain, since interjections are not conventionalized as are other forms of language. From the standpoint of reactions, however, such behavior answers as definitely and as effectively to the criteria of language activity as any other sort of language reaction. That is to say, interjectional language reactions function as means or instruments to express the conditions induced in the person by various surrounding individuals and events. What is true in the case of interjectional behavior is equally true in many other linguistic behavior situations.

At this point the question of observable and unobservable language responses arises. What shall we say of language reactions that are not observable to someone other than the linguistically reacting individual? Clearly, hidden or invisible reactions may be just as much genuine language reactions as the crudest gesture or loudest verbal speech. Once more we invoke the criterion of indirect response. Is it not just as likely that one will talk to oneself under certain conditions as to someone else? When the former is true the indirect response to things may be carried on by means of behavior hidden from the view of the bystander. For this reason, genuine linguistic reactions may occur when the auxiliary stimulus-person is entirely absent from the linguistic scene. The speech of the reacting person is a genuine language action whether or not the referee is present to hear or see the reference. The action is linguistic when the person reacts indirectly or referentially to the adjustment stimulus object. It is hardly necessary to add that the proposition made here is just as true for subvocal verbal reactions as for gestural responses of any sort.

One more point may be stressed here. The entire problem of morphological and functional language is clarified by considering the fact that some types of reference may be made in precisely the same way, although in each case the morphological character of the response is very different. Illustrative of such a situation is the same instrumental linguistic response when made with the vocabulary, accent, and stress of entirely different languages or dialects. If one can distinguish the sounds or gestures made, from the specific functions which they perform, a fairly exact distinction between morphological and genuine language is attained.

Within the field of functional language, that is to say, definite language reactions, we introduce a distinction of great importance. We may divide language into two large divisions, to each of which we apply a distinctive name, to wit, expressive and communicative language. *Expressive and Communicative Language*

In general, expressive language behavior comprises the individual's adjustments to stimuli which do not necessarily involve any direct relationship to another person. Expressive language reactions we may look upon, therefore, as in a sense the most illustrative of our indirect responses, since the exclusion of persons removes the possibility of a connection between language and any direct adjustment. But when the reaction results in leaving a record, the record may become a stimulus for some direct action and, in consequence, the original action may be considered as connected with a direct action. For example, I react favorably to a painting in an exhibition and express my admiration by writing "wonderful" opposite the catalogue number of the painting. This expression may become a stimulus (message) leading my friend to purchase the picture.

Is it not easy to see that expressive language better illustrates indirectness of response because of the passivity of the reacting individual? Expressive language activity is more of the nature of self-recording behavior, the registration of how some object, event, or person has affected us or how we should like or hope to have an event turn out, etc. Contrariwise, the communicative language reaction may take place through any number of intermediate persons as is illustrated by the passage of an order down through an ecclesiastical or military hierarchy. Certainly we can no better summarize the matter than to say that expressive language actions stand as responses only; they do not necessarily serve as stimuli for other persons as is the case with at least some of the communicative language reactions. In other words the referee is absent, or the referee may be anybody in general among a group or any sort of vague auxiliary stimulus.

Expressive language certainly is indirect, but it may nevertheless involve the elaborate employment of tools or instruments (pen, picture) for its production, but here the instruments are employed entirely to further the process of expression and not to effect some change in the adjustment stimulus object or to communicate to others the desire for such a change.

In all of this discussion let the reader note that we are not using the term "expression" in the sense of a verbal or gestural manifestation of a mental state. Such a warning is doubtless superfluous from the standpoint of our exposition but the mentalistic way of looking at the matter is so prevalent that we cannot too frequently assert our departure from that tradition.

In quite another sense we must guard against a misconstruction concerning expressive language, namely, the idea that it expresses, or is especially connected with, emotions. In some sense this view is intimately associated with the general idea that language is the expression of mental states, for here it is assumed that an emotion is the mental state expressed. Now the patent reply to such a view is the assertion that by means of expressive language the person performs actions involving what we may call ideas, desires, hopes, as well as reactions that adjust him indirectly to events past, present or future. From the standpoint of the actual adjustmental situation, expressive language is in no sense different from communicative language and in this we disagree with those who would make expressive language emotional, as compared with communicative language which is assumed to be mainly or exclusively the expression of ideas.

With respect to the morphological feature of expressive language reactions we might expect, because of the commonness of verbal behavior, that expressive language would consist to a great extent of verbal reactions. But as a matter of fact, typical expressive reactions consist to a considerable degree of gestures of various sorts, facial expressions, smirking, sneering, crying, smiling, laughing, etc.

Expressive language behavior may be divided into two types, namely, intentional and unintentional. By intentional expressive acts we refer to the indirect means of symbolical adjustment employed in the writing of prose or poetry and sometimes in talking to oneself or in uttering or writing a maxim or proverb. The intention here refers to the result rather than to the actual performance of the act, although the latter may be sometimes a definitely planned voluntary action. *Intentional and Unintentional Expressive Reactions*

The unintentional expressive reactions of which muttering (verbal response) and various non-verbal gestures are examples, are naturally more intimate responses involving no tools or other extension of the person's own organism. Not entirely different are all the reactions resulting from the intentional and non-intentional responses, for the products may be identical or similar. In uttering a proverb or maxim one may express oneself unintentionally as well as intentionally. Quite in accord with our expectation, then, we find that some expressive language reactions partake both of intentional and unintentional characteristics. Such expressive language behavior is illustrated by oaths and interjections of various sorts.

In contrast to expressive reactions, communicative language involves adjustment to some other person or persons. It consists to a considerable degree of intentional and substitutive responses [1] designed to bring about in the other person some change of an informational or overtly active sort with respect to the adjustment stimulus object or condition. We might indicate at this point that the criterion of communication depends upon the behavior of the second person rather than any result achieved by the first or stimulating individual. In plainer words, we have communicative language when the transmissive person's language reaction in the recipient. It follows, then, at this particular point that the different phases of communicative language must be determined exclusively with reference to directly observable, actually accomplished activities, that is to say, we need not consult the intentions or refer to the purposes of either person in the communicative situation. Whether or not they intended their language response to be heard or otherwise responded to is not *Communicative*

[1] Not substitute stimuli.

the problem here. But we do not mean to exclude from our observations of communicative reactions the distinction between language spontaneously addressed to another person, and language induced in the addressing person by a question or command of another. In the former case, we consider the indirect reaction to be initiated by the adjustment stimulus (the thing spoken of) which reaction is then also conditioned by the auxiliary stimulus, namely, the addressed person. The latter case, on the contrary, exhibits a reaction started off by the auxiliary stimulus (the person giving the command) which later, comparatively speaking, connects with the adjustment stimulus (the object reacted to in the carrying out of the command). It must be observed, however, that a definite purpose on the part of the first person is not essential as a characterizing feature of instrumental communicative language; it may well be that the conversational reactions in which I relate to a friend the incidents of my trip abroad will serve as an instrumental stimulus inducing him to take the same trip.

Purposes and intentions with respect to the adjustment stimulus do, however, make possible the distinction between conversation and instrumental speech. Conversational language is communicative speech in which the transmissive individual is not planning any definite, direct action with respect to the adjustment stimulus, while in instrumental communicative speech such a purpose and intention are manifest. That the purpose or intention refers to changes with respect to the adjustment stimulus and not to the actions of the speaker need hardly be pointed out. As a matter of actual practise, then, we find that in conversational communicative language action there are many adjustment stimuli or referents.

In suggesting examples of communicative language, we might mention verbal speech, and possibly song and music, as well as gestures (pointing), printing, writing, telegraphy, signaling, etc.

Poetry and other forms of literary production, when considered as language reactions, partake of both the expressive and communicative forms of language. As references to the æsthetic adaptations of persons they are of course expressive reactions. But on the other hand they serve to arouse reactions in other people in that the language responses (poems, for instance) of the first person are communicative as well as expressive. These reactions, which may be either intentional or unintentional, but not accidental, on the part of the reacting person, inform the stimulated person of some fact or condition by means of a symbolic or instrumental, that is, an indirect action.

**Receptive and Transmissive Communicative Reactions** It is very essential to distinguish, in the field of communicative language behavior, between the receptive and transmissive sorts of reactions. This distinction is made imperative by the fact that communicative language is interactional, that is, involves two persons. It may well be in many cases that we are speaking of exactly the same act or the same sort of action; but in the one case the actor communicates with someone else, whereas in the other, someone is being communicated with.  Or, we might say that in transmissive action the person's acts serve as stimuli to induce meaning reactions in a second person, whose receptive action is at the same time a stimulus to the first person to perform a meaning action, which again serves as a stimulus for the second, etc.  In general, communicative language typifies the closest and most intensive interstimulation and interresponse activity.

Among the (1) transmissive responses we may name for illustrative purposes, speaking, writing, making signs, gestures, etc., while among the (2) receptive language reactions we include hearing, touching, and seeing responses of all sorts.

As a final remark here, it is well to suggest that communicative language behavior is not necessarily more important or more complex as human performances than expressive language reactions.  Quite the contrary is true, in fact, since some expressive language reactions, such as poetry, are equally as important as any kind of communicative behavior and certainly much more complex than most speech reactions. That this point is almost obvious is seen from the fact that much expressive action may be communicative as well as expressive.

In summing up the psychological facts falling definitely under the heading of language behavior, we find a large series of reaction types beginning with shoulder shrugging and other forms of gesturing which grow by combination and integration out of non-language, expressive and manipulative actions and run up to the most complex and elaborate forms of verbal speech behavior.

Not only can we differentiate between the various stimulus-response language situations, as we did under the heading of modes, but we may also provide some arrangement for the vast amount of linguistic materials by classifying them according to the specific reaction systems involved.  Naturally enough, because of the similarities and overlappings in these reaction systems no hard and fast lines can be drawn between them; some order, however, is possible.  Accordingly, we plan to arrange a series of classes founded on the differences in communicative language, and cutting across the boundaries between communicative and expressive speech.  We base our classification on the communicative type of speech not only because greater simplicity and definiteness will thus be achieved but also because under communicative language every form of language act is represented.  Our greatest line of differentiation, then, will be that between the transmissive and receptive modes of action. *(Types of Language Reaction Systems)*

### PRIMARILY TRANSMISSIVE MODES OF LANGUAGE

Very prominent in the list of all language reactions is vocal speech. *(Vocal Speech [1])*

[1] It is not intended that this list should be arranged in the order of the importance of the reactions involved, since even in the absence of an objective standard it must be conceded that written language in complex cultural groups hardly stands second in functional value to vocal speech.

Not only has this type of language been developed as the most striking form of expressive and communicative adaptation, but it has become connected with, and instrumental to, some of the most complex behavior of which the human being is capable. Vocal speech is an integral factor in all of our voluntary and thinking action, as well as in our general social conduct. Under this heading we may place all the behavior phenomena which can be subsumed under the rubric of speech or talking.

**Vocal Gesture**

The vocal apparatus of the human individual is the instrument not only for our fully developed speech reactions, that is to say, formal verbal responses, but also for the simpler vocal gesturing, such as calling, crying, whistling, sighing, singing, grunting in infants, and other forms. Vocal gesturing, while ordinarily expressive language behavior, can also function as definitely communicative expressive language reactions. We might look upon our examples as finished and complete reactions which are coördinate with formal verbal actions; but they may also be partial and simple actions. In this latter sense they simply supply color and emphasis to verbal responses. For an illustration of this type of vocal gesturing, we may contrast the fullness of speech found in the cultured and sometimes pompous speaker with the linguistic activity of the person who offers in his speech only a minimum symbolic action of the required vocabulary. Not infrequently the richness of vocal gesturing distinguishes speakers of different dialectical groups as well as individuals of different cultural backgrounds who use the same dialect.

**Sub-Vocal Speech**

Besides overt and complete language behavior we have many kinds which are not audibly performed. Among such reactions are silent speech and reading responses and more typically, perhaps, those language activities serving as phases of what is known as "mental" arithmetic, etc. By far the most of our complex behavior (planning, brooding and various forms of thinking) includes many types of sub-vocal language. The student of language may well question whether these reactions are primarily transmissive since we can readily think of numerous instances in which they serve receptive functions, but in view of the fact that self-communication, in which they are transmissively employed is so common, we include them here.

**Non-vocal Gesturing**

Much of our language behavior goes on in the form of gestures; in fact, since we include under this rubric most of the language reactions not involving vocal or verbal behavior, the scope of gesturing conduct is very great. Such behavior comprises a wide variety of forms; here we have deaf and dumb language, shoulder shrugging, facial gesturing and movements of the eyes, arms, hands, head, etc.

Gestures function not only as primary and exclusive language adaptations to various stimuli but also as adjunct responses along with other language reactions. Thus the motions of fingers, hands and arms, the shrugging of the shoulders and numerous sorts of facial expression constitute the more or less essential accompaniments of vocal speech. So important are such accompanying reactions in many cases that without them vocal reactions carry little or no significance. A field experiment in this connection involves the observation of the degree of understanding which we derive from listening to conversation when it is both accompanied and unaccompanied by gestural responses.

Possibly it is not irrelevant to assert that gestural language represents almost every phase of human adjustment to stimuli. It may express and communicate thought, feeling, desire, the state of health, kind of disease, activity, and other forms of adjustment. By means of language gestures we perform almost every sort of adaptation that we can otherwise execute.

Very numerous are those language reactions requiring some extension of the organism's natural equipment for their execution. While vocal and bodily gesturing involve merely our own elaborate organismic equipment, other forms of language behavior comprise the use of instruments such as a pencil, pen, graver, pennants, type and paper, skins, stones, and other impressible materials as well as sound-making (telegraph) and other types of mediating tools. Such instruments are employed not only for our own personal activities but also for our complex social responses, since the most important technical and scientific information can be intentionally conveyed by the use of such instrumental reactions. It is most interesting to observe that the language reactions in which we employ tools for sign-making are not different in principle from our complex verbal reactions. The latter also involve definite autonomous tools or instruments, that is to say, sound combinations or symbols. Is not the entire set of materials with which the philologist deals formal symbolic tools employed by specific groups of individuals as media of intercourse, tools which are modified and developed to suit their own specific needs? In comparing sign and symbol language with verbal responses we find the greatest difference to lie merely in the fact that the latter are performed exclusively with our own organismic equipment. Examples of this sign-symbol class of language responses are writing, mathematical symbols, musical notes, printing, picture drawing as in the case of the cave dweller, using codes of all varieties including the employment of stamps and flowers, also wigwagging and signaling. In their respective fields many of these forms of reference making are just as effective as verbal behavior.

In considering the graphic forms of sign and symbol making, that is to say, writing and printing, we observe that special significance attaches to the fact that these reactions require for their performance an extension of the person's organic equipment. We can thereby not only extend the scope of our immediate behavior, as illustrated by the difference in transmitting information and other materials by word of mouth or gestures, but we can also obtain thereby a more permanent record. Sign-symbol language is a perpetuating form of action

**Making Signs and Symbols**

and permits of the extension and transmission of responses in the form of desires and information over long periods of time and through great areas of space. We may mention here the vast body of information concerning ancient civilizations which the people of those times have supplied to us through the instrumentality of signs on bricks, clay tablets, monuments, etc. They have communicated to us by the same means, their desires, willings, thoughts, and other manners of response as well as the things and conditions which surrounded and concerned them.

While expressive language is not excluded from this type, as witness the inclusion of picture and other forms of writing, these reactions on the whole serve to convey our ideas, wants, desires, etc., in a more formal manner than expressive behavior.

Is music language? By no means. Despite the common belief that this is the case we must utterly deny it. A possible reservation perhaps may be made in favor of so-called program music. Such means one may use to make references to various adjustment stimuli, especially of the expressive form. But perhaps insofar as such references are made we are not dealing with music but with something else. We may add, then, that all kinds of sounds including those ordinarily employed in music may be used in reference making. In this statement it is understood, of course, that we are talking of actual sound making and not sound products of any sort. In this sense we may converse by singing as well as by non-musical vocal action.

## PRIMARILY RECEPTIVE REACTIONS

While, as a matter of fact, receptive language reactions consist mainly of definite seeing and hearing responses, we may generalize all of the characteristically receptive reactions and group them under the heading of understanding. In so doing we not only generalize all the specific reactions but we separate them from the understanding reactions, which are precurrent to, or anticipatory of, final language reactions. This separation is made possible primarily by the fact that in the majority of cases the seeing or hearing acts are precurrent understanding reactions which may accompany other precurrent acts of an implicit or partially implicit nature, while the end reactions in a language behavior segment are overt responses. We might point out also that the justification for separating the understanding reactions from the rest of the behavior segment lies in the possibility it affords of a better comprehension of the whole series of factors.

Understanding responses are meaning reactions. That is to say, they function as means to the performance of some other act, and may be roughly said to consist of a realization or discrimination of the stimulus object or condition. This realization makes for an appropriate final response. The degree of realization ascribable to the meaning response depends upon whether the precurrent reactions in a behavior segment are or are not exclusively overt. As a matter of fact, the simplest sort of understanding reaction is one which involves no discernible precurrent reaction at all but only the one overt reaction system. Such a case is illustrated by the incident in which pulling the hand away is practically a part of the hearing of the admonition to "look out for the saw." Or, we might say that a simple reaction system includes the linguistic hearing act plus the reply, with whatever amount of language that involves. If the stimulus calls out definite precurrent acts, but only overt ones (as is the case when we first exclaim, "Oh, a saw," and then pull our hand away) we assume that there is a greater degree of understanding or comprehension of the situation involved. Even more understanding or comprehension of the stimulating situation must be ascribed to the precurrent receptive language reactions when they accompany or precede thinking actions. In these cases we have very complex behavior segments or behavior patterns which are a combination of thinking and language reactions. It is probably because these complex combination responses are so striking that the mistake is made of identifying language and thought. The reader must observe that in all of our illustrations we have assumed that the language reactions are indirectly adapting responses connected with direct overt and implicit responses. Such are the typical ways in which our language reactions operate, for in the final analysis they are always definite adaptational reactions and are thus conditioned by the stimulating auspices. Further, it must be observed that although in our illustrations we dealt with language understanding responses serving as precurrent functions, such reactions may themselves be final responses.

To turn now to the more specific receptive language reactions we find a series of definite types of understanding responses to a variety of different stimulating situations requiring different modes of contact (visual, auditory, etc.). Reading, for example, covers a series of responses to language stimuli seen, while audienting composes a number of responses to sound objects heard. The reaction systems operating here involve especially the visual and auditory receptor mechanisms, the optic and auditory neural pathways, localizable cortical mechanisms, all sorts of muscular mechanisms (eye, head, chest, laryngeal) and various speech processes. These different specific comprehension and seeing responses, it is well to observe, may involve different orders of action on the part of the responding individual. The stimuli of the comprehension and language reactions may be (1) intimate internal mechanisms in the sense of actual speech, or (2) partially external mechanisms as in the employment of signs or (3) mainly non-organismic mechanisms as in writing or printing.

Reading and Audienting Reactions

The term reading, let us note, covers not only the ordinary acts of perusing print but also all forms of visual reactions to linguistic

stimuli. Thus, we may speak of reading facial expressions and ges
tures of all sorts, besides lip reading in its various forms. In all these
cases reading constitutes adjustment responses, while in other situa
tions, as in vocal speech conversation, the reading of expression and
gestures constitutes auxiliary reactions either as (1) additional re
sponses to the speech stimuli or (2) as direct reactions to gestural
expressions serving as the setting factors of the vocal speech stimuli.

What is meant by audienting is more definite and familiar and re
quires no further comment except the suggestion that, just as in audi
tory reactions we find auxiliary visual components, so in visual lan
guage reactions we discover auditory components, for example, im
plicit reactions to sound stimuli. As we have indicated, we may think
of reading as a general name for visual receptive language reactions,
while the term audienting serves in a similar capacity for all recep
tive auditory responses.

**Tactual Receptive Language Reactions**
Reading and writing constitute what we may well call the normal
and usual forms of receptive language reactions. Besides these types
we find, though in unusual cases only, that tactual reactions also are
made to transmissive reactions or language stimuli. Examples are the
reactions of the deaf and blind to lip movements of other persons and
to the raised types of blind printing.

**Linguistic Implications of Verbal Analysis.**
The various implications of language phenomena may readily be
exposed by an analysis of a word or words. In such an analysis we
may hope to bring to light the multiple character of such phenomena.
First, such an analysis indicates that language activity is not only a
definite response or adaptation to a stimulus but that it may at the
same time be a stimulus for another response. Moreover, we can
easily separate the psychological facts of language from the physical,
social and other phases of speech or writing, incidentally bringing
into sharper relief the functional and dynamic character of language.

**Non-Psychological Language Words**
(a) In the first place, a word may be considered as a purely physi
cal or natural object existing in nature on a par with any other
physical thing and with the same characteristics. Here we refer to
a printed word (as it stands unread in a book) for example, or to a
vocal sound. Now, of course, in contrast to a physical object, for
example, a stone, we might say that the word as a physical object
was invented or developed through some human agency, but that the
difference between a stone and a word is only relative. Surely all of
the stones in our urban environment, at least, have been transformed
or modified through some human agency, but this in no degree
minimizes their physical or natural character.

(b) A word may be considered also as a human institution, and
now we refer to the word as a member of a specific series of language
customs. Here the word has a very different character. It is a
purely human product existing in practically all of its phases as an
artificial construction developed in the interaction of human beings
belonging to specific social organizations or cultural communities.

Such verbal or linguistic institutions may be illustrated both by acts or language things. Probably the latter constitute more striking examples since they may exist totally unused and little known. Instances of such verbal institutions are all of the words in the Moeso-Gothic Language which exists only in the Bible version made by Bishop Ulfilas. As social institutions words and their combinations may be compared with buildings, codes of statutes or customs, social organizations, governments, nations, etc.

(c) Another type of word phenomenon which belongs with the two previous classes of words, namely non-psychological data, is the word uttered under certain circumstances. Now we are thinking of the word act, the act of speaking a word, which is merely morphologically but not functionally language. Here we have random vocal actions which do not function either as expressive or communicative adaptations. For instance, there are the words uttered by a person under the effect of ether. While these are undoubtedly psychological acts instead of merely natural or physical objects they are not data for the psychologist of language, nor do they belong to the domain of psychological language behavior.

All three of the types of words we have just discussed may be considered as things and acts, but not as serving any specific language function; they are independent of any immediate language use. We will next consider the words serving in some sort of actual language situation. In this case we may be referring to the same concrete words but now they are, psychologically speaking, in some reactionalistic relationship. From a psychological standpoint it is only when words are in a stimulus-response relationship that we think of them as definite psychological data. We may differentiate then between the following forms of stimuli and response words as psychological language data. *Words as Definite Psychological Data*

Here we may speak of a printed word which serves as a definite stimulus to arouse a language response in some person, any kind of physical word which calls out an indirect reaction. This word may be regarded as a symbol, which presumably with or without the intention of anyone at this moment calls out a meaning or language response in another person. *Words as Stimuli*

Also under this division we have word acts serving as stimuli language functions. Here we include definite verbal utterances which bring about responses on the part of some person, either the individual himself or someone else. We may consider these word acts as stimuli. irrespective of whether the person intends them to be such. So we might indicate here that we have two classes of definite language function, named respectively, expressive and transmissive stimulus word acts. We may also observe that these words operate as definite symbols in the same sense as the printed word. Probably in most cases in which the non-transmissive stimulus word-act operates, the total segment of behavior will not be language. That is to say, the word voluntarily performed by the person may still not serve to elicit a definite language response on the part of some other individual.

**Words as Responses**

Here we think of the phases of the word in its functional operation as a response to some sort of stimulus, whether language or not. Now these words may be definite overt responses as in the case of answering questions, or they may be sub-vocal or other forms of verbal meaning and understanding responses. They may operate as final acts or as responses precurrent to some other final response.

In summarizing this analysis of words as language data and the differentiation of them from various kinds of non-psychological data, we repeat once more that we may be concerned with what from the everyday standpoint is considered the same word. Any given word may be both physical and psychological, and also at the same time both a stimulus and a response.

**The Analysis of Linguistic Behavior Segments**

In order to bring into sharper relief the stimulus and response functions or phases of language activities, we will find it useful to work out a few language behavior segments indicating these features. The necessity to insist upon the differences between language actions as stimuli or responses is patent, since all too frequently it is difficult to study them as distinct factors.

We experience this difficulty because in the intricate give-and-take process involved in communicative language the same action, whether verbal or gestural, is at the same time both stimulus and response, that is to say, both a response act to someone's stimulus and at the same time a stimulus for that other person's response. Not only is this the typical situation in communicative language, but the same functional conditions may prevail in expressive behavior segments, with the difference, of course, that in the latter case the action of a single person constitutes both stimuli and responses. Besides the mere differentiation between responses and stimuli in linguistic situations, it is necessary for us to study also the distinction between what we may variously call the adjustment, reference, or indirect stimuli, and the direct stimuli which are simultaneously operating. Furthermore, when we have determined the difference between linguistic stimuli and responses we must, in addition, discover whether these factors are inherently linguistic in character or whether they accidentally participate in a linguistic situation. The various distinctions between the response and stimulus phases and the two stimuli features may all be exemplified in several behavior segments.

**Segments in which Stimuli and Responses are both Language Processes**

We shall first consider a situation in which both the response and stimulus are genuine psychological language processes, making it a point to inquire whether the stimulus and response phases can be kept sufficiently distinct so that there is no danger of confusing them. In a conversation, "A" stimulates "B" by asking him a question which the latter understands. This action of understanding which is a genuine adaptation to the question as a stimulus, may be regarded as a typical receptive language reaction and therefore we have here an unmistakable language behavior segment. Because both individuals are definitely performing instrumental indirect reactions the behavior segment is indubitably a linguistic one.

Now in this illustration it happens that "B's" understanding of "A's" question involves such an overt reaction that "B's" response in turn serves as a language stimulus to "A," in the sense that "A" is informed of "B's" understanding of the former's question or of "B's" acquiescence to "A's" suggestion. The response language we may assume to be either gestural or verbal. Two possibilities are found here. "B's" receptive response may or may not be a stimulating reaction of an intentionally transmissive sort. In order to be a transmissive as well as a receptive language reaction the responding person "B" must offer "A" a definite verbal or gestural stimulus. In this case the reaction or adjustment to a stimulus itself serves as a stimulus to call out a new reaction in the originally stimulating person. The term "originally stimulating person" is applicable here only if we think of "A's" question as merely a stimulus, which we must do for the present purposes of our behavior segment analysis. But in fact "A's" question may already have been a response, since it is possible that he would not have asked the question except as a prior language reaction to "B." Whether or not this is so we can always judge from the specific situation at hand. With respect to "A's" question, which in our illustration originally stimulated "B," it would be, of course, a definite language stimulus even were it not a response to "B" but an answer made to "C," let us say, or to himself. The criterion for the stimulating character of a psychological datum is the question whether or not the action arouses a differential response, and in the case of language the response to a stimulus would necessarily have to be a definite language reaction.

We might conclude, then, that although a stimulus in the case of language is frequently also a response and vice versa, the two factors of a behavior segment can, and must be, distinguished. In the final analysis we must come back to the fundamental psychological criterion that a reaction is some differential response of an organism, while a stimulus is the correlated exciting object or condition for such a response.

Behavior segments which may be considered as only in part intrinsic language processes are exemplified by two situations. The first is that in which a person is aroused to perform a language reaction, say reading or expostulation, as a response to some natural phenomenon, while the second is that in which a response is made to some abstruse sign or symbol. In the first instance, under ordinary circumstances the natural-object stimulus precludes the behavior segment from ever being adjudged an inherently linguistic one. In the second instance, strange writing and unfamiliar language of all types

Segments in which only the Response is inherently a Language Process must not always be listed as intrinsically language stimuli for the linguistically reacting person although it is possible for such objects to be intrinsic linguistic stimuli. It is therefore only through the person's reactions at any particular time that the stimuli-objects in both cases take on language character. Besides physical objects the person's own actions or those of another person serve as such non-linguistic stimuli for linguistic response.

To a great extent, the behavior segment in which only the responses are inherently language phenomena are those in which the stimuli objects are cultural institutions. For instance, conventional language reactions such as phrases or idioms in foreign or strange languages constitute such stimuli features of linguistic behavior segments. Now while such foreign phrases may be perfectly good language reactions they cannot serve at all as true language stimuli to the person who does not know their meaning. In other words, the non-understood language phrase as an institutional fact may be a stimulus to a reaction in being the stimulus factor in a reciprocal stimulus-response situation and it is therefore a psychological fact, but the total behavior segment will not be a language behavior. Also, the non-understood phrase is, of course, a definite language phenomenon in that it is a language institution, but in our illustrative behavior segment it does not serve as an inherent language fact or any language fact at all. In no sense, however, is the foreign phrase excluded from serving a definite psychological function. It is most decidedly a psychological fact in that it elicits from the person a psychological response even of a definite linguistic sort but it is not, of course, a direct factor in a meaningful language response.

In our discussion here we are assuming that, from the standpoint of psychology we mean by language a definite reactional fact and not an institution, for it is indifferent whether the language element we take to be the non-language stimulus is a spoken phrase or a written or printed sentence. While in both cases our illustrative behavior segment involves a true language reaction to the non-psychological language stimulus, or the foreign phrase, the complete behavior segment is not a case of language behavior. And why not? Because to be genuine language behavior, the reaction must be a specifically fitting and appropriate response to its particular stimulus, and as we have seen, the language reaction to the foreign phrase could have been elicited by any sort of stimulus within a fairly large range of objects.

Our distinction between language and non-language facts can be well illustrated by comparing conversational and non-conversational language. Conversational language constitutes behavior segments in which the stimuli and responses (for there are many of each) are all authentic language stimuli and responses and all in functional interrelation with each other.

Assume that "A" approaches "B" and, under the misapprehension that the latter is known to him, offers at once to engage in conversation. To such incipiently authentic conversational stimulation "B" may be unable to respond adequately, although he may react with a verbal response. He may in fact, say, "I am sorry but I do not understand you." Here it may be observed that while "A" performs a definite indirect response with "B" as the direct stimulus and with some particular adjustment object or referent as the indirect stimulus, the activity of "A" fails on the whole to qualify as an authentic linguistic stimulus. Since "B" is not familiar with the referent in question or in other words does not know what "A" is talking about, we may say that there is no functional point-to-point correspondence between the potential language stimulus and the consequently non-linguistic reaction of "B." [1] In spite of the fact that "B's" reaction is linguistic in character it is not part of a behavior segment in which "A's" linguistic reaction is the corresponding stimulus. "A's" language response then, so far as "B" is concerned, must be considered as an ordinary psychological stimulus but not a linguistic one.

*Segments in which only the Stimulus is an Inherent Language Factor*

As in the case of all psychological activities, linguistic responses are reducible at least logically to simple ultimate units. Accordingly, upon the basis of the types of reaction systems involved, whether vocal, gesturing, vocal speech, non-vocal gesturing, etc., [2] the units of the action demand descriptive emphasis upon particular muscles, neural pattern, discrimination, attention and affective acts, etc. For example, in vocal speech the person's units of action are describable in terms of muscles, glands, nerves, cartilages, etc., involved in the expiration of air from the lungs, its direction and deflection by the diaphragm, the trachea, its conditioning by the larynx and its parts, especially the vocal cords, and the epiglottis as well as by the palate, tongue, teeth, cheeks, lips, etc. Also, in any special case the differential character of the reaction system leads to the specification of the discriminative, affective and attentional phases of the action. These features of the linguistic reaction system make for extremely specialized types of conduct. The inclusion of these factors suggests further that both when the reaction systems are transmissive and receptive the particular receptor mechanisms must be added to the descriptions. In addition to these features of verbal reaction systems are the activities of the muscles, nerves, and skeletal factors of the head in general, the neck and throat, and especially the shoulders.

*The Analysis of Linguistic Reaction Systems*

[1] This situation must not be confused with the case in which the behavior situation is a definitely linguistic one but in which the authentic referent happens to be unfamiliar to either of the two persons concerned in the language activity. In that case the unfamiliarity primarily concerns a cognitive reaction, whereas here it is the linguistic action which is incomplete.

[2] See analysis of types above, p. 221.

When the reaction system involved is a non-vocal gestural one, it is describable in quite other terms in order to include the overlapping of action which might occur. In some cases the lips and face segments appear as the primary features, in others the hands, arms, shoulders and other parts below the head. All this means that in the case of language, our approach to the intimate response datum must be entirely generalized and vague. Generalizing here, we might say that whichever one of the distinct types of linguistic reaction systems is involved, its descriptive analysis must include a series of distinct behavioristic factors.

In attempting to analyze specific linguistic reaction systems a number of problems of greater or lesser difficulty arise. Two of these we may consider, namely, one concerning the difficulty of determining what is the specific reaction system in any case, and the other the general indeterminateness of linguistic reaction systems.

First, we may discuss the difficulty of isolating the simple units of the person's action when he performs a language response. This problem may be attacked from different angles. What is the unit of action? Is it a sound or a series of sounds, a syllable, a word, or a series of words? Perhaps it may be a phrase, a proposition or a larger unit. When we are dealing with verbal reactions we run into the problem of integration, for the unification of simpler verbal elements into larger units occurs with the consequent loss of identity of the former. When we turn to gestural language on the transmissive side and to all the receptive language activities, the isolation of specific units if at all possible, is enormously difficult. In either case the attempt to mark off what might be considered a descriptive linguistic unit of action from other movements or actions occurring at the same time is far from simple or easy. We may only suggest that in speaking one must take into account whether the person is standing or sitting, whether his linguistic action is primary, or secondary and incidental to another action. For, in the consideration of these facts lies a great deal of the value of the description. Language that is vigorous and primary is different from language that is incidental and passive. Both the references and their intensity are conditioned by these facts.

Furthermore, when linguistic reactions are important and intense, the descriptive analysis of the reaction systems involves the inclusion of an enumeration and description of visceral and organic factors which in other cases may be almost entirely neglected. In language reactions performed by the person under stress of deep feeling, a description of the language units must be given which differs materially from the description to be made when the person is affectively indifferent to the referents or to the auxiliary stimulus.

Our second problem involved in the analysis of linguistic reaction systems concerns the indefiniteness of the various simple and elementary modes of the person's language actions. This problem arises from the fact that, unlike other forms of psychological conduct, linguistic behavior does not constitute a very definite mode of the organism's operation correlated with qualities or objects, either natural or contrived, or with some form of manipulation of such objects by the person. Since linguistic reactions are in every case indirect or referential modes of action, they are consequently far removed from any immediate, tangible or palpable contact with the objects responded to. When I ask someone to look at this thing I have in my hand, my action is more or less indefinite. I may point to it or perform some articulate or verbal response. Or I may perform this referential reaction by winking or making some sort of facial gesture.[1] It may be suggested further that linguistic reaction systems are, or may be, indeterminate because of the auxiliary stimulus involved, namely, the referee or the person to whom the reference is made. The fact of having two stimuli implies that so far as the reference is concerned it must be adaptable to the reacting individual. It must be an intimate or formal mode of action, an action belonging to a particular language system, national, family, or dialectal, etc., rather than to some other. In all of these different situations, the particular reactional modes of speaking or communicating will be necessarily different.

Still another point may be made here. We discover that different linguistic reaction systems are possible (when specific references function) because language responses as psychological activities are cultural in character and therefore independent of the biological make-up of the person, although in each case of action what occurs is a concrete movement or motion of the individual.

In the relationship between the verbal and gestural components of linguistic reaction systems we find evidences of their variational character. The specific shoulder and facial movement gestures which are part of the person's linguistic responses along with certain words and references may at another time be connected with other words and references.

The possible variety and types of linguistic reaction systems can be more adequately appreciated by comparing them with another condition of indefiniteness which attaches itself to implicit reactions. In this latter type of response, the indefiniteness merely refers to the circumstance whether the response shall be verbal, imagal, or some other sort. On the whole, however, the response in its fundamental or adjustment character is determined by the stimulational situation. Abstract stimuli are responded to by verbal reactions and in other ways the person is conditioned by the stimulating circumstance. In the case of language reactions the freedom and variety of action is very much greater. Implicit reactions may also be conditioned by cultural and idiosyncratic factors with the result that

[1] Whatever act I actually do perform, however, must be a conventional one so far as the two persons are concerned, if the reference is actually to be made.

they are more or less equipmental features of the individual's personality.  The person may be habitually a verbal or imagal reactor.  Quite obvious is the case with linguistic reaction systems.  Even when the person is culturally conditioned he will, because of the greater variety of linguistic institutions in any given community, be prone to exercise greater variability in action.

**Distinction between Language and Thought Conduct [1]**    As part of the recent objective development of psychology the attempt has been made to identify thought and language.  This identification was attempted in order to make thought a definite mode of psychological reaction and not an indefinite form of mental stuff or process.  Admirable as is the motive for this identification and much as we approve of the attempt to bring psychological facts out of the clouds of unverifiable assertion, we must still in the interest of the facts in the case withhold our assent from such an identification.  An intimate study of both language and thought is thoroughly convincing of the very different characteristics of the two types of psychological phenomena.  Let us proceed to a discussion of these differences.

That thought and language cannot be identified must appear a valid conclusion to anyone who cogitates for a moment about the actual behavior types represented by these two psychological terms.  Consider that the term thought when used in this identification covers a large range of psychological activities, such as planning, problem solving, judging, evaluating, inferring, [2] etc.  Can anyone meaningfully assert that these forms of complex reactions are language responses much as we may employ language behavior (though perhaps no more than all other sorts together) in accomplishing such responses?  Only a moment's reflection is sufficient to recall most convincingly that the various forms of thinking involve so many and such peculiar contacts with stimuli objects of all sorts, and with instruments for handling them, that it is impossible to call all such reactions language or even apply the term language to the typical phases of such activities.

In short, to call thinking language means rashly to overlook all the myriads of differences in the behavior situations.  To name only one fact, does not language most typically, though obviously not exclusively, constitute a response to persons as stimuli (auxiliary)?  But who would say that our thinking need necessarily have close reference to persons or human affairs?  One might possibly be misled by the prominent place which printed and written materials play in our complex thinking and planning in the form of notes and

---

[1] Because we are discussing here a conventional problem we are obliged to use the term thought in its everyday sense, leaving its more exact usage to emerge from our analysis.  It is hardly necessary to suggest that our problem here is a different one from that of the connection between actual thinking and verbal or laryngeal action.

[2] Really another type of action, but for our present purposes we overlook the differences.

records. To make the use of these verbal notes a basis for identify-ing thought and language is a grievous error. In the first place, what right have we to confuse verbal tools used in the process of thinking with that thinking process itself, any more than we have to identify with thought any other tool (of which obviously there exist a great many) used in thinking. And in the second place, such a confusion of the records of thought with the activity of thinking itself is to mistake word symbols (which are no more language than any other sort of symbols) for the actual psychological processes of language.

Furthermore, while no one can deny that language is the most useful tool for the operation and development of our thinking, there are so many other modes of action which can be used in planning, inferring, and other thinking and reasoning acts that we cannot in any sense admit any general identity between language and thought. Even if we should admit, as we do without hesitation, that in some cases (perhaps not rare instances) the thinking and planning are purely linguistic (vocal or non-vocal, overt or implicit) we yet cannot allow the general identification. Thinking and planning may consist of other kinds of reactions as well as words, or other kinds of language. And even in the present case the linguistic responses are most likely morphological and not functional language. Now as a matter of fact in all cases of important or crucial thinking (since such behavior is initiated by and operates under the auspices of very complex situations) we have a host of reactions occurring, some of which may be language responses, but others which are not.

If it seems plausible, at all, to believe that thinking is not language, even when we add that it is not always nor necessarily so, then we might see further ground for rejecting the identification in that language operates along with or in the service of other forms of adaptational behavior besides thought. For instance, in communica-tion we use language to inform others of what we desire, hope, fear, and do (in the form of overt action) as well as to make known what we think.

Up to this point we have been concerned with genuine thinking behavior. It may be objected that it is unfair to suggest that anyone would confuse such obviously different things. But this is precisely the point. Those who have identified the two types have overlooked the actual characteristics of two of our most complex types of be-havior. In justice, however, to those who have made the identification we must say that they have considered thought or thinking to be composed of simple reactions of the implicit type. It is our reply that language is no more implicit action than it is planning or problem solving. We turn then to a consideration of our problem in its different forms.

Not only can we not identify thought (as implicit action) with language responses, because each of these classes of behavior refers to what are on the whole intrinsically different adaptational functions, but we further appreciate the necessity of separating off the two types of behavior because of the different specific ways in which they operate.

Unlike language responses, thinking reactions are direct adaptations to stimuli, although some form of thought action (in the everyday sense), especially simple implicit behavior, appears to be indirect. It is this fact of the misconstrued indirectness of thinking behavior (since there are a great many of the apparent indirect types of thinking) which no doubt is in great part responsible for the misidentification of language and thought. In three general ways, then, do thinking acts appear indirect, each of which we must examine in turn in order to determine the exact relation of thought to language.

**Apparent Indirectness of Thinking as Delayed Behavior**

Because much of our thinking represents delayed forms of behavior, that is to say, because many specific reaction systems operate in conjunction with a number of different stimuli comprising the different angles of the thinking stimulus or situation, these specific responses appear as indirect, but such is in fact not the case. Let us examine the possible reasons for such a misapprehension. In the case of thinking behavior, a temporal and spatial element is involved in the complex action of responding to the various stimuli provoking the thinking response. The hit or-miss character of thinking implies such a condition. For instance, a man determining in which of many manners he can best ford a stream must probably make several movements or take several moments to decide upon the best way of doing it, but his reactions to these various stimuli are entirely direct. In language behavior, on the contrary, the one or the very few acts comprising the segment of action are all indirect actions as we have already sufficiently indicated. The temporal disparity between stimulus and response, which in thinking behavior provokes the opinion that such action is indirect, when it is really direct, is wholly lacking in language behavior where the action is always indirect.

**Apparent Indirectness of Thinking as Precurrent Action**

Again, thinking reactions appear indirect because when they are most serviceable as adjustment responses they operate as precurrent thinking or planning reactions. Such reactions pave the way for a later reaction which will result in some definite change in the condition or existence of the adjustment stimulus object. The point is that thinking either precedes an overt action, in the sense that the planning and deciding are accomplished before any actual work is done upon the stimulus objects and events, or in a single segment of behavior the thought as a precurrent reaction system precedes the occurrence of the end reaction which it conditions. In many cases, too, the characteristic of indirectness is attributed to thought reactions because no overt act at all need follow the implicit behavior. Our present interest is to point out that the implicit activity preceding overt action is in truth a direct response to the adjustment stimulus, but because this reaction has to be aroused through the intervention of a substitute stimulus the immediate reaction must be thinking or implicit activity.  But when the thinking or implicit reaction occurs, no matter how long before the overt act, it is itself a direct, though non-explicit response to the original or substituted-for object or situation.

In the case of language, on the contrary, our study has shown us that the adjustment stimulus object is frequently present when the language response is made, but the reaction to that object is referential and not direct.  This is true because the final response can only be made through the means of an auxiliary stimulus.  At this point it seems only fair to admit that possibly our term indirect does not fit language responses any better than it fits thought reactions, but there is no question concerning the fact of difference in the two cases, irrespective of the name that is employed to express that difference.

In the attempt to elucidate further the differences between the actual indirectness of language behavior and the apparent indirectness of thinking reactions, it might be well to digress a moment in order to point out that although the temporal relationship of stimulus and response is not a criterion of indirect behavior, still it is evident that the various instances of indirect reactions (language) may be differently conditioned by the temporal relation of response and adjustment stimulus.  That is to say, the degree of indirectness depends upon whether the indirect language response follows a direct response or an implicit response.  If language is associated with an implicit response, the degree of directness or indirectness with respect to the adjustment stimulus is greater than if it follows an overt reaction.  As we have just stated, it so happens that in most cases of implicit behavior the adjustment stimulus object is responded to through the mediation of a substitute stimulus function provided by something other than the adjustment object.  Thus it happens that when an indirect language response follows an implicit action the person is doubly removed from the adjustment stimulus.

This means, then, that in this instance there is a greater temporal interval between the connection of the language act and the adjustment stimulus than in cases in which the language acts follow overt responses.  If we may call any language response a response of second intention then possibly it will not be unfitting to call a language response associated with an implicit reaction a reaction of third intention.  Possibly an illustration might assist in clarifying this analysis. A person burns himself on a hot iron and his immediate and first response is a withdrawal act (reflex).  Immediately following the reflex act he makes some language responses (indirect) referring to the pain he suffered.  In this case the language activity follows an overt act (reflex) and is thus a language response of second intention. Later, this same person recalling the incident (implicit activity) communicates the details to his friend, or in other words performs a language response of third intention, since it follows the implicit activity of recalling the act of burning himself.

**Apparent Indirectness of Thinking as Implicit Action**

If thought is confused with language on the ground that the former is considered to be indirect because it is implicit action, then it is incumbent upon us to point out the error in the latter notion.

However indirect implicit reactions seem to be, they are really only incipient or other forms of actually direct responses to objects which result in no immediate change of condition or existence in the stimulus object.[1] Let us notice that the most typical forms of implicit reactions are partial or vestigial remnants of originally larger or complete reactions, as is excellently exemplified in the partially implicit visual-perceptual reaction which may be considered as the seeing part or phase, or remainder of the original seeing-touching or other whole[2] reaction system. The distinction, then, between an implicit and explicit reaction is a functional one. In other words, an implicit act may be, morphologically, exactly like an overt act, but owing to the absence of the original stimulus object no effect is produced upon that object. Now it happens that because of the absence of the original object, or because first contacts with objects produce disruptive and inhibitory conditions, the later contacts with the same objects consist of modified reaction systems. These partial or totally implicit reaction systems take on their specific character of implicitness because of the person's mode of contact with the stimulus in question and not in any sense because of their non-visibility to the acting person or someone else.

In this fact of the interdependence of response and stimulus, which of course is an inherently psychological phenomenon, we find the differentiating conditions that not only mark off overt from implicit behavior but also supply us with criteria for distinguishing one kind of implicit behavior from another. Thus when the original stimulus object is present in its customary setting, we react to it in the same overt way as usual unless some interfering condition arises. When the original object is partially present, as when we can see but not touch it, then we perform a partially implicit response. When the object is entirely absent and we are made to respond to it through a substitution stimulus we may have an implicit action which is totally different from the original act, though definitely derived from it. In case the same stimulus object substitutes for itself, which is a common occurrence, as when a person makes us think of an experience we had with him some time ago, the resulting form of implicit action can be clearly made out to be a result of responding to the person in a previous setting through stimulation of the person in a present setting.

[1] Cf. Vol. I,, Ch. X.

[2] Different, we should perhaps say here, instead of whole, because every unit of reaction is a reaction system.

Implicit action is accordingly always a direct mode of action. It only seems indirect because the original stimulus object is not present, or is not present in the same setting; but in either case, as we have previously made clear, the response has a direct adaptive bearing upon the adjustment stimulus. Our assumption is that implicit behavior constitutes direct adaptive responses in much the same way as the more striking cases of inhibition responses compose direct adaptive behavior. Contrariwise, in the case of typical language the action is overt and may result in some change in the stimulus, but the reaction is indirect because it is referential. Illustrative of such a situation is the operation of instrumental language responses.

Once more we may return to the distinguishing criterion between thought as implicit action, and language, bringing to bear upon the problem the facts concerning the relationship of stimulus and response. We suggest that while implicit responses are mediate and secondary reactions, that is to say, involve two forms of stimulation as do indirect language reactions, the contacts of the person with those stimuli in the two cases are so different that we must consider the respective actions as belonging to different types of behavior. Differences in action and name between direct and indirect responses are due to the differences in character of the additional stimuli. Now what is the exact difference? Our conclusion is that implicit behavior is always a direct adaptation in spite of the fact that for its performance a substitute or additional stimulus is required. We call the additional stimulus substitutive because its only function is to call out the reaction to the adjustment stimulus, while the response is always made to the adjustment stimulus. Quite different is the auxiliary stimulus in language reactions which must operate along with, and in synchronous addition to, the adjustment stimulus. It is a genuine auxiliary stimulus operating as an integral factor in the total language activity. This is true even when the auxiliary stimulus person is absent. Because of the peculiar non-effective character of language, such that when most effective it is instrumental or a tool, the paper, for instance, upon which one writes to an absent conversationalist is not a substitute stimulus but really a bit of material for language performance. Furthermore, we might even suggest that in the case of implicit reactions because the second stimulus merely substitutes for the adjustment stimulus, namely, the thing or situation reacted to, there is really but one stimulus object, while in the case of indirect or language reactions there are always two stimuli for any specific reaction system. We have no hesitation, then, in asserting that language is not identical with thought, either when thought is considered as planning or problem solving or when thought is regarded as merely implicit behavior.

Quite aside from the factors of apparent indirectness of implicit action, psychologists have tended to identify implicit behavior with language considered as thought because there obviously exists implicit linguistic or at least implicit verbal action. Now certainly some of our thought behavior may be considered as merely implicit action. And patently language reactions are apparently as much subject to implicit performance as any other sort of reaction, but these facts themselves contain arguments for not identifying thought and language. Observe that only a part of our thought behavior is merely implicit action, and furthermore, that we are no more justified to make implicit language synonymous with thought than with any of the numerous other types of implicit action all of which may just as well as language be considered as thought. Moreover, as we shall presently see, implicit language cannot be considered as genuine language activity. So while we might think of such reactions as thought we cannot think of them as language.

Now although implicit language may be regarded as thought, if not problem solving, we cannot accept such a fact as indicative of the identity between language and thinking, since implicit language is little, if at all, serviceable for any active thinking process. In fact, it is probably only in dreaming (day or night) that we perform implicit language activity to any extent and we need hardly comment on the striking contrast between such passive behavior and the more active process of thinking. Strictly speaking, of course, we have here only verbal or morphological language. In all other cases, except dreaming, we can accomplish many useful results by means of implicit non-language reactions (implicit construction, purchasing, etc.).

In granting that language functions most typically and most serviceably as psychological behavior when it is most overt, while thought as implicit behavior can be most serviceable to the person and operate most typically when there is a minimum of overt activity,[1] we find a further basis for disbelief in the identity of thought and language. We are convinced that language most useful for thinking must be overt handling of materials and not the pale reflection of conversation. It is really because of the overt character of language on the one hand, and the implicit character of thinking on the other, and not because they are identical, that overt language and implicit responses are so frequently operating in combination—so frequently, in fact, that it is even thought that they cannot operate separately. They cannot operate separately, it is said, in the sense that we cannot

[1] Here we must distinguish between implicit action of any sort considered as thought, and implicit thinking. The latter, of course, because of the absence of actual objects or actual problems as stimuli whether in perceptual or non-perceptual situations, is about as ineffective a form of action as we can well imagine. Such conduct is best exemplified by our action in brooding over misfortune, and in phantastic dreaming. No one, of course, will confuse such implicit thinking with actual thought that goes on in terms of implicit action, say implicit military operation, even though the latter can be contrasted with thinking in overt terms, as in the setting up of a complex original scientific apparatus. Thinking that goes on in implicit terms is an actual and important type of behavior since it is such behavior which constitutes the responses to all abstract things and objects.

think without language, a statement, by the way, which may well be true in practise, but which carries with it no implication of inflexible necessity.[1] But at any rate, if it is true that language is more typical when overt, and much more useful for thought when so operating, then it is almost obvious that we cannot identify the two.

A last refuge for the identification of thought and language is the identification of both these behavior types with sub-vocal action. Certainly sub-vocal reactions may be indirect responses and, consequently, genuine linguistic reactions. But in that case they are in no sense performing the adjustmental functions of thinking responses. Especially is this point clear when we consider that as linguistic reactions sub-vocal behavior comprises purely expressive language actions. When sub-vocal reactions, on the other hand, are merely sub-vocally performed verbal actions, they are only conventional symbols and therefore not language reactions, even if they are considered to be implicit responses. As a matter of fact, however, sub-vocal language reactions are not normally implicit actions but overt responses of expressive form.

Further evidence of another sort to establish the non-identity of language and thought (as implicit action) may be adduced from the following consideration, to wit, that the two types of action as responses to the same set of stimuli objects may definitely parallel each other without any sort of interference or conflict. Moreover, is it not true that we can think of something beyond and entirely different from the thing or circumstance of which we are speaking? This condition would be impossible if the two types of action were identical, since the person may be employing all of his language or thinking mechanisms for performing one of the two simultaneously occurring forms of response.

Still another fact militates against our identification of language and thought (as implicit action). Our language reactions, so far as their actual mode of operation is concerned, that is to say, as communicative references, are definitely acquired through social stimulation, whereas our implicit actions, though they may be symbolized, are to a great extent merely functions of our individual contacts with our surroundings. This individuality of response, it may be argued, is not any more true of thought than it is of language, for thought is also socially conditioned, but here the question arises as to whether we are not shifting our discussion from the mere performance of implicit action to the more complex forms of activity, namely, planning, or problem solving.

Neither thinking nor implicit action, then, is identical with language activity, and further, even if we agree that language is some-

---

[1] Otis, Arthur S., "Do We Think in Words," *Psychol. Rev.* 1920, 27, 339–449, has excellently described a number of situations in which thinking is doubtless a process distinct from verbal language.

times not inseparable from thought must we still say that language is the sole medium for the expression of thought or the actualization of implicit action?[1] We unhesitatingly answer in the negative and especially if the question implies any peculiar relationship between thought, or implicit action, and language responses. That thought need not be exclusively actualized through language is evident from the fact that, because thinking is planning or problem solving, the expression of the reaction more often than not occurs in the form of actual overt responses made by way of changing some object or circumstance. Similarly, implicit action, being non-effective, immediate behavior most likely has for its expression the actual initiation of some behavior affecting the previously absent and substituted for object which now has become available. Of a certainty, conditions are different in situations in which no final overt action is contemplated or possible, and under these circumstances the actualization of the thought or implicit action is achieved through the medium of language. It may possibly be argued that what we have referred to as actualization of thought is not what is usually meant by expression of thought but that what is meant is rather simple communication or telling someone of what was thought. Certainly the communication of thought, although a very frequent form of human action, does not occur with such constancy, considering the total number of possible cases of thought action, as to make any thoroughgoing concomitancy possible. Very much of the thought of the world but not all of it by far is set down in writing or is expressed by word of mouth. As a matter of fact, since language is the typical form of indirect or referential behavior, we can readily employ it in referring to our thought reactions as well as to all other sorts of actions and things. When communication occurs we must admit that we cannot conceive of any behavior that is nearly so effective for the purpose as language.

**Linguistic Stimuli and Settings**
In no type of psychological activity are investigations of stimuli so important or so involved as in the case of linguistic conduct. To be sure, the mere fact of stimulation is no more important in linguistic behavior segments than in other sorts but the particular characteristics of language activities introduce a number of stimulational complications. The very pervasiveness of linguistic conduct implies a variety and scope of stimuli objects and situations which carry with them a number of classificatory and investigative problems. How greatly varied are the different human situations in which language responses operate! We have communicative language in face-to-face contact with other persons. Or we may communicate with them through transcribed or symbolized references of all varieties. Then we perform thousands of varieties of expressive lan-

---

[1] Expression of thought is a faulty term, implying the embodiment of psychic stuff or process. When properly used, it refers to the employment of language or other action during the act of thinking or informing someone of the thinking action we have been engaged in.

guage acts, each with their own circumstantial surroundings and occasions. Moreover, we must not only concern ourselves with every variety of general human situation but we must also distinguish between those behavior circumstances in which the traditional formula of communication of ideas holds, from those in which the linguistic conduct involves references to situations which comprise primarily, feeling, desiring, believing, etc. Stimulational problems become complicated when the language is not the primary activity performed, as is supposed to be the case in the "communication of ideas," as compared with the situation in which the language is only an incidental or partial feature of a larger and more complete human situation.

In every case of linguistic behavior, it is to be vividly remembered, moreover, that we have a double stimulational situation. In other words, it is very important not only to specify the particular objects and conditions constituting the adjustment linguistic stimuli, but also to connect and correlate those stimuli objects or referents with the personal indirect stimuli in their various combinations. This fact alone introduces an important series of technicalities into linguistic stimulational circumstances.

Our primary method in isolating and analyzing the stimuli of linguistic behavior segments will be to follow the cue provided us by the separation of the adjustment or referential from the indirect phases of the stimulational functions. Incidentally, however, we find it expedient to employ other criteria in our investigation such as the communicative, expressive, transmittive or receptive character of the stimuli objects. Howsoever complicated the study of stimuli in linguistic behavior, the attempt to effect such an isolation of stimuli factors accomplishes not only a necessary descriptive purpose but adds also to our information and understanding concerning the nature of linguistic responses in general.

### ADJUSTMENT OR DIRECT LINGUISTIC STIMULI

Considering first the adjustment or referential stimuli, we need only enumerate the different classes of stimuli objects or situations to which persons react linguistically. For the specific things to which persons respond with language reactions coincide with all the possible things to which the individual can respond at all. Among the most common of our referential linguistic stimuli are concrete objects of all types and varieties. Indeed, it is sometimes said that linguistic reactions to concrete objects are in a sense primary and unique, for it is declared that in a genuine sense the use of nouns is not only the first type of language activity, but also that the reference to objects which constitutes the use of names is a central fact, since so much else in the way of linguistic action may be considered as auxiliaries and qualifiers for the references. Differences in complexity of the linguistic activity in different human communities may be symbolized

*Concrete Objects*

by the relative number of linguistic reactions performed with concrete objects as the adjustment stimuli.

Under the heading of concrete objects, we must of course include all concrete things which are not in the first instance natural objects but really artificial human constructions. All objects of art or artisanship fall into this class but do not exhaust the list. Institutional objects developed in political, religious, legal and other complex human situations must be specifically mentioned.

**Qualities and Conditions of Things**

As the next logically related type of referent, we may mention the qualities and conditions of things. As a general rule, one seldom refers to an object without including some indirect response to its qualities or conditions. Again, both in complicated and simple behavior situations we may react exclusively linguistically to the qualities and conditions of a thing on their own account. They serve thus as adjustment stimuli aside from the objects to which they belong or in which they inhere. It is recognized of course that in very simple behavior situations such linguistic reactions are limited to exclamations of various sorts, such as "Look," "Oh," etc. In gestural language, qualities and conditions are referred to by the simple act of pointing. In more complex behavior situations elaborate verbal references function as responses to this type of stimuli. In this connection it is interesting to observe how various languages differ as instruments for such referential conduct. Among some of the peoples of simpler culture the words used for qualities, conditions, and even actions are inseparable from the thing-reference reaction elements.

**Persons and Actions**

While actions are certainly not a larger class of referents than objects they nevertheless appear to constitute a prominent class of stimuli requiring separate enumeration. In general, actions of all sorts, the movements and behavior of objects, for example, may be the stimuli for language reactions as well as the concrete objects themselves. In addition we have occasion to refer in our language to actions of persons including ourselves. We find then that actions as adjustment stimuli for language constitute manipulations of all sorts, movements such as walking and running, work and play reactions of all types, and ideational and verbal responses. But not only may the actions of the referer and the referee be the adjustment stimuli for linguistic behavior, but also the persons themselves as objects. When the referee person is also the referent, then there is a coincidence of the auxiliary and the adjustment stimuli functions in the same object. It is the references made with the various combinations of personal stimuli that constitute the voice and person phenomena of the grammarian.

**Events, Circumstances and Situations**

These three types of stimuli objects along with those already enumerated doubtless constitute for most people the majority of things referred to linguistically. The responses in these cases are of course for the most part verbal and very little gestural, since any type of adequate linguistic response to such stimuli objects involves more or less symbolic forms of action. We must add here that events, circumstances, and situations are definite adjustment stimuli whether they actually exist in nature or are merely descriptive and literary inventions. In the latter case, of course, they connect up as stimuli with the abstract referents to which we turn next.

Abstract things of all sorts constitute a more limited type of referent or adjustment stimulus than any we have heretofore mentioned. Under this caption we include every possible abstract object or relation whether it actually exists or not. To a considerable extent, therefore, the referents are represented either by words, statements, pictures, or other such vehicles, or by acts in the form of concepts or ideas. In a certain sense, also, we might suggest that the conceptual abstract vehicle is originally responsible for the function of the thing as stimulus. Once the object is created, for example, a god, a round square, a scientific thing such as ether, it may be transferred and represented in verbal or symbolic form for others than the creator thereof. References to this type of adjustment stimulus are confined to limited groups of individuals, although in complex cultural societies or communities some slight contact with them by the majority of individuals is the rule. **Abstract Things**

Another type of linguistic adjustment stimuli comprises symbols of every type and variety. In a measure we might consider these to be the representative of the abstract things of which we have just spoken. This is the case when we refer to mathematical symbols, representing relations of all sorts. On the other hand, however, these symbols may be the representatives and surrogates of concrete objects, events, persons, or circumstances. **Symbols**

In the above enumeration of linguistic adjustment stimuli no distinction is made between communicative language and expressive action. An inspection of these two different classes, however, in each case informs us in what type of linguistic conduct particular types of stimuli operate. On the whole we might indicate that most of the more abstract forms of referents operate in communicating behavior segments, although in the case of the most abstruse referent, the linguistic activity involved may be expressive in character. In the final analysis whichever of these conditions prevails depends on the type of individual who is performing the linguistic action in question and the particular circumstances under which the activity occurs.

Meriting separate mention as linguistic stimuli are language elements themselves in every form, such as spoken or written words, conversation, written communication and literature in all its branches and phases. Among the typical reactions performed with respect to these stimuli are the elementary teaching of language to infants, writings and discussions concerning language and literature, literary criticism, collaborative planning about and the constructing of literary pieces, speeches, orations, dramatization, plays, etc. **Words and Literature**

### AUXILIARY OR INDIRECT LINGUISTIC STIMULI

From the foregoing study of linguistic conduct we have seen that the indirect stimulus is practically always a person. And from this fact follow the suggestions concerning the specific nature of the auxiliary stimuli. In consequence, by far the largest class of auxiliary stimuli comprises the particular individuals who are in some way connected with the referents. Either they have been present with us when a certain circumstance or event has occurred or they have some particular interest in a certain thought, or are capable of carrying out some action with respect to the adjustment stimulus object. The discussion of the auxiliary or referee stimulus may be divided according to whether it is the person spoken to, or the person speaking, who at the instant is in the foreground of the mutually interacting phases of a behavior segment. In each case the possibility for non-personal stimulation must be allowed.

**Transmissive Referee Stimuli Personal**     (a) Personal stimuli—Here we include all of the person's acts, verbal, signs, and gestural [whether facial (mimetic) or general (pantomimetic)] which function to refer us to the objects, persons, situations, etc., constituting the adjustment stimuli (referents) or the things spoken of. In general such stimuli operate in communicative language situations and naturally play a great part in all forms of conversational activities. Especially striking are these types of stimuli in situations in which one person commands or requests another individual to do something to an adjustment stimulus object, or for the speaker or the person spoken to.

(b) Non-Personal referring stimuli. Probably it is only in the expressive form of language that we can properly speak of non-personal stimuli. Certainly we may look upon pictures, words, sounds, natural objects, landscapes, seascapes, the sea, waterfalls, and other things as speaking to us or stimulating us to react to adjustment stimuli, including objects, our own attitudes, and other actions to things. It is no doubt in the field of poetic language, both spoken and written, that we find our best illustrations of language situations with non-personal auxiliary or indirect stimuli.

**Receptive Referee Stimuli**     (a) Personal stimuli. In reacting to those to whom we talk) including ourselves) there are all sorts of actions, signs, and gestures, which serve specific stimulational functions. Various lip movements, head noddings, facial gestures, etc., stimulate us to make specific types of reference to things, to intensify and detensify our speech, or to maintain silence altogether. Here the types of stimulation may be considered as existing upon different levels. Such stimulation serves to inform us whether we are making references to this person at all, that is, whether he hears what we are saying, understands the references in whole or in part, appreciates the intimate details; whether, in other terms, he is being connected up properly with the referential material.  Finally, such stimulation serves to call out responses in us which are correlated with lip movements, words, etc., serving to acquaint us with the acquiescence or refusal of the individual to carry out our request with respect to the adjustment stimuli objects.

(b) Non-Personal stimuli.  With respect to non-personal stimuli the primary function is to determine whether or not we should perform linguistic reactions to them.  Here the range and scope of stimulation is probably very limited.  We do, however, find decided cases in which we address ourselves to natural objects and phenomena regardless of the fact that we get no genuine response from them. Thus we may address the sky, the echo, some god, etc., with a complaint concerning some suffering we have experienced or with joy concerning some good fortune that has befallen us.  Here, as in the previous section, non-personal stimulation operates only in expressive reactions.  But the sort of stimulational function that we have been suggesting is at least a genuine element in our linguistic behavior situations.

There are few types of psychological activity in which the stimuli settings are such important factors in conditioning and determining the character of the activity as in the case of linguistic behavior segments.  This fact, manifestly, is due to the extremely subtle character of linguistic phenomena.  Especially in the intercommunicative situations characterizing conversational speech we find an exceedingly large number of specific nuances in the surroundings of the interacting persons which have a tremendous influence upon the actual happenings in the linguistic event.  The mere fact that two persons are in intimate relationship, especially since their activities have to do with the reference to a third thing, complicates the situation with involved settings in the form of innumerable conditions of the action and the auspices under which it occurs.  The most intricate of behavior situations are those in which the referents happen to be the reactions of the individual himself, such as his desires, attitudes, and feelings.  Hardly less complicated are the behavior situations in which the reactions of the speaker or hearer are the settings of the stimuli in question.

*Linguistic Stimuli Settings*

Let us further indicate the extreme importance of settings in linguistic behavior segments by pointing out that in such situations we have various contexts that have to be taken into account.  On the one hand, what references we make to objects, and the very fact that we refer to them at all, depend upon the conditions under which they exist, the happenings in which they take part.  On the other hand, whether or not we should make the reference to some particular individual is contingent upon the surroundings.  Also, the question as to how to make the reference to this individual so that he will do what we want him to do with respect to the adjustment stimulus,— in other words, the whole problem of understanding, is contingent upon intimate details of the individual's past biography and present

condition. It depends upon whether he has acquired particular informational reaction systems, etc., and knows just how to put them
into function at the present time.

Generally speaking, the problem of stimulational settings covers a
wide range of specific features which may be described on the basis
of whether or not they belong to the auxiliary or adjustment stimulus
or to both at the same time. When the settings pertain to the
auxiliary stimulus we must inquire whether they condition the referee
or referrer stimulus. For convenience in discussing the various
aspects of linguistic stimuli settings we will adopt a threefold division
of our material. Under the rubric of intrinsic settings we plan to
discuss the stimuli backgrounds influencing the reference reaction
itself. By the term conditional settings we will cover the influences
determining the manner in which the referential responses are made,
while the expression circumstantial settings will have to do with the
more or less accidental surroundings of stimuli conditioning the
details of linguistic reactions.

**Intrinsic Settings**   Here we have, generally speaking, the contexts or backgrounds
which are always connected with both the auxiliary and referential
stimuli in language behavior segments. So prominent are the settings
with respect to the reacting individual that they are frequently
powerful enough to determine what type of understanding response
one is to perform. If we think of verbal language as one type of
transmissive linguistic stimuli, it frequently happens that the gestures
and general conditions of the individual are sufficient to call out the
reaction of appreciating or understanding what it is the individual
would say but actually does not.[1] Frequently by observing the relationship of an individual to some adjustment stimulus object or
situation we can understand, in spite of his inarticulateness, what it
is he wants to say. Doubtless, to a considerable extent here the perspective of a stimulus is important enough to usurp in part, at least,
the function of the stimulus itself. In general the efficacy of language depends upon the equipment of the auditor or referee. This
equipment serves as an effective setting for the words of the transmissive speech of the referrer. On the whole, the points we have
been making imply the unquestionable fact that communicative, or
conversational speech at least, is always part of a larger series of
events, a personal or social situation, so that a part may be inferred
or appreciated by one's observation of the character of the whole,
which in this case is the behavior situation of the linguistic event.
Probably the most common observation in this connection is found
in the statement frequently made that the printed words functioning
in a reading language situation derive their power from the capacities,
desires, and interests of the reader. Such words must not only

---

[1] "He spoke words which, though meaningless, expressed desire." Anatole
France, *Revolt of the Angels*. What is true of desire is true of ideational and
other reactional perspectives of the linguistically acting individual.

have descriptive contexts in the written or printed material such as correspond to the facial or shoulder gestures of spoken language, but must have a background also in the behavior equipment and reactional history of the reader. The entire balance between the transmitting and the receiving individual in a language activity is closely implicated with the perspective of the stimuli involved.[1]

To illustrate the conditional background of language or the modes of response we must refer to those conditions which influence the kind of words or gestures in which particular references are couched. Probably the most outstanding setting here is the institutional character of the language that one must inevitably use for communication. Specific illustrations are the vocabulary, grammar, and syntax that one uses so far as verbal responses are concerned, and characteristic group gestures, shoulder shrugging, hand motions, etc., which are inevitable features of a person's actions but which are accidental with respect to the act of referring to some stimulus, or the type of reference made. To a considerable extent, also, the conditional settings consist of peculiarities of the individual in the form of knowledge and general capacity of expression and the use of words. Everyone is familiar with the conception that "style is the man" with reference to literary criticism. The style or manner of making face-to-face verbal references is no less a matter of the behavior equipment of the person, which is, of course, our translation of the term "man." The conditional settings appear, therefore, primarily as influences upon the transmissive feature of communicative speech, although they may sometimes serve as background or perspective influences upon expressive linguistic conduct. *Conditional Settings*

Immediate and transitory backgrounds of language stimuli condition for the most part the occurrence or non-occurrence of the language reaction or else determine the effectiveness of the function of the language stimulus. On the whole we have here a complete series of conditions of intensity of language stimuli; the sudden presentation of words, the distinctness of enunciation of speech, etc., all have some influence upon whether or not the receiving individual will hear and understand what is said. The intonation used by particular referring persons, those in authority, for example, also conditions the nature of the reference for the person. Whether or not the request or command means or requires obedience may be adequately determined by the intonation or other similar circumstantial setting. This type of stimulus setting has to do exclusively with the auxiliary stimulus function of the linguistic situation. *Circumstantial Settings*

---

[1] Generally speaking, no class of individuals has better occasion to observe the significance of contextual settings (whether of the auxiliary stimuli as the word context of a printed word or literary context of a literary stimulus, or the event, condition, or intention settings of the adjustment stimuli) than lawyers. Accordingly we find America's eminent constitution-interpreting Chief Justice saying "Such is the character of human language, that no word conveys to the mind in all situations, one single definite idea."

A somewhat more generalized type of circumstantial setting for linguistic stimuli is the perceived eagerness of the transmitting individual to say something with respect to the referent and, on the side of the referee, the willingness to hear what is being said. Here also we may add such accidental settings as the distance between face-to-face speakers, the acoustic surroundings, and the affective conditions of the speakers whether they are cheerful, excited, pleased, irritated, etc.

In concluding the discussion of linguistic stimuli settings, it is worth noting that in the infinite variations of speech conduct and situations it frequently happens that what is a linguistic stimulus in one community is a linguistic setting or background in another. Similarly, the different types of settings become interchanged in their functions. An excellent illustration is the case of the Chinese language in which intonation that is usually setting in other languages is decidedly verbal or vocabulary stimulus.

**Simpler Psychological Reaction Components in Linguistic Conduct**

So complex a form of human activity as linguistic conduct must inevitably have simpler actions of all sorts as definite phases and components. The latter are not merely smaller linguistic units associated or integrated in the larger response or pattern, such as the unit verbal actions in a sentence or phrase illustrate. On the contrary, the linguistic components to which we refer such as attention, perception and understanding on the receptive side, are essential factors of language and necessary for the performance of indirect and referential adjustments. They are not, however, themselves linguistic in character.[1] Even simple references, whether transmissive or receptive, manifestly involve perceptual responses of a variety of types. Similarly, both simple and complex linguistic actions comprise as features of their several behavior segments complex appreciation and understanding actions, memorial conduct, etc. The point is that when a person reacts linguistically, he performs actions which may be executed in entirely non-linguistic reaction systems but which may also be integral parts of the reference-making action.

Our investigation here amounts to an analysis of the types of action which the person performs as integral features of language adjustment actions. These actions, we insist, do not simply belong to reaction patterns or situations in which language also has a place. To distinguish between actual component responses of language acts and other actions that are merely connected with the linguistic reactions is of extreme importance for the understanding of the character of linguistic behavior. It is to be expected that not all reference responses have the same number of component reactions, nor will specific linguistic actions have the same type of components that other reference responses have, even when they have the same number. In our analysis, therefore, we will find it expedient to consider in general

[1] This is not a situation exclusively found in language but it operates uniquely in language behavior segments.

the activities finding a place in linguistic conduct without specifying at the moment the particular cases in which they are found or what other types of action are found with them.   In each instance, however, we are obliged to point out the precise function of the action component in speech or other types of language.   Now, as a matter of fact, we find that the different components vary in the degree of their essentiality with respect to language.   For example, because perceptual reactions are themselves autonomous types of psychological activities they may be more or less essential factors in referential responses.   Some of these reactions retain in part their autonomous character and as a result they are, to that degree, not essentially linguistic.   In our analysis it will be necessary to point out these variations both in the particular functional operations of the same type of action and in the different component action types.   For purposes of expediency it will be well to point out activities that are not linguistic component actions, but the examination of which adds to our understanding of the linguistic behavior situation.   The list of these different component and non-component actions may be developed as the analysis proceeds.

Linguistic conduct at many points includes or involves perceptual activities.   It is a distinction of perceptual responses that they are more intimately and more uniquely connected with referential responses than most other kinds of action.   In this particular case the essentially linguistic perceptions can be sharply distinguished from the autonomous perceptions since here they constitute responses to particular forms of stimuli, to wit, linguistic vocal reactions and gestures of all sorts.   The acquisition or building up of these particular perceptual activities and their performance constitute essential factors in the development and performance of linguistic actions.

**Perceptual Components**

These perceptual reactions are responses to stimuli eliciting referential actions, and not overt performances or even direct implicit actions of any type.   Another indication of the specifically linguistic character of the perceptual responses under discussion is the manner of their development.   They are acquired by the individual as definitely and exclusively referential activities.   When the person first learns to respond perceptually to referential things (whether words or gestures) his perceptual cognitions are linguistic.   This is true whether or not the stimuli objects have been previously in nonlinguistic contact with the person.

Several kinds of perceptual reactions operate in linguistic conduct.   Besides the auditory reactions to the verbal auxiliary stimuli for conversational speech we perform a great number of visual perceptual responses to written and printed stimuli of all sorts.   Nor can we exclude here the tactual responses of the blind to the raised letter or to lip movements and other gestural stimuli.   These are all on the receptive side of language behavior.   On the transmissive side we have besides the visual, tactual, and auditory reactions, perceptual responses to the adjustment stimuli. We may also have similar perceptual responses to the auxiliary stimuli as well as auditory and visual perceptual reactions to the activities of oneself as stimulus.

Generally speaking, we may divide the essentially linguistic perceptual reactions into a primary and secondary type. For the most part the reactions that we have already discussed are primary in character. They are the reactions to the main stimulational factors in speech. Besides these we have perceptions that are involved more with secondary or auxiliary speech stimuli. To illustrate, when I speak to someone the verbal reactions that I, as transmissive person, make are usually greatly supplemented by facial, arm, and trunk gestures. It is very probable that the secondary stimuli have much to do with our appreciating the reference and the general effect which the other person's speech has upon us. It is not necessary, of course, for visual stimulation to be secondary to auditory. In reading, visual stimuli may be secondary to visual and auditory may be secondary to visual.[1]

A large number of perceptual actions are involved in linguistic conduct although they are not themselves linguistic in function. These are the perceptual activities upon the development and operation of which linguistic behavior depends. Involved as they are in the various experiences or contacts with things which lead to or make possible the indirect or referential actions, these perceptual responses are connected with linguistic behavior solely on that account. Without their prior occurrence the linguistic responses proper could not occur.

Memory Components

Taking the term memory in its authentic signification there is no place for such activity in linguistic conduct. The action of speaking, as such, involves no actual memorial processes. In other words, the projection and later performance of some action has no place as an essential feature of linguistic behavior. What superficially appears as memorial conduct in such behavior situations is really learning activity. All of the acquisitional features of language, i. e., the facts involved in the building up of reaction systems that are later employed in speaking, must be considered as processes of learning. True enough, all of the linguistic capacities of the individual constitute the operation of a large and indefinite number of specific acquired verbal and gestural reaction systems. But we cannot say that the person remembers as integral features of his referential conduct what words to use or what he should hear.

Memorial activities play a large part in linguistic situations when such activities are regarded as contributory and incidental events. Here we may point out that unless the individual remembers the event constituting the adjustment stimulus or the need for referring to it he will not perform referential activity at all. In these situations all manner of deliberate projected actions may be found. But

---

[1] In all cases it is difficult to say how much of this is a case of stimulus and settings, or setting usurping the place of stimulus.

such memory reactions are all remote conditions with respect to the actual performance of language responses and are consequently not in any sense language or reference reactions. It must be observed, however, that this extrinsic memory factor operates among others as a genuine phase of complex linguistic situations. We have here, then, another instance in which we analyze complex conduct into specific features or phases, some of which are denominated the central or main actions, while others are known as the associated or contributory actions.

The performance of linguistic conduct is based upon and involves in an absolute way a great number of learning activities. At the core of these learning activities is the actual acquisition of modes of reference which are quite apart from the reaction systems operating at the time. In other words, the individual must learn the act of performing language or referential activities. Making references to things, both when the auxiliary stimulus is oneself or someone else, is a definite technique of behavior which the individual must acquire in the same way that he learns to perform any other act. Hence with regard to the original period of acquiring or learning language actions, it is not impossible to consider the technique of reference as separate from the performance of specific reaction systems. Later in the life of the individual, when the same reference can be made in different ways, as in using different national or other group vocabularies, etc., the distinction may be logically made. As actual psychological events, of course, the references are always specific acts (reaction systems) of the person.

*Learning Components*

In addition to the learning involved in the actual technique of reference making the person must, as we have indicated, learn to couch or convey this reference in particular ways. Obviously he must acquire specific words, gestures, and other vocabulary elements which are necessary in a particular group. Furthermore, the individual must acquire or learn specific modes of acting in order to conform to prescriptions and conventions. He must be selective not only in what references he makes, to what referents he reacts, in addition to particular personal auxiliary stimuli, but also with respect to his means of reference. This selective action in many cases involves inhibiting activities, and in other cases, the making of references which would not otherwise be made. These latter learning aspects of linguistic conduct may be considered as the incidental and accidental learning features of language behavior. The actual reference making responses and the use of specific vocabulary and other institutional forms constitute, from a rigid psychological standpoint, the essential learning factors in linguistic activity.

Of all the psychological actions or conditions comprising component parts or phases of linguistic reaction patterns, none are so important or effective as meaning reactions. As a record of fact, linguistic conduct is replete with meaning responses of a great many

*Meaning Components*

types. Every instance of linguistic activity comprises a large number of meaning responses which are intimate components of the actual behavior involved. Meaning responses are performed by the transmitting, as well as by the receptive, person and in each case the essential meaning reactions are primarily responses to the auxiliary stimuli. In both the transmissive and receptive linguistic actions, the numerous incidental meaning responses exclusively constitute actions to the adjustment stimuli.

Among the essential transmissive meaning reactions we may distinguish those involved with referential function from those concerned primarily with the means of making the reference. Foremost among the meaning reactions are those activities which have to do with the adequacy of the reference from the standpoint of the referent. The problem here is whether the particular language acts performed fit the referent to which they refer. Here the meaning responses call forth the appropriate language equipment of the individual in order to describe or narrate concerning the adjustment stimulus object.

Other meaning reactions of the transmissive individual condition the type of reference with respect to the referee. Whether the referee should be learned or common (vocabulary), earnest or eloquent (manner of speech) etc., is determined by the speaking person's meaning responses to the referee. To a certain extent also these meaning responses determine whether the reference should be made at all, and whether it should be made under the present circumstances on the basis of the probabilities as to whether it will be well or ill received. The presence or absence of such meaning or appreciation reaction makes the difference between speech reactions tactfully and those tactlessly performed. In actual linguistic situations, it is practically always necessary for a constant interrelationship to exist between the person's meaning responses so far as referent and referee are involved.

We may now turn to the transmissive meaning reactions occurring as intimate features of the actual communication reactions. As the person speaks he performs a large series of meaning reactions which function in the appreciation of the way the reference is to be made. This series of meaning responses is connected with the actual communicative function in that they condition the actual verbal and gestural acts in their serial form. In this sense there is an immediate control exercised by the directly preceding acts over the succeeding ones. This is essentially the problem of knowing what to say before saying it. Here we may observe the concrete word or gestural actions conditioning what particular words or gesture actions shall follow in the total process of the statement or discourse.

On the side of the audient or referee the numerous forms of meaning responses may be divided into at least two types. In the first place, we have the meaning responses relating to the actual auxiliary stimulus, in brief, the appreciation of its character. In the second place, we have the meaning responses which are reactions to the auxiliary stimulus as it relates to the referent or adjustment stimulus. The former are not linguistic meaning reactions; this characterization belongs only to the latter type.

In general, we might distinguish here between three distinct stimulus-response situations. The first is a distinctly perceptual one. Here the stimulus object which is the referrer's action or symbol calls out an appreciation or cognitive response. The person knows what the word is or what the person said. The function of the stimulus object is purely perceptual. Some part of it calls out a total reaction to the whole of it. Just how much of the original stimulus object is in contact with the person is a variable event and how much of it is necessary to be present before the stimulus function operates depends upon the person, his familiarity with the object and its character, whether visual, tactual, auditory, etc.

Next we may consider the non-linguistic meaning reaction. Now in this case the stimulus object is reacted to not as a thing with which one is simply in contact, but as a thing that has a substitute function. This object stands for something, it is a part of a statement. There is no question as to what to do with it, or what it is in its own right, but rather what its significance is, what its relatives are.

Manifestly these different reactions cannot always be rigidly held apart but in many cases this is exceedingly simple. For example, we have the case in which the stimulus object is definitely cognized for what it is but not for what it represents, although it definitely is cognized as representing something.

Our full-fledged linguistic meaning response is that in which the stimulus object elicits a referential meaning reaction. The character of this essentially linguistic meaning response may be illustrated analogously to the other non-linguistic meaning response. In this case the person perceives that a question has been addressed to him but does not perceive what the question itself is. When we think of this question stimulus-object as spoken in a foreign language, there is no doubt that it constitutes a clear case of a linguistic meaning response which cannot be performed. Probably the best examples of specifically linguistic meaning responses are those which have to do with cognizing or appreciating what one is asked to do or how to carry out in detail some request or command. The linguistic character of these responses is evident from the way they are taken over in their completion without being built up through elementary direct contacts with things, that is, through direct perceptual processes.[1] Other meaning responses occurring on the side of the audient have to do with the immediate conditioning of later understanding reactions through the operations of the immediately preceding meaning re-

[1] Thus from a psychological standpoint etymology can never give the significance of a word but only its history and usage.

sponses. In any type of extended intercommunicative conversation the audient necessarily performs a large series of distinct meaning reactions. All of the specific acts that result in a conditioning of the meaning, understanding, and answering responses which follow are included in the general class of meaning conduct.

Linguistic meaning reactions accordingly are responses to distinctly linguistic stimuli in the form of the functions of words, gestures, etc. These linguistic elements elicit the meaning responses in the audient or referee. The language stimuli here call out reference responses to things, acts, or consequences. These condition refusal, acquiescence, agreement or other responses. Further, they either stimulate or condition the transmissive response involved in saying yes or no, etc. It is needless to insist, then, that these meaning responses are of various sorts and are much more elaborate in variety than other meaning or perceptual responses. Linguistic meanings depend upon the person's general equipment when the stimuli are the common property of a group. When we speak of books, the perceptual (attached) and general meaning (unattached) responses evoked are fairly definite and pervasive. When the meaning reaction is linguistic, because of the referential character, it is more individual and private. The degree of individuality and privacy characteristic of the reaction depends upon the particular circumstances involved. In a conventional circumstance the meanings are shared by two or more persons. Depending upon the intimacy of these persons the meaning responses may be aroused by very slight substitute stimuli. Between intimate persons a word, look, or nod may speak volumes, because the persons involved have shared or participated in their contact with the referent. Manifestly such meanings may be more restricted when the referents are simple and few than when they are complex and many. The most restricted situations are those in which the stimuli call out responses that refer exclusively to situations in a particular person's experience.

It is hardly necessary to point out the great number of meaning reactions that are incidental to linguistic responses. These are concerned with the appreciation of the importance of stimuli conditions or the need for communicating with or referring to some other individual with respect to such conditions or qualities of the stimuli objects, etc. Through these incidental meaning responses we approach the full-fledged understanding responses.

Knowledge and Understanding Reactions

Although knowledge and understanding are not each inherent components of linguistic reactions, in general no complicated linguistic behavior can go on without involving them. They become an indispensable factor in pertinent, intelligent language behavior. Unless one knows what one is talking about, effective speech is not possible. Similarly without an acquaintance with, or an orientation to, particular things one cannot understand certain references to them. Knowledge and understanding responses consequently condition the character and type of speech or other language, although they are not in themselves intimate linguistic features. They involve the relationship of the speaking persons with the referents in question. Linguistic conduct, however, can go on without these adjunct activities. Language situations lacking associated knowledge and understanding responses are naturally of the simpler type.

In another section of this chapter we have pointed out the imagination functions operating in language. Here we need only add that with respect to intimate forms of conversational intercourse numerous opportunities arise to develop and create words, phrases, and sentences which constitute individual modes of reacting linguistically. This creative activity refers not only to the immediate terms or vocabulary used in making the reference but also to the character of the reference itself. A person may innovate or originate some new method of expression. In a less intimate connection with the performance of linguistic reactions we find imagination reactions functioning so as to create the referent or referential situation. Doubtless the best examples of the imaginative functions operating in language are found in the literary field. In letter writing and the creation of literature of all forms the freedom of developing new linguistic elements and functions is amply illustrated. So much for transmissive language. By implication we have already indicated in a number of places the opportunities for creative action in audienting and reading linguistic behavior. It is a well-known fact that the reader of a book sometimes gets out of the material which he reads much more than the author put in. That is to say, the auxiliary stimuli of the author serve not only a referential function but stimulate the reading individual to perform considerable imagination action also. Possibly in this type of situation it is fitting to say that the imagination responses are integral features of the linguistic behavior.

*Imagination*

The acquisition of language behavior takes place under two generalized conditions. The first involves the development of linguistic behavior by an infant in a specific native community. Such a development means the actual acquisition of references to things and the ability to communicate with other individuals. The second acquisitional situation constitutes the development of a technique for making new kinds of references and for using, as referee, the members of a community different from one's original and native one. In both cases this language acquisition is doubtless at first primarily receptive. We will refer to these different situations as the acquisition of native language, and the development of foreign language, respectively.

*Acquisition and Development of Language Behavior*

The acquisition and development of native speech consists to a great extent of the organization of specific types of vocal and gestural reaction systems by means of auxiliary stimulation. The development of language behavior is a thoroughgoing cultural process. It consists almost entirely of the acquisition of cultural modes of con-

*Native Language*

duct. Since this linguistic development takes place in the very early years of infancy we can readily observe the significant influence of mature persons upon the infant by way of stimulating and guiding him in making references to specific objects.

To no inconsiderable degree is the process of linguistic culturalization the organization of random movements of a vocal and general gestural sort into such actions as are performed by the person with immediate and intimate reference to surrounding objects. A great many instances of momentarily acquired action, therefore, are found in every case of language development. It is most incorrect to consider the process of linguistic acquisition to be one which conditions existing actions by connecting them up with new stimuli. The latter process by no means falls completely outside the domain of linguistic development. It is, however, a minor and subordinate process and has only a very limited place in the acquisition of linguistic behavior equipment.

In the course of the actual acquisition of linguistic responses by the infant the early references are primarily of a nominative sort. The first language responses are, or appear to be, references to the names of things. That this should be the case is doubtless due first, to the fact that the experiences of the individual are very limited, and second, that early linguistic acquisitions are stimulated by deliberate auxiliary stimuli.[1] The individual begins to refer to specific objects and the references are necessarily meagre and specialized. There is no question, however, that much of the simple naming action in early infancy is a result of the operation of the tradition which dictates that the elementary development of language must consist in the naming of objects. In the actual development of linguistic conduct a careful observation of the activity involved demonstrates that even if the infant ostensibly is merely learning to name objects, he is really performing complex referential responses to them—complex, that is, within the limits of the infant's psychological development.

The use of specific vocabulary responses is acquired by the infant as a series of matter-of-fact reference situations. Accordingly, no matter what specific words are found in the individual's auxiliary stimulation, they become integrated in his referential action as a part of his language behavior equipment. Illustrative of this point is the fact that infants not only obviously acquire the particular vocabularies of their national family and community groups but also that no question of complexity or simplicity of linguistic terms is involved in the process. The infant, quite as a matter of course, acquires use of certain verbal reactions no matter how complex they are thought

---

[1] This is not, of course, the exclusive or even primary form of language development, though it may be so in the very earliest years. Language, like all other behavior equipment, is acquired by subtle casual stimulation, cf. Vol. I, Chap. VI.

to be. In the development of the performance of verbal responses we have the development of behavior segments in precisely the same way as in very other type of behavior situation. The use of the vocal apparatus develops precisely as the use of the legs in walking or the arms in manipulating things.

In an hypothetical scheme we may indicate the development of language activities from the direct non-linguistic stage to the indirect and full-fledged linguistic level. We assume that the child's earliest reaction to milk as a stimulus is entirely a direct reaction, drinking for example. Such a situation has nothing at all to do with language. Next we assume that the response is conditioned by the addition of the verbal stimulus milk offered by the parent. Here the response is still the act of drinking and bears absolutely no connection with language. The reaction now can be stimulated, however, by either the object milk or the word milk. The next stage we consider to be an outgrowth into an implicit form of action. At this point the individual does not perform the overt act of drinking but the sound of the word milk may call out implicit reactions to the object. This stage of the development may be considered as going over into the actual linguistic stage. The latter consists of the performance by which the individual can react to a person who is standing near and also to the milk which is absent by crying or asking for it. This constitutes the speech reaction proper. With the increase of the person's linguistic experiences this indirect reaction to milk will take place when it is present, and when the response is expressive rather than instrumental, communicative, etc.

The acquisition of a new technique of linguistic reactions is exactly the same as the development of original native responses. Because the individual, however, has already developed such a technique a number of interfering circumstances ordinarily constitutes a feature of the new language acquisition. For this reason learning a foreign language involves a great deal of modification of verbal and gestural reaction systems as a translation of references. The new speech activity must go on in terms of the old. This point is excellently illustrated by the fact that once an individual has developed the intimate and elementary forms of a certain kind of verbal behavior he has difficulty in acquiring other types of linguistic action. The German and French person can practically never say certain words in English exactly as the native English-speaking person can. This condition may be ascribed to the fact that the original fixation of random or organized action prevents the individual from performing actions which depend upon the presence of such unorganized or random acts. *Foreign Language*

Because language as a cultural fact or product must develop at some point from individual behavior, besides later constituting the stimulational basis for the acquisition of linguistic activity on the part of other individuals, we pause a moment to consider the problem of origin. This problem at the outset falls into two divisions. The first concerns the origin of language as a psychological function and product of behavior. The other refers to the origin of specific acts or stimuli for particular linguistic activities. With regard to the first problem we clearly have no knowledge at all, since the actual human situation in which reference making behavior originated is irrecoverably lost. Probably the various speculations which attempt to locate such origins in the reference making needs of individuals located in communities are correct.

With respect to the second problem, we have all kinds of information concerning the intimate interaction between individuals in contact with language institutions which stimulate them to acquire and perform specific linguistic activities. In the history of specific languages or dialects we find evidences of the way in which peculiarities of individual reactions modify such institutional responses and products to the extent that new languages come into existence in whole or part and also of the way in which languages, considered as actions and products, change their form sometimes to the point of unrecognizability.

**Language as Individual and Cultural Conduct**

So intimately are language responses tied up with cultural conditions that the question arises as to whether linguistic conduct may be considered at all as an individual process. In origin our ordinary linguistic reactions are objectively cultural. Such conduct consists entirely of responses dictated and controlled at every point by institutional stimuli. Practically every phase of language is conditioned by the presence of permanent institutions. In the later use of language also we find the linguistic institutions appearing ubiquitously to condition and influence our linguistic behavior. Whether we think of language conduct as the general employment of modes of action existing prior to our performance of them, or whether we think of the mutual interacting behavior necessary to communicate with other persons, we have conventional actions. On the whole linguistic responses are customary actions which are rigidly and in practically every detail controlled by the group auspices under which they have developed and are used.

Nevertheless, for an exact understanding of linguistic conduct, it is necessary to insist upon the distinction between individual and cultural language. This proposition is supported by three fairly distinct considerations. First, the psychological response to a stimulus is at the moment of its occurrence a distinct natural event. Secondly, the individual belongs to many cultural groups and in consequence his eclectic performance of actions belonging to a number of groups gives his actions a personal and individual stamp. It is this fact that lends veracity to the statement that each person speaks his own personal language. Finally, it is not to be denied that the very growth, development and changes in institutional language are the work of individuals. As a result the probability is established that the person performs individual and even non-cultural conduct although it may later become cultural or institutionalized.

We must admit that whenever an individual says something, the way he says it is rigidly determined by his social surroundings. When, however, the question arises whether or not or why the person speaks we cannot in any sense gainsay the essentially individualistic character of language. For language as individual and human conduct consists of the momentary action of making individual references to particular things and conditions. Individual reference making, whether it constitutes written or spoken language, concerns the specific and intimate conditions of a particular person's life. In this sense language is or may be completely independent of its cultural character and control. At this point we must look upon any psychological event as an autonomous happening. To connect the activity of the individual at the time he speaks with historical and institutional facts of language because of the vocabulary used and the cultural auspices under which he acts is to formalize the actual linguistic situation in such a way as to miss some of its most essential features. As a unique psychological event linguistic conduct is individual and not cultural action.

A number of other conditions may be adduced here. In the first place, an individual may persist in refusing to comply with the linguistic requirements of the group in which he finds himself. Again, his linguistic responses may deteriorate and in this way come more and more to vary from the linguistic standards and conventions of his community. Or the person may move from one linguistic community to another and in this way he may become somewhat independent of the rigorous control of cultural institutions. Probably we can best determine the individuality of linguistic behavior on the basis of whether or not it is expressive. This point may be connected with the group situation by pointing out that when one's auxiliary stimulus is a person of another group the action approaches the expressive type and is mainly individualistic, while when the auxiliary stimulus is a member of the same group the reaction is probably purely cultural.

To insist here upon the cultural character of linguistic conduct because of its origin and traditions is comparable to calling language biological because it is performed by a biological organism with specific structures and functions that always operate in linguistic activity. While it is always a biological organism that speaks or refers to things the specific language act is absolutely never the function of biological structures but invariably a type of psychological event which depends upon the person's intimate and historical interactions with numerous surrounding stimuli.

The case is similar with respect to the indispensable cultural aspects of linguistic conduct. The inevitable and overshadowing cultural conditions surrounding the facts of speech do not prevent the action from being a specific, personal, interacting response of the individual with particular stimuli.

No human being misses being a member of a great number of language using groups. The various languages he thus acquires from his social, economic, professional, fraternal, and family groups make it almost inevitable that he should perform individualistic language behavior. All of these elements make up the matrix from which are derived the same kind of unique behavior products that we find in practically all invention and creation. At specific times, places, and under specific circumstances, original and personal linguistic conduct results from the use of this equipment.

The final consideration justifying the belief in individual and unique linguistic behavior concerns both the generalized fact of cultural changes, originating in individual behavior which is hardly anything but unwitting action, and the more or less intentional processes of language serving particular purposes. Certain persons who are either insensitive to the existence of social institutions or who insist upon being free of their trammels perform actions that succeed in being more or less original and, therefore, to some extent indubitably individual and not cultural. A child may persist in mumbling and pointing long after he has learned to use the linguistic behavior of his group. Some of the best illustrations are to be found in the field of poetry and other original compositions. In written language it is this individualistic character of linguistic conduct that makes for the great variety of literary styles.

**The Institutional Character of Language**

Throughout the psychological study of language as compared with the philological, anthropological, historical and pedagogical, we must constantly emphasize, as we have been doing, the absolutely behavioristic character of our subject matter. In the psychological analysis of language we are dealing always and exclusively with the actual responses of an individual. And yet as we have been forced to observe, the specific way in which this activity is carried on is conditioned by the cultural and institutional character of language. Accordingly, it is important to give some attention to the character and organization of language as institutional forms. In other words, we must take account of language behavior not only as a series of acts constituting specific adaptations to all the various stimuli objects and conditions to which, in conjunction with auxiliary stimuli, the individual reacts, but we must also take cognizance of the specific means by which these particular adaptations are carried out by individuals residing in particular groups. The study of the conventional and institutional auspices (vocabulary, grammar, syntax, etc.) under which linguistic conduct operates yields considerable information concerning the actual ways in which language behavior may be described.[1]

---

[1] This is not the study of grammar, syntax, etc., unless these studies are de-

The study of the institutional features of language that we propose [1] is extremely important as an aid to the completeness of our linguistic analysis. It reveals the fact that these institutional forms are the objects existing in the surroundings of an individual which, through casual and deliberate culturalization become the stimuli objects functioning in linguistic conduct situations. In other words, these institutional forms correlate exactly with natural objects and all their qualities that during the lifetime of the individual become the stimuli for his reactions. This point must be insisted upon in spite of the fact that, unlike the case of natural objects, these human contrivances (just as natural of course) have come into existence as the crystallizations of behavior of human beings in the course of their intimate contacts with and adjustments to their natural surroundings (objects and persons). These various institutional forms we may consider under four headings, as follows: (1) informal reactional institutions, (2) formal reactional institutions, (3) stylistic reactional institutions, and (4) tendency institutions.

The primary characteristic of these institutions is that they involve phases of action that are not easily comprehended in some formula. These language phases are not taught at all where language is deliberately taught. They are institutions having to do with the more generalized behavior of the individual. Informal reactional institutions constitute behavior that is not definitely localized as are verbal speech reactions. To a great extent, therefore, we might look upon them as gestural actions whether or not they are related to verbal, vocal action. Here we have vocal gesturing which accompanies or constitutes part of vocal speech, and other forms of gestures (non-vocal) that may or may not be independent of vocal language action. In all these cases we have action common to members of given communities, so that the new members are thereby stimulated to take on these modes of language as parts of their own language equipment and action.

*Informal Reactional Institutions*

To indicate more specifically the character of these reactional institutions we might describe them as forcefulness, explosiveness, calmness and excitability in speaking, etc. The speakers of one type of language cannot fail to be impressed with the different manner in which persons of another group carry on their linguistic behavior. The

scriptions of how people actually speak instead of enumerations of formal traditions and logical descriptions of philological materials.

[1] Our analysis can only be suggestive. To analyze actual linguistic institutions would mean to work through thousands and thousands of organized linguistic institutional units (families, national dialectal and colloquial, etc.). The student of psychology will do well, while keeping in mind the wide differences in conception concerning these institutions (psychological data are not sounds, words, sentences, signs, etc.) to read in the general philological literature for descriptions and illustrations. The following books in this connection are to be highly recommended. Cf. Paul, *Prinzipien der Sprachgeschichte*, 1898, 1909, or Eng. translation, 1898; Sapir, op. cit.; Jespersen, *Language*, 1922, *Philosophy of Grammar*, 1924; Vendreyes, op. cit., 1925.

comparative calmness and sluggishness of the conventional speech of the various Scandinavian groups must impress strongly the individuals of the Romance language groups. The same institutional conditions of rapidity, vehemence, and explosiveness characteristic of the speech of the Romance peoples in turn startle the generally calmer Northern peoples. To move from place to place over the globe is to discover thousands of concrete illustrations of the kinds of institutions we are attempting to point out.

Besides the reactional institutions mentioned we may refer also to the general accompaniment of speech with gesticulation. This type of institution refers to specific movements and actions of the hands, arms, and shoulders, that have a place in the person's conduct when he makes certain sorts of reference to things. Here we notice all sorts of gestural reactions that characterize the languages of different peoples.

Another type of informal reactional institution is the amount of referential purpose that can be carried out by simple gestures. In certain groups a nod or look carries a large understanding of what the other person refers to, whereas in other groups a greater specificity is necessary. Such institutions, of course, depend upon the simplicity and complexity of the referents and the referential situation in general. Accordingly, we expect to find such institutions flourishing in simpler human communities where referents are comparatively scarce and their details few or unimportant.

The amount of reference carried by simple gestures depends also upon the intimacy of the listener and speaker. Thus we find in intimate groups such as the family or between certain individuals that a minimum of pointing, sighing, or cooing is sufficient to refer the other person to a great deal of content in the form of things, circumstances, and conditions, which under other circumstances requires the performance of considerable linguistic action.

**Formal Reactional Institutions**

Our second division covers all of the institutional facts that involve more formal gestures, primarily those of a vocal sort, and specific verbal responses which on the whole are examples of more fixed and formal linguistic institutions. These institutions develop and persist in some local or widespread and continuous form.

And first we may consider the formal or vocal gestural institutions. Among the outstanding data here we emphasize rhythms and intonations which constitute a larger or smaller part of the linguistic activity of members of particular groups.

Intonations and pitch variations operate differently in different languages depending upon their general character. In English, for example, intonation is not a very marked feature of speech conduct. It is employed, however, in differentiating between references, rising pitch indicating a question concerning an object or event, whereas falling pitch in the same formal or verbal actions constitutes a mere declarative reference. In other linguistic groups pitch variation constitutes an exceedingly important feature of language institutions. Upon whether the tone rises, stays at a given level, or falls, depend the differences in the reference character of the vocabulary action or symbol. Tonal variation among groups employing monosyllabic words constitute the sole difference between the reference character of the monosyllabic verbal action. In Annamese the syllable or word *co* has been estimated to have no less than fifteen different pronunciations corresponding to the most widely varying references. Variations in tone constitute differences in object or event references as well as differences in time (active and passive references, for example).

Emphases of various parts of a referent action are somewhat less definite gestural institutions than those already mentioned. They are none the less formal linguistic elements. Their lack of definiteness on the whole is due to the fact that emphasis has its origin directly in the reactional character of persons rather than in formal modes of reference. An illustration of the emphasis institution is the stressing of what is considered the important or interesting feature of the referent, especially if it happens to be an event or situation. Specific institutions of this type are such as the emphasis of the kind of thing one is referring to, the place where it exists, the time it happened, or who it was who participated in the event involving the referent, etc.

Rhythmic institutions are considerably more definite than emphasis ones. These have to do more with formal linguistic activities than with the person's referential action. Immediately we think of accents upon the beginnings and endings of words, or the stress of beginnings and endings of other linguistic action units. In general, various languages have their stresses, accents, and pauses, which give rise to gestural patterns and constitute modes of action in particular groups.

When we turn to verbal reaction institutions we come to the most definite and fixed of all within the linguistic domain. Here we find action types and forms representing complex organized patterns. In the special field of verbal institutions we discover also a tremendous number of particular types of organized institutions which, when the whole series is considered effectively, divides off one set of group institutions of a particular language from its more or less similar neighbors.

Of the numerous ways in which these details may be marked out we choose a three-fold division. (a) The first includes an enumeration of specific modes of reference, the particular kind of cultural acts used in making references. This division may be said to deal with the linguistic responses as such, that is to say, in it are stressed the basis or bare means of handling the referent. The philological counterparts of these institutions are the facts of phonology, accidence and vocabulary.

In the various human groups things are referred to by means of particular qualitative verbal reactions. By means of verbal mechanisms, word sounds, reaction systems of every imaginable pattern are made. Some of these institutions vary little in related groups, such as the bread-Brot reactions of the English-German peoples. When we compare the English and Semitic groups the different psychological acts performed in making this bread reference have nothing in common.

Among this same set of institutions are included the modes or schemes of making up verbal reaction systems. Included here are various processes of forming words, such as composition, by which complex words are made up of or integrated from simpler elements or reaction systems. Examples are typewriter, doorstep, etc. Affixation is another such institutional word-forming process. Word patterns of all types are formed by prefixing, suffixing and infixing elements to larger wholes. Similarly, the modification of words is another word-making institution, like sing, sang, throw, threw, etc. These comprise definite behavior patterns of linguistic types in various groups. The duplication of verbal forms in order to perform particular kinds of reference reactions, such as so-so, yes-yes, and more remotely similar forms, also find a place in the enumeration of linguistic institutions.[1]

(b) Attention must be next directed toward institutions primarily involving actions inclining toward the referents and their linguistic treatment. Two different factors are included here. In the first place, the question arises as to what conventions exist among particular groups with respect to the amount of the referent that they specifically respond to and how much is left to be understood or otherwise referred to. In the second place, the problem concerns the precise method of organizing the specific reference acts or elements. As to the former factor the question is whether a particular language contains or stresses sex, number, and time, in addition to the reference acts having as their stimuli the thing or object, what happens to it and the place where it happens, etc. In some languages the sex of a referent is stated whether it need be or not. Other language conventions give all referents, either male or female, designation although they may be neither. This means that there is no neuter form of reference. Sometimes, curiously enough, the formal sex reference provides adequate indirect responses to objects, although as inanimate objects the referents have no sex at all. Le livre=the book and la livre=the pound, illustrate the point. Also we find the institutional condition that refers to a maiden or woman as sexless whereas the chocolate and soup she consumes are feminine and her hats and shoes are male. How the number institutions operate

---

[1] Here, as in other places, in discussing linguistic institutions we fall back upon philological terms and descriptions but the cautious reader will have no difficulty in keeping the actional and object phases of language segments distinct from each other.

may be indicated by the fact that some groups have definite institutions for two and three objects as well as one (dual, trial) although most groups use only the conventional singular and plural. With respect to time great variation is discoverable in the institutions set up by various groups. Here we need only suggest differences in refinement of reference. What kind of past may be referred to, immediate, remote, completed, uncompleted, definite, indefinite, mythical, actual, etc? Again, in the matter of time, does or does not the language comprise institutions for referring to temporal considerations such as whether something is happening or continues to happen, began to happen, happened instantly or repeatedly, etc.

Just how these references are organized in formal institutional actions is our next consideration. In some languages words or larger speech actions have a tendency to refer to special concrete features of the referent. Verbal references are simple and elemental. To a certain extent the condition here is well represented by the philological terms *isolating* and *analyzing* as used to characterize linguistic patterns. This type of linguistic institution is illustrated by comparing Chinese and English with a compounding language like Latin or Greek. Another type of linguistic organization is that in which the content or material of the referent is grouped together and compounded. Here the linguistic acts are integrated by various methods. Some types of linguistic integration involve putting together content-referring verbal action with a fair retention by the elements of their independence. This must be called from the standpoint of the formal product an associated connection rather than an integration. The philological term agglutination best represents this situation. On the other hand, some linguistic institutions constitute true integration of referential actions so that the word products are units incapable of separation. By comparing them with other referential forms, however, it may be seen how the integration has been built up. Here we have what the philologist calls the inflectional process. In this type of institutional organization the integrated actions constitute the development of entirely new forms. It is doubtless for this reason that in philological literature inflection is made to include such integrations as we have been discussing and the symbolic inflections (foot, feet) which are really new verbal acts modified from some other form.

In connection with this mention of linguistic reaction organization it may be recalled that the institution of verbal organization is connected with others in the actual performance of linguistic conduct. Thus isolating languages require intonative action to constitute actual referential conduct, while others do not. Also among the integrating languages we find degrees of fusion or integration. Some verbal organizations fall midway between the associational and integrational situations. It is in this connection, moreover, that the problem arises concerning the inclusion among a group's linguistic institutions of the particular number and types of independent parts of speech, which can be made to serve for each other as reference acts. These institutions of status extend also to the specified manner in which the substitution can be effected. Does the verb include the pronoun, is the passive formed by a verbal element or by a prepositional object, is the genitive formed in one particular way or in several ways, are some of the grammatical questions illustrating the present type of linguistic behavior conventions.

(c) With this analysis we come to the language conventions regarding the specific reactional relation of the speaker to his auxiliary stimulus. Among such conventions are the distinct language responses constituting specific linguistic relations. Here we may cite the presence and type of particular action functioning as direct or indirect address, offering and denying, commanding and acquiescing, certainty and uncertainty of reference, positive and negative linguistic behavior, politeness in form of address, etc. Illustrations are found in the consideration of the moods and cases of the grammarian. These institutions are tied up to no inconsiderable extent with the organization of simpler language into linguistic patterns. The grammarian's word order symbolizes the fact here indicated.

Stylistic Institutions

In quite a different type of linguistic behavior institution are the constituents of every person's behavior called stylistic conventions. Such conventional modes of speaking and writing differentiate various individuals of given groups. Precisely what particular convention institutions the individual utilizes is a direct reflection of the cultural complexity and cultural experience of the group in which the conventions are employed. Because of different attitudes, and different ways of looking at various conditions and happenings in specialized communities, diverse linguistic institutions arise. Stylistic conventions are very much conditioned, therefore, by the situations out of which they evolve.

A large class of more generalized style institutions are those called language idioms. Every language has its own complement of linguistic elements, having a more or less fixed form. The acquisition of these particular methods of linguistic reference involves the development of a technique for using the idiomatic mode of reference in precisely the same manner as the vocabulary and modifiers of reference are acquired and employed. Let us further note that these language forms are entirely distinct from the order and arrangement of mere vocal action, for in the case of idioms the referent plays a large place in the shaping and displaying of the linguistic style. Subtle as the distinction is, the stylistic idiom must be differentiated from the philological fact of the same name.

More restricted and specialized forms of stylistic institutions include metaphorical and similitudinous references to objects. There are many types of conventional means of referring to things in terms of other things, for example, figures of speech. The use of particular figures is correlated not only with particular national linguistic groups, but also with certain periods of time. The Renaissance period in English literature displays a remarkable use of figures and metaphors. The charm of Shakespeare's language is easily traced to his keen and pleasing employment of figures.

Probably no better illustration of the stylistic institutions of language is afforded us than the differences in speech reactions of men of different professional groups. Who is not able to distinguish the lawyer, physician, and scientist by the influences which their occupational groups have exerted upon their speech? Occupational group style is not restricted to figures, however, but extends to vocabulary and grammar as well.

Within occupational group language we discover other linguistic institutions. Suggestive here are the redundance and inclusiveness of legal languages, the exactness, crispness and symbolization of scientific speech, while the elaborateness and floridness of poetic language is self-suggestive of unique and characteristic qualities. Frequently such institutions are more apparent in written than spoken speech; in other cases the relations are reversed.

Characterizing various group tongues are such linguistic institutions as the amount and type of slang. The use of these forms indicates in great measure the degree of freedom which individuals are allowed in their departure from conventional reactions. Nor should we fail to mention the linguistic institutions involving the use of maxims, and parables in the course of referring to objects and conditions. Also the fact that in certain communities references to events, especially accidents and disease, cannot be made without constant reference to a deity of some sort, may be looked upon as stylistic phenomena. In other cases, certain events are referred to in a brooding and resigned fashion, contrasting remarkably with other instances in which linguistic references to things are made in an aggressive and confident manner. All these larger stylistic elements of language are reflected in the literature or the transcribed records of things. Thus both in belles-lettres and in other types of literature we discover particular forms of linguistic action which are based upon the types of individuals who narrate the events. It is in this sense that the old Romantic writers could find some justification for their conception of language as expressing the "soul" of the people.

Our enumeration of stylistic institutions must not be concluded without some mention of the use of characteristic statements. For instance, among the Italians we find references to the evil eye and one's safety therefrom; "God bless you," represents a more familiar stylistic institution. In this particular phase of our discussion we must insist that these modes of reference are the mere use of particular stylistic characteristics while the actual referential behavior is being performed.

Linguistic tendency institutions consist of general drifts in given directions. These tendencies or drifts can only be discerned by making comparisons between various organized linguistic systems. **Tendency Institutions**

Obviously tendencies or drifts are characteristics belonging to languages as wholes. Some languages have a tendency toward purity. There is a decided repugnance toward accepting and assimilating foreign ways of referring to things. The German language immediately appears as an example. An extreme form is Yiddish which has borrowed great quantities from various languages such as Hebrew, Polish, Russian, Lithuanian, etc. Another example of tendency institutions is the degree of resistance to change in mode of reacting indirectly to things. German again is an example of a language which has retained its inflectional character as compared with French or English. When comparing institutions of different languages we find that this drift refers to all kinds of linguistic processes, for example, use of the subjunctive, etc. A closely related drift institution is constituted of the past tendency in derivation of behavior form. These institutional drifts depend upon the contacts of linguistic groups with each other. English reveals clearly the large amount of material which it has drawn from Latin, Greek, etc.

One of the most elusive, but no less clear types of drift institutions is discernible when a person who is culturalized in one linguistic group attempts to react indirectly by means of the cultural behavior developed in another group. How difficult in large and small details is the attempt at such a translation. This situation has been considered with regard more to written than spoken language, but linguistic tendencies are none the less obstacles to the speaker. In the latter case, however, the difficulties are only compensated by means of personal gestures which are not available in the case of writing, but are not eliminated.

Among the very specific institutions illustrating linguistic tendencies in written language are the customs regarding capitalization and punctuation which differ enormously among various peoples. In general the written form of referential behavior presents a number of these specific linguistic institutions.

At the close of such an analysis it must inevitably be remarked that these institutions cannot possibly have any absolute fixity or uniformity even if we take as the unit of study some very specific dialectal unit. As we have already remarked these institutions represent crystallizations of actual linguistic conduct. No matter how rigid a fixation may be it is apparent that the linguistic conduct goes on and again liquefies the crystals which in the course of this transformation become metamorphosed. Naturally some of these institutions have greater fixity than others. For example, linguistic pattern is decidedly more fixed than the syntactical institutions or phonetic patterns. Of course, the degree of fixity depends also upon the different specific communities in which the particular institutions are found.

The fixity and rigidity of these institutions are due to a great extent to the development of writing and to the recording of the crystallization. But no matter how firmly these institutions are established by custom and usage, they are inevitably dynamic in character and so may become modified and transformed. The influence of writing and recording upon the development of institutions cannot be over-emphasized. On the other hand, the counter influence of written language upon the activities of reference must also be stressed.

Most instructive are the numerous extreme variations in the performance of linguistic reactions. Not only do they constitute peculiar, interesting and important autonomous facts of linguistic conduct but also, through their intermingling with the more conventional and common language responses in the person's total linguistic behavior, they give the individual's indirect adaptations a unique character. Like all variant conduct, definite language behavior is widely distributed over a great many specific types, some of which are related to other defects. To achieve the pragmatic purpose of indicating some of the more striking forms of defective linguistic conduct we may divide all such behavior into two large divisions, the intrinsic and the extrinsic.

**Defective Language Behavior**

An intrinsic linguistic defect from a strictly psychological standpoint consists of a variation of language reactions such as to constitute a modification in the actual fact of reference, and the way in which this reference is made. Here the individual fails to accomplish an indirect or referential act through actual incompetency or insufficiency of psychological adaptation. Or, his action may be imperfect either because of immediate insufficiency of reference or because of a more permanent personality trait or characteristic. The latter case is exemplified by the inarticulate individual who has a reference to make, needs and desires to make it, but finds himself incapable of performing a communicative referential response.

Doubtless the most striking condition in such a situation is the actual lack of any reference-making equipment, or of the kind of equipment that is necessary at the particular moment or in some specific situation. Not to know French when in Paris or not to be able to make verbal sounds in the presence of a person who does not understand sign language, is just as disastrous for the time being, and from a psychological standpoint, as total inability to evoke references.

Again the inability to make the reference, whether reactional or personal, may be due to some unfavorable influence exerted by the auxiliary stimulus. Somewhat trivial but illuminating cases are the inabilities to make references when in the presence of a rigid and perhaps hostile examiner, or of a profoundly beloved person. How frequently inefficient is the proposal of the lover even if he does manage to say what he is struggling to convey. In all ordinary situations, of course, the defectiveness of speech consists of the intermingling of total inabilities to make references and various degrees of insufficiencies of reference.

All this occurs of course on the side of the transmissive individual.

Similar total incapacities and insufficiencies of reference behavior transpire on the side of the receptive person. As in the transmissive case, the defectiveness may be regarded as involving various combinations of the double triadic relation, of which the terms are the referent or adjustment stimulus (which may be a common object), the transmissive and receptive individuals and their actions as the auxiliary stimuli, and the transmissive and receptive actions as responses. The defectiveness of language in this connection may be due to the lack of the stimulational function of the adjustment stimulus object, common to the two individuals; so that the transmissive individual's reference is not a reference with respect to the receptive individual. That is to say, the adjustment stimulus object in this case does not function consonantly for the two persons. Again, a certain type of reference as auxiliary stimulus may not be the kind that can perform the referring function so far as the receptive individual is concerned. This common situation is illustrated by the failure of the student to perform a receptive reference reaction because of the unfamiliar or incomprehensible vocabulary of the professor.

A number of conditions having direct connection with the defects of language may be referred to as factors contributory to the intrinsic linguistic abnormality. These are the conditions which involve the reference-making responses. In the first place, we may consider the general character of the personality and his equipment. The person may be characterized as generally inferior or defective. For example, he may lack that degree of intelligence required for adequate linguistic reference behavior. Or possibly he merely has not had specific experiences which would aid the particular purposes at hand. In the latter case the inability to perform language activity has its basis and origin in the peculiar reactional biography of the individual. The person may be lacking in ideas or experience connected with the defective language activity in question. These and other contributing conditions are found at the basis of both transmissive and receptive linguistic abnormality. In addition, the receptive individual may be unable to respond because of lack of attention due to engrossment with other stimuli; so that in a situation in which he is expected and apparently prepared to perform linguistic reaction, he actually fails to do so.

Extrinsic linguistic defects constitute variations in language conduct involving the mechanisms which comprise the actual reaction systems necessary for making references or for performing indirect reactions. On the whole the extrinsic linguistic defects are more palpable behavior data and in consequence may be regarded as the more frequent of occurrence. But this is merely because their more striking form brings them more frequently to the notice of those interested in language behavior. Generally speaking, the extrinsic defects concern the behavior machinery for reference making conduct. It is for this reason that the extrinsic linguistic defects are ordinarily singled out as the actual language abnormalities. From a psychological standpoint, however, although the intrinsic responses are not so noticeable, they must still be looked upon as genuine abnormal phenomena. For the psychologist's interest, of course, is in the actual adaptation and not merely in its features involving immediate structures.[1]

Extrinsic linguistic defects we divide into two sub-types. The first type constitutes the language mechanisms proper and the second, contributory actions and processes. In the former division we have language defects involving the individual's inability to perform the verbalization and gestural functions which constitute the behavior mechanisms of linguistic behavior. In detail such abnormalities comprise defects and deficiencies of enunciation and pronunciation, insufficiencies in gesture making, in verbal speech and in the graphic presentation of symbols in writing. Very common are the variants in speech behavior known as lisping, slurring of sounds, muttering, stammering, and stuttering. All of these types of defects are either reaction system deficiencies (in the sense that the difficulty may be located in the components of the reaction systems), which may or may not be correlated with structural abnormalities,[2] or behavior segment defects, namely the total lack of the necessary behavior mechanisms for reference making.

The other subdivision of extrinsic defects comprises deficiencies or variations of linguistic conduct localizable in the other component actions which may or may not be inevitable factors in the linguistic activity but which have an influence upon the actual performance of referential conduct. The difficulty, for example, may be located in the perceptual components of the linguistic conduct. The person may be unable to perceive properly visual symbols constituting the auxiliary stimulation. Or, he may not be able to hear what is said to him. Furthermore, abnormalities of this type result from the individual's failure to understand or appreciate the significance of the reference. Because of some condition of dissociation he is unable to appreciate the connection between the adjustment and auxiliary stimulus, the latter constituting the reference to the former. In the actual execution of human linguistic conduct we find a practically infinite variety of combinations in these various factors. As we may well expect, in all complex cases of abnormality of language we find intrinsic and extrinsic factors inextricably interwoven, forming all types of speech derangements. Furthermore, the intrinsic and extrinsic variations may, together, be connected up with all sorts of non-linguistic behavior defects and deficiencies so as to constitute involved linguistic abnormalities.

The actual enumeration of particular clinical pictures of speech defects indicates all types and varieties of inability to carry on lin-

[1] See Chapter on Abnormal Reactions and Psychopathic Personalities.
[2] See Chapter on Abnormalities of Behavior, p. 452.

276 PRINCIPLES OF PSYCHOLOGY

guistic behavior. Some individuals are unable to refer to things, or to refer to them by correct naming, while others are incapable of appreciating to what things names refer. We may consider these defects as involving primarily sound, syllable, and word elements on the transmissive side. Other behavior defects involve more complex actions of reference. The person may be unable to speak loudly, to speak grammatically, or with proper gestures. Again, he may be unable to read at all, to read correctly, or to read particular materials. Linguistic defects also comprise defects in writing such as inability to write at all, inability to write certain things, or to write coherently, correctly, evenly or cleanly.[1]

Considerable light is thrown upon the character of linguistic defects when we compare the actual description of diverse variants in speech with the traditional interpretations of aphasia and kindred defects. Such traditional interpretations, fostered by medical men who have practically always entertained the chief interest in such phenomena, are all handled of course in terms of an underlying nervous basis. According to this viewpoint defects of speech are merely correlated with parts of the nervous system that are accordingly presumed to be defective. Speech defects are therefore thought of either as sensory or motor in character, on the basis of a lesion or insufficiency of the functioning of sensory or motor neurons, the former being connected with the auditory mechanisms and the latter with the mouth parts. Besides these types of speech defects correlated with the sensory motor areas, all sorts of ideational or conceptual speech defects are presumed to exist on the basis of hypothetic centers located in the brain.

Influence of Language upon Individual and Cultural Conduct

It would indeed be a strange circumstance if such pervasive and constant activities as linguistic responses did not exercise a tremendous influence upon human behavior and human circumstances of all sorts. They do, of course. In a varying series of remarkable ways linguistic activities affect other forms of action for both the weal and woe of the persons concerned.

Let us turn at once to the root of the whole matter. In the fact that language constitutes a mode of referential or indirect behavior with respect to things we find one of the bases of its frequent dominance of human conduct. Immediately there is suggested here the fact that linguistic actions are usually partial and incomplete in reference whether they operate in describing or interpreting something or in requesting or directing behavior. Furthermore since description can be understood only in terms of the receptive indi-

---

[1] The reader may be referred to the medical literature in which the various para—and dysfunctioning of all sorts are lengthily described. Good summaries of these phenomena are Gutzmann, "Psychologie der Sprache," in Kafka's *Handbuch der vergleichenden Psychologie*, 1922, Vol. I, for continental literature, and Head, "Aphasia: An Historical Review," *Brain*, 1920–21, 43, 390–411, for English literature.

vidual's own experience a definite lacuna is left between what actually happens and the referential action to it.

Furthermore, language behavior is a method for and results in the crystallization and consecration of other actions, and especially of intellectual behavior. Beliefs, opinions, and other intellectual attitudes take on by the route of language such a permanency and solidity of character that they persist and dominate the individual and his group. Especially in this form do they prevent their own modification and their substitution by other and perhaps better ideas and beliefs. Scholars know that there is danger, once an idea is committed to writing, that it may appear to be final, complete, and authoritatively stultified. But of course the results are not by any means always unfavorable. For it is this same crystallization which makes language a scaffolding capable of serving in the development of ideas and their symbolization and representation when the latter are themselves too complex to be otherwise handled.

Once more, we must stress the enormous place that linguistic conduct assumes in the interrelationship between persons and different civilizations. In serving as an instrument for carrying on various sorts of human activities linguistic conduct becomes a fertile source of abuse and misdirection as well as a basis for all sorts of interconnections between human groups, and for the cultural influences of one group upon another. A similar type of interrelationship is made possible by language between persons in a particular group or between individuals of different groups in larger and more inclusive groups or communities.

Language, as an instrument of intercommunication, a means of interchanging ideas, literature, customs, and other cultural elements is obviously a unique human tool. As such it is the basis for human development, for the enlargement of cultural and social life. It is the means of transmitting everything that passes from certain human individuals to other human individuals and from group to group. On the other hand, language affords the basis for misunderstanding and controversies of all sorts. Misunderstandings arise from the incommensurability of the modes of reference so that intercommunication is impossible without some misunderstanding. Quite as many misunderstandings among individuals and groups may be ascribed to differences in language as to variations in customs, traditions, and attitudes. Symbolic of the incommensurability of language is the serious difficulty of translating from one language to another.

In many instances, too, language serves as a deliberate means of misunderstanding and imposition by the abuse of its functions and processes. Such are the uses of language for the conquest and domination of other people which are deliberately practised in diplomacy, in advertising, and in politics. How much abuse of political and economic power and authority is accomplished through the use of language which, whether actually describing and promising things, or by means of symbols or slogans, is intended to convey a deceptive idea. Not to be ignored here is the sophistic enterprise of making the worse appear the better cause through the expert manipulation of rhetorical instruments. Without a doubt the most serious misuse of language is deception in its various forms of self-misinformation and rationalization.

Abuses of language, whether or not they are deliberate and influence either ourselves or others, assume considerable prominence in the more intellectual and serious aspects of human life. The religious, artistic, moral, and scientific activities reveal numerous substitutes of words for things with resulting evil effects. Accordingly we have all kinds of magical words, and words shaping thought concerning art, moral, and religious phenomena which occasion difficulties in the knowledge and action of individuals. Especially we may cite the misuse of metaphors which mislead even the most efficient and wary of scientists. The worst difficulty experienced here is the employment of words having no reference whatsoever, thus giving rise to all types of ontological arguments and beliefs with respect to all of the complex phases of human life. Philosophers and students of the sciences in all periods of human development have taken the occasion to point out the pitfalls and treacheries contained in the linguistic conduct necessary to the pursuit of scientific work. To the linguistic influence upon the Aristotelian logic is ascribed the unsatisfactory character of that intellectual organon. In physics much error has been caused by the use of universals, such as force, caloric matter, phlogiston, etc.

Biology, with "life," and psychology with "consciousness," "instinct," "intelligence," etc., also contribute their quota of linguistic impediments to thought and genuine intellectual advance. Naturally we are assuming here that implicated with language in this circumstance are linguistic institutions as well as linguistic behavior and even non-linguistic facts. All of this is aside from the well recognized fact that, once we have made descriptions of things, we tend to overlook the other features of objects and events which were not originally included in the description, and thus are excluded from the standard knowledge and information concerning particular facts and situations.

Not the least of the influences of language upon individual and cultural conduct are the various types of insufficiences of language serving as instruments of social intercourse and thought. In quite a general sense we find that our communications cannot be restricted to methods of description and narration but must be supplemented by pictures and photographs, all of which make room for various possibilities of misunderstanding and defects in communication. Illustrative of the specialized forms of language insufficiencies are the sometimes hopeless circumstances in which a scientist finds himself when it is necessary to describe a particular type of phenomena. Linguistic activities are hopelessly inadequate in affording us the refinements of detailed references to important data. Especially is this the case in descriptions of feelings in psychology and other types of such action. Unfortunately once we have developed our descriptions in terms of available linguistic forms we find ourselves impotent in the matter of developing new descriptive elements. Perhaps this difficulty is to be ascribed more to the processes of language, namely, the processes of developing linguistic behavior, than to the operation of language activities.

Phenomena so pervasive and constant as linguistic behavior suggest on the one hand numerous methods and ways of classification while, on the other, they immediately indicate the impossibility of making a really significant classification, if one can be made at all. The value of classification, however, is so great for the light it throws upon the phenomena concerned that we cannot forego the attempt to make one. Accordingly we suggest a dual form of general classification. First we arrange language actions in a series on the basis of the way in which they are performed, that is whether they are voluntary or intentional or automatistic, etc. Secondly, language behavior may be classified according to the particular situations in which it functions. Our linguistic conduct is æthetic, intellectual, etc. To illustrate this dual classification, we choose some particular linguistic activities to serve as members of each of the two divisions of our classification. These two divisions which are of course not mutually exclusive, are represented by the terms, *behavior forms,* and *situation types.* Classification of Language Responses

## BEHAVIOR FORMS

In this class we place the gestural and verbal responses which occur perhaps as the simplest of the individual's language behavior. The stimuli function primarily as occasions for the performance of linguistic conduct. The best illustrations are exclamations and interjections. "Look," "see," "now what do you think of that," are examples in point. Although this language activity is an authentic indirect referential action, it may be considered to be in the nature of acquired reflex conduct. It is not merely a reference to verbal responses but is a genuine bistimulational action. For the most part such linguistic behavior is performed under stress of excitement and probably also in connection with genuine reflex behavior. Reflexive Language

The present group of activities includes responses that are practically as automatic as those in the preceding division, but in this case the automatistic character is due not, as in the former case, to the fact that the action constitutes personality equipment, but to the fact that these actions are intimately re-integrated with particular stimuli. Examples are the linguistic amenities that are habitually performed in connection with particular time, place, and person Automatistic or Habitual Language stimulation. "How do you do," "good morning," are illustrative instances. The automatistic character of these actions is convincingly suggested by the frequent misreactions that occur such as saying "good night" when "good afternoon" is the habit called for.

**Voluntary Action**

At least part of the language responses in conversational speech may be looked upon as definitely voluntary and intentional modes of action. Depending upon the particular situation, the individual's language constitutes deliberative and carefully chosen gestures and verbal responses. The voluntary character of language in lecturing is demonstrated without question. That the character of such language is voluntary is unmistakable when we think of how the person regulates his expressions to suit the time and occasion. How very differently we address our familiars, strangers, and persons of authority or inferiority. In like fashion we gauge our vocabulary and general mode of speech so that it may correspond with the intelligence and experience of those with whom we speak. Thus, for example, to children mothers habitually prattle baby language as a deliberate and chosen mode of behavior.

## SITUATION TYPES

**Intellectual Language Type**

When we consider language to be intellectual in character, we mean to point out that some of our references comprise intellectual modes of adaptation. This is not to say merely that these are linguistic responses functioning in, or connected with, intellectual situations. On the contrary this statement means that some of our language behavior has definite intellectual qualities and characteristics. It is not only referential behavior but it is at the same time intellectual conduct in certain cases, or artistic or some other sort, in other cases. Thus the intellectual character of language action is quite as actual and intimate a feature of such conduct as any other of its characteristics. The language activity of a scholar, as language, may be differentiated from the linguistic conduct of a poet, for example, in exactly the same way that the consumption of wholesome and needed food by a hungry man differs, as eating, from the superfluous ingestion of inedibles by the satiated visitant at the banquet board.

Intellectual language, as such, we should expect to constitute language activity, the references of which would serve as orientation responses or as means for orientation in particular fields of human activity. Probably the most striking examples of this type of linguistic conduct are the transcribing of the writings or publications of the scholar. We cannot overlook here, however, the large amount of such activity represented by lectures, addresses, orations, etc.

**Utilitarian Language Type**

Naturally the largest amount of language activity performed by ordinary individuals constitutes behavior which has a definite utilitarian character. It is activity which comprises not only referential responses but serves very definitely as adaptations for the accomplishment of some purpose or the alteration of some condition. More than any other type of language, perhaps, the utilitarian form is an extension of the individual's manipulations of things. As such it is instrumental in character in the sense that when the individual cannot reach something he requests another person to do it for him. Similar linguistic conduct in the form of requests or commands to do various things, constitutes an instrument for the accomplishment through other persons of larger types of action.

Interesting as well as important types of language functioning in aesthetic behavior situations are the reactions which comprise the materials and processes of aesthetic creation and appreciation. Unquestionably, the type examples of this form of language are the various poetry forms and similar aesthetic behavior based upon referential conduct. When the responses are genuine aesthetic actions they form an exceedingly intimate sort of gestural and verbal, or written conduct which has as its reference function the reaction to aesthetic objects. Since this aesthetic reaction is in itself a form of affective behavior and is connected with other affective responses, desires and sex strivings, etc., only affective words and gestures can be used to describe or refer to the aesthetic object. *Aesthetic Language Type*

When the linguistic action in question is transmissive, the affective language must be considered to be the activities of the individual who is the actor in the affective situation. When words are employed they are chosen as definitely belonging to this type of linguistic action. For instance, they must be especially appropriate for reference to the affective subject matter. This appropriateness of the activity is also of great importance so far as the behavior of the hearer is concerned. For it is a fact that the appreciator's reference responses when they are most adequate as reactions to affective language are primarily gestural in character. To a great extent the appropriateness, relevancy, and significance of the language used can only be discovered by an examination of the situation in which the linguistic activity is performed. Here we find that words which ordinarily could not in any sense be employed for actual descriptive purposes function admirably when they are considered as affective activities. Thus in the poet's description of birds, flowers, persons, etc., the reactions performed fit the situation and cannot be confused with other reference types.

Play activity of linguistic form neatly illustrates the differences in linguistic types of situations. Play language conduct which occurs in games and the more serious situations of love definitely shows that language behavior in its various specific qualities is a direct function of the situation in which it operates. Linguistic play behavior is unique not only in its vocabulary and accent, etc., but in the way the language operates, in the results produced, etc. Words, for example, are used diminutively. In general we find in such situations much mimetic gesturing and other actions that would not be appropriate *Play Language Type* to other situations. Furthermore, play linguistic behavior extends beyond the limits of the ordinary meanings and reference character of the same specific acts in other situations.

**Ritualistic Language Type**

Language behavior of an exceedingly specialized type is the ritualistic conduct which functions primarily in religious situations but is not excluded from social and intellectual settings in general. The special characteristic of such language is that, although it is directly functional, it must be performed in a crystallized and systematized manner precisely as though it were a solid and more or less permanent institution. Such language plainly indicates the specialized function whether it be the reverential and sacred display of religious litany or the respected rigidity of legal terminology which marks it off as a unique mode of referential conduct.

The fittingness of language indicating its situational type character is well demonstrated by the use of certain terms to suit particular occasions. Entering at this point are all the problems of style and euphuism which indicate that references have their own situational qualities as well as mere reference character. How closely interrelated the character of reference and the very facts of reference may be, can be noted from the fact that for all people at some time, and for some people all of the time, the linguistic expression or action is identical with the thing referred to. When referring to almost any abstract reference such as God, immortality, force, matter, etc., the referential fact and the reference are identical.

**Individual Differences in Linguistic Behavior**

The reader will recall that in our discussion of the individual and social aspects of language we pointed out that, while language activities in general are in many respects cultural and very closely determined by the person's cultural surroundings they are still distinctly individual reactions. Now it is our task to single out some of the details descriptive of the particular forms which this individuality of language assumes. Our method of exposition will consist of the selective enumeration of some differences which distinguish the linguistic behavior of certain individuals from others. We separate these variations according to whether they involve the referential or essential processes of language or their incidental characteristics.

Individual differences of the referential type depend in general upon the kind of person performing the language behavior and his acquaintance with or knowledge about the referent. Differences in general intelligence and capacity at once display themselves in the linguistic behavior of persons. Intelligence of linguistic action is patently indicated by the clarity, fittingness, and alertness of the speech as well as by the indication it gives of the range and variety of the person's experience. Individuals differ markedly with respect to their adaptation to the immediate referents of the language situation. In some cases the reactions appear profound, indicating a clear and deep insight into the character of the things referred to.

In others the speech is vague, hesitant, and shallow, such as follows from an inexpert and slight connection between referent and referrer. In great measure these types of individual differences are correlated with the interest which the persons take in the objects constituting the referents and in their contact with them. Superficially such individual differences in linguistic activities as performed by different individuals are manifest by the size, variety, and independence of the vocabulary employed.

The present series of qualities and conditions of reference no doubt covers a very extensive range of degrees in mode and number of references made. Not only are there differences in intelligence, expertness, effectiveness, and profundity, but also variations in relevancy, coherency, and value. It must be emphasized, moreover, that individuals not only differ from one another in these and other respects but they vary in different situations themselves with respect to different objects and different auxiliary stimuli.

Incidental individual differences are entirely concerned with the superficial qualities of verbal and gestural language behavior rather than with its referential qualities. As we proceed it will appear, therefore, that the incidental individual differences consist of a series of variants concerning the manner in which references are made. These variations constitute differences in phonetic pattern and type, intensity, perfection, pleasing or affective quality, and style of speech. As to phonetic pattern, individuals vary with regard to the pitch and intensity of their verbal action. Here we may indicate a correlation with age and sex. On the whole the language of women and children is higher, shriller and more intense in character than that of men. Language reactions differ also in fullness or volume of tone. Some individuals speak with richness and variety of volume while others have thin, flat, even, or metallic voices. An extreme degree of phonetic variation in language behavior is illustrated by what has been called the blotting paper voice. In this connection must be mentioned also the wide difference in individual behavior with respect to the amount and character of intonation. Some persons speak with painfully monotonous voices while the voices of others are replete with pleasing and rhythmic modulations. While pleasing and unpleasing speech frequently have their basis here, the qualities of reference-making attach to the timbre of verbal articulation as well as to other qualities.

Perfection and corrections of linguistic behavior include variations in the speed of speech and the amount of repetition and uniqueness in accent and pronunciation. More extreme variations of this type are lisping and ''mush-mouth'' speaking. What may be more definitely referred to as correctness of speech concerns the use of proper and fitting words and, in general, conformity to the conventions of the group in which the individual lives.

Style in speech is much more obvious in the written types of reference making but can, in no sense, be excluded from **direct** communication. Individual variations in this instance comprise the clearness of outline of speech, distinctions in words and gestures, the amount of redundancy and repetition, and in more subtle form the use of metaphors, similes, allusions and so on. Since language is so definitely a complex of many units it may not be amiss to include here syntactical correctness and pleasing quality that may be classified under other heads of individual differences. Especially under the variations of style we include the differences due to voluntary or intentional correctness and perfection as well as those which are based upon equipmental traits.

Generally speaking, it is easier to point out variations in the verbal modes of linguistic action, but this should in no wise prevent us from recognizing the fact that gestural language varies quite as much as verbal. Both as independent forms of reference making and as accompaniments of verbal speech, gestural language varies especially in form or style, such that individuals appear to act differently with respect to their gesturing. The intensity of the gesture appears striking in its variations in different individuals, so much so, in fact, that in some instances it completely differentiates the linguistic behavior of persons.

Individual linguistic differences also involve general variations comprising a complete series of activities of a linguistic type. For example, persons may be able to speak more effectively than they can write and vice versa. Again, persons may be intelligent in speaking or writing of some particular subject but not at all so when reacting to other referents. Variations in clarity, affective character, and other linguistic qualities are extremely noticeable as the behavior shifts from one type of material to another.

The psychological language perspective is exceedingly restricted and foreshortened. Linguistic psychology is in its infancy. Adequate studies of linguistic behavior as yet hardly exist. It is probably inevitable that the study of language conceived as concrete facts of psychological activity must develop and take a large place in the field of psychology, but certainly such a future is barely foreshadowed by the past history of the science.

The general development of language study indicates that this most important field has occupied very little of the attention of psychologists. Hence the correspondingly meagre development of knowledge and understanding concerning it. This is really an anomalous situation, for not only is language behavior an omnipresent feature of our conduct but it is at the same time one of the most striking types of human activity. Nevertheless it has been unwarrantably neglected, despite the fact that because of its character it might well have been made along with emotional and habit action the basis for a sound objective psychology.

What slight psychological study of language exists in any form began only very recently, in fact, in the middle of the nineteenth century. Previously, all interest in the more general features of language (theory and origin as compared with word study) was of a metaphysical character. It was this metaphysical basis in one of its forms, as a matter of fact, that shaped the character of the original psychological inquiries into language. Moreover, this psychological study began, as we shall see, more as a study of language conceived as a general capacity or function than as a series of specific activities of persons.

It was not until the development of the conception of social psychology that linguistic psychology of any form developed. Interest in language as a psychological phenomenon was first exhibited when, along with myths and customs, language came to be considered reactions or products of the general human mind. In the course of the nineteenth century great interest was developed in man, in his condition and activities. Naturally it was observed that laws, customs, myths, religions, and language, in short, all of what we have since learned to call institutional phenomena, though connected with individual psychological activities are still independent of them. Language, custom, myth, etc., while indubitably human phenomena are nevertheless independent of and prior to human individuals, and develop from age to age. From the pressure arising from such

285

problems arose the conception of the folk (-) soul or mind (*Volk-seele*) and the science of social psychology (*Volkerpsychologie*).[1]

The actual development of the psychological study of language may be traced back to the exceedingly learned and most extensive writings of Steinthal (1823–1899) who with Lazarus (1824–1903) is indeed responsible for the formal development of social psychology itself.[2] Steinthal looks upon language as one of the elements or processes of the social mind along with mythology, religion, customs, laws, etc.[3] Psychology for these writers, who in general are followers of Herbert (1776–1841), consists of the study of elements which are organized into and compose the mind. Language, accordingly, is psychic activity or process which these writers in contradistinction from their psychological authority, Herbart, consider to be independent of the anatomical and physiological nature and organization of the speaking individual.

The Lazarus-Steinthal linguistic psychology as we have already implied is concerned primarily with the origin of language. Its fundamental principle is that this origin is psychical and not historical or natural, in the sense of developing like a nation through historical events or like some organic object through natural general metabolic and ecological processes. Language for them is a sort of product of the "unconscious" interrelation of human individuals much after the fashion of the existence of individual mental stages through the mechanics and dynamics of the ideas or *Vorstellungen* in the individual minds.

The next great impetus to the psychological study of language we find in the work of Wundt (1832–1920). This writer approaches the general problems of folk psychology with the broad background of and an intense interest in physiological psychology. In consequence he studies the origin of language with an attempt to interrelate the social and individual mentalities. For Wundt social psychology with its genetic aspects of cultural development constitutes a coördinate branch of psychology with the physiological-experimental field. Social psychology for Wundt[4] therefore is complementary to individual psychology and is not especially a study of

---

[1] It is an interesting study to connect the actual development of social psychology with the cultural-historical facts preceding it. For example, the relations of Steinthal and W. von Humboldt (1767–1835) whose equally famous brother Alexander von Humboldt (1769–1859) is credited with the origination of the name Völkerpsychologie, afford us valuable information in this connection. Likewise the relation of W. von Humboldt with the general German Romanticism, and the further relations of Romanticism with Herbartian Realism are instructive for the student of language and social psychology.

[2] Steinthal, *Grammatik Logik und Psychologie*, 1855, p. 387 ff. and the references in those pages.

[3] Cf. the opening essay by Steinthal and Lazarus in the *Zeitschrift für Völkerpsychologie und Sprachwissenschaft, 1860*.

[4] Wundt vacillated considerably in his ideas on this point.

the minds of different cultural groups as is the case with Lazarus and Steinthal.

As a result Wundt opposes the Herbartian psychology with its intellectualistic mechanics, centering in the work of Steinthal and Lazarus, and brings forth his voluntaristic conception. The latter is of course connected with an evolutionary and developmental theory. According to the Wundtian conception (*Völkerpsychologie*, ersten Band, *Die Sprache*, 2 vols., 1921–22) language originates as external expression of affective mental states and then gradually develops into expression for complex ideational mental processes. Language for Wundt is not merely psychic action but rather external (psychophysical) manifestations of mental states or the social products of psychic processes.

The above proposition holds so far as the origin and nature of language is concerned. With respect to the function of psychology in actual speech, in the development of sound changes or semantic modification, etc., there is no difference between Wundt and the Herbartians. Although Wundt severely criticizes the Herbartians (for example Paul, *Prinzipien der Sprachegeschichte*, 1880) for not including psychological development in the treatment of language his work from our standpoint is precisely like theirs in this respect. Aside from the problem of linguistic origin, Wundt merely takes philological data and attempts psychological explanations in hypothetical terms of psychic processes and developments.

Partially an outgrowth of the Wundtian doctrine of language development is the conception of language as a series of significant or symbolical acts. These symbolic acts or gestures are presumed to develop in a process of mutual give and take between individuals (cf. Mead, "A Behavioristic Account of the Significant Symbol," *Journal of Philosophy*, 1922, XIX, 157-163). In this type of viewpoint language consists of gestures or acts which are or have meanings. But on the other hand, language is not treated as actual responses for specific sorts of indirect adaptations. The behavior function is confined to the development of meaning in a conversation of attitudes.[1] To a great extent this viewpoint constitutes a limitation and an improvement of the theory of language development as a general human function. It does not, however, concern itself with the

[1] This viewpoint may be connected with a larger intellectual movement which concerns itself with the general development of meaning and cognition in social processes. Besides Professor Mead's own writings typified by such papers as "The Relation of Psychology and Philology," *Psychol. Bull.*, 1904, I, 375–391, "Social Consciousness and the Consciousness of Meaning," ibid., 1910, VII, 395–405, "What Social Objects must Psychology Presuppose?" *Journal of Philosophy*, 1910, VII, 174–180, and "The Mechanism of Social Consciousness," ibid., 1912, IX, 401–406, the movement embraces the writings of Baldwin, "Mental Development in the Child and the Race," 1895, "Social and Ethical Interpretations in Mental Development," (3) 1902, etc.; and Royce, "Psychology" (1903), and probably goes back to a Schellingo-Hegelian type of philosophical idealism.

manner in which the individual acquires modes of referential action which as significant or referential was developed entirely without his contribution or effort. The individual's ordinary language action consists entirely of the performance of a referential action irrespective of the way in which it was developed. The person uses language as an action tool which he finds available in his group just as he would use a canoe. His language learning is exactly like his paddling learning. He does not make language that involves in any sense deliberate constructions or any special reference to himself as a factor in the process. As a matter of fact, as we have indicated, the person acquires the reaction as a direct result of institutional stimulation. The existence of the institutions are only in part psychological phenomena and so the facts of language, insofar as they are the data of the philologist or anthropologist, possess their characteristics, in part at least, independently of psychological conditions. We are unalterably opposed to the view that language, as a fact in nature, is exclusively a product of psychological processes. The actual character of verbal activity as psychological phenomena has been lost sight of, while language as intimate specific modes of conduct to particular stimuli has not been considered at all.

Very interesting and important developments in language have been worked out recently by ethnologists and anthropologists. These developments consist of the attitude toward and description of language as very definite functional activities in the lives of cultural groups or communities. Illustrative of this type of development is the work of Boas (*Handbook of the American Indian Languages* 1911, Part I, ''Introduction'') ; Marrett *Anthropology*, 1911, ''Chapter on Language'') ; Hocart ''The Psychological Interpretation of Language,'' *British Journal of Psychology*, 1912, 5, 267-280) ; Malinowski (''Problem of Meaning in Primitive Language,'' in Ogden and Richards, *The Meaning of Meaning*, 1923). While in all of these studies the functional character of language is stressed there is of course no adequate psychological handling of such activities. There is in other words no treatment of language as concrete bistimulational individual responses.

In striking contrast to these conceptions of language either as (1) mental states called meanings, which are transferred from one mind to another, or are aroused in one mind by another through the medium of speech, (2) verbal or other physical or psychophysical manifestations of various sorts of mental states, or (3) meaning gestures or symbols developed in a social process, or (4) social conduct, stands the viewpoint of the present work according to which psychological linguistic phenomena are concrete indirect adjustments to bistimulational circumstances or situations. According to this conception language activities may be studied and described precisely as they exist, as types of the person's everyday responses to concrete stimuli around him.

So much for language as individual referential reactions. When our interest centers in comparative problems, differences in speech, we have the problem of investigating the origin of the specific modes of referring to things and conditions. Here we find that the particular form of language behavior depends upon the particular human situations in which the speaker finds himself. It depends upon the kinds of things to which he needs to refer in different cultural communities and, in addition, upon the cultural behavior institutions that condition how references can or must be made among sets of particular people. Furthermore, we require only the examination of the actual behavior of persons to discover how, through their various interactions, the language institutions change and thus in time come to be variations in the speech of a given community. In turn these altered linguistic institutions serve as original linguistic forms for later generations of speakers.

# CHAPTER XXIV

## INTERPERSONAL REACTIONS

**General Description of Interpersonal Conduct**

One of the most unique of all types of psychological behavior is that which we may name interpersonal action. It possesses marked adaptational characteristics distinguishing it from the other types of activity in the psychological domain. At the outset, we might indicate that the fundamental characteristic of interpersonal responses is a type of dynamic spontaneity which marks the individual, as not only responding but highly responsive. This spontaneity of behavior depends upon the fact that the stimulus object is a person endowed with an exceedingly large number of stimulational functions. Now, this stimulus object or person may, at any particular time, stimulate the original reacting individual in almost an infinite number of different ways that may not be predictable. We do not imply that the individual cannot frequently predict what another person's responses will be under certain specific circumstances. Sometimes, indeed, we know practically every kind of activity we will eventually be called upon to perform in response to some other individual as a source of stimulation. Nevertheless, we deem it a mark of characterization of these activities that the responses are of the unforeseen type, and not of the standard variety easily predicted or observed. For, after all, what specific stimulation and what specific response will be displayed by an individual at a particular moment and in a particular order, cannot possibly be known beforehand.

Essentially, interpersonal reactions are responses occurring in situations in which the individuals concerned have mutual influences upon each other. In this sense their activities are spontaneous and are functions of the moment because of the stimulational possibilities resident in the persons as stimuli objects. Imagine an intense series of activities on the part of a pair of lovers. At the first approach, especially when the relation between them is not of long standing, the original activity stimulated by one's own prior expectancy as to what the other's attitude is, may become decidedly different as soon as the actual meeting takes place. Possibly this is due to the other person's change of attitude resulting from the discrepancy between the realization and the expectation. Or, the person may have just undergone some thrilling or terrible experience which affects the second individual's actions which are the stimuli for the first person. Let us consider also the intimate personal responses which the two individuals mutually elicit as a result of the behavior equipment each has previously built up with respect to the other as stimulus. In this situation we have the most marvellous interplay of behavior —changes in attitude, belief, hope, expectation—as well as in immediate delight, information and disappointment occuring under specific circumstances. In all of this interplay of action the point to be emphasized is the immediacy of the stimulation and the momentary and spontaneous responses occurring like the infinite changes in the play of kaleidoscopic color. Such interpersonal activities are easily observable in various types of behavior situations. They are discoverable in conversation, fighting, playing, and sex conduct, in short in every type of behavior situation where give-and-take reactions are prominently present. Perhaps the best example of the advantageous performance of such behavior is the teacher-pupil interaction in the most effective type of teaching and learning. In such a situation the stimulational necessity to meet a new and important circumstance reveals intellectual behavior in an efficient and serviceable manner.

The foregoing analysis must not mislead the reader. Because we have characterized interpersonal reactions as responses to persons as stimuli, the principle of division between this type of action and other conduct is not necessarily that a person always serves as a stimulus. In other words, the presence of a person does not mean that the behavior is always interpersonal. Persons as stimuli are not, as our study has often emphasized, different from any other kind of stimulus object or situation. Rather, when persons as stimuli elicit from each other intricate and subtle responses to the variety of their stimulational functions, we have the clearest examples of interpersonal behavior. When one merely responds with an action of admiration to a beautiful person, the situation is not necessarily an interpersonal one. The person in this case is in principle no different as a stimulus object from a beautiful flower or tree. But if in addition this beautiful person who speaks, desires, criticizes, and formulates ideas, etc., elicits in the other individual a series of immediate and spontaneous reactions corresponding to those stimuli, the situation is decidedly of interpersonal character.

Moreover, objects of all types that are capable of displaying various stimulational functions and of being endowed with new stimulational functions at the time, may constitute the stimuli for the individual's interpersonal behavior. Such objects naturally are those which have rapidly changing characteristics. While in contact with these types of stimuli objects the person may, at least in many cases, perform the rapidly changing spontaneous action we characterize as interpersonal behavior. The suggestion, furthermore, forces itself upon us that persons in interaction with animals are well fitted to perform a great series of these interpersonal types of behavior. In many instances our contacts with active and intelligent animals in their playful and hostile aspects provide us with innumerable occasions for the kind

292 PRINCIPLES OF PSYCHOLOGY

of interactional behavior we are sketching; here it is not rare for such action to be genuinely reciprocal.

It must appear clear that interpersonal behavior is always constituted of, or at least is invariably involved with, contingential activity of all sorts. Its contingential character in fact gives it its characteristic spontaneity and general dynamic character. We might point out further that in complex interpersonal situations the individual's equipment of reaction systems may be drawn upon at such length and in such quantity that his entire equipment is heavily taxed and frequently found inadequate. Accordingly, the interpersonal behavior situation may be regarded as one in which the individual is constantly acquiring new modes of action on the basis of his equipment, and the stimulational circumstances to which he is subject. These newly acquired responses are not necessarily reaction systems which become permanent features of the individual's equipment. They may merely serve as reactions to immediate temporary circumstances surrounding the person, as in the behavior acquired in immediate interpersonal situations during the course of a game or in the play of repartee.

But if interpersonal behavior is contingential and spontaneous it may nevertheless be action which takes place over a period of time. In other words, it may constitute mutual interchange of responses which require delay of performance, either because the action cannot be immediately performed, because of some difficulty of stimulation, or because the persons involved are in different places. In the former case, the individual has to consider and reflect upon the activity of the other individual before he can formulate or develop a response action. This type of condition is illustrated by the activity of debate and argument. In the other case, namely, in the absence of the stimulus person, the behavior of the responding individual has to be transmitted somehow to the stimulating individual. Thus the mutual interaction of the person must necessarily wait upon the process of communication. It is clear, of course, that since interpersonal reactions are not responses to persons as such, one of the interacting individuals may be absent, so it is readily understood that in discussion or debate the participants may be far removed in space. Hence the activities may be wholly implicit.

Interpersonal reactions are contingential primarily as a condition of the response circumstances. This does not exclude the fact that the responses, when they occur, may be idiosyncratic or cultural and even superbasic in character. The point here is that the mutual interactions of individuals in very simple situations constitute spontaneous developments of behavior on the basis of immediate situations involved and the superbasic equipment of the individual. In some more complicated situations, and in situations of about the same degree of complexity as others, much cultural equipment comprises the basis for the spontaneous interpersonal reactions. We frequently observe how the most intimate mutual interactions of some individuals are based entirely upon cultural and conventional modes of equipment. Such persons we call unbending and formal, since they allow practically no idiosyncratic behavior to seep into their interpersonal conduct. In still more complicated behavior, the activities may consist primarily of idiosyncratic equipment and of immediately developed activities of the idiosyncratic type. Here it might be added that the interpersonal reactions are of all degrees of complexity and include, of course, volitional and voluntary behavior.

From the nature of interpersonal behavior situations we readily appreciate that in such circumstances a great number of new stimulational functions are developed. Since human beings play the most striking rôles in the activities called interpersonal we find an inexhaustible and fertile source for the development of these stimulational functions, especially under the immediate, indeliberate, and mutually interactional circumstances constituting the most typical forms of this type of conduct. It would be a grave mistake, however, to assume that it is only between human persons that such behavior occurs. This type of behavior can be performed as well by some types of animals in interaction with each other. Accordingly, it is quite possible to make certain that interpersonal reactions comprise a type of behavior not confined to human beings. We repeat, then, that no special significance attaches to the circumstance that we are concerned with human interpersonal reactions. It is only because we are especially interested in human behavior that we need not apologize for the use of the term interpersonal. But this use of the term interpersonal behavior should not be considered as symbolizing anything but the facts with which we shall deal in this chapter.

An exceedingly important point in the description of human interpersonal behavior is that in certain situations the two or more individuals involved may deliberately assume certain characteristics, as possible and even necessary stimulational functions, in order to elicit the desired response in the other person. Thus, an individual who desires the friendship and intimacy of someone may simulate qualities which he does not have, or may actually proceed to develop them for the purpose of becoming more attractive to the other individual. At once we think here of the behavior of the hypocrite, sycophant and the fair admirer and follower of good example. This situation constitutes an exceedingly great elaboration or complication of behavior, which in its simpler phases is found among lower animals. The differences, however, between the two types of conduct situations must be emphasized.

An obvious accident of human life and behavior is the fact that interpersonal conduct takes place upon the level of, and is mediated by, linguistic action. We have already indicated that a typical example of interpersonal conduct is conversation. We add, then, that even when the essential interpersonal behavior is not referential in character, referential conduct may constitute the central and most important form of behavior that the organism performs in the interpersonal situation. By language in this circumstance we understand not only verbal speech but all types of reference function. It must be insisted that linguistic behavior, however, is not by any means an exclusive type of interpersonal activity but that almost any type of action may be involved in this form of behavior. Interpersonal conduct is therefore a type form of action. In fact, we may consider it more in the nature of a behavior situation in which, whatever specific reaction systems are performed, depend upon circumstances which cannot be specified in general but must be adduced from the happenings as they occur.

Generally speaking, the linguistic type of interpersonal behavior, or interpersonal action involving linguistic actions, are the grosser and more explicit interpersonal forms of action. On the whole, the linguistic forms bespeak a lack of the essential intimacy that is characteristic of interpersonal behavior. The most intimate interpersonal forms consist more of the subtle interchange of behavior, of silent and even non-gestural (in an overt sense) understanding and communion. Persons in thorough interpersonal behavior relationship need not make references but stimulate each other nevertheless. Mutual desire, personal knowledge, feeling, and willing responses are interpersonally performed with only a touch or an exchange of glances as the intermediary contact, or even completely without such effective accompaniments as are observable by any third person. Indeed the two individuals concerned (for in the most intimate situations only two are involved) cannot well inform others just how the interpersonal activity proceeds. The stimulation in these cases consists of facial expressions, and other personal gestures that are casually perceived by the responding person. Thus we find various degrees and levels of interpersonal behavior primarily on the basis of the intimacy and complexity of the stimuli reactions involved. Actions of the interpersonal type in which a number of individuals are concerned are, of course, the least intimate and least complex of all.

As a final note in our introductory sketch of interpersonal behavior we might suggest more definitely than heretofore that while the most subtle and unique of the interpersonal reactions are performed when there is a one-to-one relationship between the interacting individuals this is not the exclusive form of interpersonal conduct. A marked variation may be recorded as taking place when there are three or four persons in intimate interaction. In this instance each individual, we assume, constitutes a basis for stimulational and responsive action with respect to each of the other individuals in the group. This type of interpersonal situation often results in the performance of behavior which is exceedingly intricate but not so intimate as in the one-to-one situation. An informative example is that in which three or four representatives of companies or nations meet to negotiate with one another and with the expressed desire on the part of each to achieve an advantage for himself or the cause or country he represents.

Quite a different type of situation with resulting differences in specific details of behavior is that in which we have a one-many relationship. Here we assume that the interacting individuals are evenly divided. One individual serving as the source of the interpersonal stimuli and responses constitutes the party of the first part, and a set of individuals standing over against him as the party of the second part comprises the opposite source of the interpersonal stimuli and responses. These two sides may be considered as hostile or friendly and either side may function as the primarily stimulational or primarily responsive side at the time. For example, when a group of students listens to a professor we may consider the latter as the party of the first part who provides the primary source of many interpersonal stimuli and responses. Namely, he stimulates questioning, doubting, etc., which overbalance the responses he performs to the stimulation of the listening individuals who may overtly question an occasional statement. For the rest, stimulation on the side of the student group or the party of the second part elicits very slight changes in mode of speech and kind of subject matter introduced into the lecture.

As an illustration of the one-many interpersonal situation with the many side as the party of the first part and constituting the primary source of stimulation, is the case of a group heckling a political speaker. In this give-and-take process, the speaker may be on the defensive and may find his audience an unexpected source of stimuli calling for puzzling, surprising, and even confounding action. The speaker, on the other hand, may stimulate only vigorous and denunciatory ideas and questions as the surrogate of a hopeless and unpopular cause, or with respect to himself as a fair prey to a politically blood-thirsty pack.

Our final type of interpersonal situation is that in which both parties consist of several or many individuals ranged on two or more sides of advantage or disadvantage. A good example is the situation in which a group of lawyers is constantly developing new ideas and answers as responses to the stimuli of another set of attorneys. The responses of the first set of lawyers serve, in turn, as new and startling stimuli for the reactions of the individuals on the other side of the controversy. Suffice it to say that complex human circumstances supply us with all possible varieties and types of spontaneous and exigential modes of interpersonal behavior.

As we might expect, then, the specific varieties of interpersonal conduct are exceedingly numerous. For our purpose which is primarily illustrative, we can choose with a view to our expository problem a number of types that display the primary characteristics of the present type of behavior. These types are isolated on the basis of

Types of Interpersonal Reactions

the stimulational origins of the activities involved. We deem this an adequate basis since it will be recalled that the spontaneity, immediacy and profuseness of interpersonal behavior are due to the rapid engendering of stimulative functions by persons and things. As to particular instances and examples of such behavior, we must when we face the problem of nomination, realize once more the unfortunate inadequacy of language. No matter what act we refer to as operating in interpersonal situations, none is exclusively interpersonal. Rather, in each case,—whether laughter, play, imitation, love, suggestion, fear, argument, teasing, sympathy, flattery, etc.,—the behavior may be non-interpersonal as well as interpersonal. That is to say, these names stand for generic or family types of action, the individual members or instances of which cut across a number of different classifications. For examples of interpersonal conduct we may take any activity which answers to the distinction we have isolated as descriptive of such psychological phenomena. We may indicate the specific characteristics of four large divisions of interpersonal behavior, named as follows: (a) autogenic, (b) homogenic, (c) heterogenic, and (d) reciprogenic interpersonal behavior.

**Autogenic Interpersonal Behavior**

The essential characteristic of this type of interpersonal behavior is that the specific spontaneous activities that the person performs are directed toward and remotely stimulated by various objects and persons which possess their particular stimulational functions because of the reacting individual's own interpretation and evaluation of those objects and persons. To illustrate, an important type of interpersonal behavior is that in which the individual interacts with a god as the stimulus. Now the individual's performance of his acts of humility, awe, reverence, and solicitation in their various prayer forms is done just as though the stimulus interacted with the individual and directly stimulated his action. The fact of the matter is, however, that the responses are self-stimulated on the basis of what the individual has heard and learned concerning a god as a person with whom he must interact. Likewise, a person may follow the precepts of someone whose stimulative qualities he has himself engendered. In a similar way, individuals may initiate and be subject to the suggestions of social, political or professional groups, or other aggregates of individuals. The member or officer of an organization interacts with the group by way of developing a great deal of spontaneous and immediate behavior on the basis of what he supposes and presumes is expected of him and on the ground of his imagining that he is being watched, suspected, checked up, etc. Whatever behavior he performs is, however, due largely to his ascription of stimulational qualities to the group or organization with which he is in interaction.

Not entirely different from this type of activity is the behavior of the individual who himself suggests and exhorts a group of persons to do various things, because he looks upon the group as interacting with himself. Thus his action, presumably stimulative of particular behavior, may have no such effect whatsoever because the activities are autogenic in their stimulation. Despite the fact that our illustrative individual ascribes particular qualities to the members of his group, such that it is necessary to exhort them or suggest to them to do things in the way that he considers necessary, this behavior on his part is self-stimulated. Moreover, his conduct whether in its direct performance or in its previous planning may be performed entirely out of the presence of the group. Ordinarily we expect that the spontaneity and immediacy of the behavior development would be greater when the stimulus is present, but this is not always the case. Depending upon how much the individual creates his universe of interaction, he develops more or less interpersonal behavior in situations in which he is not actually in contact with the stimuli.

Let the reader not be misled by our illustrations. The stimuli for autogenic interpersonal behavior need not at all exclude single individuals. Our interpersonal conduct of the autogenic type may consist of spontaneous and variable activity performed after endowing a particular person with stimulational qualities which call out interpersonal behavior. Accordingly, we develop all kinds of *ex more* and pleasing conduct deemed by us requisite at a particular time in order to interact with a particular person, a superior, perhaps. In more intimate situations interpersonal behavior is performed to a member of the family in order to avoid suspicion or accusation, but instead of the other person's actually responding to us by way of legitimately stimulating us to the kind of action we have indicated, he may know nothing about the circumstance involved or be only vaguely aware of the total interactional situation. In this type of autogenic interpersonal behavior situation it is well to point out that the endowment of the interpersonal stimulus object with stimulational qualities may be based upon a more secure foundation than in the case of interacting with a group. This means to say, in our actual illustration there is ground for definite suspicion on the part of the other person which must be waylaid, but it may not be so intense or exaggerated as the behavior of the interpersonally responding individual indicates.

Interpersonal behavior of the autogenic type may also consist of responses to animals or objects. In the case of animals we have very definite inter-stimulational situations. Especially is this found in cases in which we are hunting the animal. In such instances we plot against and stalk the animal to a great extent on the basis of possible behavior it might perform. Who is not acquainted with some example of the proverbial spinster who performs intricate solicitous activities with respect to some pet animal as a result of ascribing to it all types of personal traits of pity, fear, love, shame, remorse, etc.

Interpersonal behavior with natural objects as stimuli probably requires a very primitive personality equipment and behavior milieu. Anthropological literature is, of course, replete with descriptions of the interactions of individuals with natural phenomena of all varieties which are interacted with as though they had the qualities requisite for the spontaneous and immediate development and performance of give-and-take behavior. The obvious example is the worship and adoration of some natural object as a deity, or the emulation of some of the qualities of natural inanimate objects and animals. Among the numerous activities of children we likewise find most intense interpersonal behavior of the autogenic type. Objects are endowed with every conceivable type of interpersonal stimulational quality on the basis of the child's partial or complete personality equipment.

**Homogenic Interpersonal Behavior**    The central mark of distinction of this type of behavior is the fact that the primary interactions are with the reacting person himself. Succinctly put, an individual interacts with himself as the source of the stimulational functions which call out the typical dynamic interpersonal conduct. To a considerable extent the actual behavior mechanism here is like that in the autogenic type, especially in the sense that the individual endows himself with various sorts of stimulational properties to which he forthwith develops and performs responses. This, however, does not by any means exhaust the situation. The person may in an entirely legitimate and authentic way stimulate himself to perform the spontaneous and profuse activities constituting the essential features of interpersonal behavior. Typical of such genuine homogenic interpersonal conduct are the activities of criticism and self-accusation, which the individual performs through his own stimulation. In similar fashion he may stimulate himself to self admiration and flattery. The main point here is that such narcissistic behavior represents action correlated with stimulational functions that are not ascribed to the person himself as the stimulational interacting individual. But they really occur as stimulational qualities in the person.

Probably the most typical and striking form of homogenic interpersonal conduct is self-conversation. This doubtless forms the very center of some of the most important and complex behavior that the individual performs. Closely connected with this type of activity is the introspective and retrospective type of reflection constituting the core of contemplative intellectual conduct. To anyone who performs this type of behavior no further descriptive details are necessary. In fact it is quite difficult to do other than point to this type of activity as it actually occurs in order to refer to it. Despite the difficulty in the actual description, there is no doubt that this is a very genuine form of conduct.

Typical of homogenic interpersonal behavior is the type of action commonly known as rationalization. Here the person is bent upon convincing himself that the reaction which he performed, or is about to perform, is entirely just, proper, and best fitted for the circumstances at hand. In detail, the process of rationalization consists in stimulating oneself to discover and evaluate evidences which authenticate and make more or less completely satisfactory the action performed. This type of rationalization might be considered as a form of pseudo-reasoning although sometimes it is entirely well founded and securely based upon facts.

Very similar is the homogenic behavior process in the activities of self-justification. In this case the person stimulates himself in a more definite way concerning his own good judgment with respect to the action he is performing. Self-justification differs, therefore, from rationalization in that in the latter case the individual argues with himself that the activity performed was proper in a more objective way. In other words, he attempts to induce in himself the intellectual attitude of accepting as an excellent coördination of ends and means the situation in which he is involved. In rationalization the person declares that the action performed is right regardless of who did it. In self-justification, however, the person is more concerned with his own particular action and its rightness or wrongness as a personal self-centered type of behavior. Both of these types of action may involve self-defence and fortification. The person fortifies himself usually by stimulating himself to assume intellectual attitudes which keep him inviolate with respect to some intimate situation. To a great extent we find this type of intellectual attitude illustrated by a person who accepts some sort of moral attitude that fortifies him or defends him in his general contacts with other persons. A prominent character here is the important academician who adds to his moral strength as a competitor of the productive scholar by the pious promise of some day writing a great book or by convincing himself that he really does not want to write a book but would rather do laboratory work or inspire students orally when he can escape the onerous duty of teaching.

Self-hypnotization constitutes one of the best illustrations of heterogenic interpersonal conduct. Under this general heading we include all activities in which the person induces or suggests in himself various modes of activity to meet particular conditions and circumstances. Falling into such a classification are all sorts of desires, feelings, and other kinds of non-cognitive or non-intellectual modes of behavior. For the most part we have been stressing in all these illustrations the more serious forms of action. We need therefore to add that this type of behavior comprehends the less serious and trivial activities as well, such as the responses of laughing at oneself, joking at one's own expense, etc.

An enormous number of interpersonal activities are of the type in which the stimulating individuals are for the most part other persons. In other words, the characteristic interpersonal mode of behavior is definitely stimulated by the constantly changing characteristics and circumstances of individuals. The intrinsic characteristic of this type of conduct, is that those persons who genuinely

Heterogenic Interpersonal Reactions

enough stimulate immediately developing contingential behavior are not aware of their function in providing what very frequently is a great mass of closely connected stimuli. Thus the responding individual whom we are describing may definitely observe activities performed by the other individual which may or may not have a bearing on his own situation but which still constitute stimuli for the performance of interpersonal behavior. An obvious illustration is supplied in the consideration of the mutual interaction of competitors in some particular situation but in which the activities of each person in his stimulational capacity are not definitely correlated with the responding individual.

Illustrative of the present type of behavior are the complex and intimate plannings and plottings which individuals perform as direct responses to the activities of other individuals in whom they are interested or with whom they compete. Especially should we stress here the fairly rapid and clearly discernible changes and progressions of behavior stimulated by swiftly changing conditions or activities on the part of the stimulating individual. Here we must visualize the intense and busy activities of a person who is planning a campaign against another individual, although the latter may have no definite awareness of the influence which the changes of his behavior will have upon the person whose heterogenic behavior we are describing.

A situation of a very different type but illustrating the same point is the heterogenic interpersonal behavior of a scholar scrutinizing, criticizing, and marshaling objections to the work of another scholar of a very different type of school of thought. In this case, we assume that the actual conduct and changes of the stimulating individual are mediated by his writings, which if they are voluminous, offer sufficient possibilities for a protean transformation of characteristics. The search for these elements, either as a means of ultimately pointing out inconsistencies or for the purpose of harmonizing them in order to constitute the butt of a rigid criticism, sufficiently emphasizes the rapidly changing and cumulative development of the typical interpersonal mode of behavior.

There is no better illustration of heterogenic interpersonal behavior than that in which the women of a community, quite innocently but for the fact of blindly following custom, through their various manners of talking, dressing, and acting stimulate men to perform much reflex, desiring, affective and ideational behavior. The heterogenic stimuli in other cases are located in the unpredictable and unstandardized behavior of the men which calls out corresponding reactions in the women. Such behavior is clearly not all sexual in character but it occupies a central place in the total conduct on each side.

One further point must be cited to indicate the character of heterogenic behavior. It is in this class of interpersonal activities that we find the most fertile field for the performance of intellectual conduct. The constant and profuse stimulation of one individual by another makes possible a great many changes in intellectual attitudes, in opinions, beliefs, and other intellectual conditions with respect to the heterogenically stimulated person.

In the fact that the heterogenic stimulation functions need not be known to the stimulational individual, we find the basis for the circumstance that the stimuli here may be animals as well as people. In consequence, a great mass of stimulational functions are performed by animals which result in heterogenic behavior by the reacting individual.

Similarly, the stimuli for heterogenic interpersonal behavior may also be individuals as members of certain communities. The reactions then constitute changing and accumulating responses to the groups as a whole rather than to the particular individual, although the individual provides the particular stimulus occasion.

Our final division of interpersonal conduct may be considered as the most typical of all, since it exhibits in most exaggerated form the special characteristics signalizing this type of human conduct. The primary principle here is that we have a very definite mutuality of interstimulation and interresponse. When two individuals are involved both are definitely aware of themselves as the source of stimulation for the other individual and as responding to the stimulational changes resulting in each other. Such behavior as we have already suggested constitutes a very large list of activities. It follows, therefore, that interpersonal conduct of this type operates in all of the different situations in which individuals find themselves and includes all kinds of behavior, feeling, desiring, willing, imagining, knowing, flirting, etc. These activities arrange themselves in a hierarchy of complexity and intimacy, the complexity for the most part being a function of the conditions and circumstances involved, especially when something is at stake in the behavior situation. The intimacy, on the other hand, depends primarily upon the type of behavior indulged in, as for example, in mutually affective conduct. *Reciprogenic Interpersonal Behavior*

In this division of interpersonal behavior we may suggest as an illustration the very subtle interrelationship of individuals found in sympathetic conversation. The predominant note of such a situation is a sharply defined mutual commingling process. What is more, the behavior represents a developing and progressive series of activities. In the course of conversations, individuals can enter into each other's interests and general behavior status. Still more than this, however, is involved. Not only do these individuals share and communicate their interests, desires, and other behavior conditions, but at the same time they heighten and intensify these interests and conditions. Our interest in this mutual interchange of stimulus and response is especially concerned with the augmented commutuality and reciprocation of behavior, with the constantly developing responses to rapidly appearing and unforeseen stimuli. While in particular conversations a general trend can be discerned in the development of the mutual behavior, on the whole we have here a typical unforeseen development of human activity.

It remains now to differentiate most sharply this conversational reciprogenic behavior from actual language. Namely, reciprogenic conduct is not concerned especially with any referential function which it superficially resembles. We may point out that when language actions are of the type we call communicative or conversational they constitute most typically instrumental activities. Namely, they serve as preliminary responses for persons who wish to bring some action about through the instrumentality of some other individuals. Thus, linguistic activities are decidedly indirect and referential, whereas the reciprogenic situation shows us very definite direct activity of the mutually interstimulational type. Whatever language occurs, therefore, in combination with reciprogenic interpersonal behavior is instrumental and incidental| to the main interpersonal situation. Quite frequently the same exact referential responses may result in entirely opposite results. They may add to mutual understanding and love, or misunderstanding and hate, on the basis of the deeper interrelationships that result.

Discussion as an interpersonal type of behavior founded upon linguistic conduct is likewise an important illustrative form of action presenting innumerable interstimulations and responses, on the basis of the different individuals' information, rememberings, and articulateness. Each individual develops simultaneously numerous specific forms of action as elements of attack and defence. In many cases they are entirely unexpected by the opponent and in each instance depend upon his interest, attention, and alertness which stimulate new and different types of action in the other individual. The complexity and frequency of the changes are conditioned by the type of subject matter or the universe of discourse involved, as well as by the degree of disagreement existing between the individuals and the interest each may have in making his own point prevail against the other. In such interpersonal behavior a victory or similar achievement is the distinct end in view.

Explaining, persuading, and pleading are terms which immediately suggest exceedingly important and frequently very subtle types of interaction designed to induce in others specific kinds of intellectual attitudes or other particular kinds of behavior. In these cases we assume, as we have indicated, that the interacting behavior is divisible into two aspects. On the one hand, one individual or party of the reciprogenic behavior is attempting to bring about a particular kind of change in the other individual, whereas the latter's behavior consists of resisting or rejecting or otherwise making ineffective the activities of the first person. On the side of the first party, the activities may consist of supplying the other person with evidence or at least statements which make certain facts plausible. To a considerable degree, then, the process of explaining consists of determining and discovering what kind of statements of facts will satisfy the other individual. When these points are determined by the first individual, he attempts to present and impress them upon the second person. The latter thereupon performs a large series of actions, not necessarily counter presentations of facts, which are presumed to allay the statements of the former, or to discredit them, or possibly to reject his assent to the performance of a particular kind of overt activity.

In the interpersonal behavior that we call convincing, proving, and demonstrating we have action by the party of the first part consisting primarily of an attempt to show the other person that he actually entertains intellectual attitudes quite like or similar to the supposed new stand which the party of the first part wants him to accept. In other words, the process of convincing and demonstrating consists to a considerable extent of unifying the other person's intellectual responses with various things and conditions. The first person assumes as his task the process of organizing the other person's information already possessed and bringing it to bear on the new facts toward which the intellectual attitude is to be taken.

The process of proving consists primarily of the application of objective facts as a basis for the acceptance of some intellectual attitude. The person who proves attempts to show that certain events and conditions are evidences which establish and point to the intellectual attitude in question. Here sometimes, however, instead of organizing the actions of the other person, the first person may really attempt completely to overthrow all the intellectual attitudes the other person already possesses; because, as he argues, the facts in nature are evidence of conditions which make it necessary to assume another type of intellectual attitude concerning such facts. Partially we have here the situation in which the first person is attempting to show that there is a coincidence between the thing to which the intellectual reaction is to be taken, and the evidence thereof. Now this does not mean entirely that the person is actually shown the event as it occurs, but he may be induced to believe it or to take some attitude toward it by being shown the report of an experiment upon such an event, or a demonstration of the fact in question.

By the term argument we shall designate a form of reciprogenic interpersonal behavior in which the mark of distinction is the thoroughly equal vigor and power displayed by both parties in performing the actions constituting the interpersonal situation. All types and varieties of specific action are found in such situations. Both parties may be attempting to induce intellectual reactions or attitudes in the other person, or to persuade each other to do something which each believes ought to be done by himself or the other, or by both. Some specific actions are conditioned by the desire of one person to induce an intellectual attitude, for example, by virtue of the first person's manifestation of the belief in the facts concerned, and by his express desire to have the other person agree with him. Again, the basis of the interaction may be the certainty of each concerning the facts involved in the case. Furthermore, in the process of arguing and disagreeing each individual may attempt to induce action in the other quite aside from any actual evidence or attempt to organize the other person's present intellectual equipment. Each essays then to induce in the other the attitude in question on the mere basis of authority and persuasive power or perhaps by means of arousing some sort of feeling attitude on the part of the other.

In this type of situation it may very well be asked how, when the individuals are both serious and honest, such a great amount of interpersonal behavior is possible. Why is it that individuals cannot see things in the same way or in the same light? When doctors disagree it is exceedingly interesting to ferret out the basis for such disagreement. Frequently, of course, one or the other of the concerned individuals may be duped by a fallacy, but this is often not the case. Accordingly, we plan to examine a number of important situations which may lie at the bottom of this type of behavior.

Generally speaking, the vigor, amount, and type of spontaneous interactional behavior found in argumentative conduct or in Socratic discussion may be said to depend upon the differences in the intellectual and other relevant equipment of the individuals concerned. This difference in behavior equipment serves as a definite resistance and as a basis for the minimization and rejection of the other person's stimulating attitudes. Significantly enough, it is the mere fact of having the attitudes which is the basis of the resistance. The evidence for this is that the resistance is just as strong when the person has no basis for his attitude or has forgotten what it is, as when the important foundation of his attitude is ready at hand. Normally this resistance is correlated with the equally groundless acquiescence in an attitude because of desire or feeling rather than actual persuasion by the facts. The eloquence or sincerity of the other person may also count for much. Personal and private desires, envy or anger as responses to some person may make us especially susceptible to the conviction of his lack of worth. Or, again, the pliancy of attitude may be dependent upon the authority of others who accept and hold certain attitudes or are willing to perform certain actions. These among many other weighty and trifling conditions determine how strongly one clings to the attitudes or ideas involved in the interactional process. A further strongly influencing factor in the interactional process is the question whether the result of the argumentative procedure is the performance of an action that may have considerable consequences. Besides these more intrinsic influences, we may consider the circumstances which constitute the settings surrounding the behavior conditions.

Important elements in the spontaneous and developmental interaction of behavior enter when each individual has hold of a particular, true, and valid principle, but assumes that his particular set of facts is the whole truth and therefore irreconcilable with the other's. An illustration is the violent interaction between those who hold the wave theory and those who maintain the corpuscular theory of light. In each case the argumentative conduct is, or may be, definitely conditioned by the fact that both parties overlook the possibilities of a common ground which may yet be discovered. In this illustration we are assuming that both types of activity are based on actually demonstrated and acknowledged facts. The development of interpersonal behavior becomes more pointed when each individual is acting on the basis of a different interpretation of some common fact. The point is that each one interprets the fact on the basis of his own training or general system of ideas which may be entirely incompatible with that of the other.

A very important basis for heterogenic interpersonal behavior is supplied by the circumstance that an individual is confirmed in his own intellectual attitude concerning certain phenomena by the discovery of some fact made while holding to a particular hypothesis. It is likely that an hypothesis that has been rejected overtly but which one has implicitly held has really been the instrument for the discovery. At any rate, it is such a circumstance that constitutes the foundation for complex argumentative behavior. Similarly, the hypothesis that psychology is a science of measurable things may be considered as a strong basis for oppositional interpersonal behavior although what one has really measured may not be a psychological fact at all. Not seldom, of course, there is much faith in one's hypothesis for some personal reason. Thus a psychologist may presume that it is a psychological achievement to discover that large type should be used in the printing of school books.

Worthy of our attention is the fact that each individual insists upon carrying over into the domain of his opponent what is true in his restricted field, or upon considering it as true in general. Accordingly a biologist, impressed (overimpressed perhaps) with certain genetic data, may insist upon transferring those principles into other fields in which such facts cannot possibly apply. Another striking example is the attempt to carry over the elementary notion of the survival of the fittest into other fields. Similarly, individuals impressed with the power of statistical manipulations and laboratory experimentation necessarily find opposition when forcing such techniques to fit the wrong type of data. Hence, the stimulation of much interpersonal behavior in those who are interested in types of phenomena to which these statistical techniques do not apply. Such interpersonal activities are very much intensified when an individual merely borrows some of these techniques from another field without really understanding how they are applicable to the present circumstances. Closely connected with the situation we have just described is the adherence to some principle which is valid but which is wrongly applied. Thus, while the idea that one must be scientific is generally valid, one may apply the principle in such a way that the attitude inevitably meets with a tremendous reactional opposition on the part of individuals possessing better orientation. The "scientific" attitude may be made to cloak an infinity of unscientific things, not the least of which is bare enumeration which, in some cases of inquiry, corresponds to house wiring in physics. Again, one may start with the correct attitude that food does not exist without a feeder and insist upon translating it to mean that the existence of food (now the natural object, corn for example) does not exist without a reaction, either feeding or knowing.

Misinterpretation of the opponent's interpersonal stimuli is a potent source of strong antagonism. Because our opponent does not believe in a narrow mechanism we hold him guilty of a senseless vitalistic attitude. Or, if he gives up a metaphysical vitalism, his opponent concludes that he is a crude mechanist. The failure of each side of the interpersonal situation to state his position adequately may sometimes be found to increase the probability of the counteraction.

Merely because we find our most telling illustrations in the field of controversy and oppositional interaction we cannot be blinded to the fact that these are merely illustrations, which in no sense monopolize the field of such behavior. We find just as important and characteristic activities when the interacting parties agree with one another and when their behavior mutually stimulates intellectual and other cognitive forms of rapport. A stark example of this sort of intensification and closeness of individuals in interpersonal behavior occurs when the interacting individuals come together because of only an apparent agreement between them. Thus a scientist who merely rejects a crude form of mechanism, and a most sentimental mystic may ostensibly find themselves in harmony although there is no basis for this agreement. Again a shallow littérateur who has never in any manner intensively cultivated a technique of rigid thinking may find himself at one with the critical scientist who rejects some faulty conception in his field. In this situation both may find themselves agreeing but their basis for agreement is not to be found in the manifest interpersonal behavior. That is to say, the interpersonal behavior has an undercurrent of commutual sympathy aside from the intellectual attitudes involved.

Thus far we have been emphasizing reciprogenic interpersonal situations, founded upon linguistic behavior. The latter, it may be added, has played a large part in the situation both for weal and for woe. Misfortune in plenty is the wage of him who permits himself to fall into the trap of using different descriptions for the same thing in interpersonal behavior of the argumentative type. But as we have already seen, reciprogenic interpersonal conduct consists of all types of action that individuals can perform. We might therefore consider at somewhat greater length the affective activities which on account of the intimacy with which they are performed, in many cases constitute special interpersonal forms of behavior. In brief, the interpersonal reactions of this type may be of two general descriptions, namely, sympathic or dyspathic. In the one case the actions involve a close and intimate mutuality of feeling; in the other, although the activity may be just as close and intimate, it is of the type which separates off and divides individuals. Among the sympathic actions we suggest exceedingly interpenetrative activities of mutual faith, respect, admiration, and simple pleasure that individuals induce in each other through a rapid shift of behavior at any particular moment of immediate contact, or through more remote activities performed when the persons are not so near in space and time. These sympathic interpersonal activities have all kinds of foundations and correlations. They may be performed between individuals of opposite sex or with a decided sex basis for the action. Such being the case, considerable stimulation from the biological features of the individuals is involved or the action may be merely the result of each others' conduct stimulation.

Contrariwise, mutual sympathic behavior may be based upon qualities and activities of the individual which are not sexual in character at all. Such conduct takes place between persons of the same sex because of actually working together in a coöperative enterprise and as a result of discovering in each other a constant play of behavior changes and qualities which stimulate admiration, approval, fealty, deference, reverence, and other types of action. Especially is such activity found in circumstances in which individuals are coöperatively employed in perilous enterprises such as exploration and war, or in constant teamwork such as business partnership, domestic and family life, etc.

Among the numerous dyspathic responses we may consider activities under the class names of mutual domination, anger, quarreling, and humiliation. Clearly these terms already imply that whatever affective behavior is involved is very closely connected with, if not indeed entirely founded upon, business, domestic, economic, or general social competitive conduct. While our purpose here is to emphasize affective conduct it is quite as illustrative of our point that dyspathic interpersonal activity is involved with action that is not especially affective in character. Throughout the behavior we find a great deal of subtle stimulation such as the suggestivity of innuendo, winking, cryptic remarks, clandestine and mysterious conversation, puzzling gestures and other proceedings observed by one individual in the conduct of the other.

In quite a separate class we put the interpersonal activity known as laughter, teasing, and joking. It is plain that these terms denominate behavior with a considerable degree of similarity in their actual performance. Some distinction is present, however. Easily differentiated is the type of conduct in which individuals willingly enter, such as mutual conviviality and laughter, from conditions in which the stimulation of the other person is resented and resisted or simply not encouraged. The latter type of case perhaps is more sharply defined, on the surface, at least. It is necessary, therefore, only to suggest the behavior picture of the very intense activity in which the individual who is being teased or roiled, exhibits a spontaneous and energetic protest and resistance. On the other hand, we have just as definite a situation, but perhaps not so clearly observed, in the circumstance in which two or more individuals are very actively engaged in a situation of jesting with each other or calling forth peals of laughter. In the latter instance, the process may be thought of as involving to a certain degree the implicit bringing of each other into a situation in which the desirable action of amusement and mirth is quite manifestly stimulated.

An especially interesting, and for illustrative purposes very instructive, type of reciprogenic interpersonal behavior is the situation we may describe as the performance of wit activities. Display of wit, it is redundant to say, finds a place in all phases of human behavior. Superlative examples are found in the intense and absorbing interpersonal behavior of keen adult play. But no less informing are the examples drawn from resisting and retaliation situations.

Here we must contrive descriptions couched in terms of thoroughly obvious mutual antagonism and intense penitent behavior. Imagine two individuals engaged in some sort of diplomatic game. Each is exceedingly intent upon concealing his motives and desires even to the point of hiding his responses in the form of gestures or facial expressions which might serve as stimuli for the other person's information reactions concerning the former's attitude. Primarily the main object in this activity is not to give oneself away or not to afford the other individual any intelligence with respect to what one is planning or doing. A very enlightening exemplification of this type of behavior is found in the slighter interpersonal action between two hagglers in an oriental mart.

Similarly, various friendly games in which persons are intent upon bluffing each other illustrate the same point. Besides acting in a concealing manner and shielding oneself behind a screen of cryptic and mysterious remarks the individuals may attempt to mislead each other by actual overt misrepresentations of various effective types. The main point to observe, of course, is the constant flutter or scramble of each to provide new and strange stimuli that the other cannot respond to, and thus to overwhelm and overcome one another.

Our illustrations perhaps are sufficient to suggest the character of each of the types into which we have divided interpersonal be-

havior as well as the general nature of such behavior taken as a type
of human conduct.   It remains to be pointed out that in complicated
interpersonal situations all of the different types operate in some
combination or other.

Such unique behavior as interpersonal activity could hardly have escaped some attention in psychological literature. These responses, however, have never been actually isolated and described as they operate in human interaction. The behavior involved has been noticed but its description has resulted almost always either in some incidental use of it for some other purpose or the activities have been confused with quite distinctly other forms of behavior.

The perspectival placing of our description of these responses can therefore only be made by indicating some types of misinterpretation which have been formulated concerning them, whether or not they have been completely or satisfactorily isolated.

Probably the most flagrant confusion of interpersonal behavior with other types of action has been that in which they have been made into cultural behavior. In other words, the characteristics of interpersonal action have been implicitly considered to be the subject matter of cultural or social psychology. Quite unintentionally these activities have been presumed to constitute all the phenomena which really consist of the acquisition of cultural equipment through culturalization processes. This misinterpretation has been possible because cultural or social psychology has been interpreted as consisting of activities in which persons are stimuli. Now it is clear that the facts of cultural behavior are comprised of entirely different sorts of phenomena. Also persons as stimuli have no special significance either in cultural phenomena or interpersonal behavior. In no sense is interpersonal action a mere fact of human contact. As we have seen, interpersonal behavior can be performed between a person and an animal or even a natural object.

Another confusion of interpersonal behavior with other types of activity is the conception of it as consisting of reactions in which individuals work together or coöperate in some way. Manifestly interpersonal activities do find a place in coöperative situations of all sorts and for no surprising reasons. Hardly any kind of relationship between persons can be excluded from the activities that are performed in human situations. But interpersonal behavior has nothing especially to do with the facts of persons being together. Rather, it comprises a specialized and unique form of action. Especially is this the case since the person himself may be a stimulus for his own interpersonal behavior.

Interpersonal conduct has been most effectively treated in the type of thinking to which we have referred in our notes to the chap-

ter on language behavior. In explanations of the origin of language
and meanings and in descriptions of the interactions of individuals
(with the consequent development of certain stimulational qualities
in acts and things involving interplay between persons) the description of genuine interpersonal behavior has been exceedingly well
done. Especially is this the case in the articles of Mead referred
to in the bibliographical notes just mentioned. We consider, however,
that the emphasis upon the products are entirely misplaced. In the
descriptions referred to, stress is laid upon the development of meanings and significances as the products of the interactions between
persons. That view, as we have already intimated, constitutes a
commendable suggestion concerning the naturalistic origin of the
significance of symbols, even though it is connected up with an
equivocal conception, from a psychological standpoint, concerning
the nature of consciousness in general and consciousness of self.

While interpersonal behavior may result in behavior products or
behavior techniques, at least in a very limited way,[1] the fact of resulting products has no characterizing significance so far as this
type of conduct is concerned. When interpersonal behavior is looked
upon as a technical process of social creation it is a very different
sort of thing. Usually interpersonal action is completed in the mere
play of action performed at the moment. When a product results
it is an entirely incidental phenomenon. For the most part genuine
interpersonal behavior, as it occurs in its various specific circumstances, is usually too brief and contingent to result in any kind of
product, no matter how unimportant or insignificant.

Furthermore, interpersonal behavior is not necessarily face-to-
face conduct. The contacts between the interpersonally acting individuals may occur through comparatively long separations in
space and time. To be classified as interpersonal, the reactions need
only have the extempore and spontaneous characteristics which we
have signified.

---

[1] We distinguish here between behavior developed from previously performed
behavior and behavior techniques as deliberate or non-deliberate products of
action.

## CHAPTER XXV

## THE NATURE OF VOLUNTARY CONDUCT

Charac-<br>teristics<br>of Volun-<br>tary Reac-<br>tions

Voluntary conduct consists essentially of behavior segments chiefly characterized by the presence of a preferential response or choice. The main principle of a voluntary reaction is that the person is in some situation in which he may or may not perform some particular type of response. In plainer words the individual is in contact with objects or persons to which he might perform a certain activity but chooses not to. In detail, the individual attends to and perceives several objects, each of which might become a stimulus to a further response, but only one of them actually elicits an additional and definitive reaction.

Voluntary action, then, involves alternatives of conduct. These alternatives may be of different varieties. Possibly the question arises whether of two actions, "a" should be performed and "b" not, or vice versa. In complex situations, of course, the preference involves the inhibition or rejection of more than one action because many possibilities of response are present.

The preference of voluntary action may be considered in two ways. In the first place, as we have seen, the preference refers to which response the person shall perform, in other words to the behavior side of the situation. But the preference may also be directed toward the stimuli objects. Of two objects that have been actualized into stimuli through attentional reaction the person chooses one to perform a further stimulational function.[1] Thus, this one object performs two stimulational functions, while the other object, which might have some claim upon the individual for a different reaction does not become a stimulating object in this second instance. It is in this sense that one of the objects is preferred as a stimulus to another object or to several others.

The division of voluntary action into two general types, mainly a reaction choice and a stimulus preference, does not point to two different kinds of action. Rather it stresses the fact that we find either the reactional or stimulus side of the voluntary behavior segment emphasized. Even in view of the fact that in the final analysis all such behavior constitutes choice or preference responses we find it to our advantage to specify on which factor the emphasis

[1] The voluntary action accordingly refers to a response correlated with a second stimulational function of the respective objects. This is true since whenever an object is attended to it is already performing a stimulation function, since a stimulus is merely a functional phase of a behavior segment.

312

is placed. For although we may consider the object to be the preferred element we cannot describe it as preferred unless it is coordinated with a preference response. This preference response stands out clearest when we observe that the preference of one action involves an inhibition of some other, or an interception of the behavior system or pattern to the rejected object.

The problem of voluntary behavior becomes therefore the investigation of the specific guiding and determining principles for the preferences manifested in specific voluntary behavior segments. As a record of fact we sum up and describe these guiding principles or determinants under the term of consequences. That is to say, the person's conduct is guided or influenced by the consequences either to himself and his interests, or more remotely to some other person or situation. Naturally the consequences must be looked upon as dominant or purposing stimuli even if they have no embodiment in an actual event or object, and are not natural circumstances or events.

Now we may point out that the essential and characteristic feature of voluntary action is, that what we do or do not do to the objects and persons around us is influenced by some condition or circumstance other than the qualities or proximity of the persons and objects involved in the behavior situation. Ordinarily our reactions to things and persons depend merely upon their qualities and relations to us and upon our particular personality behavior equipment. In voluntary action, however, these two factors are only partial determinants. In addition to these, the results and expected or possible outcome of our action are definite conditions for the operation of our behavior. Such results or consequences may be considered as immediate behavior determinants or as more remote conditioning factors. In other words, the consequences are immediately involved in the very performance of the act, as in taking the wrong road, or saying the wrong thing, or they may be more remote. The latter situation is illustrated by the consequences of following the wrong plans in a military campaign. It is easy to distinguish between the immediate and more remote consequences by calling the former results rather than consequences. Also it might be useful to point out that, on the whole, remote consequences are connected with voluntary conduct in which acts are stressed, whereas immediate results or consequences function more commonly when the preference for stimuli is employed.

Possibly the character of voluntary action can be satisfactorily illustrated by pointing out that such conduct is found among practically all the more complex forms o. human adaptation. To begin with our everyday activities, we must show preferences of all sorts in connection with things we purchase, and the route by which we travel, also the things we say, the time we say them, and to whom we address them. Among this group of actions are many that are unimportant as social behavior and which require very little time for their performance. Again, in more complex situations we have choice of occupation, preference of husband or wife, and other situations involving behavioristic crossroads, with a final action of preferring one of two or more alternatives and the inhibition of others. Very easily illustrated are voluntary actions involving complicated moral and other forms of cultural behavior which the person is frequently called upon to perform.

It is exceedingly important at this stage of our description to notice that the consequences of acts need not be actually known or thought about by the acting person. It is only necessary that the results operate to influence the reaction. This condition works out in the following manner.

In the first place, lest we forget how it is possible to have our action determined by things we do not definitely know about, we must be reminded that knowing in the sense of what is popularly called self-conscious appreciation of things, is different from the ordinary sensitivity to objects characterizing psychological phenomena. Psychological sensitivity, we recall, merely means that whenever we react to an object, our response is differential in the sense that each kind of thing elicits its own unique response. This kind of phenomenon, if it is called knowledge, is clearly and completely different from the more elaborate overt knowledge processes involving complex language intercourse with oneself. These two forms of phenomena must never be confused.

More positively we may state the situation in voluntary action with respect to knowledge when we point out that our preference reactions may be performed upon the basis of conventions and group or class ideals. How often we refuse to do something because of the incongruity of such behavior with our cultural trainings! This type of preference situation contrasts markedly with the situation in which we deliberately reason out a preferred way of acting. Whether the modality of our contact with the consequences as determiners of our voluntary conduct is personalistic or subreactionalistic, we are in implicit contact with them.

We observe, therefore, that the reaction side of the voluntary behavior segment consists of a definite final action of some sort which is preceded by precurrent reactions of various degrees of complexity. The precurrent reactions determine or influence the identity of the final action, that is to say, influence its preferential character and determine that it should prevail, and assist in the inhibition of other possible reactions. The nature and complexity of the precurrent responses determining the final action depend upon the stimulus situation and the general personality or behavior equipment conditions of the acting person.

**Differentiation between Voluntary and Volitional Behavior**

In our study of volitional behavior we have already had occasion to point out that such action must not be confused with voluntary conduct. Especially when the former is exceedingly complex, as it sometimes is, it very much resembles voluntary conduct on the surface at least. Volitional action, however, constitutes on the whole a very different, if not simpler, type of activity.

In the first place, as we have seen, voluntary action involves very definite preference activity and corresponding inhibition of non-preferred responses. Not so in volitional activity. Here the fundamental principle is the determining of the final reaction by other intermediate and intervening responses. No preference or problematic situation is involved. Voluntary action in consequence requires definite delays and postponements of action which are not features of the volitional type of behavior.

Secondly, the actual specific circumstances in each type of action are different. In volitional action the determining and auxiliary responses are necessarily fortuitous because the objects reacted to are unstable and shifting; whereas in voluntary action the most complex and acute behavior may be performed with respect to perfectly fixed and completely stable conditions. When voluntary action involves such shifting circumstances, the latter merely complicate and maximize the difficulties in the action, but the inconstant and mutable factors are not essential features of the behavior segment concerned. Furthermore, unlike voluntary conduct, the primary emphasis in volitional action is not at all upon consequences. At this point of course we are comparing the more closely related of the two types. Differences are more marked in other instances. Also we must not overlook the fact that in complex behavior circumstances volitional and voluntary action occur together in various inextricable combinations.

In the third place, voluntary action involves on the whole a considerable number of social and cultural factors. In point of fact, our most typical voluntary responses concern social or conventional consequences. Accordingly, the entire behavior picture is tinged with social or institutional character. Volitional conduct, on the other hand, is most typically concerned with natural objects or circumstances. Hence voluntary action is singularly a type of humanistic behavior belonging most emphatically among the more definite anthropological modes of psychological phenomena. The value and significance of a description of voluntary action, varies directly with the proportion in which it is concerned with specific human circumstances and conditions.

Our fourth differentiation refers to another fairly diagnostic difference between the two types of action. Namely, volitional behavior does not so frequently involve the acting person as a stimulus factor, and when it does, not so completely and intimately as in voluntary action. In the latter type of behavior situation, because of the consequences serving to condition the whole action, the acting person is most frequently the center of the entire situation.

The
Analy-
sis of a
Volun-
tary Be-
havior
Segment

So complex are the units of voluntary responses and so much activity is involved that they really constitute situations. In consequence our attempt to analyze voluntary behavior segments forces us to be constantly and carefully upon our guard to the end that we may isolate the facts of voluntary action proper, from the factors making up the larger situations in which it is found and from which it is almost indistinguishable. Notwithstanding the fact, however, that a complex voluntary action involves a large variety of behavior material, we may still bring it into the focus of our analytic attack. That the unit of voluntary behavior, despite its complexity, is still a visible and calculable quantity is manifest from the fact that the whole series of behavior circumstances embraced by voluntary action are held together by the character of the consequences or results involved, even if we are somewhat uncertain of the exact identity and number of the stimuli. For instance, from the object of ambition attained as a result of voluntary behavior we learn the nature and significance of the acts involved in the particular adjustment. As a matter of fact, however, knowledge of the consequences and results informs us accurately of what the stimuli are in particular voluntary actions. Thus we are able to keep in view the unity of the action.

An actual analysis of a voluntary behavior segment reveals to us first a final response, in other words, a definite adjustment act constituting the intrinsic and central feature of the behavior unit. This definitive response we have already seen is always determined by some preceding behavior of a more or less complicated sort; either it is the outcome of a previous choice of action or choice of object to which to react. In either case the prior determination of what definitive response shall occur is a process which is itself determined by the character of the consequences or results involved in the behavior situation.

What precise form of action this definitive response takes is a function of the total circumstances involved and naturally varies enormously in details. In a number of very different voluntary behavior situations the final action may be a definite overt or even an effective response of some sort, such as the act of purchasing something or refusing to purchase it. Also, this final reaction may consist of a more complex form of conduct which may be looked upon primarily as overt but which really contains a great deal of complicated implicit behavior. An example is the construction of a bridge after having determined upon or preferred one form of action to another as a result of the particulars concerned. In many instances, however, the final reaction in a voluntary behavior segment is a purely implicit one. A judgment or decision about some situation or person constitutes such a final activity. Clearly it may be called informational in character as over against the overt form. In this case of course we must observe that it is the acceptance or the formulation of the informational or intellectual action which is the telling factor of the voluntary action and not the mere performance of the intellectual response. In either case this definitive final action may comprise a great series of subordinate activities which may or may not be closely conditioned and controlled. The degree of complexity which a voluntary activity may attain is gathered from the fact that innumerable subordinate actions may be part of the response requiring a long time interval for their actual performance.

Having thus depicted the nature of the final reaction we may next consider its precursors in the behavior pattern which are, generally speaking, of equal importance. These anticipations of the final action are forms of psychological behavior which aid the individual in eliciting facts or constructing possible conditions in order to establish the preference of a final action. Therefore, they are based upon and operate in direct conjunction with the consequences of the person's preference or choice; that is, they serve as a guide to a standard of the person's action. For instance, one must consider the consequences of one's act to oneself or to other persons. Thus depending upon the kind of consequences involved, we have specific forms of precurrent reactions. In simpler types they consist of the direct perception of the situation, and an immediate inclination toward one or the other of the alternative stimuli objects or situations. For example, when choosing a road at the turn, we may prefer one course of action to another on the basis of the immediately perceived situation. Perhaps the smoothness of the road from where we stand attracts us and inclines the behavior beam in its favor. When confronted with more complicated situations the person's preceding precurrent reactions take the form of implicit behavior of all sorts including intricate problem solving activities of various degrees of complexity.

In general, we may add that, in voluntary behavior segments a great deal of language activity takes place. In many instances the choice reaction is decidedly determined by such behavior. But the outstandingly prominent factor in voluntary behavior segments is the operation of large portions of the behavior equipment of the person. In fact, it is impossible to speak of consequences of action unless we take into consideration the knowledge, intellectual attitudes and skills possessed by the person functioning in the precurrent phases of the voluntary behavior pattern. Indeed voluntary action, because it is a preference form of behavior, involves much more of the individual's total personality equipment than most other types of behavior. No doubt, in its most complicated forms voluntary conduct is determined by personality equipment, just as much as the most involved problem solving activity. To take a concrete example, the consequences of the person's actions may be dependent upon his needs. Some immediate necessity may be discerned by him, such as securing a position, or arriving at some destination. Again the consequences involved may point to the adherence of the individual to some ideal of a moral, æsthetic, or intellectual sort, or the development of such an ideal. In this latter case, the necessarily poignant study of the situation by the person involves his performing the most intense forms of action comprised in his behavior equipment.

A further analysis of voluntary behavior segments reveals the large number of variations and modifications that are possible in these behavior patterns. So numerous in fact are these particulars of action that no formula of voluntary behavior can possibly be marked out. Not only may the order of the specific component actions be widely varied but the character of the patterns may have few, if any, reactional elements in common. This situation is exactly what we should expect in view of the fact that in the various instances of voluntary action the stimulational circumstances are flexible and shifting in their operation. As a consequence the individual's activity shifts considerably. No complex voluntary action occurs without comprising a great many trial and error procedures as integral features of the individual behavior segments. Under such circumstances naturally the total action of the person cannot work out on a prescribed or even smooth pattern.

It is especially to be noted that voluntary action may be truncated in various ways. For instance, after all the preliminary activities are performed and the final choice of action determined upon, the latter or definitive reaction may not occur. What happens in such a case is of course that some other and different type of action comes in to replace the final or definitive activity. This is only one type of truncation which occurs. In other cases all varieties of shortcuts are possible. Such shortenings of the pattern may occur in the precurrent deliberate actions or in the final or definitive part of the pattern, or in both at once in various combinations.

**Types of Voluntary Behavior Segments**

In casting about for some scheme of ordering or classifying voluntary behavior segments, we may always depend for a ray of light upon the general character of the behavior studied, howsoever feeble it may be. Thus, we may hit upon the variations incidental to the varying degrees of complexity as a mark of differentiation. Naturally in simple voluntary types the preferential behavior is determined or influenced by comparatively simple precurrent reactions. Whether or not we perform a certain preferential reaction is determined entirely or mainly by our information concerning the requirements of the situation viewed in the light of the consequences involved. This preliminary informational behavior constitutes a cognitive orientation with regard to the relative merits of the competing alternative stimuli objects, and always occurs in addition to the numerous attentional and perceptual responses marking the actual contact of the person with the objects involved in the behavior situation. Clearly the voluntary behavior segments that contain these informational responses are more complex than those involving only perceptual activities. In contrast to informational behavior segments perceptual voluntary reactions are based upon conditions immediately available and seen, or otherwise observed. Such instances of voluntary action may very reasonably be included under the heading of knowledge voluntary action. Still we must not be oblivious to the large series of more intricate activities including informational actions of varying degrees of complexity. Our differentiation may be made upon the basis of more or less intense direct acquaintance with the elements involved in the voluntary activities.

More extreme forms of voluntary action are those based upon more complicated psychological phenomena. For example, our choices of action cannot be made at once without some definite problem solving conduct or reconstructive actions which more or less completely modify and transform the original behavior circumstances. Other instances require reasoning behavior as an aid to voluntary adjustments. We are assuming, of course, that a problem solving action, for example, is more complex and involved than one in which we merely act upon information, but we do not overlook here the great complexity to which informational behavior sometimes attains. If we can keep these two types separate, which obviously in practice is not quite feasible, we may consider them as different types or classes of complex voluntary conduct. Of a surety we find many cases falling in between these two types and others consisting of combinations of several of them.

In another class we place these voluntary activities which include responses termed by popular psychology self-conscious action. That is, the person definitely stands at the center of the situation realizing as fully as possible what position he takes in the total situation and the precise consequences of the action to himself. In other words, he plays a very prominent part as a stimulus factor in his decision or deliberation concerning what his preference response shall be.

Quite a distinct class of voluntary behavior segments is that in which an individual finds it necessary to resolve a genuine conflict between competing stimuli. The difficulty and effort of the activity along with the complexity and many-sidedness of it is a definite outcome of the conflicting stimuli circumstances. As a result the individual is obliged to investigate and discover the relative merits of the stimuli and to evaluate and compare them. On the other hand, the conflict may be located more definitely on the side of the person. That is to say, the evaluation of the competing stimuli fairly definitely favors one of them but the action which it elicits is in disharmony with the individual's personality make-up, so that a difficult situation must be overcome. Sometimes such a conflict is resolved only after a long period of time, even years. Not until the person's personality equipment changes can the conflict be harmonized and the definitive response of the voluntary behavior allowed to operate.

Somewhat along a different line of behavior circumstances are those complex actions in which the precurrent responses are not so elaborate or so serious as to involve either the type of self conscious action we have been describing, or problem solving or reasoning. Instead, this particular type of voluntary action comprises musing, reflection, and cogitation. In general, the balancing of fairly immediate and apparent circumstances calls for a large series of these less intricate implicit actions. While it is possible for such activities to reach a high degree of complexity, the general conditions nevertheless are not so weighty as to involve more trenchant and more critical action. So incomplete and variable a list of voluntary activities suggests, of course, more types than we have space to isolate. Yet our survey is not unsuggestive of the number and kinds of such activity.

**Psychological Foundations of Voluntary Action**

In simulation of all complex activity voluntary behavior is also based upon several more elementary forms of psychological activity. Or at any rate we may say that the performance of voluntary conduct involves some characteristics of action that are quite as distinct as they are essential. Hence we may analyze three elementary forms of psychological behavior which may be considered as fundamental to voluntary action, namely, inhibition of action, delay of response, and meaning.

As a preferential type of action, voluntary conduct clearly involves a series of inhibiting actions. It is these inhibiting responses which are at the basis of the selective and judicious discrimination of the stimuli objects and circumstances competing for a chance to perform an action-eliciting function. The superior potency of one object over another to bring about the performance of a definitive response is at the level of complex behavior a definite result of inhibiting action. Naturally the inhibitional function is very complex and operates in a large behavior situation which includes immediate desires, interests, and other actions as well as cultural and idiosyncratic behavior equipment of all sorts.

Connected closely with the process of inhibition in voluntary action is the principle of delayed behavior. Whenever the problem of inhibition arises the selective activity extends over a period of time. Thus the performance of the definitive action is delayed. In other words, there may be a considerable play of waxing and waning of potency on the part of stimuli objects. For example, a particular object, say a flower on a neighboring hillside, appeals to a person and he may desire it; on the other hand, he may be on his way to keep an engagement. Clearly the plucking of the flower must be inhibited. But even in this simple case where the decision is genuinely predetermined some delay in action has occurred, namely, the original response has been delayed in execution because a weak or impossible alternative has arisen. More delay of action is manifestly the rule when the flower, for example, makes a strong appeal as compared with the engagement. In such a case, considerable time may elapse until the issue is determined by such factors as the person's fatigue or the approach of nightfall. We have already seen that in complex voluntary situations this delay occupies a very considerable period of time, possibly weeks and months or even longer. Generally speaking, in all situations where actual conflicts of interest and desires of different people are conditions of the voluntary action a long delay is an intrinsic factor in the total behavior segment. When such voluntary action is delayed because of the failure of two or more possible stimuli objects to develop a prepotency over the other or others, we have a condition of difficulty or effort.

At another point entirely than in the deliberative stage of action does delay of behavior appear as a prominent phenomenon. Since voluntary action involves all sorts of human circumstances the actual consummation of the behavior may require an extremely long time. Thus, if I decide to abstain from some kind of work or pleasure a long time elapses between my original stimulation and final performance. At this point, however, the delay of behavior may prove to be a case of continuity of action but nevertheless this feature of the behavior must be included in our description. Clearly whether the person completes the action or not is a part of the circumstance of voluntary action. If an individual wills to go to college his choice of action continues throughout the years involved. If he changes his action and does not complete his term, we discover that another voluntary action has been performed which discontinues the first. In behavior circumstances, then, which have normal limits or periods we consider the action delayed or continued until it is completely consummated. When behavior situations have no such limits or periodicity the delay element can only be ascribed to the deliberative phase of the voluntary action.

Preferential conduct, such as voluntary action is essentially, must likewise be based upon meaning activity. As complicated forms of differential and discriminative behavior, meaning reactions are indispensable bases of the selective and rejective functions of voluntary conduct. As we have seen, it is the interplay of meaning responses which make possible, influence, and determine the character of the definitive voluntary reaction system. In fact, the complication of the voluntary action is primarily due to the number of precurrent meaning reactions functioning in the behavior segment.

Now, while all voluntary behavior is based upon meaning responses as a foundation this fact is most clearly discernible in the simpler activities. Accordingly the place of meaning responses in voluntary behavior can most favorably be seen in the delineation of its development. Thus, it is only in simple voluntary situations that the preference or choice rests merely on the fact that the stimuli conditions induce preliminary reactions in the individual serving as meaning responses, that is to say, responses determining the nature and facilitation or inhibition of the final reaction. The determination of the final response on the basis of preceding meaning activity is the starting point for the development of very complex voluntary actions.

The latter, which constitute the most definitely purposive of all human conduct, include meanings that have become extraordinarily intricate and may be termed knowledge and informational activities.

In view of the great variety of types and instances of voluntary conduct, it is certain that the stimuli for such behavior consist of all kinds of objects, circumstances, and situations. But it is especially worthy of emphasis that it is not objects and situations directly which perform the stimulational function but rather these objects considered from the standpoint of the activities performed with respect to them. The stimuli functions for voluntary action, therefore, are rather remotely connected with the objects around which they center. Thus the true stimuli functions reside in the results, the worthwhileness of the action to be performed with respect to the objects concerned. They have to do with situations or relations in which the objects are located. It is to be expected, of course, that the consequence or value of the actions with respect to particular stimuli objects includes all types. Most frequently perhaps they refer to the person performing the action. The question here is whether the action should be performed because of an advantage or disadvantage it may afford the acting individual. Or the action may or may not be in consonance with the dignity or standing of the reacting person as a parent, official, scholar, or what not. Similarly, the consequences may have to do mainly with some other person. Would this action hurt his feelings, impoverish him, or be an injustice to him? Or the actions may be decided upon or rejected because of the results to some object. Will this act destroy or injure the object or reduce its usefulness? In both these cases, namely, whether the other person or the object is the locus of the stimulus function, the activity of the voluntarily acting individual may have no further reference than to the conditions or results affecting them. On the other hand, the individual's decision may be founded upon some remote result to himself. Very often the criterion of action concerns the fittingness of the conduct from the standpoint of a general scheme of behavior. To do or not to do a certain action may disturb the harmony of a situation or destroy its æsthetic unity. Furthermore, we may stipulate that the criteria for the performance of a voluntary action may be its economic consequences, or they may involve and be associated with ideals and social standards which are closely connected with and concern the reacting individual.

Objects as stimuli for voluntary actions play a decidedly minor stimulational rôle, since they are found only in the most elementary types of action. Observe, however, that when objects are the stimuli for voluntary activity the competitive circumstances connected with them are based upon the comparative strength of their relative qualities to induce in the individual the problem of alternative behavior. As we might well expect, objects serve primarily as stimulational functions in connection with other kinds of stimulational factors. Music or paintings may be stimuli not only as things by themselves but as things which determine a comparison and discrimination leading to the action of going to the concert hall or art gallery or remaining at home or going to one place rather than to the other.

An extraordinarily large number of voluntary stimuli functions reside in events and situations both of natural and human types. The question arises as to whether one should or should not enter into a particular situation or relationship. The decision is influenced by the determination of whether or not one of these competing situations is the lesser of two evils. In this case we assume that some compulsion or restraint is present to force a voluntary action. This need not always be the case, however. Sometimes the decision is made merely on the basis of the presence of two alternative situations, or the possibility or feasibility of doing something, or getting into some situation rather than not. Situational types of stimuli are of course complicated by various forms of institutions. The question of whether or not one should enter into some type of situation is conditioned by the presence of opinions, laws and customs in the community in which one lives.

Probably the most complex and compelling voluntary behavior is stimulated by persons and their conditions. It is in our relations with human beings that we are palpably confronted with conditions calling for preference reactions. Familiar to all is the large series of conflicts arising between our own wishes and those of others, or perhaps the conflict between other persons challenges us to choose to enter into some kind of action with respect to them. We might decide to harmonize their opposition, or to bring about a settlement by lending the weight of our authority or power to one side or the other.

Let us pass now to the most complex voluntary actions that are performed, namely, responses in which the individual himself and his own actions serve as stimuli objects. The person must choose and decide whether or not he will perform a reaction with respect to himself or his own conduct, as the center of the stimulational situation. Is it fitting, the individual must decide, to perform this kind of action in view of his own qualities and characteristics? In other words, many complex voluntary actions demand the determination and decision to do or not to do something on the basis of the analysis of one's own traits of behavior and character. Hence one may come to the conclusion that with such characteristics the action cannot be done. The alternatives are not necessarily complex. Possibly they merely imply the bare physical strength of the person. To illustrate, a problem arises whether to undertake some kind of work or competition with a certain individual. Thus one proceeds to make a comparative study of his own and the other person's qualifications. In other instances, this type of consideration possibly involves an analysis of the person's social or cultural traits, intellectual attainments, and so on.

The main point, therefore, is that the individual knows himself and examines his characteristics in exactly the same way that he knows and reacts to other objects and persons. Such knowledge of himself and his behavior make-up offering the basis for decision and acceptance of alternatives of behavior, the individual acquires in precisely the same way as he acquires knowledge and information about everything with which he is in contact. Knowledge of himself we may very well suppose has a series• of stages of development. At one period it is very vague, but with increased contacts and considerations the individual comes to know himself rather well and is thus able to perform expert problem solving action with himself as the chief stimulus factor. We certainly find here a situation analogous to that of the individual's knowledge of some specific action, such as his speech. The vague knowledge of himself we may compare to knowledge of his language when he does not appreciate that he speaks prose. His later and more complex knowledge of himself we may compare to the individual who not only knows the grammar and history of his language but also has a thorough acquaintance with his linguistic reactions in all their psychological aspects, both individual and social. In this sense the individual may be cognizant of his strength and weakness, his relative powers and capacities, and even his value as judged by objective standards as well as by personal attitudes of his acquaintances and associates.

Whatever object or situation can be a stimulational factor for voluntary action may likewise function as a setting or background. What is more, perhaps no other types of action are as much conditioned and modified by settings or backgrounds as are voluntary responses. These settings or backgrounds which ordinarily might be considered as indifferent factors in behavior situations may decidedly incline the balance toward one kind of object as stimulus rather than another. The question as to whether to go abroad or to the mountains may be decided in favor of the latter because the former entails crossing the ocean. One profession rather than another is chosen because of the remuneration or the leisure connected with it. This is indicated when we recall that voluntary action stresses stimuli selection as well as action preference.

Furthermore, the necessity for preference reaction is frequently made stringent and compelling because of the circumstances in which the stimuli conditions are placed. For example, the choice of whether to subscribe for some cause or other is made exceedingly urgent because of the public opinion setting which sensitizes the individual to the circumstances. Even the most intense moral action is modified and changed because the final decision one makes and the reaction following upon it will be known and criticized by one's acquaintances. Equally important as settings for voluntary action stimuli are the person's own cultural and idiosyncratic behavior equipments as well as his immediate reactional circumstances.

Our summary review of the stimuli factors in voluntary behavior clearly indicates its extensive range. To begin with the simplest type, preference behavior is performed in elementary situations on a perceptual level. In such instances the alternatives and consequent behavior are trivial and of slight, if any, importance. From these trivial situations the range of voluntary behavior extends to the most complex human circumstances which perhaps occur to individuals but once in a whole lifetime, the choice of a profession, a career, a mate, etc., as well as our determinations when confronted with crucial and absorbing moral issues. Because such behavior circumstances involve a finality and irretrievability of action they are the source of considerable agitating and even tormenting conduct. How full of fears, thrills, dejection, and dispiriting agony is the person impelled to do something that will compromise his social and moral ideals or the legal code, the rejection of which will leave him morally integrated but bereft of all that is attractive, successful, and harmonious.

Naturally, these more extreme limits of voluntary behavior imply the performance of all kinds of activity intermediate between them. In sum, voluntary activity covers the whole range of human action when the individual is sensitive to his surroundings and his place in them. A common form of abnormality of behavior occurs when an individual performs voluntary conduct in situations which really do not require such complex behavior for purposes of adaptation. In thus considering the ranges of behavior we observe sufficiently that the consummatory responses constitute actual ways of eating, speaking, writing, dressing, voting, playing, etc. The most striking types, however, involve the performance of knowledge and intellectual behavior. In such situations the person must determine what he shall learn, know, and believe.

Like the other intricate and complex types of psychological adaptations, voluntary behavior segments naturally involve in an important way many simpler component actions. By these simpler component responses we mean, of course, something beyond the omnipresent and indispensable precurrent attentional and perceptual actions found in all behavior patterns. Our study of voluntary action components with one exception, then, will not include the latter types. For a long time, it has been recognized that attentional responses play a unique rôle in voluntary behavior. But we hasten to point out that these attentional responses are more complex than the simple actualization of a stimulus. *(margin: Simpler Component Actions in Voluntary Behavior)*

Ordinarily we think of a voluntary action as an effective performance of some sort. In other words, the consummatory response looms up as the primary one, although we can never lose sight of the preceding determining action. And, in the operation of such precurrent activities we find a great deal of implicit action which is the component of that type of action in the voluntary behavior segments. Chiefly this implicit behavior fills in the period of delay before the final action occurs.

On the whole, implicit reactions in voluntary behavior segments serve to place the individual in contact with objects and situations not immediately present, but exerting an influence upon the nature and operation of the deliberative and final reaction phases.

With respect to the deliberation features of voluntary action we may distinguish between the complex and more simple situations. In the former, implicit behavior influences the inhibition and preference of responses or stimuli objects by bringing the person into contemplative contact with the consequences of his action. Clearly the consequences cannot be overtly present until the final action is complete, and must, therefore, be reacted to implicitly. The actual process by which this is done is of course the substitution of some object (an actual thing, printed or written matter, or the person's own action) for the consequences in question.

Again, it is possible for implicit action in the deliberative phase of voluntary behavior to place the individual in implicit contact with features other than the consequences. For example, it may serve to connect him with the detailed phases of the act to be performed or the probable or best place where the action can transpire. How great a complexity these implicit deliberative responses attain may be surmised when we recall that the deliberative process is exceedingly complicated and involves a great deal of problem solving with respect to objects and consequences not present. Also in this manner much of the person's past actions and their results can be passed in review in order to throw light on the present behavior situation.

In less complicated deliberative processes (we might with greater propriety term them voluntary precurrent activities, since not all precurrent activities are deliberative), the implicit actions serve merely as guides to action by way of representing alternative objects that function as stimuli to action. Here we illustrate the situation by referring to the comparatively simpler functions of implicit behavior employed in simply remembering or recalling the nature of the issue.

The simpler functioning of implicit activity in the precurrent phases of voluntary action suggests a corresponding occurrence of implicit behavior in connection with the final adjustment. When we have decided to go to Europe we still have to preperceive our exact route. Possibly the value of our suggestion lies more decidedly in observing a hierarchy of deliberation or at least precurrent actions, the major ones of which have to do with the consequences and the lesser ones with the actions themselves. On the other hand, however, if the final action in our behavior segment is itself implicit, then the operation of implicit responses requires no further elaboration.

When voluntary action is complicated and operates in intricate situations it is decidedly constructive as well as preferential. These terms do not refer to entirely different kinds of action; on the contrary they serve merely to emphasize the fact that in complex situations the preference action involves a modification and reconstruction of his past behavior procedure. It follows then, that imagination responses may constitute a considerable portion of voluntary behavior segments. Especially when consequences are serious and actions are difficult of accomplishment, it is necessary for us to construct plans and procedures to effect our final adaptation.

Not to one phase of voluntary action only are imagination responses restricted but they are involved in every phase of the various behavior segments. They may refer to the construction of the whole consequence factor or its details. In other words, they are employed to determine what are the alternative situations and the relations between them, and also to decide upon the particular one to be made the basis of action.

Again, in the actual organization and formulation of the final action after the decision is made much constructive activity may be required. Similarly it is frequently necessary to perform imagination reactions for the purpose of actually carrying out whatever final response we have determined upon. In most cases of voluntary action probably the ideal mode of adjustment would be one in which the decision was made upon an impartial examination of all the factors in the behavior situation. This, however, is far from being the actual way in which our voluntary behavior is performed. Many coördinate responses of different character play their part in our decisions. We find that feeling attitudes loom large in this connection, in many cases acting as a major determinant of conduct. Hence, the preferences we show for the alternatives connected with the performance of the final action are strongly influenced by appeals made to us by things, persons, and places. Our affective behavior may indeed be the weightiest element in any given situation.

Especially do our affective reactions lie at the basis of the tastes, judgments and inferences functioning in voluntary action. Many of our prejudices for or against persons and things are built upon a definite affective foundation. Either of three things may happen. Our intentions and decisions may be formed because the affective reactions induced in us by primary stimuli objects are the strongest determiners, or because the setting of the stimuli situation proves most influential; or finally, because we may perform some voluntary action as a result of the fact that the affective response elicited by some object is more or less closely connected with the principal stimulating factors.

By no means must we consider affective influences upon voluntary action as interfering factors or even extreme determiners. They do not at all serve in this capacity. It is only in particular and perhaps infrequent situations that affective reactions completely influence the person to decide a behavior situation otherwise than the objects and relations in the situation seem to dictate. Most frequently perhaps, affective factors serve as coördinate and harmonic influences upon the decision and performance phases of voluntary action. They are, in short, not only actually occurring but also legitimate factors in our complex choice or preference activities.

For a long time psychologists have been attempting to discover a very close relationship between voluntary behavior and attention responses. In fact it has been frequently asserted that the entire matter of preference may be reduced to the fact that whatever idea is attended to and kept in the field of attention, will go over into action. Now, setting aside the mentalistic implication, this observation holds to a certain extent. That is to say, frequently our preference of one stimulus over another depends upon the sustained presence of a particular object so that we attend to it frequently or constantly; but this is true, of course, only for very simple functions. To make all voluntary action simply a matter of attending to a stimulus, for this is what the view really amounts to, is to oversimplify the circumstances beyond all reclaiming. Such a view overlooks the fact that especially in complex action what we are interested in, and attend to, depends upon some prior preference reactions. It is of course unnecessary to reject the viewpoint on the ground that it embraces a mentalistic conception implying a diremption of psychological phenomena into a mental and physical factor, either in the form of making voluntary action consist of a bodily movement following a mental state, or merely a bodily movement such as eye movements. That view is self condemnatory and self excluding.

Furthermore, it must be insisted upon that attentional action in complex voluntary behavior constitutes reactions not only to stimuli objects but also to the actions that one is about to perform or is performing and to the great number of details having to do with the consequences of the action either to the person himself, or to others. The person attends to the advantages or disadvantages of the behavior involved, as well as to all other features of the situation. Clearly, many and complex attentional reactions are here requisite.

From the standpoint of an actual study of voluntary conduct, therefore, almost every case of such action is much more complicated than the view which depends upon the attentional function either in its original or any emended form implies. Hence we conclude that attention responses operate in voluntary action by way of selection and sustained action exactly as in other complex behavior situations. While the importance of attention in any kind of behavior and especially in voluntary action, cannot be mitigated it never amounts to a controlling condition in voluntary conduct.

Conditions Determining Voluntary Action

Is it possible for a student of psychological phenomena to reach the subject of voluntary behavior without being impressed with the essentially concrete human situation surrounding such conduct and constituting the particular behavior event? Every detail of the intrinsic voluntary event and of the circumstances surrounding it is replete with specific conditions and circumstances which make the activity what it is. While we shall attempt to point out a fairly large series of such surrounding and constituting circumstances which very definitely are conditioners or determiners of the occurrence of the voluntary act and its specific behavior picture, we need only insist that these facts are correlated with particular details of the person's activity and are not in an essential sense the causes of the latter. We must point out, however, that these conditions, whether they are thought of as determiners or as mere correlates of what occurs, are genuine instances of the principles of such behavior and not mere records of the empirical happenings when a person performs a voluntary action. That these two, namely the principles and the description of voluntary conduct are subject to confusion is doubtless due to the fact that there exist innumerable types of voluntary action.

Our enumeration of conditions, therefore, must consist primarily of the statement of generalized situations which pertain more or less to most of the types of voluntary behavior. Be this as it may, we submit that the conditions to be enumerated are representative of such generalized principles. Most of the situations or conditions determining choice and preference and the carrying out of the preferred action can be clearly enough divided into two divisions. On the one hand, we have definite psychological factors, which can be subdivided into (a) conditions involved with the response and stimuli constituting the immediate voluntary action, and (b) those conditions pertaining especially to the person, his equipment, and behavior surroundings, both individual and cultural. On the other hand, a series of non-psychological conditions play their part in influencing what actions shall be preferred and performed at any particular time.

Foremost among the immediate response determiners of voluntary behavior are the individual's motives directly related to the behavior circumstances in question. In other words they form the immediate behavior set of the individual. The motivation responses then represent the individual's immediate purposes. In a very simple situation I am motivated with respect to some stimuli situation, say the purchase of a necessary article. Being on my way to carry out this purpose I inhibit reactions to stimuli which, if I responded to them, would deter me from carrying out my original motive of purchasing something. Similarly, the individual may perform desire and wish reactions of all sorts which operate as deterring or facilitating determiners of particular choices and performances.

What frequently appears to be an indispensable condition of voluntary action is the knowledge activity which individuals perform at the time. Without awareness of certain circumstances and conditions one is unable to perform voluntary behavior at all or one performs a different type of action than would otherwise be the case.

All the stimuli corresponding to these immediate responses influencing voluntary conduct must also be listed as conditioning factors. It may be suggested that the objects and conditions functioning as stimuli in these cases are not to be looked upon as the settings for the more specifically voluntary action stimuli, although in some instances they may appear to be such. It is probably more accurate to consider them as entirely different kinds of factors of behavior.

At this juncture considerable emphasis must be placed upon the presence of persons and their activities in the surroundings of the voluntarily acting individual. Because of the different attitudes and beliefs of other persons, the acting individual finds it necessary to choose between actions which he may prefer, or acts the other person makes necessary or likely. An outstanding set of examples offers itself in the consideration of moral situations which challenge the individual to perform preferential reactions. The interaction of the person with other individuals constantly results in various alternative situations calling for choice behavior. This is true when the person is not directly in contact with other persons but finds it necessary to take sides in their conflicts.

An extraordinarily large amount of voluntary conduct is conditioned by the person's own behavior as stimuli. Even his simple reflex responses may excite him to action having a large influence upon his voluntary conduct. Food and sex responses especially stimulate the individual to perform actions which result finally in choice or preference responses or the need for them. No less, of course, do such responses condition the types of action than their occurrence. Naturally what is true of such simple actions must in similar circumstances likewise be true of more complex behavior. Motives, desires, fears, etc., are in this sense stimuli in complex voluntary behavior situations.

In speaking of personality influences upon voluntary reactions we refer, of course, to the equipment of the person. In other words, what actions are preferred and performed, and what objects will be chosen as voluntary stimuli, depend upon the individual's informational and skill equipment. It is often entirely impossible for a person to perform a voluntary reaction unless he has some behavior equipment serving as a basis for the determination of which one of two alternatives should be performed. One cannot decide to do something unless he has the behavior or skill equipment which the action requires and can perform the choice and final action intelligently. That is to say, an individual's capacity for voluntary action and the conditions determining its specific character depend upon his intimate reactional biography.

This involves not only the private and idiosyncratic equipment of the person but his cultural equipment also. The latter, moreover, may be the more important in complex voluntary action. We recall that in the course of culturalization the individual acquires certain habits of action. When drawn into alternative behavior situations these character factors serve as very significant influences in the determination of the individual's choice of action. It is these cultural equipments, moreover, along with the other personality elements, that affect the formulation of his intentions, motives, and purposes with respect to the many intricate and conflicting conditions of everyday living. Thus the individual's various equipments operate both immediately and mediately to condition and determine the type of behavior under discussion. As exemplifications of such conditioning of voluntary action, we need think only of the way in which an individual's religious or intellectual training alters his decisions in a voluntary situation involving issues or alternatives of conduct.

Our exposition naturally leads us to a consideration of institutions of all types as voluntary behavior stimuli. An intimate study of the voluntary conduct of particular individuals makes necessary a study of the kind of institutional surroundings in which one has become culturalized. Thus, for example, to discover why a person wills to destroy property or to enlist in the army one must discover the institutional conditions under which he has grown up. A most effective example here is the willingness of some individuals to undergo martyrdom. This is often largely explained by the type of cultural institutions in contact with which the individual's personality equipment has been acquired.[1]

Non-psychological conditions exercise quite as much conditioning and determining influence upon voluntary action as psychological factors. For example, my preferential reaction toward some object, as in the case of purchasing a watch, may be determined by the availability of various makes and models. Many a purchase action follows a large and serious investigation of possibilities and weighing of alternatives because of the mere existence of different types of timepieces or the belief that there are differences in those present. In cases where only one type of object is available, only the alternatives of buying or not buying are possible. In such complex activities as voluntary behavior these factors may seem trivial in the mentioning, but they nevertheless claim a large place in the behavior situation.

Again, the availability of resources both for the initial purchase and later upkeep, in short, one's economic conditions, determine the choice and final action. Thus, we find innumerable æsthetic, professional, social, natural, and other circumstances operating as determining and conditioning factors upon our voluntary behavior. We might consider that this determination operates upon the person both directly, as a factual or natural accident, and indirectly as a remote condition of the voluntary behavior situation through

[1] Here we need take account both of the original and permanent institutions of the individual's group and the more temporary institutions constituted of or based upon propaganda of various descriptions.

some influence upon the psychological processes. For instance, a physical or cultural condition might influence a person to accept a certain belief which in turn will affect his preferential behavior. These suggestions merely indicate once more the truth that complex behavior, like voluntary action, is firmly set in an intricate human situation as a matrix. Directly in proportion to the number of such facts which we can correlate with voluntary action, do we succeed in describing it effectively and in penetrating to its essential nature.

**Classification of Voluntary Action**

That classification in psychology is difficult, especially in the complex domains, is a truth which we have frequently discovered and no less frequently remarked upon. To attempt the coördination and organization of different types of voluntary action is an enterprise which is inevitably blocked and impossible to carry out. Still, because of the understanding of the present phenomena that we obtain from such an attempt we may once more essay such an organization. We observe at once that in this particular instance our classification must be based upon the consideration of three factors, (a) the stimulating conditions, (b) the response conditions, and (c) the consequences of the action. The last member of our criteria is exclusively characteristic of voluntary behavior and marks the present classification as a unique one.

Our first type of voluntary action is characterized by a stimulus condition which is very intense or compelling. A person has a particular thing to do, and may be fully equipped with the skill or information necessary to perform the activity. Furthermore, he may be desirous of performing the act in question. But, as it happens, the consequences of his behavior loom up either as extremely doubtful or as positively forbidding. The result is a very common and conflicting situation. In many cases of our voluntary action, especially those involving social and moral conduct, we must describe ourselves as suffering keenly under the circumstances the pangs of a temptation stimulus which must be resisted.

A second type of voluntary conduct represents the case in which we have at least two very compelling stimulating situations. With regard to behavior equipment, the person is equally well prepared to do the one as the other. In addition, no personal ideal or information especially favors the performance of the one or the other. Similarly, the consequences are equal in weight. Hence we have a typical situation of external conflict. The difficulty and uncertainty of the person in making a decision between the two situations depends upon the importance of the specific stimuli and the general behavior circumstances.

A similar type equally calling for inhibition or preference involves the situation in which the alternative stimuli conditions are equally compelling, that is, equally favorable and unfavorable. The consequences of performing or not performing the respective actions in this circumstance also are of the same weight; but on the other hand, the ideals, desires, and knowledge of the person are extremely vigorous and important. Here we have what we may call an internal conflict. On this account the activity is very difficult to carry out.

Another type comprises two stimuli of equal importance and compulsion, namely, two unfavorable and unsatisfactory behavior situations. So far as our knowledge and desires are concerned, these are both of equal unfavorableness. The consequences, however, are such that one of them has to be performed. Thus the poignancy of voluntary activity comes in when we must determine which is the lesser of the two evils, and perform an action accordingly.

A very different type of voluntary activity may be isolated according to the predominance in it of situations in which the primary factor is on the response side. Let us suppose that the person is very eager to perform some particular kind of activity, either for some need or because of some ideal, and of which the consequences would be favorable, if not compelling. Perhaps the achievement promised by the performance of the act in the way of gaining the good opinion of people, or attaining some advantage for oneself, is very striking. But unfortunately the stimulating conditions, that is, the objects or persons concerned in the action as stimuli, introduce such difficulties of accomplishment that the person cannot come to any conclusion as to how to carry out his activity. Such a situation is keenly illustrated by the futility and baffling character of unconsummated behavior, such as moral or social failure. We need only add here the comment that all varieties of combinations of these three main factors are possible. In the aggregate the series gives us a large number of varieties of voluntary behavior situations.

Because of the great complexity of voluntary action and the fact that it involves the operation of the person's whole behavior equipment, we expect to find a wide range of variation in voluntary conduct; more, perhaps, than in other forms of action. Moreover, for the same reasons the voluntary actions performed by any particular individual at different times are different. These variations concern the frequency and quality of the activities, their rapidity, and the circumstances in which the person performs them. Some illustrative instances of such individual differences are quoted in the following paragraphs.

Some individuals differ in that they seem to have a very definite control over the details of their voluntary activity while others have little or none. The first individual performs activities primarily of the sort in which the personality factors are of account as over against the stimuli conditions, while in the case of the second person the stimulational conditions are more potent in the decision and choice of action. That is to say, the voluntary action of some individuals is characterized by more purposiveness. This purposiveness is, of course, entirely a function of the individual's personality equipment and reactional biography. Persons vary therefore because of the

Individual Differences in Voluntary Action

number and types of behavior they are capable of performing with respect to both skill and information.  These variations may be due to the larger opportunities some have•of performing voluntary action or developing the necessary knowledge, techniques, and facilities for such behavior.  Easily recognized is the value of travel, education, and the contacts facilitated by residence in a large environment, as a result of which some persons have a better and stronger hold on their surroundings than others.

Very closely connected with the qualities of purposiveness and control is the actual worth of the voluntary activity.  In other words, in some cases individuals actually have expert deliberative capacity. They have greater appreciation and knowledge of the existence and value of voluntary situations and of their consequences.  Accordingly, when the final activity occurs, it is entirely or nearly satisfactory for the situation and circumstances at hand.  In other instances there is no very definite certainty that the final action will be suitable for the situation.  Moreover, individuals differ in the degree to which they permit their deliberation to be determined and conditioned by extraneous circumstances.  This condition is closely related to that of the degree with which the individual projects himself as a factor into the voluntary behavior situation.  Both of these circumstances of individual variation are related to the question as to whether the person actually deliberates before making a choice, or only substantiates his choice by deliberation after it is made, even though he is ready to discard it.

In similar fashion individuals vary in the rapidity with which they come to a decision concerning preference objects or preferred activities.  Some are exceedingly rapid whereas others are very slow. This fact gives rise to the popular designation of some individuals as impulsive, in contradistinction to others who are obstructed in their voluntary activity.  Both these individual differences refer, in fact, to such extreme varieties of behavior that both types of individuals may be very inadequately adapted to their surrounding conditions.  For instance, the impulsive individual may perform a final reaction before any adequate deliberative process has taken place. Equally disadvantageous is a too extended deliberation so that the final action, when it occurs, is no longer necessary or fitting.

An additional series of individual differences is based upon the relationship between the precurrent action involved in deciding upon the performance of an action and carrying it out.  The question arises as to whether, even after a person has made a choice, he will carry out the connected final action or whether he can or will inhibit it.  Very frequently the quality of a voluntary behavior and its adaptability depend upon the modification of the decision as the circumstances vary.  This modification must sometimes extend also to the final action.  But some individuals refuse to modify their choices.  Once they make a decision they cleave to it, no matter how many changes are demanded by the varying conditions. Such individuals maintain their original decision even against their own interests and without regard to the opinions of other people. The other extreme is represented by the person who is so sensitive to variations in stimulating circumstances that he can hardly be said to have come to any decision at all because the decision is not fixed enough to go over into action. Here we have an exceedingly large amount of vacillation and inability to persist in any sustained mode of behavior.

The discussion of individual differences leads by a natural and easy transition to the problem of training in voluntary action. Just how this can be done we have already implied, since individual differences all depend in great part upon the behavior equipment of the person. To sum up, then, we may say that the training of an individual consists of the acquisition of responses of various sorts necessary to meet the types of situation with which the person is most likely to come into contact. These reactions to be acquired consist of informational and skill behavior of various sorts.

Even under the most rigid mentalistic régime psychologists have refused to accept a particularized mentalistic interpretation of voluntary action. In this sense we have a unique perspectival background for our study of psychological phenomena. Although the term "will" has persisted in psychological literature there have been many positive arraignments of the idea that this term stands for some definite mental state. Even now this conception has not been wholly given up. It was not infrequently argued for even on experimental grounds. But the general trend of psychological thinking has been toward the extrusion of such an element from the psychological domain.

To account for this anomolous situation in psychology is a difficult matter. A suggestion is found in the fact that the extreme complexity of voluntary behavior has prevented its interpretation in terms of mental states in the same sense as perceptions (sensations) or feelings. In the first place, there seemed to be no way of connecting such complex phenomena with the simple operations of the nervous system despite the heroic effort of James. In the second place, voluntary activity seemed to be so obviously an interaction with complicated surrounding objects or persons that little plausibility attached to its interpretation as simple mentalistic elements. We find in psychological literature, therefore, not only that voluntary action is not made into an element of consciousness by structuralistic psychologists but, as we have already said, that it is not conceived by the functional psychologists as any kind of mental process. The latter have been inclined to interpret voluntary action as the operation of other mental states, such as the play of ideas in attention, and to say that the will is the whole person acting.

In the observation that voluntary action constitutes a complex type of responses to persons and things we see that a possibility was present of regarding such conduct as genuine interactional behavior. Indeed the conception of will as the whole person active is decidedly a step in this direction. But naturally in a mentalistic milieu this achievement could not have been possible. Not only were psychological phenomena not regarded as behavior, but because voluntary action was always connected with the problem of freedom, the psychologist could abstain from a rigorous study of such conduct which he regarded as belonging to the philosophical rather than to the psychological domain.

That the complexity of voluntary behavior and the consequent lack of a neural concomitant are not the only reasons why psychologists have not interpreted it as simple mental states is evident from the fact that, were this the case, thinking would likewise not have been thought of as the operation of mental states. Accordingly we look for another suggestion to account for this circumstance in the fact that voluntary activity has been carefully fostered by the ethicist. This has traditionally been the case because ethical conduct has always been construed as a deliberate form of voluntary conduct. We may indicate, then, that in contrast to the case of thinking in which the logical influence has been rather detrimental to the psychology of thinking, the influence of the ethicist upon the psychology of voluntary action in the present instance has been salutary, in the negative sense, at least, by preventing its being interpreted as simple mental states. We suggest once more, then, that if the psychologist could have conceived of himself not as a student of mental states but of conduct, these ethical influences upon his thinking at the point of voluntary action could conceivably have resulted in an organismic position such as that outlined in the present chapter. For the observation of the choice and deliberation which one performs in moral situations must lead to the interpretation of voluntary action as the specific interactions of an individual with his surrounding stimuli. We add then that, although ethicists have so frequently sought for the springs of action in innate mentalities and in human nature, in their descriptions of deliberation and choice of conduct they have certainly shown the way to an organismic interpretation of voluntary conduct.

# CHAPTER XXVI

## LEARNING CONDUCT: A TECHNIC OF BEHAVIOR ACQUISITION

**The Problem of Learning**

Within the realm of psychological phenomena we may distinguish between two fairly distinct types of reactional processes. As one type we may divide off the ordinary adaptational responses occurring whenever the person comes into contact with adjustment stimuli either directly or through the intermediation of substitute stimuli. Now these may be sharply set off from the technical or contrived action of which learning is the most typical and the best example. In learning activities the person is technically and sometimes deliberately getting into contact with objects in order to acquire responses to them.

The learning activities are especially unique and easily differentiated from other forms of technical and contrived action. The adaptations achieved by learning conduct comprise the development of the ability, possibility, or capacity to perform other particular actions, as compared with such adaptations as seizing some object or property, transforming it, knowing it, having some feeling with respect to it or perhaps coming into some immediate better relationship with one's surroundings. The technical character of learning consists essentially, therefore, of the process of acquiring behavior, of furnishing or refurnishing one's behavior equipment, or of adding new elements of behavior equipment to the catalogue of personality endowments existing at any particular time.

Learning behavior in consequence constitutes some of the most important and constant types of psychological activities that the individual may perform—important, because in the human organism, at least, the exigencies of even ordinary living under the simplest conditions of cultural existence are such that the reactional growth of the individual is an imperative and rigorous eventuality—constant and frequent, since the organism from the instant of birth must acquire all the innumerable forms of action necessary for adaptation. It must learn to walk, to talk, to feel, to think, to make things, and so on, and each of these activities involves thousands and thousands of actions. Furthermore, the individual must develop an indefinite number of skills in the making of tools and instruments. Especially in complicated civilizations an individual must adapt himself to an indefinite number of objects and events implicated in his work and play. In short, a great deal of the life time of an active and pro-

338

gressive person is devoted to the contrived, if not deliberate, process of acquiring new modes of behavior, fresh ways of doing things as equipment to meet the exigencies of the changes in older situations, or of the new circumstances constantly arising in his surroundings.

Not alone is such acquisition sufficient. The human person in his cultural milieu must develop a great mass of behavior equipment in order to adapt himself to the social conditions in which he finds himself. He must acquire all those acts of politeness, responses of social grace and the severities and amenities of behavior demanded of him as a member of various social aggregations. In addition, in any kind of intricate civilization an individual is constantly moving from one group where certain social practises and activities prevail, to other groups where correspondingly different practises and activities operate. To these new techniques he must develop behavior and learn to adapt himself. Then, there are the innumerable skills and techniques of an occupational or professional sort. Think only of the skills of the engineer or physician which actually mount up into thousands of specific reaction systems.

Nor can we overlook all of the myriads of particular behavior equipments of an informational or knowledge sort. Activities of this character are the essential basis for all the numerous cognitive orientations the individual is constantly called upon to make during the course of his daily activities. Such activities are acquired chiefly through book learning but also include activities which the individual attains through observation of the surrounding objects and circumstances with which he is in direct contact. Or, he may have acquired such behavior through the imparted materials derived from other individuals who have themselves made observations or acquired them in some indirect way. It is appropriate to add here the special skills involved in transmitting such information. Plainly we are including the development of all the techniques for handling knowledge and information, and in performing general cognitive orientational activities.

Fundamentally learning behavior may be characterized as a restricted form of general psychological action. As a form of acquiring or organizing stimulus-response connections, learning activity is very much like the general fact of psychological conduct. For, it is clear that learning, like psychological behavior in general, is a process of coördinating responses with particular objects, persons, and events, so that the objects at some later period provoke responses which have been built up in connection with them. Nevertheless there is a general difference discernible at this point. Namely, whereas in the case of psychological behavior as a whole the coördination of stimuli and responses is general, depending only upon the contact of the person with the object (that becomes a stimulus and later performs a stimulational function), in learning activity some sort of contrivance of connection between the person and his

The Nature of Learning Behavior

objects (which become stimuli objects) is arranged. In many cases this is a thoroughly deliberate procedure. The child is brought into direct and necessary stimulational contact with some kinds of objects, as for instance, the materials of reading and writing. In other instances, of course, the procedure is not deliberate in this sense, but still some elements of contrivance and technical connection are discernible. Such learning activities are therefore not entirely casual but depend upon a certain amount of indirect stratagem and artifice. An example here is the process of casual culturalization in which the child necessarily learns certain types of action but only because the stimuli objects that are instrumental in the learning activity are cherished and preserved. As a consequence this situation constitutes an undeliberate contrived contact of the individual with such stimuli.

**Psychological Foundations of Learning Behavior**

From our general description of the learning type of psychological action we may well expect that it depends decidedly upon general psychological principles. All learning is deeply rooted in the fundamental psychological characteristics, namely, differentiation, variability, modifiability, inhibition, integration, and delay of reaction. The activities involved in each specific learning case are based upon the particular stimulus response relationship indicated by these terms and upon the degree and particular manner in which these characteristics operate. For instance, the differences in learning capacity between human and infrahuman animals are rooted in the fact that in the latter animals the characteristics of integration and delay are not prominent, if they occur at all. Accordingly, infrahuman animals are unable to acquire certain behavior in any degree or are able to do so only in a very inferior way.[1]

Not only are these elementary psychological characteristics the basis of learning activity in the sense that they symbolize every type of object (stimulus) and person or organism (response) coördination, but also because they are types of processes which bring about the necessary connections of the learning organism with the stimuli objects to which he is acquiring behavior. For example, we may count upon the characteristics of variability to constitute the source for the trial and error procedures which are always essential factors in learning and of extreme importance, if not indispensable in particular learning situations. These fundamental characteristics of psychological conduct, therefore, constitute the simple foundations for learning.

In addition we may enumerate more complex psychological conduct operating in learning situations. For example, the facts of association summing up the relationship between the individual and surrounding objects as well as the connection between the objects

---

[1] This illustration must be taken only as a symptom of, or a general reference to, the total series of differences making animal conduct an almost entirely different sort of thing from that found in the human animal sphere so far as actual essential details are concerned.

themselves play an indispensable part in learning behavior segments. Similarly, attentional conduct and the ideational form of implicit behavior must be included as factors in the operation of all kinds of learning activities. Our plan, then, is to discuss these various bases in order.

Differentiation as a basis for learning consists of an historical process constituting the progressive contact of the learning individual with objects toward which he is acquiring new conduct. As a basic psychological contact with objects the differences in the qualities of things, whether tactual, visual, or of any other sort, call out an elementary differential response. This fact of differentiation in the first instance comprises a case of momentarily acquired conduct. In this sort of situation the learning is undifferentiated from the mere psychological process. Now, in addition to this situation we may or may not have the acquisition of other or more complex reactions. If no further differential reactions are developed, no learning situation or problem is involved. When additional differential responses, however, are acquired by the object or situation in question we have a more definite learning situation. Whether or not a learning situation is present depends, as we have already suggested, upon the question as to whether or not the acquisition involves the technical connection of objects and the person. When the individual's contact with prospective stimuli objects involves this technical factor we have learning, both when the individual acquires to the same object different simple differential responses which replace one or more than one previously acquired differential response, or when he acquires an entirely new differential action.

Such is the account we must give of the simplest circumstances in which the differential principle operates as a basis for learning. In more complex circumstances we have many widely varying differential responses developed toward the same object. These differential responses may all be primary in the sense that they represent reactions on the same level of acquaintance or contact with the object. On the other hand they may be in part primary and in part secondary in that they are based upon previous reaction acquisitions. The latter type of situation leaves the level of direct effective or manipulative action and approaches, or is quite identifiable with, cognitive or orientational behavior. Moreover, the complex acquisition may depart from the simple acquisition in that the former involves contacts not only with simple objects or situations but also with such objects and situations in various degrees of complex relationship. Here too the responses may be for the most part primary or intermingled with secondary responses.

So far we have considered the principle or character of differentiation as basic to, or constitutive of, the learning process. We may now turn to the rôle of differentiation in learning when it is a process. In this instance it functions as a process of identification of new or possible elements in a situation and as the basis for the contact resulting in the technical acquisition of behavior. Differentiation of this type operates either as very simple effective actions of the exclusively overt type, or it consists of the more complex, semi-overt, full-fledged perceptual reaction systems, or still more complex implicit cognitive responses. To the writer it appears certain that the processes to which we are now referring, comprise and exhaust the immediate and remote controls (kinæsthetic and visual sensations) of the older psychological literature. Illustrative of at least the simpler points we have made are the various available observations of the processes obtaining in an experiment when an organism learns to perform some type of discrimination. In learning to enter a door in an apparatus that is marked with a color associated with food, and to avoid the entrance marked with another color sign associated with some type of punishment, the animal's conduct reveals the connection between certain objects and the changes taking place in its reactional equipment as well as the functional modification in the stimuli objects.

The act of persisting in varying the contacts with an object until some satisfactory relationship is established contributes a definite basis for the learning of skill and knowledge. It will be recalled that the principle of variability is primarily a persistence in maintaining a contact with an object until the action with respect to it is satisfactory, complete, or fitting. Accordingly the result of such action is a new status or relationship between the learning individual and the object serving as stimulus. This status, of course, consists of the acquisition of new types of responses to the object or situation with which the person is in contact. In this contact situation we find the stimuli objects operating with their original properties to which the individual may not yet have a satisfactory or fitting response. Or the object may present different properties from those with which the individual has formerly had contact.

Variability probably more than any other characteristic of psychological phenomena consists of an identity of function, in its constitutive and process features, as they operate in learning situations. This fact is immediately recognized when we recall that the principle of variability in learning is the basis of the universally familiar trial and error activities that we find as essential factors in at least all complex learning. Variability, as a process, operates as the repeated contacts of the individual during a series of trials which result finally in the building up of a particular type of response-stimulus coördination. Every learning experiment excellently illustrates the process of variability when it is referred to as trial and error learning. Thus it is universally recognized that the kind of learning in which trial and error procedure is possible is more effective than any other type.

As a basis for learning, the characteristic of modifiability functions primarily to change one's present equipment in order to profit by some present contact with a stimulus object or situation. By modifying one's action some alteration is achieved either in a previously acquired reaction system or in the individual's personality equipment by the replacement of some previously acquired equipment. In detail the modifiability basis for learning activities involves a definite elimination of reactions appearing as unadaptable or unsatisfactory with respect to objects with which the individual is in contact or concerning the development of equipment for reactions to new objects. Modification in its various forms is undoubtedly of fundamental importance as a basic feature of learning behavior.

When viewed as a process the modifiability characteristic serves primarily to change the individual's conditions of contact to the end that some problem may be solved or some new kind of adaptational response developed. Such a process throws into relief the activities that require elimination if the learning action in question is to take place. Both as basis and process the modifiability principle is exceedingly well illustrated by the case of an animal which is learning a maze. Here the modifications in action and especially the elimination of unnecessary responses is shown in great profusion in even a moderately complex maze problem.

In a much more obvious manner than most of the other psychological principles, integration of action serves as a basis for learning. Essentially, the present activity results in the organization of older simple reactions to form more complicated new ones. The newer responses, indicated by contact with the stimulational object, provide more satisfactory and effective forms of behavior in the situations involved. This type of integration basis or constituent of learning activity occurs of course in simpler situations. In more complex circumstances the integration principle operates as an organization of new simpler reactions that are now in the course of acquisition into larger parts of behavior. That is, the integrational action definitely exhibits a prospective aspect, since the conditions of the problem not only determine the organization of reaction systems previously acquired but also those in the process of acquisition. In the literature on learning the integration of simpler reactions into more complex ones has become a classic illustration of learning processes. In learning, such skills as typewriting, telegraphy, writing, or drawing, the progressive organization of simpler reactional elements into more complex ones, is an obvious subject of observation.

Taken as a learning process integration affords the organization of stimuli conditions in such a way that by this very action we provide a technical contact of the individual with stimuli objects. Thus a new combination response is dictated by the situation and is accordingly developed. In this contrivance of circumstances for learning, the integration of stimuli elements may result in the development of behavior in the form of new reaction systems or in the organization of a series of reaction systems to constitute a new and complex pattern of behavior.

Delay of action forms a further basic psychological characteristic for learning reactions. Its chief rôle is to provide the opportunity and condition for the organization of action resulting in the apportionment of the behavior on the basis of the characteristics of the stimuli objects. Such apportionment of behavior consists essentially of the postponement and delay of action until some other behavior has first been performed. Activities in which the delayed principle constitutes a basis may be generalized as process reactions. At any rate the activities having delay as their basis consist for the most part of a process response such as arithmetical reaction operations, the operation of a machine, or driving a motor car, etc. In complex situations this delay principle as a basis for learning produces various forms of memorial conduct as integral factors of the learning action.

When delay operates as a process in learning it does so primarily by way of introducing difficulties and apparent possibilities into the learning situation. This procedure forces the individual to postpone his final adjustment reactions until he has made a survey of the situations at hand and developed various combinations of activities in order to meet the difficulties presented. In the end the individual is forced to develop some form of fitting adjustment. The use of the delay principle in learning results in the acquisition of complicated precurrent and final reaction systems in complex patterns of acquired responses. The details of the procedure consist for the most part in the serialization of objects and conditions serving as stimuli. Through such an arrangement and variation of stimuli conditions the modification of precurrent and final reaction systems in complex patterns is brought about. Illustrative of learning activities in which the delay principle is a prominent factor are all the instances involving complex manipulation of tools, instruments, or objects, as in the case of puzzle box experiments and the acquisition of skill in handling any kind of apparatus or puzzle.

As a basic principle in learning activity, inhibition serves as a check of particular acts which the individual possesses as part of his behavior equipment, in order to give preference to some other activity better fitting the situation at hand. In typical instances of learning involving inhibition we find that the contacts between the individual and objects are modified so that an action which the person has previously developed with respect to an object is made to wait upon another action that is deemed more suitable for adaptation to the particular object or situation functioning as the stimulus at the particular time. This principle of inhibition may operate merely as a temporary condition or the learning may consist of the induction of a total and permanent inhibition of a particular type of action.

Functioning in the form of a process the inhibition principle affords the introduction of alternatives in the stimuli conditions.

Naturally a learning situation of this type very definitely calls for inhibition of reaction to it so that the learner strengthens his acquisition of reactions to a new object by the contrasted inhibition to the other type of response. Generally speaking the inhibition process consists of employing various kinds of methods to eliminate wrong or useless activities. This is the center of the inhibition function in learning situations. The use of punishment and reward conditions in learning experiments well exemplifies the employment of inhibition as a process in the acquisition of learning behavior.

Quite as fundamental a basis for learning behavior as the simpler psychological characteristics is the more complex behavior phenomenon of association. It will be recalled that not only are associational processes at the basis of ordinary stimulus-response coördinations but they constitute the functions for the connections between objects and situations which make learning possible and effective. Still further important ground for learning is found in associational activities connecting up simpler responses into more complex forms of behavior. It is such connections of reactions which provide the basis for complex pattern making in both the precurrent and final factors of behavior segments.

By way of summarizing the various conditions in learning situations brought about by the utilization of the fundamental psychological principles as processes or by their operation as bases, we may enumerate a series of changes that take place or result from the learning. Quite naturally these changes may be divided into those that take place in the individual and his equipment, and those that transpire in his surroundings or the objects and circumstances constituting those behavior surroundings.

In the first place, we notice a very fundamental change in an object in that through the learning process it becomes a stimulus object. This change may be stated as providing a functional value for the object in the sense that it takes on some form of specific stimulational capacity. In various ways this process goes on. We may acquire a completely new reaction so that the object or condition in our surroundings, which previously had no stimulus function at all, now comes to have the capacity to elicit a new response. Or its stimulational function is such as to arouse a response similar to one which was prompted by some other kind of stimulus object. In short, we may consider that a person transfers a stimulus function from one object to another whether or not the stimulus function in question remains in the original object or not. So far as the particular function is concerned it may call out a manipulative reaction, an affective response, or some type of cognitive orientational reaction. More specifically, the response may be some information as to what one can do with an object, how to open it, or otherwise manipulate it or modify it in some way or make it go or stop.

Another type of change is that brought about in some object which already has stimulational function for the individual, but which takes on a new capacity, either replacing the old one or constituting an addition to the former stimulational function. These different stimulational functions in the object exist in various ways. On the one hand, the new and the old functions may compete so that the specific conditions in the settings of the objects and the particular circumstances and needs of the individual at the time are required to dissolve the competition. This is done by the inhibition of one reaction and the functioning of another. On the other hand, the stimulational functions may not compete at all but each operate without regard to the other. In such cases the objects are normally found in different settings and the types of contact are more or less inevitable.

A third type of change in objects resulting from the learning activity has to do on the whole with more complex conditions. In our two previous types of conditions the changes were fairly definite. This would naturally be the case with simpler types of objects and learning situations. For this reason the stimulational functions are definite in the sense of calling out particular reactions. In complex situations, however, the changes occurring in the objects or situations result in a series of more or less indefinite stimulational functions. Accordingly the reactions to such objects are in the form of complex manipulations or orientational attitudes because of the number and indefiniteness of the stimulational functions. Here the reactions on the whole may best be described as experimental. The particular types of action comprise combinations of previously acquired reaction systems and entirely new ones. Just how the responses operate is contingent upon the particular relationship of the objects to the individual. In other words they stimulate him in different ways at different times and according to his desires and interests at different periods. The present situation may be illustrated by the example of a person who takes on all sorts of stimulational functions for us so that the way in which we react to him at any particular time depends upon which of the stimulational functions operate on the basis of that person's various and varying conditions. Similarly, complex phenomena which undergo more or less constant change, stimulate us to perform only indefinite and speculative forms of action.

Changes in the person corresponding to those in objects and resulting from contacts of individuals with objects, lend themselves to a similar summarization. To begin with, the individual may develop a completely new form of response without any definitely visible modification of previously acquired responses. He acquires an entirely new way of doing something which correlates with a completely new stimulational function. For the most part this new type of action is correlated with contact with the new object, although this is not entirely necessary. In their simplest forms these early and simple acquisitions are of course merely reaction systems constituting movements, coördinations, and controls of what is primarily the biological organism. With the increasing development of the individual these acquisitions become larger and more complex activities. As a fairly definite intermediate stage we may consider the acquisition of discrimination or sensing reactions and the beginnings of verbal speech.

Another type of change in the individual refers to the elimination from his reactional equipment of some action that has been previously acquired and performed. On the whole this change consists in the passive lapse of action as the result of avoidance of contact with some object having the stimulational function of eliciting the response in question. Or it may be the positive act of not doing something or the inhibition of an action when the individual does come in contact with an object possessing a stimulational function for him.

Probably the most common form of change in the individual resulting from the learning process is the modification of old action in greater or lesser degrees. The stimulational functions in such cases elicit an action, which is quite definitely a simple modification of an old behavior, to meet some variation in the object or situation. An illustration is found in the slight variation in one's reactional equipment necessary in changing from one automobile to another in which the gear shift is different. An equally prominent form of modification involves the use of an old reaction in a new way. That is to say, so far as the reaction system itself is concerned, it does not undergo any new change but it functions in different adaptational situations. The fundamental principle here is that the reaction becomes attached to a new type of object which takes on the same stimulational function as another. As a final change ensuing from the acquisition of a new response in the learning process, we mention the combination of old responses into new more complex ones. Learning a language involves such a process to an extensive degree, especially in the organization of separate words into sentences.

Since the results of learning activity are always the acquisition of new equipment or reactional resources, it is not difficult to classify learning activities on the basis of these acquisitions or products. On the whole we may look upon these products as reactional capacities or techniques which function in later contacts of a person with objects in former contacts with which this reactional equipment has been developed.

Classification of Learning Situations

As the first type of product of learning behavior we mention the orientational activities, those knowledge or information responses to the different objects and situations concerned in the learning circumstance. Under this division we place all types of cognitive reactions, intellectual attitudes, meanings, etc., which go to make up the individual's orientation with respect to his surroundings. Here we add also the person's various abilities to state and describe things. This linguistic feature of orientational reactions may be considered a specialized form of behavior product and not necessarily a factor of cognitive or informational types. It is quite possible that one may be able to perform cognitive reactions with respect to knowledge objects and at the same time not be able to formulate and state his knowledge.

Informational acquisitions are of two distinct sorts, information of acquaintance and information concerning objects and things. Information of acquaintance consists of knowledge acquired through direct and immediate contacts with the qualities and conditions of objects. Information about things is orientational equipment acquired mainly through secondary implicit response to things. Knowledge of the former type cannot be acquired without actual overt contact with things, whereas in the other type of knowledge our equipment is derived in a secondary way by hearing or reading about the objects and conditions concerned. It happens to be true, as a matter of fact, that most of our orientational equipment comes from the indirect type of contact with things.

What is by far the largest division of learning products are the equipmental activities to which we give the name adaptational learning. In this division we include all the particular types of action serving as concrete adaptations to particular objects or situations. The range here is exceedingly large beginning with comparatively simple movements and running up to the most complex types of action. Specifically, the adaptational learning product enables an individual to make his way through the various mazes of objects in his surroundings and to perform complex techniques of a mechanical or artistic type. A particular characteristic of these adaptational types of action is the fact that they may or may not include an awareness or appreciation of the action at the time. When an individual has acquired the learning product he is merely able to do certain things in particular ways. One of the best illustrations of this characteristic is the often quoted illustration of the expert cloth dyer who in spite of his mastery of the technique is unable to impart his capacities to anyone else. To a great extent we may look upon such learning acquisitions as practical rather than theoretical and especially when the simpler activities are in question. In all complex adaptational activities both of these features are naturally combined. Strictly speaking practical learning might be confined to primarily overt actions while behavior consisting mainly of implicit responses may be nominated theoretical. Wisdom naturally will not be warred with in holding too drastically to such a crude distinction.

We must include as products of the adaptational type of learning not only all the capacities and skills which the individual performs as particular individual and personal reactions, but in addition also the cultural behavior he performs in common with other members of his groups. Especially we suggest here the various customs and manners which constitute particular adaptations in definite behavior situations. It is primarily as an instrument for the teaching of manners, conventional mannerisms, social accomplishments and specialized custom techniques that the so-called finishing schools exist as over against the book-teaching colleges.

A type of learning product of no slight importance in the general personality make-up of the individual, though very seldom mentioned as a form of learning activity, are the affective responses of various sorts. A great many of our contacts with stimuli objects and situations of a technical learning type result in the individual's acquisition of reactional equipment which is entirely affective in character. In such contacts with things the person acquires various likes, dislikes, and in general, what is commonly called, his tastes. These affective reactions are acquired with respect to persons, kind of work, places, and all kinds of things. Affective attitudes must also be included as learning products. Optimistic and pessimistic types of affective attitude are learned in the same way that the performance of arithmetical problems is learned. Probably the fact that affective learning is primarily of the casual sort is responsible for the general overlooking of these types of learning products. Not always, however, are affective reactions acquired in the casual way. In our efforts to instill what we are pleased to call patriotism in our schools and under the guise of moral teachings at home, individuals are definitely induced to acquire loves, hates, fears, and other types of affective behavior equipment. Persons must in general acquire affective responses that are appropriate to specific occasions. Plainly the acquisition of affective responses is decidedly an integral part of every person's culturalization or domestication.

Indispensable components of all complex personalities are those types of learning products consisting of all the more or less complicated skill or process reactions. Learning products of such character consist of complex organizations of both informational and effective adaptational reactions. By means of these behavior acquisitions the individual is enabled to perform a series of indefinite activities in order to adapt himself to situations which he has not yet had contact with, but to which he can react because of their inclusion in some system. Very common illustrations are the processes of spelling, reading, or arithmetic. Once we learn the general process of reacting to additions and multiplications we can perform responses to many types of problems involving them. Other examples of this general type but not so definite are the skill acquisitions of complex artisanship, for example that of the machinist. We may include here also the various techniques of judging and discriminating which find a place in the carrying out of one's profession whether it primarily involves contacts with things, as in engineering, or with human beings as in the practice of law or medicine. The important point is that the individual develops various methods of organizing precurrent and final reactions to the end of accomplishing some kind of adaptation to a complicated stimulus situation. In all of these reactional acquisitions it is worth noting that the stimulating situation with which the individual works, remains fixed throughout the whole process of adaptation. In this sense, the activities are contrasted with the type of learning next to be described.

Under the caption of experimental learning products we may subsume all of the activities we learn involving intricate responses to shifting situations. Because the stimuli conditions for the experimental types of learning behavior change more or less rapidly the type of learning acquisition cannot be very definitely described. Generally speaking these actions consist of responses in which the individual is required to fit a response to the new aspects of the shifting stimulus situation. This type of learning product, therefore, can only be described as capacity or wit, or in more common situations, general intelligence. It is not untrue to say then that we can learn insight reactions as well as habits of effective action. In more complex conditions the learning product constitutes a means of contriving reactional experiments in order to seize hold of the law of variation in the stimuli circumstances. We may refer to this general learning product as rationality or intellectual alertness. Obviously such learning products are by far the most complicated we acquire and naturally enough they are the most difficult to develop. Also we may say of them that when they are acquired they render the person into the most effective type of adapting individual. Whatever specific type of learning product is present—whether wit, intelligence, intellectual capacity, or rationality—the activities operate both in practical and theoretical situations. Shifting circumstances may constitute the indefinite and immediately developing circumstances in carrying on an engineering enterprise, or they may consist of more elusive and varying conditions in some theoretical type of scientific work.

**Conditions of Learning**     Learning behavior like all other psychological phenomena is conditioned by a number of circumstances which definitely affect them. From the nature of learning behavior it follows that frequently these conditions are of more importance and have greater influence in learning situations than in others, since in learning behavior the products are of extreme importance. In general, the conditions of learning affect its rapidity and ease as well as its value. This last point refers, of course, to the product or the equipmental acquisition resulting from the learning behavior. All of these learning conditions can naturally be organized on the basis of whether the condition is primarily on the side of the reacting individual or on the response side, that is to say, whether the conditions concern mainly the stimulus material or the things being learned, or still further the relationship between the person and the material, in other words, the character of the contacts between the person and what he is learning. Accordingly the various conditions of learning determine (a) the kind of material an individual can learn, (b) the amount or profundity of the learning, number of details or intensity of learning, (c) the ease with which the learning takes place, (d) the length of time that the individual can retain the reactions learned, and (e) the facility with which the person is able to make use of the reactions he has acquired.

To turn first to the personality factors we may indicate how the specific features of the person's previously acquired behavior equipment exert their influence on various learning situations. Consider now the general equipment of the individual developed in his previous contacts with his surroundings. It is plain that an individual who already has a large behavior equipment is more capable as a learner than one who has a scanty equipment. The student of logic already starts in any learning situation with a previously achieved equipment which enables him to appreciate the nature of perceptual materials presented, insofar as they have a logical organization and structure. In the same sense the previous acquisition of biological knowledge and principles of study is an excellent preparation for the pursuit of medical studies. Historical and political science makes for quicker and easier, and more profound learning when the individual comes into contact with law and politics. Similarly, in technical and vocational learning the individual having the appropriate background, including similar elements of various sorts, is the effective learner in situations involving skills and techniques. Moreover, it is such previously acquired equipment that enables him to see into the new learning situation and to develop effective equipment as a consequence.

Still more general behavior equipment conditions are the previous acquisitions of knowledge with respect to the use of past equipment and the manipulation of new materials that have to be learned. The person who understands from his past experience how to study and how to intensify the various features of the learning activity inevitably turns out to be the individual who has acquired the most material in the most profound manner and who has learned most eagerly, etc.

Habits of study, investigation, and work, when they are of a certain type are especially conducive to the rapidity and general satisfactoriness of the learning, whereas learning habits of more unfavorable quality interfere tremendously with the individual's present learning activities.

Among the more special equipmental traits influencing present learning processes are the interests of the individual. When uninterested in what one is learning, the process is a very slow and ineffective one. Such interest is distributed first over the materials to be learned, and secondly over the results of the learning and the processes involved. In all cases interest in the material at hand helps the individual to achieve learning products. This is perhaps more true in the case of informational learning. In the learning of skill reactions the interest is primarily directed to the learning process itself, since in this instance the acquisition constitutes a series of manipulatory processes. The interest in the product of learning may be a temporary interest in what is being learned at the time, regardless of whether or not the individual will be concerned with such a learning product in the future.

An outstanding phase of interest is directed toward someone whom the present learning will please. In other words, the learning activity of the individual is conditioned by whether or not he is attempting to satisfy or please someone who is interested in having him learn.

Intellectual attitudes of various sorts with respect to the material to be learned, and the individual's capacity to learn are further conditions of learning. When the individual believes himself to be capable and has confidence in his own abilities, learning is proportionately simplified and furthered. In the same way the judgment that the materials to be learned or the skills to be acquired are not worth while has the opposite influence upon learning behavior.

A determining feature of learning of no mean importance is the question whether the material is going to be asked for, or whether it is merely an exercise which goes on for the moment. This has a great deal to do with the condition previously discussed, namely, interest. It has been definitely determined that when students expect that the information they are acquiring will be called for later, they are more effective in acquiring and retaining it, whereas without expectation of such a demand they do not learn so quickly or retain the material so long.

Closely allied to such an influence is the effect of any competition or rivalry present in the learning situation. The rapidity and general effectiveness of learning is often a direct outcome of the individual's complement of competitive and rivalry equipment. The person who is working against his own or somebody else's record is far more zealous in the acquisition of the learning activity than someone not so stimulated. Whether this rivalry and competition makes for greater accuracy is a question depending upon the individual, the learning material, and the peculiar situation. No absolute or general rules can be here formulated, with the exception perhaps that incentives of all sorts have a large place as learning determiners.

Next we turn to the conditioning influences of the learning material itself. First we give our attention to the kind of materials involved. What is meant by kind of material depends of course upon the individual concerned. Some individuals learn more easily and more rapidly in the field of skill reaction, while others acquire learning products of an informational nature with greater ease and rapidity. No matter what type of person is concerned, however, some material is in itself simpler and more attractive than others. Certain material is essentially difficult and complex, comprising a large number of more or less heterogeneous elements that do not easily fit into any particular kind of organized system. On the other hand some things are seductive and tease the learner, drawing him on to effective and rapid learning. Other materials necessarily halt the individual's progress in the learning process. Furthermore, the type of material learned has a direct bearing upon the length of time the learner can perform the reactions acquired. Generally speaking, process or principle reactions, when practised, are more or less permanent. After learning to read or calculate one can always do these actions, and as we have intimated the more frequently one attempts to test the stability of the learning, the more stable it becomes.

Conditions involving the contact of the person with learning stimuli may be referred to as learning reactional experience. Here we have such factors as the frequency with which the individual is in contact with the learning stimulus and the recency with which he has had such contacts, their pleasantness or unpleasantness, etc. Extreme cases of the latter situation are the rewards and punishments which are part of experimental learning. Also an important problem here is the question whether the individual is able to complete a contact with the stimulus object in the sense of finishing a problem, so that the whole situation is apparent, or whether he can complete it only in part. Especially is this a significant factor when there are a great number of elements in the learning process.

Reactional experience in learning situations, especially in contrived learning, may be referred to as the type of presentation of material. Both ease and accuracy depend considerably upon the way the material is presented to the individual. By presentation of material is meant its distribution, whether it is presented to the individual as a whole or divided up into portions. No absolute rule of course can be considered for this operation; it is contingent upon the length and kind of material, and possibly the person's interest in it. Again the material for learning may be presented all at one time or distributed in various time units. Questions arising in this connection refer to which sort of presentation is better. Probably the most valuable although the most general rule that can be formulated here is that the presentation of materials must be adapted to the specific situation at hand.

All learning, as we have said, may be conceived of as a technical mode of behavior. Namely, the activity comprises contrived connections between the person and objects resulting in new behavior acquisitions. Ordinarily, of course, while such behavior is technical in the sense we have described, it need not be deliberate or even known to the individual. The element of contrivance perhaps is manipulated by some person other than the learner, but even this contrivance on the part of an observer is not an essential feature of the psychological activity of learning. It is quite clear, then, that

The Nature of Experimental Learning

the extreme type of learning behavior is the experimental contrivance and procedure designed to control the learning processes in the laboratory. It is well worth distinguishing such extreme manipulation of the learning situation from the ordinary conditions of technique and contrivance which are characteristic marks of all learning in general. This distinction is necessary since it is apparently true that a limit must be placed upon the technique or the control of the stimulus response coördinations. All the more necessary is it to study and reflect upon the differences between natural and laboratory learning because much of our information concerning the learning process is derived from the learning performed under laboratory conditions.

In the first place, learning done under rigidly controlled laboratory conditions must be thought of as constituting a very distinct and unique type of behavior. Without a doubt there is no kind of activity which is not somewhat affected by the imposition of laboratory conditions. In the case of learning these conditions are always intensified. Even if no complex apparatus is necessary which places the individual in a very specialized type of setting, the learning activity is done under conditions that are no wise comparable to those under which the individual actually operates in his everyday life. For one thing, in contrived learning situations it is almost impossible to take adequate account of important individual differences. Accordingly we expect that laboratory learning is performed more or less rapidly and thoroughly than in normal situations involving the same type of materials. It follows, then, that no generalization derived from either laboratory or natural learning observations will be directly applicable to the other type, certainly not without a great many extreme qualifications. This is quite apart from the fact that the results of experimental learning must be handled as averages or summations of the activities of one or more persons. From the standpoint of rigid control and definiteness of data, actual learning results must be considered as mere records of individual achievement and the learning contrivances as mere pedagogical devices. From our standpoint, however, the discovery of details of individual variations in learning, whether in different persons or the same individual, constitutes an unmistakably scientific achievement. This is especially true when some principle of variation can be established on the basis of coördinate circumstances.

Since the differences in behavior may be ascribed to modifications and specializations in the settings, it is worth pointing out that these conditions may have a tremendous influence upon learning conduct. In general we might characterize laboratory settings and conditions as exceedingly artificial. This term in itself does not, of course, convey a tremendous lot of meaning but if we consider that this artificiality refers to very definite conditions which have a marked influence upon the learning behavior, its influence upon the actions involved cannot be underestimated. That settings do affect learning activities has been definitely demonstrated by experiments on children whose work is found to undergo a change upon the introduction of even the fairly remote condition of competition with other children.

Because learning experiments must be so contrived as to produce results which, as data, are simple enough to make it possible to use them as comparisons and numerical statistical investigations, a very definite condition of an unusual sort is introduced into learning situations. This condition is nothing less than the contrived connection of the learning individual with materials which are not only artificially simple but are not comparable with materials to which the individual ordinarily adapts himself. To illustrate, in studies on memorization, thought of as memory activities, the kinds of material used are nonsense syllables or lists of arbitrarily chosen integers. These are supposed to be learned in series. Clearly these types of materials are very different from anything to which we have to adapt ourselves in our normal behavior situations, so that the learning activities here are hardly comparable to those we have in actual life. Furthermore, the nature of the processes employed are such that they can scarcely be used as bases for the interpretation of normal learning processes. Not only are such materials and the way they are reacted to not typical of memory situations but they cannot be taken to be typical cases of learning at all. And why? Because the conditions of the experiment are such that what actually happens is that the individual trains himself to develop a serial form of verbal behavior which is quite independent of the material as stimuli. The reaction is as much an adjustment to time of presentation, that is to say, the interval and rhythm, as it is to the actual material involved. It is observed in performing these experiments that unless there is ability to reinstate in the form of verbal responses the total series one can hardly report any memorization results. Accordingly it is better not to make use of any visual cues but merely to get into the swing of the rhythm, using the first syllable in the series as the stimulus for the total serial response. The other members of the series do not function, therefore, as stimuli in any sense. Furthermore, it is noted that if any interference with the rate and regularity of the exposure occurs, the total reaction is broken up and the memorization is practically nil. This interference with the total serial response is also brought about by a momentary unreadiness to respond when the experimenter is about to start the presentation of the materials.

When we turn to skill reactions of various types we again find that the type of activity lending itself to rigid control for experimental purposes is at considerable variance with ordinary activities that individuals perform. Although skill activities are so numerous, it is difficult to discover some suitable type which lends itself to the contrivance of laboratory study.

The contrivances for the learning processes themselves have to be so specific and definitely circumscribed that it is hardly ever possible to obtain valid data for any but the particulars studied. In other words, the introduction of a very specific and rigid form of contrivance makes the experimental learning entirely different from any kind of technical contact of the individual with stimuli in his ordinary activities. In short, it is the artificiality of the contrivance and the technique of learning which marks off this type of learning from normal activities.

Since experimental learning is a distinct type of psychological activity different from the learning which occurs in the ordinary circumstances of an individual's life, it can only throw light upon and be compared with the ordinary process of learning insofar as there are common elements in the two situations. That such is frequently not the case we have already amply indicated. In drawing conclusions from experimental learning, therefore, one must not be too much influenced by the sense of informational power that such studies appear to offer.

**Causes and Stability of Learning**

Often the problem arises as to what is the cause of learning in the first place and what makes the learning persist once the individual has acquired it. This question may be genuinely asked from the standpoint of what conditions of a very specific sort are correlated with the processes constituting the learning action, and with the particular types of acquisition which result from and are the products of the learning behavior. Unfortunately, however, this question as usually put, does not refer to these elementary and empirical facts. Instead it points to a condition which is supposed to be more fundamental than the mere contact of the individual of a certain equipmental status with objects that appeal to or attract him. In general, the question overlooks the fact that both the stimuli for learning and the learning person are found in a situation that makes it humanly necessary for the person to acquire certain equipment and to use it later when the situation demands. Nevertheless we observe that even after such considerations have been passed in review, some people still ask what causes the learning. For this reason although learning has always been considered as acquisitional process, it has not forced psychologists to a thoroughly objective view of psychological phenomena.

It is no secret in the history of psychological thought that this question arises from the inability to disassociate oneself from the conception of a faculty or a mental process as underlying the whole activity of the individual. Accordingly when the observable facts are passed in review such a person inevitably insists upon asking for something else in the way of an explanation of learning. This something else, of course, is never forthcoming. In more recent times when the faculties and mentalities became translated into nervous functions and mechanisms this "something" has been sought in some connections of the nervous organization. But since obviously the nervous system as such cannot be isolated from the total operations of the organism and therefore cannot be a primary basis for learning or for any other kind of activity, the question still remains a perennially unanswered one.

That is to say, we urge strongly that whatever actual basis there is for this question finds a very definite answer in terms of the correlated conditions of the learning as we have outlined it. By way of an instructive analogy we suggest the question aiming to discover why a particular man has married a certain woman. Now if one seeks for information in the psychic contents of the individuals or in the functioning of their nervous systems, obviously the question is meaningless and never can have any rational answer. On the other hand, we need look for no more definitely scientific cause or explanation than is contained in the facts superimposed upon or following the original meeting of these individuals. And what are these facts? None other than the equipment making them congenial, such as their similarity of tastes, added to their constant or frequent togetherness; so that their mutual or apparent compatibility appears on the surface. Furthermore there are the economic circumstances that make marriage possible, and the continuity of conditions that make their being married plausible. Anything else than such factual details offered in the way of a cause or explanation whether for our illustrative event or for any learning fact has no place in a rational investigation. We should consider insistence upon any other cause to be nothing but a *damnosa hereditas* which requires ruthless abscission in order to allow for a proper view concerning the facts in question.

In every learning situation, a similar set of circumstances is discovered and referred to as the cause or explanation of the proficiency of the person's learning processes and of the length of time the products of the learning remain as part of his equipmental endowment. Conditions involved here are the kind of materials from the standpoint of the learning person. It is clear that certain kinds are more agreeable and congenial to the individual. A student finds that informational materials can be learned more stably than manual operations of some type. Also furthering the stability of learning is the practise and use of the material acquired. Similarly the importance of the material to the individual has a decided effect upon the firmness of his learning acquisition. Quite naturally the completeness with which he learns has a telling influence upon the stability of his learning conduct.

The ever present individual differences in psychological activities find no better illustration than in the case of learning behavior. In fact they are nowhere else so prominent or so extreme. Every individual varies from every other in his learning capacity and general adaptibility to specific types of learning situations. These individual variations, it must be emphasized, are relative to very particular learning materials and learning circumstances. All such specificities

**The Relativity of Learning**

of learning capacity and learning performances and adaptability depend directly and definitely upon a number of concrete conditions. These conditions have their foundation in the differential equipments of persons acquired in their previous behavior circumstances. Also such conditions concern the person's general type of experiential background for the particular learning situation at hand. Moreover we must never ignore what is a most important fact, namely that individual variations in learning ability are dependent upon the availability of stimuli objects and conditions and the person's access to them, as well as his interest and general hygienic conditions.

Reflection upon the bases for individual differences in learning reveals that the infant's obvious incapacity to learn is due to its insufficient learning background in the sense that he lacks behavior equipment not only for the immediate type of learning situation at hand, but for general adaptability to learning situations. Adults, therefore, have a double advantage as compared with children. The former not only have a set of similar reactions in their equipment but also have built up in their past experience various forms of adaptations to general learning situations. The whole matter may be well described by pointing out that learning actions represent intensifications of learning adaptations; that is to say, the more one learns, the more intense becomes one's capacity for learning. On the other hand, we see why it is that children who have some equipment which is helpful with regard to some specific learning or to learning in general, have an advantage over one whose equipment may be much greater. For the first child possesses a particular set or trend of learning in contrast to a broader and more scattered learning acquisition. A corresponding disadvantage, however, is present at the same time, for such an individual is not as open to new types of learning situations and on the whole is more fixed and inclined in certain learning directions.

These considerations concerning the nature of individual differences bring us to the problem of how we should conceive of learning. More specifically we might ask what is the meaning of the fact that some individuals are not able to learn at all. In other words, is learning an absolute capacity which underlies all learning behavior? Our exposition has already indicated the impossibility of such a conception. If we look upon learning as an absolute capacity independent of learning situations we inevitably make of it an utter abstraction unrelated to any actual psychological fact. Without question such a conception can be of no service whatever to students of psychology. But here we come again to the problem of abnormality. Certainly we have all degrees of learning capacity even to the point of finding individuals who fail to learn at all. Leaving aside the latter, we find that the various degrees of learning ability constitute intensification of learning on the basis of past experience, whether in the form of contrived and deliberate or casual contact with objects and situations that become learning stimuli. So far as abnormal individuals are concerned we discover of course some who are defective in the sense of being undeveloped, and, who, insofar as they are defective, are excluded from participating in learning behavior.

By a gradual transition we are led by the consideration of individual differences in learning to consider the problem of limits; in other words, we ask how much can a person learn? The present writer is convinced that from a theoretical standpoint no limit can be placed upon the amount and type of learning the individual can acquire. In every case it is discovered that whether we take a specific individual or groups of persons the actual limits are prescribed only by the human contingencies and circumstances surrounding the learning individual. Were it not for these practical and cultural limitations the individual could develop until he would become an entirely different type of human individual. That is to say, actual observation on the psychology of learning reveals the fact that it is in no sense necessary for us to draw up our principles on the basis of what we actually see happen in the way of learning in schools and under present general human conditions. Our study of learning, therefore, should take as much account of the possibilities of learning as of the actual observations based upon technical and cultural limitations of all types. In no sense can this be considered a teleological suggestion. The fact is that we must not allow ourselves to be misled by artificial conditions that are really not necessary at all.

For example, simply because our educational procedures, constituting our most effective and common mode of contrived learning, are based upon various preconceptions of what the child requires and upon the conditions of our particular civilization, we must not assume that individuals learn only what they can or that there is any relationship in fact between what they might learn under entirely different circumstances and what they are acquiring at present in the way of learning equipment. Our suggestion is, therefore, that when we draw up our principles on the basis of the individual who is learning, rather than on the formal conditions set to his learning, we achieve an entirely different conception of the nature of human learning capacity.

For the most part it is fair to say that our teaching institutions and instruments are designed for the purpose of adapting individuals to given and existing situations. Learning activities on this basis consist mainly of acquiring particular techniques of action. Starting with the mechanics of reading and writing the individual is carried to the point of acquiring information about various things. Very little, if at all, is the learning patterned for the purpose of de-

veloping new capacities and new growths. Our currently predominant ideas concern the unfolding of powers latently resident in the
individual, for adaptation to existing conditions, rather than the possibility of the individual attaining hitherto unknown powers. The
difference here is between a standard of learning with a preconceived
goal and one without any fixed goal whatever.

Like several of the other types of activities the study of learning has always had in it the basis for an objective psychology. As the other subjects, too, this promise of objectivity remained a germ which never came to fruition. For here as elsewhere, the observed responses and their interconnection with stimuli objects and situations were still thought of as an external feature of the datum correlated with some internal mentalistic process. So that, although in modern times learning activities have been studied ever since the time of Reid, who divided behavior into intellectual and active powers, an objective viewpoint has nevertheless not resulted. This situation is all the more remarkable in view of the fact that in the classical studies of Ebbinghaus on memory his work was precisely that of learning. Here the promise that lay in the consideration of learning as definite connections of responses and stimuli could very easily have been fulfilled. But this promise did, of course, not materialize. Even though in all of this work the complicated psychological process of memory was for experimental purposes translated into external activities, the connection between such procedure and an objectifying viewpoint was never realized, much less established. This situation, as much as anything else in the field of psychology, shows us that our interpretations and even our observations must wait upon cultural changes before their form and significance alter. Because the mentalistic tradition was firmly established and dominant in the field of psychology, the fact that the process of memory was falsified and made into simple learning activities, did not urge a transition to an objective form of psychology.

Some of the methods of correlating observed objective behavior in learning with mentalistic processes consist of the connection of the objective learning conduct with interests and purposes presumed to be mentalistic influences or counterparts of the objective action. In this way the learning activities, so far as the observable objective action is concerned, are thought of as being habits connected with internal processes. Still another way in which the actual objective conduct of learning is connected with mentalistic processes is illustrated in the conception of apperceptive mass. According to this view, which was primarily associated with cognitive activities, learning consisted in the assimilation of mentalistic elements to a complex of previously connected mentalistic factors. This latter complex was thought of as the apperceptive mass. Instead of the whole process,

361

whether involving acquisition of an informational sort or responses of an affective type, being interpreted as an acquisition of definite reaction systems in contact with specific stimuli, such acquisitions were thought of in terms of mentalistic elements.

# CHAPTER XXVII

## GENERAL CONDITIONS OF PSYCHO-LOGICAL BEHAVIOR

No proposition in the entire domain of science is more firmly established than that the data of the various branches are all interconnected. Quite obviously all the facts constituting the subject matter of the different sciences are derived from a factual continuum. Accordingly, we find that in many cases the data belonging to separate sciences are not only closely related and correlated with one another but are in fundamental interdependence upon each other. In the early chapters of this work we have already indicated with telling illustrations that psychological facts in particular do not occur in a vacuum. In detail we have aimed to point out that because a psychological response is at the same time the action of a biological organism that the data of psychological science are to a certain degree identical with the data of biology. All of this has to do with more or less specific interconnections of data. In addition we have similarly indicated in several chapters the way in which particular reactions are influenced by facts and conditions, only some of which are strictly psychological in character but all of which exert fundamental influences upon the existence and operation of psychological facts.

*The Problem of General Behavior Conditions*

In the domain of psychology this interconnection of facts must be asserted and firmly adhered to, inasmuch as perhaps here as nowhere else does this fact constitute an element in the appreciation of the fundamental character of the data. It is our particular problem in the present chapter, therefore, to investigate the specific interrelationships of data which constitute the basis for the existence of the natural phenomenon which we know as a psychological fact. Could we know all of these circumstances we could undoubtedly give a complete statement of the origin and existence of this type of natural event.

Notwithstanding the fact that this view may in some sense be wholly acceptable, still the student attuned to the undercurrents of psychological and general scientific thought cannot but be impressed with the lingering doubts and irresoluteness of understanding which persist. Psychological phenomena are still wittingly or unwittingly thought to be or to contain, factors of an inscrutable and unknown type. There yet remains the notion that psychological data cannot be exhausted in such descriptions as the natural scientist makes. This is only an extension, of course, of the same questions and doubts with respect to biological phenomena. *X*'s of various sorts are not completely extruded from any domain of science, although the character of the data of physics has traditionally allowed for a greater certainty and confidence in their scientific observations and interpretations.

Our present aim, then, is to survey the more general conditions underlying the development and operation of psychological facts. Essentially this is a generalized problem which, while handled in concrete terms, involves the consideration of the character of a psychological datum when considered as a general fact in nature. Primarily our purpose is to emphasize and bring into sharper relief than we have formerly done the fact that no loose ends exist in the description and interpretation of psychological data, such that a residual problem exists as to the concrete nature of such phenomena. We propose to indicate that specific psychological data have their definite and final origin in certain conditions that may be definitely observed and thoroughly accounted for. Naturally our study, though unquestionably methodological, as a generalized problem, is still scientific and not metaphysical in character in the accepted usage of these terms. In other words, we have no suggestions as to why psychological processes and phenomena have come to exist and periodically transpire. Such questions moreover are abstractions from and conceptual misreactions to the concrete data that do exist; they only arise in the interest and by virtue of intellectual traditions unrelated to the data and problems at hand. Our problem rather consists of an attempt to survey the different specific conditions influencing existing psychological phenomena both with respect to their particular form of existence and operation.

Since psychological phenomena comprise an enormous number of specific facts, it is impossible to consider these conditions without organizing our materials into as definite a form as their nature permits. Both the variety and number of these specific facts, and at the same time the suggestion for their isolation are indicated by the circumstance that psychological phenomena involve, on the one hand, highly complicated and delicate biological organisms and, on the other, intricate and in many cases, subtle functions and operations of the organism to many different types of conditions. The total series of facts may be summarized as follows: in the first place, we have the problem of origin which concerns the original general acquisition of psychological actions. Next comes the problem of types of action which the organism acquires and is able to perform. Then we have the question as to how the particular actions or acquisitions operate. And finally we face the problem of the total complement of activity the person performs, in other words the kind of personality he is. This summary includes the complete natural history of the interactions of organisms with their environing conditions. Starting with the simple organism and natural objects the history continues up to a complete social and cultural personality on one side, and things, on the other, to the natural properties of which have been added all kinds of ascribed qualities. We may proceed, then, to isolate some of the types of phenomena commutual with these psychological data.

At the outset we must draw a line between those conditions determining the development of psychological activity and those conditioning the operation of such events. This preliminary isolation of influences or conditions is basic to all other handling of the phenomena. Accordingly we place on one side a great many conditions correlated with the development of personality equipment, while on the other, we arrange the circumstances conditioning the operation of such equipment after it has been acquired. The very existence of a particular type of psychological fact may be looked upon as correlated with a number of circumstances which impede or accelerate the development or lack of development of behavior systems into what we might call an organization of empirical potentialities (persons). Similarly, the actual occurrence of certain events in the form of behavior is also correlated with a number of specific conditions which may be looked upon as making possible or impossible the actualization of a potential behavior circumstance (action). Upon the basis of this general distinction between influences we may isolate the particular types.

Among the more specific problems we can isolate (a) conditions influencing either the total individual or some specific activity or series of activities. Certain influences produce exceedingly large effects or are correlated with them, whereas others produce only slight modifications in the development or operation of the personality. That is to say, some of the conditions that affect the individual are localized in a few particular acts; others influence the development or operation of the greater portions of the person's behavior. Because of definite circumstances the person develops one or more reaction traits peculiar to himself. Still other situations give the entire personality a particular slant or direction. A second set of conditions influencing psychological phenomena may be isolated according to (b) whether they are psychological or non-psychological in character. When these concomitants are psychological in each case we characterize our influence or condition on the basis of whether it is a response, or some equipmental factor previously acquired that has an influence on the development of the person or the performance of some of his actions.

Further investigation of influencing factors reveals to us (c) whether they are direct or indirect conditioners. By direct we mean of course conditions having an immediate effect upon the operation or development of a person's psychological conduct. Contrariwise, indirect influences produce their effect upon some extrinsic condition of the individual or of his surroundings, which in turn causes a modification in the person's development or performance of action. Or the influences modifying his development or particular action can be isolated on the basis of (d) whether they affect primarily the response or operate predominantly upon the person's psychological environs. As a last set of conditions we mention those that (e) function permanently or temporarily. That is to say, they may remain as constant modifying circumstances of the individual's development or action, or they may merely operate at some particular time and have no further effect. It will be expedient in our discussion of the various psychological influences to follow distinctions made above though in no set order.

## CONDITIONS AFFECTING THE DEVELOPMENT OF PSYCHOLOGICAL PHENOMENA

Our first investigation is given to the consideration of conditions which in themselves are definitely non-psychological but which provide the possibility for the existence and development of psychological facts. Arising at this point are the most fundamental questions concerning the origin and possibility of the existence of particular psychological phenomena. Our cue for the discussion at hand lies in the fact that we have in the world of nature what we refer to as a continuity of life processes, such that the offspring of a pair of organisms are like the parents in their essential biological details. Now it is a fact that in the processes of biological evolution animals have appeared which are capable of performing what we call psychological action. That is to say, we find developed in the world of nature organisms performing reactions on the basis of differentiation, variability, etc. Whenever such an organism is born, therefore, we have a potentiality for the development of psychological behavior. How complex the behavior will be depends also upon the fact of the evolutionary development. Animals differ in that they are more or less capable of performing psychological behavior. In whatever line or species with which we deal we find the processes of continuity. This fact has been responsible for the development of all sorts of misconceptions in the sense that organisms are presumed to inherit psychological behavior. The misconception here is glaring. All that we actually have is the obvious evolutionary development with the processes of continuity involved. In every case it must be noticed that whatever development or actual performance of psychological behavior occurs is dependent not only upon the organism's place in evolutionary development, the species, genus, etc., to which it belongs, but also upon the mass of specific circumstances which constitute, along with the evolutionary processes, essential conditions of the psychological fact.

Having already reviewed the bases or coördinate circumstances of the evolutionary sort for psychological conduct we must now consider the commutual factors first, on the side of the organism, and secondly, on the side of the environing conditions. Among such factors we must notice the organism's actual anatomical and physiological circumstances. In the first place, we find here the specification of the kind of potentiality we have for the development of psychological facts. In other words, not only do we discover that the particular anatomical organization of the animal as a member of a particular species influences the complexity and specific types of behavior performed but we also find such influences as the height, weight, length, and other anatomical features.[1]

On the basis, then, of what kind of organism we have and its correlation with particular kinds of psychological phenomena we must consider the stage of maturity of the organism. Whatever possibilities originally exist in a certain organism for the development of psychological phenomena we find that the specific development of its behavior circumstances is tied up with the individual's stage of maturation. The immature individual is unable to do various things which the mature organism is especially well fitted to perform.

Once more we must give heed to our intellectual defenses. The maturation of the organism must in no sense be thought of as an actual biological basis for psychological phenomena whether the latter are assumed to be mental powers or processes, or actual responses to stimuli. Especially must we eschew any suggestion that psychological phenomena are functions of the biological structures. It is impossible to disregard the fact that biological variations and conditions can only affect biological conditions. At this juncture are to be marshalled the facts of the independence of psychological behavior of the size, weight and shape of the brain, of the sex of the individual or his color, etc. In consequence our point concerning maturation amounts to the circumstance that only when the organism as a biological mechanism reaches a certain development can certain responses be built up and performed. In plainer words, it is only when the organism can walk that it can skate and do similar more complicated acts. Thus the lack of biological maturity, such as the absence of a normal heart or other organ, is a condition in no wise unlike the absence of a stimulus or the occurrence of some accident. Bear in mind that we never have a sheer biological organism becoming able to do a psychological action. But all the time we have biological and psychological activities performed by the same organism.[2] The more complex psychological action develops out of less complex psychological action. But naturally such developments must wait upon biological maturation.

We must be especially alert here to guard against the injection of

[1] Cf. A number of such details we have already treated in Vol. I, Chap. III.
[2] The correlated biological and psychological properties of an organism in contact with its surroundings are precisely analogous to the mechanical and chemical properties of a piece of marble in an acid.

a false potentiality into the situation. Psychological literature is gorged with the conception that this maturation means a gradual unfolding of latent mental powers waiting to be developed. Nothing can be further from the truth. At this point we may distinguish between a true and a false notion of physiological limits. This term may refer to an upper limit of this mental unfolding, or it may signify the limitations placed upon the development and performance of action by the character (structure) of the organism (one cannot do anything that requires three hands), or by the particular stage of maturation. An example of the latter condition is the ability or inability of the individual to walk without supports at a given age. Can there be any question concerning the relative merits of the two conceptions?

Upon several occasions we have already pointed out that the abnormality or normality of the organism, both with respect to its biological character and its orderliness of maturation, is an important commutual factor with the development of psychological characteristics. For instance, if the organism is not perfectly formed or has been injured either before or during birth, it is clear that the truncated organism resulting from such injury is not able to develop a personality which will be in every respect equal to a normal or uninjured individual. What the limitation in development will be, and how extensive, as well as the particular type of failure of development, depend upon the particular type of injury. That is to say, if the person should be born without legs and with no other injuries so far as this particular condition is concerned, the individual will not be defective at all with respect to book learning, and other achievements that do not involve the use of the legs. Similarly, any injury to the end organs or other anatomical features of the organism constitute a disadvantageous condition for the development of the individual.

Much the same interference with the development of behavior results from the character of the person's physiological functioning. No doubt the accelerated operation of certain glands has an influence on the advantageous or disadvantageous development of the psychological personality. Closely related to such circumstances are the individual's hygienic or health conditions. The development of the number and kind of his behavior traits which the person can acquire are often direct outcomes of his health circumstances. Diseases all too frequently have their influence upon an individual's total development, or otherwise merely condition the lack of development of some particular type of psychological activity. These conditions, of course, are observable not only in infancy but at all times throughout the person's whole development of psychological conduct.

Every pediatrician and almost every parent is poignantly aware of the havoc caused in the child's biological and psychological development by permanent and temporary diseases and derangements. Deficiencies in the metabolic functions alone account for innumerable cases of both mere backwardness and total insufficiency in psychological development. Numerous other dysfunctions of the organism, whether due primarily to structural conditions or environing circumstances, have a similar influence upon particular individuals. How much psychological development trouble can be set down to the account of gastritis alone is doubtless unknown but that it is a great deal, we can be confident.

So far we have been considering the facts on the side of the organism more or less independently of the environing circumstances in which the organism is found. This neglect of the environing conditions is obviously impossible, since no biological fact may be considered as anything but the mutual interaction of the organism and the environment.[1] The environing conditions in connection with psychological facts are of two types, indirect and direct. Indirectly, environmental factors are reciprocal circumstances with psychological facts in that the character of the organism and its hygienic circumstances are functions of the surroundings of the biological individual. This influence may extend even to the existence or preservation of the animal. It also has a great deal to do with the organism's normality. When the environing circumstances make for the normality of the organism, these circumstances constitute influences upon it in the sense that the development of psychological facts is not interfered with from the side of the environing features.

Turning to the direct influences of environmental facts upon psychological conduct we find that the presence of objects in the surroundings conditions the development or at least makes possible the development of certain types of behavior. Without these objects and conditions in the environment the development of the organism would be entirely different and the existence of certain psychological phenomena not possible. It is impossible to overlook the fact that the development of elementary differential reactions and their number depend absolutely upon the natural properties of objects which through this development become stimuli objects, and in general, psychological data. Furthermore, the importance of these environing things cannot be overstated when we recall that the reactions acquired through early contacts with objects have a great influence upon later acquisitions.

Under the direct environmental influences upon human conduct we must include not only the factors ordinarily and properly called environment in the sense of biological conditions, but also human phenomena of an anthropological and sociological character. These constitute, along with the natural environing circumstances, the commutual events existing alongside of and determining the development of psychological facts. For illustrative purposes let us refer

[1] The psychological correlate of this fact is that even a reflex action depends in its origin and operation not only upon the biological mechanisms of the individual but also upon the environing objects.

to the important environmental influences upon the individual of hi
family circumstances, the kind of people and objects they include
of his companions later in life, and the congeniality and uncon
geniality of his human surroundings. For the latter point conside
the difference between a native and a foreigner in a particular plac
with respect to their specific developments. Think, then, of the grea
effect of economic surroundings upon people. The presence of op
portunities to carry on various activities not only gives the individua
chances of getting into contact with objects and conditions servin
as stimuli for the development of behavior, but it operates to en
courage the individual and to serve as a support which helps him t
acquire certain traits, such as courage and self assurance. In sucl
a way he is aided in building up traits of all types. On the othe
hand, an individual living under economic and other circumstance
which are uncertain, finds in these environing conditions many de
terrents to the development of behavior of many sorts. Also, the
serve to make him build up various fear responses and timidities whicl
have a generally bad effect upon his whole development.

On the whole we might say that the clemency or difficulties of one'
environment make for the person's general stability or instability
As a rule, one who is constantly shielded from all difficulties build
up a type of personality lacking the behavior elements which protec
him from various oppositions and disappointments arising later in hi
life.

Let us turn now to the anthropological conditions affecting th
existence and development of psychological facts. It is these conditions quite as much as the types of species to which the animal belong
or its evolutionary status which are correlated with the existence and
development of psychological phenomena. No individual is capable
of developing psychological behavior that is absolutely foreign to his
anthropological surroundings. For example, it is inconceivable that
a primitive individual should acquire ideas or other kinds of psychological activities which could only have been developed in the milieu
of a more complexly civilized individual. It is unnecessary to argue
that no primitive black could possibly have developed the ideology
of a European philosopher or the engineering skill of a man living
in an industrial civilization. In this connection we might consider
a specific illustration. Sometimes in psychological and anthropological literature we find such a suggestion as this, that if Edison
had lived in a different type of civilization he would still have been
an inventor. Now setting aside the frivolity of the conception that
there is such an entity as Edison instead of a concrete individual
developed and living in a particular set of human circumstances, the
question arises as to whether or not this attitude is based upon a
conception of inventiveness as an entity that always exists but mani-
fests itself differently under different circumstances. We urge that
the inventiveness and other psychological phenomena of creation and

ransformation are functions of the particular facts of the person's mechanical and general human situation in precisely the same sense hat any person as an organism is a function of biological circumstances (conception, gestation, metabolic and secretory developments, tc.). No other scientific conception seems to be acceptable.

In this sense we assert that what is called a primitive or a medieval mind is a direct function of the particular circumstances under which he psychological behavior designated by these terms has developed. n this sense any particular psychological activity, such as the behavior of a scholar, or a good or inferior thinker, is a set of concrete phenomena correlated with other sets of actual conditions. In a imilar way we can easily divest ourselves of the belief in entities such s intelligence, genius, insanity, etc.

Telling illustrations of the influence of cultural surroundings upon persons are found in the equipment of æsthetic and moral appreciaions and sensitivities. These cultural conditions for example determine the individual's æsthetic tastes; what the Oriental or the native African considers subtle or beautiful music, the Occidental may fail ltogether to esteem. How profound an influence this is, may be gathered from the fact that eminent psychologists have held to the opinion that certain appreciations of harmonies and fusions are innate, natural properties of the hearing individuals. Relevant here lso is the fact that a Hindu or Japanese lacks the appreciation and he æsthetic gusto which are among the Europeans' equipmental reactions to the Venus de Milo and the Apollo Belvedere.[1]

Our next task is to consider data correlated with the existence of psychological phenomena which are themselves psychological in character. Here we have facts of a psychological sort which make possible the existence of other psychological phenomena.

To begin with, we observe that the reactions which are especially favored in their development, either because they are themselves based upon the biological factors of the organism, such as reflex action, or because they are very early developed, such as momentarily acquired behavior, have a very definite and direct influence on the later acquisition of the individual. Thus the type of mentality (behavior) developed receives its character from previous behavior acquisition. We have already sufficiently pointed out how our behavior equipment may be thought of as developing in a hierarchical order. The foundation reactions come first; the basic which are without any very special biological basis, are built upon the former, and influence what we have called societal conduct which we may think of in this connection as capping the total behavior equipment. Such acts of the behavior type account for the existence and development of ad-

[1] For a more general discussion pointing to a reversal of the popular conception that cultural phenomena depend upon psychological facts see Kantor, "Anthropology, Race, Psychology, and Culture," *American Anthropologist*, 1925, 27, 67-283.

ditional favorable or unfavorable psychological phenomena. Account
ing for behavior acquisition in this manner excludes most rigorousl
the falsifying powers, drives, and instincts that constitute competin
and replacing "causes" of the existence of mind or mentality.

Hence psychological correlates of psychological phenomena compris
equipmental influences upon the development of specific facts, whic
in their totality constitute psychological data. Nor must we over
look the effect of particular psychological actions which have only
temporary existence but which nevertheless exert a tremendous in
fluence upon the development and existence of psychological facts
Consider the effect upon a person's total behavior of his yielding t
some temptation at some particular moment. In this peculiar situa
tion the person may put himself into such a human circumstance tha
he turns out to be a hunted fugitive deprived of all opportunities o
self development, whereas under other circumstances he might hav
been a statesman, scientist or some other type of valuable personality

### CONDITIONS AFFECTING THE OCCURRENCE OF PSYCHOLOGICAL PHENOMENA

In our investigation of the circumstances existing along with an
conditioning psychological phenomena we must consider also the par
ticular occurrences of reaction as well as the existence of the individ
ual's equipment. To a great extent our exposition here follows th
outline of the equipmental conditions. Indeed in certain instance
some of the commutual circumstances enumerated also function i
connection with the specific operations of the individual. It may b
necessary, therefore, to repeat some of the points that have alread
been made.

Prominent non-psychological conditions correlated with the oc
currence of psychological phenomena are the anatomical factors o
the organism. These are, for the most part, correlated with the ac
tual possibility of existence of such psychological facts at a particula
time rather than their efficiency or serviceability. In other word
while some types of facts interfere with the effectiveness of psycho
logical behavior, the kind we are now discussing have to do with th
total inhibition of some types of action. Losses and dysfunctionin
of various anatomical parts have a destructive influence upon, or ar
concomitant with a total inability to act, or a defective or inefficien
form of responding. Injuries and losses of anatomical features o
the organisms have a distinct influence on every type and variety o
psychological fact. The grossest movements and the most subtl
thinking are alike conditioned.

A necessary warning justifies digressing for a moment. We ar
not indicating here an influence of a change or loss of an organ upo
its function. Such is far from being the case. This conceptio
dominates medical thought and frequently brings about a wide dis

agreement between the medical and psychological attitudes concerning the facts in question and so is a great detriment to an understanding of them. Because psychological action is the behavior of a biological organism, any destruction, degeneration, or dysfunctioning of the structural make-up means ipso-facto an interference with the person's actions.

Turning now to the physiological or functional conditions of the organism that are concomitant with the existence or operation of psychological facts, we may first consider diseases of various sorts. Especially fevers and other pathological conditions as well as unhygienic circumstances of various types very soon interfere with the functioning of either all or only parts of a person's behavior equipment. Some of these effects and influences upon behavior are merely temporary. With the cessation of the disease (headache, fever) or fatigue the person's capacity to perform psychological action is renewed. That is to say, psychological phenomena are prevented from occurring for only limited temporal periods. In other cases, however, the dysfunctional circumstances are permanent and thus prevent the individual from performing certain types of behavior at all. But it is not only disease in the sense of extreme dysfunctional circumstances which influences the performance of psychological activities but also the slighter derangements which may be considered as difficult normal functions of the individual. Examples here are the unusual behavior of persons during menstruation and child bearing which sometimes amounts to a more or less complete dissociation of the individual.

Fatigue which represents a very definite lowering of functional capacity may directly modify the operation of the individual's behavior. Loss of sleep definitely alters an individual's behavior. On the whole it prevents him from performing his actions in anything like the ordinary manner; it interferes with his critical attitudes and processes. Fasting, thirst, and overeating also exert marked influences on the person's conduct, for the most part preventing activities from occurring, although in some cases the direct effect is to heighten the individual's adaptation to particular stimulational conditions and objects.

Exceedingly numerous and common events concomitant with the occurrence and operation of psychological phenomena are the functional conditions of the organism under the influence of drugs of various sorts. The effect of such drugs as cocaine, morphine, opium, etc., on the psychological actions of the individual, although not subject to specific scientific formulation is in no sense a debatable proposition. It has always been asserted that alcohol in various forms has an effect upon the individual in action. Apparently when taken in moderation alcohol has a tendency to increase the functional capacities of the individual, but on the other hand, there is no question that the constant use of alcohol, especially in large doses, must

have a detrimental if not destructive influence upon behavior. In
this connection it is common observation that certain individuals
under special conditions are exceedingly influenced in their action
by teas, coffees, and other stimulating beverages.

Up to this point we have been discussing mainly those influences or
concomitants of psychological phenomena causing a direct modification of the individual's behavior and hence exerting an immediate
influence on his adaptation to various stimuli. But the influence of
drugs, alcohol, and other stimulants also have an indirect influence
in the sense that before modifying the individual's psychological activity, they have some effect on his physiological functions, and increase or lower his resistance, improve or reduce his energies, etc.

The non-psychological concomitants of psychological phenomena
on the environmental side offer quite as many circumstances and
situations correlated with the possibility or impossibility and with
the effectiveness or ineffectiveness of operation or occurrence of
psychological facts at particular moments. To take some striking
illustration, a war situation affords overwhelming evidence of the
concomitance which makes possible the performance of moral, political, military, and domestic conduct of many varieties. The achievement of economic independence makes it possible for the individual
to do all kinds of actions which otherwise would not be feasible. On
the other hand, various human situations and circumstances as well
as natural phenomena constitute commutual occurrences with the temporary or permanent absence of certain psychological events. For
example, a man who cannot afford to purchase materials is unable to
carry on some kind of activity requiring such materials. Again cli-
matic conditions, especially temperature or humidity, have considerable influence upon the person's permanent or temporary operations
Also these factors considerably affect the efficiency and possibility of
the individual's performing particular activities.

As in the other cases we have already studied, so here, these influences are more or less direct. In other words, the dysfunctions of
the organism which affect the psychological activity may themselves
have been brought about by other psychological behavior, so that
concomitants of various types operate in a circular fashion.

The strictly psychological concomitants of the occurrence and immediate existence of psychological phenomena are exceedingly
numerous. Hence their variety extends over and includes practically all of the features of the reactional and stimulational conditions. The concomitants on the reactional side may be divided off
into those psychological conditions concerning the equipment of the
individual, such as good and bad habits, correct and incorrect information, etc., and those constituting immediate performances of
behavior of particular types. Without doubt equipmental activities
comprise a fertile source of psychological concomitants. For it is the
peculiar complex of psychological equipments and responses which

make the person's actions what they uniquely are throughout his reactional biography. Previously acquired behavior equipment sometimes interferes with, and hinders the operation of, particular activities. To illustrate, the person who has acquired timidities and fears as part of his equipment is at some particular moment unable to perform behavior requiring self assertiveness and courage. On the other hand, the development of exaggerated forms of activity such as fool-heartedness and recklessness interferes with the appearance of calm and deliberate behavior. Obviously the equipmental concomitants are not limited to particular actions which interfere with other conduct. But the existence or operation of particular actions at stated periods are without doubt functions of the person's previous acquisition of such equipment.

Other psychological conditions do not comprise equipment but may be considered as responses immediately occurring. Feelings are such concomitants. For example, a person under great strain of a feeling sort, or who is abstracted in some problem, is unable because of this condition to operate with very common and habitually functioning activities. Thus one who is melancholy, exceedingly preoccupied or worried over some problem, is unfitted for intellectual work or in many cases cannot even respond properly to vehicles in the street. Likewise a person while performing an inspiration or purposing response stimulated by some object or person is greatly influenced and conditioned in the present performance of some other particular response. In this range of conditions we may place also the facts represented by the anecdote of Demosthenes who became the supreme orator while conditioned by his compensatory reaction to the stuttering stimulus.

Our study of concomitants of psychological events would be hopelessly incomplete without the suggestion of the great influence that particular psychological settings have upon the operation of psychological phenomena. The main suggestion at this point involves the fact that even when equipment is present and occasions are otherwise favorable, the actual occurrence of certain types of psychological phenomena are interfered with because of the untoward conditions of the setting of the stimuli objects. Contrariwise, in other situations the setting factors are decidedly responsible for the occurrence of some action that under other circumstances would not have transpired at all. A very important type of setting is comprised of the person's own psychological conditions. Not only the person's intelligence, affective and intellectual states, influence his actions by serving as a setting for his stimuli objects but also his moral and political ideals influence him to act one way rather than another in specific circumstances.

With these suggestive illustrations we undoubtedly have touched upon the general circumstances which may be considered as the causes and conditions of the actual existence of psychological phenomena.

In the total enumeration of these types of conditions we firmly believe are exhausted all the conditions and determiners of such events. No other kinds of determiners exist. As we have already suggested so frequently, the enumeration of these different conditions of psychological phenomena leaves no room for any occult or mystical explanatory elements. This is not to deny, however, that even in the simplest type of situation the actual concomitants which operate along with psychological phenomena are exceedingly difficult to isolate. Moreover, the certainty of having given an exhaustive statement of the essential particulars of any event is problematic. This situation, however, is so typical of all psychological occurrences that in the simplest circumstances no one is sure that only a limited number of empirical conditions are operating. Probably the greatest fault one might find with our organization of facts is the generality of the enumerations and suggestions. The most valuable type of analysis, though it is practically impossible to achieve, is an actual discovery and enumeration of the specific conditions and circumstances which correlate with the development and operation of a particular person's psychological activities.

# CHAPTER XXVIII

## THE BEHAVIOR OF THE ORGANISM DURING SLEEP, HYPNOSIS, AND WHILE DREAMING

Our investigative approach to the phenomena of the present chapter impresses us at once with their uniqueness and specialized behavioristic character. Especially the facts of sleep and hypnosis point to what appear practically as states or conditions of the organism rather than exertional activities. Certainly in their occurrence they are not productive of any decided results or effects upon the surrounding objects and conditions of the acting person. And yet they are definite overt performances howsoever they may differ from other actions in the overt class. With respect to dreaming behavior we have again a singularity of happening. In this case we find a pronounced performance of implicit action but lacking the order and effectiveness which is traceable to a close contact of the acting person with his behavioristic environment. A careful study of these three types of psychological phenomena results, of course, in their description as definite modes of interaction of the organism with its stimuli. Accordingly, our exposition is divisible into three parts in each of which the particular stimulus and response circumstances must be indicated.

### Behavior of the Organism While Sleeping

What the organism or person does while sleeping constitutes just as specific a type of conduct as any other. The necessity of emphasizing this point arises from the circumstance that the person or organism during sleep acts very differently than when performing other types of behavior. Although while sleeping the individual is ordinarily quiescent, subdued, and not subject to spatial translocation, we must still look upon such action as he does perform as definite behavior conditioned by specific types of contacts with his surroundings. The description of the behavior of the sleeping individual is accordingly based upon the assumption that he is performing psychological action in principle similar to all other types. Our descriptive procedure, therefore, involves emphasis of the differences in essential details.

*Nature of Conduct Sleeping*

Let us begin with the more general descriptive features. We may look upon sleeping conduct as a general suspension of most of the person's psychological activities. To a great extent sleeping action

377

constitutes a restriction and limitation of the behavior which the organism performs at the time. In the precise degree in which the person is or is not restricted in his behavior we may speak of him as psychologically awake or asleep. This restriction and limitation of conduct naturally extends beyond the functioning of the person's responses, to the stimuli objects in that the latter no longer perform their customary stimulational functions. Thus the person becomes reduced in the number and type of actions he performs with respect to surrounding objects. Correspondingly the objects remain as stimuli objects only, without exercising their ordinary stimulational capacity.

Sleeping conduct is a type of dissociated action. When the person is asleep he is out of behavior contact with the various objects and situations constituting his usual surroundings. It is this condition which is the essential fact of his quiescence and which contrasts so markedly with his waking activities, in which he is in intimate relation and contact with specific environing objects and persons.

Entering more intimately into the conditions of sleeping conduct we find that it is decidedly less differentiable. The sleeping individual cannot single out certain objects to react to. This means that he is responding at once with whatever of his behavior equipment that is operating at all. In other words, the entire psychological organism is responding as a totality to whatever objects or conditions are reacted to at the time. We do not expect to find, therefore, any specialized reactions directed toward particular objects. It is this undifferentiated behavior that is describable as rest and relaxation. Acting in this way the person is actually performing very few responses that may be singled out as effective adaptations or adjustments to complex things or situations.

On the side of stimuli objects the dissociation of sleep includes an almost complete absence of differentiation between them. The qualities and conditions of things do not stand out with sufficient strikingness. Hence objects are not adequately differentiated one from another to be in contact with the person or to elicit specific reaction systems. Thus when the sleeping individual performs complex actions they are not only of the implicit type but the responses, not being effectively conditioned by immediate objects and circumstances, are erratic and confused so that things, places, times, persons and conditions are responded to as interchanged, transformed and reconstructed. In other words such complex implicit actions, i. e., dreams may be exaggerated, phantastic, or grotesque.

The dissociation of the sleeping person may be looked upon as primarily a condition of being transported from one set of stimuli to another. That is to say, the person becomes dissociated from the objects, things, and circumstances constituting his ordinary surroundings and responds only to those stimuli which bring about the functioning of visceral and other so-called organic reactions. This fact is easily observed when we study a person who is about to fall asleep. In making such observations we see him changing from re-actions to objects in visual and auditory contact around him, until he becomes an individual reacting only to the undifferentiated objects such as the air which induces the automatic operation of the respiratory functions, pressures which stimulate restless movements, and temperature modifications stimulating simple changes in the position and exposure of the organism.

Because sleeping conduct consists of the dissociation of the individual from most of the objects and conditions surrounding him, we might very well say that during sleep he approaches as closely to a mere biological organism as is possible. In our ordinary psychological behavior we find that although psychological individuals are obviously biological organisms the biological processes of the person are integrated into and lost in the total psychological response. Not so in the case of sleep. Here the person's psychological activity, because of his being in minimum contact with objects and persons, is thrown back into the lowest types of his behavior. This point must not be carried too far, however, since the performance of a great deal of dreaming behavior indicates that the person is by no means limited exclusively to the performance of simple actions resembling biological behavior.

It is interesting to note that the sleeping conduct of the person may be analogically compared with the biological phenomena of hibernation and æstivation. Just as the biological organism becomes dissociated from the natural environment and consequently enters into a condition of lowered biological functioning, so the sleeping individual through his dissociation from his psychological surroundings becomes a psychologically reduced organism. Still further the analogy goes between the two types of phenomena when we take into account a series of biological changes discoverable in the person while sleeping. The list includes prominent modifications in the respiratory and circulatory functions. Sleeping individuals show marked slowing down of the respiratory action and general changes in the configuration of the respiratory curves (deeper breathing, shorter expiration, etc.). Further changes have been observed in the circulatory functions, including variation in blood pressure and volume. In general, blood pressure falls, pulse rate decreases, and the blood distribution varies. During some periods of the sleeping condition, the volume of blood in the periphery increases with a possibility of a decrease in the cerebral circulation.[1]

Because our interest in sleeping behavior is after all an interest in a type of psychological action, it must be pointed out that the suspension of behavior involved is subject to a great extent to the caprice of the acting person. The person cannot entirely control whether or not he will suspend his behavior, but within wide limits

[1] The authority here is Howell, *Physiology* (9), 1924.

he can determine the length of the suspension and also postpone
sleeping for comparatively long periods of time.

Since the primary factor in sleep activity is the individual's lack
of direct contact with or his dissociation from his ordinary stimuli
objects, it is important to consider some of the intrinsic behavior
modifications arising from this contingency. As we have already
pointed out, our clue to the number and nature of these changes is
found in the fact that during sleep the person performs practically
no adaptational responses to surrounding objects. Accordingly, the
behavior picture of the sleeping individual is quite different from
that of his waking activities. In detail, the sleeping person is performing visceral or interoceptive and, to a lesser extent, exterocep-
tive reflexes. Of the latter the individual performs both the localized
and general types.[1] So far as the actual operation of the various
reflex actions are concerned, these need not be less active and less
productive of results than in the ordinary waking state, although on
the whole the organism is much less active. Especially is it noticed
that the sexual reflexes may operate in as effective a manner as in
the waking state. Possibly combination reflexes, such as the sexual
acts, which are stimulated by implicit behavior stimuli, are more
powerful and operate to a greater extent than other kinds of action.
In the case of other reflex responses, however, for instance the digestive reflexes, a similar fairly effective functioning probably occurs.
Whenever there is food present in the alimentary tract it serves to
incite the organism to metabolic action.

Let us not be misinterpreted as minimizing the extent to which the
sleeping person is actually in contact with external objects, for there
always is some contact of this sort. It is a common observation that
the organism performs reflexes to external stimuli in much the same
way as in the waking state. Also we cannot overlook such phenomena
as sleep walking and sleep talking which are stimulated either by
some other person or by the acts of the individual himself. But
such activities as these, of course, have their characteristic traits or
qualities when performed by the sleeping person, and so we might
say that when such actions occur during sleep they are practically
automatistic and not indicative of the same spontaneous and intimate
appreciation by the person of the stimulating conditions as is true
in the waking state. In general, while sleeping, reactional contacts
with objects are automatistic in character. This means there is always a lessened appreciation or awareness of objects and the manner
of one's response to them. In plainer speech, the sleeping person,
even when he is performing a relatively complex action at the same
time, does not know what he is doing and doubtless in most cases
would not be willing to do it if he did know. Convincing examples
of such behavior situations are the performance of various climbing

[1] Cf. classification of reflex action, Vol. I, p. 135.

feats one does in sleep walking, and the kind of information one gives while sleep talking.

That the sleeping individual is by no means completely out of contact with his surrounding objects but is in uninterrupted interaction with his stimuli, is satisfactorily demonstrated by another change in reactional condition. Namely, the sleeping person becomes increasingly sensitive or hyperæsthetic to particular kinds of stimulating objects and conditions. In fact, the person may be more definitely sensitive to certain stimuli which in the waking state do not produce such an effect upon him. Doubtless much of the basis of the particular kind of implicit behavior (dreaming), which the individual performs, is to be accounted for on this basis. Cold stimulation may induce dreaming of frigid experiences. The point here is that because the individual is dissociated from the great mass of objects and conditions forming the milieu of his waking activities, he may be more in contact with some particular stimuli that during the waking state are crowded out by more important or more striking stimulation. The abnormal field affords us some remarkable illustrations. Observations made upon hysterical patients indicate such changes of their activities as they go from the waking to the sleeping state that they drop out their inhibitions and are able to overcome their paralyses, anæsthesias, and contractures. It is only the reactions to auditory stimuli apparently that are exceptions to this situation.[1]

The specific conditions resulting from the general dissociation of the person from his environing stimuli are probably best investigated by consulting the changes in the components of reaction systems. To begin with the muscular functions we find generally that muscular action is greatly minimized. By the physiologist this fact is spoken of as a diminution in muscle tone. Similarly, the glandular components operate in a noticeably lessened manner. Because most of the observations upon sleep phenomena have hitherto been made by physiologists the tradition has grown up that it is due to the lack of muscle tonus that the sleeping individual is inactive. It is said, for example, that the relaxation of striped muscles produces the closure of the eyelids, and the divergence of the eyeballs. Now while this condition may possibly be true, as in the case of the muscles losing their tone because of a toxin, or some sort of fatigue effect, still, from a psychological standpoint, we must insist that the relaxation of the muscles is the result of the dissociation of the individual from his surrounding stimuli. Evidence for this latter statement is found in the observations of the anæsthetist who can observe the gradual lessening of the tone of muscles as the etherization or other anæsthetic process proceeds. Here as elsewhere in the field of

---

[1] Cf. Hurst, A. F. *The Psychology of the Special Senses and their Functional Disorders.*

psychology, to hit upon some one change in a component function of the organism's responses as the sole cause of his behavior is to misinterpret completely the psychological facts.

What is true for the muscular and glandular reaction system components can be just as well observed in others. Accordingly in sleeping behavior we find also the receptor functions greatly modified. While the various neural action components are not as readily observed it is impossible to do otherwise than to assume that they are likewise changed in correspondence with the other factors and the total reaction systems of which they are components.

Just as significant a metamorphosis occurs in the affective, conative, and differentiative components of specific reaction systems. So far as the affective components are concerned we find that the sleeping individual is less alive to affective qualities in things. As a consequence he is not calmed, excited, pleased, or displeased, etc. In the same way we may ascribe to the lessened action of conative factors the unreadiness of the person on the whole to actualize stimuli objects into full-fledged stimuli functions. The facts concerning the differentiative functions have already been sufficiently suggested in discussing the general characteristics of the phenomena of sleep. It remains only to suggest that all of these changes we have been describing are functions of the more general interactions of the person with surrounding objects.

**Methods and Conditions of Sleep Induction** If sleeping behavior consists essentially of a process or condition of dissociation we should expect that the activity of going to sleep or of putting someone else to sleep would involve a fairly definite series of methods and conditions. We discover that the transference of the individual from the waking type of stimuli situations to the sleeping ones involves two types of methods and conditions. In addition to the general methods of sleep induction, holding more or less for all individuals, there are certain specific processes which are effective only for certain individuals and at certain times. Both of these types of methods just as definitely illustrate the dissociation process. The enumeration of these methods and conditions of sleep induction accordingly falls into two broad divisions, namely the general, holding for all persons, and the special, comprising the idiosyncratic methods and conditions of particular individuals. In each case the methods and conditions of sleep induction involve the comparative prominence of reactional or stimulational factors. Generally speaking, by methods we mean the processes employed in inducing sleep in oneself or in some other person, whereas the term conditions refers to the contribution of the surroundings. In the following exposition we shall employ a special name to indicate whether the sleep is induced primarily by the response or stimulus factors or by a method or condition.

## General Methods and Conditions of Dissociation

It is fairly easy to see how important in the inducing of sleep is the letting down of behavior in the sense of lying still or sitting quietly and not performing what we ordinarily call work of an overt sort. On the whole, relaxation means merely the cessation of effective activity to as great an extent as is possible. The person actually accomplishes this by selecting some non-exertional type of behavior. What one does, then, is to lie or sit passively in a fixed position. This relaxed activity often takes place as a progressive elimination of the grosser movements up to the point where only the very subtle effective reactions remain, such as are involved in keeping covered, etc. **Relaxation**

Another method involving primarily the reactional factor of behavior is the gradual elimination of implicit responses to stimuli objects and conditions of one's actual everyday life. As long as one continues to think over the day's events or some anticipated action, sleep will not occur because obviously this is a very definite means of keeping the individual in contact with situations and things of the waking state. To bring about a process of inhibition requires a strenuous effort in many cases. Sometimes the individual has to grip his hands, hold on to something, or for a while otherwise substitute for implicit action. Later by the gradual cessation of both overt and implicit activities the desired result is obtained. **Inhibition of Implicit Action**

What is frequently an exceedingly essential method of inducing sleep and practically always a condition for its continuation is the rhythmization of action. The very process of making rhythmic one's respiratory and other visceral reflexes means a translation of the individual from the waking type of stimulational condition into the sleeping one. In fact, this process definitely disconnects the person from the objects around him and attaches him to the conditions supplying endogenous stimulation. By this means the inhibition and suspension of behavior to external objects, which constitute sleeping, are easily brought about. A practically absolute demonstration of the function of rhythmization in the induction of sleep is found in the process of putting a child to sleep. The actual method of inducing the rhythmization involves tapping and patting the individual at any point which still remains in direct contact with waking-state stimuli in such a way that the fundamental rhythmic action of the individual is not disturbed by the stress of responding to an external stimulus. The main purpose, therefore, is to prevent the person from performing any uneven reactions. For example, if the hand or foot moves it is those parts of the organism that must be patted or stroked in order to make of the individual a completely rhythmic actor. In the case of infants the rhythmization process is induced by rocking or shaking. **Rhythmization of Action**

**Fatigue**

Probably the most powerful determiners of sleep on the reactional side are the conditions of fatigue themselves. No matter what the individual desires to do, or what he may consider expedient, he cannot go on for an indefinite period without sleep. Here the physiological processes and conditions assert themselves and the person may fall asleep in the midst of whatever work he is doing. Thus soldiers fall asleep during march and only wake up occasionally to find themselves surprised at their own lapses of association with things about them. In other situations the eyelids droop, the head nods, the whole body may sway and one may be unable to persist in what one has been doing up to the present point.

**Absence of Stimuli**

Turning to some of the stimuli conditions governing the advent of sleep we note at once that in accordance with our previous statement, these conditions are the influences on the sleeping person of his surroundings. For instance, it is generally impossible to induce sleep in oneself or another without first cutting off the light so that visual contact with objects is prevented. In like manner, sounds must be removed so that we create an overt dissociation of the person from his surroundings. This removal of stimuli itself consists of a transportation of the individual from one type of object to another. For example, the removal of one's clothes and the general change of situation from contact with objects while standing and walking, to conditions of lying down, are decidedly favorable for the initiation of sleeping behavior.

Oftentimes one finds oneself naturally removed from stimuli objects. If alone on a plain or in the woods where no sounds or movements occur, and darkness falls, one very soon falls asleep provided, of course, he does not substitute for absent stimuli his own revery actions or feelings of fear and nervousness.

Very closely allied with the absence or removal of stimuli objects from the sleeping individual is his adaptability to those objects that necessarily have to remain. The more accustomed one is to his surroundings, his bed clothes, and his bed, the more easily is he disintegrated from them. The person who simply cannot go to sleep the first night in a strange place is typical in his lack of adaptation to objects around him. Thus, he is prevented from bringing about the dissociation necessary for sleep. Especially is this adaptability factor operative in the case of auditory stimuli. For, since sounds cannot in the majority of cases so easily be removed, we are forced to fall into the habit of dissociating ourselves from them by merely becoming adapted to them.

**Monotony of Stimuli**

Our adaptations to auditory stimuli afford an easy transition to the observation of the effect of monotonously presented stimuli on the person undergoing sleep induction. The rhythmic and constant continuation of any type of stimulation accelerates the individual's adaptation to it and quickly induces slumber. For example, the

prolonged auditory stimulation of the humming of an engine or
some other piece of machinery offers a very favorable condition for
the person's dissociation.  Similarly, repeated stroking of a child's
or even an adult's head will produce the necessary transference of the
individual from the waking state.  And not unrare are those persons
who must be "read to sleep."  Of course, in cases like these we assume that there are no other stimuli objects available which can serve
to distract the person from the monotony of the rhythmic stimulus.
In the absence of such interfering stimuli, the person easily becomes
dissociated and goes through the various typical sleeping activities.

A simple and very effective method of providing the proper stimulation for the dissociation of the individual from his ordinary surroundings is that of hypnosis.  Some other individual in this case
becomes the sole stimulus object or the center of all the stimuli functions for the time being.  As part of the means of putting the other
person to sleep, the operator narrows down the person's field of
action, that is, reduces the person's number of stimuli and behavior
conditions so that gradually the objects around are eliminated from
contact with him.  Because this process of inducing dissociation in
the individual by another is accomplished primarily through verbal
means, the hypnotic method is usually referred to as suggestion.  The
monotonous presentation of the stroking and reading stimuli referred
to above, may be considered as one of the variant components of the
general hypnotic method.

**Hypnosis**

The application of anæsthetics of all varieties (ether, chloroform,
various gases, etc.) constitutes a powerful method and supplies unusually favorable conditions for the induction of sleep, especially of
the sound or intense type.  In this case the conditions operate by
inducing profound and far-reaching changes in the biological conditions of the organism.  Similar conditions are supplied by the injection of toxins of various sorts, the smoking of opium, the chewing
or snuffing of drugging substances and by indulgence in the use of
alcohol.  In all these ways the person may put himself into a more or
less profound sleeping state or reactional contact with his surroundings.

**Anæsthe-
sia**

Doubtless all of these anæsthetic phenomena are very closely linked
up with abnormal or endotoxic conditions in the individual.  That
is to say, when fevers or infections of various sorts produce auto-
intoxications, they bring about a sleeping condition.

An exceedingly effective condition for the promotion of the sleeping-
action is the disoxygenation of the atmosphere in which the organism
happens to be at the time.  Whenever there is a lack of oxygen in the
atmosphere or a superabundance of carbon dioxide, as in the case of
sitting in a poorly ventilated room, the person is bound to become
drowsy and lassitudinous or sufficiently dissociated to fall into profound sleep.

**Disoxy-
genation**

## Special Methods and Conditions of Dissociation

In addition to the above general methods and conditions of sleep induction there are innumerable special processes and particular conditions that are necessary for the disorganization of certain individuals. These particular processes consist perhaps of ways of lying. Some people have to be in a certain position which for others would mean constant wakefulness. Other individuals require a light burning somewhere in the house. And familiar as well as amusing is the individual who must first go through a series of actions such as locking windows, making the rounds of the house, looking under the bed, etc., before he is prepared to relax for sleeping behavior.

Whether or not the individual desires or decides to go to sleep, greatly affects the advent of his dissociation. Such a conditioning factor takes the form of voluntary action of some type or of other sorts of activity depending upon the person's needs and wishes. Possibly the individual recognizes the urgent necessity of sleeping in order to be prepared for some kind of effort on the following day. This condition prompts not only the act of going to sleep, but also the use of a particular method to induce the person's disintegration. That is to say, the person may deliberately stop thinking about things and cut off his various stimuli.

**Specific Types of Sleeping Behavior**

Our exposition of the facts and conditions of sleeping behavior has already revealed that, howsoever dissociated from the stimuli the organism may be, it is impossible for it to be completely removed from the objects and conditions constituting its milieu. It remains therefore, as we have seen, for the organism to perform such actions as are stimulated by whatever objects with which it is still in contact. As we have suggested such reactions as the sleeping person performs belong primarily to the two great classes of reflex and implicit behavior. These, however, do not exhaust the sleeping person's conduct. We will, therefore, pass briefly in review the comparatively few types of action performed by the person while sleeping.

**Reflexes in Sleep**

In addition to the points already made concerning reflex action during sleep, we may suggest that the person continues to act for a comparatively long time without doing anything else but respond reflexly to primarily internal stimuli. This fact is well illustrated by the activities of persons in a cataleptic condition. Cataleptic and catatonic individuals are able to exist for a long time while performing only such simple reflex actions as suffice to keep them alive in their alimentary or respiratory surroundings. Such sleeping states as these are not necessarily of the deepest sort. At least they need not continue to be such but may vary in depth or profundity during the length of time that the sleeping goes on. Furthermore, it may be observed that psychological behavior of the catatonic or cataleptic sort may be called sleeping conduct because the individual is dissociated from his everyday conditions and performs only the simple types of action indicated. In other words, we may look upon the activities of the cataleptic individual as aids in defining the nature of sleep rather than as conditions discoverable in sleep.

Our study of sleep has already revealed the fact that the implicit behavior of the sleeping individual is of a particular type, namely, that which does not require any direct or controlled substitution of stimuli. The best example, of course, is dreaming behavior which is probably a universal feature of ordinary sleep. At this point we need only remark that the peculiarities of sleeping dreams with all their crudeness and grotesqueness are due to the fact that the substituting stimuli consist to a great extent of the person's implicit reactions which continue to function from the time in which he is in contact with the adjustment stimulus until the time of dreaming.

*Implicit Behavior in Sleep*

Aside from the reflexes and dreaming implicit responses the sleeping individual performs action belonging to different classes of behavior, although all are performed in an automatistic or subreactionalistic manner. Sleep walking and talking occur to us immediately. Such actions frequently take on considerable complexity. Talking activities especially appear to be highly involved responses, since it is possible to carry on a limited conversation with a sleeping person. In the latter type of actions, however, the person never goes beyond the performance of habitual verbal actions. Even in the lighter forms of sleeping conditions, such as drowsiness or lassitude, the individual is unable to learn or acquire new types of conduct. In deep sleep such action is entirely out of the question. Among the actions performed in the sleeping situation are to be mentioned the more or less mechanical activities of marching, and various manual operations provided they are not carried on too long or that the sleeping condition is periodically interrupted.

*Other Behavior in Sleep*

Considerable illumination is reflected upon the nature of the psychological conduct of sleep by inquiring into how completely transformed the individual is from the waking to the sleeping behavior milieu, or how complete is the person's dissociation. These various degrees of the individual's transformation or dissociation are commonly referred to as the intensity, depth, or soundness of sleep.

*Soundness of Sleeping Conduct*

In general, there are two ways of inquiring into the soundness of sleep. The first involves the question as to how deep is the final dissociation the person reaches. Here any concrete evidence is difficult to obtain but doubtless the farthest stage of dissociation is reached through the method of anæsthesia. The anæsthetist must be on guard lest his patient becomes so far dissociated as to be out of contact even with the endogenous stimuli for visceral reflexes.

The second type of inquiry into the soundness of sleep concerns the measures required to arouse the sleep or dissipate the dissociation. For the most part the problem concerns what kind or intensity of stimulus object is necessary to re-connect the person with objects around him. For this purpose the employment of various types of sounds proves a feasible method. Considerable positive evidence is available indicating that the soundness of sleep varies at different periods of the normal state of nocturnal sleep.

Depth of sleep apparently differs also for particular objects with particular persons. A classic example is the sleeping mother who is lost to all stimuli objects except the cry of her child. Similarly sleep talkers may be insensitive to all but a particular kind of word or question. In these latter examples we find a test of depth or soundness of sleep in terms of the relative qualities of stimulating objects.

**Stages of Sleeping Behavior**

Howsoever difficult it may be to define such a condition, there probably exists a particular point of normal maximum dissociation. This we may consider to be the full-fledged sleep of the person at a particular time. But we need not waver in our certainty of the existence of different degrees of the person's dissociability at various periods. These degrees constitute phases of the normal situation of going to sleep and waking up. For the present we shall attempt to differentiate practically between five stages of such dissociation. Because these do not represent clear cut steps in dissociation we must expect them to involve much overlapping. Also they must not be looked upon as being stages through which the person inevitably and regularly goes in being transformed from the waking to the sleeping situations. Rather they are types of dissociation of the individual from his surroundings which can be arbitrarily placed upon a scale having as its end points what we ordinarily call being completely awake and completely asleep. Furthermore, we must observe that each of these various sleeping periods themselves comprise a number of degrees of dissociation. To these different stages of sleep or dissociation we shall apply names taken from the language in general but which will be given specialized connotations.

**Lassitude or Languor**

In this condition the dissociation involves principally the negative reaction of the individual to objects which ordinarily provoke overt action. In other words, the individual may be in complete contact with his surroundings so far as perceptual responses are concerned but the final acts connected with such actions never occur. The individual seems inert although he may be perfectly aware of all that is going on. Moreover he can engage in conversation with someone, but the directness and aptness of his reply are not quite as effective as in other cases.

**Drowsiness**

When drowsy the individual is in such a state of dissociation that in general he is in ineffective contact with his surrounding conditions. The dissociation here involves not only overt forms of action but also perceptual and even more subtle implicit forms of behavior. As compared with lassitude or languor, drowsiness is a much more pervasive form of behavior condition, inasmuch as it involves practically all of the person's activities. But the complete negation of activity characteristic of lassitude is not a feature of this type of dissociation. The drowsy person cannot do anything well but he can do practically everything even though his action is dragging, halting, and requires more effort than is normally the case.

The person in the hypnagogic state is in fairly definite contact with his surroundings but the latter seem to be completely disorganized with respect to his reactions to them. The individual may be aware of the presence of objects but is not able to distinguish them adequately or otherwise respond to them properly or effectively. Things appear confused, disorganized and distracted, throwing the individual out of his usual orientation with respect to them. Delusions and other perceptual misreactions are characteristics of hypnagogic states. In a genuine sense the hypnagogic condition may be considered a definite mid-point between the maximum disorganization or dissociation we call sleep, and the minimum dissociation of the waking state. Hypnagogic states may be considered to be stages in the dissociation process of normal sleeping and waking life or a more or less lasting period of twilight existence connected with an unusual situation such as the deliria of fever or anæsthesia. Hypna-gogic State

The phenomenon of torpor represents merely a more profound form of drowsiness. In general, the individual is more helpless. All of his actions consist of decided fumblings because of his detachedness from things. The torpor state begins to be a decided condition of negativity in which actions even when they are started are not carried out to completion. Torpor

In its most intense form this condition amounts to a practical cessation of all the person's actions. The stuporous individual is never in any but a tenuous contact with external objects. A fairly typical condition in stupor or catatonia is illustrated by the case of the artist who, while apparently showing no signs of reaction to external things still reported after his recovery that all the while he was projecting images upon the white wall opposite which he lay. Also in such cases the patient probably continues to have what we ordinarily call reveries or day dreams and in general is not so far removed from objects around him as is the case in complete sleep. Stupor or Catatonia

As we have already indicated, we consider this condition of the person to be the stage of most complete dissociation. For practical purposes we will assume that all sorts of things are in the person's surroundings. He may be in the midst of a variety of happenings but in none of these does he participate. Hardly anything more than this may be said in characterizing so variable a phenomenon as sleeping behavior. Normal Sleep

Sleeping behavior is no exception to the general rule of psychological phenomena in the matter of irregularity of occurrence. Many extreme and less extreme variations of performance occur to disturb normal sleeping conditions. These variants or irregularities Anomalies and Irregularities of Sleeping Behavior of sleeping conduct concern both the manner of going to sleep and the way the sleeping activities are carried on. In both of these phases there are many types of individual differences.

Anomalies of sleeping behavior manifest themselves as functions of particular times, places, and situations. For example, some individuals cannot sleep in the daytime. They appear to be adapted exclusively to night sleeping. On the contrary, however, others can go to sleep more readily in the day than in the night. At the basis of these facts we discover the condition of wont and usage. Because of previous adaptation some individuals cannot dissociate themselves from their day life stimuli, while others are as tightly bound up with their nighttime milieu. Similar variants are found in the requirements of particular persons for certain special conditions as a possibility of going to sleep. For example, they cannot relax in a light room; others require some sort of illumination, or cannot continue to sleep unless they lie in a certain position. Some individuals are indifferent and can sleep in what appears to be the most uncomfortable and disturbing condition possible. They go to sleep, for instance, while standing up or all bent and twisted. Further illustrations of variations of sleeping conduct are the inability of certain persons to sleep in any but a familiar place. To others this makes no difference at all. Some demand the assurance of safety afforded by locked doors and windows, in contrast to those who are able to sleep in the most easily accessible of places. Obviously these variants and peculiarities of sleeping behavior depend upon the person's intricate life activities and his immediate and remote experiences.

An especially interesting individual variation of sleeping conduct is afforded us by the person who does not require any attendant ceremonies as over against the one who can go to sleep only as a deliberate and definite process. Illustrations of these respective differences are found in the anomalous manner in which some persons can sleep while carrying on a type of mechanical work as contrasted with him who cannot even have a light in the room, to say nothing of not being in customary night clothes with all other conditions at their most favorable point. A common example of unceremonious sleeping is that of the nurse who sleeps perfectly well between duty calls. In a sense, sleep walking and talking illustrate anomalies and unceremonious sleeping, although in these instances the anomaly is that the action takes place while sleeping, rather than that the person sleeps while performing such action.

Among the sleep anomalies constituting actual defective behavior is the conduct called insomnia. This is essentially a situation in which the person is unable to detach himself from his waking surroundings and to become associated with his sleeping environment. Very frequently insomnia issues from excitement of some sort in which case it is only a temporary and mild condition. On the other hand, it may be a more or less permanent defect that has the result of totally controlling and perhaps disrupting the individual's life. Doubtless insomnia of the more lasting and stubborn type in many cases has its origin in a general bad adaptation to one's surroundings. But it is just as certain that in other circumstances it has its foundation in the generally poor organic or biological functioning of the individual.

What is clearly the most serious defect of sleep is the condition known as actual sleeping sickness. The central feature of this event is the total inability of the person to keep himself connected with his surroundings. The result takes the form of long periods of sleep correlated with serious disturbances in the individual's general life conditions. Sometimes as in "African sleeping sickness" this condition can be definitely connected with parasitical infections (*Trypanosomes*) mediated by the tsetse fly. In other forms of this disease, for example *encephalitis lethargica,* apparently the trouble is caused by a very definite bacterial infection of the streptococcus group.

From our study of sleeping behavior as a condition of the individual's dissociation we may conclude that because of the great variety of circumstances under which this dissociation occurs that sleeping behavior is classifiable into a number of fairly distinct types. Hence we may differentiate between normal sleep constituting a periodic dissociation which results in the re-energizing of the individual or the removal of toxic elements from his organism, and hypnotic sleep, a superficial form primarily induced by some deliberate method on the part of the sleeping person or some other. One more type of dissociation that has not been suggested in our previous study is the cataleptic sleep, following an epileptic fit or convulsion. In this instance we have a dissociation coupled with a very definite condition of exhaustion succeeding a high type of excitement. The cataleptic form of dissociation indicates an important differentiation from other types of sleep in that the individual becomes cut off from his surroundings rather suddenly. Unlike the normal condition of dissociation therefore, in the cataleptic situation the exact period of transformation from one stimulus milieu to another can be definitely observed.

Naturally such a constant and important form of psychological phenomena as sleep, calls out a great series of theories designed to explain and account for its occurrence. For the most part these theories are exceedingly inadequate, useless, and far removed from any descriptive relation to the observed phenomena. For example, among psychologists the views have developed that sleep consists of or is caused by the sublimation of attention, a quietism of apperception, and a contraction of the field of consciousness. In all cases these theories consist essentially of metaphorical statements which are presumed to sum up the phenomena under investigation. If taken seriously, such theories are practically an admission that there exists such entities as

*Theories of Sleep*

attention, consciousness, or apperception that have some sort of function in human activity.

Physiologists and anatomists have been exceedingly fertile in developing theories concerning the nature of sleep. Ordinarily their theories have been formulated in terms of some localized organ or restricted function of the organism. To illustrate, one theory maintains that sleep is caused by anemia of the brain, another, that it is due to a stasis of blood in the thyroid gland. Still another accounts for sleep as the filling of the ventricles of the brain. It is to be expected, of course, that some types of theories make use of the nervous system for explanatory purposes. Accordingly, it is asserted that sleep occurs when the neurons are dissociated by the contraction of the dendrites and axones. A modification of this viewpoint suggests that the retraction which takes place is in the neuroglia instead of in the nerve cells themselves.

A different set of theorists operate with the conception that sleep is due to certain chemical changes in the organism. They believe that sleep results from an impoverishment of oxygen in the brain or that there are fatigue products in the blood or accumulations of toxins in various tissues. The absence in these theories of any very definite explanation has led theorists to assert that sleep is merely an instinct, that the organism has an instinct to sleep, and there they have allowed the matter to rest.[1]

In commenting upon these various theories, one is constrained to remark that if there is any basis of fact in them at all, it comes about because the particular author of the doctrine merely takes one phase or condition discoverable in the sleeping situation and makes of this partial fact a theory to account for the total activity of sleep. Unfortunately, also, the sleeping condition is presumed to be an abnormal condition of the individual. For our part we believe that no special theory of sleep is necessary. It suffices to describe the actual conditions of the individual that are observable when he performs this type of behavior, precisely as in every other case of psychological action. The descriptive features of sleep, however, naturally involve both biological and psychological factors, but this is merely a variant in degree and not in kind of psychological description.

### The Behavior of the Organism During Hypnosis

**Nature of Hypnosis**     The hypnotic behavior of the person, quite like his sleeping conduct, consists primarily of a very specialized type of relationship or contact with stimuli objects. During hypnosis, however, in contradistinction to the sleeping condition, the person is not dissociated from his stimuli but uniquely and unusually in contact with them. It is this close connection of the individual with some of his stimuli

[1] For a summary of theories concerning sleep, see H. Piéron, *Le Probleme Physiologique de Sommeil.* 1913.

that really amounts to a partial dissociation. That is to say, the person is so closely connected with some of his stimuli that he is perforce out of contact with the other objects in his surroundings. It is the condition of close connection, however, that must be emphasized, for it is that factor which is at the basis of the specific action of the hypnotized person. Also, in contradistinction to sleeping behavior, hypnotic conduct is especially active and positive, so much so in fact that the person makes himself passive and subordinate to the very point of dissociating himself from his surroundings and going to sleep.

Hypnotic behavior may be described as action performed by the individual as a result of transferring himself to a particular behavior environment. Since in typical cases the stimuli to which the hypnotized individual is transformed are centered in another person it appears, first, that the transference is due primarily to that other individual who may be called the operator, and secondly, that the person undergoing hypnotism is entirely inactive. The former point is negated by the fact that interpersonal hypnotism is only one form. Autohypnotic phenomena are just as authentic as interpersonal ones.

As a result of the condition that the hypnotized individual is more directly and closely connected with some specific stimuli, the total behavior of the person takes on a special characteristic. Generally speaking we may describe this characteristic as a loss of spontaneity of action. This means that the individual's behavior lacks insight, criticism, keenness of observation, and even general behavioristic orientation. On the whole, the person seems best able, and to a certain extent even exclusively, to respond to suggestions of the operator. In connection with this lack of spontaneity and general contact with surroundings a number of striking, special conditions are always found. It is such prominent conditions that have been most emphasized and that have, consequently, colored the ideas generally current concerning the phenomena of hypnotism. It is our plan to consider at present the main facts of such behavior in the following order. *Reactional Changes in Hypnosis* [1]

Distinctly characteristic of hypnotic behavior is the fact that the individual may be made to perform various sorts of actions that are possibly ridiculous, far fetched, or at any rate extremely noticeable, in comparison with his ordinary conduct, but which, nevertheless, he will not remember that he has ever done. This quality of his behavior depends in great measure upon his lack of observational efficiency. The situation is similar to that of the individual who, upon being told to select all of the red disks from a heap containing disks of many colors, is not able later to say how many other colors the heap contained nor whether the list included some particular color or not. The lack of observational efficiency is not only the basis of *Diminution of Observational and Recollective Action*

[1] For the data of hypnotic phenomena consult A. Moll, *Hypnotism*, 1890, G. M. Bramwell, *Hypnotism*, etc. 1903.

hypnotic amnesia but it may also be considered as an independent characteristic of the hypnotic individual. Thus the hypnotized person seems to be in a trance and unresponsive to the various things around him. He acts as a complete automaton at the mercy of the operator. Because the person is so conclusively in contact with the stimuli centered in the operator, he is oblivious to the presence and activity of other things.

**Hypnotic Anaesthesia and Hyperaesthesia** Precisely what reactional modifications occur in an individual's behavior are well illustrated by his anæsthetic and hyperæsthetic activities. So closely associated may the person be with the stimuli centering in the operator that the everyday objects surrounding the patient do not perform their ordinary stimulational functions. For example, pointed or sharp objects or burning things which ordinarily stimulate the person to discriminate their painful qualities do not do so because the hypnotized individual inhibits the corresponding reaction systems through the displacement effect of the operator's stimuli. And so the person's tissues may actually be injured and still the object will not perform its usual function. On the other hand, as a result of suggestions of the operator, objects ordinarily lacking the capacity to arouse a pain response may now do so. In other words, some object which usually does not elicit pain reaction under these circumstances calls out an exceedingly violent form of response.

Hypnotic anæsthesia is of course not confined to pain stimuli and responses but involves all forms of sensing and perceiving stimuli and reactions as well. A similar condition exists also with respect to the more elementary feelings. In this field of action likewise the inhibition of responses and the lack of stimulational functions to operate can be traced directly to the more intimate attachment of the individual to particular stimuli and his relative detachment from others. All of the phenomena suggested here are amply authenticated by numerous actual cases quoted in the literature on hysterical personalities. The inhibition of action as the basis of anæsthetic conduct appears plausible enough. But how account for hyperæsthetic behavior? Our suggestion is that the hyperæsthetic individual merely performs responses in his equipment on the basis of substitute stimulation. The suggestions of the operator serve as substitute stimuli for the reaction systems in question. Thus the operator's verbal actions take on the substitutive function ordinarily belonging to the objects of the sensing and perceiving actions. An enlightening analogous situation is that of the child beginning to learn to read. When he is especially eager to read and to know what is printed he finds himself sometimes in an uncontrollable process of supplying word responses for which no printed stimuli exist.

**Hypnotic Hallucinations and Delusions** Many phenomena closely connected with those just discussed are to be found in the behavior of the hypnotized individual. Hypnotized persons are subject to various forms of implicit and semi-implicit response abnormalities. The individuals perhaps see animals and persons not actually present, or believe themselves to be in the presence of danger, etc. On the other hand, on the basis of suitable verbal stimulational conditions, the person may create for himself beliefs which materially change his ideational circumstances from his actual ones. These delusional activities are often connected with and greatly influence various other actions. Believing himself to be the possessor of great wealth the hypnotized individual might, for example, approach a government official with the offer to purchase a public building or a town.

Great disturbances are also induced in the hypnotized person's overt responses. For example, his dissociation is manipulated in such a way as to make him unable to walk, to utter certain sounds, or otherwise to perform simple overt actions. In this fashion various sorts of cataleptic attitudes are induced. On the other hand, the individual under hypnotic conditions may be made to perform actions of which he ordinarily believes himself incapable. In other words, here as elsewhere persons are deprived of their inhibiting functions, and thus are capable of doing various activities which they usually prevent themselves from executing. But beyond this, it is fairly certain that a person under hypnotic condition is not able to do things that in his normal condition he is absolutely unable to perform. Briefly, unless the individual has the equipment for some action he cannot perform it under hypnosis. For in the hypnotic state there is no process of developing behavior equipment; rather what is ordinarily inhibited behavior is performed without hesitation. **Hypnotic Transformation of Overt Behavior**

So well do most of the phenomena of hypnotism answer to what is commonly called suggestibility that it is hardly necessary to say that the suggestibility of the hypnotized person is tremendously increased. It may be mentioned, however, that the mere fact of being hypnotized means that an individual puts himself entirely under the stimulational dominance of some other particular person. To be sure, there may not be consent, whether tacit or otherwise, to become stimulationally dominated by the other individual, but the general relationship, at least, must not be resisted. Once such a relationship is effected, the line of the person's action is conditioned by the other person up to a certain limit. The operator may suggest anything that is not too violent to the integrity of the other person's personality or does not transcend his capacity and likelihood of action as conditioned by the details of his personality equipment. The avoidance of acts leading to crime and shame points to the essentially active character of the person in hypnotic situations. **Hypnotic Susceptibility to Suggestion**

As a result of similarities in the behavior situations the problem of engendering hypnotic conduct parallels the problem of sleep induction. In both cases we have to deal not only with the facts of the actual behavior as it goes on but there is a further problem of how the behavior begins. Apparently, this is true because each **How Hypnotic Behavior is Engendered** of these types of behavior marks a practical discontinuity of the person's action.  Hence the appearance of the person entering into a state or condition.  Hypnotic phenomena differ, however, from sleeping behavior in that the former primarily involves the individual's connecting himself firmly with a stimulus situation rather than dissociating himself from stimuli.  Naturally this characteristic allows for more differences in reactional details.  The precise mode of engendering hypnotic action depends, of course, upon the type of stimulus situation to which the individual attaches himself.  It will serve our purposes to divide these modes into two general types, namely autohypnosis and interpersonal hypnosis.  Because they represent only the most extreme forms of hypnotic phenomena they are deliberate types of action but they need not be such at all.  For the more subtle and everyday forms of hypnotic behavior the modes of induction are less organized and complex.

Hypnotism, as we have seen, involves mainly a limited stimulus situation and a corresponding diminution of response.  The autohypnotic process of engendering this circumstance, therefore, is the manner in which the individual, himself serving as operator, attaches himself to some particular kind of stimulus situation at the same time that he dissociates himself from other stimuli.  The type of activity here is of course of a very limited sort since it is impossible for the individual to subject himself to his own limiting stimuli.  Either of two things happens.  The person may hypnotize himself to perform actual sleeping behavior.  In other words, he may engender a type of action which amounts to a lowering of his activity in general.  Or, his cessation of action need not necessarily be ordinary sleeping but may constitute what is ordinarily known as a trance.  The autoinduction of these two forms of hypnotic behavior may be correlated in each case with a particular method.

To induce hypnotic sleep the method involves primarily the manipulation of one's own conduct.  Effective in this connection is the process of directing one's behavior toward some form of implicit action.  That is to say, the individual tries to respond implicitly to nothing in particular, or to the absence of some definite object.  This is really nothing more than an intentional and deliberate method of going to sleep.  As such, the process reduces itself to the elimination of the possibility of stimulation and the consequent narrowing of the person's field of activity.  If one is unable to react to sheer vacancy, or the absence of objects, one may merely substitute implicit actions for overt ones.  Thus the individual begins to "think" of some particular event or person.  Gradually he eliminates these objects in turn until by the time they have all disappeared he is really sleeping.  Not infrequently the continuation of the implicit action merges into dreaming.  With particular individuals the specific process of limiting the field of action varies.  In some cases rhythmic action must be introduced, such as counting numbers or sheep, and so on.

The induction of the trance type of hypnotic behavior is in general simpler.  In this instance the individual merely focusses his attention upon some particular object, a brightly colored patch on the wall, or a glass or a crystal object.  The engendering of such a hypnotic state begins with the projection of images, or at least the performance of considerable imagal conduct.  This continues until the person enters into a situation in which one image reaction serves as a stimulus for the performance of another image response, so that throughout the duration of the hypnotic activity the person continues to perform one subdued implicit reaction after another with an absence of any kind of exertional form of conduct.

The interpersonal method of inducing hypnosis does not entirely differ from the process just described.  Either the individual himself, or some objects to which the operator directs the attention of the person undergoing hypnosis, serve as the limiting stimulus.  But in this case, of course, the induction of the hypnotic condition leaves the person open to the performance of all types of activity suggested by the operator.  The precise methods of inducing the hypnotic condition are unlimited.  The individual to be hypnotized may be asked to gaze upon some object, in other words, to make it the sole stimulus at the time until he detaches himself from all other stimuli objects.  At other times, he is touched in some way, pressure being exerted upon the eyes or some other localized part.  Again, hypnotism may be induced by merely keeping up a stream of verbal suggestions in a suitably modulated tone of voice until the desired effect is reached.  Just what particular method is employed depends upon a number of special conditions, for example, the kind of activities one wishes the person to perform after hypnosis is induced, or upon the character of the person.  Some individuals are not able to inhibit resistance to verbal suggestion, whereas others find it difficult to limit themselves to the performance of action to a bright object on the wall or some instrument in the hand of the operator.

Both the process of inducing hypnotic behavior and the actual performance of such conduct are surrounded by various conditions making for the ease and smoothness of the particular reactions as well as providing the possibility of their occurring at all.  These conditions are the circumstances on the side of the person and the stimuli respectively. **Reactional Conditions of Hypnotic Behavior**

On the response or personal side is first the question of agreeing to, or resisting the attachment.  These reactional conditions of agreeing to or resisting hypnotic attachment to stimuli situations are not necessarily deliberate or intentional.  On the contrary, they may belong to the lower ranges of behavior, even down to the automatistic level.  This point merely emphasizes the common and pervasive character of hypnotic behavior. Probably no one any longer believes that hypnotism can be induced only in abnormal persons. The fact is not only that everyone is subject to hypnotism but that a great many of our activities are hypnotic in character. We have already described that behavior fact. Especially is this true, for example, in the case of our various beliefs. Our confidence and belief in the existence of certain things and in the value of particular actions are based upon the process of confining our attention to particular stimuli objects to the exclusion of others.

Many of the methods of salesmen reduce themselves to this process, especially in the absence on the part of the purchaser of any knowledge or counter beliefs which might serve as the basis for resistance to the suggestions offered. A person contemplates the purchase of a particular kind of automobile. The salesman so extensively explains the merits of the particular car, that he detaches the purchaser's attention from the merits of other cars. In this way the merits of the particular car receive a value and importance quite out of proportion to their actual character, and as a result this car is purchased instead of some other. Because of the absence of such a basis of resistance in some matters, or in all, there are individuals unfortunate enough to lack the power to resist hypnotic influence in any degree, especially if they are subtly brought into contact with it. Just the opposite is the person who can meet such suggestions with a resistance founded either on knowledge, general indifference, or positive refusal. When such resistance is available, no individual is subject to hypnotic influence.

In general, the activities of an hypnotic sort cover all types of human behavior. We have hypnotic conduct in the realm of intellectual responses. We may be hypnotized in the direction of volitional behavior. What is ordinarily referred to as mob or crowd action consists to a great extent of the performance by individuals of a great deal of complex behavior of the intellectual, affective, and volitional type, through a process of mutual hypnotization. In the case of the typical mob bent upon some sort of definite activity, individuals wittingly or unwittingly hypnotize each other with respect to particular stimuli in the forms of objects and actions, with the result that certain concrete purposes are achieved.

Besides resistance as a negative condition of hypnosis we may cite also the restlessness and the general expansiveness of the person's behavior. As we have repeatedly observed the exclusive attachment to some kind of stimulus situation means that in general the individual's behavior is lessened in variety and scope, and that he is in a subdued condition. As a result, if some circumstance prevents this subdued situation from occurring the hypnotic process is interfered with. One would not think of attempting to hypnotize a person who is at the time under great affective or emotional excitement. Especially one who is exceedingly joyful on account of some good fortune could hardly be made to compose himself sufficiently to withdraw from the objects and conditions constituting the joyful situation and to attach himself to some restricting stimulus.

On the stimulus side the advantageous or disadvantageous conditions of hypnotization include such qualities as the pleasingness and attraction of the attachment stimulus object. Some object that has great attraction for, or is interesting to, the individual will offer the optative conditions for the attachment process. Similarly, the operator who appears to be competent, authoritative, and confidence-inspiring may expect much greater success in bringing about a hypnotic condition than if he did not appear so. The attractiveness and interest of the stimulus, however, must not pass beyond a certain limit. If an object is of the sort that has too great an attraction for the individual, if it presents many sides of interest, the restricted and subdued behavior characterizing hypnotic conduct is decidedly prevented. If the operator's suggestions, for instance, are in form or content too interesting or reminiscent of exciting experience, they obviously do not serve the purpose of the operator. Hence the verbal suggestions for hypnotism are usually monotonous repetitions of some sentence which may be considered to be definitely directed toward certain desired results.

Regarding stimuli conditions in general, the problem of advantageous or disadvantageous conditions refers primarily to the direction in which the person's behavior is supposed to tend. As a consequence, the stimulus object may turn the person away from an attachment to it. An object serving to recall a painful or unpleasant experience naturally induces one to avoid it. On the other hand, the attraction of such an object may interfere with the person's attaching himself to some other object with which he might desirably connect himself.

Among the most striking features of hypnotic behavior is that referred to as post-hypnotic suggestion. This is essentially a situation in which the individual attachment to a stimulus situation involves the performance of an action at a time removed from the original contact with the operator. Deferred hypnotic action for the most part occurs only in interpersonal hypnotic situations. The operator may suggest that at some later time, hour, or day he shall perform some particular action. Now this deferred reaction has always appeared as a very mysterious sort of condition. Upon consideration, however, we observe that it is merely another instance of the ordinary deferred or delayed reaction. The mystery appears to enter because we are not able to state what is the substitute stimulus for the deferred action when it actually occurs. While as a matter of actual practise, we cannot often determine what the exact substitute stimulus is, there is no question that it is always present and operative. Deferred hypnotic behavior in principle, therefore, is not different from ordinary memorial conduct, and as such involves

*Delayed Action in Hypnosis*

no different problem. Possibly the only instance of delayed behavior in autohypnotic situations are to be found in the case of individuals who are able to arouse themselves from sleep at any particular time. To look upon this type of psychological behavior as an instance of delayed autohypnotic action may cast a ray of light upon hypnotism in general.

### The Conduct of the Person While Dreaming

Nature of
Behavior
Dreaming

Dreaming behavior consists for the most part of the performance of more or less uncontrolled implicit responses.[1] These reactions are performed so far from any intimate contact with adjustment objects that the actions are not organized and controlled as are either overt and effective actions or ordinary implicit responses. It is hardly necessary to discuss dreaming responses with relation to overt behavior. But when compared with other implicit reactions we might say that dreaming conduct bears a different relation to the substitute stimuli involved. In all implicit behavior with the exception of dreaming, substitute stimuli objects and situations function to condition orderly and even effective responses to adjustment objects. Not so, however, in the case of dreaming implicit behavior. Here the substitute stimuli objects as well as the previous implicit responses functioning to arouse further implicit responses are so few, that the connection between the person's activities and the original stimuli objects is extremely mediated and attenuated.[2]

To specify in detail the uncontrolled character of dreaming behavior is to point out that no definite specifications as to what kind of behavior will occur are discernible in the person's situations. Accordingly, such activity is free in the sense that it is unrestricted with respect to time. Events are lived through which have no definite relationship to the individual's past experience or to the phases or periods of a particular unit of dream conduct itself. Events are confused and confounded through the failure of the dream responses to constitute a coördinated series of acts. Likewise for the same general reason persons and objects are mixed in the most heterogenous disarray. In general we may conclude that the dreaming person is able to change his status completely and be in contact with individuals with whom in the non-dreaming state it is impossible.

[1] That dreams consist essentially of implicit behavior although called by other names has been recognized for centuries. Hence, the conventional belief that dreams are imagination states (reactions).

[2] This is not to say, of course, that one cannot perform orderly and effective responses (solve problems, for example) when performing what is ordinarily thought of as dreaming, but here no doubt we have simply called the action dreaming because the individual was asleep. The details of the action are so different that this kind of behavior should not be called dreaming. We must distinguish between solving a problem when dreaming and dreaming that we have solved a problem.

In similar fashion one can accomplish results ordinarily unachievable in one's non-dreaming condition.

At the basis of the disconnected and unrelated character of the implicit responses of dreaming conduct lies the general detachedness of the individual while performing such behavior. Dreaming occurs when the person is not in intimate behavior contact with his surroundings, when he is relaxed, when he is not performing practical adaptational adjustments to his actual natural and human environment. Now it is just this sort of practical detachment of the individual from his concrete surroundings which enables him to be ever so much more active (implicitly) than he could be were he constantly performing practical adjustments. It is only such detachedness and freedom that make possible the elaborate and intense implicit action of which dreams are woven.

Naturally such intensely active and detached modes of behavior comprise a great number of different types of action. They involve familiar and unfamiliar objects and events; they are more or less related to the person's everyday life; they are longer or shorter in duration. In general, they vary in essential or unessential details. In point of fact, dreaming responses are so numerous and varied that it is hardly possible to correlate and order them in any sort of significant arrangement. We may make, however, a practical and tentative classification. *Types of Dreaming Conduct*

First, we may consider such dreaming activities describable as an implicit living over or review of the events of the ordinary waking and detached day. Individuals are constantly repeating in their dreams the actual activities of the previous day or days. In most cases such activities are those in which the individual has been in actual contact with important or striking situations. As a consequence when the ordinary business of the day ceases or during lapses of activity, the person lives over and repeats in dreams the actions that occurred under those significant and pronounced circumstances. In this way he reparticipates in situations which, on the one hand, are stimulating because of their pleasantness or satisfactoriness, and on the other, because of their dangerousness, striking, or unpleasant character. This type we may consider the most passive of all dream behavior in the sense that the person is a spectator of actions and events that are clearly past and irrecoverable. *Review Dreams*

Not only does the dreamer review the activities that he has previously performed and relive situations that are past, but also in his detached implicit behavior he anticipates future events and actions. Among the more striking instances of this type are the dream activities in which the person prelives some action which he expects to perform, or an event in which he is to participate, both of which are about to happen. How frequently in his implicit detached responses the person who is an applicant for a position foresees or foretells in his dream what will be the result of his application! *Anticipatory Dreaming*

Similarly, one may anticipate some personal or financial disaster in his dreaming action. In many instances individuals are actually influenced in their concrete actions by events and conditions met with in the dream process of anticipating actions and situations.

**Compensatory Dreaming**

Many dreams constitute quite definite reactional compensations. While we are detached and free in our activity we accomplish implicitly many achievements which are impossible for us to attain in our ordinary actual contacts with objects. Thus in our dreams we act out situations in which we are richer, more handsome, more agreeable than it is possible for us to be in our customary human relationships. In similar fashion the struggling poet in his dreams enacts a drama in which he plays the part of a renowned celebrity. The artist compensates for his poverty and neglect by becoming a famous artist whose pictures are in great demand at fabulous prices.

**Escape Dreaming**

Closely related to the above type are implicit activities in which individuals escape from persons and situations that in actual life oppress them or prevent them from living the kind of life they would choose or desire. This type of dream not only removes the individual from unsatisfactory or disturbing situations but in numerous instances forces him in his dreams to return to a galling or dissatisfied condition in which he found himself at some previous time. Here the very fact of realizing that one is happily removed from the original undesirable circumstances prompts one to dream that he has returned to them in the same way that the constant annoyance of dissatisfying conditions prompts the person to dream that he has escaped from such actual situations.

**Satisfying or Wish Fulfilling Dreams**

Things desired or wished for in actual waking life may be received or accomplished when the person is dissociated from the reactional conditions in which these things are located. The desiring circumstances of course are of every possible type and description. They may be exceedingly personal, referring to changes in the person's normal surroundings. Among the more personal of these dreams are the satisfaction of some desire for a particular object, the improvement of one's financial status or the change in relationship between oneself and others. Similar satisfaction is obtained in the course of dreaming with respect to travel, the promotion of one's professional rank or social status, etc. In recent times, the psychopathologists have made much of wish fulfillment of an intimate sexual sort. Doubtless many dreams are occasioned by the general unsatisfied sexual needs of the individual or the desire to have intercourse with some particular person which is impossible under ordinary conditions. So impressed have these physicians been with the force of such unfulfilled desires that they have attempted to interpret all dreams as being wish fulfillments and even wish fulfillments of a sexual sort. Nothing is more certain, however, that sexual wish fulfillments are only one type of wish fulfilling dreaming behavior and that wish fulfilling in general constitutes only one among a great many types of dreaming conduct.

Among other satisfactions achieved in dreaming activity are modifications and changes in objective surroundings to which one may be personally indifferent, but which one desires as generally worth while. For instance, one may dream that the capital is located in another than its actual place, because one wishes it to be there as a matter of necessity for the better conduct of the nation's or state's affairs.

Very frequently dreaming reactions take the form of repeating some condition that the individual may have experienced or heard of. So far as the dreamer is concerned he may have little or no interest in the situation, either in his waking or dreaming period. Sometimes the mere contact with a particular sort of situation is sufficient to result in a dream centering about it. Hearing or reading of a new type of machine or someone's success in some kind of situation, the individual gets into contact with the circumstances after becoming detached from the stimuli objects ordinarily monopolizing the stimulational functions of his conduct. **Occasion Dreaming**

Probably the most striking type of occasion dream is the activity known as nightmare. In this sort of phenomenon the person participates in a situation of an exceedingly exciting character which brings about in the dreamer a reaction of fear or perhaps terror, culminating in a violent awakening and a reintegration of the individual in his everyday surroundings.

These representative types of dreaming conduct may be considered to be a fair sampling of the exceedingly numerous forms that dreaming behavior take. Essentially these must be considered as types of which there are a great number of varieties in the dreaming history of any particular individual. It is well to notice here also that these different dream forms represent a process of descriptive differentiation between types that makes for distinctness of the dreaming conduct. Probably in almost every case an actual instance of dreaming constitutes some form of combination of two or more of these different types. One would hardly expect that so dissociated a form of behavior as dreaming conduct could in any sense be a definite and clear cut form of action. Dreaming conduct therefore is decidedly intermixed in almost every instance.

Since dreams are such tenuous and fleeting activities and on the whole exceedingly difficult to reconstruct we expect them to be disorganized and disjointed. However, we discover that our dreaming goes on in some fairly definite form, and has some orderly manner of arrangement. Accordingly we attempt a classification of dreaming activity on the basis of what we may call the content or the outstanding way in which particular dreaming behavior goes on. **Types of Dreaming Processes**

By this term we refer to a type of dreaming conduct that is on the whole activity duplicating in practically every respect the person's **Veridical Dreaming** ordinary actions and situations. What is meant here, then, is that the dreaming conduct is very much like what is performed in the waking state. The only difference between the dreaming and ordinary everyday conduct is that the person is not actually adapting himself as he dreams he is doing. Furthermore, no environmental control is present.

**Transformation Dreaming**

In other dreaming conduct the person transforms or confuses actions and situations from the standpoint of his everyday conduct. Instead of delivering a lecture at the place where he actually does in his waking situation, he substitutes other institutions or modifies in his dreaming the type of audience with which he is in contact. This form of transformation amounts either to a mere substitution of one actual situation, which one knows in his concrete experience, for another, or it involves the transforming of the actual conditions into unknown and unfamiliar objects and persons. In this case, too, the dreaming activity starts with some features of the person's actual life but transforms them in a way which is not actually possible. The result is a predominantly fabricated and unusual dream content.

**Symbolical Dreaming**

In the course of many dreaming activities the objects and persons constituting the content of the dreaming situation may be entirely symbolical. In this case the dreaming behavior corresponds to the euphemistic and symbolic methods of expressing oneself in language situations. For some reason or other, perhaps unknown to the dreamer, the content of his dream comprises a set of symbols of events and persons which the individual does not admit either into his overt or implicit waking actions. Appropriately here we may refer to the psychopathologists who have undoubtedly discovered cases of dreaming behavior in which the individual's action is a ·hidden and symbolic substitution for a kind of action he would not allow himself to perform when not dissociated from stimuli objects and circumstances. The point is namely, that the person who is subject to various inhibitions with respect to sexual conduct and situations, in dreaming about such things always symbolizes and suggests them rather than faces them outrightly and interacts with them in their natural form. In many cases, also, the symbolic type of dreaming process occurs as a means of shielding the individual from some feared object or condition he cannot bring himself to accept or have dealings with.

**Phantastic Dreaming**

Unique in the entire field of dreaming processes is the type in which the individual indulges in all sorts of phantastic action. In chaotic fashion his dreams are filled with various grotesque objects possibly not having any significant content whether known or unknown to the individual. In fact, in such dreaming behavior situations there may be no definite relationship of the dream processes or materials to any condition or situation of the person. Its phantastic or grotesque character may be ascribed to the presence in the surroundings of the person of some kind of subtle stimulation.

Coupled with this fact is always the exceedingly active character of the detached or sleeping individual. Under these conditions, then, the implicit or dream content comprises a series of exceedingly phantastic situations. Objects, if they appear in the dream, are malformations of actual or imagined things. Events are so misshapen and modified that they bear not the slightest resemblance to any kind of actual condition of the individual. An excellent way to derive an exact idea of what phantastic situations and events are like in such dreams, is to examine the peculiar drawings and paintings made by individuals who are ordinarily in a dissociated or disorganized condition. The drawings and paintings of the insane with their grotesque combinations of color and shape give a good idea of the possibilities in phantastic dreaming.

The complicated and tenuous character of dreaming in turn makes **Frequency** for extreme difficulty in the observation of such behavior. Hence **of Dreams** arises the question as to how frequently individuals perform such conduct. This question is often asked in its most extreme form, namely, whether some particular persons dream at all. It is not difficult to find individuals who assert that they never perform such behavior. Usually, however, it is found that such reports, while representing the person's honest belief, have no basis in fact. It is generally found that the individual has merely not remembered. Because dreams are so difficult to report, only exceptionally striking activities of this sort are actually remembered and described.

Recalling that dreaming conduct constitutes the sheerest form of implicit behavior activities which are performed when the individual is dissociated from his everyday environment, it seems difficult to believe that there are any individuals who do not dream. It is possible, however, that certain individuals participate in so few striking and important situations that there is no continuation of their activities in implicit form nor in their dissociated or sleeping condition to compensate or allow for escape from difficult and undesirable circumstances. Certainly it is true that some individuals have more frequent striking dreams which are reportable than others have. In no field of human behavior are individual differences so pronounced and so variable. We should expect that the stolid, insensitive person would actually perform very little activity of the sort we call dreaming, whereas, on the other hand, the sensitive individual must be constantly having all sorts of dreams. Again, the person who is active and ordinarily has many vital experiences may be expected more frequently to carry over his activities from the waking to the sleeping situation than the person whose behavior is limited in this direction. We have here a situation analogous to that which we find in the field of imagination behavior. Everyone knows how great are individual variations in the matter of creating new objects and situations and the projecting of new circumstances into their daily actions. It is precisely such differences that we find in their dreaming behavior.

Generally speaking with regard to the total behavior of the person we should expect that no individuals fail completely to perform some kind of dreaming behavior at some time, and further that some persons always do so when occasion permits. But these dreaming reactions may be so lacking in definiteness and strikingness that they make no impression upon the dreamer. That all individuals can dream appears evident from the fact that all persons can and do perform implicit actions. We observe also that when dreaming conduct is discussed with a group of individuals those who insist at first that they do not even know what dreaming is, report later that they dream frequently and that their dreaming behavior is rather distinct and definite.

**Diurnal and Nocturnal Dreaming** Ordinarily when dreams are spoken of it is nocturnal behavior which is referred to. This is true no doubt because in night dreaming the person is definitely asleep or in other words he is definitely dissociated from his behavior surroundings. Nocturnal dreaming undoubtedly was also the first to attract the notice of behavior students and the first to be studied. As a matter of principle, then, the distinction here is really between dreaming in the waking and sleeping state. Just here we may point out that there cannot be any sharp distinction drawn between dreaming conduct, whether we divide it into day or night dreaming, or waking and sleeping dreaming. Dreaming conduct we must repeat once more is the primarily implicit behavior we perform when we are partially or relatively dissociated from our ordinary living circumstances.

Howsoever little variation may exist in dreaming behavior regardless of the circumstances under which it may occur, there are observable certain variations that are the rule in general but which may not hold for specific individuals. For example, it is probably true that the night dream is more subject to phantastic content and organization than the day dream. On the other hand, day dreaming probably involves more prominently activities of a wish fulfillment nature and the attempt to accomplish what one ordinarily cannot do. Day dreaming or waking dreams are more constructive and connect up more closely with the person's daily activities. It is for this reason that the consequences of day dreaming may be fraught with graver consequences for the person. No matter how phantastic or grotesque nocturnal dreams may be they are inevitably limited in time and their occurrence is well marked off from other activities and situations. In the case of day dreaming on the other hand, the constructed situations may be so lasting and fit in so closely and firmly with the person's other activities that he may perform behavior which as a result is unbalancing and thoroughly abnormal in character.

Diurnal dreaming in its most marked differentiation from night dreaming is constructive and creational. The dreamer builds up for himself a new and distinct world peopled with individuals different from those actually met in life and containing situations that are the products of his own imaginative conduct.

Day dreaming perhaps may be more closely characterized by the fact that the constructive behavior is to a great extent anticipatory. The person plans new experiences and new modes of life. Planning and developing new conditions comprise decidedly the central method of looking forward to new conditions that may or may not be improvements of present circumstances. In all of this planning and anticipating of other conditions and circumstances there is undoubtedly an element of constancy of effort. The person persists in carrying on the process as soon as he is sufficiently dissociated to permit such behavior to occur. In many cases too the person may be said to be constantly dreaming so that dreaming constitutes a large part of all of his activities.

A milder form of constructive action characterizing diurnal dreaming is revery. So mild in fact is this type that it may not be considered constructive at all, but merely a passing in review of situations and conditions that have been pleasant and important to the individual. To a considerable extent the revery phase of day dreaming is retrospective. The person attempts to live over and over situations which have appealed to him. Revery dreaming is probably more preservational than constructive. It merely slows up the life process of the person and keeps him for a longer or shorter time among current or past, pleasant or attractive circumstances.

Dream behavior, no less than all other human actions, is conditioned by a series of definite situations. These conditions determine not only the occurrence of dreams but also their particular mode of operation. As in all other cases of psychological conduct these conditions are distributed among the reactional, stimulational, and other factors ordinarily influencing the conduct of the person. Conditions of Dreaming Activity

Many of the determining factors of dreaming are centered in the individual's actual behavior equipment. In precisely the same way as in all other kinds of actions, only those individuals can dream who have a certain amount and type of behavior equipment. Furthermore, the richer and more varied the personality's behavior equipment, the more complex and interwoven his dream activities.

Similarly the stimuli conditions of dreaming conduct constitute very important and essential determiners of the kind and duration of dreaming activity. There must always be particular stimuli conditions to put the person's equipment into action, for dreaming behavior in common with all other psychological activity constitutes interactions of the person with specific stimuli. The fact that the person is dissociated from his workaday stimuli conditions does not argue for lack of stimulation but rather for less common and more subtle inciters to the peculiar form of action which dreaming comprises.

Dissociation from the kind of stimuli conditions that surround ordinary behavior throws into sharp relief the setting for dreaming conduct. Here not only do stimuli settings constitute effective determiners of action, as in other types of behavior but, since the person is removed from his usual surroundings, these settings themselves may perform definite stimulational functions. Among such setting-conditions influencing dreams and their contents are position in bed, amount and kind of clothes one wears, strangeness of room, etc. Under experimental conditions these setting determiners of actions consist of tightening and constricting of various parts of the organism.

Naturally the depth or the degree of the individual's dissociation enters as an extremely prominent conditioning of his dream behavior. Specifically it conditions whether the dreaming activity takes on characteristic nocturnal or diurnal character. It also influences the phantastic nature of the dream content. All this follows from the fact that the degree of dissociation is the primary basis of the occurrence of dreaming at all. Dreaming behavior quickly assumes an abnormal character when it becomes such a prominent and permanent mode of the person's contact with his surroundings that he is unable to distinguish between the constructions of his dreams and the situations common to him and other individuals. Some individuals are dissociated to such a high degree that their lives on the whole consist of dreaming instead of activities which are alternations of dissociated and associated states. In many types of insanity and especially in paranoia and dementia præcox, the individual is so out of touch with his actual surroundings that he is unable to distinguish between the inventions he is himself responsible for, and the workable constructions and manipulations constituting his workaday activity.

The Stimuli for Dreaming Conduct

Stimuli situations are perforce different in the case of dream reactions than in other kinds of behavior since the essential factor of dream activity is the dissociation of the person from his ordinary surroundings. We find, therefore, that in many instances dream behavior is stimulated by a type of object or condition not closely related to the dream activity, in other words, a remotely removed substitute stimulation. So remote may the actual stimuli be that they are discovered only with great difficulty, if they can be discovered at all. In other cases, however, the actually correlated stimuli conditions can be easily traced out.

This situation prevails, as we have already suggested, because the stimulational conditions for dreaming are very like the situations in all sorts of implicit activity. Dreaming behavior, however, differentiates itself sharply from ordinary implicit conduct in that the former is less subject to specific control. In contradistinction to dreaming conduct, implicit action for the most part involves more definite connections between the adjustment and substitute stimuli. This situation is of course to be expected since the adjustment stimuli for dreaming conduct are so vague and dissociated from the individual.

The stimuli for dreaming behavior, then, are decidedly substitutional in nature. In fact, we may think of the activity as having originated through the operation of substitutional stimuli which direct the individual toward what would ordinarily be the adjustment objects and situations. This is in striking contrast to the ordinary implicit behavior situations in which the adjustment stimuli are the primary factors and the substitute stimuli merely replace them functionally and serve to bring the person into reactional contact with adjustment objects and conditions. In enumerating and describing the stimuli for dreaming behavior we may, as in other cases, divide them into objects, conditions, and actions. In the present connection, however, the terms have a somewhat technical significance. They carry the meaning of type of stimuli rather than particular things.

When objects constitute the stimuli for dream action they necessarily have to be fairly vicarious substitutes for ordinary stimuli. To illustrate, if some portion of the body is uncovered, the individual may dream of arctic exploration and other conditions involving coldness or temperatures in general. Because the stimulus is functioning vicariously in substitute fashion the line between what constitutes an object and a condition is very hazy. Other things serving prominently as substitute stimuli for dreams are sounds such as wind, whistles, blankets, lights, etc. How these stimuli operate may be gathered from the suggestion that it is the freedom of the stimulus object, the reclining position and the absence of tight day clothing which stimulate dreams of flying, etc. For the most part these are features of the person's surroundings while he is dreaming. In other words they are features of his environment to which he has become attached after being dissociated from his ordinary environing circumstances. Not that this is the exclusive situation with respect to object-stimuli for dreaming behavior but it is certainly a common one.

Among conditions serving to stimulate dreaming conduct we place in a prominent position the contingencies and necessities of the individual's daily existence. These initiate trains of implicit behavior which operate continuously and finally become full fledged dreaming conduct. We assume that from these conditions and circumstances the person is unable completely to dissociate himself. Such stimuli accordingly are more definitely adjustment situations themselves than are the stimuli previously described. Hence, the stimulus comprising, as it does, an actual condition of the waking state is not nearly so vicarious. Correspondingly the dreaming activity is much more definite. It is not so likely to be phantastic as only transformative, if it is not merely the "living over" type. In many cases the dreaming which such stimuli initiate takes the form of a review of the person's general circumstances throughout the day or some particular event that has taken place at some former time.

So far we have been discussing primarily the conditions stimulating nocturnal dreaming conduct. Different situations exist of course with respect to day dreams. For them much more definite persons or objects become substitute stimuli for an elaborate operation of implicit behavior. For this reason the stimulus activity in the day dream is more like the ordinary case of memory although the controlled factors here are lacking. In the case of night dreams the checking and control of the normal waking state are more or less absent.

The person's own behavior serves not by far as the least prominent or important form of stimulus for dream activity. Starting with the simplest type we find that various reflexes elicit reactions to other persons, as in sex dreaming, dreams of feasting, etc. Again, desires, hopes, fears, and other sorts of feeling activities which undoubtedly are carried over into the state of dissociation serve very definitely as stimuli to call out corresponding reactions. Dreams prompted by reactions of this sort can be classified mainly under the heading of review, though a great deal of dreaming conduct of the transformation type is elicited by this type of stimulation. Moreover such stimulation may be regarded as belonging both to the associated and dissociated surroundings of the dreaming individual.

**The Continuity in Dreaming Behavior** Although dreaming reactions are most clearly activities of dissociation, actions involving the removal of the person from his everyday surroundings and his transportation to another set of conditions and situations, still the continuities found in such behavior must not be overlooked or underrated. These continuities are of two sorts. We have already found sufficient evidence to show that dreaming activity constitutes a prolongation or continuity of the person's ordinary behavior. This situation may also be established upon more remotely observational grounds. Since dreaming reactions must after all be performed with such behavior equipment as the individual has, the reactions performed are necessarily continuous, since the person's equipment remains with him constantly. Moreover, it is hardly probable that dreaming conduct is performed with reaction systems that operate exclusively in dreaming responses. Again, when the person is no longer able to use this equipment in dreams it is likewise lost for every kind of situation. Furthermore, there is evidence that it is precisely dreaming conduct that is the most strikingly continuous of all types of behavior. Cases exist on record of abnormal individuals who in spite of the fact that they have a very definite alteration of personality still dream of things in their normal condition. In fact, some of these individuals have been reintegrated primarily through their dreams. That is, their total behavior has been synthesized by making them see on the basis of the dreams they reported that they had had experiences different from their present ones and that really belonged to an environment other than their immediate abnormal setting.

The second type of continuity in dreaming behavior is the interdependence which exists between dreaming activities of different successive periods. Persons may carry on dreaming behavior involving the same situations, persons, and events at any particular time that they enter into the dissociated condition. Dreams continue in series from night to night or from sleeping period to sleeping period. When such continuous dreamings are confined exclusively to the sleeping or dissociated state they simulate the behavior constituting one personality, or one phase of a personality, of dissociated abnormals.

It is an unfortunate circumstance of psychological history that the phenomena of this chapter have always been treated as abnormal. The damage incurred by such a procedure has been no less than the obscuring and retarding of our knowledge and understanding of some exceedingly interesting and important types of psychological reactions. This unfortunate handling of these reaction types has of course been varied. In each case, however, it has resulted in the same inadequate treatment.

Sleeping behavior during many centuries has been misinterpreted as a state of condition of the organism not unanalogous to living death. Numerous simple theories to account for such a condition have already been suggested. At best, sleep has been interpreted as a type of physiological activity. In this way such phenomena were farthest removed from interference with intellectualistic conceptions concerning psychological data.

It is an innovation, therefore, to consider sleeping behavior as minimal and limited action performed under particular conditions. As such, sleeping activities take their place among the remainder of the psychological behavior of the person. And what is no less important is the fact that to handle sleeping phenomena in this way does not interfere with the study of it also as physiological activity. For an excellent summary of the present status of knowledge and opinion concerning sleeping and dreaming conduct consult the chapter of de Sanctis (Psychologie des Traumes) in Kafka's *Handbuch der vergleichenden Psychologie*, vol. 3, 1922.

Studies in hypnosis have a long history. The descriptions and interpretations of this phenomenon, continuous with that of our own day, may be traced back to Mesmer. The record of all this history consists for the most part of the discussions of the nature of the hypnotic state (hypnosis is thought of as a state), and the way it can be brought about. Particularly, hypnotic behavior study runs through animal magnetism, the neurosis and abnormality stages, to the stage of suggestion. Unlike sleeping conduct hypnotism behavior has for a long time been considered a psychological phenomenon. The perspective of this study may be easily and well surveyed with the aid of Moll, *Hypnotism*, 1890) and Bramwell (*Hypnotism, its Theory, Practice, History, etc.*, 1903). The latter is also illuminating with respect to the therapeutic employment of hypnotism. Generally speaking the hypnotic studies of recent years lend themselves readily to interpretation in terms of definite responses to stimuli.

The most ancient interpretation of dreams has persisted down to the present day. This attitude, namely, that dreaming must be interpreted and elucidated instead of described as an event in nature, as it is more vigorously held by the Freudian psychopathologists, continues the old conception of dreams as bizarre and occult phenomena. That the latter look upon dreams as merely the symbolic self-revelation of sexual desires does not minimize the obscuration of the ordinary implicit adaptational character of such activities. Indeed, to think of dreams as the manifestations of subconscious desires (Freud, *Interpretation of Dreams*, 1913) is to render impossible the studying of them as definite personal responses of individuals to their more unusual and irregular stimuli conditions and circumstances. Even if dreams are not conceived as exclusively sexual phenomena, the same obfuscation of the facts of dreaming conduct results when they are not studied as specific types of psychological adaptations. A type of study adhering more closely to the actual facts in the case is represented by the work of de Sanctis (*Die Traume*, 1901). Recent attempts at the experimental study of dreaming are reported by Mourly-Vold (*Ueber den Traum*, 1910–1912).

# CHAPTER XXIX

# PSYCHOLOGICAL ANALYSIS OF COMPLEX BEHAVIOR SITUATIONS

The Problem of Situation Analysis

In consonance with the mood and temper of this work already frequently indicated, we attempt in this chapter to analyze in detail some of the extremely complex behavior situations. It is our purpose, in making this analysis, to isolate the psychological factors involved, whether individual or cultural action and to indicate their exact place in the behavior complex. By making such an analysis we are enabled to appreciate the nature of the psychological phenomena operating in such intricate circumstances and to observe the influence and functioning of such behavior (among other equally essential factors) in the complicated situations of psychological life.

Attention may once again be directed to the general attitude of this work in which we are strongly opposed to confining our studies to the simple facts of psychology such as the description and enumeration of the very simple reactions. In order to present in any sort of effective form the principles of psychology we must draw upon the facts of complex human life as well as upon the elementary types of reactions that the human organism performs in making its adaptations. This means that in distinctly human behavior we cannot confine ourselves to simple individual reactions but must consider in addition complex cultural conduct. Just what this kind of analysis involves is revealed by referring to our study of language. In that analysis we had occasion to suggest the coördinate occurrence of psychological and non-psychological events although in that study we were obliged to confine ourselves to the behavior factors. That situation exists because the generality of linguistic activity prevents us from stressing very effectively the character of the human situations in which linguistic conduct is performed. In the present study, however, we shall have ample opportunity to take account of the larger phases of the behavior situations involved, for we shall choose for our investigation those activities especially adapted to particular prescribed kinds of human circumstances.

Stressing as strongly as we do the complex behavior of human beings, does not imply an under-evaluation of the simpler forms of action. As we have had occasion to remark, all psychological phenomena constitute elements in a series which is entirely continuous and the members of which vary only in details. We have also implied that it is impossible to underestimate the value of the simplest forms of behavior because it is only those simpler types that lend themselves to experimental investigative techniques. Thus, the less intricate behavior earns for the whole series the evaluations of actual and verifiable phenomena. The value, nevertheless, of verifying and demonstrating the existence and character of the simpler forms of activity is somewhat diminished unless such establishment of facts and principles is carried over to the complex behavior actually constituting the subject matter of human psychology. Psychology, therefore, can only consider itself half grown and ill formed unless it takes account of complicated conduct.

When we inquire into the causes for the universal neglect of the extremely important phenomena of complex human behavior we probably find that, aside from the physiological tradition in psychology which confined the subject to elementary reactions, the great difficulty is in actually making such a study. But we naturally expect our involved æsthetic, religious, and scientific conduct to be exceedingly difficult to isolate and analyze. How difficult this analysis really is, is manifest in the task of separating off such different behavior as the religious from the scientific, or the moral from the religious, with which they are very closely intermixed. It is manifestly equally difficult to separate off what are actual æsthetic behavior facts for example, from the nonæsthetic. For instance, how can we segregate our æsthetic appreciation responses of a novel from our prejudice for or against the writer and his attempt at moral preachment? This condition, however, should not deter us from making the attempt to add to our psychological descriptions the discussion of such indispensable forms of behavior.

That the analysis of complex human behavior is not impossible is demonstrated by the fact that we have already succeeded in beginning an isolation of the various types of involved conduct. In separating from each other the four types of societal action we have already achieved considerable progress in the performance of this task. In contrast to the study of societal conduct, however, we must now emphasize not the types of responses but the kinds of situations involved and the relative influences of all the various factors occurring in these behavior complexes. Not only must we describe the intricate circumstances under which the individual behaves, but also the influence upon each other of the various factors contributing to the total make-up of the behavior situation. Unlike the study of societal behavior in which the personality is stressed with its equipment of behavior in all its types and origins, we emphasize now the large complex of institutions, natural phenomena, traditions, and social organizations of all sorts that play prominent parts in the behavior circumstances of complex conduct.

In the field of psychology two great principles may be assumed to govern the operation of all of the facts comprised in this particular domain. These principles are, first, individual differences, and second, the intermixture of actions and situations in all complex human behavior phenomena. The first principle has been amply discussed and demonstrated throughout the body of this treatise. Accordingly it devolves upon us in this division of our work to amplify what have previously only been suggestions for the differentiation between the various factors inextricably interrelated in complex human behavior situations.

At the outset we must differentiate between what is and what is not a psychological fact. Necessarily then we distinguish between actions of individuals and the things and conditions with which these actions are involved. In complex behavior situations this distinction is not always obvious. To take the most difficult case, in religious situations we find a neglect of the difference between what is an existing historical fact and a thought or belief which is a psychological action, either dynamic as an actual immediate response, or staticized in the form of a habit or tradition of behavior. The latter activities of a complex behavior situation must be isolated from all kinds of things that are not action, for instance, from natural objects and cultural objects or institutions. Probably the most requisite distinction here is between the actual behavior of individuals and the statistical or historical activities which may be thought of as action too, but action of a group, state, government, or other sociological or humanistic entity.

Another distinction is immediately suggested. We must mark off psychological actions from the materials and products of such actions. Both the materials and the products may of course themselves be psychological actions but in that case they are different from the actions at the center of our immediate interests. This distinction is especially necessary in the kinds of complex actions in which the psychological responses are creative or transformative. The materials in such situations may be thought of as the stimuli objects or actions which elicit and condition creative and transformative responses. When these activities have been performed or are completed, the objects and actions which constituted the stimuli and the materials may be looked upon in their transformed status as the products of the actions in question.

Next, we find it expedient to mark off natural objects from humanistic objects both of which play important rôles in complex behavior situations. Probably the greatest difference between these two is the fact that one exists in nature independently of any action of the individual, while the other is a product of, or at least connected with, such human activity and circumstances. To illustrate, in the case of scientific situations we must distinguish between natural phenomena which are independent of the behavior of the person (upon our first contact with them they are crude data such as natural objects and events), and data that are the results of the activity of scientists, such as descriptive or traditional materials (scientific facts). In short by natural conditions we mean actual facts in the world of nature as over against the products of the psychological behavior of individuals. In the field of art this distinction is remarkably clear when we try to differentiate between beauty as a natural fact to which one reacts and beauty as a result of traditional beliefs or arbitrary standards. So far we have suggested distinctions between things in nature and institutions. The former are entirely independent of any action performed upon them; the latter are the results of behavior. In the same way we can distinguish between a human event as a fact in nature, and a historical fact as a traditional description constituting the result of the psychological reactions (whether personal or cumulative) to the natural event.

Coming to the differentiation between individual and cultural behavior that occurs in complex interconnection with intricate behavior situations, we discriminate between specific activities of the individual that are due more or less to his own development and experiences, and the same type of personal reactions arising from and imposed upon him by the institutional stimuli among which he lives. Thus in artistic situations the individual's responses may be actions performed merely because of the existence of æsthetic traditions of various sorts, whereas other of his acts are definite results of his own personal development and contacts with æsthetic objects and circumstances. The former or cultural type of action has more to do with conventional appreciation responses to art objects or objects of natural beauty, while the latter or individual conduct is concerned more with the development of new techniques, new objects, etc.

Whether or not our analysis will be successful, the urge to make it is stimulated by one of the most important and imperious of scientific stimuli, namely, the absolute methodological necessity to keep as clear and distinct as possible the data with which we deal. Unless we keep our different types of data isolated and distinct, we can never hope to master their details or give them proper description and interpretation. It is not an unusual occurrence to find students of psychological phenomena utterly confusing certain data, reactions with institutions, and acts with their stimuli, especially when the latter are also acts. For our part, we must absolutely hold distinct that which is psychological from that which is not. We must keep separate stimuli from responses, etc.

And finally, our emphasis is upon analysis. Complex human behavior situations are too complex to offer us the hope of being able even to describe fully the person's actions. In lieu of this circumstance, then, we can only attempt an analysis and isolation of the various factors involved in these complex situations. It is because psychological behavior is so difficult to describe and interpret that we must include the enumeration of the non-psychological or nonreactional data. Through the mention of the non-psychological facts we may expect to obtain light bearing upon the psychological factors.

Thus, what we cannot achieve directly we may attempt to accomplish through the correlation of the behavior phenomena with the objects and circumstances with which they are related.

In this type of analysis that we are about to make we must forefend ourselves against numerous pitfalls of language which unfortunately serve to confuse the investigations with which we are concerned. Any slight contact with such complex phenomena indicates immediately that we not only use different names for the same type of things and the same names for very different types of facts, but also allow names to confuse things and actions. Of all the complex human situations in which human behavior is involved we shall study for illustrative purposes the ethical, political, æsthetic, scientific, and religious situations. The examination of these selected types will serve to illustrate the psychological conditions with respect to all types of complex behavior.

### ÆSTHETIC BEHAVIOR SITUATIONS

In analyzing an æsthetic behavior situation we discover at once that it is composed of the workings of two sets of objects and conditions. In the first place we meet with the behavior segment involving the individual's performance of a specific æsthetic response to a particular æsthetic stimulus. This behavior segment is based upon and begins to operate in a milieu which involves on the one hand a particular person or individual with a unique background of development and personality make-up, and on the other a set of objects and circumstances of natural and cultural types. These circumstances make possible and afford the basis of operation of the æsthetic behavior segment. With these two elements of the æsthetic situation as a basis and with their two phases supplying the cues we may proceed to analyze the detailed features of the æsthetic situation.

The Æs-
thetic Be-
havior
Segment

Considering first the response factors we find that a behavior segment may be of any one of a number of types, each of which by itself or in combination with some other, constitutes the psychological action side or element of the complex behavior situation. Among these response factors we are able to single out four outstanding types of æsthetic conduct, namely, the creation of some art object, the appreciation, the criticism and the evaluation of a work of art.

Creative activity comprises the development of a conceptual response to some object of beauty and the consequent performance of a number of technical operations resulting in the final production of the object thus conceived. Prominent in creative activity we find, as we have already suggested, the performance of a great amount of implicit action. This is operative not only in the conception of the work of art but in its detailed development. Imagination activities of all sorts likewise function predominantly in the creative process. It may be well to point out that the creative action here is not unlike the creative response operating in any kind of productive situation. But in the æsthetic situation the detailed differentia have direct and immediate reference to the development of some beautiful object.

Such, in brief, are the suggestions concerning the actual conceptual and manipulative activities performed in the production of some object constituting an adjustment stimulus for the type of æsthetic reaction we have been indicating. The enumeration of acts and processes, no matter how large and complex, can only be partial and incomplete unless we include all of the various contributing actions which in a sense precede and parallel the actual creative manipulations by way of directing the type and manner of response leading to the result of producing or creating a particular kind of object. Among such contributory activities we discover the desire or need for expression. Here we have a very active type of response in the form of an urge or desire to produce some object or to externalize and materialize some conception that one has developed in one's general activities. Clearly the type of æsthetic behavior we are now mentioning is a specialized form of activity only found in individuals whose surroundings and previous experiences have led to the development of the particular reaction systems which make possible the carrying out of an æsthetic activity. That is to say, is the person capable of being æsthetically stimulated so that he performs the kind of expressive and materializing behavior we have been suggesting? Has he taste and talent, æsthetic capacities and technical craftsmanship?

Certainly in each case of æsthetic behavior the activity of any particular individual at some specific time is influenced and developed under very specialized circumstances. Although the activity is all classified as æsthetic behavior, this term denotes nothing of the individuality and uniqueness of the particular responses in each case. These differences of behavior are sometimes slight. Assuming that the stimulating conditions during the course of the individual's reactional biography and immediate stimulational circumstances are similar the actual fact is, however, that the stimulational causes and conditions of æsthetic conduct do not ordinarily coincide. For this reason the activities are unique in the sense we have just indicated. In performing æsthetic reaction accordingly, individuals make or enjoy particular kinds of art objects, particular subjects, and particular manners. As our exposition will sufficiently indicate, the specific causes and conditions of the performance of æsthetic reaction considered as responses merely, and the existence and stimulation of particular objects, are determined by the individual development of the reacting person in his social or cultural surroundings, and by the natural and anthropological circumstances constituting the person's human milieu.

The appreciation type of æsthetic activity involves a minimum of creative performance. On the whole it is a fairly passive action of enjoying and contemplating some object as it exists. Doubtless there is a large element of affective behavior found in every appreciative situation. The passivity of such conduct is made possible by the fact that the individual is merely performing behavior reaction systems that he has acquired during the course of his past reactional development while in contact with the object to which he is now reacting or to similar objects. To a great extent we might contrast the appreciative and creative type of æsthetic reaction by pointing out that the stimuli for the appreciative reaction are not only objects created by or contrived by persons but natural objects of beauty.

The æsthetic responses we call criticism are not only reactions to æsthetic stimuli objects themselves but also to the development and background of works of art and nature as well. The critic of an æsthetic stimulus performs a reaction to the comparative merits of works of nature and to the methods and techniques involved in the production of works of art. The art critic responds to the technique and method of the creator of the object as well as to its surroundings and the success or failure of the producer to attain a certain standard of excellence for the particular kind of work. Furthermore, the responses of the critic have as their stimuli the detailed subject matter and material of which the art object is made, in addition to the technical capacities and performances of the art producer. The literature on art criticism is exceedingly instructive with respect to these points. And especially when we observe the confusion in such writings resulting from the failure to distinguish the works of art from the worker, and its qualities from his capacities and performance.

A fourth type of æsthetic response we have referred to as the evaluating of æsthetic objects. This type of activity is to a certain extent non-æsthetic in character, involving the economic placing of an æsthetic object, but this reaction must be considered as also including an æsthetic appreciation and criticism of the objects in question. All of the reactions and attitudes taken toward a certain æsthetic object no matter how inclined toward economic and other behavior modes, cannot but be æsthetic in character when the stimulus is an æsthetic object. This is true of course, only when the reaction is one of evaluation and estimation. In other cases the response may be æsthetic only to a slight degree, if at all.

In the isolation of the distinctive responses in such cases we have of course emphasized differences. But it would be defying good counsel to believe that these reactions are all sharply divided off one from another. This is clearly not the case. Furthermore we may be certain that a number of common elements are to be found in all of the different types of responses. For example, simple knowledge of the beautiful and some æsthetic feeling of delight or the more extreme ecstatic conduct are found in some degree in every æsthetic activity. So common is the latter observation that it has led to the unfortunate conception that an æsthetic reaction is a feeling or an emotion and that an æsthetic object is an expression of such a feeling.

Turning now to a consideration of the stimulus for the æsthetic behavior segment we must point out that here we have a distinct stimulational function. We may immediately apply to it its distinctive term, namely, beauty. The term refers to the qualities of existence in the object performing the stimulational function which elicits the appreciative, creative, evaluative, and critical reaction. Probably in no place in the entire psychological realm is it as necessary to insist upon the unique and independent existence of the qualities of an object as those we call beauty or the beautiful. The establishment, strictly speaking, of the existence of objects possessing such qualities as beauty should not be any more difficult to accomplish than in the case of an object which has the quality of redness or sweetness. It is an historical fact, nevertheless, that our thought concerning psychological phenomena has become traditionally incrusted with convention so that in quarters where we least expect to find it so, it is believed that beauty is a quality of things in some way dependent upon the activity of the individual. This, of course, is far from being the actual case although it is true that, unlike a reaction to the color red, the response to a beautiful object itself is always based to a great extent upon a cultural behavior situation. In other words, whereas the simple reaction to a color or sound may be purely universal, the reaction to such a complex object as a work of art or beauty in nature is heavily conditioned by the individual's cultural experiences. Howsoever strongly intrenched this subjectifying idea may be, it is still far from representing the actual fact. Strict regard to the actual facts in the case indicates that the objective character of beauty is not minimized even when the beautiful thing-stimulus is entirely a product of craftsmanship. It is impossible to make progress in our psychological thinking with respect to æsthetic situations without accepting the object of beauty as the autonomously existing thing it actually is.

All varieties of objects and things are capable of performing the stimulational function of arousing an æsthetic reaction. As we have already suggested, we may consider here all kinds of objects of nature such as landscapes, seascapes, or objects of diverse sorts, such as stones, rivers, animals, plants, etc. Also we include persons and various parts of the human figure. Actions of many types, especially the movements of animals and human beings, as well as those of objects in space, constitute beauty stimuli.

As in all cases of human behavior of every sort of complexity the stimuli objects bear an exceedingly close relationship to human activity and human contrivance. Ordinarily we seldom fully appreciate that what we call natural objects as the stimuli for our conduct are most thoroughly shot through with human modification and change. Our ordinary natural stimuli are unquestionably touched with cultural alteration or individual transformation. Much the same condition prevails with respect to æsthetic stimuli. Perhaps the actual, natural beauty-stimuli objects are not so much as other kinds of natural objects transformed through the medium of human contrivance. The addition to them of human qualities is due to a great extent to mere reactional contact with them. Thus the added characteristics are more of the appreciative sort, namely, liking or preferring the thing as a natural object.

On the other hand, the field of æsthetic stimuli is very much taken up with completely contrived objects, products of æsthetic activity developed and created by other individuals as well as by the person himself, and which after production and creation, serve to stimulate the individual to perform appreciative æsthetic activities. Obvious stimuli of this type are of course the ornamentation and decoration of buildings, pictures, paintings, statuary, music, throughout the range of what are commonly called art objects. That the scope and variety of these contrived and product-stimuli objects are extremely extensive is easily seen from their inclusion of all the decoration and embellishment added to any kind of object of common use having an æsthetic quality.

The Æsthetic Milieu    The term milieu in this exposition signifies the total general circumstances and conditions surrounding the person's development of equipment for æsthetic action, and the immediate surroundings which make æsthetic behavior possible, and influence its occurring in a particular way at a given time. So far as the personality equipment is concerned, æsthetic conduct depends upon the development of specific techniques, and in general, special æsthetic modes of behavior. Under the heading of techniques we include all of the reaction systems involving the conception of an art object and situation and the overt types of action performed in order to bring the object into existence. Further, we must consider here the personality equipment resulting primarily in the appreciatory type of æsthetic reaction, such as the development of special æsthetic discriminations and the training of perceptual reactions for complex æsthetic stimuli as over against the perception of more elementary natural objects (and other non-æsthetic objects whether complex or simple).

Nor must we ignore the development and operation of all types of affective responses which go to make up what are commonly known as the sensitivity and refinement of character which play a large part in appreciatory and creative activities of æsthetic behavior. Then we may isolate the activities that can hardly be more definitely and accurately described other than by generally referring to them as taste. To a certain extent the personality equipment we call taste is made up of the kind of reactions we have already suggested. But we should like to submit the proposition that taste constitutes a unique type of expertness and efficiency in the appreciation and construction of art objects or in general for the reaction to æsthetic stimuli. That the activities of taste are unique as over against the other reactions we have indicated, may be accepted in view of the fact that taste is not only affective and manipulative but also involves cognitive elements of various sorts. In addition, discriminations and comparisons enter into the general behavior constitution of the reactions we have denoted as taste behavior equipment. Æsthetic interest is a further type of æsthetic personality equipment which plays a large part in the general æsthetic behavior situation. By interest we mean of course a kind of curiosity and at-homeness or familiarity with æsthetic objects of all sorts. It is a type of behavior equipment that sharply differentiates the artist or æsthete from other types of individuals.

Exceedingly prominent among non-personal factors in the æsthetic milieu are the conditions and circumstances to which we may generally refer as standards. In creative functions especially individuals respond æsthetically with very direct reference to the standards of art of the particular period. The range of construction with respect to beauty stimuli is remarkably large and what particular kind of activity occurs at a given time is done with direct regard to current art standards. Marked variations from this situation exist, of course. Then we have art activity which is original and unique. But even in this instance the originality is relative. To suggest only one striking illustration, let us point out how prevalent was the religious standard governing the æsthetic products of the medieval and early Renaissance periods. This particular factor in the æsthetic situation, as we shall see, constitutes an important stimulational feature and connects up with the non-psychological condition of the æsthetic behavior situation that we will refer to later as the general human circumstances finding a part in complex behavior situations.

Art standards as stimuli for the development and functioning of æsthetic reactions likewise have their place in the appreciation of art. Here as well as in the creative case the reaction is performed with a keen regard for the prevailing art standards. As we have already implied, the phenomenon to which we refer as the art standard correlates with the circumstances we previously canvassed on the side of the personality factor of the æsthetic milieu. Let us suggest once more that it is these stimulational factors that exert a great influence upon the occurrence of æsthetic reactions. Further let us note that while the personality factors in the milieu have to do more with the technical production and actual appreciation responses to æsthetic stimuli, the non-personality factors influence more the specific kind of art product that results from the reaction and the degree of approval, disapproval, or acceptance of the specific form and pattern of æsthetic objects to which the individual reacts.

Perhaps no less important as a feature of the æsthetic milieu on the non-personal side is the large set of cultural institutions which although they are not directly æsthetic in character, nevertheless determine in a very precise manner what the nature of the æsthetic activity will be. For example, it may be a cultural or institutional stimulus for individuals of a particular group to emphasize plastic art as over against architecture; or they may perform reactions in which architectural objects constitute the æsthetic stimuli. Institutions are more specialized in their operation when the nonæsthetic factors in the milieu condition specific details of the æsthetic activities and of the objects which play a part as stimuli in the æsthetic behavior segment.

**Non-psychological Factors in Æsthetic Situations**

Non-psychological factors influencing æsthetic behavior segments consist of human circumstances of various sorts which have a general effect upon the behavior of individuals living and acting among these human conditions. At once we think of the economic situations notably modifying the æsthetic behavior of individuals and groups of persons. Plainly the appreciation of art in the case of some individual can be traced definitely to the fact that he is financially able to come into contact with art influences. As in every other psychological domain, the performance of æsthetic reactions must wait upon learning and training. Also for the same reason certain individuals can achieve the leisure to indulge in such activity and to purchase art works and in other ways put themselves in a condition for building up and performing æsthetic activities. Similarly in national groups the flourishing of æsthetic conditions and conduct parallels the rise and fall of the economic status of the group. In this connection we suggest at once a number of other conditions which influence a set of individuals composing a group. For instance the practise of æsthetic behavior is intensified or originated through contact with other groups, either through commerce, war, or some other agency for the interaction of states or nations. A quickening effect upon æsthetic behavior is likewise traceable to religious, political and other human conditions. To be added here also are the essential conditions for developing and performing æsthetic reactions. Among these conditions are the availability of objects and situations capable of stimulating æsthetic conceptions and the materials to be made into art objects of all varieties and descriptions. A study of the æsthetic behavior of various groups indicates the direct influence upon such activities of the materials to be found in the group's national or cultural surroundings.

## THE SCIENTIFIC SITUATION

Scientific behavior in its large sense occupies an extensive place in complex human life. It functions in all of the comprehensive situations involving achievement and accomplishment. Scientific behavior may be said to have its roots and its greatest function in practical issues although it represents a continuity of behavior which carries over to the most abstruse situations in the lives of individuals. In the latter case scientific conduct is not so much a matter of practical achievement as it is one of orientation among and penetration into the meanings and significance of things.

From the psychological standpoint scientific activity as distinguished from the merely rational and logical, may be considered in great measure as effective and expert sort of behavior.  In these activities the individual functions as a skilled and highly efficient manipulator and interpreter of the objects and conditions with which he is in contact.  His response relates the objects and conditions with which he is involved and brings to bear upon them other actions that have been serviceable and important in other situations.  This phase of scientific behavior constitutes what may be called the person's scientific equipment, including the corpus of information and techniques employed and found serviceable in similar previous activities.  From this standpoint we might well look upon scientific behavior as a decided outgrowth and development from simple techniques and general means of meeting conditions and resolving problems found in the everyday necessities of making satisfactory contacts with environing objects.

Viewed in such a light scientific behavior tends toward intellectual and cognitive activity, although it has its roots definitely in manipulative and practical factors.  When scientific conduct reaches a high stage of removal from practical immediate manipulations it becomes abstract, theoretical and generally orientative.  As such, it is no longer transformative and adaptational but rather contemplative and appreciative.  At every stage of the work the activity is in some sense of course abstract and removed, involving as it does intricate implicit activities.  These constitute for the most part concepts of concrete and abstract things and relations such as fit into specialized situations.  In passing it will be noticed, too, that this type of activity from a psychological standpoint is not necessarily rational or worth while.  These qualities may or may not attach to such behavior.

Following the lead of the discussion of the æsthetic situation we shall also find it expedient in this case to divide our inquiry into two divisions, one, stressing the actual scientific behavior with its two phases of the behavior segment, and the other emphasizing the consideration of the general scientific milieu that provides the conditions and circumstances making the behavior segments the particular types they are in individual cases.

Reactions of a scientific type may be differentiated into two general forms.  On the one hand, we have the technical or intrinsic responses constituting the behavior of an essentially scientific type.  On the other, there is a great mass of behavior having great influence upon technical scientific responses but which in themselves are more general and to a certain extent extrinsic. *The Scientific Behavior Segment*

Generally speaking, technical scientific activity, as we have already indicated in our general description, consists of knowledge and cognitive reactions of all sorts. Probably the mainstays of scientific conduct are intellectual responses. Certainly it is such conduct that operates in the scientific situation which is properly speaking orientative in character. Scientific behavior is carried on probably for the most part through problem solving activities and reasoning conduct. By means of these types of action adaptations are made constituting the adjustmental features of the scientific behavior situation.

It must already appear evident that scientific activity is the kind of behavior which involves the use of ideas, meanings, and knowledge as the primary tools and techniques for the manipulation of objects and the development of orientative attitudes toward them. We might also add that the person's activities in such a case constitute behavior in which the ideational tools employed are manipulative according to the specific exigencies of the situations, which means they operate in a way contingent upon the specific involved circumstances, both those on the side of the stimuli and those on the side of the capacities and scientific standing of the person. Such behavior is also performed according to general rules and formal standards which we may refer to in the aggregate as the logic of science or methodology.

The intrinsic or technical scientific responses divide themselves into two types. The first we may consider as field work. Here we have primarily observations upon phenomena which throughout the whole series of activities exist as independent objects that may be perceived through various methods by the use of all kinds of instruments such as telescopes, microscopes, etc. The ensuing reactions, therefore, are made to things which remain the same throughout the complete course of response, and the reactions accordingly consist of an attempt to become cognitively oriented with respect to them as they exist and operate in their own natural conditions and habitations. The range of such activities is very large. It runs from observations of astronomic phenomena through the study of plants and animals in their natural milieux, on up to the study of complex human conduct consisting of one's own reactions and the behavior of other individuals in personal, economic, and social circumstances.

The second type of intrinsic behavior consists of activity involving manipulation and transformation of objects in an endeavor to learn what they are, their constitution and method of existence and operation, as well as their relation to other things. Necessary for the accomplishment of such behavior are various manipulations and the use of apparatus and contrivances of all sorts in order to achieve a variety of specific purposes. Experimentation may consist of the manipulation and control of objects as a mere aid to observation. Things and processes are checked or modified in their growth and development in order that it may be made certain that the observations which have been made are valid. In other cases manipulations of the laboratory type constitute behavior designed to verify certain observations, check them up, or in other words to satisfy oneself that the observations are accurate and reliable. Still an additional type of intrinsic laboratory or experimental behavior comprises the attempt to discover which of a certain type of knowledge actually constitutes the fact in a particular case. This form of behavior involves the designing and carrying out of a crucial experiment which, when accomplished, provides the desired information.

A variation of manipulative behavior is designed to achieve the establishment of some new principle which perhaps was originally suggested by some form of accidental discovery during field observations. Such manipulations, of course, are very highly specialized and applicable to particular circumstances. The successful issue of them consists of the formation of a new principle and knowledge status with respect to some distinct kind of phenomenon.

Turning to the extrinsic or general human responses operating in scientific behavior situations we may enumerate a series of activities which occur when persons perform responses in the general scientific behavior situation. First, our attention is given to curiosity responses. Individuals performing scientific work are responding to stimuli which arouse their thirst for knowledge and require considerable manipulation before the activity is carried out to its completion. Similarly, scientific work demands many interest reactions. These prompt the individual to make various manipulations in order to carry on the interest responses with respect to the identity, function, and similarities of things as compared with other things.

Again, we may point out that scientific responses in their extrinsic form consist merely of activities which although they constitute laboring and occupational procedures and keep the individual interested and occupied, still belong to a leisure situation. The responses performed are desirable on their own account and are not irksome and compelling.

Certain scientific responses take on the nature of adventure conduct, since the various manipulations and techniques employed involve voyages of discovery, as is actually the case in geographical, ethnological, and biological expeditions, excursions into the unknown as when one's work consists of laboratory studies of objects and situations which are manipulated and transformed in the course of laboratory experimentation.

Finally we note that extrinsic scientific reactions comprise activities of personal achievement and power. Individuals perform actions which give them a grasp upon things through a greater appreciation of the nature of these things and a method of controlling phenomena through the discovery of principles which enable the individual to predict the behavior of certain things under definite particular conditions. Other scientific behavior may be mere occupational action, doing things to keep busy or make a living, while in still other scientific work the activities are indulged in as factors leading to one's superiority over other persons. Such extraneous activities as we have been pointing out here, we may add are not excluded in some form from the other types of complex behavior situations.

The stimuli for scientific behavior both of the intrinsic and extrinsic sort cover the whole range of human environment and conduct. The expert handling and orientational adjustments to stimuli include responses to all kinds of things, conditions, and circumstances. The result of such behavior is the identification and isolation of the stimuli things and conditions, the discovery, enumeration, and transforming of them, the classification or relating of them in various ways to other objects and circumstances as well as comparing and contrasting them in order to discover the likenesses and differences in their quality and of their action.

By way of characterizing the various objects eliciting specific scientific responses and their components as over against any other type of behavior we may describe scientific stimuli as possessing special qualities which bring them into the particular behavior segments of complex behavior situations. Among these qualities are the necessities of objects and situations. Objects may force themselves upon persons as being necessary for identification or control. A failure of a crop creates the necessity to have a particular kind of farm product. Thus there is a challenge to the individual to develop techniques and manipulations for the development of such a product.

Scientific stimuli also possess the quality of strikingness or unusualness. Any condition or circumstance very different from the ordinary or usual becomes at once a stimulus for the development of responses tending toward the identification and placing of these things in the general perspective of the individual's surroundings. At other times, the objects and circumstances serving as stimuli for scientific responses are problematic. Such objects have the characteristic or quality of presenting some complexity of a condition or situation which needs to be overcome or resolved. These situations baffle the need or desire of persons to control and predict such circumstances and therefore they take on the problematic quality of stimulating investigation of a scientific type. Similarly the quality of unknownness of objects and circumstances brought into the range of an individual's scientific conduct through some type of substitution stimulus provides a large scope of stimuli for scientific reactions.

**The Scientific Milieu**    Among the personalistic factors constituting the basis for scientific conduct we place first the behavior equipment of a knowledge and informational sort which makes it possible for the individual to be in touch with scientific stimuli and to perform responses with respect to them. The execution of any type of scientific work presupposes a definite status of knowledge and information on the part of the person performing such an activity. These knowledge or informational equipments constitute the most effective tools which we have already suggested as operating in scientific behavior situations. Furthermore, the effectiveness of scientific reactions depends upon the directness of the acquisition of these equipments with respect to actual situations having a likeness and similarity to the stimuli objects and conditions with which the individual is now in contact.   The personal behavior features of the scientific milieu lead to and connect with another equipmental basis for scientific reaction, namely, the interest of the individual in the character of his surroundings and the improvement of his orientational status with respect to the world in which he lives.

Next we might consider equipment of the individual to which we refer as the desire for knowledge and control over situations constituting the immediate stimuli for his scientific behavior.   Such desire of knowledge of a certain sort to a great extent constitutes the main features of what we might call a scientific personality.

It is impossible to overestimate the value of intelligence as a factor in the personalistic milieu for scientific behavior.   Whether or not an individual can perform scientific work effectively, if at all, depends upon his development and performance of intelligence behavior, both in the immediate situation or as a general quality of his personality make-up.   It is in great measure the equipment which makes for intelligent conduct that conditions the expertness and efficiency with which the scientific work is carried out.

These various equipmental conditions may be looked upon as intrinsic personalistic factors.   They do not, however, sum up all of the personalistic factors which actually exist.   Many other milieu factors of an extrinsic character always find a conditioning place in the performance of scientific behavior.   Among these may be suggested the general equipmental responses of self assertion and the characteristic of achievement and conquest.   Still others that under ordinary circumstances do not constitute such commendable conduct but which aid in the fostering of scientific work are the reactions of seeking praise and compensation for work accomplished.

Among the environmental factors of the scientific milieu we suggest first the traditions and institutions of a knowledge type.   In certain communities there exists a definite knowledge status which affords the basis for a great deal of scientific activity, in exactly the same way that traditions of a religious or æsthetic sort existing in some community condition the development and operation of much religious and æsthetic conduct.   Human individuals forming particular groups may be governed by conditions or institutions of exactness and definiteness which in turn lead to the performance of scientific conduct.   Conditioning surroundings of such nature belong to particular occupational or professional groups or to national communities.   As we have implied they determine whether scientific conduct is to be performed at all.

Additional environmental circumstances for the performance of scientific behavior are supplied by the standards of scientific achievement. These standards function as determiners of the type of scientific work to be performed, and set the pace for the kind of investigative methods that shall be utilized, both with respect to the kind of things to be investigated and the methods by which the studies shall be brought to completion. We find in certain communities especially when they are considered from the standpoint of time succession that particular materials are the standard things to be investigated. So we have physical periods in scientific work, biological periods, or humanistic and sociological epochs. In support of this notion we call attention to the fact that certain eras of human societal development are scientific periods, while others are not especially characterized by such qualities.

With respect to modes and methods of investigation, scientific work is very definitely and closely determined by methodological principles and logical rules governing such work at particular times and in particular communities. In fact these methods of investigation become standard and absolute and have great influence upon the work done even to the point of determining that certain necessary operations are not permissible because of the establishment of contrary institutions. In such a rôle investigative methods often operate as unyielding and even harmful determiners of scientific conduct. For example, at a certain time in the history of scientific behavior all work follows the standard set by an evolutionary hypothesis, a condition contrasting markedly with pre- or post-evolutionary periods. This circumstance may, as we have indicated, be either extremely salutary or detrimental for carrying on scientific behavior. The great value of the evolutionary conception for biological pursuit and all its branches is a matter of common knowledge. On the other hand, the introduction of this conception into investigations of specific human behavior and culture has not been of great advantage. In the science of psychology itself we observe how standards of investigation have conditioned the determination of scientific work for good or evil. Accordingly, as we have had occasion to indicate, the influence of standards set by chemical investigations have been responsible for the performance of responses leading to the "mental states" psychology. In another period under the influence of biological conceptions the psychological responses were concerned with the mind as a function of biological organisms.

Among the standards for scientific work are listed the ideals of simplification and complexification. During certain periods and certain types of scientific work these various standards condition the performance of scientific activities of particular types. At one time the thoughts and manipulations of science tend toward the simplification of phenomena, while at other times the data are made into as complex facts as possible.

Many are the non-psychological factors conditioning scientific work. Influences of no mean prominence are the particular methods of industrial and military circumstances which introduce particular kinds of investigative reactions and manipulations. Such factors make especially for the copious development and occurrence of scientific activities of all sorts. Other conditions of a non-psychological sort providing the possibility for the performance of scientific reactions are the conditions in which positions are created for people who can and in many cases do perform scientific work as their particular tasks. In many instances scientific work is fostered and carried out not because of scientific or social needs but because of the desire to give people work to do.

Very prominent and effective conditioning of scientific behavior by circumstances entirely non-psychological are the various influences upon the methods and subject matter of science by political and religious authorities of all sorts. The classical illustration is the interference with experimental work when the authority of the schools based upon political and social circumstances is thought to be opposed to such work.

Similar influences involve the direction which psychological responses are made to take through the influence of the system of discipleship prevalent in all human society. Many kinds of scientific work are never attempted because the masters do not approve of it and are able to control the scientific output. Thus they allow only the kind of work which can be performed by their own disciples. Anyone familiar with the political organizations and practises found in all scientific domains, whether located in academies or operating under other auspices, fully appreciates how greatly scientific reactions are conditioned and controlled by deliberate and enforced or non-deliberate and casual non-psychological (scientific) factors.

## RELIGIOUS BEHAVIOR SITUATION

Religious behavior situations [1] are unique in being the most difficult to handle. Generally speaking, the difficulty of analysis and the uncertainty of the isolation of data may be traced back to the general scientific conditions and traditions surrounding the investigation of such facts. Religious phenomena have always been sacred territory not to be trespassed upon by the curious investigator. And for the most part the study of religious phenomena has been made from the standpoint of those interested in religion as such, and not from the standpoint of students of human conduct. Fortunately the study by the anthropologist of religious institutions and the religious behavior

[1] For our purposes we consider current religious conduct. It is not our purpose to discuss the history and genesis of religious behavior nor to make a study of comparative institutions existing in some particular group or in different groups.

of more primitive civilizations constitutes a happy exception to this rule and provides us with considerable information and many valuable points of view in undertaking this kind of analysis.[1]

Whatever conditions are responsible for the present unsatisfactory status of the study of religious behavior phenomena, it is a fact that the data involved are very difficult to get at and on the whole present a formidable resistance to the inquiring student. It is safe to say that for the most part the term religion and religious phenomena represent a very complex unanalyzed mass of behavior of various types, some of which are exceedingly different from some of the others grouped under the same general categories.

In view of this general situation it is especially true in the study of religious behavior situations that our analysis must consist mostly of a separation of the various kinds of conduct and behavior conditions involved in it. To single out from its behavior matrix the genuine religious conduct is a much larger task, and perhaps a much more important one, than the attempt to describe the nature and peculiarities of religious conduct as such. To succeed in differentiating, however meagrely, the various different activities coming under the general heading of religious behavior allows us to obviate considerable controversy concerning its nature. Symbolic of the unsatisfactory confusion existing in religious studies is the fact that writers on this theme state that religion is a summary and totality of human conduct and attitudes. Such a statement, of course, when taken to mean an inevitable and unchangeable condition is nothing more than a confession of ignorance of the behavior facts in the field and the inability to work them out.

For the psychologist the guide to action is very clear. He must attempt a differentiation between characteristic types of conduct and their stimuli in order to distinguish as sharply as possible religious from non-religious behavior. Unless this differentiation is both possible and actually achieved in some sense, we cannot expect to form any scientific attitude toward any of the phenomena called religious behavior or genuine religious behavior itself. Today perhaps this attitude can at most be only a partial and tentative one.

First and foremost, religious behavior must be distinguished from *magical* conduct. The latter may be described as a series of manipulations in the form of handling objects in a particular way in order to bring about a certain result. Or various non-effective actions and verbal linguistic responses are performed as a means of accomplishing some purpose. In this case the desired results are more often than not presumed to occur through the agency of some power or potency. Magical behavior may be designed to cure some disease, as when the magician smears blood or mud on a wound and applies

[1] In this matter, as in others, the sharp distinction maintained between the so-called primitive and civilized phenomena has been restricted in overlooking important likenesses and differences between them.

to it some herb or other object.  Or, it may be the execution of a dance or fasting with the aim of introducing some change in atmospheric conditions, making it rain for example, causing the crops to grow, or a sterile woman to bear a child.  Probably it is quite unnecessary to point out that these manipulations and activities go on with a total disregard of their impotence to bring about the desired change of circumstances.  In other words, there is a gross ignorance of causes and relations in general.  On the other hand, the magical behavior may be what it is because of the ignorance on the part of the magical actor of some particular relationship involved, so that some feature of the magical action may be perfectly logical or rational but not closely related to the total result.  In this latter sense magic extends to scientific interpretations involving the most complex techniques of scientific work as when some type of action is performed which has absolutely no relationship to the results one desires to achieve.

In contrast to the magical form of behavior, religious conduct at this juncture may be said to be decidedly non-manipulative.  It is more of an activity of appreciation and adoration and when it does involve effective action the responses are manipulative only in the sense that they carry on some form of worshipping and appreciating technique.  In this worship all sorts of symbolic material may be employed.  How closely interwoven these activities sometimes are is exemplified by the fact that prayer, when it is an actual attempt to achieve something through the intermediation of some superior power, is magical in character, since praying involves an expectation that some worshipped power is of such a character as to bring about the needed or desired situation.

*Mystical* conduct is not religious.  Rather it stands out as a type of behavior in which the individual thinks or knows himself to be a part of a larger whole.  This form of action presupposes that the person looks upon himself as an isolated unit having affinities with and really belonging to some larger unit describable as the world-all, the whole, the absolute, God, the cosmos, Nature, etc.  Preëminently mystical activity is an intellectual or orientational response based upon traditional or cultural conditions although it does not exclude feeling attitudes of dependence and isolation.  As in the case of magical conduct it is not difficult to distinguish mystical action from that of worship and awe which we call religious.  Although we should not lightly pass over the similarities between these two different kinds of behavior we should at the same time recognize that such resemblances merely stress what is common to the two kinds of activity and thereby throw into relief their wide variations.

Religious conduct is not *mythological* behavior.  The latter we view as activity constituting the explanation and interpretation of natural phenomena in terms of arbitrary things and conceptions far different from those based upon objective investigations of the phenomena. It is a type of explanatory conduct which is designed to satisfy either a serious informational interest or merely a casual curiosity concerning cosmic affairs or any specialized natural phenomenon. A classic illustration is the attempt to account for the presence of fire among human beings by developing a myth about it instead of investigating the situation, or professing ignorance concerning the actual facts of the case. To a great extent mythological conduct is speculative activity, while in the same proportion it comprises the exercise of poetic activity and imagination in bringing about the adaptation of the individual to the circumstances involved. We must add, however, that mythical conduct may be practical and effective in its connection with some power which by that act is construed to exist and to have certain qualities. This means to say that mythical behavior need not be verbally explanatory but may be performed through asking something of, or promising and giving something to, some naïve personal or impersonal being. It is hardly necessary to contrast this type of behavior with the activity we have already signalized as religious conduct.

Prominent in the mélange of complex religious behavior we find an æsthetic element which must also be distinguished from the more definite religious behavior. Here as elsewhere the basis for differentiation lies in the isolation of the stimuli functions. Now while we can on this basis separate the characteristically different responses, we find that in the actual behavior of individuals the various types of conduct are intermingled. It may therefore be no easier to separate off the æsthetic from the magical or mystical actions of particular individuals.

For the psychologist, and especially under the present analytic circumstances, it may not be amiss to differentiate between genuine religious conduct and the forms of behavior frequently associated with it. Here are to be listed various formal and conventional actions such as praying, church going, persecuting, confessing, etc., which are performed as habitual responses along with the members of the religious congregation or the social groups, or as deliberate activities deemed necessary for the maintenance of one's social or business position.

From the actual religious behavior must also be kept distinct the peculiar intellectual attitudes and activities which have a distinct religious tinge. In this group of actions are placed the study and investigation of religious phenomena and religious traditions as in theology, in its branches and related subjects. While these activities are motivated by and connected with religious attitudes they are not themselves entirely religious action, though they may be considered to be extreme variants in the field of religious behavior.

Finally, religious conduct is marked off from *divination*. In this case we have a generalized activity serving functions in all types of human situations. We need only remind ourselves of all the different circumstances in which divination has a part. A general consults a seer demanding information concerning the outcome of an impending battle. A father desires to be foretold the destiny of his newly born child.  In similar fashion the seer or prophet is called upon to foretell the fate of nations or groups as a result of the immoral or unwise conduct of the people.  Such activity is found to contrast very decidedly with religious conduct.  If common factors are present in the two types it indicates no more than in other cases the intertwining of human conduct in complex behavior situations.

Having thus isolated religious phenomena from these very closely connected behavior techniques we may turn to a description of the religious behavior segment and milieu which will throw into relief the characteristic factors of such conduct.

The responses of a distinctly religious type as we might expect are very numerous and considerably detailed in form.  But, as we have indicated, the main activity centers around the actions to which we may refer as reverence, awe, and worship responses. **The Religious Behavior Segment**

By awe reactions we mean activity primarily of an affective sort. Specifically it takes the form of self belittlement and self effacement in the presence of some great force or power, some baffling or incomprehensible circumstance or situation, or a representative thereof. With respect to the reverence response we find a relationship of the individual to the stimulus, implying a distinct, highly appreciative, and exalted evaluation of the character, power, and function of the stimulating object.  The reverence reaction also contains numerous elements of an attractional or loving sort.  Worship responses may be described as propitiatory attempts to make peace and be in close harmony with the stimulus object, or to form a compact with or request something of, a higher or more powerful agent.

Probably as components of the three forms of activity we have described, though still somewhat independent activities, are the depression and exaltation activities constituting features of religious conduct.  On the one hand, the individual responds with depression and despairing behavior in the presence of overwhelming forces and powers which leave him weak and insignificant by contrast.  On the other, there is the element of exaltation or self estimation issuing from a sense of communion and commonness with the unknown and powerful stimulating forces.

Religious behavior no doubt also includes a reaction of dependence. Especially when the individual is impressed with his impotency and lack of power to bring about changes in his circumstances or to achieve certain objects which his behavior conditions require, he is induced to lean upon what he considers the strength and power of some higher agent.  Closely connected with this affective response of dependence is fear behavior.  Not infrequently a person's religious reactions are colored by an element of fear and trepidation in the presence of unknown and overwhelming surrounding powers.  To be sure, this fear is not localized, as in the case of ordinary fear of some object which one definitely knows about and the presence of which is a concrete fact. Rather, religious fear is an implicit reaction to a much larger and always a more indefinite type of thing or circumstance. Nor is this ordinarily a positive fear, such as avoiding some dangerous object, but a fear attitude based more upon the negative condition of inefficiency and lack of power to meet certain circumstances. Fears of this type answer well to what are popularly called superstitions.

A very familiar component of religious responses may be described in terms of thrill and ecstatic appreciation. The element of thrill consists mainly of the libration and palpitation arising from supposed contact with a powerful force or circumstance, or a gigantic tremendous situation. The appreciative activity or the faith response on the other hand, refers more to the realization of one's contact with some worthy and exceedingly magnificent and supreme type of object condition, or circumstance.

All these qualities and factors of the religious reaction we have been describing we consider to be intrinsic responses, that is, direct actions to actual religious stimuli. In plainer words, they are reactions to adjustment stimuli which always have to be mediated by substitutions of various sorts. These substitute stimuli are ordinarily common circumstances or frustrations of all sorts, misfortunes, and on the other hand acts of heroism, or sublime or magnificent scenery among a vast host of other things.

Quite different are the extrinsic components of religious reaction those features contributory and additional to the strictly religious response. These activities are directed toward the substitution objects that take on some of the stimulus function of the truly religious objects. Description here fails us somewhat, but we may point to the activities of solemnity, hushedness and abashedness made in the presence of the unknowable and in the quiet and beauty of the temple or cathedral, or to the various feeling responses which they inspire the worshipping and awed individual to perform. Sometimes these extrinsic reactions may be thought of as genuine religious responses that have become conditioned by the substitute stimuli for the adjustment religious stimuli. In part also we look upon them as additional actions induced in the individual on the basis of an anticipation and preparation of the actual religious responses that are somewhat in abeyance because of the absence of the adjustment stimulus and the consequent necessity to substitute for it. Generally speaking, the distinction here issues from the different methods by which the religious stimuli come into play. The difference between the intrinsic and extrinsic religious reactions therefore is a result of the particular medium which the individual adopts to bring himself into contact with his religious stimuli.

Religious responses, both of the extrinsic and intrinsic types, are further distinguished on the basis of whether they are primarily individual or cultural in character. The former are derived from more personal and individual contacts with various types of objects and human conditions stimulating religious responses. Cultural religious reactions, on the other hand, are elicited by stimuli that are based upon very definite institutional circumstances and in general conditions that are independent of an individual's personal contact with things. Cultural religious reactions stress, therefore, the behavior which the individual acquires through a process of culturalization. Reactions of such a nature are not so intimate and personal although in other qualities and respects they are precisely like all other religious types of conduct. Probably our distinction can be made more explicit by adding that on the whole the individual type of religious reaction represents a higher degree of behavior. For such conduct is generally more deliberate and involves a more profound appreciation on the part of the individual of what his behavior means and signifies. Such conduct, however, may be entirely beyond the control of the person in both cases, but on the other hand, the individual behavior is always more likely to be somewhat more reflective and deliberative and less automatic and blind than cultural religious action. Moreover religious conduct of the individual type is less tied up with cult and ritual and thus not so extensively involved with dogma and myth and more connected with a free and spontaneous expression of an individual's attitudes in the presence of unknown and majestic forces and conditions.

As we should expect, the stimuli for religious conduct comprise decidedly unusual and extraordinary circumstances and objects. Especially is this true for the adjustment stimuli that are all important and more markedly different from the substitute stimuli operating in conjunction with them than in non-religious situations. Religious reactions are made to incomprehensible forces and conditions met with in human behavior, such as death, the helplessness of man in the face of nature and other like circumstances. These qualities accrue to objects and conditions which baffle individuals and transcend their ability to handle and understand them. The exact nature of these qualities differs, of course, with different individuals. In many cases such characteristics are ascribed to situations and conditions not really possessing them. In this manner adjustment stimuli become created through the activities of the individual who is in contact with objects and circumstances he does not know and which, as a result, have an untoward influence upon him. The projected qualities of things, therefore, take on stimulational functions eliciting worshipping and awing responses.

Objects and circumstances constituting the adjustment stimuli, once they come into the reactional environment of the individual, are named in various ways. Conventional terms suggest themselves, God, the Sacred, the Divine, the Absolute, the All, the Unknowable, etc. When not couched in impersonal terminology as forces, powers, etc., these adjustment stimuli are conceived of in personal

terms after the manner of human beings, activities, and conditions.

To further our investigative study of religious conduct and at the
same time enlighten its character we must dwell on the frustration
and balking of individuals in carrying on their schemes of life. The
inability to achieve what one desires and the thwarting of knowledge
easily lead to reactions to higher powers which we call responses of
awe, fear, and worship. In many instances these responses drift
into an appreciation of fate or an overwhelming and superhuman
force or power supposed to govern and control all the circumstances
surrounding individuals. Again, in what is perhaps a higher form of
religious conduct, the frustration activity terminates in a conception
of a stream of external and permanent values existing in the universe
and constituting the essence and significance of seen and unseen
powers, forces, and objects.

Quite apparent are the stimuli for religious conduct comprising
actual and natural objects, such as persons and things to which are
ascribed qualities and conditions calling out typical religious conduct. In these cases we have a close coincidence between adjustment and substitution stimuli. Sufficiently illustrative of this type of
religious stimuli are the parents and other persons who are worshipped and reverenced as the typical objects functioning in religious
life.

**The Reli-
gious
Milieu**
Among the personalistic traits and conditions favorable for the
operation of religious conduct we note a strong inclination toward
affective conduct and in general toward the type of equipment characterizing the individual as tender-minded and sensitive to his surroundings. Religious conduct rests clearly upon a general equipmental foundation of pliant and yielding traits. The individual who
is all reliant and full of extreme self confidence is much less likely to
be impressed by his natural circumstances, to the point of developing
reactions of awe and worship to them. Not that we can draw hard
and fast lines here. But certainly within limits we can make distinctions between types of equipment which are or are not fertile
ground for the acquisition and performance of religious responses.
For example, the more self-reliant individual who is still sensitive
to the world about him, may indeed perform religious conduct, but
it is probably of the primarily cultural sort which is accepted entirely
on the basis of culturalization stimuli.

From the standpoint of an individual's reactional biography, on
the whole, the religious person is recruited from those individuals
who have been in contact with such circumstances and conditions of
life as to have made them sensitive to the shortcomings and frailties
of themselves and other individuals, as well as to the deficiencies in the
human circumstances and natural conditions around them.

In the milieu of religious conduct we find cultural and traditional
forces operating more strongly than in any of the other complex be-

havior situations. This is due of course to the fact that here we do not have reactions to natural phenomena but to contrived cultural circumstances. This situation varies, as we have already pointed out, with the complexity of the individual and the responses he performs. Accordingly religious behavior is very much influenced by the presence in the person's group of institutions that have an influence upon religious activity. The existence of strong religious traditions in an individual's behavior milieu more often than not determines that person's type of religious conduct. In certain communities the economic and industrial situation is such that there is little left in the form of a thoroughgoing religious attitude or conduct. What religion there may be is strongly bound up with some of the other types of human behavior situations we have been delineating.

On the other hand, the individual's behavior milieu may possess great possibilities for the building up and performing of religious conduct of the more genuine and typical sort. This latter type of human surroundings is less stable and certain in character and allows greater play for the development of religious adaptations. Genuine religious attitudes and practises flourish in situations where economic, social and political life is discordant and disturbed. In non-spiritual communities religion comes down to a crude sophisticated attitude and sentiment of blindly accepting faith because it probably pays, and because on the whole it has a favorable influence upon one's personal achievement and success.

Environing conditions and influences upon religious behavior coincide very closely with non-psychological factors. It is therefore very difficult to make sharp distinctions between the two. In general, however, we may consider non-psychological factors to be the general geographic and economic circumstances that are at the basis of a complex, industrial and highly artificial mode of living. Under such auspices religion in only a crude and practical form is possible. Since specific descriptions of these general non-psychological conditions are scarcely possible, we can only point out that in general they comprise the impersonal and general circumstances surrounding religious behavior situations. *Non-Psychological Factors in Religious Situations*

A more personal and perhaps more specific type of non-psychological influence upon religious conduct involves the isolation of an individual, such that he either finds himself more drawn toward religious stimuli or less so. Being securely placed as a member of some human community may mean that he will thereby conform to prevalent religious activity in a docile and unreflective way. On the other hand, the sense of isolation possibly has the opposite effect. The secure individual may not need any contact with or protection of unseen forces or powers, and thus does not perform religious behavior. A still more particular type of human condition influencing religious conduct is the actual help one receives in a practical manner or the spiritual guidance resulting from contact with a church or a priest who is present under all circumstances to provide the needed sympathy and advice.

### THE ETHICAL BEHAVIOR SITUATION

The isolation and description of the psychological conduct involved in moral behavior situations are not much less difficult to achieve than in the previous types. In essaying, then, the discovery of what is of interest to the student of psychology in the moral situation we find it expedient first to distinguish sharply between conduct that is sheerly customary behavior and activity having a distinct moral flavor. In other words, we must determine what are the minimum characteristics that distinguish moral conduct situations from other types of human phenomena. Generally speaking, we mean by the moral situation those activities of the person which are performed in direct relation to standards of right and wrong. Moral conduct is behavior involving the good or the evil, as distinguished from the merely approved and the bad or harmful.

It is manifest also that we are concerned only with the intimate behavior of a particular person and not with the status of certain conduct rigorously determined to be a condition of right or wrong or in accordance with a proper standard of good and evil. Our study is one of individual morality only, and not of situations constituting reflections upon and logical determinations of what is an appropriate code of moral behavior. Not that a person's behavior is absolutely independent of such rationally determined codes but from the psychological standpoint we are only interested in the actual activities performed. The right and wrong or good and evil must always refer to some particular action which involves the determination of what to do, or how one's activity is connected with the standard so that it may afterwards be judged as having been correctly determined and properly performed.

Further to specify ethical psychological action we may distinguish between genuine moral conduct and the activity of performing an approved or disapproved response. In the determination of whether an action is or is not a moral response the criterion of whether the indivdual is to be praised or blamed for his action is not a valid method of judgment. The moral reaction is simply the response made upon the basis of an ought or ought-not standard and is entirely independent of whether it is approved or disapproved, or even whether or not it is a desirable type of action.

**The Ethical Behavior Segment** In essence the response of a moral situation consists of a final reaction performed after deliberation. In other words, the moral response is always a voluntary action of a special and typical sort. Moral conduct, then, on the response side comprises activities the performance of which must be decided upon with direct consideration of right and wrong or it must be determined whether or not an act should be performed at all, or whether it is proper or improper action in view of the particular circumstances.  Such a behavior pattern involves considerable intellectual and choice behavior as precurrent to the final response performed.  In performing such actions of course, the individual makes use of a great many component activities in the sense that he must be aware of the situations and circumstances involved.  He must know or be oriented to those circumstances to the point of having some expertness in judging situations.  Again the morally acting person performs a considerable amount of thinking and problem solving conduct.  All of this means that the individual must be cognitively responsible and effective in his behavior both with respect to the particular activities to be performed and to the standards of action governing him in the present situation.

Moral behavior patterns may be of the most complex and intricate type of voluntary behavior that occurs.  And yet in every case we may consider it to consist of the elements of voluntary conduct.  No matter to what complexity moral conduct attains, it may be summed up in terms of intellectual thinking, problem solving, and reasoning action with some sort of final response which constitutes the consummation of the behavior pattern.  It must be added that moral conduct described as we have been indicating, constitutes what might be called the technical and intrinsic features which, however, as human facts or features of a complex human behavior situation, must not be considered to be more important than the anguish, suspense, and general suffering-affective conduct that has a prominent and perhaps a predominant place in many complex moral behavior situations.

Only when we consider the comparatively simple and unimportant problems in human life, can we think of a voluntary behavior situation as consisting of the technical responses of deciding, choosing, and then performing some consummatory activity.  Recall only some important situation involving a series of grave consequences to an individual and our description of the moral conduct must include a great series of affective reactions which in many cases cover a great portion of the catalogue of affective behavior.  Without having before us a particular case, we cannot offer a more detailed description of the affective responses which occur.  At this point the student of psychology must avail himself of the help offered us by literary artists in depicting the crucial, soul stirring dramas of moral conflict and human incompatibilities.

Stimuli for moral conduct are for the most part situations of various sorts.  Depending upon the complexity of the circumstances in which these stimuli play a part they are more or less complex and involve greater or lesser consequences for the person performing the behavior.  On the whole the simpler stimuli situations arousing moral conduct involve various non-personal conditions and circumstances.  Typical of such comparatively simple stimuli are the problems as to how much money or time should be devoted to a particular cause, whether one should enter into some kind of contract, accept some sort of position, or move to a particular place. In such situations certain consequences or conditions define the alternatives, and force a deliberation resulting in a voluntary performance of some sort of behavior.

Naturally, the more complicated moral behavior situations involve persons and personal relations as stimuli. Common examples are all the situations in which the reactor has contracted some kind of obligation with respect to an individual or toward persons in contact with whom one is expected to perform some sort of behavior, or from whom some kind of right or return obligation is claimed. As combinations of personal and non-personal situations we might propose the conditions which may be called temptations and enticements.

**The Moral Behavior Milieu**

As we should expect, the personal factors having a place in moral situations are exceedingly numerous and intricate. The great complexity and importance of ethical conduct and the extensive differences in the actual operation of types of such behavior bespeak a complexity on the part of the equipment of the individuals performing such activity, and innumerable resulting individual differences. Accordingly, it is possible to enumerate a series of facts concerning behavior equipment and their effect on moral conduct. A typical moral behavior equipment contains an ample degree of knowledge and information with respect to one's obligations and rights in particular situations. In addition the individual possesses knowledge of various kinds of situations in which moral problems arise and which call for deliberation and choice. Furthermore, we must consider here the equipmental factors comprising likes, tastes, intelligence and other intellectual attitudes toward circumstances. Especially requisite for such behavior are various equipmental traits describable as expertness in understanding human situations, and the capacity to withstand social pressure, as well as stamina necessary in analyzing conditions and situations in the presence of urgent and overwhelming needs to act promptly. Not to be ignored also are equipmental qualities and traits comprising inhibitions and suppressions of conduct when necessitated by specific circumstances.

A personal factor taking a prominent place in the milieu of moral behavior situations is the individual's reactional biography. Especially must due regard be given to the practise the person has had in the performance of moral conduct. This means not only experience in performing deliberative and choice responses to moral stimuli but also the training the individual has undergone in making judgments, choices, reasoning and problem solving reactions of all sorts in general human situations.

With direct view to the appreciation of the individual's performance of moral conduct on the basis of some level, we must consider the culturalization processes through which he has passed. Thus, according to his culturalization the conditions of his moral behavior are determined, its complexity and general character, in the sense of whether it represents a high type of human activity, or functions on a very simple plane of human interaction. Despite the fact that moral conduct in its essential nature is idiosyncratic and operates on the basis of an independent consideration of the involved circumstances and an expertness of analyzing and appreciating the consequences to ensue, still the moral behavior situation is replete with institutional factors. No matter how idiosyncratic and independent an individual's moral conduct, it nevertheless must go on in a very definite human situation. It is clear that our present point concerns the existence of the standards and foundations of right and wrong, of good and evil, which constitute the criteria and the determiners of what particular acts should take place at some specific time in a given human situation. It is impossible that individuals should be insensitive to the general trend of environing establishments which imply what is right and wrong. The question even arises in a moral behavior situation as to the existence of any kind of right or wrong. In other words, it is questioned whether or not a certain situation can be a moral one at all in view of the presence or absence of a criterion for the determination of whether one ought or ought not to do a certain act. Now while this criterion of right or wrong is, to a great extent, a development and projection of one's own personal experience, it is nevertheless tremendously influenced by current standards historically developed in the acting individual's environment. For instance, in a milieu in which a monogomous union of the sexes does not prevail, questions of faithlessness cannot arise between two particular individuals. Also in situations in which private property is not a cultural establishment the individual cannot perform conduct involving the determination of when he should or should not appropriate for himself certain objects.

In contradistinction to the other complex types of behavior we have been describing, the suggestions for non-psychological influences and circumstances in moral behavior situations are more easily made. As a rule it is quite readily appreciated that the presence or absence of land and water courses and objects of various sorts alter complex ethical situations. Likewise the presence or absence of persons, the smallness or largeness of a particular group and the existence in it of certain persons with particular functions offer a fertile situation for the performance of action based on right and wrong standards.

*Non-Psychological Factors of Moral Behavior Situations*

## THE ECONOMIC BEHAVIOR SITUATION

So much of the behavior of human beings is concerned with making a living and so many of the interests of persons have direct bearing upon their economic crises and circumstances, that it is extremely difficult to mark off an economic situation from any other situation of complex behavior. This predicament has led to various erroneous ideas concerning the basis and influence of economic life upon all of the other kinds of circumstances having to do with human living.

So far as we are concerned, of course, the economic features and circumstances of any complex human situation are only a part or phase of the total human predicament. Each separate phase must be considered as a partial feature only of the total behavior complex and for investigative purposes must be isolated and analyzed out in order to aid the designs of observation and description. Not only are the economic circumstances of human life inextricably interwoven with other types of activity and in many cases predominant over them, but, because they are so prominent a feature of practically all forms of human society, we find that their specific psychological factors are so varied that mere enumeration of them would entail an enormous task and probably could not be satisfactorily accomplished at all. It is not for us to forget that a psychological fact must be thought of as a very distinct and unique form of interaction of an individual with a particular kind of stimulus object or situation. Now if we permit ourselves to consider certain types of action found in some particular society as the psychological paradigm we should of course introduce a serious error into our thinking. What is an economic psychological behavior complex in a white industrial civilization has no parallel probably in some simple form of black society in which even agricultural conduct is not essential and accordingly lacking.

The statement of the difficulties is tantamount to the description of economic behavior. We may add, therefore, that in contradistinction to the religious, scientific, æsthetic and moral situations that we have already attempted to delineate, the economic activities lack practically all characteristics of individuality and personal detail in performance. Economic conduct is most intricately fused with cultural and social facts, including of course economic circumstances of a statistical sort. To differentiate, then, the psychological behavior features is enormously difficult. Furthermore economic behavior is distinguished by its intermixture with many non-psychological facts. This is not to deny of course that distinctly psychological economic activities exist. Nevertheless the task of extracting them from their common human matrix is an unenviable task.

At this point we must make the most of the conception of type action which has explicitly or implicitly been featured so much during the course of our entire description and general handling of psychological phenomena. When we come to economic activities we cannot get into any kind of close connection with the specific detailed responses occurring. Acordingly they must be handled in the form of suggested types. The problem of isolation grows so acute that the bounds of scientific description become strained to the uttermost. Since the conceptualized handling of responses is prevented by their thorough interfusion with the general complexes comprising the situations in which they occur, our only resort is to an abstract form of pointing to such responses or making referential suggestions, rather than of offering any sort of thoroughgoing description.

To point out all these difficulties as we have said is a positive form of description of such conduct. In no sense is the statement of the recalcitrancy of these phenomena an apology for any incompleteness of analysis or insufficiency of description. Rather it is a positive attempt to focus attention upon the character of a particular type of psychological phenomena and to demonstrate the utter futility of attempting to achieve a quick and easy psychological solution of economic problems. If it is so difficult even to distinguish the psychological from the other features certainly one cannot discover any simple psychological principles to account for the existence of economic phenomena whether of a behavior type or some sort of statistical fact.[1]

A safe if not satisfactory methodological suggestion for carrying out our present purpose is to shift the scene of our inquiries from the infinitely complex circumstances of present industrial civilization, to the simpler types of human situations where economic conduct is less intricate. It has already been implied that this procedure will in no sense mean a simplification of the facts of the case. It will merely make possible the isolation of a few typical psychological facts and their relation to other facts in the behavior complex. The results will be applicable to more complex situations by the simple process of multiplication.

Responses classified as features of economic behavior situations may be further subdivided into a series of type forms having special reference to particular phases of the economic life of human individuals. These types may be denominated as ownership or acquisitive conduct, saving or retentive behavior, making and producing of articles necessary for self maintenance and the carrying on of various play and worship activities, the exchange or barter, use or consumption reactions, and transport and delivery conduct. All of these are maintenance activities in the sense that they provide oneself and others with food, clothing, shelter, and the objects and processes necessary for carrying on the domestic, aesthetic, and religious behavior of human existence.[2]

*The Economic Behavior Segment*

Under the heading of ownership and acquisition, and saving and retention behavior situations are included all of the various responses which have to do with the specific manipulation of objects and the performance of processes which stress the accumulative storing up, preserving, and defending of objects and things one requires or desires

[1] How much less possible is it to discover psychic principles such as instincts to account for the dissatisfactions in industry and the more definite phenomena such as strikes and labor wars.

[2] In making these abstractions we may still avoid the kind of simplified thinking which reduces the intricate and involved behavior of human individuals to simple activities of biological organisms.

for certain occasions and purposes.  It is clear that we have before
us a series of activities possessing no distinctness of description or continuity of action except as they fall into the general human scheme of
carrying on what we call economic activities.  Precisely what the individual does in the form of specific reaction systems in performing
this behavior depends upon the time, place, circumstances, and persons
involved.  Although no further specification of what occurs is possible, we may reiterate once more that so far as our psychological study
is concerned we must confine ourselves to the intimate personal responses made to specific things with which the individual is interacting.  How exceedingly varied are the specific behavior segments and
reaction systems performed by the individual in an economic situation is easily conjectured when we recall all the various planning and
problem solving activities necessary for making and defending the
accumulation of objects, the inhibition of activities which would les-
sen or reduce the store, all of the evaluating activities representing
and distinguishing objects that should or should not be added to the
accumulation, as well as the scheming and stealing necessary to make
the collection.

In a similar manner we include under the heading of work and play
all of the performances and manipulations that are unified by their
inclusion in the economic situation.  In this class fall the activities
pertaining to agriculture and industrial processes, the digging of
ground, the ensnaring of water and land animals, and their preparation, the acts of making pottery, bowls, and other containers for the
preparation and storage of food, the making of instruments and tools
of every description and the performance of all kinds of work in the
form of personal action directly involved in food getting, clothes, shelter, and instrument making, whether for barter or use.

The term exchange we use to represent all the necessary or unnecessary activities for exchanging either products or one's services.  A
large number of different human reactions suggest themselves.  Exchange behavior involves an enormous number of activities involving
the sheer transfer of things, the development of schemes to induce
others to trade with one upon one's own terms, the persevering conduct occurring in the attaining of advantages or preventing one from
sustaining some disadvantage, the activities of announcing and advertising one's goods and their merits, and the ceremonials of all degrees of elaborateness which have a place in the economic conduct
primarily concerned with the exchange of things.  The complexity
and specific character of these activities of course vary enormously
when the exchange is of articles immediately desirable and useful or
when it is a matter of achieving advantage and increasing one's own
store and accumulation.

On the side of use and consumption we have an infinite series of
specific types of responses pertaining first to the desires, wants, and
needs of individuals for particular things, and their consumption and

employment when attained, in addition to the specific processes of preparing and apportioning objects with respect to one's different periods of use and on the basis of the distribution among the members of one's household or economic unit. It is at this juncture in economic activities that we have a great series of connections and complications of economic responses with others of an æsthetic, moral, and religious type.

Our enumeration would scarcely be complete without mentioning the acts, processes, and manipulations necessary for moving or transporting oneself and one's goods in the course of bringing about a better set of relations between oneself and stimuli objects and situations. Without taking into consideration specific instances and types of culture, it is impossible to give any further specification of the responses involved here but we need only suggest the different media, such as land, water and air in which this transporting behavior occurs.

As our analysis has forewarned us, the stimuli for economic responses do not lend themselves to a precise specification of their nature because of their commonness and pervasiveness. The only alternative is to repeat the names of objects and situations which have already been suggested in the discussion of economic responses. We may add, nevertheless, that the stimuli for economic conduct consist of objects of all types and varieties, especially those that assume specific human qualities and functions. For instance, objects in nature, as well as persons, take on specific economic functions regardless of their original natural properties, structures, and relationships. The same thing may be said for events and circumstances of all types. Situations and circumstances primarily developed and built up as play, æsthetic, political, or moral conduct may through the activities of individuals take on an economic function in the same way, of course, that original economic activities and objects assume play and religious functional capacity for stimulating conduct of a religious or play type.

It is probably needless to suggest that the stimulational functions in economic situations attain to various degrees of complexity. Exceedingly prevalent especially in more complicated types of economic behavior are substitutional stimuli of all sorts, as well as all kinds of universal, individual and cultural, adequate and partial, endogenous and exogenous, unit, constellation, and serial stimulation of innumerable varieties.[1]

The milieu factors which first take our attention center in the personality features. Economic conduct has its roots in the various types of behavior equipments of the acting individuals. Immediately suggestive are one's various capacities and skills, capacities to enjoy, to produce and to trade, skills of making, developing, and generally manipulating things having close connection with the production of various objects, and the modification of economic circumstances.

*The Economic Behavior Milieu*

[1] Cf. Volume I, pp. 49 ff.

The equipments of the individual which comprise avarice, envy, and other similar responses condition the performance of various kinds of economic behavior and the energy with which such activities are carried out. Likewise, fears, apprehensions and trepidations as behavior traits of the individual play a not insignificant part in the function of that person's economic conduct and especially of the acquisitive and accumulative types. The development of industrial arts in practically every type of economic behavior situation sufficiently indicates the rôle that the æsthetic equipment assumes in the carrying on of economic activities.

Exceedingly important in the milieu on the personalistic side is the general reactional biographies of individuals. Not only do we find a basis here, as everywhere, for the development of personality equipment but in the previous performance by the individual of contingential behavior we find an influence upon present economic conduct. Whether one has observed or experienced comforts and plenty or has known nothing but want and penury, conditions the kind of behavior he is now willing or urged to perform in the economic domain.

On the non-personalistic side a tremendous importance attaches to economic institutions as factors in and determiners of economic behavior of all varieties. If a particular group does not have institutions of saving and private property there is present an entirely different kind of economic conduct than if such institutions did exist. For example, the existence of such institutions means that appropriation of economic objects may be brought about by stealing as well as by the laborious manipulations involved in construction. Whether one is diligent in the performance of economic responses has much to do with the presence of the institution of the equal or unequal distribution of the economic objects and functions in the particular group. The existence of personal or industrial slavery as an acknowledged or unacknowledged economic institution in a certain group exercises considerable effect on the number, quality, and types of economic activity which prevail, in addition to the fact that they determine whether the activities will be purely economic or intertwined with aesthetic and religious factors. Our list of suggestions may be extended by the addition of style or fashion institutions in any group. These constitute exceedingly rapid modifications of standards of work, dress, and eating, etc., and cause wide variation in the amount and quality of work, transportation, and the use of things and processes constituting economic objects. Lastly, the existence of monopolies, whether or not permitted and avowed, as well as economic organization in the form of trade or workers' guilds, exert a tremendous influence upon the course and quality of economic conduct of every description.

**Non-Psychological Factors in Economic Behavior Situations**

Probably in none of the complex behavior situations is there precisely the same medley of natural and human circumstances playing a part as in the economic. Natural circumstances and phenomena of varied types are interconnected with human facts of organization, number, and size of groups as parts or features of general situations properly denominated economic for our purposes. So interrelated are these different types of fact that more frequently than not it is difficult to separate them for investigative purposes.

To start with simple natural phenomena, we might take into account the geological and geographical conditions of the group in which the individual lives. We must consider the presence of minerals and other sub-soil resources, also the actual character of the soil, as well as the topographic features of the country. Closely related to such natural features is the presence or absence of water, rivers, lakes, or ocean, the proximity to desert regions or to fertile plains. Of indispensable consideration in this connection is the flora and fauna of the particular location where the behavior transpires. Somewhat different types of natural phenomena are the sudden changes and modifications occurring in the environment of individuals, such as fires, floods, earthquakes, cyclones and other untoward or advantageous influences modifying human behavior.

Among the distinctly human circumstances having their share in the total complex economic situation are changes and modifications in the natural conditions surrounding the individual. The development of water courses, roads, railways, and inventions of all sorts for the tilling of soil and travelling are human efforts of a distinctly economic character. Also may be added those circumstances centering around migrations, military movements, conquests, and changes in control of resources. Likewise fitting into the general economic behavior situation are the quite different circumstances comprising historical and statistical facts closely related to institutions but still either independent, or at the basis of, such institutions. The significance of such cultural phenomena as the existence of tools and implements for various purposes is illustrated by the importance of machine development in economic behavior and in fact the general psychological circumstances of human beings. Not to be excluded here either are historical monopolies, ownerships, the preëmption and domination of natural resources, and the general conditions and circumstances having a central place in all human economic behavior situations.

Our studies in the present chapter constitute a reaffirmation of the principle that we must abjure simplification when it interferes with the descriptive functions and interests of psychology. If, as is practically always the case, the psychologist meets with exceedingly complex data, he should not ignore them in order to confine his domain to simple phenomena capable of statement in abstract terms, or describable as abstractions. This proposition is plain when it means merely that in order to make his work significant, the psychologist must treat complex behavior which is really the essential content of human psychology. But it really means more; it means that the psychologist must study such complex phenomena in conjunction and contrast with the complex non-psychological situations in which they always occur. Our chief perspectival note consists in pointing out the almost complete failure of psychologists to honor this prescription.

In mitigation of this circumstance we may say that both of these activities were impossible to carry out prior to the development of an objective viewpoint in psychology. Only when psychological phenomena are conceived of as actual responses to stimuli can simple and complex activities be studied and described as similar phenomena differing only in degree of complexity. Even the most complex behavior of human organisms may be investigated as partial phenomena belonging to a large human setting exactly as the simpler conduct belongs to smaller human settings or perhaps simpler or animal situations. As a matter of fact, even simple human phenomena are hardly different in the reactional details of organisms than are the most complex. The difference lies more in the participation of the organism and its behavior in higher and more intricate situations.

Under these circumstances we may consider as one of the merits of this analysis of complex behavior phenomena the methodological lesson it gives us concerning the value of analysis in all psychological situations. To follow out such an analysis even with a comparatively simple reaction such as color discrimination would add much to our enlightenment concerning that type of action. For example we could distinguish the strictly discriminative features, consisting of the interaction between the organism and the object, from the specific physiological changes in the organism. Both of these could then be set off from the physical phenomena of radiation and from the mechanical, electromagnetic and other properties and conditions of the stimulus object. Again, all of these various psychological, physical, and physiological facts could be analyzed from the standpoint of the influences upon them of other physical, physiological and psychological factors. At present it is safe to say that, howsoever well some of these phases are now known, their understanding would thus be enhanced, and the appreciation of the total set of activities as a psychological datum would be for the first time mastered.

Let us turn to another illustration of psychological analysis which must add to our general acumen in matters of human behavior. This time we consider a type of action which must be analyzed out of a series of different human situations in order that its true character be made known to us. Such an example we find in the laughter response. Instead of assuming that laughing is a simple form of action occurring under various circumstances we find through this analytical procedure that it is really a function of the situations in which it happens. Thus there are many types of different actions with perhaps a surface identity in organic components comprised under the single term laughter. There is the laughing response to an incongruous object which is a very different action than the one performed to the dissimilar stimulus of being tickled. The stimulation for the latter action involves both physiological sensitivity of the skin and a cultural factor. Now it is only the latter quality of the stimulus which is in any sense comparable with that of the incongruous stimulus object. Laughter is also a reaction built up as a defense adaptation against ridicule or frustration. Then there is another kind of laughter response which involves reciprogenic interpersonal stimulation and occurs in mutual enjoyment situations. In this kind of action we should distinguish the delight factor from that stimulated by a non-personal stimulus object. And finally we may mention the kind of laughter which one wittingly or unwittingly performs to please some other person, sometimes for an ulterior purpose of one's own.

Of the extant literature concerning the behavior of complex human situations, we must make the same assertions as we do for many of the much simpler responses. Namely, our descriptions are patterned more after the work of literary artists and anthropologists than the analyses of anatomists and physicists. This is not because the latter have no jurisdiction over complex human phenomena but rather because their descriptions fall short of the minimum complexity necessary for the identification and interpretation of such multiplex data.

# CHAPTER XXX

ABNORMAL REACTIONS AND PSYCHO-
PATHIC PERSONALITIES

The Prob-
lem of Re-
actional
Abnor-
mality

An almost inevitable concurrence with the fact of extreme variability in human behavior is the presence of reactional abnormality
and psychopathological personalities. Concomitant with the circumstance that no two people are precisely alike or perform exactly the
same sorts of reactions there exists the fact that some individuals and
their reactions are beyond the range of desirable or reactionally effective limits. Let us recall that all human actions are dependent
upon so many specific factors that they differ enormously in various
particulars. At the source of this variability lies of course the fact of
individual differences in personality equipment. No two people, as
we have seen in our study of personality, can have precisely the same
set of reactional equipments. Furthermore, for the same individuals
particular contacts with immediate surrounding conditions are
fraught with a great many possibilities of reactional variations.

Now it is these constant variations in reactional performance that
lead us to envisage the more compelling problems of abnormality. So
extreme are such variations that there is much miscarriage and futility
of behavior. Individuals are not able to do the things they desire, or
to perform actions that are expected of them nor are they able to meet
conditions and circumstances which constantly surround them or
periodically arise in their various interactions with persons and
things.[1] Every day we see how ineffective and even hopeless some
persons are in attempting to make adjustments to their surroundings. Worse still, if possible, is the fact that a great many persons
are not only unable to orient themselves satisfactorily or to shoulder
their behavior responsibilities with success, but their very existence
is miserable and exceedingly irksome. Persons exhibiting such unadaptable reactions we may classify as psychopathological.

Just here an extreme difficulty arises. As long as we remain content to handle abnormality as a vague, general, and practical problem
all is smooth sailing, but when we attempt to define strictly and
describe exactly what constitutes an abnormal reaction and a pathological personality in any given situation, the entire matter becomes
exceedingly difficult. Especially is this true when we try to make
our determination on a strictly psychological basis and not upon a
conventionally social or moral standard.

[1] The types of behavior treated in this chapter are primarily then the reactions
which are distinguished for their ineptness and disserviceability rather than for
their superiority or supernormality or for their mere singularity.

Furthermore, as long as we take obvious cases in which we have a failure of adaptation, such that the person endangers his own life or that of others, we have a fairly definite pathological criterion. When we consider instances, however, with less obvious harm observable to the acting individual or to others, the question of abnormality is not so easily settled since in that case we have no such simple definable condition. Criteria of violence and destruction, for example, apply only to extreme cases but do not help at all for diagnosis of slighter abnormalities. And here we find that the answer to the question of what kind of action constitutes an abnormal one, and what kind of personality is normal, depends upon whatever specific criterion one adopts. On the whole, it is true of human situations that the criterion of abnormality is never an absolute or fixed one but must be considered as entirely arbitrary except from the standpoint of a particular interest. Such is no less the case, we wish to point out, even when the simple problem of biological maintenance or survival forms the basis of our standard of abnormality, for in that instance one must assume that maintenance itself is always a valuable or desirable circumstance.

Still further to complicate the problem of a standard for pathological conduct arises the consideration that even when we do accept the mere failure of maintenance as a criterion, it still gives us no satisfactory basis for determining who is abnormal. For not every condition that constitutes a failure of maintenance for one individual need be even as much as an unusual or disturbing condition for another, since some individuals may be and frequently are, able to make particular compensations. In other words, abnormality is decidedly an individual matter. Again, what is an abnormality for one person need not be so for another because the reactional biography of each individual makes necessary entirely different kinds of conduct. Certainly in the matter of variation psychological science must concern itself with individuals. The closer we keep to unique particularized phenomena, the nearer we are to actual facts. Thus since each individual necessarily represents a variation from every other individual, it is by no means an easy task to separate off one person from another in order to call him normal, even if his reactions are decidedly exaggerated from the standpoint of some other person.

For the more practical purpose than a scientific understanding of extreme reactional variations we find criteria established which are based upon certain conventional standards. These standards in the final analysis practically involve the more or less serious failure of the person to adapt himself to social and general human conditions. Now, while these standards have no fundamental scientific foundation, criteria of abnormality have to be adopted because of the harmful and destructive character of many of the abnormal reactions. While facing the general problem of behavior standards it may be well to consider briefly some of the practical determinations of what constitutes abnormality.

In the forefront of such conventional criteria we find the standard of the medical tradition which is based upon the inability of the person to carry on his biological functions and to participate in the ordinary economic processes. Then there is the standard of the lawyer who is likewise forced to attend to the extreme variations of behavior, because in many cases is involved the person's liability for acts resulting in his own injury and that of others, as well as the destruction of property. Again, the sociologist establishes a criterion for abnormal conduct on the basis of the failure of the individual to adapt himself to social requirements. Without doubt all of these undesirable circumstances of the individual may be involved in what we call abnormal conduct.

However, as we have already indicated, none of these criteria is based upon definite and accurate scientific principles; that is, such criteria serve only the practical purpose of segregating individuals who are victims of undesirable human circumstances (behavior troubles) from others involved in other noxious human eventualities, such as economic, social, military or hygienic difficulties. For example, a man's failure to maintain himself biologically might not at all be due to his abnormal psychological behavior but rather to his lack of immunity to disease germs or to his social misadaptations traceable to changes in natural conditions (crop failures, mine explosions, etc.)

Very far indeed, then, must such criteria be from an exact psychological basis. In none of these various attempts to formulate criteria of abnormality is there any attention paid to the actual behavior problems concerned. In other words, such criteria give us no classification on the basis of different psychological or reactional characteristics. And it is from the standpoint of the actual stimulus-response situations involved in the specific behavior circumstances of the individual that the psychologist must formulate a standard or criterion of abnormal behavior.

And yet in spite of the fact that the practical criteria of abnormality are far removed from definite psychological principles, we cannot overlook the truth that their mere connection with human conduct is sufficient guarantee that they have considerable psychological implications. The implications we may consider as being focussed in the lack of adaptation. For after all we may observe that the individual's general maladaptations constitute failure not only to maintain himself in his biological or sociological surroundings but also to respond properly to his psychological stimuli.

The problem of a psychological criterion for abnormality then, difficult as it is, is not insurmountable. In the very fact of failing to adapt oneself we can discover intricate and important psychological conditions which define and localize conduct abnormalities.

To make our abnormality studies exact and our determination of abnormality valid, we may follow out a set of definite investigations.

In the first place, we must assure ourselves that we are dealing with individual maladaptations and not mere conventional descriptions. In other words, the question must be answered whether the person's actions are not suitable for him or do not meet his own behavior needs, or whether it is merely in the esteem of others that he has failed. We must, however, observe carefully that not infrequently it is a definite psychological maladaptation not to win or hold the esteem of some person or group of persons, when for example, we are dealing with social adaptations. But social adaptations, of course, do not constitute all or even most of the individual's behavior situations.

For a precise determination of abnormal conduct it is necessary also to investigate the reactional history of the individual, for it is only in this manner that we can be certain that the individual's conduct is or is not the proper thing for him to do. Unless a person has built up reaction systems of a particular sort we cannot expect him to be able to respond to the objects with which such a reaction system is correlated. For example, we find among abnormal individuals many who have been so protected and sheltered that the slightest contact with actual affairs finds them unready to respond effectively, if at all. From such developments there result many failures of response and many complete or almost complete behavior breakdowns on the part of particular persons. On the other hand, an individual who through his contacts with objects and persons builds up a particular type of reactional equipment must be expected to act accordingly, regardless of whether the ensuing conduct is for his own or anybody else's advantage or disadvantage. In fact, very frequently such behavior occurs because of early equipmental acquisitions that force upon us copious sources of disastrous behavior results.

Still another inquiry for the determination of abnormality and its extent or degree, consists of the study of the person's immediate behavior surroundings, with especial reference to his reactional biography. Of course, it is to be expected that no matter what the person's development of behavior equipment has been, a tremendous crisis of some sort, or some absolutely new situation, finds the individual unprepared for adequate adaptation to them. But here as is not the case in other pathological situations, the difficulty may be localized in the extraordinary circumstances to be reacted to, and not in any lack of behavior equipment in the individual unless indeed one expects that a person should be so equipped that he can perform adequate responses to all possible situations. Through this inquiry we may observe whether the individual can compensate for his behavior lack in the course of time and whether he can at all modify his conduct equipment or acquire new behavior equipment to meet new situations.

Most emphatically we conclude therefore that an adequate psychological criterion for pathological behavior conditions must be specific and particular—one which is derived from an intimate study of an individual and his reactional conditions, and not from any type of statistical data concerning psychological conduct. The study of reactional pathology, then, is an extremely individualistic problem. Consequently we cannot have fixed generalized methods of handling all cases indiscriminately. Since each individual must be studied as a particular case each pathological reaction is a unique investigative problem for the abnormal psychologist.

**Pyschological and Psychiatric Attitudes toward Abnormal Phenomena**

Especially instructive for the study and interpretation of reactional abnormalities is the comparison of the different kinds of interest evinced in abnormalities on the part of the psychologist, the physician, and the psychiatrist. This comparison may be considered from the standpoint of two stages in psychiatric development.

From the standpoint of the earlier period of psychiatric development [1] the psychological attitude contrasts markedly with that of the psychiatrical, in that the latter was far removed from the study of reactional abnormalities as behavior at all. Insanity and feeblemindedness as blanket terms for most abnormalities were treated as forms of disease and in accordance with the conditions of the period under discussion, search was made in all cases for symptoms that would symbolize some particular disease entity. Accordingly, most of the work of the psychiatrist was concerned with the classification of patients on the basis of the specific types of disease entity they represented. How futile this technique of classification was, how unsatisfactory from the standpoint of the actual handling of patients, is a matter of the unenviable records of medical history.

By way of criticizing this psychiatric attitude toward abnormal behavior we might point out that in general it continues the pre-scientific doctrine of the "possession" of insane patients. This criticism is justified even though physicians attempted to discover the seat of the disease entity in such a tangible element as the nervous system. The whole attitude may be more particularly criticized because of its failure to carry out the obvious function of the physician, namely, to cure the patient. It is clear that because the most definitely determined cases, those in which organic lesions could be discovered, such as dementia paralytica, idiocy, etc., and which were not subject to improvement, were set up as patterns, other cases which probably were subject to improvement were not handled in a manner calculated to bring about this effect, although in them there were no gross lesions or biological defectiveness. Such was the case, for example, with the myriads of individuals who were classified as dementia præcox and hysteria cases. For the most part under the domination of such an ideology as we have indicated, physicians could merely perform the office of putting their patient safely away so that they would not harm themselves or others or be a burden to anybody.[2]

---

[1] Clearly this reference to period is not intended to point out chronological divisions since the two views subsist side by side.

[2] Although we are here criticizing a faulty psychiatric situation we do not in

A second and decidedly more advanced stage in psychiatric development we consider to be that in which the attitude of mere classification gave way to the notion that the insane must be considered as peculiar biological manifestations, that is, individuals having abnormal life histories.   This view finally developed into the attitude that the insane patient represented an abnormality of behavior.   It is from this attitude, which represents a tremendous improvement over the previous one discussed, that we may distinguish the psychological attitude.

Briefly, the psychiatric attitude toward abnormality is a far more practical and limited one than the psychological.   The psychiatrist is primarily concerned with the cure of the patient much after the analogy of curing and preventing disease, say, tuberculosis, whereas the psychologist is interested mainly in an understanding of the phenomena involved.   The latter is eager to know precisely what happens in detail when persons react abnormally.

Because the psychologist is concerned with a more detached and thoroughgoing analysis of reactional objects, he is bent on the investigation of the intimate, specific details of the development of reactional equipment on the part of the person studied and the use of that equipment under specific conditions of stimulation at later times.   On the other hand, the psychiatrist, being primarily interested in achieving better adaptations of the individual, confines himself in consequence to a limited set of activities.   To a certain extent this means that the psychiatrist is interested more in the immediate circumstances of the individual as a member of society, whereas the psychologist studies the person as placed in the whole set of circumstances having an influence on the abnormal behavior situation.

As another concrete example of the difference between the psychiatric and psychological attitudes toward abnormalities, we may cite the fact that frequently the psychiatrist not only cuts himself off from the internist who studies the non or mal-functioning of the physiological machine, but he sometimes goes farther and divides his field off from that of the neurologist who deals with what are presumed to be bodily as compared with mental difficulties.   To make such a distinction between neurological and psychiatric (mental) disturbances indicates of course that one is not clinging to a thoroughgoing behavior viewpoint. [1]   When the psychiatrist stresses behavior attitude it is

the least believe that in the same period the psychologist could have handled the situation any better.   As a record of psychological history the psychiatric conditions that we have been describing are correlated with the prevalence of an exceedingly faulty conception of psychology.   Indeed the erroneous psychological ideas obtaining at the time were responsible for the unsatisfactory status of psychiatry.

[1] It is in effect making reactions like memory perception, thinking, etc., into mental action or manifestations of mental action as over against walking, reaching, talking, and other responses instead of considering them as more or less refined forms of differential responses to stimuli objects and situations.

apparently only because of the indicated needs of the cases and not because there is a fundamental psychological attitude assumed toward the phenomena studied. In consequence of this fact the psychologist, unlike the psychiatrist, does not overlook conditions in the nervous system, musculature, or any other localizable facts involved in behavior defects. It is an imperfection in the view of some psychiatrists who are interested in failures of adaptation, to assume an attitude of neglect toward biological conditions in individuals, as though the latter did not occur or affect the total behavior situation.[1] Such a view no doubt arises from an over-emphasis of the mentalistic aspect of the mentalistic-physiological dualism, even though the observations and treatment of cases are accomplished at least partly through behavior studies.

On the whole we might indicate that when the student of abnormal phenomena works with an authentic and adequate psychological conception he is interested in every form and variety of unsatisfactory or exaggerated behavior. He is interested in activity correlated with or involving the loss, disease, or malfunctioning of a specific organ or organs or the malfunctioning of the organism as a whole, as well as maladaptations resulting from environmental conditions. Again, fortified by a workable psychology the psychopathologist includes among abnormals, persons whose conduct difficulties involve cultural, social, moral, legal, and economic maladaptations. Among such individuals may be mentioned those who are unable to build up economic reactions necessary to meet the exigencies of current economic life. Also included here are those persons who have not the moral and legal ideas and customs permitting them to get on with their neighbors. In brief, the psychological study of abnormality calls for the inclusion of all exaggerations and singularities of behavior whatsoever.

**The Problem of Classifying Abnormal Phenomena**

Reactional abnormalities and psychopathological personalities are numbered by the thousands and tens of thousands. No imagination is too poor to picture the innumerable variations of psychological dysfunction which mark the efforts of human individuals to adapt themselves to all the natural and human or cultural conditions surrounding them. The problem arises accordingly as to how we are to arrange the facts of abnormality for the purpose of surveying the field. Suggestions are to be found in the fundamental psychological principle involved. Namely, we may search for the basis of abnormalities in the nature and types of the person's reaction systems (reaction system defects), in the type of personality equipment of the person (personality difficulties), and in the connections between the individual's reaction systems and the correlated stimuli (behavior segment difficulties).

---

[1] Hence arises the obnoxious situation in which the mentalist with his doctrine of the psychogenic origin of mental disease stands over against and fights the physiologist who believes that mental diseases have their definite neural or at least bodily cause or basis.

Let us consider first reaction system defects. We find many persons doomed to perform abnormal or pathological action because reaction systems are lacking, have been lost, or are out of function. For the most part we localize the basis for reaction system defects in the malformation, loss, or lack of development of one or several factors of the reaction system. Usually the localization can best be made with respect to reaction system factors which may be correlated with some anatomical structure or set of structures. But this does not mean that the localization cannot be traced to some of the other factors, such as the discriminative, affective, and attentional phases which have no special, anatomical structures correlated with them, unless we think of the total biological organism (anatomical and physiological organization) as the structural correlate of each of such reaction system factors.

Reaction System Defects

Among the abnormalities based upon reaction system defects we must place all those defective conditions which exist because the person has never had the possibility of performing certain reactions. Because of the congenital malformation of some organ or its early loss, the individual has never been able to acquire certain reaction systems. The maldevelopment or loss of an arm precludes the development of manual activities. Similarly, the loss of an arm, foot, or other organ results in an inability to perform certain actions which were once a part of the person's behavior.

Besides actual malformations and losses of various structural parts we must note also that the mere non-functioning or malfunctioning of some part or the whole of an organism results in the non-development of reaction systems or their inability to operate once they are acquired. In studying the details of reaction system defects we must look out for diseases and affections of particular organs of the individual or of the whole individual which unfit him for the acquisition of behavior equipment or for its later use. The diseases and dysfunctioning of the glandular mechanisms, for instance, are excellent illustrations of how the failure of the entire organism to develop properly, results in the development of defective reaction systems, if any at all. Cretins and mongolian idiots may be considered as personality types belonging to this division.

Under the equipmental sources of abnormal reaction phenomena we find abnormalities of conduct arising either from the lack of necessary equipment of reaction systems or from the acquisition of unsuitable ones. The former situation is found in the case of the so-called feeble-minded. Among the specific behavior troubles based upon unsuitable equipment we may cite personalities who are not equipped to adapt themselves at all. Such persons have equipment developed in contact with a psychological environment which makes them unable to react properly to their present surroundings. Persons who find themselves foreigners to the customs, language, and laws of another cultural group than their own original one, illustrate this type of case. The

Personality Equipment Defects

extreme relativity of equipment and psychological surroundings is in
evidence here.

Again, individuals develop behavior equipment incompatible with
the rest of their personality, either that which has been previously
developed or which will be later acquired.   In this way all sorts of
incompatibilities of action are brought about and result in all kinds
of dissociations or inefficiencies of conduct.   Other reactional abnormalities having their source in equipmental conditions are inequalities
of traits or interests.   Persons who develop too many reactions of
some kind or too few, thereby become unfit to meet the behavior needs
of particular situations or of all situations.

Many of the equipmental abnormalities are of the type in which a
discrepancy occurs between the equipment of the person and his
immediate behavior needs.   Difficulties arise here when conditions
make it necessary for the person to perform actions which do not comport with his behavior equipment.   For instance, an individual who
has built up the personality of a scholar or an engineer drifts into a
business life.   As a result of this incompatibility between his personality equipment and his present conduct, he may feel estranged
from life in general, become unstable, doubtful, and apprehensive.
As consequences of such conditions the person may develop unsatisfactory behavior compensations or break down entirely.

**Behavior Segment Defects**   The behavior segment difficulties fall into a great variety of types.
In the first place, a person may build up strange behavior segments
so that his behavior is different from that of others either with
respect to natural or cultural objects.   In effect this means that the
individual develops such reaction systems that the objects correlated
with them take on unusual or unsatisfactory stimulational functions.
Various phobias illustrate the development of behavior segments in
which objects assume for particular persons very extreme stimulational capacity.   In other words, the responses built up are very far
from suitable for the natural objects in question, or the behavior does
not comport with that of others in the group and hence terminates in
more or less serious maladaptations of the person.

Another type of behavior segment abnormality is that in which
reaction systems built up for one kind of object operate only as
responses to other kinds.   This type of situation is illustrated by the
normal illusions and hallucinations of ordinary life which in complex social situations may be highly exaggerated and become very
serious.

Probably the most common abnormality found in the entire field
of psychopathology are the cases in which normally developed and
satisfactorily operating reaction systems to stimuli fail to operate
when the stimuli objects are present.   We may say that the objects
fail to perform their stimulational functions although the requisite
reaction systems exist for them.   Classic examples are the great
varieties of hysterical amnesias, paralyses, aphasias, etc.   In such

cases, things, words, etc., which have taken on particular functions for the person, in that he has acquired particular reaction systems to them, do not any longer call out those responses, either at the moment or at all.

In general, we might point out that the reaction system defects correlate more or less well with what the psychiatrist calls organic, mental disease, while the behavior segment abnormalities are referred to as functional defects. An exceedingly important difference must be noted, however. Whereas the medical term organic refers only to conditions in which some actual lesion of anatomical structure or physiological maladaptation is present this is not at all the case with the psychological reaction system. Possibly an abnormality, in which the reaction system factors are correlated not with a specific anatomic organ but with the entire organism, is always called something other than organic.

Upon the basis of these principles of abnormality classification we may attempt to organize abnormalities of behavior with some moderate degree of success. This success, however, lies in the fact that while at the same time we achieve some type of classification, we do so without overlooking the specific conditions involved in each abnormal situation or the possibility of several of them belonging together in the same patient. In other words, in our attempt to group abnormalities into general classes we must avoid the pitfall of robbing them of their very specific and individual behavior characteristics.

For practical purposes we might place all of the cases of abnormality into three main divisions with a number of subdivisions under each. The purpose of the divisions is to point to a number of possible ways in which abnormalities develop and operate. In no sense is the classification intended to be a scheme of exhibiting types, for, as we have so frequently asserted, no such abnormality types exist. Every investigation of abnormal conduct worthy of the name must under all circumstances start with a person and his conduct. The three divisions of behavior abnormalities we shall call (A) unusual behavior, (B) unadaptable conduct and (C) defective or pathological behavior, the same terms, of course, designating the personalities performing this behavior.

*The Organization and Characterization of Abnormal Phenomena*

## UNUSUAL BEHAVIOR

By the term unusual we refer to the conduct of individuals which is clearly an extreme variation from the behavior of other persons but which may not be unadaptable. In other words, such behavior may not interfere with the ordinary adjustments of the individual to his natural or social milieu. In some cases, however, these unusual reactions variously called queer, eccentric, etc., prove to be disastrous to the individual's adaptability. When we consider the per-

sons who perform such actions we find them distinguished from their
fellows.  They stand out either as superior to others in some trait
or capacity, or else comparatively inferior.  Such personalities we
group into three divisions on the basis of the number of unusual
reactions they ordinarily perform.  Accordingly, our classification
runs: individuals having: (a) some reactions unusual, (b) many or
most of their reactions unusual, or (c) the total personality may be
said to be unusual.

**Some Re-actions Unusual**

Here we turn immediately to the reactions called mannerisms.
Almost every individual has certain forms of activity that do not
fit in with the rest of his own behavior, or with the behavior common
to the individuals among whom he lives.  These mannerisms as
typical of such peculiarities of behavior may belong to any of the
particular situations of the individual's life.  He may have eccentric
ideas, or feelings of a religious or moral sort, or peculiarities in
his speech, dress or gait.  Again, he may be restless, "nervous,"
timid, shy, etc., or possess decided likes and dislikes for certain
things and persons.  Marked interests of various sorts similarly fall
into the category of actions which stamp as unusual the person
who performs them.  For instance, it may be unusual for an individual to be intensely interested in history, or science, especially when
a person's life generally seems to exclude such an interest, as in the
case of a butcher being absorbed in the Thirty Years' War and
collecting a library on the subject.

**Many Re-actions peculiar or Different**

In this group we place individuals whose activities represent a
numerically greater amount of the same sort we have just been
describing.  A typically queer or distinguished individual is the
foreigner who comes to a particular group with entirely different
language capacities and actions, or a person who has decided accents
in his speech.  Most striking examples of peculiarity and unusualness are the persons whose moral variations and religious practices
differ greatly from those of other people.  One is readily convinced
of the unusualness of a person's reactions, when they are not merely
immediate responses but constitute equipmental behavior, that is,
more or less permanent modes of the person's actions.  Moreover,
the individual is accounted a confirmed abnormal when he persists in responding to stimuli in his own way rather than taking
on the behavior ways of others around (becoming assimilated with
them).

In this connection we must observe that in a very decided way
we find that our so-called maladaptations depend upon established pre-
cedent, customs, and institutions of particular groups.  In other words,
they are primarily conventional in character.  It is especially important to notice here the relativity of adaptation, namely, that what
is a perfectly normal form of activity and adapts a person in some
particular group, is not so in other groups.  Students of psychopathology have never fully appreciated the extreme importance of

the social condition and the necessity for social adaptation as factors in abnormal situations. For the most part, our ideas of abnormality and maladjustments have been based on obvious difficulties which people have in adapting themselves to natural phenomena, although as a matter of fact probably most of our abnormal phenomena have to do with reactions to social situations and not to natural conditions.

When we speak of the total personality as being unusual we mean, of course, that so many reactions are peculiar that the whole individual seems to be very different from other persons. Or, the individual may have a certain limited number of exaggerated activities that overshadow all his other reactions so that he appears decidedly different from the usual kind of person, or extremely anomalous from the standpoint of the rest of the people in his surroundings. *Total Personality Unusual*

In this group we place all those individuals who appear to be abnormal because of their temperament. They may have such powerful feeling reactions to certain conditions and persons that they are unable to get along with other people. On the other hand, they may be exceedingly easy to get along with, so easy in fact as to be constantly taken advantage of and mistreated. Frequently such individuals seem to be very lively and joyful, so irrepressible that they absorb in themselves all the mirth and gayety available. Closely connected with the latter type of abnormal individual is the happy-go-lucky person, the one who cannot see anything wrong or disadvantageous in the universe. In the same classification we include those other individuals who cannot find anything in the world that offers a saving grace from the miseries and troubles to which men are heirs. Here we find the dreamer, the individual who transforms the whole world of things and persons into some sort of introspective content, the man who contemplates and cannot act. Closely related to this type is the thinker, the person who is constantly understanding things, trying to get at the bottom of all phenomena. In contrast we have the man of action, the individual who is ever doing something, perpetually trying new stunts with or without successful achievement. As a last sample of the individual whose total personality seems unusual, we cite the genius of all sorts—the man who stands out as a peculiar or distinguished on the basis of his achievements whatever they may be or because of his constant or exclusive application to some peculiar kind of situation, event, etc.

## UNADAPTABLE REACTIONS

Under this heading we study the behavior of those who are unable to adapt themselves to their social or natural surroundings. Briefly, these individuals perform actions which do not aid them in getting on or which interfere with their general welfare.  Such behavior may make them undesirable neighbors, prevent them from earning a living, or bring about general unsatisfactory living conditions.  One feature of these abnormal individuals must be remarked upon.  They are not in every respect unadaptable; however, they perform enough unadaptable responses to make them definitely incapable of getting along in their particular environmental situations.  Of course, a cumulative development of reactional inadequacies may at any time totally unfit them for life in their particular communities.  This statement merely indicates the processes whereby one type of abnormality develops into another.  As we have so frequently implied, the lines drawn between cases are not very sharp and do not completely separate off any particular individual from another, nor do they absolutely locate an individual in some particular class of abnormality.  Furthermore, abnormal persons may not only deteriorate in their conduct so that they must be placed in a group with more serious defects, but they may also improve and so either call for reclassification into a less seriously defective group, or be removed from the class of abnormals entirely.  Although in this division we cannot differentiate between those individuals who have a few, many, or all of their reactions of an unadaptable sort, we can still differentiate between the more or less serious cases upon the basis of the particular types of action they perform.

**Bashful and Bold Personalities**

Beginning with the simplest class of unadaptable individual we need hardly suggest that it probably includes everyone at some period in his life or in some particular situations.  Typical examples are the shy, bashful, and retiring persons who cannot meet people on an equal plane or face them squarely.  Such unadaptable modes of conduct have a more or less great influence upon the person's total behavior.  Whatever the effect upon his general behavior circumstances, such traits of conduct constitute decided instances of unadaptibility.  In this same group we place those persons whose conduct interferes with the privacies and intimacies of others.  The traditional book or insurance agent with his insolent and blustering approach and unreserved insistence, in disregard of the prospect's convenience and dignity, illustrates one of the extreme types.  While in many cases such modes of conduct sometimes work out to the complete advantage of the person who performs them, we must consider such behavior from the standpoint of the manners and conventions of social life as an anomalous type of action.  The variations in such forms of conduct are extremely large in number and in almost all cases where the term abnormal applies at all are decidedly prominent.

**Reserved and Effervescent Personalities**

Two contrasting types of unadaptable persons are the effervescent individuals who are intimate kin with all the world, and the lonely shut-in individual whose shrunken contracted personality cuts him off effectively, if not completely, from his fellow beings. All varieties of the expanding personality are constantly met, ranging from the individual who is merely willing to exchange confidences with any-body, to the person who forces his views and powers upon others. The extreme form is the braggart and swashbuckler who makes himself either conspicuous or obnoxious. These maladaptational responses can be of any type, including manners and gestures as well as language responses of all sorts.

At the other extreme stands the type of individual who not only does not meet others with spontaneity but, on the contrary, turns away from them and remains withdrawn and alone. Typical behavior of the shut-in and withdrawn personality are the reticent, unexpressive and uncommunicative attitudes that constitute unsurmountable bars to intimacy, and result in the general avoidance of such persons by others. The specifically maladaptive character of such action lies in the fact that it prevents the individual from entering into any sort of necessary personal association with other people. Furthermore, such unadaptive personalities are perhaps on the way to building up much more serious behavior traits. From an unadaptability to social and personal situations these individuals develop the incapacity to respond even to their natural surroundings and conditions to the extent of not carrying on effectively their essential biological adaptations.

We constantly meet a type of unadaptable individual whose typical conduct is that of the protestant and critic. Among the extreme forms of this personality type are those individuals who disapprove of their surrounding conditions and circumstances. They are constantly condemning the appearance and actions of persons as well as the larger activities of the group, such as political and social institutions. Such critical and protestant conduct may have as its stimulus some particular kind of object or situation such as the moral or religious practises and beliefs of a group. Or the critical responses may be more widespread, that is, cover a wider series of conditions. It is the measure of the extent of the individual's protestation which marks the degree to which he is unable to adapt himself and live comfortably. *The Protestant Personality*

Various conditions may be considered as conducive to this sort cf unadaptability. For instance, the incapacity of the individual to agree with his neighbors with respect to moral and religious activity may be due to the fact that the person has but recently come into a new social milieu. Accordingly, he belittles his new surroundings and protests against them in favor of his former conditions. Familiar examples are the artists of all types who, because of the freedom they enjoy in the creational activities of their art, cannot abide the moral and conventional restrictions of social intercourse. In still other cases the individual may have been originally stimulated by actual difficulties and inconveniences of his surroundings and in consequence may have become unadaptable by constantly referring to those conditions. In other words he may carry over his disapproving attitude to other situations.

Another basis for the development of the critical personality is the acquisition of various personal and individual principles and ideals which cannot be reconciled with the practises of one's group. Illustrative of such persons are the radicals who make violent protest against current political, intellectual and artistic practises. Here we have the striking example of the conscientious objector who, because of various scruples, cannot participate in the war activities of his group, and as a result finds himself in a very serious state of unadjustment.

**The Criminal Personality**  Countless books have been written about the non-adaptability of those supremely unconforming individuals labelled criminals. In most of such writings, however, the bias of social conventions has successfully interfered with an adequate consideration of the psychological features involved. Many writers have failed to make allowances for the opportunities that the favored criminals have to compensate for their unadaptable behavior so that they escape the brand and taint of inferiority, and as a result these writers have created the false belief in inevitable and even hereditary criminal traits in the more humble law breakers. As a matter of fact, however, the actual criminal personality is merely one who is badly adapted to the modes and laws of his groups, so that his life, freedom and sphere of social intercourse are curtailed.

From a psychological standpoint, then, a criminal personality is an individual who has built up personality traits either of the negative type of non-conformance or the positive sort of exercising his own reactions and desire without regard to the rights and privileges of others. In making this statement we are clearly distinguishing between the person who merely commits a crime on some specific occasion and the one whose criminal action is the result of equipmental development.

Criminal behavior  equipment may be acquired through the sheer necessity of one's living circumstances. The exceedingly impoverished individual seeing things around him which he cannot procure through the ordinary conventional means of bargain and purchase takes what he wants irrespective of group disapproval and the consequences of his act. In other cases, a person may find himself in circumstances in which it is necessary to develop defense and attack reactions in order to cope with hostile individuals and thus he develops criminal responses against persons. Criminal types of another sort are those individuals who acquire conduct which is entirely approved of by the group and which results in no inconvenience or harm to the individual unless the activities are not successfully carried out, or accomplished on a large enough scale. It is this type of criminal conduct that indicates most clearly the behavioristic basis of criminality.[1]

It remains to be added here that the maladaptability of the criminal does not always represent failure to achieve a satisfactory existence in a social group (such as social ostracism or imprisonment) but it may constitute a failure to adapt oneself to one's own standard of conduct or ideals. The defective behavior then consists of a too great indulgence in dissatisfaction with oneself and in the sufferings incidental to remorse and self accusation.

Under this heading we consider individuals who have built up anxieties and worrying reactions which prevent them from adapting themselves effectively. Prominent in their behavior are reactions of uneasiness and unendurableness to all kinds of stimuli situations. Such individuals are constantly disturbed and alarmed about the possible occurrence of untoward conditions and are in a permanent state of fear lest some disaster come to them. In extreme cases each changing circumstance stimulates the person to expect some new impending difficulty or calamity. For instance, such individuals are perpetually afraid that they will catch a cold or some disease or that some monetary loss will occur to them. Probably the most familiar of these anxious personalities is the fretting mother who is permanently in expectation of some disaster befalling the child who for the moment is out of her sight.

Anxious and Worrying Personalities

The less extreme types of anxious personalities are those who cannot be called actually pathological since they manage somehow to get through their days in spite of the extreme strain and effort required. But they are certainly unadaptable because they cannot go through a single day without great difficulty and alarm.

With the suggestion of these different types of unadaptable personalities we may consider that the psychology of such irregular behavior phenomena is sufficiently indicated. In no sense, of course, is such a brief presentation of a few cases to be thought of as anything but an indication of the number and varieties of such conduct irregularities and insufficiencies. Thousands in number are the unadaptable personalities. Others that might be mentioned are the overcurious, the too easily satisfied, the moody, the intrepid, the jealous, the indiscreet, the flighty, the unindustrious, the overzealous, the opinionated, the avaricious, etc.

Once again we must emphasize the lack of absoluteness existing between the two types already considered and between these two and the third to which we shall presently turn. Now while we should expect to find real differences in the actions and equipment of the persons studied, it is possible that in some cases we have in our three divisions merely degrees in the exaggeration of conduct as

[1] Crimes committed by individuals because of lack of intelligence cannot in a psychological treatment be considered other than unintelligent activity since our psychological criterion is different from the social or legal one.

compared with normal activity. For it must always be insisted upon that conduct abnormalities are mere exaggerations of behavior. In the final analysis, of course, we must repeat that what is an unadaptable situation for one person may constitute an extreme defect in another and vice-versa. Or, it may amount only to a harmless eccentricity. We might suggest also that to a certain extent we find that cases of the first (unusual) and second (unadaptable) divisions primarily comprise irregular behavior with respect to social stimuli objects and conditions, while the third pathological division concerns irregular conduct primarily with respect to natural objects and situations. But here again we must always go back to the person whose behavior is studied and to his particular reaction conditions.

## DEFECTIVE OR PATHOLOGICAL PERSONALITIES

In this division we consider the cases of persons who are not only decidedly irregular in their behavior, but unfit as well. The actions are not only very different from those taken to be normal but they constitute actual deficiencies or pathological modes of responding to objects and conditions surrounding the pathological individual. Among such defective or pathological behavior is the failure of particular reactions to operate when they are required because of inhibition or because they are not a part of the person's equipment. An example of the first condition is the case of the person who has learned to speak and is now stimulated to ask or answer a question but cannot respond at all, or cannot respond in an intelligible manner. The second condition is illustrated by the person who never has been able to acquire, or who never has acquired, some necessary or desirable mode of behavior.

Because of the generally more serious character of the abnormalities in this division and because of their greater complexity on the whole, we must discuss a number of detailed conditions involved in such abnormal circumstances. First, we must take note of the number of reactions included in the defectiveness of the individual. The question arises as to how large a number of the person's actions are pathological. Are they few or many? In many cases the person's defects may be partial, only one type or a few different types may be missing or out of function. When sufficient activities of certain types are defective, we think of the person as totally defective. Of course, this does not mean that the person stops acting entirely or even that he cannot perform any psychological action. The classification, however, may be taken to mean that the person is pathological as a psychological organism. Such a circumstance clearly indicates the now familiar relativistic attitude which we must take toward psychological abnormalities. In our discussion we will treat those cases in which few responses are pathological as reactional defects, while those cases in which many or all reactions are defective, we will refer to as personality defects.

Before we proceed to our detailed examination of pathological conduct, it would be best to point out the other considerations which must be taken account of in the study of extremely abnormal cases. In the first place we must consider the temporal conditions involved. The question arises whether the difficulty is present only for a short period of time or whether it goes on always. For example, a person may experience a temporary inability to speak or walk or he may be permanently unable to perform these reactions.

Again, we must consider whether we are dealing with a mere immediate behavior defect or a personality or equipmental condition. Is the defect one which has to do with a particular act only or does it concern a condition of development of the person which affects a whole type of action? It will be observed that this condition involves a distinct temporal element but one which is somewhat different from that just considered.

The question whether a defect is reactional or equipmental connects closely with the problem whether the defect is due to equipmental conditions (development of reaction systems) or to circumstances entirely external to the person. The question here concerns the pressing, intolerable, and overwhelming situations which may occasion abnormal conduct. Or, the abnormality may originate from disease or injury to the biological organism. Now 'while, as we have said, the subdivisions of this pathological section will be organized on the basis of the number of reactions involved, we will attempt to give due place to these other points.

As we might expect, the specific forms of reactional defects are many in number. From this number we may select four illustrative types for the purpose of exposition. As names for these types we will employ the terms (a) deprivational defects, (b) injury defects, (c) acquisition defects, and (d) regression defects. **I. Reactional Defects**

Behavior defects in the sense that persons are unable to perform some particular reaction or group of reactions may be due to the fact that such persons have been deprived of the opportunity or possibility of developing such reactions. A typical example is the individual who lacks some end organ or receptor (whether by malformation or injury) or whose muscular system or some other factor of anatomical organization is out of function, and who, as a consequence, cannot develop reaction systems to particular stimuli objects and conditions. The main fact of the deprivation is that the individual is bereft of the contact with objects necessary to develop adequate behavior toward them. The absence or loss of the receptor or some other part of the organism results in the lack of some essential condition for the building up of required behavior. It must be carefully observed, how- **Deprivational Defects** ever, that this condition need not be exclusively located in the organism. Exactly the same results follow, of course, when the stimuli objects are absent. Furthermore, when a lack of objects prevents the person from developing necessary reaction systems we have precisely the same kind of abnormality occurring. For we must repeat again that the defectiveness here is a behavioristic defect, a lack of behavior and not an injury in the organism. The latter is indeed a type of abnormality but one which is not included in our study. What we are interested in is the fact that the person does not have a response to a stimulus which he is expected to have or which it is desirable for him to have.

**Injury Defects**

Injury defects consist of the inability to perform reactions because of some injury to and partial destruction of the biological organism. In contrast to the deprivational defect in which the individual has never been able to acquire particular types of reactions, in the case of injury defects the individual may have previously acquired certain reaction systems but because of some injury is made incapable of performing them, either temporarily or permanently. That is to say, a person who suffers from injury to his legs or arms or some other part of his body, loses thereby some reaction systems which he had previously possessed. Here again we must be clear that it is not the anatomical injury that constitutes the defect. To be sure, the biological injury is quite an essential feature of any abnormal behavior situation in which it has a part but the reactional defect can be otherwise produced; that is to say, it may result from the fact that the objects concerned have lost their stimulational functions. Many pathological situations of this type constitute exaggerations of the ordinary situations in which objects lose their stimulational functions; the distastefulness of olives, or the exciting and disturbing qualities of certain colors, will serve as examples. In these cases the reactions are lost, not as a result of some biological condition but through some kind of circumstance affecting the relationship between the object and the person. The individual's interest in the thing may be lost or some other reaction may be inhibited because of a too frequent contact with the objects in question.

**Acquisitive Defects**

Abnormalities of conduct of the reactional type constitute definite forms of acquiring specific unadaptable responses to particular stimuli objects. Thus, an individual may develop an extreme affective response, say of fear or disgust, toward some particular object or person. In these situations the person acquires effective responses to particular objects which are more or less intense and desirable than the situation actually demands. Many of our acquisitions of violent likes and dislikes, exuberant enthusiasms and absorbing interests illustrate these acquisition reactional defects. Prominent examples of abnormality, when it concerns only some particular action or set of actions, are the various commonly known phobias such as fear of high places, fear of water, of particular persons, etc. Many of the superstitions and behavior inhibitions which seriously interfere with our behavior welfare may be traced to such acquisitions of defective reactions.

As we have pointed out in the other description of reactional defects, here also the behavior difficulties may be correlated with some biological disturbance. In this type of abnormality we frequently find an exceptionally vigorous functioning of the biological mechanisms or a decrease in the energy with which the person acts. Probably the biological conditions have to do with the well-being of the organism in general or with the optimum functioning of the glandular mechanisms in particular.

Attention must be called also to the great influence of stimulational conditions upon the acquisition of untoward and defective reaction systems. Both the presence of natural objects and conditions of all sorts, and the social circumstances of the person are conducive to the building up of specific reactional defects.

Reactional defects may be due to the modification or gradual deterioration of the person's reaction systems. The particular activities we call defective may have been normally developed and may have operated normally up to some particular moment, after which they no longer functioned in a satisfactory manner. Certain conditions conspire to bring about an undesirable or unsatisfactory functioning of behavior. For instance, the individual may have some kind of progressive desire which interferes with the normal operation of his reaction. Most familiar is the regressive defectiveness in visual responses resulting from the impairment or disease of the eyes or from some injury to the optic cords or visual brain. Such impairment or regressive conduct of a visual, auditory, or other sort may result from or accompany diseases and degeneration of the organism as a whole and not some special organ or segment. Persons suffering from epileptic seizures suffer regression of their previously normal conduct; their speech becomes defective; their gait and general walking responses are modified to the point of deterioration. *(margin: Regression or Modification Defects)*

Deterioration of conduct develops from the gradual disappearance of objects from the person's behavior surroundings. As a consequence actions having to do with such stimuli objects become less and less effective in their operation and may deteriorate entirely. Consider the case of the person who leaves his own native land and cultural group and as a consequence finds himself in the course of years with a set of deteriorated language reactions, which if they do not entirely disappear, become very defective indeed.

Since the individuals who are classed in the subdivision of personality defects have most of their actions defective, or have so many defective actions that the whole personality operates abnormally, we refer to them as pathological persons. As in the case of our other divisions here also we group our pathological personalities into special groups according to certain outstanding features of the behavior con- *(margin: II. Personality Defects or Pathological Personalities)* ditions involved. These conditions, as in the previous treatment, include source and type of origin of the abnormality, the limits of the behavior concerned, the specific kind of action that is abnormal, and the results or effects of the abnormal conduct. Once more we submit that the classifications and divisions are pragmatic in character. They are made and used only for the practical purpose of orientation with respect to a particular kind of psychological phenomena. In a thorough analysis of abnormal individuals we seldom find their actions susceptible to a single rigid and logical classification. On the contrary, every abnormal person performs actions which throw him into several classifications. As a matter of fact, we have been able, without doing too much violence to the facts studied, to divide our pathological cases into seven different divisions or types. The names applied to the various groups of personality are as follows: (A) undeveloped or non-developed, (B) abnormally or defectively developed, (C) disintegrated, (D) dissociated, (E) degenerating or degenerated, (F) disorganized, and (G) traumatic or truncated.

**A. Undeveloped or Non-Developed Personalities**

The primary principle of classification here is that the persons concerned have been unable to build up a necessary or suitable behavior equipment to meet the needs of their behavior surroundings. This lack of equipment refers to behavior deficiencies for particular present surroundings or a conduct milieu with which the person might have been in contact. Obviously this lack of personality development is a relative condition and is dependent upon the particular human being concerned, as well as upon the behavior circumstances in which he finds himself. Furthermore, the types of pathological conditions vary enormously. At the bottom of the scale stand those pitiful human beings who have never built up enough equipment to adapt themselves to their most elemental natural conditions. They have not developed walking responses, are unable to move from one place to another, cannot eat properly, or take care of their simplest needs as animal organisms or as creatures in contact with their surroundings.

No whit less pitiful are such creatures who, although somewhat more complexly developed, are unable to speak properly or at all, to remember, to learn, to appreciate things, or to develop and carry out desires and voluntary reactions with respect to objects and persons around them.

In order to provide specific or case illustrations of the undeveloped or non-developing persons, we may indicate that in this group fall all the persons who in the medical and psychological literature are called feeble-minded. Making further use of the medical classification, let us note that it is the individual labelled as an idiot who shows the least development of personality equipment. Next in the scale is the imbecile with more and a higher type of reactional equipment for adaptational purposes. And finally, those persons included under the medical terms of moron and borderline cases may be thought of as having more and better personality equipment actually reaching the point of sufficiency.

Howsoever necessary it may be for us to use as illustrations of the undeveloped personality the terminology developed in medical practise, it need hardly be suggested in view of our general conception of abnormality, that the psychological conception is very different from that of the medical tradition. It must be noted primarily that to a considerable degree the different terms of classification for feeble-minded individuals have conventionally represented absolute abnormalities in the sense that each term was presumed to represent specific disease or abnormality entities.

From the psychological standpoint, then, the types of personality quoted under the general heading of feeble-minded represent only a series of types of individuals who have failed to achieve satisfactory, permanent, personality development. From the psychological standpoint, therefore, the failure of development of equipment in any type of behavior situation constitutes an abnormality. Thus, for example, individuals who are generally called normal must be placed in our category of undeveloped individuals if it happens that they find themselves unequipped with reaction systems to meet particular situations. A physician or engineer who, in a situation different from the everyday run of conditions, finds himself lacking in the necessary informational or technical equipment, must be placed under this category of abnormality.

Naturally the conditions attendant upon the failure of personality equipment to develop should be carefully enumerated. Accordingly we group the under-developed personalities into two large divisions for the purpose of more closely identifying them and their pathological circumstances. These two divisions are, (1) reaction system abnormalities, and (2) behavior segment defects.

In this subdivision we place all of the cases of personality non-development in which the defect can be localized definitely on the side of the organism. For instance, the non-development may be due to the person's inability to acquire reaction systems either because of a failure to come into contact with the necessary objects and conditions or because of some inability to acquire reaction systems even when in contact with such objects. In the latter case the non-development is practically inevitable and for the most part correlated with some sort of biological insufficiency or defect.

*(1) Reaction System Non-Development*

Consider first the fairly accidental reaction system non-development. Possibly the person has not the opportunity to be stimulated by the objects to which he must build up reaction systems. Or, he may be absorbed in other things and disinclined to develop reactions which he now requires or will need later. On the whole such non-development has to do with more complicated forms of activities which may be compensated for or in a measure retrieved later in life.

When the non-development is inevitable and has a biological correlate we are able sometimes to analyze out specific failures of development, while at other times we observe how the undevelopment is fairly general involving a great deal of the person's behavior or lack of behavior. In some cases the localization is such that the failure of some equipment to develop is definitely due to the absence either anatomically or functionally of part of the organism. The defect, maldevelopment, or loss of one or both eyes, ears, hands, or other parts means that the individuals cannot have the behavior equipment that other persons have. Such persons lack visual, auditory, manual, or other modes of responses.

Again, we have generalized developmental abnormalities correlated with total malfunctioning of the organism. Such cases are exemplified by individuals called cretins, mongols, and amaurotics, in some of which we can trace out specific biological conditions, such as the glandular secretion insufficiencies or hyperfunctioning of the glandular mechanisms. Then there are the cases in which the organism is broken or injured at birth (traumatic amentia), or the biological development is not normal (microcephalic idiocy), or in which some disease condition is present (hydrocephalic, syphilitic, encephalitic, meningitic, or epileptic amentia of the medical tradition.) [1]

(2) Behavior Segment Non-Development

Not only may the failure to develop personality traits be correlated with some defect or degeneration of the reaction system factors, but it may result from conditions having to do with the relationship between the organism and the objects and conditions in the surroundings. Probably the most outstanding behavior segment sources of personality non-development involve the deprivational conditions. Here the primary condition is the absence in the individual's surroundings of particular objects and situations as a result of which he is unable to acquire reactions to them. Later the fact that he does come into contact with such objects indicates his lack of equipment and hence his definite abnormality. Such behavior segment personality non-development is among the most common of the more extreme variations of human behavior. Its most striking example is the peculiar case of Kaspar Hauser which we reproduce from Tredgold's [2] description.

"On May 26, 1828, a youth, apparently about sixteen or seventeen years of age, was found near one of the gates of Nuremberg. He was unable to give any account of himself, and inquiries failed to discover how or whence he came or who he was. He was 4 feet 9 inches in height, very pale, with short, delicate beard on his chin and upper lip. His feet were tender and blistered, and showed no signs of having been confined in shoes. He scarcely knew how to use his fingers or hands, and his attempts at walking resembled the first efforts of a child. He could not understand what

[1] For a standard medical treatment of these types of abnormalities consult Tredgold, A. F., *Mental Deficiency*, (4), 1922.

[2] Op. cit., pp. 332 ff. Reprinted with the kind permission of William Wood and Company, New York.

was said to him, and replied to all questions by a single phrase: 'I will be a trooper, as my father was.' His countenance was expressive of gross stupidity. He appeared to be hungry and thirsty, but refused everything offered to him except bread and water. He held in his hand a letter stating that the bearer had been left with the writer, who was a poor labourer with ten children, in October, 1812, and who, not knowing his parents, had brought him up in his house, without allowing him to stir out of it. This was regarded as being intended to deceive. Upon a pen being placed in his hand, the youth wrote the words 'Kaspar Hauser.'

After an official inquiry—which, however, revealed nothing—he was adopted by the town of Nuremberg, and Professor Daumer undertook his education. He was found to be extremely childlike, and to have no knowledge of the most simple facts of everyday life. But he had a remarkable faculty of smell and for seeing things in the dark, and under the instruction of Daumer his mind expanded in a wonderful manner. In fact, probably as a consequence of its sudden awakening into activity, he became ill, and his education had to be discontinued for a time.

He was taught the use of language, and after a time was able to record his recollections. He said that he had always lived in a small, dark cell, continually seated on the ground. He had had no covering, except a shirt and trousers, and had never seen the sky. When he awoke from sleep he was accustomed to find near him some bread and a pitcher of water, but he never saw the face of the person who brought them, and he had no knowledge that there were any other living creatures besides himself and the man who brought him food. This man eventually taught him to write his own name, and finally brought him to the Nuremberg gate.

For a time mental development took place with great rapidity. . . . He was taken under the protection of Lord Stanhope, and he was subsequently employed in the Court of Appeal, but he showed little real capacity for work. On October 17, 1829, he was found bleeding from a slight wound which he said had been inflicted by a stranger. On December 14, 1833, at Anspach, he met a stranger by appointment, on the promise that the mystery of his birth would be revealed. During the interview he was mortally stabbed, and he died three days afterwards. . . .

The mystery of Kaspar Hauser's birth and death attracted widespread interest, and has never been solved. It was contended by Earl Stanhope and the Duchess of Cleveland that he was an impostor, but this view was strongly combated by both Professor Daumer and the eminent Bavarian Jurist, von Feuerbach. The latter considered that Hauser was heir to a princely German house, put out of the way to favour another succession."

Here we have a case in which the deprivation was fairly complete. But there are, of course, all degrees of such abnormalities, all varieties of the amount of equipment which persons fail for one reason or another to acquire. These failures of development of personality equipment comprise also individuals who are lacking in types of activities, that is, are short on intellectual actions, feeling conduct, originating or social behavior, etc.

Another class of individuals who have failed to develop adequate equipment of some or all kinds are those whose difficulties may be traced to a preoccupation with, or absorption in, other behavior.

Individuals who develop one type of behavior first do not in consequence acquire reactions of other types. We may speak of such persons as having interest or behavior slants of particular kinds. Illustrations from the familiar range of behavior phenomena are those persons who devote themselves wholly to business and therefore cannot develop general æsthetic responses. The case of Darwin is often cited, concerning his lamentation that his naturalistic preoccupations left him incapable of appreciating poetry and the other arts. Typical also are the traditional artists who are so incapable of responding properly to their economic and social surroundings that they require a guardian. We observe that the lack of personality development may be dated from any period of the person's life. Doubtless the earlier the date at which the lack of development begins, the more serious the case, since when an abnormal development starts it always has a cumulative effect.

In discussing the behavior segment personality undevelopment we must point out the exceedingly important temporal factor that is practically always involved. In other words, in most of these cases we may expect that where the failure to develop is not so far-reaching that it does not involve a great deal of equipment, the condition may be overcome in time. In such cases the undevelopment may be considered as a case of underdevelopment or retarded development, all of the deficiencies of which may be surmounted. When the lack of development is far-reaching, however, the possibility for overcoming the abnormality is not possible. This is true because obviously the equipment of an individual is acquired by a series of chronologically graduated stages, so that once having failed to acquire certain responses to objects, the individual finds himself deficient in his ability to develop other behavior corresponding to similar objects and conditions that appear to him later in life. Illustrative of these chronological stages of development is the condition of the individual who, failing to acquire behavior equipment with respect to elementary mathematical processes, cannot as a consequence adapt himself to more complicated mathematical objects and situations.

The behavior segment failures of personality development suggest also the fact that in many cases, and especially with respect to the more complicated conditions of human life, compensations are possible in the sense that an individual overcomes his deficiencies by performing entirely different kinds of behavior. Thus, an individual who has failed to develop his elementary mathematical equipment may turn to another kind of work. Possibly from a social standpoint such a necessity for compensation may not be considered as even unusual, but when the problem arises concerning the failure of behavior equipment acquisition, the psychological judgment decrees that we have abnormality of behavior. This is the decision even though from an economic standpoint perhaps an individual may prove to be a more effective personality than he might otherwise have been.

We cannot leave this part of our material without considering once more the inheritance problem in psychology. For it is frequently asserted that at least some of the abnormalities here treated are inherited or are due to a heritable factor. Immediately we are called upon to inquire whether by an abnormality is meant an action, or some quality, power, or entity. If the latter is meant, then, of course, the certainty of its non-existence absolves us from inquiring concerning its hereditary connection with a person. On the other hand, if by the term abnormality one intends to refer to a behavior fact or situation, then the study of the actual facts involved indicates the impossibility of the presence of any heritable factor since behavior cannot be inherited. The problem becomes even more clear when we consider that to a great extent the abnormalities concerned are not behavior situations in which undesirable or improper action of some sort is performed, but rather conduct in which certain responses are lacking.

Next we may inquire whether there are inherited structural defects which account for an individual's failure to develop psychological reactions. Here we must differentiate between the conception that transmissible structural elements exist in the individual determining and conditioning his development of psychological behavior and equipment, and the fact that when the biological organism is in some way defective, that organism may not be able to acquire certain types of behavior, if any type at all. Let us consider what is involved in each case.

To accept the conception that there exist certain hereditable structures which determine the development of behavior abnormalities means that we adopt a rather generalized and precarious idea. Are there specific structures determining the development of particular psychological actions?[1] Are we not merely asserting that a structure must exist in order to account for whatever specific kind of behavior the person does develop and perform? How much less plausible is it to believe that structures are inherited which determine that certain actions should not be acquired. Less plausible still is the belief that the individual can inherit a lack of structure which, as a consequence, precludes his developing certain forms of behavior.

The question still remains whether there is such a transmissibility factor for the general normality of the person. A moment's reflection indicates clearly that normality is not a quality which an organism has or has not but it is a name or conception referring to the completeness or satisfactoriness of the development of an organism. As a matter of fact, this degree of development when it is not complete or satisfactory, covers a great range of differential developments. It must not be overlooked either that completeness and satisfactoriness of development are not standardized, but greatly varying conditions.

[1] See our discussion of general inheritance problem in psychology, Vol. I, p. 172.

We come to the conclusion that there are no hereditary factors in our first type of abnormality. So far, then, there is no problem of heredity involved in abnormal conduct. It is left to us to consider, therefore, the precise circumstances involved in the fact that there are organisms which, because of their lack of satisfactory biological development, cannot interact with their surrounding objects and conditions as other organisms do, and are in consequence to that extent pathological. There is no doubt at all that many abnormalities of psychological conduct are to be accounted for by the fact that the organism is biologically defective and hence cannot get into contact with objects necessary for the acquisition of psychological equipment. Just what these biological defects are, and how they originated, are facts in no manner to be determined by reference to mysterious hypothetical heredity. On the contrary there are clear indications that we must study the complex and important conditions influencing the specific development of any particular organism. Such a study will undoubtedly yield us valuable information concerning the pre-psychological development of the organism which carries over to its later psychological evolution.

**(B) Development of Defective Personality**

The principle of classification here is that the individuals concerned build up such particular features of their behavior development, or such a totality of wrong behavior equipment, that they are not able to adjust themselves to their natural and cultural surroundings, and hence are abnormal.[1] The primary emphasis here is upon the positive development of undesirable or unadjustable behavior equipment. For it is the possession by the individual of this developed unsuitable behavior equipment which characterizes his abnormality. More specifically we may point out that the abnormal behavior equipment may unfit the individual to react to some particular kinds of situations or to all of his surroundings. To illustrate, the person may build up so many unadjustable reaction systems that he will be unfitted to adapt himself to any kind of situation that constitutes the normal environment of human beings. Of the countless individuals belonging in this group we may characterize several types, using for convenience of reference names derived from the psychiatric literature.[2] The basis for the organization of the cases involves the kind of faulty action performed, kind of situations in which

[1] How narrow the line is between normal and abnormal conduct is clear from the consideration that frequently when the acquisitions are socially successful, no matter how incongruous, they make of the person a hero rather than a lunatic in the esteem of his fellows.

[2] Here the reader is warned that although we must use terms derived from the medical literature in order to refer to and illustrate groups of individuals, we must not be thought of as accepting along with the names any of the conceptions that ordinarily go with them. It should be unnecessary to point out that we can only use such names as referring to forms of action and not as marking off unique types of persons. In no case do we find any person referred to by one name who does not perform behavior belonging to persons of other classifications.

such action occurs, origin of defective conduct, its permanence, etc.

In this group we place a great series of individuals who do not Delin-adjust themselves properly, if at all, to the legal, social or conven-quents[1] tional and moral institutions constituting parts of their cultural sur-roundings. In other words, the legal, moral, and social institutions which ordinarily stimulate individuals to restrain themselves and otherwise control their conduct do not with the delinquent individuals function in this capacity. Such persons develop and perform ac-tivities of various sorts that alienate them from other members of the communities in which they are found. For the most part, as we might expect, the reaction equipment unfitting these individuals to adapt themselves properly to their surroundings has a definite form. That is, they may be responses to particular kinds of stimuli and so, for example, we have individuals who are primarily sex of-fenders. That is, they have built up responses resulting in sexual excesses. Others perform sex activities so unappraised as to be called perversions. The latter may range from looking into the windows where live persons of opposite sex to the practice of mutilating (hair-braid cutting) and otherwise injuring contrasexual individuals or persons of one's own sex. In this same group may be placed homo-sexuals, for here we have individuals who have acquired sexual and other modes of action which unfit them for association with their fellows and otherwise prevent them from adjusting themselves to their human surroundings and circumstances.

Other examples of the persons in the present group are those called pathological liars and swindlers. The former are individuals who have built up habits and other reactions of non-truth telling. They simply cannot function adequately in their personal relations with other people. The lies they tell are of every manner of description, referring to experiences they have never had, acts of prowess per-formed, or relations with persons they have never really been in. Sin-gularly enough, the lies are not always to the advantage of the latter nor are they intended to be. Quite as frequently such falsehoods show the person to be undesirable and unworthy. These pathological liars simply acquire the equipment to act in a certain way; they frequently neither intend to accomplish anything in particular by such action nor are aware of the uncertain quality of their behavior. In this sense they differ from persons whose lying actions are phases of plans for definite accomplishment.

Pathological swindlers ostensibly plan to accomplish something by their abnormal conduct but in reality this is not the case. The specific abnormal reactions acquired by these individuals have to do with schemes of all sorts. They are constantly organizing societies, associations, and business corporations to exploit their own talents or various natural resources, as well as to accomplish various other sorts

[1] For descriptive material relevant here cf. Healey, *Pathological Lying, Accu-sation and Swindling*, 1915.

of desirable or undesirable results. Of primary interest here for us is the fact that the conduct displayed constitutes a cumulative development of an aggressive and organizational form of action. While in form very similar to action comprising the legitimate behavior of business men, the activities of pathological swindlers are not based upon certain or probable resources found in former situations. In abnormal situations such activity merely mirrors the expansiveness and, at least, partially, the obliviousness to reality of the acting person.

Just what specific stimulational circumstances condition the inception of the undesirable or genuinely abnormal types of behavior equipment must be sought in the specific behavior surroundings of the persons concerned. Similarly the question as to why the development of such abnormal behavior should begin at any particular time can only be answered by consulting the particular reactional biography under consideration. Suffice it to say that probably no two cases are alike or have similar conditioning circumstances. In other words, each case is a unique development and is probably also uniquely differentiated from similar more normal individuals.

Paranoiacs [1] The term paranoiac symbolizes for us a group of persons who have developed a stock of behavior equipments primarily intellectual in character, which marks them off from the rest of the individuals in their respective communities. While the behavior defects may be localized in abnormal intellectual activities, the actual abnormal responses of these persons cover a very wide range of behavior. Paranoiacs respond abnormally to any and every mode of human circumstances and surroundings. Paranoiac behavior consists of mechanical, inventional action, beliefs, metaphysical and philosophical thinking, attitudes of a scientific or political sort, or modes of thinking concerning practical and domestic problems and situations. A characteristic of paranoiac thinking is that, in spite of the superficially localized range of the behavior, such conduct usually dominates the operation of the whole personality and makes him unfit for carrying on his ordinary life activities. It is precisely this domination of the person's total behavior which distinguishes the paranoiac from the normal individual. Probably there is no person whose behavior equipment does not include some paranoiac behavior which in its broadest sense is merely intellectual action based upon wrong or unsound premises. For this reason it is probably in the field of paranoiac abnormalities that we find the principle best established that abnormalities of conduct are merely smaller or larger exaggerations of what is called normal conduct.

While it is unwise to attempt too closely restricted generalized descriptions of abnormal conduct or pathological persons, we might still indicate a few valid generalizations concerning the individuals placed

[1] Cf. Bleuler, *Textbook of Psychiatry*, 1924, 509 ff.; Bianchi; *Textbook of Psychiatry*, 1906; Kraeplin, *Lectures on Clinical Psychiatry*, (2) 1906; this latter work may be generally consulted for behavior pictures of abnormal personalities.

in this group. At least we might say with a degree of confidence that a prominent form of behavior here is an exaggerated manner of self evaluation. Paranoiacs tend greatly to over-evaluate or under-evaluate themselves. They develop beliefs and opinions concerning their nature and actions, having little or no basis in objective fact. These intellectual reactions are developed as compensations or escapes as well as weapons of offense or defense.

Among the persons in the paranoiac group are those whose entire energies are directed toward the invention of some mechanical contrivance, the solution of some problem, or the explanation of some fact or event all upon the basis of wrong or imaginary principles. Typical instances are the hundreds of individuals who have worked upon perpetual motion machines. Every patent office is replete with records concerning persons who have attempted to make such machines, without abiding by the mechanical laws and principles involved.

Abnormal problem solvers are well exemplified by the long line of exotic mathematicians who have attempted to square the circle or perform similar feats of mastering problems. Much more numerous are the illustrations of the aberrant interpreters of things. It is a common phenomenon to observe how persons explain with borrowed or invented reasons their own behavior and conditions as well as other facts or alleged facts. Their own poverty is explained by the cruel and unjust deprivation on the part of other persons. Their failures are attributed to the machinations of mysterious cosmic or human influences. In a similar way impersonal conditions are given interpretations not derived from actual natural conditions.

Belief forms of intellectual responses constitute a large portion of paranoiac conduct. Common varieties are the persons whose conduct is defective because they believe things are more important, persons more gifted or more wealthy than they really are. The most striking examples are those persons whose beliefs constitute an identification of themselves with historical characters (Napoleon, Christ, Cæsar, kings, or queens or other members of royal families), with the various members of the trinity, or with some criminal. With others of this group the beliefs concern circumstances or events in which they have participated in the accomplishment of some feat of strength or intellect or the persecution of some enemy. Paranoiacs also frequently believe themselves to be greatly beloved by persons (one or many) who are in fact entirely oblivious to their existence, but who are none the less interfered with or annoyed by the abnormal individuals. More normal abnormalities of this type are the supreme beliefs in the value of democracy, monarchy, equality, etc.

These illustrations typify the defectiveness localizable in the intellectual responses, but it would be erroneous to assume that these false and defective intellectual reactions are not intermingled in chaotic mixtures with other behavior in any given case. As a matter of fact, in our everyday surroundings it is difficult for an individual who acquires one type of defective intellectual action not to involve himself in others.

The seriousness of the paranoiac modes of behavior is frequently conditioned by the number of forms of false beliefs and attitudes the person has developed. For it is this range of wrong reactions to many things and persons that often determines whether the individual will act out his beliefs and, if so, with what untoward results. Again the seriousness of paranoiac behavior depends upon how long it has been developing. If the abnormal development has not been going on for a very long time, its progress may be checked and the development of the person directed into normal channels. Should the defective development of the person be a condition of long duration, however, the abnormal features of the personality become so interrelated with that person's psychological behavior conditions that he may never be able to function normally in his ordinary surroundings.

To a certain extent the duration of abnormal personality development depends upon the importance or strikingness of the situation that is determined to be the source of the trouble. This proposition may of course be taken to be corollary to the proposition that the abnormality in the first place and its specific form are direct functions of the person's stimulational surroundings. The importance of any situation is, of course, relative to the particular individual concerned. Such relativity is easily recognized when we consider that not a single individual is by nature of his development completely free from some defective elements of behavior equipment. But in many cases the person remains normal and is able to adjust himself to his surroundings because the situation to which his abnormal reactions are developed are of little consequence to him or to his welfare.

A very important form of faulty intellectual reaction, overshadowing and making abnormal the total personality, is the occasional type. Under this heading we refer to abnormal or hysterical reasoning, thinking, and belief which occur under stress of some crisis or conflict. When war comes to some nation individuals lose their sense of values and are unable to think correctly with respect to the enemy's nation and its citizens. This condition is very similar to situations in which the individual himself suffers a severe loss or indignity. Immediately he develops faulty intellectual and reasoning behavior and is no longer able to adapt himself properly to his social and cultural surroundings. In the case of a large number of persons simultaneously developing such faulty personalities, some compensation is automatically developed, but from the standpoint of the damage done to one's own intellectual integrity and to other persons' peace and property the abnormality is not thereby mitigated. Moreover in such cases, no other phase of a person's behavior need be affected by the abnormality unless it is very closely related to the actual abnormal situation.

**Stuporous and Catatonic Personalities** [1]　Here is a group of abnormal individuals whose acquisition of faulty

[1] Excellent material is contained in Hoch, *Benign Stupors*, 1921.

reaction systems consists primarily of feeling responses that are on the whole negativistic in character. The personality equipment becomes progressively and predominately one of disinterest. Such individuals accordingly lose the behavior alertness resulting from an intimate contact with the things that ordinarily arouse the individual or depress him. With the catatonic-stuporic personalities, however, the behavior is dominated by apathetic activity which, if it progresses far enough, gets to be a comatose or stuporous form of behavior. Very frequently the person's apathetic behavior is coupled with depressive and melancholic affective conduct, but the development of the person is decidedly toward the indifferent and apathetic mode of action.

How far the development of such disinterested and apathetic conduct proceeds may be indicated by the fact that stuporous individuals have no interest even in themselves or their surroundings so that they will not even take care of their elementary biological functions. Nor are they concerned with the rules and conventions of social life, much less with adapting themselves to their natural surroundings. In many cases they lie in bed or wherever else they are placed much as though they were physical objects. Also their behavior simulates that of a sleeping or hibernating animal.

In the above descriptions of this group of abnormal cases we have stressed only the striking variations in the behavior of the individuals concerned. Obviously they do not on the whole act in the same way, for their specifically abnormal conduct is tied up in each case with different behavior equipments in their reactional biographies. Also each person has his own individual set of surrounding conditions with the result that his behavior case history is unique. The reason that the members of this class may be so easily and so effectively grouped is because they perform in common an exceedingly striking and unmistakable type of action.

With these terms we label individuals who acquire behavior equipment appearing to the observer as a progressive detachment [2] from the environing world of work and responsibility. At a certain moment in their psychological careers, individuals who may appear as tremendously well oriented in their social, intellectual, economic, and artistic situations, begin to fall away from their surroundings. Such abstractions and withdrawal from their usual occupations and responsibilities may seem to contrast greatly with the person's previous behavior status. A brilliant young collegian, absorbed in his work, busy with his effort to maintain his scholastic study and secure his academic rewards, becomes listless and indifferent and finally loses all

*Schizophrenic or Dementia Præcox Personalities [1]*

---

[1] Meyer, "The Nature and Conception of Dementia Præcox," *Journal of Abnormal Psychology*, 1910, 5, 274–285. "The Constructive Formulation of Schizophrenia" *Amer. Journal of Psychiatry*, 1922, 78, 355–364.

[2] This is always a more positive form of action situation than the indifference behavior of the stuporous and catatonic personality, which see.

contact with his former life save the persistent performance of some mannerism or gesture reminiscent of his former activities.

Although here, as elsewhere, the clinical pictures of abnormality descriptions differ tremendously in detail, still a fairly common basis for grouping persons in a class is afforded and suggested by the shrinking from responsibility and the generally difficult conditions surrounding such persons. For the most part the original stimulational sources for the development of such behavior equipment are the hopeless and fearful situations by which the person comes to be overwhelmed.

Probably in no case is the abnormal conduct of the schizophrenic to be accounted for other than by a long drawn out development beginning early in his reactional biography. Some persons very early in their lives begin to diverge from other individuals as the result of a certain difficulty which they cannot face or which seems impossible to them. In their premature stages they are merely shy, timid, shrinking, and withdrawn, and do not participate in the same activities as others. Later, they may be very tightly shut up within themselves and even build up, by means of their own imaginative responses, worlds which are peculiar to themselves and which replace the actual things and conditions around them.

Among the specific types of human situations and conditions influencing the development of such defective and pathological personalities, we might mention serious economic or social difficulties that appear to handicap the person. The inability to compete with others in the economic or artistic world makes these individuals willing to give up the battle. Not that there are any such absolute conditions existing, but they appear so to persons who have not built up behavior equipment necessary to combat with whatever adaptational opposition they meet. To a not inconsiderable extent, the development of disserviceable equipment is a negative process, that is, the building up of behavior equipment not found serviceable in critical situations.

It is not unlikely that at the basis of the development of schizophrenic personality there exists a general functional inferiority of the biological individual. Such a functional inferiority may in two ways be the condition primarily responsible for the pathological personality development. Namely, it may either result in an inferior psychological personality, or may act as a stimulus for the individual, leading him to build up withdrawing and detaching behavior.

**Eccentric and Pervertive Personalities [1]** Conspicuous variations from other persons are the queer and eccentric individuals for whom various group customs and situations function very differently in the way of arousing behavior.[2] These individuals acquire behavior equipments marking them off from the

---

[1] Here we may immediately think of the women who must dress and act like men.

[2] Exceedingly valuable material will be the reward of those who search in Southard and Jarrett, *The Kingdom of Evils*, 1922.

rest of the associated population. The milder type of such behavior variation we will call the eccentric or queer individual; those possessing more marked eccentricities of behavior may be classed as perverted personalities.

Among the former types we cite those persons who acquire conduct appertaining to modes of living opposed to those ordinarily existing around them. Familiar are the vagabonds and wanderers who do not dress, eat, or sleep in the manner prescribed by conventional, civil society. Moreover, such persons may have in no wise acquired the desire and respect for property and its rights which are considered as essential behavior forms of persons. Nor do they hesitate to act out their widely varying behavior by not accumulating property or using it as others do.

In this division of abnormal individuals may also be placed the misers and hermits whose conduct is extremely glaring in its contrariety to and contradistinction from the other members of the community. Similarly, the dreamer and the social critic build up an unusual personality and either do not fit in with the practical adaptations of those around them or find the ways of acting and living of others extremely irksome and disturbing.

As pervertive personalities we label those whose behavior equipment of an odd and pathological sort is more specialized and therefore on the whole shows a greater degree of exaggeration. Such individuals may thoroughly disregard the more fundamental behavior customs of the group, even to the point of non-compliance with hygienic and self preservative behavior. Striking examples here are the inebriates and drug fiends who not only do not make any pretense to avoid excesses of living, but seek exotic modes of action even in spite of their ultimate and rapid dissolution. Other examples are the so-called sex perverts, those who build up sex action in no wise according with the regulations of their group or any human group. Specific examples are those called homo-sexuals, sadists, masochists, sodomists, the incestuous, etc.

Neurasthenical and invalidal personalities are familiar types to all of us. Their acquisition of pathological behavior equipment has to do principally with health stimuli situations in some form. Because of certain specific circumstances discoverable in their behavior surroundings, they develop responses of fatigue and exhaustion. In general, this amounts to an inability to cope with their everyday situations. Probably the most exaggerated form of this type of pathological personality is the invalidal person who is not only unable to carry on his everyday activities but may be obliged to confine himself to his bed for a longer or shorter period. *Neurasthenical and Invalidal Personalities [1]*

On the whole these persons require much care and service; many of them might well be called rest-cure personalities. They must be constantly pampered, guarded from disease conditions and protected

[1] Cf. Bleuler, loc. cit. pp. 556–559, 571–572.

from their own hygienic fragibility. In tracing out their more or less detailed development we discover that they are highly suggestible as far as hygienic conditions are concerned. They are exceedingly fearful of germs and of overtaxing themselves. In every thing and place there lurk for them grave and threatening dangers. Every contact with a strange or different object or situation is approached with a torturing self-questioning and self-urging. For in such cases the imaginative activity of the person is constantly employed.with the creation of difficulties in surrounding objects and corresponding incapacities and unfitness in themselves.

In the course of the building up of these neurasthenical and invalidal personalities we discover a series of movements around a vicious circle. At first, perhaps the contact with a disturbing situation stimulates the acquisition of an invalidal reaction. This situation in turn makes these individuals less able to carry on their regular work. Their days are spent in constant watchfulness over their well-being; they cannot sleep and accordingly their nights are given over to unceasing agitation. As a consequence, they build up more and more responses of invalidism. The end point in this pathological process is of course the development of so pain racked and so incapable an organism that the person becomes a hopeless valetudinarian. This means that he has finally acquired the most extreme form of pathological behavior of this class.

When compensations are lacking and persons cannot remove themselves from the noxious situations that originally give rise to the neurasthenic development, they frequently do away with themselves. A comparatively large number of suicides are thus recruited from this type of pathological personality.

As in all cases of pathological personality development, so in the present instance, the specific conditions favoring the particular acquisition of behavior equipment are many. We may, however, point to some very striking situations which seem to provide fertile soil for neurasthenic and invalidal development. Without question the development of general invalidism of some sort of a localized incapacity, such as eye weakness (inability to react effectively in a visual way), hardness of hearing (inefficiency of auditory responses), frequently serves as a protection against and an escape from the criticism and censure of others and of oneself for not accomplishing more and for not carrying out one's own future promise or meeting the expectation of others. Not that this compensatory fact is explicit in any sense (probably no invalid would care to acknowledge what he is doing) but the situation is none the less a genuine one.

**Impulsive and Compulsive Personalities**[1] Conspicuous among pathological personalities are those individuals who have built up behavior equipment which, when performed, marks the reacting individual as one who has no control over his actions. As a result such persons perform behavior without premeditation and

[1] Bleuler, C. C., pp. 560–564.

which has unsatisfactory or even disastrous results. What makes these activities especially pathological is the fact that they occur more or less suddenly when the individual comes into the presence of some particular stimulus. Furthermore, the person performs these actions with great determination and energy at the moment but later fully appreciates the folly and the inappropriateness of his conduct. For in many cases such actions are in direct conflict with the rest of the individual's equipment. They may be totally antagonistic to the moral scruples of the individual and the conventional prescriptions of the person's social group which he accepts and by which he desires to abide.

In this type of defective behavior we have additional evidence that some pathological conduct is derived directly, and by a very easy transition, from normal behavior. For the most part the types just discussed may be considered as extreme exaggerations of the individual's ordinary behavior. However, the extreme forms of these pathological activities are decidedly impressive because of the disastrous results which they entail.

Within the field of these particular pathological activities we accept as expedient the distinction between impulsive and compulsive behavior on the basis of whether the primary conditions for such activity can be located in the stimulating object or in the behavior equipment. Impulsive individuals are those who perform reactions primarily because of the influence upon them of stimuli objects and conditions, while the compulsive personality performs such action mainly because of his behavior equipment.

As examples of pathological conduct depending primarily on stimuli conditions we will consider the various *manias* prominent in psychiatric literature. Here we may instance *kleptomania*, describable as the inability to resist taking some article whether one needs it or not and in spite of the fact that the person has plenty of money to purchase it, if he so desires.

The *pyromanic* individual cannot prevent himself from setting fire to some object or building, the mere presence of which means that he carries out his maniacal behavior without regard to consequences. Not unfamiliar nor uncommon is the *dipsomanic* personality who cannot resist drinking when in the presence of spirited liquors. In the same way *sexually manic* individuals are irresistibly stimulated to perform various types of sexual behavior some of which result in violence to other persons. Here, we also find individuals who are unfortunate enough to acquire *homicidal* and *suicidal manic* conduct, so that they may be driven by themselves or by others to commit murder or suicide. Suicide frequently results from a sense of the unworthiness of oneself or others. Again, these maniacal individuals cannot conceive of being burdens either to themselves or others; that is, they cannot endure the thought of suffering or making others suffer.

Suggestive of the easy transition between the decidedly pathological forms of conduct and our ordinary everyday behavior situations is the extreme imperiousness of certain stimuli, such as a spot on the tablecloth which one cannot resist touching, even though the action may cause extreme embarrassment to one's hostess and oneself. Again, the same condition is found in the tremendous influence upon us of the conditions of our home when we are about to leave it. We are driven to a reëxamination of doors and windows, although we are certain we have securely locked them.

As illustrating the compulsive form of pathological behavior we may mention the extreme moral scrupulousness characterizing the person who must perform particular acts of charity, even if by so doing he puts himself to great discomfort in helping someone who perhaps is not in need of help at all. Other individuals are constantly doubting everything, even to such a degree as to be unable to carry on any kind of action without elaborately questioning its propriety and value. The same type of compulsive individual may carry over his doubting to practically all information that is brought to him.

Quite a different form of compulsion reaction comprises the various fears built up by individuals, which dominate all of their behavior. Psychiatric literature is replete with descriptions of persons who have developed pathological fears of other persons and things, of dirt, contamination, high and narrow places, of lightning and other natural phenomena, as well as fear of being unjustly dealt with, etc.

**Prison Personalities** [1] An exceedingly specialized type of pathological personality is the prisoner. Here is an individual who because of the particular conditions ensuing from his incarceration builds up certain types of defective behavior. The pathological conduct developed is directly traceable to the circumstances that have brought him into his present plight, and to his immediate and future prospects. The prisoner does not only refer back to the circumstances connected with his prison experience, but his whole behavior is very definitely determined by that experience. It is solely for this reason of the availability of the individual's abnormal conduct for definite study and analysis that we put him into a class of his own even though his conduct may not be unique.

Very prominent among the specific activities of prison personalities are the developments of ideas and beliefs concerning their innocence and the unfortunateness of their conviction and present retention. These personalities weave elaborate webs of imaginary facts about the circumstances of their crimes, their trials, prison treatment and future pardon. Not infrequently do they consider themselves martyrs suffering without cause for crimes they have never committed.

Another type of conspicuous prison conduct are the reactions of excitement and depression that appear to follow from the realization

[1] Excellent descriptions and references to literature in Glueck, *Studies in Forensic Psychiatry*, 1916.

of one's undesirable condition. Thus prisoners rage and fume at the bars which hold them so securely and which rob them of their liberty and freedom of action.

Probably the most typical conduct of the prison personality is the incessant and vigorous querulousness and grumbling concerning conditions as they are. To a great extent the time of the individual is occupied with protestations and railing against his undesirable predicament and arguments for his release.

It is impossible to suggest more specific features of the conduct of the prison personality without making a direct analysis of some particular case. The significant cause for a consideration of this type of personality is that it provides us with data concerning the occasional development of a special type of pathological equipment. Such a consideration is exceedingly suggestive of the fact that any kind of overwhelming and extremely unusual condition, such as being drafted into the army, may result in the individual's development of pathological modes of behavior.

Individuals of this type represent an exaggeration of the unadaptable type of reaction. Essentially, they build up responses of anxiety and dread with respect to particular kinds of situations. When the anxious and expectant forms of reaction are extremely intense they dominate the total life of the individual to such an extent, in fact, that he is unable to carry on his normal functions as a member of a particular community. **Anxious and Expectant Personalities[1]**

The cases we are now considering resemble, to a great extent, some of the behavior abnormalities we discussed under the heading of the unusual, but with this difference, however, that the anxious and expectant behavior traits are thoroughly ingrained in the person's equipment and do not occur only on some specific stimulating occasion. The individuals then are not reacting pathologically to particular situations but are constantly living upon the ragged edge of impending disaster.

So defective in their psychological conduct do these individuals become that they absolutely dread to perform many kinds of action. They cannot bring themselves to the point of meeting people. For this reason they find themselves hopelessly morassed in a set of living and working conditions which are obnoxious to them but which they are absolutely powerless to change for fear that they may further reduce themselves in their social and economic circumstances.

Just as some abnormal individuals are characterized by ideas and other actions pointing to an excessive over-evaluation of their personalities, we find other defective persons with a corresponding depreciation of themselves. Inferior personalities comprise in their behavior equipment intellectual attitudes which place them far below their **Inferior Personalities**

[1] Good material for the next three types of illustrative cases may be found in Frink, *Morbid Fears and Compulsion*, 1918, and in Hitschmann, *Freud's Theories of the Neuroses*, 1917.

proper position in their own esteem and in general comparison with other persons. As a result such individuals become humble and servile and are unable to carry on their everyday activities in a satisfactory way. In detail they consider that they have lost ground in competition with others, or they think they are in an absolute sense unable to keep up with their particular job or profession. Hence, life becomes for them hopeless and not worth while. In many cases the result is self destruction.

As in other instances, we have here the building up on the part of inferior personalities of various attitudes which amount to a rationalization of their activities and conditions, and serve as protections against and defenses of, their failings and weaknesses. Typical of these rationalizations are the eschewing of ambition and the general under-evaluation of the accomplishments that the individual finds himself unable to achieve.

**Inhibited and Vacillating Personalities**

Correlated at least roughly with impulsive and compulsive personalities are those individuals who build up reactions characterizing the total personality as indirect and inconclusive in behavior. A typical picture of this sort is the individual who hesitates lengthily before performing an action, considers it in all its details, questions the necessity for doing it, speculates about the consequences, and even after working out an elaborate problematic situation where none is actually necessary, perhaps does what was originally indicated by the stimulating situation. Or, he may completely inhibit his action.

In general, we find all degrees of vacillation and inhibition in various persons. But in all these individuals, we may locate the essentially defective behavior in an unwillingness to commit themselves to the indicated action. Either they dread taking an intellectual stand, performing a decision reaction to the stimuli involved, or plunging into a more explicit performance of a given type.

In great measure we may trace the beginnings of this vacillating and inhibiting behavior equipment to some particular condition in the individual's early behavior life. Perhaps as a child he was constantly admonished and criticized. Because of the continuous fear of dissatisfying the parents a child may acquire responses of timidity and hesitancy which form a nucleus for the development of more and more behavior of the same sort until it dominates his total personality. In other cases, the source of the hesitant and vacillating behavior is located in a disaster that at some time befell the person when he was about to perform an action, or just after he had performed it.

**(C) Disintegration of Personality**

In this subdivision we place individuals whose conduct displays evidences of the breaking up of the integrity which usually characterizes particular personalities. In the most striking forms of disintegrated action the behavior picture involves an explosive disturbance of the individual that practically amounts to a violent discerption of his behavior equipment. No one who has ever seen a person go through a fit of epileptic behavior requires a verbal elaboration of the disintegrational activity.  The observation of the delirious and convulsive action of the epileptic behavior situation constitutes both an excellent and an effective introduction to the facts of behavior disintegration.

We may further suggest that when a diremptive and sejunctive action is occurring, the person's more or less slight contact with stimuli objects and situations depends upon and can be measured by the degree of his equipmental disintegration.  In other words, the greater the disintegration, the slighter the contact of the individual with the stimulus object.  When a person is disintegrated, he is not presenting to his stimuli surroundings a solid front as a unified and complete psychological organism.  His reaction in mild situations is halting and uncertain, while in more intense circumstances it is repetitive and indifferently appropriate with respect to behavior circumstances.  In the most extreme cases the person's disintegration means almost complete inability to make use of any action equipment in a psychological manner so that his behavior is almost entirely confined to biological functioning.

From our description of disintegrated action it is evident that the pathological conduct of this class concerns a status of the person's existing equipment.  Hence, there is a definite distinction between the pathological behavior of this division and the two preceding ones.  On the one hand there is no failure of behavior equipment involved.  It is not improbable that in some cases at least the fact of disintegration at a particular time reverts back to the person's failure to acquire equipment which might have prevented this condition from occurring.  On the other hand, the disintegrations of personality are not cases of building up specifically wrong behavior equipment, although here again the actual disintegrational actions may be traced back to the fact that the pathological person has passed through a particular development of reactional acquisition.

Disintegrations of personality are exceedingly great in number and extremely varied in type.  Without a doubt the greatest typical difference between the cases in this division is that marking off the individuals whose disintegrational action involves external objects and situations as conditions, from those whose disintegrative behavior is connected most closely with physical or general biological conditions.  In order to illustrate the varying forms of disintegrational action we will now consider one type each of the three most typical forms.

Probably the most striking instances of disintegrated behavior are those actions referred to as epileptic seizures performed by persons called epileptics.  Here we have in the extreme forms, at least, complete and utter disintegration of the individual's behavior equipment

Epileptic Personalities [1]

[1] Consult Bleuler, loc. cit. 445–465, Rosanoff, *Manual of Psychiatry*, 1920, 205–214, and Clark, "A Psychological Interpretation of Essential Epilepsy," *Brain*, 1920, 43, 38–49.

resulting in a total lack of reactional adaptation to surroundings. In other cases just as serious but not so complete, we find the person acting, but in an exceedingly violent manner. Here we refer to the manic forms of personality disintegration, behavior situations in which the person runs wild and commits all kinds of horrible deeds. A fundamental descriptive feature of such action is the person's utter lack of control of his activity; he is completely at the mercy of stimulating objects around him and the organic situations contributing to the development and operation of the disorganizational behavior.

Epileptic forms of sejunctive conduct cover an exceedingly wide range of behavior descriptions. Aside from the most violent and striking type we have just mentioned, there are other forms less disturbing and upsetting. These consist primarily only of extreme vertigo and orientational instability with respect to surroundings. A mark of distinction, however, which admirably differentiates epileptic and all other types of disintegrational behavior is that the epileptic forms of conduct are pathological response conditions very intimately involved with the person's biological status. The circumstances which initiate the epileptic conduct may be traced either to various temporary disturbances within the organism, or else to some permanent functional disorder in the individual's biological mechanism. Among temporary and immediate biological disturbances are acute indigestional difficulties, while permanent biological conditions involve disturbances of cerebral circulation, general malfunctioning of the organism because of toxins or infections, etc.

**Manic-depressive Personalities [1]**

While the epileptic personalities display the most extreme and most typical form of disintegration, they are not as illustrative as are some other cases of the intimate psychological conditions involved. For the purpose of showing how disintegrations of actual psychological equipment work out in detail, we will turn to the behavior called manic-depressive in psychiatric literature.

In the very fact that the manic-depressive individual shows a marked stage of exhilarated conduct contrasting with his own later or earlier depressive and subdued behavior, we observe a distinct sign of personality disintegration. These differing forms of alternate conduct, appearing as they do with persistent constancy, show us that the person is not responding with the reactional consolidation that is the usual mode of human behavior. When the so-called excited state appears, the individual does not respond with the inhibiting and conservative conduct he has at one time or another acquired. Similarly, in the depressive stage the manic-depressive personality responds without the spontaneous and buoyant reactions which, in practically every personality, are prominent parts of the behavior equipment.

[1] Consult Rosanoff, loc. cit. 267–291, Kraeplin, *Lectures on Clinical Psychiatry* (2), 1906.

But such evidences of disintegration point only to the most generalized forms of diremptive behavior. For specific descriptions of this type of disorganization we must attend to the intimate details of the manic-depressive person in action. We find, for example, that the individual does not respond in an organized way with his ideational or informational responses. He does not have connected intellectual attitudes toward things, not even toward his own surroundings and hence, he appears completely disoriented. Again, with respect to language, the person may be hopelessly confused or disorganized. The result is frequently an unintelligible verbigeration consisting of a mass of words without distinct or significant references. In less exaggerated cases the person's linguistic behavior may not be completely devoid of meaning but the words uttered are more or less confused in reference.

The disintegration of the manic-depressive type of personality is further characterized by the utter lack of interest on the part of such individuals. They show no constant succession of organized adaptations with respect to their surroundings. Their reactions are haphazard and without the apparent purpose that ordinarily accompanies a familiarity and constancy of intercourse with one's social and natural situations.

Considering a still more intimate and detailed form of behavior subject to disintegration, we find that diremptive personalities are incapable of any degree of sustained attention. They jump from one thing to another like birds in pursued flight, being at rest and in contact with particular things only long enough to allow another object to come into their field of conduct.

As an indication of the degree of disjointedness of the pathological individual we may consider the utter suggestibility of manic-depressive individuals. Anything in their surroundings may be suggestive to them of something else with a consequent new flight of action. In fact every object indifferently serves as a substitute stimulus for some other object. For instance, a man wearing a black suit of clothes stands for Dr. Black (a substitute for an actual physician) who is supposed to have injured them or one of their children.

The specific forms of pathological behavior performed by the manic-depressive provide occasion for many differing types of equally plausible interpretations of such conduct. An interpretation especially instructive is that which looks upon the manic-depressive person as a reversion to an infantile mode of existence. Accordingly, it is pointed out that manic-depressives split up on a chronological plane. The individual is presumed to throw off the action built up as a grown person acquired in his socializing situations. He is no longer reserved but becomes unhesitatingly frank and even descends to a purposeless garrulity.

The query as to what conditions bring about the behavior of

manic-depressive reactional pathology elicits a large number of different answers. Contributing causes may be psychological or non-psychological; they may be hygienic in character or connected with circumstances far removed from the health conditions of the person.

Among psychological conditions is the influence of surrounding circumstances which present the individual with the necessity for action and which he cannot effectively meet. Exceedingly overwhelming conditions may lead directly to a disjointed and disintegrated condition of the person. Great disappointments or tragedies in the individual's life easily induce personality disintegration. Again, changes of a striking sort in the person's general biological functioning and health have similar results. Childbirth and the great transformations involved in sexual maturation and decline of the organism frequently cause personality diremptions.

**(D) Dissociated Personalities**

A set of individuals whose behavior is disrupted and disjointed, somewhat like that of the persons in the disintegrated class, are the dissociated persons. We have just seen that disintegrated individuals, in their partial use of behavior equipment, display a reactional picture of disturbance and distraction. In the case of dissociated persons, on the other hand, the partial functioning of equipment proceeds in a very orderly way. The individual, even though he may appear to be doing extraordinary types of action very unlike his normal conduct, still does them with a smoothness and calmness which completely conceal the pathological character of his conduct. Thus, for example, an individual whose dissociation works out as a definite alternation of personality may perform behavior that to the observer does not seem at all unusual and disturbing.

Another unique characteristic of dissociated behavior marking it off from other types of disjointed conduct, is that it may be permanent. That is to say, the breaking up of the equipment into parts is not a spontaneous and momentary condition but constitutes a general abiding characteristic of the individual. We note accordingly that dissociations of personality have their source and origin in the general personality development. In this sense we find that dissociated personalities have a very close connection with the cases we have described as a building up of wrong behavior equipment. The difference, however, between dissociated individuals and those we have labelled as the wrongly developed, is that the former do not build up specifically wrong activities constituting the dissociation. Rather, they develop in such a way that the occurrence of dissociation is later possible.

In detail, what happens is that an individual grows up in an environment in which the various objects and persons do not constitute a homogeneous unity. The result is of course that the person builds up equipment which does not therefore hang together very well. Later, under stress of some particular circumstance his various behavior equipments separate along definite lines of cleavage, and in their operation constitute alternations and dissociations of personality. All of these suggestions concerning dissociated individuals may be well made out in the classic description by Prince of the case of Miss Beauchamp.[1]

Pathological dissociation must then be thought of as a type of behavior condition in which the reaction systems of the individual are left in abeyance and do not function when the objects which ordinarily perform the stimulational function are present. It is this condition of abeyance characterizing the action systems that constitutes the fundamental fact of dissociation. Dissociation, then, is a condition of the non-functioning of part of the individual's behavior equipment. As we survey the various types of personality dissociation we find that on the basis of the number of reaction systems functionally idle we can separate the dissociated individual into two general classes. Those who have only some specific reaction systems out of function we call hysterical, while others who have great numbers of their reactional equipments non-operative at different periods we term alternating personalities. Our attempt at a description of dissociated individuals will comprise the two general types just mentioned.

In this class we point to individuals whose dissociations constitute partial breakdowns and losses of reactional equipment. In each case we find that the individual is unable to perform certain types of activity just as though he never had acquired reaction systems for responding to particular situations. It is for this reason that we characterize these individuals as having lost some of their behavior equipment although it is one of the special characteristics of this type of abnormality that the so-called lost equipment may be very readily reinstated, and become functional again. Our organizational and descriptive purposes will be well served by a brief description of some striking forms of behavior systems lost by such individuals. **Hysterical Personalities[2]**

First, let us consider a great variety of amnesias, losses of memorial reactions. Some hysterical personalities are unable to remember certain events, certain people, or to respond to any fact or condition circumscribed within a given period. Ordinarily these memorial disintegrations are connected with some particular event, some personal difficulty, or an injury of some type. So complete may the memorial disintegration be that the individual is unable to remember anything. He may not even recall his own name, his relations to his own family, or the place where he lives.[3]

Dissociations of a perceptual type are exceedingly common among hysterical personalities. Striking examples are the individuals who

[1] *Dissociation of a Personality*, 1906.

[2] Consult Janet, *Major Symptoms of Hysteria*, 1907, and Hurst, *The Psychology of the Special Senses and their Functional Disorders*, 1920.

[3] For other points concerning the abnormalities of memorial conduct, see chapter on memory.

cannot see particular objects or persons, or perform visual perceptual responses at certain periods of time. Other dissociated personalities become totally blind and remain so until they recover from the hysterical abnormality. The same general points apply to smelling, tasting, hearing, and other forms of perceptual reactions. What appears as an exceedingly startling form of hysterical dissociation is the analgesic defect; namely, hysterical individuals lose the differential responses to pain stimuli so that they may be cut, burned, and stuck with needles without performing pain responses.

A much studied type of dissociational loss is the linguistic defectiveness of individuals. In various hysterical personalities we find all sorts of language deficiencies. Individuals are unable to pronounce certain words, to recognize them when they see them in writing or in print, or they may not be able to speak and answer a particular question, or any form of inquiry whatever. Again, hysterical personalities drop out of their behavior equipment reactions of a syntactical form, so that they are unable to speak correctly or grammatically. Briefly, there is no kind of language response that may not be found lacking in some form in disintegrated personalities.

Turning now to the great mass of overt performances, we find that these either drop completely out of the personality equipment or disappear along with the other types of actions we have just discussed. The disintegration in some individuals involves the loss of walking responses, or the ability to make particular movements. These activities may all be considered under the general heading of disintegrational paralysis.[1] Such disjunctional conditions are more or less permanent. In other words, in any particular individual they may last for a certain length of time and then completely disappear. It is interesting to observe that the dropping out of performance reactions generally belongs to the more organic types of action such as are represented by disturbances of alimentation, respiration, etc.

In considering the details of the personality disintegrations we have just been describing, we find that any type of sejunction may occur. Such personality losses are due, as we have intimated, to stimulational conditions of various sorts. The specific surrounding circumstances responsible for the development of the abnormality, condition what specific form the disintegration assumes. Therefore, the particular kind of defect, whether it is a loss of overt performance or a perceptual, memorial, or linguistic activity, correlates with the particular stimulational conditions responsible for the abnormality in the first instance.

Again, the disintegrational loss may be conditioned by the individual's knowledge of some weak point in his organic make-up or by

[1] The study of abnormalities from an objective psychological standpoint may be expected to yield in the near future descriptive terms derived from the observed behavior conditions rather than from the neurological (medical) or mentalistic (psychological) traditions.

the general character of his biological organization. Thus hysterical blindness or deafness are considered as simulating injuries to end-organs while paralyses resemble injuries which individuals may suffer to their nervous systems or musculatures. In this connection it is interesting to observe that paralyses and anæsthesias of various types occur very frequently in a form which matches more the knowledge of the individual than his actual anatomical and physiological organization. Accordingly, we find that disintegrations take place on the basis of geometric patterns rather than according to some nerve distribution. Here we have the so-called glove, sock, or sleeve anæsthesias, etc.

A descriptive peculiarity of the disintegrational defects we have been reviewing is that to a considerable degree they consist of activities developed by the individual. In other words, disintegration may be based upon the fact of acquiring disserviceable and defective behavior equipment. Accordingly we find in disintegrated individuals certain modes of pathological conduct which are not essentially losses of functions but rather acquisitions of abnormal behavior. Instead of becoming anæsthetic an individual grows exceedingly sensitive, and so it is not improbable that most disintegrated individuals exhibit some symptoms of hyperæsthesia or hyper-sensitivity to pain stimuli.

An exceedingly prominent and commonly observed form of personality dissociation is found in the cases in which individuals do not lose a part of their equipment but apparently use their equipment only at alternate periods. In consequence we find that at stated intervals these disintegrated individuals act entirely differently than at other times and under other circumstances. In the famous Ansel Bourne case a preacher left his house and, going to another part of the country, became a merchant on a small scale. A peculiar condition is that in some cases the alternating personalities are not aware of each other. In this situation there are of course more than two personalities, that is to say, multiple personalities. It is possible that a single person may dissociate in such a manner and with such a degree of defectiveness that at different times he assumes as many as eight types of personalities.

*Alternating Personalities* [1]

The line of division between the personalities and the way the alternations occur depend upon the original development of the personality. The main point is that during the course of the individual's development, the different reaction systems forming the material of his personality may develop under entirely different auspices so that they are not subject to the same fusional process that characterizes what we ordinarily call the normal individual. In the situation responsible for the alternation we find the specific circumstances which

[1] Sidis and Goodhart, *Multiple Personality*, 1905. Binet, *Alterations of Personalities*, 1896, and Prince, *The Unconscious*, 1921.

bring about the particular behavior details of the personality dissociation.

**(E) Degenerating Personalities** [1]

In this subdivision of abnormal conduct and pathological personalities we place all of those individuals which show a definite progressive degeneration. They may have developed normally and in a fully definite manner and in no sense include in their personality equipment undesirable or defective traits of conduct. At some particular point, however, in their life cycle they begin to deteriorate and in a more or less rapid fashion become defective in action, in the sense that they irrecoverably lose some particular kind of equipment or all of their equipment. This deterioration is so rapid in some instances that individuals reach a stage of total dissolution in a period of months, or the degeneration may continue over a period of some years. Here we may consider a few varying forms on the basis of the psychiatric classification.

**Paretic Personalities**

Individuals to whom this term or its synonym dementia paralytica applies, exhibit behavior pictures indicating a very definite and in the course of a short time, a very complete degeneration. In short, these persons lose their orientation. From their equipment are dropped out the informational reactions which orient them with respect to the ordinary conditions of human life. They do not know where they are, what their situation has been or is, nor in any definite sense, what is happening to them. In like fashion they are affected with an unmistakable loss of capacity to react to objects and events in a memorial way. Nor are the elementary performances free from marked deterioration. All of their action in fact becomes uncertain; they cannot do anything without tremors and other prominent disturbances of a like character. For example, they display unmistakable degeneration in their gait until they are unable to walk at all. Activities like writing and talking decline in functional accuracy and serviceability. Along with the more circumscribed losses and deteriorations of action these individuals on the whole become displaced in their ordinary environment and circumstances. In clinical descriptions they are described as performing hallucinatory and delusional conduct with rapid alternation of agitated and depressed states. Probably the best indication of the sort of condition we have here is found in the fact that these abnormal personalities are not only psychologically but also biologically degenerating.

**Senile Personalities**

Indicative of the behavior abnormalities belonging to the present class are the cases psychiatrically classified as insanities of arteriosclerosis, presbyophrenia, and senile dementia. As contrasted with the condition of paretic personalities the degeneration here is not definitely progressive. The individuals do not deteriorate with such a marked tendency toward dissolution nor is the degeneration so

[1] For literature indications of the following types of pathological personalities consult any of the standard psychiatric treatises, a very useful bibliography of which is found in Bridges, *Outline of Abnormal Psychology*, 1921.

rapid. In the senile personalities the pathological conditions are more diffused from the standpoint of the general central organization of the deterioration. Furthermore, the degeneration is or may be peripheral in character. Frequently there are degenerations of reaction functions which are more or less distantly removed from the reactionally central or most important features of the personality.

To a certain extent the difference between the paretic and senile personality degeneration may be indicated by the appearance in the paretics of an immediate and rapid deterioration of the individual, whereas senile cases appear more like cessations of development, although this cannot be mistaken for a condition of non-degeneration. Aside from the central descriptive differences between these cases and the paretic personalities, we find marks of degeneracy such as general disorientation, all sorts of behavior lacks regarding interaction with the surroundings and accompanied by hallucinations and illusions of all sorts, as well as restlessness, weaknesses of various varieties, incoördination, and tremors.

As in paretic abnormalities the biological conditions of senile pathological personalities are prominent factors. But in contrast to the former case in which the organized degeneration can be correlated with degeneration of centralized tissues, that is to say, the neural structures, we find in the case of the senile that the immediate source of anatomical degeneration is some more peripheral structure. For instance, the vascular tissues or other peripheral organs may be the seat of the localized biological deterioration although here, as everywhere else, nothing less than the total organism undergoes the degenerative changes.

While the typical and most striking cases of personality degeneration are those in which the biological as well as the psychological organism is involved, this is not at all an absolutely necessary condition. From a strictly psychological standpoint the same general personality degeneration occurs when the person is merely cut off from the objects and conditions constituting his normal behavior surroundings. The person who is taken away from his business and put into an entirely different kind of life, as in the case of military conscription, may become completely degenerated, especially if this enforced removal from his ordinary surroundings lasts for a long time. When the degeneration is not of a very long duration the person may become reconstituted again and resume his normal behavior.

By disorganization of personality we refer to persons whose behavior consists of such responses as clearly reflect a condition of definite disjointedness. While they are not entirely prevented from acting, their responses are inaccurate; they fail to connect up with stimuli objects; their performances fail to strike and in general are exceedingly ineffective. Disorganizations of personality are pathological conditions which have nothing at all to do with the process of building up equipment nor with the kind of equipment the person **(F) Disorganization of Personality**

has acquired.   Rather the difficulty is located in some condition which
incöordinates the person and makes him loose in his action.   The most
typical cases of the pathological behavior we place in this class are
the intoxications.   These disorganizations are entirely familiar to
everybody.   An excessive indulgence in alcohol so disorganizes and
dissociates the individual that he is unable to walk or talk or perform accurately and integrally even the crudest overt performances.
Seeing double is the classic symptom of such disorganized behavior.

The disorganization conditions induced by alcohol may be considered as due to an exogenous poison.   Other such poisons having
similar effect are morphine, opium, hashish, and mescal.   Now we
wish to point out that all of these exogenous toxins constitute only one
type of condition responsible for pathological behavior.   Numerous
other toxins of an endogenous sort have the same effect.   Here we
may suggest that any kind of fever, infections, or other condition of
the individual, involved with auto-intoxications, may bring about
more or less violent conditions of personality disorganization.   The
medical literature is full of material indicating disorganization effects
that can be traced to the malfunctioning of the glandular apparatus
with an accompanying toxic result.   Naturally these disorganized
personalities perform all sorts of misplacing implicit conduct.   They
are described as delirious, which means in effect that they are not
capable of any very definitely organized perceptual and ideational
conduct concerning persons and things surrounding them.

Disorganizations of conduct are not at all confined to the comparatively simple types of behavior situations we have been indicating.
The examples given stress the disorganizations involving modifications in the individual himself.   We turn next to behavior situations
in which disorganizations constitute maladaptations to all sorts of
complex distracting and disturbing stimuli circumstances.   Hence we
stress the individual's activity with respect to specific surrounding
conditions.   Accordingly we find that behavior disorganizations may
consist of the lack of coördinated conduct with respect to moral, social,
economic, and other types of situations.   Typical examples in this
connection are the individuals who become disjointed with respect
to their moral surroundings.   Persons who, before they become disorganized, conduct themselves with propriety become degenerate
from the ethical standpoint.   Their whole activity is morally blunt.
They do not carry out promises and apparently have no regard for
any of their social or economic obligations.   The point to be
especially emphasized here is that the person is completely disjointed
and uncoördinated.   Bleuler quotes the case of a disorganized individual who because of some disappointment while attending a dance
hanged himself and upon being cut down immediately began to
dance again.

Such individuals likewise display disorganizations in their intellectual behavior; that is, they become disoriented in the sense that they

confuse their surroundings.  They mix up in haphazard fashion the various places they occupy in society.  One moment they look upon themselves as outcasts and irresponsible individuals, while the next they behave as though they thought their position in society was a fixed and prominent one.

Worry situations may completely distract and disorganize a person's conduct.  Misfortunes of various sorts, fear conditions such as the fear of detection of some crime one has committed, or fear that some enterprise will turn out disadvantageously, are all effective sources of disorganization.  Conditions involving jealousies which form an exceedingly prominent feature of an individual's behavior phenomena constitute a further potent source of personality inco-ordination.  Extreme poverty and general economic disadvantages, especially when they have pronounced effects upon the individual, result in just as serious an abnormality as though the whole organism were charged with the disturbing influences of a poison.

As a final illustration of pathological personalities and defective conduct we may consider the behavior of persons who are broken up or destroyed in part.  The main point here is that the individual, considered as a biological unit, is destroyed or truncated in the sense perhaps that an organ is lost or put out of function, and in consequence is unable to perform activities involving in an important way the use or operation of the lost or injured organ or part. (G) Traumatic Defects and Injured Personalities

These deteriorations, truncations, or losses are obviously of every degree, kind, and variety, and upon the specific character of the injury or destruction depend the particular kind of personality defect and pathology of conduct.  On the whole, however, for descriptive purposes we might differentiate between two types of traumatic personalities which we call generalized and specialized traumas.

Under the first rubric we place all abnormal personalities whose behavior difficulties involve some trauma, disease, or destruction which is strategic and centralized in the sense that whole classes of behavior are affected and the person is cut off from the performance of complete types of adaptations to particular stimuli situations. For example, injuries to the brain or other parts of the central nervous system result in the inability to perform any activity of a particular class.  Similarly, degenerations of muscle tissue or other organs occur, with the definite result that the individual is unable to perform specific types of action.

Our division of specific truncated personalities embraces those individuals whose behavior difficulties involve particular organs or localized defects.  Among the commonplace instances of such localized defects or injuries may be mentioned the loss or destruction of one or both eyes, hands, or feet, resulting in blindness, deafness, ageusia, anosmia, the inability to walk, hold, or throw things, etc. The less common injuries or defects involve organ inferiorities or superiorities, which lead to insufficiency or the absence of certain specific forms of behavior or to the too prominent or vigorous performance of particular actions. Illustrative of organ inferiority insufficiencies or hyperfunctionings are the defects of the ears, eyes, or other receptors, and the exaggerated or inadequate functioning of the sex or other glands. When considered as elements in the detailed performances of specific responses, these localized defects and injuries must be considered as reaction system defects, but we are assuming here that the general results are that the personality as a whole is put out of function.[1] In the latter case, of course, we may definitely place the abnormalities under discussion among the pathologies of personality.

Occasion has already been found several times to point out that in all of these descriptions of abnormal conduct and pathological personalities we have been able merely to offer suggestions taken more or less at random from the various angles of the total personalities involved. In no sense is it possible to give connected behavior pictures which adequately and completely represent specified abnormality conditions or personality defects. Here we must repeat again that what we have been interested in is the psychological investigation of particular persons. All schemes of organization and classification are merely of account insofar as they help in an understanding of the particular personality and his difficulties. The classifications are all worthless unless they can be of some use in throwing light upon our understanding of pathological individuals. At most our classifications and descriptions can only provide items of reference for the consideration of abnormalities.

**The Conditions of Abnormality**

Throughout the discussion of the various types of abnormality we have found it necessary to specify some of the conditions responsible for the exaggerations of conduct. We might still profitably consider in a more specialized form some of the conditions influencing the development of defective personality and the operation of pathological behavior.

In the first place, we must refer to the biological conditions involved in abnormal conduct. Since the psychological personality is always a biological organism we naturally expect to find a great number of biological factors involved in the operation of abnormal behavior. We have already seen that such abnormalities may be connected with anatomical losses, malformations or injuries. Pathological conduct also accompanies all types of unusual physiological functions of the organs or of the organism as a whole. Here we find pathological behavior connected with failures of physiological functionings, insufficiencies and hyperfunctionings of all varieties. Once more we must utter a solemn warning that in no sense should it be considered that there are biological conditions which are correlated with certain

---

[1] Frequently the pathological personality is really built up in the form of compensations for the lack of an organ (paranoia or delinquency of the deaf and blind) or for its inferior functioning.

mental disturbances, since we have absolutely nothing to do with the operation of a mind or mentality correlated with biological processes.[1] What we are concerned with is the biological mechanism which fails to develop or has developed particular kinds of reactions to specific stimuli objects and conditions. The relationship between psychological conduct and the biological features of the organism is well illustrated by the fact that psychological conduct may be responsible for the person's biological conditions. How many of the distinctly feminine and masculine biological traits are due to psychological behavior? And are not the biological characteristics of people that enable us to tell their human circumstances the results of the kind of actions they perform?

We turn next to a set of conditions at the basis of pathological conduct which we call definitely psychological in character. Here we refer to all sorts of behavior equipment such as fears, faiths, beliefs, which may be entirely normal and fitting for certain circumstances but which, when the person meets with new and strange situations, become the sources of the development of pathological conduct or constitute the basis upon which the individual is split and disintegrated. A concrete illustration here is the fact that the psychological development of the individual may later make it possible for him to develop disintegrations. To illustrate, a child who is not induced to build up behavior of discipline and inhibitions of various sorts, must perforce find himself disintegrated when he later meets with strongly resisting human conditions. Another case is that of the person who builds up equipment only for the tranquil surroundings in which he ordinarily lives, and who becomes hysterical and shell-shocked when violently transported to a turbulent environment such as is always connected with war situations.

Another set of conditions favoring the development of pathological conduct comprises the various types of natural and human environments. Very common even in the most advanced civilizations are the circumstances compelling persons to live under exceedingly poor natural surroundings. The result is that individuals develop under bad hygienic and biological circumstances that inevitably produce pathological psychological personalities. Strikingly illustrative of such situations are the common circumstances of isolation in which persons live without the benefits of human resources making for hygienic and adequate human life. Such natural conditions are always involved in the development of so-called degenerate personalities. In our own country the districts, where whole settlements of individuals have not enough to eat and where they are all diseased with hook worm and malaria, are prolific sources of the degenerate type of pathological personality.

[1] In no sense must we confuse the grosser forms of action of the person with biological facts while the more refined and subtle responses to stimuli (thinking, remembering) are called mental or psychological facts.

The social conditions under which human beings live afford further ground for the sources of abnormal conduct. Persons are always surrounded with diverse kinds of complex living conditions. These lead to the necessity of keeping up an appearance of conformity to the dictates of the group. Thus we have the basis for building up beliefs and ideas concerning one's superiority or inferiority, or the prejudices against certain members entertained by other members of the community. Such community life leads also to conflicts of desire and ambition which, if they get beyond the control of the individual, cause him to develop abnormal and defective reaction systems. The slightest reflection shows us to what an enormous extent human conflicts within a community are productive of pathological ways of behavior.[1]

A prominent type of abnormal conduct fostered by social organization and traditions comprises the extreme differences society permits and encourages in different individuals. A striking illustration of this condition is the feeble-mindedness of women that many human groups insist upon. These developments of abnormal conditions are also fostered on the basis of color and lines of craft and technique. Thus in all complex human societies decided differences in personality equipment and development with respect to knowledge, information, and general intelligence are encouraged. Still another intricate series of conditions conducive to abnormal behavior development are the economic circumstances of our present industrial and social organization. The completely uncertain conditions of economic dependence in which most persons find themselves coupled with reactions of insecurity and fear concerning their future welfare, provide a tremendous amount of possible situations for building up defective personalities and dissociations and disintegrations of all types. Typical of our American economic organization are the shifting conditions in industrial life. Persons are not in control of the crafts in which they are employed. The factories where they work may be closed down or moved away entirely without any obligation or notice to the workers. Or the workers may find themselves thrown out of jobs under conditions which make them economically helpless and insecure. The fact that so large a percentage of pathological individuals is found among foreigners indicates how quickly the disconnectedness of persons from the world in which they live causes the development of reactional defects. In short, stormy and unsettled human conditions of any character are always the bases for the development of abnormalities of all sorts. Here we might instance the great public manias quoted by various writers which have occurred in connection with crusades, war hysteria, etc.

[1] Among the most informative facts of the psychology of abnormality are the insanities of non-conformity. An illuminating example is that of Chidley, the Australian (Sydney) sophic and cynic, cf. Havelock Ellis, *The Dance of Life*, 1923, pp. 79–82.

As a final indication of the kind of conditions conducive to the development of psychological abnormality we might consider the personal or domestic relations. How much wrong personality development is initiated and developed by acute family dissensions and the serious incompatibilities of domestic life. So familiar are the serious disorganizations induced by unhappy love and sex situations that it is necessary only to refer to them.

PERSPECTIVAL AND BIBLIOGRAPHICAL NOTES

Traditionally, the complete interest in and the handling of abnormal reactions of psychopathic personalities have been relegated to the physician. Probably the reasons for this circumstance are found in the fact that any difficulty or peculiarity of the person had to be studied and handled by those individuals in whose care lay the diseased and injured.

A second contributing condition which is doubtless very closely related to the first is the fact that psychologists were interested in the analysis and description of mentalities. These so-called mentalities did not lend themselves readily to association with the kind of peculiarities exhibited by psychopathic individuals and their behavior.

It is only in comparatively recent times that psychologists have been developing an interest in abnormal phenomena and primarily through the fact that physicians themselves have been forced to develop conceptions concerning the psychic (psychological?) origin and character of "mental diseases." (Cf. Janet, *The Major Symptoms of Hysteria*, 19, Lecture I; Hart, *The Psychology of Insanity*, (3) 1916, Chapter I). Accordingly, psychologists have in turn been practically forced to concern themselves with psychopathological phenomena. But even under these conditions progress in this direction has been very slow.

Because of this traditional situation in the field of psychopathology the study of abnormal psychology has naturally followed a fairly devious development finally leading up to our present psychological conception of abnormality (a development which may be crudely described as beginning with the tradition that abnormalities of conduct are all caused by or center about some physiological or organic condition).

In the very earliest period of scientific handling of abnormal psychological phenomena, the viewpoint prevailed that any anomaly or abnormality of conduct could be traced to some type of lesion in the nervous system. This view undoubtedly had its basis in the fact that physicians, because of their training which has always stressed disjointed physiological and anatomical facts, attempted to find in every type of abnormality some anatomical lesion as the factor responsible for unusual or abnormal function, such as inability to remember or general disorientation. This view was no doubt based upon the formula that every psychosis is correlated with a neurosis and upon the idea that malfunctioning of digestion for example is

correlated with some malformation or injury in the digestive structure. In more recent times the failure to discover anatomical lesions
has been responsible for enlarging the parallelistic conception to
include toxic conditions and the general malfunctioning of the organism as organic bases and causes of "mental" disorders. This
stage we may refer to as the first or physiological period in the
scientific (medical) handling of abnormalities.

With the development of observations concerning the influence of
suggestibility and hypnosis in the causation and cure of behavior
difficulties, physicians were led to the conception of a mental etiology
for the development of (at least what are called the functional) behavior abnormalities. As a consequence, they formulated ideas which
led to the institution of various systems of psychotherapeutics. These
at first utilized prominently suggestive treatments and hypnosis and
in our own day have been followed by a great variety of psychoanalytic movements.

That both of these types of views concerning psychopathic individuals and abnormal conduct do not accurately take account of abnormal psychological situations is evident from the fact that in very
recent times physicians themselves have arrived at the conception
that what they must treat is not either the physiological organism
alone nor the so-called purely mental functions, but the individual
as a totality.[1]

This change of attitude undoubtedly represents a much more practical position than either of the other two, but it is still very far from
constituting an adequate position from a psychological standpoint.
Furthermore, to a considerable degree this view has been developed
into a medico-sociological conception according to which the human
individual is presumed to be a unit of both mental and bodily structures or factors, and functions.[2] But the behavior of the individual
in both its normal and abnormal aspects is still accounted for by either
mentalistic or organic conditions or both.

As contrasted with such conceptions the treatment of abnormalities
in the present work is thoroughly psychological in all its phases. In
brief, the psychological conception implies that abnormal conduct
constitutes extreme variations of the same kind of intricate interactions between persons and their surrounding objects and situations
as comprise the subject matter of the science of psychology. This
view we may designate as an organismic or synthetic one as over
against any analytic position which deals exclusively with the person

[1] This is the case of the various psychiatric movements which stress persuasion, or the psychoanalytic types of psychiatry which, starting from the
study of the sex disturbances in people, have carried over to a larger range
of defective conduct.

[2] Here falls, for example, the psychiatric work of Meyer, Adolf, and his
pupils (published in *Mental Hygiene*, and elsewhere), that of Myerson (*The
Nervous Housewife*, 1920) and Southard and Jarrett (*The Kingdom of Evils*,
1922), and much of the Freudian materials.

more or less independent of stimuli conditions and situations, or with the mental or physiological aspects of a total human stimulus-response situation.

To be sure in the present chapter we cannot go beyond the general principles of such abnormalities. We can furnish only suggestions concerning the conditions and circumstances operating when abnormal conduct is in question. Nothing else is possible without a concrete and intricate study of specific cases, specific abnormal individuals and their behavior. For example, in studying personalities constituting wrong personality development, it is essential to investigate particular cases in order to ascertain what specific type of conduct the abnormal individuals actually do build up. Or if the abnormality is a failure of personality development it is necessary to learn what is the precise detailed behavior status of the individual concerned.

In the present chapter, then, we are concerned with the actual psychology of abnormality, with the psychological principles involved in the peculiar and undesirable (widely varying) behavior which makes for so much unhappiness and despair in human life. We are not attempting to offer some psychiatric descriptions to the student of psychological behavior irregularities. Certainly we are not concerned with pointing out the histology of the tissues found in individuals who perform irregular and unusual conduct. What we are interested in is the actual behavior persons perform, and under its own peculiar conditions, according to which it assumes the particular character we observe it to have.

It is of some importance also to place our work on abnormality in perspective with what has recently been called the academic psychological standpoint. The latter is nothing but the orthodox psychological attitude as it is employed by psychiatrists. Represented by practically all of the standard psychiatric literature, headed for example by Kraeplin (Psychiatrie 4 vols. (8) 1909–15) this viewpoint is responsible for the symptomatological attitude toward abnormalities. It consists of the enumeration of an exceedingly long list of so-called mental symptoms which are presumed to be organized into syndromes or mental disease entities. Because these syndromes are treated as impairments of faculties or mental functions (inability to remember, illogicality, mental cloudiness, etc.) the psychiatrist failed to notice that each so-called symptom is really a specific form of behavior with respect to particular conditions. No person has just delusions; such activities are always wrong reactions originally conditioned by specific surrounding circumstances and operating in a particular way because of such stimuli-surroundings.

From the standpoint of the present work all abnormalities must be treated as we have already explained, as deviations from others called the normal. Accordingly our cases need not be sought exclusively among the hopeless inmates of insane asylums. Every person presents us with data concerning some or many specific types of psychological abnormalities. Furthermore, we need not test a person for an abnormality on the basis of some formal laboratory performance but can study his actual conduct in the actual coördinate surroundings in which his behavior is found. How common the pathologies of conduct are we may gather from the fact that many very serious defects of behavior may be studied in the negations, hesitancies, excitements, tantrums, and disorientations of children.

**END OF VOLUME II.**

# INDEX

511

and statistical behavior, 416; historical action, 416; natural vs. humanistic objects, 416; individual vs. cultural behavior, 417; complex æsthetic behavior situation, 418 ff.; æsthetic behavior segment, 418; creative activity in, 418 ff.; appreciation or contemplation of art object, 419; criticism of art object, 420; evaluation of art object, 420; stimulus for æsthetic behavior segment, 421; personality and non-personality factors of æsthetic milieu, 422; non-psychological factors in æsthetic situations, 424; complex scientific situation, 425 ff.; nature of technical scientific behavior segment, 425 ff.; religious vs. mystical, 426; stimuli for scientific behavior segment, 428; the scientific milieu, 428; complex religious behavior situation, 431 ff.; religious vs. magical conduct, 432; religious vs. mythological behavior, 433; extrinsic and intrinsic religious behavior, 436 ff.; stimuli for religious conduct, 437; the religious milieu, 438; non-psychological factors in religious situations, 439; complex ethical behavior situation and nature of moral phenomena, 440 ff.; ethical behavior segment, 440 ff.; the moral behavior milieu, 442; non-psychological factors of moral situations, 443; complex economic behavior situation and connection with social and non-psychological facts, 473 ff.; acquisitive conduct, 445; work and play, 446; exchange, 446; use and consumption, 446 ff.; moving and transportation, 447; stimuli for economic behavior, 447; economic behavior milieu, 447 ff.; non-psychological factors in economic situations, 448 ff.

Compulsive personalities, 486 f.

Concepts, use of in reasoning, 190; and language, 216.

Conditions of psychological behavior, divisions of, 359; interrelation of scientific data, 363; conditions commutual with psychological data, 364; conditions affecting development of phenomena, 366; biological evolution and psychological potentiality, 366; anatomical and physiological circumstances, 367; maturity of organism, 367; abnormality and normality of person, 368; physiological functioning, 368; environmental influences, 369 ff.; direct and indirect, 369; anthropological and sociological, 370 ff.; psychological conditions, 371 ff.; conditions affecting occurrence of psychological phenomena, 372 ff.; loss of anatomical parts, 372; dysfunctional circumstances, 373; fatigue and drugs, 373 ff.; non-psychological concomitants, 374; psychological concomitants, 374 ff.; equipmental conditions, 374 ff.; psychological settings, 375.

Conditions, of sleeping behavior, general, 382 ff.; special, 384; of hypnotic behavior, 397 ff.

Conductive reasoning, 193.

Confusion of actual and imagined, or witting and unwitting imagination, 76.

Conjecturing behavior, 143.

"Consciousness" and memory, 117.

Constructive reasoning, 193.

Constructive technique of problem solving, 180 ff.

Contingential behavior, in interpersonal situations, 292.

Continuity of species doctrine, and emotions, 18; and inheritance of psychological qualities, 366 ff.; 477.

Continuous activity, see Memory.

Controlled imagination, 61.

Controlled learning, 353 ff.

Conventions, stylistic, 270.

Conversation, as actual language, 222; as interpersonal behavior, 298 ff.

Conversational vs. non-conversational language, 232 ff.

Convincing responses, 138 ff.; as reciprogenic interpersonal conduct, 303.

Cravings, 48.

Creation of art object, 55 ff., 418 ff.

Creative or imagination responses, 54 ff.

Cretins, 474.

Criminal personalities, 502.

Critical reasoning, 194 ff.

Critical thinking behavior, 169; requirements of, 170.

Criticism, as homogenic interpersonal behavior, 295; as a phase of constructive activity, 420.

Criticizing as thinking behavior, 160; requirements of, 160 ff., 170.

Croce, 210 n.

Cultural or "tender" emotions, 8, 13; in children, 17.

Cultural language conduct, 207, 262 ff.

Culturalization, as basis of problem solving, 186; and voluntary behavior, 330 ff.

Cultural influences, upon desires, 42 f.; upon language, 278 ff.; upon idiosyncratic conduct, 293; upon voluntary reactions, 315.

# INDEX

517

conduct, 73 ff.; fallacious popular notion of, 72.
Otis, 243 n.

Paramnesia, 112.
Paranoiac behavior, 480 ff.; self-evaluation, 481; mechanical invention, 481; problem solvers, 481; beliefs, 481; hysterical thinking, 482; reasoning, 482.
Paretic personalities, 498.
Passions and emotions, 11.
Pathological behavior, 468 ff.
Pathological liars, swindlers, 478.
Paul, 265 n., 286.
Paulhan, 84.
Perceptual phase, of emotional behavior segment, 6; of language responses, 253 ff.
Performative memory acts, 94.
Personal identity, memorial basis of, 102, 103.
Personalities, abnormal types of, 464 ff.
Personality equipment, see Reactional biography; defects of, 459 ff.
Personality influences, upon voluntary conduct, 330 ff.; upon learning, 351.
Persuading and pleading as reciprogenic interpersonal behavior, 302 ff.
Perverted personalities, 484 ff.; inebriates, 485; sex perverts, 485.
Phantasy, 61; dream, 404 ff.
Philological language data, 207 ff.
Philosophic imagination, 78.
Physiological functioning, as general condition of psychological behavior, 367; and sleep, 412.
Physiological influences upon psychological behavior, 368.
Physiological structure—function action contrasted with psychological activity, 367 ff.
Pieron, H., 392 n.
Planning, as thinking conduct, 159; as interpersonal behavior, 300.
Play and imagination behavior, in children, 69; and problem solving, 177, 178.
Poetry as language, 222, 281.
Political and social imagination, 82.
Post-emotional behavior segments, first proximate, 8 ff.; second proximate, 9 ff.
Postponed reactions, see Memory.
Practical and theoretical reasoning, 196 f.
Practical problem solving, 174 ff.
Practice, in imaginary conduct, 64 ff.
Precurrent reaction systems in emotional behavior, 6 f.

Predicting, and memory, 102; as thinking conduct, 165 ff.
Pre-emotional behavior segments, 6.
Preference behavior, see Voluntary action.
Primary or violent emotions, 5.
Primitive or mediæval mind, as function of circumstances, 371.
Prince, 495, 497 n.
Prison personalities, 488 ff.
Problem solving conduct, characteristics, 173; three types of practical, 174 ff.; two types of theoretical, 176 ff.; indifferent problem solving, 177 ff.; techniques and methods of, 178 ff.; analysis, 178 ff.; synthesizing, 179 ff.; conduction, 180; hypothesizing, 180; transformation, 180 ff.; inference, 181; construction of techniques, 181; trial and error or experimental technique, 182; stimuli for, 183 ff.; individual differences in, 185 ff.; idiosyncratic problem solving vs. institutionalized form, 186; logical vs. psychological study of, 201; and voluntary conduct, 319.
Process reactions, 349 ff.
Products, of language, 207; of learning, 347 ff.
Projective memory acts, 94 f.
Prospective or planning action, 159.
Protestant personalities, 465.
Proving, as reciprogenic interpersonal conduct, 303.
Psychiatric conception of abnormality, 449 ff.
Psychoanalytic view of the Unconscious, 118.
Psychological action, contrasted with structure-function event, 367 ff.
Psychological acts and act products, 416.
Psychological concomitants of occurrence of psychological phenomena, 374 ff.
Psychological conditions of psychological development, 371 ff.
Psychological criterion for abnormality, 456.
Psychological language data, 210 ff.; characteristics of, 211 ff., 229.
Psychological vs. logical behavior, 222 ff.
Psychological vs. psychiatric attitude toward abnormal phenomena, 456 ff.
Psychological settings, of psychological events, 375.
Psychopathic personalities, see Abnormal reactions.
Psychopathological theory of wish fulfillments, 402 ff.

# 524 INDEX

volved, 152 f.; and language, 154 f.; conditioned by knowledge and informational equipment, 155; types of, 156 f.; judging, 156 f.; planning, 159; analyzing and synthesizing, 159 f.; criticizing, 160; deciding and choosing, 161 f.; abstracting, 164 f.; predicting, 165 f.; explaining, 166 f.; estimating, 167 f.; speculation and reflection, 168 f.; variations in critical quality of, 169; distortions in thinking, 169 f.; in animals and children, 171; stimuli for, 171 f.; apparent indirectness of, 238 f.; as delayed, 238; as precurrent, 238; as implicit action, 240.

Thought and language, 216 ff., 236 ff.

Thoughts as logical products, 202.

Torpor, 389.

Training of imagination, 64; of memory, 109; in voluntary conduct, 335.

Trance, as type of hypnosis, 397.

Transformation dreaming, 404.

Transformative or imagination responses, 54 ff.

Transforming techniques, as most intricate problem solving techniqne, 181.

Transmissive language, 223 f.

Traumatic defects, 501.

Tredgold, 474.

Trial and error, as a problem solving technique, 182.

Unadaptable behavior abnormalities, 463.

Unadaptable reactions, 463 ff.

"Unconscious," the, and language, 287.

Uncommonness of reasoning behavior, 197.

Uncritical reasoning, 194 ff.

Understanding reactions, as receptive linguistic responses, 226 ff.

Undeveloped personalities, 472.

Unusual behavior abnormalities, 461.

Unwitting imagination, 75 ff.

Use and consumption, reactions, 446.

Utilitarian language type, 280 ff.

Utilitarian theory of emotions, 13.

Validity, of reasoning, 199.

Vascillating, in believing action, 133 ff.

Vendreyes, 210 n., 211 n., 265 n.

Verbal institutions, 267 ff.

Verbal responses, 215.

Veridical dreaming, 403.

Vico, 210 n.

Vocal, speech, and gesture, 223 ff.

Volitional conduct contrasted with voluntary behavior, 314 ff.

Voluntary reactions, and language, 278; nature of, 280; alternative stimuli for, 308; reactional choice and stimulus preference in, 308 f.; consequences in, 313; and knowledge, 314; final action in, 314, 316 ff.; precurrent reactions in, 314; differentiation from volitional behavior, 314; analysis of voluntary behavior segment, 316 f.; overt and implicit definitive responses, 316; language activity, 317; behavior equipment involved, 317; modifications and truncations of, 318; classification of voluntary behavior segments according to degrees of complexity, 318; dependent upon preliminary reactions, 318 f.; psychological foundations of, 329 f.; based on inhibiting, delayed, and meaning behavior, 320 ff.; stimuli of, 322; as influenced by stimuli settings and backgrounds, 324; range of, 325; simpler component actions in, 325; affective components of, 327; interpreted as purely attentional process, 328; determining conditions of, 328; and motives, 329; personality influences upon, 330 f.; classification of, on basis of stimulus and response in, 333 f.; traditional treatment of, 335 ff.; ethical influence upon, 336.

Von Humboldt, 210 n., 285.

Wanting, 51 f.

Watson, 215 n.

"Will," 335, 336.

Wish fulfilling dream, 402 ff.

Wishing, 51.

Wit activities as interpersonal behavior, 308.

Witting imagination, 75.

Wolff, 117.

Women, heterogenic interpersonal behavior of, 300.

Words, use of in imagination, 59; analysis of, 228 ff.; as social institutions, 229; as psychological data, 229; as stimuli, 229, 247; as responses, 230.

Work conditions of imaginations, 66.

Work and play, 446.

Worry, 10.

Writing and printing as language, 225.

Wundt, social psychology and conception of language, 286.

Yearning, 51.